THE AGE OF CHARLES I

Also by David Mathew

Surveys

Specialised Studies

Biography

Novel

ENDYMION PORTER

From a portrait by William Dobson in the National Portrait Gallery

[*Frontispiece*

THE
AGE OF CHARLES I

by

David Mathew

EYRE & SPOTTISWOODE
London

First Published *1951*
Reprinted *1951*

*This book is printed in Great Britain
for Eyre & Spottiswoode (Publishers) Ltd., 15 Bedford Street,
London, W.C.2, by Hazell, Watson & Viney, Ltd.,
Aylesbury and London.*

In memory of
JOHN,
sixteenth and last
Lord Arundell of Wardour

ILLUSTRATIONS

PREFACE

THIS study of the Caroline period in England is a survey
of English life during those years of the personal rule of
Charles I which terminated in the Civil Wars. Under another
aspect, it is an examination of the state of England in the decade
when the Court of King Charles and his Queen was the centre
of authority until this was submerged on the outbreak of the
conflict. The period of rule without recourse to Parliament has
particular significance, in that it provides an indication both
of the authority of the Crown and the influence of the example
of the sovereign. In spite of the presence of those forces which
would in time precipitate a conflict, the dominant impression
of the period is one of peace: internal peace in the sense that
until the last years opposition was not manifest, and external
peace because the King could not go to war unless he was
prepared to call a Parliament, which alone could vote supplies.
The last period of King James I and the first four years of the
new reign had been dominated by the figure of the Duke of
Buckingham, who belonged wholly to the Elizabethan tradition
in its Jacobean guise. For this reason *The Jacobean Age*, to which
this study is a sequel, ended with that favourite's assassination.
With his death the little wars were over, and in the quiet time
that followed it is possible to assess the consequences of the
Tudor century.

In the first place, the results of the Elizabethan Settlement
had largely worked themselves out. After seventy years, the
impact of the Anglican tradition upon urban and rural life
had profoundly modified the relations between the monarchy
and wide sections of the people. The quality of authoritarian
ecclesiastical thought and doctrine was peculiar to England,
its influence on kingship was more explicit than was the custom
in Catholic Europe. The note of reverence for the Throne, which
is associated with the name of Dr Laud, suggested the attitude
exhibited towards the Prince by Lutheran Consistories. In a
sense it was these Lutheran affinities that aroused the intense
dislike of those who traced their own descent to Knox or
Calvin. In spite of King Charles' very careful foreign policy,

were still valued for the fighting quality of their opposition to the Roman system. In a more homely fashion, the Calvinist households were regarded as a preservative. Young men who went to France would note the places in which they could stay with "one of the Religion". As a matter of duty, the visitor would attend the preaching at the new Temple which Salomon de Brosse had built at Charenton; the English layman (though not always the English cleric) encouraged attendance at Calvinist services when abroad. As a result, Lutheranism meant very little, and the special position of Gustavus Adolphus as a Lutheran was not appreciated. The political outlook of a Lutheran and Imperialist prince seemed inexplicable and, when grasped, appeared hardly more sympathetic than that of a Roman Catholic. In general, it may be said that throughout the first half of the seventeenth century the English occupied with such affairs tended to see the Protestant Cause in Europe in the light of their fragmentary knowledge of the Calvinists.

It does not appear that the travellers, or, indeed, even the envoys, gained any serious knowledge of the political development of the European monarchies or of their legal systems. Studies such as these were what Lord Chesterfield would map out for Philip Stanhope. In another field the secular influence of France, which would endure among the English ruling classes until the French Revolution, was by this time manifest. It can be traced in architecture, decoration and a taste for the amenities. It was, as yet, a question of what men admired rather than what they would wish to transplant; the streams and waters of the Luxembourg, the shady groves; the fountains in their marble basins between the mulberry avenues of the private garden of the Hôtel de Richelieu; the cabinets of ivory and porcelain and coral. French practices in the art of horsemanship were accepted as standard, as were the customs then governing the code of the duel.

It is worth noting that the foreign influences which were held to characterise the French Queen's life in England did not, for the most part, come from her own country. Thus, an Italian inspiration lay behind that contrivance of the masque, which Queen Henrietta loved. The palaces and chariots and cloud machines, the effect of moonrise and of the sun's rays, were the fruit of Florentine experience and of the manipulation of the engines and vessels long in use at the Gonzaga Court of

Mantua. In another field it is difficult to over-estimate the effect of Vandyck's work after he settled in London in 1632. There were constant echoes of his Genoese period. In a sense, he imposed his flattering conception, delicate and Mediterranean in its inspiration, on the ladies and youths of the Stuart Court. The ancestry of his English sitters is well known to us, and also their, in many cases, robust inheritance. It is hard to believe that he did not attribute to them an unreal fragility. Surely there was a tendency to depict them in terms of their Queen's qualities.

It was those elements in the Caroline world which were national that proved most durable; the King's attitude to his Anglican Faith; a realisation of the presence of the King's enemies within the nation, which was to become a Tory legacy; the beginning of the parson-squire relationship; the idea of a Civil Service which could, even if in fact it did not, survive changes of government. And in the sphere of personal relations there was the rapid growth of the idea of privacy; that form of intimacy which made the Court the private circle of the sovereigns and the sense of the private life of individual families. The letters of Dorothy Osborne, who was growing up during these years, reflect this new development.

In public life a slow change-over was now taking place from official to private patronage. The gentleman of leisure would for the first time have his dependants. This had developed gradually throughout the century, since the last of the great households disappeared in the Essex Rising. The antiquary and the man of curious knowledge were emerging; Sir William Camden was one of the King's younger contemporaries. Unlike the verse of the Caroline poets, which normally circulated in manuscript, historical and antiquarian collections remained buried until the date of publication. Thus, Spelman's *History of Sacrilege* and Dodsworth's collections of the *Monasticon*, although compiled in these years, were not published until much later. In every field there was a broadening of the scope of interest; this was the time of John Aubrey's boyhood, and that of the others who would later found the Royal Society.

The years before the Civil Wars saw the development of a lateral movement in the general strata of the English social scene. Country-house visiting for purposes of pleasure, as described in the Verney Letters and in George Garrard's

The enormous development of the coal trade had been manifest now for some twenty years, and coal was used in the growing industries. These latter, and especially the soap-boiling and alum trades, were associated with those monopolies which Laud opposed. The price levels, which had been rising steadily, tended to fall towards the end of this decade. There was a sharp decline in the prosperity of the cloth trade in the west of England.

In the present study, an examination of the reign and of the characters of the King and Queen, is followed by a survey of the European scene as viewed from England, and of the rival foreign policies within the kingdom. The work of the Queen of Bohemia, the King's only sister, and that of Laud and Strafford, are placed within the setting of a foreign and domestic policy. The religious and educational trends are then discussed, and aspects of the idea of property are investigated; an attempt is made to describe their impact on the different income levels. A study of the Royal Navy suggests the degree to which a Civil Service, or, indeed, a class of professional officer, had as yet crystallised. Some of these problems have been touched on in the Ford Lectures, delivered in 1945 and printed as *The Social Structure of Caroline England*.

The present study ends with the outbreak of hostilities, and will be followed by another book on *The Genesis of the Civil Wars*, which will examine the various forces that brought about the liquidation of the Caroline world. The complex situation in both Ireland and Scotland in the years before the conflict will be studied in the later volume. The development of life in Wales in the first half of the seventeenth century has a unitary character. It was little affected by James I or by Charles I in the years of peace. There were no marked external changes in the period between the failure of the Essex Rising in 1601 and the raising of the levies for the Civil War. Welsh affairs, also, are therefore reserved for later treatment. The working of Conciliar Government and of the Prerogative Courts can best be seen in the light of the views of their supporters and opponents. They are therefore linked with the development of the parliamentary opposition and of the religious opposition, in so far as this was political, which will both be considered in the next book as part of an attempt to analyse the situation which developed in the years between 1642 and the King's death.

The majority of the manuscript sources mentioned in *The Jacobean Age* have also been used for the present volume, and I am happy to repeat here the grateful acknowledgments already made. In respect to early Catholic libraries, I express my gratitude to Lady Agnes Eyston for an opportunity to study the seventeenth-century volumes at East Hendred, and to the trustees of the Mapledurham Estate for a similar opportunity in regard to the Blount library at Mapledurham House. I am grateful to the Marquess of Lothian for permission to make a further study of the Coke MSS. in his possession, and for enabling me to visit Breedon Church, and to Mr W. A. Pantin for the opportunity given to study seventeenth-century Oxford inventories in the Bodleian Library, and for showing me the monuments at Lydiard Tregoze. I would wish especially to thank the Curator of the Gallery in the Ducal Palace at Mantua. My thanks are also due to the Rev. Geoffrey Soden, to Dr F. Sherwood Taylor, and to the late Dr Wilhelm Schenk, whose recent death is a grave loss to students of the early Caroline period.

Finally, my brother Gervase has worked out the whole book with me and has helped me in every section.

DAVID MATHEW

WOBURN SQUARE.
June, 1938.
MOMBASA.
October, 1949.

CHAPTER I

INTRODUCTION

A STRANGE tranquillity marks that period of the reign of Charles I before his personal government failed under the strain and the nation slid into the Civil Wars. The first three years from his accession in 1625 were overshadowed by the personality of the Duke of Buckingham, to whom his reticent sovereign gave that affectionate and in time spontaneous confidence which it was not in his nature to bestow again. But Buckingham was a legacy from the lavish Jacobean world, and the characteristics of the early Carolines did not come clear until King Charles and Queen Henrietta had emerged from the many entangling commitments into which the favourite minister had led his sovereign.

To the Caroline Age belongs the Laudian experiment, Wentworth and the King's government; a certain religious temper in the Anglican Church and a variety of social forms; an outlook on life which was to characterise both Falkland and Thomas Browne; a literary tradition which was highly individual and separate; the approach of Vandyck and Le Sueur and various architectural forms; a transient Court Catholicism and, much more permanent, the spirit behind Maryland. In the country, and among the squires and farmers, a way of life inherited from Elizabethan times went on unaltered. The middle classes in the towns moved forward with an even and non-political development; for before and during the Civil Wars England was filled with neutral citizens. The reactions of the town workers are necessarily very difficult to determine. In the country the labourers seem to have remained unmoved until the landlords started to recruit them. Puritanism and the political implications, which were inseparable from its traditions, had of course a great significance. It coexisted with the Caroline spirit, and was its solvent.

It is most difficult to define the limits of any period, but there is a certain unity attaching to the short stream of years between the death of Buckingham and the outbreak of the Civil War.

So far as the King's life was concerned, the containing dates would seem to be 23 August 1628, and 22 August 1642. The first of these dates is that of the assassination of the Duke of Buckingham, who was at once his chief minister and the sole confidante of his solitary spirit, and the second marks that setting up of the royal standard at Nottingham which declared the opening of the wars.

From a constitutional point of view, a special character belongs to the eleven years of the King's rule in which no recourse was had to the Lords and Commons between the dissolution of the third Parliament of the reign on 10 March 1629, until the meeting of the Short Parliament on 13 April 1640. Two events which had a wide repercussion throughout the country as the carriers brought down the news from London were the arrest of Sir John Eliot on 23 March 1629, in consequence of his actions in the House, and the impeachment of the Earl of Strafford on 23 March 1641.

Although the actual negotiations with France and Spain were both delayed, there was for all practical purposes a state of peace with foreign powers from the time of the surrender of the Huguenots in La Rochelle some two months after the death of Buckingham. Only the possessing classes were directly affected by the constitutional struggle, but the whole nation felt that rather strained tranquillity which arose from the absence of external war. These years saw the high-water mark of the hierarchic power of the Church of England; a great archbishop's rule at Lambeth and an Anglican polity. It was a strange situation, and one which Queen Elizabeth would not have welcomed; nor was this Church power to be tolerated by the great secular oligarchy of the eighteenth century, nor yet even by the Restoration world.

At the same time, the ecclesiastical authority, which lay so heavy on the non-conformitants, lent a particular character to these years. They were the hey-day of the *Pax Anglicana*. George Herbert went to Bemerton in 1630 and Nicholas Ferrar to Little Gidding in 1625, the first year of King Charles' reign. An answer made by Ferrar in a dialogue with his tutor Augustine Lindsell at Clare Hall very perfectly reflects the spirit of the Anglican Caroline tranquillity. "Nay, Tutor," said the young Ferrar, according to the account in his brother's life, "you are to answer to God for this. Why did you commend

unto me, & made me (being so young at College, as I was) to
read the Lives of all the Holy men of old time, & Saynts of God,
the good Fathers of the Church, & of those good Men, in our
later times, even in the Church of England, the Saynts & Holy
Martyrs, was it, that I might only know the good things that
they did? & what was that to me, if you intended not, or that
I should not endeavour, to fitt & frame my life in all I could,
by the assistance of Almighty Gods good grace & Spirit, to doe
& to live as they did, as much as was in my poore power to
doe."[1]

The men whose names are most closely associated with this
devout spirit of peace died before the conflict: Herbert in 1633,
Bishop Lindsell in 1634 and Nicholas Ferrar in 1637. At the
same time, the Anglican parish life, even where the Laudian
mould was firmly set, went forward far on into the Civil War.
The Universities suffered their changes in 1643 and 1646, and
the actual ejectment of ministers in the country districts came
still later. Although Crashaw was expelled from his fellowship
at Peterhouse in 1643, it was not until 1647 that Robert
Herrick was forced to leave Dean Prior and that the community was dispersed from Little Gidding. It was only with
the King's surrender to the Scots in May 1646 that the continuity of the Caroline way of life in rural England was really
broken.

In so far as the literary tradition is concerned, certain strains
survived until the Restoration. It was only then that they gave
way to the new spirit which was under different aspects so
robust and classical. That pastoral religious world which
coexisted with the Court of Charles I by far survived it, and a
direct descent leads down from Herbert to Traherne.

If the quotation from Ferrar shows this spirit in its hey-day,
the natural term of its repose is in the *Centuries of Meditations*. "When I came", wrote Thomas Traherne, "into the
country, and being seated among silent trees and meads and
hills had all my time in mine own hands, I resolved to spend it
all, whatever it cost me, in search of happiness and to satiate
that burning thirst which Nature had enkindled in me from
my youth. In which I was so resolute, that I chose rather to live
upon ten pounds a year, and to go in leather clothed, and feed

[1] A Life of Nicholas Ferrar, from the Baker MS., printed in the *Ferrar Papers*,
ed. B. Blackstone, p. 82.

upon bread and water, so that I might have all my time clearly to myself, than to keep many thousands per annum in an estate of life where my time would be devoured in care and labour."[1]

The spirit of Traherne is marked by quiet and by a translucent moderation. The imagination lies in repose and in simplicity. "And God", he continues, "was so pleased to accept of that desire, that from that time to this I have had all things plentifully provided for me, without any care at all, my very study of felicity making me more to prosper than all the care in the whole world."

This was the century of Quietism which in England grew naturally among those who desired a retirement which the Laudian conception of Church order did not itself provide. Such Quietism would find a friendly soil in the deep belief of the Caroline churchmen and in their well-grounded resignation. The religious conceptions of all parties were singularly clear-cut, and that note of studied reasonableness which came to the Anglican Divines of the later part of the century was as yet hardly apparent. The *Laws of Ecclesiasticall Politie* was admired at Lambeth, but the country clergy of the years before the Civil Wars had not very much in common with Richard Hooker's legal and strictly Elizabethan moderation.

It is impossible to set a boundary to the spirit of any period. The simpler forms of expression (so particularly associated with the early Carolines) are seldom found until the reign was well advanced. They were overtaken, and in a sense defined, by the strange thought and vocabulary of the Independents. At the same time, the influence of the Jacobeans, with their heavy-laden imagery, is manifest in much of the writing of the time of Charles I, and especially among those who professed concern for the philosophical notions which threaded in and out of Bacon's thought.

Two quotations suggest in their different ways that secular Caroline spirit which was the counterpart to that of the divines. The first is from *Urne Burial*, a passage well known but so characteristic, which in spite of its later date breathes that atmosphere of reflection which had come to its author in the years of peace. "They made use", wrote Sir Thomas Browne, "of Musick to excite or quiet the affections of their friends, according to different harmonies. But the secret and symbolical

[1] Thomas Traherne, *Centuries of Meditations*, Third Century, No. 46.

unit was the harmonical nature of the soul; which delivered from the body, went again to enjoy the primitive harmony of heaven, from whence it first descended; which according to its progresse traced by antiquity, came down by *Canæ* and ascended by *Capricornus*."[1]

The second and less familiar example of the Caroline approach is contained in one of Viscount Conway's letters. Here there mingles the distilled philosophic process which had come down from Bacon with the beginnings of that cruder interest which was to mark the Restoration. "The Lord Chancellor, St Albans," so runs this passage, "sayth that the great leisure and want of busines, brought forth in the monkes those subtiltyes, that for theire fine spinning are like spiders webs, and fit to be swept away; mirth is oposite to seriousnes as levity is to gravity. Laughter in the face of a statesman is like a cat in my Lord Cromwell's breeches, and a paper of verses in his pocket is an abhomination like a pigge in a Jewes poke. All things in heaven and under the moone keep theire order, the starres goe not out of theirs spheares, and the elements keepe theire places."[2]

The seventeenth-century Englishman had little real interest in astrology; but there was, among those in high places in Church and State, a sense of immutable stability which could only be increased by the teaching of such doctrines as Passive Obedience and Non-resistance. The conviction of the security of the State appears marked in both Laud and Strafford. It was not in their case an instance of undue reliance upon the Prince; for it seems probable that both men possessed a clear and not altogether sympathetic view of King Charles' character. But the possibility of the interruption of the functions of the monarchy would have seemed incredible, and this applies with equal force to all the King's adherents and to a great extent to most of the members of the Opposition.

That hardening of the regalian conceptions in the Tridentine polity which had resulted in the clearer definition of the power of the Bourbon and Hapsburg monarchies can be found reflected in the English State. King Charles came naturally to those doctrines as to the extent and preservation of his Regality,

---

[1] *Urne Burial*, Chapter IV.
[2] A letter from Viscount Conway, dated 14 July 1636 (Cal. Portland MSS., vol. iii, p. 36).

which had given to King James I self-conscious pleasure. His royal duty was as manifest to the sovereign as was the impiety of those who in his later life would attempt to curtail what God had given. The enemies of the Church of England were in his eyes never free from the shadow of the guilt of sacrilege. Again, the nexus between the King and the Established Church gained an additional strength, since it arose from the essentially English character of shared responsibilities. Yet this bore heavily upon a sovereign who would have been ridden by scruple had he possessed imagination. The years after the death of Buckingham gave him in some respects a deceptive impression of his power. Across the State papers of his firm advisers he would write: "Let it be done. C. R." It was part of the tragedy of King Charles' life that later he was oppressed by his responsibilities, and then could not fulfil them.

In the political field the mark of the years between 1628 and 1640 is the practical outlook of the men who, to so great an extent, controlled the royal policies. There was nothing visionary about either Laud or Strafford. As far as the affairs of England were concerned, both men, and especially the Archbishop, had clearly defined and possible objectives; they were markedly without extravagance, and the churchman was limited in his imaginative grasp. The years without a Parliament were realistic in their political intention. A lack of money set the bounds to a programme which was for the most part unambitious. Laud, walking in his garden at Lambeth or sliding over in his barge to the Star Chamber or the Court, applied his unrelenting energies to the business of each day. He was always at full pressure, and his mind worked as smoothly as a piston.

The policy of Thorough, associated with Laud and Strafford, was one of short views reduced immediately to practice. A curious element is the close character of their partnership. Wentworth entered Dublin as lord deputy in July 1633, and Laud was promoted to the See of Canterbury just one month later. They were very soon so bound together that one could not politically survive the other. The enemies of both could bring down either, and they never took the slightest step to minimise the chances of disaster. A passage in a letter dealing with an Irish Committee, which had just been set up in London, indicates the *tempo* of their joint work. "But I am not to trouble that Commission", wrote Dr Laud, "with any Church affairs, but only such as either His Majesty or myself shall doubt of, if any such occur. And by this means I shall be able to make you the quicker despatch at all times of these my businesses, when they are to attend no man's leisure but my own."[1]

There is here a resemblance to the approach of Richelieu and to the servants of the great Monarchy; though to Laud's eyes the kingship which he served was bound up with certain theocratic elements. On its political side it was a more independent approach than that of the Tudor ministers, of Thomas Cromwell or even Gardiner. And with it went a sustained courage. An answer written by the Archbishop in the Tower after his fall is alive with vitality and with this quality. "For of all simulations or dissimulations, that is the basest," he declared, "when a man, for poor, temporary, fading ends, shall shift his religion or his judgment concerning it, with the time if not with the tide, as if at all times he had somewhat to seek before he would express: whereas it is most true which St Hilary speaks in matter of religion, *Non opus est intervallo aliquo inter cor et os:* 'There's no need of a distance between the heart and the mouth; as if a man were to bethink himself of some faithless ambiguity, before he would speak that which belonged to the profession of his faith.' "[2]

This was written in the leisure of imprisonment, but throughout Laud's active years there is an impression of a determined will with little taste for reconsideration and a rather dour intention to carry through an allotted quantity of administrative and financial labour. His architectural work thus represented a relief from this severity.

A memorandum of the benefactions which he intended to complete includes his plans "to build at St John's in Oxford, where I was bred up, for the good and safety of that college". Against this sentence, as in the case of most of the others in this short list, he has entered the one word "Done". There is something characteristic of the man and of the time in the achievement of so much fine stone-work. If Peterhouse Chapel so well suggests the ordered Laudian quiet, it is the Canterbury Quadrangle, with the pillars and the high frontispiece, which brings back the reign of Charles I in its full glory. The statues

[1] Laud's *Works*, vol. vii, p. 66.   [2] *Ibid.*, vol. vi, pt. i, p. 84.

by Hubert Le Sueur, so often reduplicated, are truly characteristic of a stereotyped magnificence.

A certain quality of grandeur based on seventeenth-century
conceptions of the dignity of kingship is characteristic of what
may be called the Court architecture of these years. There was
relatively little private building in the grand manner. Hatfield
and Audley End and the Jacobean parts of Wilton had come
down from the previous reign, and their palatial dimensions
were now outmoded. It is rather the piazza at Covent Garden
and certain college quadrangles, official architecture in fact,
that is associated with the early Carolines. Statues of the
sovereign, anticipating those which were to be cast in later
years in honour of Louis XIV, formed an accustomed element
in this decoration.

This is very well brought out in the correspondence between
Balthasar Gerbier and Lord-Treasurer Portland, who was
arranging for statuary at Roehampton House. After a visit to
Roehampton "to settle a place for *Carolus Magnus*", during
which an arrangement was suggested for the garden calculated
to make the statue appear to best advantage, certain letters
were exchanged.[1] These included instructions to the scrivener
for an agreement between the Lord Treasurer and Le Sueur
for casting a horse in brass for the figure of His Majesty. It was
stipulated that Le Sueur in making his model was to take the
advice of the King's riders of great horses for the shape and
action both of the horse and of His Majesty's figure on the
same.

Here is a well-paid—for the statue was to cost £600—and
calculated magnificence contributing to that external manifestation of the royal dignity by which King Charles set so great
a store. It is the same sense to which the canvases of Vandyck
ministered. Here we have, for the first time in English history,
the phenomenon of the fashionable painter, urbane and yielding. Sir Anthony Vandyck had gained a sensitiveness to the
requirements of his sitters. In his early days in the Archdukes'
dominions he made his own the conceptions of that rich
merchant class which desired a record that was architecturally
faithful. The portrait of the Burgomaster of Antwerp, now in
the Hermitage of Leningrad, has such a background—the
dome of the city hall rising blue into a light sky away in the

[1] State Papers, Dom. Charles I, clviii, 48, 54 and 54, 1.

distance far beyond the figure by the table, with its onyx-
headed paper-weight and the vague suggested statuary.

Yet Vandyck's success during his nine years in England,
between 1632 and his death in 1641, was to come from a
familiarity with the desires of the ladies of the Court, which
was at once easy and penetrating. In this setting it was not so
much King Charles' taste as that of his consort which was to be
the deciding factor. Surely the favourite painter must have
seized very perfectly the texture and the limits of the Queen's
imaginative vision.

In this connection his portrait of Paola Adorno in the Frick
Museum has an especial interest, representing, as it seems to do,
the Vandyck conception at its farthest limits. It is true that the
costume, the nine rows of gold braid on the white satin, the
curling golden pattern on the wide falling sleeves, and the light
cap sewn with diamonds, suggest the Genoese patriciate rather
than a Stuart background. But in this painting of Donna Paola
the clear awareness and the pure colour, and above all that
small, sophisticated, regal head, bring back the Court ideal of
the mid-century and, very probably, the type of character that
Henriette Marie aspired to be. The Vandyck approach represented an amalgam of magnificence lightened by sophistication;
it was easy and expensive, and gave instant pleasure.

To this long line of the Vandyck women from the first
portraits of Queen Henrietta to that of Lady Clanbrassil with
the trailing caught-up draperies, there was a literary counterpart which in effect appealed to those conceptions which these
paintings satisfied. Much more than Edmund Waller, so sympathetic to the Court taste, it was perhaps John Cleveland who
reflected most completely that world of the royal circle with its
simple classical allusions and the rather unspontaneous gaiety.
In *Mark Anthony* the spirit of that Court life lies mirrored: the
circumscribed elegance; the theme to which convention led
them; the tended and idyllic measures.

> "Wanting a glass to plate her amber tresses.
> Which like a bracelet rich decked my arm,
> Gawdier than Juno wears when as she graces
> Jove with embraces more stately than warm;
> Then did she peep in mine
> Eyes humour chrystalline
> I in her eyes was seen,

> As if we one had been,
> Never Mark Anthony
> Dallied more wantonly
> With the fair Egyptian Queen."

This line of appreciation went in Queen Henrietta's case with a gaiety which was conscious and innocent, and a rather careful and regal virtue. But this was no defence before the Puritans. Nor was it of value to recommend the foreign consort to the country gentry and the merchants, whether Royalist or Parliamentarian.

Any introductory consideration of this period must include a brief discussion of the wife whom King Charles so deeply loved. Beyond her trammelled frivolity there lay a French sense of the royal autocracy, which was reinforced by Austrian values. She was the first and only English queen to inherit in a near degree the blood of the House of Austria. The scene against which she moved through the peaceful years was lavish and mannered and pastoral. All her portraits contrive to indicate a desire for stateliness and a sense of carriage. She was capable of a driving, fragile energy. It was only the coming storm which would reveal her lucid and narrow understanding and her hard and brittle mind. One is left principally with three impressions— the directness; the ignorance; the diamond quality.

The Queen's political action has been examined and re-examined, but it is not this that was significant. Her knowledge, even of the English language, was never adequate, and her interventions seem always guided by a very rigid opportunism. She had nothing towards which to polarise the swinging needle of her husband's mind. In the calm years King Charles' line was fairly constant, but in a crisis his hesitant decisions were accustomed to slip free of all advisers. It was rather in the social field that Queen Henrietta's rôle had more importance.

With women she made a few friendships held to with tenacity, while she seems to have reserved her intimate affections for her French ladies, Mesdames de Motteville and St George, and at one stage for the Countess of Carlisle. But for the gentlemen of the Court, and for those who accepted this new influence, she set a fashion reflected in the writing of the period which was amenable to a stylised form of elaborated gallantry. She exercised a certain transient fascination over those who would have found themselves at home in the Restoration Court.

It was perhaps this that riled the Puritans, together with her
uninquiring virtue. Unlike her husband and so many of his
subjects, she was incapable of moral indignation. The dis-
couragement of wits and libertines formed no part of that high
tradition of the Court of France and Navarre. The Queen had
no concern for the moral reputation of other people, and her
own was protected by the courtiers' prudence and by her own
imperious chastity.

Each element in the situation must have struck the contemporary English observer as exotic and in all respects
unhealthy. It was so remote from the accustomed life in
England which was both rooted and acquisitive. This new
mode was carried forward in that idiom which Habington
attempted to acclimatise.

> "When I survey the bright
>   Celestial sphere;
> So rich with jewels hung, that Night
> Doth like an Ethiop bride appear."[1]

The world of Queen Henrietta's Court vanished completely.
It had something of the character of a masque with its formal
movements. It had no touch with common life, and it was
fitting that it should have ended in the loyal city in the tamed
and unreal setting of the Merton Grove.

[1] From Habington's *Nox Nocti Indicat Scientiam.*

CHAPTER II

THE KING AND THE QUEEN

THE character of Charles I was singularly ill-adapted to the growth of that hearty popularity which had been of a great, though over-rated, assistance to the House of Tudor. The Elizabethan legend appears in sharp contrast with that of the Royal Martyr, which in its final analysis was cold and tragic. It was hard, not only for the mass of his subjects, but also for his courtiers, to grasp the workings of their sovereign's mind. Charles I appears always to have been burdened by the responsibilities of kingship, and these were never freed from their religious implications. It is not unreasonable to suggest that King Charles was such an isolated figure just because he considered that this isolation was divinely ordained. He was a crowned and an anointed King, and this was the standard by which he would judge his royal actions.

It seems probable that it was this factor in his outlook which led King Charles to accept all men into his service. He must admit that all men might return to their bounden duty, and give him that obedience which was so manifestly his right. Similarly, his duty to the Commonwealth forbade him to move from his course to save a servant. It was the Archbishop of York who assuaged his conscience when he was troubled about the sacrifice of Strafford. A strange belief in the efficacy of his actions as a sovereign was one of the most potent of the influences that led King Charles forward from stage to stage.

Different interpretations are placed on the effect produced upon the King by Buckingham's murder. There seems good reason to suppose that with his death he lost something of his power of developing an intimate relationship. His spontaneous and unhampered confidence was, perhaps, never again given to any man. His counsellors were henceforward to be aware of a certain cold and official character which lay at the core of the most proven friendship. This is especially notable in the case of Laud. The King in certain respects leant much upon the Primate whom he had created. He was grateful to God for placing at his side such a strong and gifted coadjutor. But after the Archbishop's imprisonment and when he could no longer fulfil the duties of his high office, he seems to have slipped quietly from his sovereign's memory. The case of Strafford was not dissimilar. And here there came into play King Charles' tenacious and royal remembrance. Everything alleged to the disadvantage of his ministers would lodge in that considering and retentive mind. He remembered all those who had brought down the Duke of Buckingham, and before thirty his capacity for confidence was atrophied. He was the King and must receive them all, his courtiers and councillors. In a sense they must all equally be the objects of his concern and of that reserved religious service which his Coronation Oaths had bound upon him.

He was not so much disillusioned as unexpectant, and other things disturbed him besides a lack of loyalty. No great reward could surely be expected for the fulfilment of a simple duty. All those with whom he came in contact were his subjects, though they might be recalcitrant. That great position which he held from God did not permit him to have supporters. This facet of his outlook was notable in his later years, when he would not admit that men by supporting him had gained a claim to be rewarded, and his mind stretched out to consider those with whom his own followers were contesting. He could not have had that realist and constricted outlook of the Hanoverians; he could have led no party of King's Friends.

From one point of view those many interviews when King Charles was a prisoner of the Army or the Scots were the explorations of a tenacious mind into the problems of men's allegiance. He was perfectly inconsiderate and sincere as he pursued through life his rigid doctrine. He did not admit that he could lose his claim to his subjects' service. There is no evidence that he considered that there could be another loyalty than that which bound men to the anointed King.

Charles I would bestow peerages and marks of favour with a graciousness which was in effect and manner stereotyped. The low and pleasant voice captured the hearer. He had almost every gift of royalty; but his mind was far away. That memory and the courteous attention were at his subjects' service, it was his confidence that remained unanchored. But during his middle years these traits had not come so clear. In the decade without a Parliament his enemies lay off. It was with the impeachment of Strafford that they gathered again.

King Charles had reticence and a wide tolerance of social types. He could put up with almost any collaborator who would do him service, and he had that grave and regal courtesy which almost concealed his own indifference. In Strafford and in Laud he found two ministers who both had come to hold his own exalted view of kingship. It was principally this factor that led him to promote and for a period to maintain them. It is not realised that his support was proof against the fact that both men believed in a theory of sovereignty while having a rather weak esteem for the reigning monarch. This circumstance did not deter King Charles I, who was immune from the vagaries of men's affection.

He was sensitive to the reactions of those about him, but he noticed rather than responded to them. He had given all he had to give to Buckingham. In other respects, too, he was separated from his courtiers. The ordered piety and the fastidiousness which meant so much to him kept at a distance all those who frequented his father's Court. King Charles was singularly proof against the growth of intimacy. It was not only the continual dignity which would not be put by. It was rather the perfection of his manner; the quiet gait; the entrances which held so much of majesty; that grace so restrained and yet so sumptuous; the angle at which he held his silver cane.

He had that taste for ornament which Vandyck valued, the occasional diamond and the Mechlin lace. In general, his taste was sure but too impeccable. With grave attention he would examine the cabinets and the range of pictures. Unlike the *Grand Monarque* he had not the surroundings which would enable him to be Olympian, neither did he possess his garish sense of theatre. It was rather to Italian than to French models that his feeling led him. Inigo Jones contrived the setting within which the Court life played. It was reminiscent of Vicenza in its scale and pattern, and of the Basilica Palladiana in that city with those tall colonnaded windows and the wide arcade. There was a desire for balance and for moderation. The courtiers, used to heartier times, could not but dislike their King's preoccupation with that perfection of form which the *Seicento* was to admit so easily.

HENRIETTA MARIA

From a painting ascribed to Gerard Honthorst in the National
Portrait Gallery

Yet King Charles himself was very insular. It was only the setting which was rather foreign. Travel he disliked, and his one experience on his Spanish journey had left him with a lasting distaste for continental influences. He was both withdrawn and incurious. He had none of his father's admiration for the Courts of Europe. Only his mastering sense of obligation compelled him to receive and maintain in England Marie de Médicis, the Queen's mother. His agents would bring him cameos, and the crates of pictures would arrive from Italy and from Flanders to adorn his galleries; but these were the appurtenances of his regality. They were fit ornaments for the Crown of England.

There was, however, no way in which the King was more profoundly national than in his outlook on religion. He had a desire for prayer such as his father does not seem to have experienced, and his devotional observances chimed well with a decorous and moderate ceremonial. He truly loved the Church of England. The mental climate of the Laudian tradition, which derived from Andrewes, was that in which he felt at home. A religious faith and sense of obligation both reinforced this deep attachment. His nature was at once tempered and obdurate. He was singularly secure in his own certitudes. The King sat through the great sermons which Dr Laud made in the royal presence. A strengthening virtue was imparted by these deep, cool expositions.

"For though there be many 'pillars'," declared the Bishop of Bath and Wells at the opening of the King's first Parliament, "yet there is but *unus* Rex, one King, one great and centre pillar; and all the rest in a kingdom do but 'bear up' under and about him."[1] "And indeed", he was to hear on a later day, "moral justice alone cannot possibly be enough for a Christian King. Religious and pious 'justice' must come in, too. He must take care for the souls, as well as for the bodies and goods, of his people."[2] Then, leaving the question of the sovereign's duties, the carefully provoked sentences would turn upon the Church of Rome, to which the King had never felt attraction.

"And now", said Dr Laud, "I cannot but wonder what-word Saint Paul, were he now alive, would use to call back 'unity' into dismembered Christendom. For my part, death were easier to me, than it is to see and consider the face of the Church of

---

[1] Sermon for King Charles' first Parliament (Laud's *Works*, vol. i, p. 104).
[2] Sermon for King Charles' Inauguration (*ibid.*, vol. i, p. 205).

Christ scratched and torn till it bleeds in every part, as it doth to-day; and the 'Coat of Christ', which was once spared 'by soldiers because it was seamless', rent every way, and which is the misery of it, by the hand of the priests: and the Pope, which Bellarmine hath put into the definition of the Church, that there might be one ministerial head to keep all in unity, is as great as any, if not the greatest, cause of divided Christianity."[1] As far as Rome was concerned, this very succinctly gives the King's own outlook.

At the same time he was sharply divided from the Puritans by his high sacramental theology. He came easily to the Laudian view. A prayer, preserved among the Archbishop of Canterbury's private devotions, will indicate King Charles' doctrine. It was composed for recitation before the reception of the sacrament. "O Lord God," it runs, "how I receive the Body and Blood of my most blessed Saviour Jesus Christ: the price of my redemption, is the very wonder of my soul, yet my most firm and constant belief upon the words of my Saviour. At this time they are graciously tendered to me and my faith: Lord make me a worthy receiver, and be unto me as He hath said. Amen."[2] This description of his approach may serve to explain how it was that the King always remained so far immune from the influence of the Bishop of Mende or the Queen's Capuchins, and so aloof from his convert courtiers. Conscious of his office, he would turn naturally and rather impersonally to his Fathers in God. The calm Anglican phrasing came to him as reassuring.

In this matter of religion he would not admit discussion. After all, King Charles I was almost thirty when he first turned to his wife with that affection which was to burn so steadily. Reserved and chaste, he was singularly unmoved by women. It was not within Queen Henrietta's range to influence him in questions of divinity. He had his duty as a sovereign, which he did not dare neglect, and his ministers like Portland, Laud and Strafford. The management of the Court, its *tempo* and its fostered sympathies, he left to his young Queen. A touch of melancholy, which was both dignified and a trifle uxorious, had settled down on him. With the years he turned increas-

---

[1] Sermon before King Charles' third Parliament (Laud's *Works*, vol. i, pp. 105–6).

[2] Portion of the prayer "Eucharistia" (*ibid.*, vol. iii, p. 75).

ingly to lean upon this marital affection and to enjoy the family life which gave him peace. For the rest he was detached and acquiescent; the Queen would bring around her the courtiers whom she chose.

King Charles was thus doubly insulated from his English subjects, and this fact explains why the Cavalier legend so seldom traced its roots to those who had been in his peace-time service. This sovereign's personality was hardly known, and he affected his people very little except through the enactments to which he gave assent. Some illustrations will serve to indicate how remote was the sentiment of the Stuart Court from that of the mass of seventeenth-century Englishmen.

There was about the Queen's circle an atmosphere of softness which was bound to prove repellent to the King's robust supporters. It is perhaps in the correspondence of Lord Goring, Her Majesty's Master of the Horse, that this quality appears most charged with a saccharine and skilful courtesy. Two letters sent to Sir John Coke, who was at the time in attendance upon the King as Secretary, will give the character of this approach. "All I can say from hence", wrote Goring from Greenwich where he was in waiting upon the Queen," is that, since our blessed Master left our incomparable Mistress, she is in sad extremity which we that are of little other use must strive to divert, though never hope to expel till that happy return. And so," he concluded, "it being very late and I very very weary I humbly rest your faithfullest humblest servant, noble sir, Goring."[1] Such words were surely as alien to the older Cavaliers as they would be to the lords of the Opposition.

Within a few weeks a second letter was composed in the same vein. "Yesterday", began the Master of the Horse on this occasion, "I presumed to give you [the Secretary of State] thanks for the infinite honour you have done me in giving me the opportunity to make so many inestimable presents to the Queen my Mistress from His most excellent Majesty, my most gracious blessed Master, whereof we had no small need considering how disconsolate she hath been."[2]

It was, perhaps, the playfulness of such subservience which

[1] Letter from Lord Goring to Sir John Coke, dated at Greenwich 18 May 1633 (Cal. Coke MSS., vol. ii, p. 10).

[2] Letter from the same to the same, dated at Greenwich 3 June 1633 (ibid., vol. ii, p. 16).

made this affectation so distasteful to the great squires of the Country Party. With minute verbal workmanship much trivial information was conveyed about the Queen's new preferences: her "very pleasant change of air" at Richmond; her liking for strawberries and certain fish; her custom of an afternoon siesta. And on the frame there was embroidered the detail of her Catholic piety, which Goring would approach with reverent courtesy. "May she be pleased", he wrote of the Queen in the same summer, "not to use her needle so much as of late she hath done, which gives her overmuch leisure to muse, and whereof I said I would complain by you Sir, to His Majesty, had she not feed me to the contrary with the coronation piece of gold."[1] It was a quiet and placid flattery, partly French and wholly mannered. The carp rose to the still surface.

The peculiar airlessness of the Court in its inner circles seems in part due to the Queen's calculated charm and to her virtue. The former quality attracted men of gallantry who remained anchored to her, while her devotion to the King and her light and prickly dignity rendered their approaches in time insipid. She had certain women friends, whom she cherished warmly; but they were appanages to her male admirers.

Her French background had been in almost all respects so very different. With a nice and perfect dignity and sense of honour, the system of the French Court did not require, nor indeed comprehend, the domesticity which King Charles loved. The description of Madame de Chevreuse given in the *Memoirs* of Cardinal de Retz, however objectively unreliable, suggests a very different world from that in which the Stuart King moved, so careful and inhibited. "Her being devoted to her passion," writes the Cardinal of this first great friend of Queen Henrietta's, "in which she might be called constant though she changed objects, did not hinder but that the least thing diverted her from it: but she came always to it again with transports that made her distractions appear agreeable. No person was ever less attentive to danger, and never woman had a greater contempt for what is called scruple and duty."[2] This is the spirit of the *Mémoires du Comte de Grammont*; it is hardly translatable into King Charles' idiom.

[1] Letter from Lord Goring to Sir John Coke, dated at Greenwich 22 June 1633 (Cal. Coke MSS., vol. ii, p. 22).
[2] *Memoirs of the Cardinal de Retz*, vol. i, p. 150.

In every way the *tempo* of life in England was quite distinct.
The mortal verbal contests, which in London were confined to,
or disguised as, theology, were personal in her own country. In
this connection the well-known opening sentence of de Retz's
account of Mazarin could surely never have been penned in a
Court grouping on which convention had begun to weigh so
heavily. Fortified by a social and theocratic solidarity, the
bishops of the Church of England thundered and slumbered
beneath an angel roof. Already there were the things one could
not say. De Retz stood out in vivid contrast. "Cardinal Mazarin's character", so runs the passage. "was quite the reverse.
His extraction was mean and his childhood infamous."[1] The
Coadjutor of Paris and the Queen both had a French-Italian
mixture of descent. The possibility of such phrasing throws a
light upon the young Henrietta's hot, and natural, and long,
resentments.

At the same time the Queen of England came from a Court
which had a sense of hierarchy, more graded, more tedious and
more elegant than that to which the Stuarts could aspire. A
quotation from St Francis of Sales will serve to indicate the
traditional element in that political environment. "And because", wrote the Bishop of Geneva in an account of the Duke
of Mercœur's funeral, "my father, grandfather and great grandfather had been brought up pages to the most illustrious princes
of Martigues her [Marie of Luxembourg, Duchess of Mercœur's]
father and his predecessors, she regarded me as an hereditary
servant of her house; and made choice of me to preach the
funeral sermon in that great celebration, where there were not
only several cardinals and prelates, but a number of princes
also, princesses, marshals of France, knights of the Order [of the
Saint Esprit] and even the Court of Parliament in a body."[2]
This is an outlook which in its varied elements would seem to
link Alexander of Parma with the *Roi Soleil*. It suggests the
heavy-weighted texture of the Tridentine world, at once feudal
and military and not oligarchic. The support for the Crown
was singularly close and unquestioning, except for spasms of
rebellion. The France of the Great Monarchy was coming to
its birth.

A strict religious observance, and the practice of spiritual

[1] *Ibid.* vol. i, p. 66.
[2] Preface to the *Treatise on the Love of God*, ed. Mackey, p. 13.

guidance and direction, bore down upon the *Enfants de France*. St Francis' influence was close in to the French Court as Bossuet's was to be. The note of sensitive feeling, very warm and flowing, which marked Queen Henrietta's pilgrimage to the gallows tree at Tyburn thus traces itself to Monsieur de Génève. His *Philothea* came from a Catholic family of the League, and few spiritual writers have possessed such a wide, partial, faint discipleship.

It is noticeable that the Queen was on the whole not unsuccessful with Archbishop Laud. She never failed to treat him as a very serious politico-religious figure, and she invested him with the prerogatives of the high prelates of the Church of France. It was, in fact, less difficult for the Queen to meet the King in regard to his friends than it was for her husband to be at ease in his wife's circle. Even when times were calmest, Charles I does not seem to have expected much. With his outward hesitancy and his weak sense of humour, he was more at ease with the strongest characters, such as Strafford, whom he never liked, or Dr Laud.

There is little evidence that King Charles possessed imagination. He would respond to the Archbishop's heavy sallies, and his written comment on a proposal made in the Primate's report on the province of Canterbury for 1633 makes a deep impression. In these lines the sovereign's readiness for platitude and his graven sense of duty are alike so manifest. The sentences were added in response to Dr Laud's suggestion that the dark corners of the diocese should be lit by worthy ministers. "C.R.", so runs the royal note, "if there be Dark Corners in this Dioces, it were fitt a true Light should Illuminat it: and not this that is falce and uncertain."[1]

The King was very sure in his convictions. It was his trust in persons that was imperfect, and it was for this reason that he lacked the power to arouse the confidence of his own councillors. An entry in Laud's Diary, made in 1636 at the height of the Archbishop's favour, will show the sense of insecurity that remained in the nearest of the King's supporters. "*An.* 1636. Oct. 14.", the entry runs, "I dreamed marvellously that the King was offended with me, and would cast me off, and tell me no cause why."[2] This is just the record of a dream, but it is the comment which proves revealing. "*Avertat Deus.* For cause I

---

[1] Laud's *Works*, vol. v, pt. ii, p. 320.   [2] Diary, *ibid.*, vol. iii. p. 227.

have given none." All those who came to him, once Buckingham was dead, would feel this except his wife. It was even the case with his nephew Rupert.

Under these circumstances one of Lord Goring's postscripts sounds menacingly through the sugared phrases. The courtier was speaking of the King's first Scottish journey, which had taken place in 1633 at the time of the earlier sequence of letters. "The happy example Scotland hath given will", he wrote from Richmond, "be prosperous, I doubt not here when the good hour comes. Never was there private family more at full peace and tranquillity than in this glorious kingdom, for we hear not of the least disorder therein from one end thereof to the other."[1]

[1] Letter from Lord Goring to Sir John Coke, dated at Richmond 2 July 1633 (Cal. Coke MSS., vol. ii, p. 242).

CHAPTER III

THE EUROPEAN SCENE

APPRECIATION of European politics in the second quarter of the seventeenth century was affected by the transfer of the storm centre to Prague and the Rhenish Palatinate and to High Germany. For more than a hundred years the rivalries of the Courts of France and Spain and the interaction of both upon the states of Italy had been a commonplace of the diplomatic scene. The English Court had never underestimated the significance of the Low Countries, and a long life-time had passed since the establishment of the United Provinces under the general guidance of the House of Orange.

In comparison with the close knowledge of France and the Low Countries and Italy, the position in the German lands was very little understood in England. The shifting mosaic of rival princes was confused and indistinct, and very hard to visualise. English envoys had long studied the French and Spanish policies, but the Imperial Court at Prague was shadowy, especially during the reigns of the last two quiescent Emperors of the elder line of the Austrian Hapsburgs, Rudolf II and Matthias. On the death of the latter in 1619 the imperial crown had passed to the Archduke Ferdinand of Styria. The new ruler, Ferdinand II, was the son of the Archduke Charles, who had sought the hand of Queen Elizabeth at the beginning of her reign. He was a true prince of the Counter-Reformation, King of Hungary in so far as the Crown lands of St Stephen had not been conquered by the Turks, elective King of Bohemia, and soveriegn of the hereditary duchies of the House of Austria. With England he had no personal contact, interest or sympathy. His only link with English politics was as a cause of the misfortunes of the Palatine family.

There is always a temptation to detect in this earlier period the outline of that eighteenth-century Germany of the princes which did not, in fact, take shape until the early part of the reign of Louis XIV. The English merchants went to the Han-

seatic cities; but there was no contact between England and
the smaller German dynasties; no envoys; no traders; no casual
travellers. It is true that Scottish and Irish soldiers of fortune
served abroad in considerable numbers, but, except in the case
of a few Lowland officers, no news of their experiences came
back to London.[1] Low Germany, in fact, was unimaginable. In
England there was no picture of that sullen land, or of the
wooden northern cities in the snow, Berlin or Wolfenbüttel.

As far as literary sources are concerned, a certain impression
of the German borderlands had been conveyed by *Coryat's
Crudities*, a travel book published in 1611. Against this must be
remembered the limited circulation of the work, which in any
case only dealt with a single journey from Strasbourg to
Dusseldorf, and thence through "Cleveland" into the Dutch
Provinces. Thomas Coryate's few details about the country-side
are vivid: the walled towns guarded against bandits; the
halberdiers before the gates of Durlach; the chestnut trees and
the elm-shaded roads; the arched wooden bridge across the
Neckar[2]; the vineyards of the Moselle country.

The impression of the cities is less distinct, for the writer
spreads elaborate description. At Heidelberg he celebrates the
façade of the new palace, and the effigies in milk-white alabaster
with gilded armour in the chapel of the Electoral House. The
concentration upon Heidelberg in *Coryat's Crudities*[3] is perhaps
related to the fact that the year before the book was printed
King James' daughter had set out for her new capital. In
England it was, in consequence, the one town that was well
known in Western Germany. There seems to have been no
contact between Charles I and his German relatives on his
mother's side, the Mecklenburg and Holstein princes, but his
only sister, Elizabeth, had been married since 1610 to Frederick
V, Elector Palatine.

This was a marriage which was held to accord with what the
politically vocal section of English life regarded as the Elizabethan tradition. It was the first occasion on which an English
princess had formed an alliance with the Protestant continental

---

[1] There were also a few English soldiers of fortune. Sydenham Poyntz was
perhaps the most remarkable, but he did not return to England until 1645. *The
Relation of Sydnam Poyntz* was not printed until 1908.

[2] *Coryat's Crudities*, vol. ii, pp. 205-7. Durlach is called "Turlowe" in Coryate's
narrative.

[3] Coryate, *op. cit.*, vol. ii, pp. 207-30.

system; it was also popular as against the Spanish marriage which James I tried to achieve, and the French marriage which he actually did achieve, for his eldest son.

It was, perhaps, considered less as a German association than as a compact with that Calvinist world in Western Europe which was headed by the bridegroom's uncles, Maurice and Frederick Henry, successive Princes of Orange and the Duke of Bouillon. Among the Elector Palatine's first cousins was Charlotte de la Tremouille, who, as Countess of Derby, was responsible for the defence of Lathom House, and the future Maréchal de Turenne. This *bloc* was bound together by a Calvinism which was French in its inspiration, and used that language as a vehicle. At Heidelberg French was the court language; the Electress Palatine never learned German. It was an element in the situation that the feeling in England for the unity of the Reformed Religion looked always towards Geneva, to the faith of Knox and Coligny and William the Silent.[1] To those trained under the old Queen, the Princess Elizabeth and her husband were associated with a cause which was both practicable and glorious. Throughout her hard career the Queen of Bohemia, as she would become, was seen in England as a defender of Western rather than German Protestantism, and as an anti-Spanish rather than an anti-Austrian champion.

These points are set out in some detail because it does not appear that there was at that time any real understanding in England of German policy as such. No English envoys were accredited to the Electoral Courts of Dresden and Berlin, or to the Ducal Court of Munich. The lesser princes were known in London as mere names and titles barely decipherable. In this connection S. R. Gardiner has made no allowance for the two planes of knowledge—the immediate Stuart comprehension of the policies pursued in Paris or the Hague, and the ignorance of what lay beyond the Rhine.

As a background to the situation in King Charles' reign the

---

[1] An interesting comment on this point of view is made by Thomas Coryate, himself a beneficed clergyman. In regard to the Elector Palatine he wrote: "Hee was a singular nutritius and foster-father of the Church. For hee professed the same reformed Religion that wee dooe in England". But in reference to Strasbourg he has this note: "The present religion professed among them is not altogether conformable unto ours in England. For they embrace the Lutheran doctrine, wherein they differ something from our Church of England" (Coryate, *op. cit.*, vol. ii, pp. 194 and 226).

career of the Elector and Electress Palatine should be set down. In 1619, after a period of negotiation, Frederick V accepted the Crown of Bohemia offered him by the Protestant nobles. This was the signal for the beginning of the Thirty Years War, but within eighteen months the new sovereigns were driven from Prague by the army of the Emperor Ferdinand II. Their German possessions were also occupied—the Lower Palatinate by Spanish and the Upper Palatinate by Bavarian forces. The pressure of English public opinion in favour of action on behalf of the King of Bohemia was very strong. A small English contingent under Sir Horace Vere was sent out to occupy Mannheim and Frankenthal in his name. The last fortified place in his dominions to acknowledge King Frederick's sovereignty was Frankenthal, from which the English garrison was withdrawn in April 1623. Charles I appreciated that the fact that his brother-in-law should be dispossessed of his hereditary lands was not in accordance with the dignity of the English Crown. It was his consistent intention until his own troubles overwhelmed him to obtain a partial or complete restitution of the Palatinates, first for his brother-in-law and, after the latter's death in 1632, for his eldest son, Charles Louis.

It does not appear that Charles I was interested in the Thirty Years War save in connection with this problem of the Palatinate. He had no personal experience of such distant sovereigns as the two cousins of the House of Vasa, who ruled in Sweden and Poland respectively. There is little to show that the Court of St James had either concern for, or understanding of, the fluctuating policies of the Saxon and Brandenburg Electors, or of Maximilian of Bavaria. The world of the mercenary generals, which may be held to include in their very different fashions both Mansfeld and Wallenstein, was one which Charles I could never focus. Certain aspects of their actions struck at his belief in sovereignty. The whole concept of a mercenary was unpalatable to him, and he was never at his ease with those Scottish soldiers, like Alexander Leslie, who had passed a lifetime in Swedish service.

This has a bearing on his attitude towards the campaigns of Gustavus Adolphus, which aroused so much enthusiasm among his Protestant subjects. The French support for the Swedish king, which was made explicit at the Treaty of Barwalde in February 1631, held significance and aroused suspicion. This alliance provoked Charles I to a milder variant of the profound distrust which it awakened in his sister's mind. He was at a disadvantage with no envoys to report to him from Dresden or Munich. The King of Sweden's victories and marches between his landing at Usedom on 4 July 1630, and his death on the battlefield of Lutzen on 16 November 1632, produced a deep impression in London and an almost wild enthusiasm among the inheritors of the Elizabethan policy. King Charles met the situation by allowing the Marquess of Hamilton to raise a force of seven thousand men to aid the Swedish king. Hamilton was to have a certain independent status, and his immediate allegiance to King Charles was safeguarded; it was an arrangement which would prove both decorous and ineffective.

After the death of Gustavus Adolphus, interest in England faded. In September 1634 the defeat at Nordlingen ended Swedish participation in the struggle, and in the same month the Marquess of Hamilton sailed for home. Henceforward it was a relatively simple conflict between the House of Austria and those of her German enemies who were maintained by the French Crown. Two years later an ornamental mission, under the leadership of the Earl of Arundel, was sent to the Emperor to propose the restoration of the Palatinate to the King's nephew. The fruitless journey only served to prove how remote the two Courts were from one another. This situation had resulted from many causes. In the previous generation Prague had been the imperial residence; it was to Prague that Philip Sidney went. The Hapsburgs of the Styrian line were only beginning to reoccupy Vienna very gradually. Neither the painters nor the architects had yet begun to travel to the Austrian capital. There was no polite traffic across the war-scarred German lands. Again the Court of Austria was neither welcoming, nor interested, nor accessible. The Jesuit setting, centred upon the Emperor's confessor Father Lamormaini, was uncongenial to the envoys who had renounced communion with the Roman See.

This is evident in the account of Arundel's mission which was provided by one of his train, William Crowne.[1] On the arrival at Linz ten coaches were sent to attend on the ambassador, who

---

[1] The title runs as follows. *A True Relation of the remarkable Places and passages observed in the Travels of the right honourable Thomas Lord Howard, Earle of Arundel and Surrey, Primer Earle and Earl Marshal of England, Ambassadour Extraordinary to his sacred Majesty Ferdinando II Emperour of Germanie, Anno Domini 1636*. It was printed in London in 1637.

was met by the Marshal of the Court. On the next day the
High Steward and the imperial confessor paid visits of respect.
The audience took place on the third day.[1] "His Excellence",
it is explained, "stayed nineteen dayes, and all the time at the
Emperour's charge, and served only by his Majesties servants;
in as much state as he himself; at the first course the Drums
beat up, and at the second, musicke with voyces."[2] The account
leaves the impression that the careful and staid courtesy was
very nearly emptied of all meaning. On his way home Arundel
met the Emperor and Empress for a second time; they were at
Mainz for the ceremonies connected with the anniversary of
the coronation; there were religious processions and Court
sermons.

From Linz and Vienna the party had gone on to Prague,
where the Emperor's son, the King of Hungary, held a form of
viceroyalty. They were shown the stables lately built by
Wallenstein, with marble mangers and thirty-eight red marble
pillars. "The most noble collection of the Emperor Rodolphus"
was displayed; "the cupboards of coral, porcelain and mother-
of-pearl, the amber cups and basons, the crystal and ivory cups,
the cabinets." They viewed the little chests of pearl and all the
skins of the Indian horses whose pictures hung up in the
masking room.[3] This old-fashioned and rather gaudy state
had little relevance for Stuart England. The Imperial House
itself appeared encased within the conventions of the second
period of the Counter-Reformation;[4] there were no serious
marriage projects to advance on behalf of English princes or

[1] Details in Crowne, op. cit., p. 17.

[2] Ibid., p. 21. The account of Arundel's visit to the Queen of Hungary at Vienna
shows the degree to which the official hospitality was coloured by Jesuit influence.
"From hence he went to severall houses of the Jesuites, the first was a University,
where was presented to his Excellence a kind of Comedy by young Schollers in
masking attire, and one of the house playing on an instrument like a Virginall,
severall kindes of musicke" (ibid., p. 23).

[3] Ibid., p. 31.

[4] The conventions of imperial portraiture indicate the remoteness from the
English world. In the gallery of the Palazzo Ducale at Mantua there are two
portraits, both by Lucrina Fetti, of Eleonora Gonzaga, second wife of the Emperor
Ferdinand II. They were originally placed in the convent of Sant' Orsola at
Mantua. In the first, dated 1622, the dress, with its deep gold pattern worked on a
silver ground, and the elaborate square jewellery seem almost as remote from
contemporary English taste as does the manner of the later portrait, in which the
Empress holds the orb and sceptre and wears the cross-surmounted imperial
crown. In the second portrait the Empress is given a leaden-white complexion.
The effect of both pictures is curiously hieratic.

princesses. To the English mind of this period there was a vagueness and even a sense of unreality about Vienna.[1]

Meanwhile Charles I and his advisers were bent upon observing the political reactions in Paris and Madrid and in the Hague. It is significant that it was only through the action of one of these Western Powers, or perhaps of two of them in combination, that the King envisaged the achievement of his dynastic intention. The Spaniards might procure the cession of Heidelberg and the western portion of the electoral lands as the result of diplomatic pressure; the French might include this among the objectives of their Rhenish policy; the Dutch might take part in a military effort. It was the first of these methods that King Charles preferred. It is difficult at this date to discover the real purpose of these obscure and tangled negotiations, or the price that he was prepared to pay to gain his object. It certainly seems very doubtful whether Charles I ever intended to enter into a military alliance with the Spaniards against the Dutch. It was an axiom with the Spanish foreign minister, Olivares, to make his terms intolerably high as a means of precluding the fulfilment of a bargain which he felt to be onerous. Too much weight need not be attributed to proposals which never advanced, and perhaps were never meant to advance, beyond the stage of drafting. It could be no part of the policy of the King of Spain to restore the Elector Palatine. As the years went by, the regaining of the Palatinate became not so much an item of Stuart policy as one of the King's habitual preoccupations. Charles I was already dead when the Peace of Westphalia at length brought his nephew, Charles Louis, back to Heidelberg.

The situation in regard to the United Provinces was complex. The twelve years' truce with Spain had expired in 1621, and the reconquest of Holland was the explicit major objective of Spanish policy. Preparations had long been in train, and the occupation of the Hapsburg lands in Alsace, and also of the Lower Palatinate, was bound up with the establishment of a route to bring the Spanish forces north from their training and recruiting grounds in Northern Italy. The first years of the

---

[1] There is evidence that the Catholic squires under the Restoration were always mindful of the House of Austria. The following entry occurs in the common-place-book of William Blundell of Crosby, "Obituaries: The Lady Haggerston, the Roman Empress" (*Crosby Records*, ed. Rev. T. Ellison Gibson, p. 304).

renewed struggle saw certain Spanish victories, and also some
English military aid for the Prince of Orange. This phase was
concluded before the death of James I. Later the Dutch made
progress, taking the citadel of Maestricht in 1632; in the East
Indies they made war upon the settlements which the King of
Spain had obtained with the Crown of Portugal. As far as the
Low Countries were concerned, the conflict was wasting and
intermittent. One factor brought the rulers in Brussels and The
Hague closer together. The Governors of the Spanish Netherlands had followed the attitude of Madrid in relation to French
policy. As the years passed, a fear of Cardinal Richelieu's
intentions dawned on the Prince of Orange and his advisers.

In England the Elizabethan school still favoured a Dutch
alliance, but another current of opinion could be detected in
the circle of the great merchants. Trade rivalry was growing,
and indignation had been aroused by the murder of English
traders at Amboyna, in the Spice Islands, by the Dutch colon-
ists. This massacre took place in 1623, but details were not
known for some twelve months. The disfavour into which the
Dutch then fell had something to do with the concentration of
enthusiasm upon Gustavus Adolphus. English merchants concerned with seaborne trade were also inclined to favour peace
with Spain, so that their shipping might be safe from the
Dunkirk privateers.

In some ways it is surprising that the German struggle was
not followed more closely, seeing how many of King Charles'
subjects were engaged on one side or the other.[1] But far the
greater number were either Scots for whom their sovereign had
little sympathy or Irish for whom he felt but slight responsibility.
For the most part this soldiery maintained or adopted Calvinist
or Catholic principles. In the Court itself there was scant
liking for the hero-worship aroused by the King of Sweden,[2]

---

[1] Cf. a reference to Lord Arundel's journey. "The same day the Countess of
Tyrconnel an Irish lady, and Sir Griffin Markham an English gentleman dined
with his Excellency, and many Scottish and Irish Colonels hath visited his
Excellencie and dined with him likewise; and they say a great part of the
Emperours Army bee the Kings subjects" (Crowne, *op. cit.*, p. 47).

[2] This standpoint is reflected in the work of Major-General Robert Monro, who
wrote in 1637: "He [Gustavus Adolphus] set light by his owne life in Dutch-land
that they might keepe theirs . . . he brought the keyes and open'd their Church
doors that were closed by the Anti-Christian Idolaters so that the Devills doctrine
was banished again out of the Pfalz" (Robert Monro, *His Expedition with the Scots
Regiment*, p. 165).

and none for the conspiracies that eddied around Wallenstein. There was small esteem in London for the mercenary calling. Few details have come down to us of the lives of the English soldiers of fortune, but a sentence in Sydenham Poyntz's *Relation* is telling. It was written in 1636 when that officer was staying with Sir Lewis Tresham.[1] "Now winter did salute us, every Regiment was sent to his Garrison. I desired my Captain to give me leave to travel further, who yielded to my request and gave me a discharge, and away I went to Amsterdam where I found some of Mansfields souldiers under Sir James Lesly who had two or three regiments, under whom I tooke pay and so to Germany."[2] There was an immediate contrast between such campaigning and that of the expeditions sent out to the Low Countries in the reign of Elizabeth. In Scotland the matter was seen differently, but in London these years can serve to mark the beginnings of a long indifference to the Englishmen who went out to serve some foreign sovereign.[3]

In Germany through this troubled time the predominant note was insecurity. A progress such as Lord Arundel's could very seldom be repeated, and even on this carefully guarded journey two of the ambassador's train were killed by bandits. The ceremonial coaches were not as yet intended for long-distance travelling, but rather for receiving envoys and for a movement from one palace to another.[4] Drawn up with the

[1] Sydenham Poyntz, who became a Catholic through the influence of an English Franciscan friar at Vienna, was formerly described by his brother as "an absolute Protestant in the Unity with the Church of England". Cf. *Historical and Genealogical Memoirs of the Family of Poyntz*, by Sir John Maclean, pt. ii, p. 160. Sir Lewis was a Recusant married since 1602 to Maria de Recalde, the Spanish stepdaughter of Alderman Moore (Cal. Clarke Thornhill MSS., pp. 133 and 147-8).

[2] *The Relation of Sydnam Poyntz, 1624-1636*, ed. Rev. A. T. S. Goodrick, Camden Society (1908), pp. 46-7.

[3] On the other hand, Sydenham Poyntz's brother was very conscious that his life was associated with the royal service. "I was", wrote William Poyntz, "then in the West Indies, Commander of a shipp of the Right Honble Earl of Warwick; and a little before in H.M. service in the Isle of Re in France; and before that in H.M. Service at Cades in the Kingdome of Spayne; and before that in the service of the Lordes of the States in the Netherlands on the behalf of our late deceased Sovereign Lord King James of famous memorie, with the Right Honble Lord Robert Earl of Essex in the Service of the Queen of Bohemia" (Chancery Proceedings, Charles I, P.p., Bundle 21, No. 60, printed in Maclean, *op. cit.*, pt. ii, p. 160).

[4] In addition to the coaches sent by the Emperor, three coaches were sent by the Duke of Neuburg to Lord Arundel's lodgings at Dusseldorf, and coaches belonging to the Queen of Bohemia awaited the English party a mile outside The Hague (Crowne, *op. cit.*, pp. 1 and 4).

ELIZABETH QUEEN OF BOHEMIA

From a painting by M. J. Van Miereveldt in the National Portrait Gallery

gilded crowns upon their roofs and with the emblazoned royal
arms, they formed a part of the approach to the residence of
their own sovereign. They belonged to the apparatus of ceremony, along with the halberdiers upon the staircase, and the
guards in the courtyard with their long plumes. For the actual
road journey wagons were used Lord Arundel and his party
needed eighteen, and every fifth wagon displayed the English
colours.[1] Both coming and going, the ambassador's train went
by water when this was practicable. "We tooke", wrote Crowne,
describing the passage from Cologne, "a Boate drawn with nine
horses and went up the Rhine by many villages pillaged and
shot downe, and many brave vineyards on Mountains along
the rivers side."[2] These details serve to indicate the unimaginable quality which marked the German lands.

On the level of commercial intercourse English merchants
and factors possessed an adequate knowledge of Lübeck and
Hamburg; they were established in the Low Country ports and
in certain trading centres on the coasts of Spain and Portugal.
There were defined lines of travel across Italy as far to the south
as Naples, but it was only in France, and to a lesser extent in
the Netherlands, that Englishmen passed and repassed continually. To the merchants and the envoys there were added
those who travelled for pleasure, or for health, or in a general
sense for education. At the beginnings of what would develop
into the Grand Tour, the journeys were specifically intended to
equip a young man for the life of Courts. The royal residences,
their layout and construction, were conceived as set-pieces;
they were annotated and described.[3]

A point may be made here. There was little contact with
the houses of the great families of France, Italy and the
Netherlands as opposed to the often merely formal Court
visits. It was not as yet the custom for the nobles on the Continent
to entertain the English traveller of their own rank. The
inconveniently large company with which persons of quality

---

[1] Ibid., p. 3.　　　　　　　　　　　[2] Ibid., pp. 5, 6.

[3] The descriptions extended to gardens. Thus, under 19 June 1641, there is an
account of the garden-house built by Christian IV of Denmark at Gluckstadt—
"The gardein stands in a square plott of ground, encompassed with a quicksett
hedge or wall, the best that I have seen, making most delightful walks" (*The
traveles of Peter Mundy in Europe and Asia, 1608-1667*, ed. Sir R. C. Temple, vol. iv,
p. 119). In Crowne there is reference to "another very large stately garden of the
Empresses neare unto the citie [of Vienna] called her *Favorita*" (*op. cit.*, p. 24).

then travelled would militate against the development of the practice. Besides, in the unsettled France of the years before the Fronde, a man of prudence would hesitate to invite a foreigner to his house unless he knew that he was acting in accordance with his sovereign's wishes. For this reason, even envoys would make use of the public inns.

An interesting account has survived of Sir Paul Pindar's journey overland from Venice to Calais on his way home from his embassy in Constantinople.[1] The ambassador had a party of twenty-four with him. At Venice, a palace in Canareggio had been hired for him, and at Turin they lodged in "a house of the Duke's".[2] Elsewhere nothing in the shape of official hospitality was offered. Between the Adriatic and the Channel they were five weeks on the road. At Lyons they reached more familiar ground,[3] and in regard to Gien there is a note that Sir Paul stayed in a Protestant's house[4]; this searching out of Calvinists is a recurrent feature. In France a system of post-horses was already well established. The relatively good roads made travel by coach practicable; nor were the charges for hiring exorbitant. For Sir Paul Pindar's journey coaches were hired for the stretch from Paris to Calais at forty crowns the vehicle. This was considerably cheaper than the prices which obtained on the road northwards from Lyons.[5] Considering only Northern Europe, it seems probable that the best-organised routes of travel were those between the Channel Ports and Paris

[1] Some of the inns visited by Sir Paul Pindar in 1620, the *Golden Star* in the Piazza della Paglia in Padua, the *Auberge La Tour* at Brescia, and the *Three Kings* at Milan, survived through the seventeenth and eighteenth centuries (*Travels of Peter Mundy in Europe and Asia, 1608-1667*, ed. Sir Richard Carnac Temple, Hakluyt Society, vol. i, pp. 99, 104 and 106). The *Star* at Padua cost five livres *per* man *per* day (*ibid.*, vol. i, pp. 98-9). As a comparison, Richard Symonds in 1649 paid *en pension* terms—"lodging and eating at the *Rosa Rossa* at Turin three dayes at three livres a day of Turien" (printed *ibid.*, vol. i, p. 235).

[2] *Ibid.*, vol. i, p. 111. This was before the close association with the Court of Turin which resulted from the marriage of Henrietta Maria's sister with the Duke's heir.

[3] When Coryate visited Lyons "the *Three Kings* [was] the fayrest Inne in the whole Citie, and most frequented of all the Innes in that town, and that by great persons. For the Earl of Essex lay there with all his traine before I came thither" (*Crudities*, vol. i, pp. 211-13). Sir Paul Pindar stayed at the *Three fflowers de Luces* (*op. cit.*, vol. i, p. 119). Richard Symonds lodged at a cheaper house—"*Le Feu de France* at 50d. a day" (*ibid.*, vol. i, p. 235).

[4] *Ibid.*, vol. i, p. 123.

[5] The charges on this stretch amounted to two shillings for each horse for a post-stage of some five English miles (*ibid.*, vol. i, pp. 119 and 132).

and between Ostend and the Spa.[1] The harbours favoured for
the sea crossing were Calais, Dunkirk and Ostend, and on the
English shore Dover,[2] probably because the Customers were
established there. By the shortest route the passage took five
hours, varying according to the wind and tide; the price
charged was five shillings. A market boat sailed from Dover to
Calais on the Tuesdays and Fridays of each week.[3]

Throughout Mundy's account it appears that all Sir Paul
Pindar's staff had good accommodation, perhaps because they
formed part of an ambassador's suite. The reference to Edward,
the footman, suggests how early the idea of the travelling valet
had developed.[4] During these years of peace in France and Italy
the volume of overland traffic was increasing, even though so
many merchants still preferred to go to the Spanish and
Italian ports by sea. With the commercial decline of Antwerp,
and with Amsterdam developing as a rival to English enterprise,
attention was concentrated upon Paris. Madrid was inaccessible
and unappealing and Rome was suspect, but in Paris there
could already be discerned the outline of the European capital.
The influence of the Huguenots made sections of the English
gentry feel that they would be at home there; for others, Paris
was the unquestioned centre of military elegance. It was the
true exemplar of the code of honour and the courtly life.

[1] There was always fairly good travelling between Ostend and Brussels, and as
far as the Spa, near Aachen. Coaches could also be used with ease throughout the
United Provinces.
[2] Both Sir Paul Pindar in 1620 and Richard Symoncs in 1649 lodged at the
Greyhound at Dover. Symonds, however, has this note: ' Iff ever I passe agen to
ride to the *Queens Arms* at the peere, for many reasons, especially for the convenience of being neare the botes and sparing expense" (*ibid.*, vol. i, p. 218).
[3] These details are also taken from Richard Symonds' account. His own crossing
lasted from nine in the morning until two in the afternoon.
[4] The party included Edward described as a footman, Thomas Humes a Scot
and Teodore a Muscovite. Among senior members of the company were Henry
Faro a tailor, Robbin the cook, Rice Davies, John Curry and William Pennington
(*ibid.*, vol. i, pp. 42-3). With this may be compared the provision for Sir George
Douglas' journey as ambassador-extraordinary to the Kings of Poland and
Sweden in 1634. He took with him five coachmen and two cooks, a butler, clerk of
the kitchen and "chasser," three pages and seven other servants whose duties are
unspecified. It was estimated that clothes for the three pages would cost £30
apiece. He set out with a new coach, a cast wagon and a wagon. Cf. an early
seventeenth-century bill for extraordinaries. A note contributed to the *E. H. R.*,
vol. xlv, pp. 626-30. Other details of embassy expenses of this period are printed
in "Embassy of the Earl of Leicester to Denmark 1632 ', by the Rev. Reginald
Cant, *E. H. R.*, vol. liv, pp. 252-62. Lord Leicester was to receive £8 a day for his
personal expenses (*ibid.*, p. 257).

More prosaically, young men would go to Paris to learn the language. It may be held that in these quiet years, when the Revocation of the Edict of Nantes was not in question, Paris meant more to the English gentleman of fashion than to his sovereign.

In London no one doubted the significance of the policies of the Courts of France and Spain; but here again there is evidence of King Charles' insularity. Louis XIII was the Queen's brother, and Philip IV of Spain her brother-in-law, but neither made a personal impression upon Charles I. It cannot even be said that the visit to Madrid to seek the hand of the Infanta had aroused any dislike of the Spanish King; in fact, the English Court toyed gently with the idea of a marriage between Don Baltasar Carlos, the heir to the throne of Spain, and his first cousin, the Princess Mary. In the case of both the Western monarchies, it would seem that Charles I gave a remote, almost doctrinal, support to the position of his brother sovereigns. He was not greatly interested in the ministers that they chose to employ. Thus there is reason to suppose that King Charles, although not his advisers, consistently underrated the crucial rôle of Cardinal Richelieu, who was chief minister of France throughout the peaceful years of his reign. In this matter his judgment was reinforced by the Queen's dislike for the great prelate. To Olivares, a matter in this case of less importance, he gave little thought. Such respect as he accorded to Pope Urban VIII was granted to him as a brother temporal sovereign.

The years under consideration showed little change in political leadership in Western Europe. There was a certain effect of immobility due to the fact that the same rulers and their ministers continued to guide the policies of the different states. Louis XIII and Richelieu, Philip IV and Olivares, Frederick Henry of Orange[1] and Aerssens van Sommelsdijk, Pope Urban VIII and Cardinal Francesco Barberini, were all either ruling or in office when Charles I came to his father's throne, and there was no change among them during the seventeen years prior to the outbreak of the Civil War. Relations between England and these powers were also governed by the King's determination, which seems manifest after 1629,

[1] In this case Charles I succeeded on 27 March and Frederick Henry on 23 April 1625.

to remain at peace; a war could not be undertaken without the support of Parliament.

There was constant contact between the Western nations, but no personal intercourse between the sovereigns or the ministers. It is perhaps these last factors which account for the effect of insulation. This was mitigated in the case of France, on account of the special links which bound the actual Court circle in England to the capital of the Queen's brother. Even so, there was more understanding of the life reflected in the portraits of Philippe de Champaigne than that of the Hôtel de Rambouillet. Superficially, certain Italian modes had been adopted, and in particular, the masque scenery and conventions which had been initiated in the Lombard duchies. In the drama there were long-established Italian and more recent Spanish models. If a distinction may be attempted these were the Renaissance or Renaissance-Baroque elements. It was on such a level that Velasquez was so acceptable. Still, there was little exchange of thought and idiom with the Spain of Calderon and Zurbaran or with Bernini's Rome.[1] The Stuart Court had affinities with France and the Low Countries, but it remained impenetrable to ideas which sprang from a pattern of life in the Tridentine mould, which was then dominant in Southern Europe.

[1] These diverse figures were very exact contemporaries—Bernini and Zurbaran were born in 1598, Velasquez and Vandyck in 1599, Calderon in 1600 and Philippe de Champaigne in 1602.

CHAPTER IV

THE RIVAL FOREIGN POLICIES

THE death of Buckingham had made the continuance of the desultory war with France an unattractive proposition even to his royal master. The dissolution of Parliament in 1629 made war impracticable. The need of money which dominated all these years made peace imperative. The Duke had been killed in August 1628, and by mid-October La Rochelle had surrendered. The relief of the French Protestants, whose resistance was centred in that city, had been the avowed object of the war. The peace made between King Louis XIII and the Huguenots deprived the conflict of its purpose. On 24 April 1629 the French war was closed by the Treaty of Susa. In November of the following year the Treaty of Madrid ended the state of hostilities with Spain, which had lasted for years without actual battle.

All parties in England had concurred in one or other of these treaties. At the same time, there was almost universal support among his subjects for King Charles' determination to obtain the restoration of the Palatinate. The acceptance of the crown of Bohemia by the King's brother-in-law, the Elector Palatine, had resulted not only in his expulsion from his new kingdom but in the loss of the Upper and Lower Palatinate. The Upper Palatinate had been occupied by Bavarian forces since 1621, and the Lower Palatinate, with the capital Heidelberg, had been garrisoned by Spanish and Imperial forces since the failure of Count Mansfeld's expedition in 1622. In so far as he had a persistent object in foreign policy, King Charles desired to regain the Palatine dominions for his sister's family.

Considerations of prestige weighed with him. From his accession in 1625 until the birth of the Prince of Wales on 29 May 1630, the heir to the throne[1] was his sister, the Queen of Bohemia, and, after her, his nephews, Prince Frederick, who died in January 1629, and Prince Charles Louis. The restitution of

---

[1] With the exception of 13 May 1629, which saw the birth and death of Henrietta Maria's eldest infant son.

these hereditary lands appealed to King Charles' affections, and still more to his sense of dignity and order. Their retention, against the will of England, was an affront to him. It was vexatious that his sister and her husband should have to live at the Hague or in Rhenen as importunate pensioners.

It does not seem likely that he was moved at all by the religious question. He was remote from that side of English feeling which now for half a century had supported the continental Protestants. He had a distant and insular appreciation for the Lutheran conceptions and for the heavy-kneaded theology of the *Confessio Augustana*. Still, one factor must have been present to his dry and accurate memory. In both areas of the Palatinate it was not the Augsburg Confession but the Calvinistic ministers who would gain by the Elector Frederick's restoration.

An element of jealousy tended to complicate the situation. The Queen of Bohemia had been devoted to his elder brother, Henry, Prince of Wales. With her impetuous and long-sighted charm, she had little in common with King Charles. Meanwhile, all the support for a policy which could be called Elizabethan, as drawing its inspiration from the great Queen's reign, gathered about her. She could not but be the heroine of the Puritans, as of all who wished for a forward and aggressive action.

In his own way King Charles was as remote as his father had been from such heroics. The ambassador of his choice was Rubens, who was at this time at his Court representing the Archduchess Isabella. It was a characteristic of the Caroline spirit that it suggested a new world. Here, where the King and Queen moved with their circle, there was no room for out-at-elbows soldiers with Dutch sympathies, for martial tavern talk or breast-plate hopes.

Remaining always within the framework of diplomacy, the King took a grey view of the European scene. He had no sympathy for the King of Sweden, and rather less for Cardinal Richelieu. Madrid was an unfortunate memory, the Hague aroused distaste. He looked out on the possibilities as on a chessboard. He had no feeling for one piece beyond another. King Charles had a clear sense of gratitude, but little loyalty.[1] In

---

[1] Cf. despatch from the Venetian Ambassador dated 8 January 1631, "He [the King] does not trust many, and when he conceives a good opinion of anyone he does not let it fall". The King gave his gratitude where he had already given his affection. The relations with Strafford were always on a purely business footing.

fact, he kept his loyalty for God and his royal duty. Thus no tie bound him to the Dutch, but he remembered all his life the service which the Marquess of Hamilton had done him in levying volunteers for the King of Sweden's cause. This is, perhaps, the explanation of the readiness with which the King would enter into schemes to aid the Spaniards against the Dutch and the Dutch against the Spaniards, plans that were mutually exclusive. Not caring much about the issues, he advanced his pieces simultaneously and then cleared away the board.

Throughout King Charles' life an absence of hope, approaching to disillusion, was close to the surface of his mind. His attitude in his nebulous foreign policy can best be interpreted along these lines. He had small expectations, and the event did not deceive him. Throughout he was limited to diplomatic measures. He knew that these could not be backed by force, except at a price he would not pay. This may account for all the changes of project accepted by a sovereign who was normally singularly persevering. It seems that he avoided giving thought to his expedients. He hoped little from them and, in fact, obtained nothing. Unless he called a Parliament he could not go to war.

Within the circle of the royal advisers the terms "French" and "Spanish" are applied freely throughout this period. The "French" party was very complicated in its personnel and motive, the "Spanish" was simpler. As a term of abuse, the latter expression was convenient since it recalled the Spanish pensioners of King James' reign and the ascendancy of Gondomar. In fact, it covered those who, like Lord-Treasurer Portland, favoured peace and economy. Opposition to the extravagance of the Court would lead a minister into the "Spanish" camp. Strafford belonged to it through these years; it was at the core of Royalism. The sections of opinion favourable to an alliance with Spain recognised that any military expedition to the Continent would be impracticable for the time being; the King would be dependent upon Parliament if ever he were once involved in a foreign war. All those who were in a direct sense servants of the Crown were in agreement upon this matter. Carlisle and Portland, Cottington and Strafford, had a similar outlook on this policy, Laud, in so far as he was concerned with foreign matters, took the same view.

It does not seem that the supporters of this policy could expect that it would crystallise into action. The Anglo-Spanish alliance was a paper scheme, and its merits were largely mythical. The chief supporters of this policy were isolationists in effect. They did not forget that the financial situation was inevitably precarious; their approach was pre-eminently sober and realist. With the exception of Sir Tobie Mathew, who was in and out of Roehampton House, there were no Catholics of repute among the active members of the "Spanish" party.

The "French" party was very different. It included, for diverse reasons, the adherents and the entourage of the two Queens. It was favoured by the party of action, and drew a measure of support from anti-papal sentiment. The alliance between Cardinal Richelieu and the King of Sweden meant that those who saw Gustavus as a Protestant deliverer were drawn towards this party. The inheritors of that Elizabethan tradition, which still moulded the thought of the King's envoys, desired to see a vigorous policy implemented. Both Secretary Dorchester and Sir Thomas Roe were of this mind. A rather curious fact may be noted here. A number of those who were Queen Henrietta's intimates, and the strongest adherents of a "French" policy, came in time to give at least a qualified support to the Parliament which would oppose her husband in the field.

For a consideration of the working out of the rival policies, it is simplest to begin with the Carlisles, the husband a leader of the "Spanish" party and the wife the Queen's chief intimate. In the few months after Buckingham's assassination James Hay, Earl of Carlisle, then abroad in Italy on a diplomatic mission, was regarded as his destined successor in the royal favour. The idea passed. No one could come into the King's life and fill the place which had been occupied by his one confidant. Still, Carlisle, now ageing, remained a personage of consequence, considered in some fashion as an elder statesman in King Charles' rather rigid scale of values. The cadet of a great Scottish family, he had long been anglicised and separated from his own countrymen. He belonged to no caucus. He did not serve the Parliament or the English peers, but only his own interests and the House of Stuart.

The careless legendary extravagance of his maturity had given place to a heavy uneven intake of wealth which was the

devoid of all religious prejudice and had let these things go by.[1] He was, in those days, happiest down in Sussex with the Northumberlands—"sitting in his withdrawing-chamber, within the parloir at Petworth, in the window where that table is", or moving across the bowling-green or pacing in the birch walk or in "the garden where the roses are".[2]

From time to time he would go to London, and when Thomas Carey was appointed ambassador to Venice, Carlisle took his house in the Strand at an unfurnished rental of £150 a year. Since his early manhood he had accumulated a great experience. He had been a disciple of Robert, Earl of Salisbury, and he knew the trend of every movement. His friends had grown up into different camps. Sir Francis Nethersole, once his secretary, was now the Queen of Bohemia's solemn agent.[3] Sir Isaac Wake, the envoy at Turin and soon to go ambassador to Paris, had been "his right hand and most faithful follower".[4] He had made contact with the young men of the future, not only with George Con, but with George Goring. "Never poor boy was so much bound to a good old man", declared Lord Goring, "as is my son to your Lordship."[5]

All these links were within that closed circle of the Court and the high officials, the air to which he was accustomed. Principles and sober lines of thought were alien to him. He had a feeling for the brave and lavish. This was the side of his character which attracted the Queen, this and his elegant mastery of her own language. "The Queen my sacred mistress", wrote her Master of the Horse to Carlisle, "is beyond measure yours."[6] But on the Queen, and on those who depended upon the Court, he had a greater claim than that of elegance and ageing courtesy, for he was the husband of the Countess of Carlisle.

The Queen had always had a penchant for elder women.

[1] A letter from Sir Robert Kerr to Lord Carlisle in favour of Dr Echlin throws a light on this matter. "In a word he is Mr John Echlin's brother and has no fault but that he is a Papist, but such a one as will be in Heaven as soon as he is dead" (ibid., vol. cxxxvi, p. 68).

[2] References to Petworth in Penshurst MSS., printed in Letters and Memorials of State, ed. Arthur Collins.

[3] The Oxinden Letters, p. 27.

[4] Letter from Francesco Correr, Venetian Ambassador in Savoy to the Doge and Senate, dated 10 December 1628 (Cal. S. P. Venetian, 1628-9, p. 428).

[5] Letter from Lord Goring to the Earl of Carlisle, dated 19 June, 1628 (Cal. S.P. Dom., 1628-9, p. 169).

[6] Letter from Lord Goring to the Earl of Carlisle, dated 29 September 1628 (ibid., p. 297).

Her ardent and gay temperament responded to the stimulus of the adventurous Duchesse de Chevreuse during the years before she settled down to easy marital relations with King Charles and to her years of child-bearing. She had been only a girl of sixteen when she first came to England, and had shown a hero-worship for the "fair and painted" Marie de Chevreuse. Courage always won her admiration. In that time between her marriage and the favourite's death, she had been kept too close to the Buckingham associations. The Duchess and the old Countess of Buckingham and Lady Hamilton, and above all, Lady Denbigh, had been constantly around her. With the latter she was eventually to form a constant friendship; but the whole situation had been forced on by the King. "Grant", we find in a list of His Majesty's gifts in the February after his wedding, "of a pavilion of tawny damask with a chair, cushion and footstool suitable to the use of the Countess of Denbigh."[1]

Lady Carlisle had a skill in tricky situations, and a talent in manœuvring around the seat of power, passing and repassing. She was on the scene in all those years which linked the two diverse ascendancies of Buckingham and Pym. The Duke she attracted and his wife she agonised. Ten years older than the Queen and a daughter of the ninth Earl of Northumberland, she had been married since 1617 to Carlisle, then Lord Doncaster, the old King's favourite. This marriage had brought her an independent great establishment (or rather a high fashionable rate of living) and opportunity. The type of influence she exercised was then only possible to a married woman.

It was with Lady Carlisle that the Queen found refuge from the Villiers women, and from her own difficult relations with the Duke of Buckingham. Like Madame de Chevreuse, she breathed the very air of politics. She must have had a fascination, for she exercised great power over the men to whose political fortunes she became attached. Sir Tobie Mathew's account suggests that Lady Carlisle was in no way passionate. Combinations appealed to her, and the management of affairs. She had affinities with the *grandes dames* of the Fronde. To the Queen, with her Bourbon traditions, it was no disadvantage that her new friend should be *intrigante*. Sensitive and very brave, and yet with mild abilities, the Queen was captivated by her wit and swift intelligence.

[1] State Papers, Dom. Charles I, appendix of Grants under 25 February 1626.

From the first she had her own position, and by 1627 the Duchess of Buckingham had noted how great she was in favour. In August of the next year, when the favourite was murdered, Lady Carlisle was left in temporary supremacy. She had passed that summer through an attack of smallpox, attended at Penshurst by Sir Theodore Mayerne. "Your lady", wrote Sir Robert Ayton to Carlisle at this time, "has recovered both her health and beauty beyond expectation. She is still the only woman in the Queen's affection."[1]

On this situation the Carlisles' position hinged. As the husband came slowly back from his embassy to Venice during the autumn and winter of 1628-9, there were rumours of his new "Spanish" affiliations. He had been received with distinction at Turin, and he brought back from the Duke of Savoy a sword valued at £10,000. A gentleman attached to the Ducal Court accompanied him to England.[2] At Brussels, Carlisle paid his respects to the Archduchess Isabella, and at each stage Venetian envoys reported on these journeys made to the powers hostile to France and Venice. Rumours of his point of view reached England. "The Queen", wrote the ambassador in London, "who has heard of the ideas disseminated by him [Lord Carlisle] against France will do him no good."[3] Lady Carlisle wrote urging his return.[4] She explained that he was thought hugely Spanish. In reality his ideas seem to have been limited to an elderly desire to help his friends and a rather high view of the treatment due to him. Consideration for the King's ambassador was the only measure by which that century could gauge the sovereign's peaceful glory. It was the first of these purposes which led him into the territory of the United Provinces.

He was there joined by Sir Thomas Roe, and they made their way to the Hague so that Carlisle could visit the Palatine family with whom he had links dating from the old King's days. "The Earl of Carlisle", the Venetian secretary at Zurich had reported as he passed through, "seems very obsequious and

[1] Letter from Sir Robert Ayton, dated 3 September 1628.
[2] Cf. letter from Mr Beaulieu to Sir Thomas Puckering, dated 21 January 1629, printed in Court and Times of Charles I, vol. ii, p. 8.
[3] Letter from Alvise Contarini to the Doge and Senate, dated from London 2 February 1629 (Cal. S. P. Venetian, 1628-9, p. 516).
[4] Letter from the Countess of Carlisle to her husband, dated 22 December 1628 (State Papers, Dom. Charles I, cxxiii, 6).

beholden to the Queen [of England] and eager for a change in the fortunes of the Queen of Bohemia."[1] But by mischance he arrived in Holland only in time to learn of the accident which had befallen the Prince of Bohemia and to acquaint the Queen with the news of the death of her eldest son. "The Prince," we read in the account in a contemporary newsletter, "going with his father from the Hague to Amsterdam to see the ships of the West India prize, was drowned by the way in the Haarlem Sea, with nineteen persons more of their company, by the unhappy encountering of their boat with another that was stronger, laden with beer, whereby, being splitted, it was presently filled up with water, and sunk."[2] The Prince's vessel sank on to the sands and grounded on an even keel. The boy was lashed to the mast by his attendants, but was frozen to death in that wintry weather.

This was a considerable check to the hopes for the Palatinate. It was said that the dead heir was "a prince so admirable, both for his natural parts and learning in those young years, being but fifteen years old, as that the eyes and hopes of all the afflicted party were already fixed upon him". It is not difficult to detect the note of panegyric. Still, one point is clear. Apart from the child Rupert and his nursery full of brothers, there only remained the weak and unconvincing King and, after him, his son, Charles Louis, an undeveloped, fickle boy. Yet these facts might serve to strengthen Carlisle's conviction that nothing could be gained for the Palatines save by the way of negotiation. Anxious for peace with Spain and ready for a peace with France, Carlisle returned as a supporter of a cautious policy which would necessitate the avoidance of all adventure.

To implement such a policy there were two officials, Sir Francis Cottington, who was despatched to negotiate with Spain, and Sir Dudley Carleton, who had become Secretary of State on Lord Conway's retirement in December 1628, and had been raised to the peerage as Viscount Dorchester. He came of the lesser gentry, very conscious of his descent; a man of fifty-six, acutely ambitious and long inured to disappointments. Some twenty-five years earlier he had been secretary to

---

[1] Letter from Girolamo Cavazza to the Doge and Senate, dated from Zürich 4 December 1628 (Cal. S. P. Venetian, 1628-9, p. 424).

[2] Letter from Mr Beaulieu to Sir Thomas Puckering, dated 21 January 1629.

Lady Carlisle's father, Lord Northumberland, and he had suffered when his patron was imprisoned after the Gunpowder Plot. He had recovered from this setback, but he had been seared by his repeated failure to attain to office. When Sir Ralph Winwood died, and at each subsequent vacancy, he had angled for the Secretaryship of State. In 1622, when his father-in-law, Sir Henry Savile, died, he would have been content to succeed him in the post of provost of Eton. He was the most experienced and the senior member of the then undeveloped foreign service, and for the last twenty years had been in charge of embassies almost continuously; first four years in Venice, then nine years at the Hague, a spell in Paris and then the Hague again. He must have had an acute nostalgia for London, for his great series of newsletters, all carefully preserved, reflect month after month of detailed gossip. Yet in spite of his voluminous correspondence, the lines of his character are not clear. No convincing portrait emerges as in the instance of his colleagues Coke and Conway.

Lord Dorchester appears primarily as the expert diplomatist —the adviser who is prepared to advocate a policy, and then to direct the means by which it can be implemented. Solid as were his views, he had a veneer of suppleness. He had the old King's phrasing, he was of his time. Buckingham, who had shown him no great liking, turned to him in the end, determined to rely on his *expertise*. It was through the favourite that he was made a peer, and promised the reversion of the secretaryship when arrangements could be made to displace Conway.[1]

There was at this time an almost complete division of functions between the two Secretaries of State, Sir John Coke, who held office from 1625 until 1639, being solely responsible for the home department. Dorchester's field of action covered all diplomatic matters, and his position was in some ways the nearest approach that England was to experience for many years to what we now know as the Foreign Secretary. It seems that his general ideas were Venetian, and he is always praised by the envoys of the Serene Republic. He favoured peace with France and an aggressive policy in Germany. His comments on the Church of Rome were always acrid, perhaps because he

---

[1] He had been created Lord Carleton of Imbercourt on 22 May 1626, at the time of his mission to Paris, and was advanced a step as Viscount Dorchester on 25 July 1628.

had burned his fingers long ago. He relied on the engine of that Protestant sentiment with which he, to some extent, concurred. Buckingham had required a policy of adventure, but the Duke was murdered before Dorchester took office. In effect, his suggested line of action was pigeon-holed. This, and blood-pressure, may account for the note of weariness which is marked throughout the two years of his term as Secretary.

A few points may be noted. Without much evidence of wit Dorchester belonged to the school which loved to display familiarity with the current phrase-making of Europe. He brought into his letters Spanish and Italian turns of speech.[1] The sentence in which he refers to St Ambrose as "the old Divus tutelaris of the Milanesi" brings us back to Essex's days.[2] He loved to regard himself as an expert on European travel. When Secretary of State he urged the young Duke of Lennox to settle down at Saumur in Touraine ' to pass the dog days", and recommended Spain for its winter climate. Dorchester was all his life a collector of Spanish books. One trait is less attractive. His letters against Sir Thomas Glover, then envoy to the Porte, suggest that he could pursue an enmity with rancour.

For eighteen months before his promotion he had been a widower and childless. His private means were small and he sought a stabilising alliance. There had been rumours that he would marry Lady Villiers, by birth a St John and the widow of the Duke's brother, Sir Edward, who had been President of Munster. The advantages of this match were largely political. Lady Villiers had eleven children and Dorchester needed an heir. It was, perhaps, Buckingham's murder which enabled him to choose a younger bride.

The month before the assassination, the first Viscount Bayning, a merchant of very great resources and in the prime of life, died at his house in Mark Lane in the City of London. There was a certain opposition among Dorchester's friends to the alliance which this event made possible; but in June 1630 the Secretary married Lady Bayning. She belonged to the inner circle of the great families, a daughter of Sir Henry Glemham and, through her Sackville mother, a first cousin of

[1] Cf. letter from Sir Dudley Carleton to Sir John Digby, dated 22 February 1610: "I cannot but give you the *para-bien*" (Correspondence of Sir John Digby, Cal. Wingfield Digby MSS.).

[2] Letter from the same to the same, dated 8 February 1612 (Cal. Wingfield-Digby MSS.).

Lord Dorset's. She had a married daughter, Lady Newark; three younger daughters, all well portioned; an only son. She brought with her the administration of large estates acquired by her first husband as an investment and the possession of Bentley Parva Hall in Essex; both during her son's minority, which had some seven years to run. Lady Dorchester's personality hardly emerges. It is clear that she was a decided Anglican, rather attached to country life. At the time of his second marriage, the Secretary of State bought back his grandfather's little estate, Brightwell Manor, in Oxfordshire, which had passed to a recusant landowner, Sir George Simeon.[1]

Dorchester planned his life carefully, was business-like, a little formal. These qualities are revealed in a correspondence with Dr Brian Duppa, then Dean of Christ Church, in regard to the entry into the University of his stepson, Lord Bayning, who was now turned fifteen. The Dean explained that he had entered Lord Bayning's name as a commoner at the Canons' Table, where his diet would be very good, "though not at that height it was lately grown to, three or four good dishes being now the ordinary".[2] His tutor would be Mr. Chaworth, younger brother of the Viscount of that name. There was nothing lacking, but a lodging; perhaps the Bishop of Peterborough would place his set of rooms at the Secretary of State's disposal. These notes complete the rather meagre impressions of Lord Dorchester's background.

Throughout his life the new Secretary had a certain restraint in action. Seriously he accumulated the necessary data. In this respect his period as Foreign Minister foreshadows the coming of the high bureaucracy. This is seen in the way in which he meets those correspondents who write to him upon affairs of State. Bred in the Elizabethan Age in the days of thrust, the favourite method of his own last years was to become the act of parry. His assumption of office, however, was made after the old style.

"I cannot", he wrote to Lord Carlisle from the Court, "make a better entry into a secretary's place, which His

---

[1] Letter from Secretary Dorchester to the Bishop of Oxford, dated from the Court at Farnham, 9 August 1630. This letter deals with the construction of a pew for Lady Dorchester in Brightwell Church (State Papers, Dom. Charles I, clxxii, 40).

[2] Letter from the Dean of Christ Church to Secretary Dorchester, dated at Christ Church, Oxford, 12 April 1631 (ibid., clxxxviii, p. 49).

Majesty hath conferred upon me, than by paying your Lordship the first fruits of my letters, as they are the first I write in that quality, not by commandment, for your servant hath his despatch already by other hands, but out of a due respect to your person and service, with acknowledgment of many and very weighty obligations renewed unto me.[1] . . . I must", he continued, "be true to myself in retaining always a grateful remembrance, and rendering your Lordship my most humble thanks for those good offices which I know very well how to value. Every one walks within the circle of his charge, and His Majesty's hand is the chief, and in effect the sole directory."

From the very first, Dorchester's freedom was quite trammelled, and his prediction verified that the King's hand was "in effect the sole directory". King Charles was at this time between the tides. He had lost Buckingham, and he had not yet given himself to that combination of the friendship of Laud and the guidance of Strafford which was to mark the years after 1633. It was Buckingham's confidence and not the King's which Dorchester had gained after his efforts. Besides, King Charles was always tempted to that policy of reinsurance among his own officers which has often tended to mark a personal monarchy. He would listen to Portland and send Cottington to Spain to carry through the policy of rapprochement. Faced by this financial stringency and by the activity of an ambassador who might so easily supplant him, Dorchester grew weary. A letter to his predecessor Conway very clearly indicates the situation.

"The affairs of the world", wrote Dorchester in the summer of 1630, "are grown ripe with the season. The Duke of Mantua has capitulated for himself and a few men, the rest of his town being sacked after a long siege. The Duke of Savoy dead after having seen Saluces lost before his eyes. The King of Sweden has entered Germany which divertisement is like to make the peace of Italy.

"Now the great ones have eaten up the less [the Austrians the Mantuan and the French the Savoyard], a pill composed of plague, famine and war being ministered to them by Mazarin, a Spanish doctor, they are like to vomit again. At Farnham their tents [those of the Court] are set up like Tartars, and they

---

[1] Letter from Secretary Dorchester to the Earl of Carlisle, dated 19 December 1628, printed in the *Court and Times of Charles I*, vol. ii, pp. 1-2.

hunt before and after noon like Indians, as if they should dine and sup on nothing but what they kill."[1]

It was clear that the Secretary of State was reduced to the rôle of an observer, deprived of power to act upon the situation. He could record with pleasure that the Hapsburg powers would suffer from the Swedish "divertisement", but he could do no more. English diplomacy was in the doldrums through this eventful year. On 26 June 1630 the King of Sweden landed on Usedom. The Day of Dupes was to witness the final establishment of Cardinal Richelieu's power within the Bourbon monarchy. Dorchester's letter mentions the appearance on the European scene of the second of the great Cardinal-Ministers of France. He is right in attributing high influence to the Papal Envoy to the Court of Mantua, a man supple and very *fine* and only twenty-eight, so young for such distinction. The Secretary already spells his name in the French fashion, Mazarin. In England the landing of Gustavus Adolphus was seen as most significant; it created a revolution in English feeling.

[1] Letter from Secretary Dorchester to Lord-President Conway, dated from the Court at Farnham, 7 August 1630 (State Papers, Dom. Charles I, clxxii, 34).

CHAPTER V

THE QUEEN OF BOHEMIA

BEFORE tracing the effect of the King of Sweden's invasion upon English policy, it is worth while considering the orbit within which the envoys moved. There had been now for many years a resident Ambassador at Constantinople accredited to the "Grand Signor". The Turkish control over the Balkans made the embassies at Galata the focal-point for the development of Eastern European policy. There was, of course, an English envoy at Venice and another at Vienna. But in all the great tract of Europe south and east of Poland and the Germanies, and in Italy south of Turin and Venice, there was no other permanent diplomatic establishment maintained by the first two Stuart kings. The kingdom of the Two Sicilies was in the hands of Spain; the States of the Church were technically hostile territory; there was no regular resident at the Court of Tuscany.

Portugal was still at this period under Spanish rule, for the re-establishment of national independence under the House of Braganza did not take place until the winter of 1640. This would only leave the Hague and Paris as permanent diplomatic posts, with an eye kept on Brussels for the Spanish Netherlands. For the rest, envoys trailed in the wake of the dynastic system. Kings would send missions of congratulation or condolence on accessions and funerals to the members of their own family. Their envoys with the royal children would jealously guard against appeals for help. Thus, as an example, the relations with the Court of Turin were fairly close because the Duchess of Savoy (Madame Royale) was Henrietta Maria's sister. The Queen of Spain was their sister, too, but she had left France before Queen Henrietta could remember.

There was an envoy during parts of the Thirty Years War with the princes of the Protestant Union, and the two Scandinavian Courts received attention from time to time. In its more serious aspects, the situation swung upon a London-Paris axis. From the beginning of the dominance of Richelieu until the Treaty of Utrecht in 1713, the Government of France supplied that vitality which really created a continental policy. The Hapsburg power, with its centres at Vienna and Madrid, appeared remote, amorphous and unfriendly. From Paris alone there radiated a system of alliance; close with Venice, intermittent with the Hague, in play with Sweden. The English envoys were, in a sense, the friends of France before her time. Those bred in the Elizabethan tradition were irremediably opposed, not only to King Philip II and his descendants, but to all the House of Austria. This constant enmity, self-confident and righteous, was a permanent factor in opinion throughout England. Such a strong national sentiment was at the base of the position in English life held by the Queen of Bohemia and by the King of Sweden.

In the spring of 1630 the Queen of Bohemia and her husband were at Rhenen hunting in the woods beyond the villa that the King had erected in the planned Dutch gardens out of the proceeds of the sale of his lordship of Lixheim in Lorraine which had fetched one hundred and thirty thousand rix-dollars. Their coaches, each with six horses, making that royal show which the Queen required so urgently, passed and repassed between Rhenen with its Italianate facade[1] and the house at the Hague which had been placed at the disposal of the exiles by the States of Holland. These two houses were crowded with all the furniture that had been rescued from the Schloss at Heidelberg, and had been brought in wagons from Sedan. The wall spaces were covered by the stuffs taken from the great iron-bolted trunks. There was careful arrangement of the chairs of state sent over from the Court of England.

One thousand pounds a month for the Queen and five hundred pounds monthly for her husband, representing allowances from the English Crown, were not likely to suffice for their style of living. "The music at our repasts", so runs an account of one of the Queen's journeys, "was composed of a spinnett, a viol and two voices; the Escoutette and one of the burgomasters trilling and drinking, drinking and trilling, to the tune and measure."[2] Still, this was only a rustic diversion.

[1] The King of Bohemia described the house as Palazzo Renense. Correspondence between the King and Lord Dorchester on 8 August and 10 September 1630.

[2] Journal of a voyage in North Holland preserved in State Papers, Holland, 1625. It is attributed reasonably to Mistress Crofts by Mrs Green in her Elizabeth of Bohemia, p. 245.

It was at home that the real business of maintaining state was practised. The gold plate was in position, the woven arms of the Bohemian kingdom, and all the *insignia* of that royal rank by whose acknowledgment Elizabeth and her husband set such store. There were sixteen or seventeen little dogs and monkeys,[1] both species equally thought of as pets both elegantly playful and in the mode. Against this background the Queen of Hearts played out her policy.

She had great courage, a dislike of compromise and a clear detestation for the House of Austria, and for the whole Tridentine scale of values, which earned the admiration of her English contemporaries. She spoke French easily, and her letters are sown with French expressions, some of them unknown in her native country. *Voix de chapitre* is a case in point.[2]

The Queen of Bohemia had a jollity which belonged to her royal father and a love of horseplay which was very far from the delicate taste of her younger brother. "Thou ugly, filthy camel's face,"[3] she began a letter to Lord Carlisle. It always amused her to call him "Camel's Face", the phrase recurs. In this connection it is perhaps worth noting that the members of the oligarchic society in England did not expect their royal family to maintain their own high standard of a grand and careful manner. The Queen of Bohemia had a cheerful, chiding way with her brother's officers. She was prudent enough to write to Sir Henry Vane, whom she did not trust, as "Honest Harry".

This was her favourite expression, "honest", and she took very easily all the admiration and all the praise that came to her. She had the capacity for fire, and could coin an expletive as in her phrase on Cardinal Richelieu—"but this ulcerous priest was not then *Son Eminence*". Yet her position was made by the men whose loyal devotion she inspired, for it is certain that men fell for her. She was bold and chaste and welcoming. "Honest Tom", "Honest fatt Thom", she wrote to Sir Thomas

---

[1] Letter from Sir Dudley Carleton to Lady Sedley, dated 9 February 1622.

[2] On the other hand, the Elector Palatine spoke a French which has that naïve and touching quality which was to prove so attractive in the House of Brunswick. His reply to those who complained of his extravagance in building Rhenen—*C'est toujours un divertissement*—is reminiscent of George II.

[3] Letter from the Queen of Bohemia to Lord Carlisle, dated from The Hague, 2 June 1630 (State Papers, Holland).

Roe, the most influential of her supporters, and she was wise to lean on him. While she created her own legend, it was Roe who laboured and worked over her policy. This policy should have been very clear, although its application was impeded by the Queen of Bohemia's tempestuous energy and by the way in which she would call to her aid her royal dignity.

It is characteristic of the diplomatic action of this period that Sir Thomas Roe should have maintained an interest in the fortunes of the German Protestant Union while holding the post of ambassador to the Ottoman Porte. He had been a close adherent of the Queen of Bohemia and of her brother, Henry, Prince of Wales, since they had first appeared in public. He had belonged to the very last period of the old Queen's reign, and had been one of her esquires of the body. Sir Thomas Roe had kept himself aloof from the Jacobean world, a great adventurer. Coming from a city family and related to the Greshams, he had an understanding of Elizabethan policy in its commercial aspect. As a young man he had gone to South America in search of gold. He had spent four years on an embassy to Jehangir, moving with the Mogul Court to Ajmir, Mandu, Ahmadabad.

In all his posts he showed the same ideas, a high insular maintenance of his King's greatness and a negligent, slighting attitude towards the Latin world. A quotation from Roe's despatches from Ajmir, in which he dismissed the alleged peaceful intentions of the King of Spain, bears immediately upon this point. "Only an Italian poore Jesuite", wrote the ambassador, "had enformed the Prince [Jehangir] that Portugall would be quiett—a brave securitye."[1] After his embassy he had gone back to England by way of Persia. From 1621 Sir Thomas Roe had been ambassador at Constantinople, anxious to return to England, but maintained in his post by the representations of the Levant Company and of the great English merchant houses who trusted in him.

He was forty-seven when he eventually reached home in 1629, and for the rest of the period until the Civil Wars he was the foreign minister designate of an alternative government. His voice was that of the Elizabethan Age, which Charles I was

[1] *The Embassy of Sir Thomas Roe to India*, ed. Foster, p. 124. This contains an excellent account of Roe's relations with Father Corsi. Since 1580 the Kings of Spain were sovereigns of the Portuguese dominions in the Indies.

unwilling (and perhaps too prudent) to attend to. A certain consistency and elevation of character comes out clearly in Roe's line of action. One can understand how Wentworth valued him and how Laud wished to bring him into office. He was, perhaps, the greatest among those figures in the history of English foreign policy who were destined to remain all their lives in opposition. His personal ascendancy is very manifest, and one gains the impression that the King and his advisers were never for a moment unaware of his presence. In rich language he would set out the old aggressive purposes. He hankered after action and a Protestant alliance which seemed to him to offer the sole constructive policy. Wentworth and Laud would wish to make the King obeyed; Roe was concerned that King Charles should be glorious. It is therefore not surprising that he should have been captivated by the Swedish King.

He had crossed over from the Low Countries with Sir Dudley Carleton after leaving a memorandum with the Prince of Orange which sets out his point of view most lucidly. His opposition to the House of Austria comes out as strongly as does the maritime bias of this policy and his firm defence of the Dutch alliance. In this paper he was speaking of that domination of the northern seas which might accrue to the Imperialists from their recent victories. "The loss of the free trade of the Baltique Sea", he explained, "is more dangerous to the kingdome of England and to the United Provinces than any other prosperity of the House of Austria, being the Indyes of the materialls of shipping, and, consequently, both of their strength, riches and subsistance."[1] His style is so cumbered and expressive ". . . the Indyes of shipping". No man could gain King Charles' austere sympathy with all this ornament.

"Ther is no way nor meanes", he then goes on, "so ready and powerfull to affect this, and consequently to give breathing to the afflicted parts of Germanye, as by uniting the Kyng of Sweweland and the Prince of Transilvania. Of these truths I suppose no practised man will doubt."[2] This is the essence of Sir Thomas Roe's policy. Madrid and Vienna must be hampered and harassed. He had done all he could with the Grand

---

[1] *Sir Thomas Roe's Mission to Gustavus Adolphus*, documents printed in *Camden Miscellany*, vol. vii, p. 2.
[2] *Ibid.*, p. 3.

Vizier to labour against the peace which the Sultan Murad IV had signed with the Emperor. "Lastly", he wrote in this connection, "all the ministers of the Grand Signor know and confess their dishonour and disadvantage by this peace, to which they were constrayned to yield by the Asian War."[1]

With this background of experience, Sir Thomas Roe was sent abroad to Danzig a few months after his return to England. His errand was to assist in making peace between the King of Sweden, who was already meditating intervention in the field in Germany, and the King of Poland. It was a mission in which Roe was carefully fettered; that calm influence at Whitehall, which the Lord-Treasurer personified, steadying him always away from action. He was instructed to assist both the King of Sweden and his "Austrian" Catholic cousin, Sigismund III of Poland. His orders from King Charles[2] included a statement in regard to a somewhat petty prince, which shows how determined his sovereign was to keep his actions in a minor key. "There is a Prince in those parts, the Duke of Curland, with whom we have allyance and particular friendship." A letter to Lord Dorchester from Sir Thomas Roe when he was setting out for Danzig on this mission shows that he felt how much his hands were tied. "My truncks and servants are gone," he explained, "the ship at Margrett ready; the playne truth is, as if it were a sickness incureable, we doe all things too late."[3]

The negotiations at Danzig, where Roe remained from the early autumn of 1629 until just before the King of Sweden landed at Usedom in the next summer, are beyond the scope of this study. They are only relevant in so far as they build up Sir Thomas Roe's political doctrine and throw light on that line of action which he came home to advocate for England. A letter to the Queen of Bohemia bears on this subject. "The substance of our miserable treaty," he wrote in September, "Mr Carleton will relate to your Majestie."[4] He was always candid with her, and in her eyes he had the root of the matter in him: he distrusted the French; he loved the Dutch and Swedes; above all, he detested the House of Austria.

[1] *Ibid.*, p. 4.

[2] Instructions of King Charles I to Sir Thomas Roe (*ibid.*, p. 19).

[3] Letter from Sir Thomas Roe to Lord Dorchester, dated June (?) 1629 (*ibid.*, p. 9).

[4] Letter from Sir Thomas Roe to the Queen of Bohemia, dated from Danzig, 21 September 1629 (*ibid.*, p. 40).

Very soon his letters began to come in to King Charles and his advisers, all beaten out in that grand enduring manner. They harped on the one theme, and all bore the same burthen. "Yet I may say", he wrote to his own master, "I have seen a brave king and glorious capteyne that hath high Pyrrhean thoughts which he wilbe ready to act in your Maties and the publicque service."[1] "It were a sullen reservedness," Roe explained to Sir Robert Carr, "and a betraying of truth to forbeare to tell you that their brave king . . . must have some noble dessigne then to wast idle, or in this corner of the world."[2] And then he came to that demand for financial assistance and alliance which was found so galling. "He [King Gustavus] is a prince highly ambitious of glory and dominion and hath no object before him but the war in Germany, whither a little reall encouragement from England would transport him." To Dorchester he wrote on the same theme— "And ther is nothing wanting but a little reall encouragement."[3] Roe was committing himself far and irretrievably, and the Queen of Bohemia's letter to him was timely. "Assure yourself," she wrote so free and jovial, "I will ever be constantlie honest fatt Thom's true friend in spite of the divelL"[4]

It was not in King Charles' nature to like the Vasa. The rude strength and vigour that marked Gustavus was as uncongenial to the Stuart sovereign as was the Renaissance quality of his learning and his swift statecraft. The seventeenth-century spirit, coming up from France and Italy, conditioned the English Court, but it had not yet reached to Sweden. That spirit was only to reach Stockholm in the succeeding generation with the sledges that brought Descartes into Sweden in Queen Christina's time.

Meanwhile, it seems clear that Charles I disliked his Vasa cousin, the great form so heavy and inelegant, the short tawny hair of *il re d'oro* (as his Italian soldiers of fortune called him), the stoop from the strong neck, those light-blue, near-sighted eyes; King Gustavus, with his great bold forehead, declaring:

[1] Letter from Sir Thomas Roe to King Charles I, dated 30 September 1629 (*Sir Thomas Roe's Mission to Gustavus Adolphus*, p. 45).

[2] Letter from Sir Thomas Roe to Sir Robert Carr, dated 28 October 1629 (*ibid.*, p. 50).

[3] Letter from Sir Thomas Roe to Lord Dorchester, dated 13 October 1629 (*ibid.*, p. 49).

[4] Letter from the Queen of Bohemia to Sir Thomas Roe, dated at the Hague, 9 November 1629 (*ibid.*, p. 53).

"I fear stupidity and treachery more than force."[1] It was not the English policy to embark on any continental venture and the King of Sweden was alien to all that King Charles represented. Willingly he left him to Cardinal Richelieu.

From Elbing and Danzig Roe sent two letters to Sir Robert Anstruther. "Now he [King Gustavus]", exclaimed the ambassador, "is armed, his bloud warm, the expense of leavies borne, his soldiers veterans *ad oram Rubiconis*. Yet he is so wise a prince that he will not pass over unless his friends build the bridge."[2] "He is", he writes again, "both *caput* and *cor regni*; he is all, and worth all."[3] Such words were not tolerable to the King of England in the mouth of his own servant. Sir Thomas Roe returned to his country, but not to new employment. He sailed homewards through the sharp late spring of the northern waters. It was April when he passed into the Sound, away from the waste of those green Baltic seas and anchored off Elsinore. He was coming back to spend his life in opposition.

Roe's treatment on the completion of his mission indicates the difficulties of public servants in an age before pensions were established and when the method of remuneration by sinecure, which the Whigs developed to so fine a point, was still rudimentary. Nevertheless, in this case a sinecure was found eventually, the chancellorship of the Order of the Garter, but the ambassador had to wait for seven years.

There is good reason to suppose that Roe was very ignorant of the Court feeling; proconsular in his approach; insensitive to atmosphere. He was quite genuinely chagrined as he waited in his hired house in St Martin's Lane and nothing came to him. He had that wide, unorganised vision which is associated with the earlier time. He had been ambassador, but he could cast his eye about on all preferment. "Late mortalities have opened the way to ambitious suitors; as, to Wales, Portsmouth, the Stannaries, the Rolls, Justice in Oyer."[4] There were so many possibilities. They would not come amiss to a royal officer.

---

[1] Cf. *The Thirty Years War*, by C. V. Wedgwood. This book, which is by far the most valuable modern study of this subject, gives an admirably balanced account of the King of Sweden's policies and of all the events which followed from the Elector Palatine's original acceptance of the Bohemian crown.

[2] *Sir Thomas Roe's Mission to Gustavus Adolphus*, p. 69.

[3] Letter dated 8 April 1630 (*ibid.*, p. 80).

[4] Letter from Sir Thomas Roe to Viscount Wilmot, dated at Stamford, 2 August 1630 (State Papers, Dom. Charles I, clxxii, 10).

Always his language was Elizabethan. To the Queen of Bohemia he exclaimed [1] that he observed all men's advancement before him and above him, as astrologers do comets; for the fixed stars and the highest are the least observed. However mathematically accurate, this surely showed a poor psychology. His mind led him, surprisingly slowly, to the true answer. In August he was asserting that the Court was a labyrinth of which he had not the clue. [2] In October he had found: "Our Court is constant. The Lord-Treasurer only is able to open and shut." [3] He had realised the power of the Earl of Portland.

Roe made a final effort by way of the Earl of Holland, who had the Queen's ear and a share of favour. The approach is almost in the nature of a political testament, and it has this value—that it makes clear the alternative around which views could crystallise. Sir Thomas entreated the Earl to cast his nativity and to counsel him whether he might prove acceptable to the King and fit for these times. [4] If he received no mark of His Majesty's grace, he would seek the sunshine on a green bank where poor men enjoy it as warm as King's favourites. Drake's ship, which was docked at Deptford, had more honour than if she had gone to sea and perished. He concluded by declaring how unseasonable and impolitic was such a proposition as that of peace between Spain and the States of Holland. "We can make no fruitful confederacy but in the north, nor recover our reputation but in our own element the sea."

Against a background of partly bitter comment on his position, Sir Thomas Roe drew out for the Secretary of State, Lord Dorchester, and his friend, Sir Robert Anstruther, the lines and even the small miniature detail of the ancient policy. Thus in October 1630 he is found setting out the proposition that the restoration of the Duke of Courland's family concerns his Majesty in power, religion and reason of state. [5] Like so many Englishmen, Roe's attitude to foreign politics

[1] Letter from Sir Thomas Roe to the Queen of Bohemia, dated from St Martin's Lane, 14 July 1630 (ibid., clxx, 53).

[2] Ibid., clxxii, 18.

[3] Letter from Sir Thomas Roe to Sir Robert Anstruther, dated 29 October 1630 (ibid., clxxiv, 101).

[4] Letter from Sir Thomas Roe to the Earl of Holland, dated from Stamford, 20 September 1630 (ibid., clxxiii, 49).

[5] Letter from Sir Thomas Roe to Secretary Dorchester, dated from Stamford, 3 October 1630 (ibid., clxxiv, 10).

was marked by a single-track enthusiasm. His hero was the King of Sweden and his panacea an Anglo-Swedish-Dutch alliance. "That King", he wrote to Sir Robert Anstruther of Gustavus, "does not rely upon the French, and it matters not what they do for a bigotry governs them."[1] He was persuaded, he went on in the same letter, that "any papist-blinded estate[s] are Egyptian reeds". In this connection the Queen of Bohemia maintained, with more vivacity, the same position. She always found the "Monsieurs" insincere, and feared lest the French should play her brother *un tour de Breton* or some other trick.

It was in this atmosphere that the middle period of the reign drew to a close. During 1630-1 there was but little alteration; Roe constantly demanding an alliance which the King and the courtier-diplomats found unacceptable; the Secretary of State now ailing; King Charles careful and distant. The Bohemian sovereigns stayed at Rhenen. "Thanks to God", wrote Roe to their agent, Sir Francis Nethersole, "for the continuance of his blessing to that brave King who must do good for us against our wills."[2]

By April 1631 Secretary Dorchester's health became precarious. He had had forewarnings of a fit, and sat in his house at Westminster attending to Dr Mayerne's prescriptions. At Court the Earl of Portland, as Roe had noted, held such confidence as the King admitted and all the power that he could seize upon. For the men of the old *régime* it was a period of disillusion. It was at this time that Dorchester wrote to Lord Holland that, if he should be cut short and should follow his old master (King James) in his end, as he already did in his diseases, he would be able to leave his friend *nihil præter lachrymas* after his long and expensive services.[3]

In that summer the Secretary of State wrote to Sir Thomas Roe that the Chancellor of Sweden had termed him the *auctor et impulsor* of King Gustavus' German undertakings.[4] Sitting in his "cell" at Bulwick through the ensuing winter, Roe

[1] Letter from Sir Thomas Roe to Sir Robert Anstruther, dated 29 October 1630 (*ibid.*, vol. clxxiv, p. 101).

[2] Letter from Sir Thomas Roe at Bulwick to Sir Francis Nethersole at the *Golden Stirrup*, over against the New Exchange in the Strand, dated 31 December 1631 (State Papers, Dom. Charles I, cciv, 108).

[3] Letter from Secretary Dorchester to the Earl of Holland, dated 30 April 1631 (*ibid.*, clxxxix, 63).

[4] Letter from Secretary Dorchester to Sir Thomas Roe, dated at Woodstock, 19 August 1631 (*ibid.*, cxcviii, 46).

would descant upon the rumour that he had received a missive from the King of Sweden written in letters of gold. It was poor recompense for unemployment. Two sentences which date from that winter set the tone of events in London. A letter from one of the Grooms of the Bedchamber describes the Court as being like the earth, naturally cold and reflecting no more affection than the sunshine of their master's favour beats upon it.[1] In the same vein a newsletter sent to foreign parts remarks that "the Court is like a swarm of bees, a confused hum amongst all".[2] At about this time an unnamed Swedish intelligencer wrote to his master giving the rumours current in the outward Court, and in the Stone Gallery at Whitehall, and in the walking council of St Paul's. There was little to comfort the King of Sweden from these quarters.

The year 1632 ushered in changes. Secretary Dorchester was failing. He was only fifty-eight, but quite exhausted. There was an estate worth £700 a year to maintain his family. His wife was enceinte. The period of office had brought Dead Sea fruit. He was leaving after all his active life so little to the heir he hoped was coming.[3] It was mid-February before the Secretaryship of State at length fell vacant. "Lord Dorchester," wrote Sir Thomas Roe, "as he walked rightly in life, died manly and christianly, and rejoiced and recommended the King of Sweden: and so, like a swan sang his own funeral."[4] Roe concluded by explaining to the Queen of Bohemia's servant, Mr Dyneley, that he dared not guess at Dorchester's successor, but divined that the Lord-Treasurer would for a time supply the service.

The anti-Swedish party now made some headway around the calm, uninterested Stuart King. These were the men who were attuned to the Vandyck mood. They were supple and eager to assuage the southern Courts. The old Elizabethan framework seemed to them as barbarous as it was unnecessary. Their lines ran out to Paris or Madrid, perhaps to Rome. Sir Henry Vane,

[1] Letter from William Murray to Sir Henry Vane, dated at Whitehall, 18 December 1631 (ibid., cciv, 72).

[2] Newsletter dated 30 December 1631 (ibid., cciv, 107).

[3] In fact, the posthumous child was a daughter, born in June 1632 and dying six months later. Lady Dorchester survived her only son, Lord Bayning, and her great fortune went to her four daughters, one of whom was the mother of Barbara, Duchess of Cleveland.

[4] Letter from Sir Thomas Roe to John Dyneley, dated from London, 22 February 1632 (State Papers, Dom. Charles I, ccxi, 74).

the present ambassador to the Court of Sweden, a man whose significance will be considered later, was for the moment their chief figurehead. Such men were light in hand and even in intention barely serious. A letter to Vane from Sir Tobie Mathew contrives to give the key to this approach. Yesterday night,[1] he explains in this despatch, he had waited at supper on Lord Carlisle and had conversed at large with Sir Jacob Ashley,[2] a worthy gentleman and a great lover of the Marquess (of Hamilton) and Sir Henry. Sir Jacob had spoken highly of the courage and intellectual and experimental abilities of the King of Sweden, but Sir Tobie had never heard any man totally exclude from him covetousness and arrogancy and inordinate ambition. Sir Tobie never apprehended a man who had no issue male, nor multitudes of subjects, only auxiliaries, but just as he would apprehend a storm.[3] He rejoiced that the Lord-Treasurer still stood at the same height in the King's favour, and that he and Lord Cottington were very dear. These matters were in a sense trivial because Sir Tobie was so distant from them. It was of more consequence that he could report that the Lord-Treasurer was now in a better and clearer air of greatness than ever Vane saw him in. These were the times of Roe's dejection.

Just at this period the Queen of Bohemia was herself weighed down by those acute Lutheran and Calvinist dissensions which in England and among the English supporters of the Reformed Religion found so little echo. Those who had desired an aggressive Protestant policy had always thought in terms of those forces which immediately or more remotely drew their inspiration from Geneva; the French Huguenots, the States of Holland, the Elector Palatine. They were now for the first time to experience a Lutheran conqueror. Thus it was not only the position of vassalage to the Swedish Crown which galled upon the titular sovereign of Bohemia, it was also the special place which

---

[1] Letter from Sir Tobie Mathew to Sir Henry Vane, dated from London 25 March 1632 (*ibid.*, ccxiv, 64).

[2] Ashley would seem to be a transcriber's error for Astley.

[3] It is interesting that Sir Thomas Roe reached the opposite deduction from the same premises. "If this King", he wrote, "had a settled posterity it were great wisdom to stay his career and limit it; but when we see he is . . . rather a torrent than a live spring, that all his glory and greatness depends upon his own virtue and life; and that in case of sure mortality it is certain that all this inundation will dry up and return to the first channel of moderation, it is merely folly to object him."

King Gustavus claimed for the adherents of the Augsburg Confession in the estates of the Palatinate. This religious question was in turn the outward symbol of the Vasa political predominance.

King Frederick was borne down by scruples, but it seems more likely that the Queen was wounded in her persistent and yet eager pride. Through 1632 the King of Bohemia grew worn from these anxieties. He had, indeed, no other resource save in the King of Sweden, who was "so hard to content". His German advisers could not but be discontented by the Swedish victories, which received such welcome from their English friends. On 7 September 1631, Gustavus Adelphus had defeated the Imperialist forces at Breitenfeld. On 21 March following, he entered Nuremberg. "We will not", wrote Roe, "give the King of Sweden leave to conquer like a man by degrees nor human ways, but we look he should fight battles and take towns so fast as we read them in the Book of Joshua, whose example indeed he is."[1]

In the summer Wallenstein was recalled to the Emperor's service, and the tide slowly began to turn. Late that autumn Frederick, titular King of Bohemia and Elector Palatine, visited his brother-in-law the Duke of Zweibrücken. Though only thirty-six he was a broken man, old before his time, and so worn with care that even his own brother did not recognise him. There was plague at Bacharach on the Rhine as the King rode homeward. At Mainz he was taken ill,[2] and there he heard of the death of Gustavus at the battle of Lutzen, which had been fought on 6 November. Dr Spina, the Court Physician from Darmstadt, was sent out to him, and detected the pustules of the plague. On the 15th the patient became delirious. He was far from his home at Rhenen, where his house stood beside that great, high, springing church tower which overlooked the morne flat country. There were his wife and the survivors of his thirteen children, the youngest boy, Gustavus, just ten months old, and the youngest girl, Sophia, the mother of George I, a child of two. Their prospects were unhopeful; their state penurious. After four days of delirium King Frederick died at

---

[1] Letter from Sir Thomas Roe to Sir Edward Horwood, dated from Bulwick, 28 May 1632 (State Papers, Dom. Charles I, ccxvi. 92).

[2] S. R. Gardiner, who is usually accurate on such points, states in error that King Frederick died at Bacharach (History, vol. vii, p. 207).

seven in the morning of 19 November, in the Archbishop Elector's territory of Mainz, in his hired lodging.

With the two kings now dead, the possibility of aggressive English policies had vanished. Both the Bohemian cause and the Swedish legend took their place in the mythology of English sentiment. Swiftly they came to their enduring place. "Never", wrote Sir Symonds D'Ewes, "did one person's death in Christendom bring so much sorrow to all true Protestant hearts—not our godly Edward's, the Sixth of that name, nor our late heroic and inestimable Prince Henry, as did the King of Sweden's at this present."[1]

King Charles invited his sister to England, but she preferred to stay in the Low Countries. There was nothing to impede the rather artificial peace between the Court of St James and foreign powers. The scene was set for the short Vandyck years. "All", wrote Roe to his mistress, "goes one way, and I know not the wit of it."[2]

The periods in English seventeenth-century history are very brief, and the political personages of each phase crowd one another. There were now present in the background, not only the figures of the new opposition, but the survivors from King James' time and those whose mould remained Elizabethan. In Holland there was growing up the most vivid member of the Palatine family—the boy Prince Rupert. Among the many elements that made up the very varying cavalier approach, some were remote from, and indeed hostile to, the atmosphere of King Charles' Court. In addition to the Scots who had fought in the continental wars, there came now the German contribution to the English struggle. Prince Rupert was never to know the Vandyck world. His sense of kingship and of German noble knighthood, that immense resilient courage and that high mind which was to be so starched and curious, were slowly developing at Rhenen. At both ends of the reign of Charles I we find the spirit of the Queen of Bohemia.

[1] *Autobiography of Sir Symonds D'Ewes.*
[2] Letter from Sir Thomas Roe to the Queen of Bohemia (State Papers, Germany).

CHAPTER VI

THE EARL OF STRAFFORD

THE position of Thomas Viscount Wentworth is cardinal to the political structure of Caroline England. His career has been examined and re-examined, and each political action in the last year of his life has been subjected to interpretation. The nature of his intentions and the elements responsible for his fall have been canvassed and explored. Yet his general standpoint has been approached too often by historians imbued with the severe prejudice of the quiet Victorian century, and he has been judged in the light of the Whig principles which triumphed in the Revolution of 1688. His abiding influence is the more remarkable because, for seven years from July 1633 until April 1640, he was absent in Ireland as Lord-Deputy, and was only in London for brief visits. It was not until January 1640, a short eleven months before his impeachment and arrest, that he was given the earldom by whose title he is known. The documentation relating to Strafford's public life is copious, but the papers in Lord Fitzwilliam's collection may throw much new light. Certain facts are, however, clear.

In the first place he was attached to kingship and not to the King. Close as they were to one another, Strafford's respect for Charles I veered always towards dislike. There was never between the two men that confidence which makes it hard for a sovereign to sacrifice his minister. From the beginning Strafford stood apart from the royal fabric, outside it and upholding it. He went singularly free from his own social environment. His views were high and popular; he had nothing in common with the opposition lords. On the contrary, he belonged to that type of statesman who always offers his services to monarchy. That was his chosen road and it was only the presence of the favourite Buckingham which had blocked his normal hopes. He tired of opposition before the way was cleared for him by the Duke's murder; but in any reign he would have come to serve the sovereign. He was authoritarian, and thus loved the exercise of delegated high authority.

Strafford's name has become almost the symbol for unbending force. He had a mind tenacious and not quick, with an easy heavy humour, no lightness of touch, no turn of speed. He was quite self-confident, very hasty, generous and unsuspecting. There was much in his make-up which was close to the roots of life in England. His religion, his nationalist views, his insularity, alike reflected a range of opinion which had now crystallised among the landed gentry. It was part of his weakness that his principles were by current standards so *sound*. He held so many wide convictions that no one in the main stream of English life would disagree with; there was an element of the obvious about much of his thought, his views on foreign policy, for instance. His character had, of course, great strength. From his royal master to that master's remotest enemies, no one in that brittle world could fail to be afraid of Strafford and of the iron in him. There he stood, as in the Welbeck portrait, with the dark-knit brows and that free, grave composure. He was brusque and stern, and alike conventional and intimidating.

He was, as his most recent biographer, C. V. Wedgwood, has remarked, very emotional. He was sanguine and North Country. A belief in the power of leadership remained with him. Since he was born to great wealth, he suffered from the disadvantage that things came to him too easily. He did not realise the cross currents and the shoals. In this matter he was enlightened by Archbishop Laud, the prelate who had given him his friendship when they had both set out to serve the doctrine of authority. It is clear that this was an association in which Laud, the man who had climbed, brought to the layman his own bruised, worldly wisdom.

"My Lord," he declared in a letter written during his first autumn at Lambeth, "when I say the less assistance the more merit, I did not put you off with a compliment, for my answer was real. 'Tis true, able and well-affected men are brave associates, and great services are done at ease by such instruments. But wot you what? Where many are employed at once, and all very able, there usually proves to be in some a fretting cankerworm of ambition, and that for particular aims makes such a division, as gives far greater impediment to the greatest affairs, than any want of sufficiency can make."[1] One can see

---

[1] Letter from Archbishop Laud to Viscount Wentworth, dated 14 October 1633 (Laud's *Works*, vol. vi, pt. i, p. 302).

that the Primate felt the duty of imparting to Lord Wentworth that clear view, tinged with acerbity, that he had come to hold in regard to all those who seek preferment. Both men were sensitive, but it was only the younger who was confiding. There was something protective in the attitude of the old bishop, who had never been tempted to look for "brave associates". "And therefore," he concluded, "by your Lordship's leave, the conceit which you express, of all able, and all hearty, and all running one way, and none caring for any ends so the King be served, is but a branch of Plato's commonwealth, which flourishes at this day nowhere but in Utopia, and thither I have no purpose to send your Lordship." On this text the friendship of the two men can be studied.

In age they were some twenty years apart, and Strafford was approaching forty when Laud came to occupy the chief place in his life. He had always had few friends, an intimate dependant here and there, like Christopher Wandesford or George Radcliffe, but none like the Archbishop. Many years before, he had made a short-lived child-marriage with Lady Margaret Clifford, and had lately, in the autumn of 1631, become a widower for the second time through the death of Arabella Holles, to whom he had been devoted. He was now friendless and very desolate. His brother-in-law, Denzil Holles, was a leader of that party of the opposition squirearchy which he had left. It was to be some time before he would swim into Lady Carlisle's orbit, he was for the moment between the tides. In all that world the new Archbishop alone sustained his high exacting view of the nature of those who wield authority. Very readily he made him his confidant and poured out to him his plans and hopes. A study of his letters makes it clear that he gave to William Laud that devotion which his own direct nature would have wished to lavish on his master. In some respects this friendship, which on the side of the younger man was so intense, must have proved galling to the sovereign, for in time King Charles' insufficiency became a link between his two chief ministers.

They had neither the King's subdued vitality nor his fastidiousness. Their force had made them boisterous with a boisterousness that was a shade unreal. Together the Primate and Lord-Deputy made merry, bandying jests and quips. Their mutual enjoyment of the obvious and the commonplace only served to underline their deep respect for one another, and their firm affection. Laud's side of the correspondence, in particular, throws light upon his noisy, serious and loaded humour. "And what do you mean to do", he wrote to Lord Wentworth in the summer of 1632, "for your journey into Ireland? Will you stay till August be past and put yourself upon the flaws of September in that broken sea? You may find more danger in a ship to Ireland than over the Thames in a skuller. Did ever Brutus or Cassius do thus or thus at Tiber?" The references to Plutarch are interesting, as is the pressure at which Dr Laud maintained his heavy and questing wit.[1]

Strafford's Cambridge days provided another subject for this raillery. The friends came from the St John's Colleges in the two universities. "A St John's man," the Archbishop wrote in reference to Dr Boyle of Waterford, "you say he is, and of Oxford; your Cambridge panniers never brought such a fairing to the market?"[2] "As for Bishop Howland," he wrote again, "you never heard of him. What? Nor of Jeames' wife neither? Good Lord, how ignorant you can be when you list. Yes, but you have taken St John's Ox, *flagrante crimine*, and I put you to your memory." He was always fond of these quips about the churchmen who had come from Strafford's college.

There was between the two men a genuine confidence in religious matters. Strafford was of that way of thinking which the Elizabethan Settlement had formed among the gentry. The Established Church was logical, inevitable and necessary. It gave him satisfaction to see Law well administered, while for the rest he gave adherence to a generalised Biblical Protestantism which owed much to the divines of Calvinistic principles who had taken root in Cambridge in the old Queen's time. "I pray," the Archbishop wrote again to him, "what means this Johnnism of yours, 'till the rights of the Pastors be a little more settled? You learned this from old Alvey or Billy Nelson."[3] This is a good example of Dr Laud's jesting style

---

[1] Letter from Bishop Laud to Viscount Wentworth, dated 30 July 1632 (Laud's *Works*, vol. vi, pt. i, p. 302).

[2] Letter from Archbishop Laud to Vscount Wentworth, dated 14 May 1634 (*ibid.*, vol. vi, pt. i, pp. 374-5).

[3] Letter from Archbishop Laud to Viscount Wentworth, dated 14 May 1634 (Laud's *Works*, vol. vi, pt. i, p. 373), The references are to the Elizabethan divines, Richard Alvey and William Nelson.

through which can be perceived his security and his deep contentment.[1]

There was no possibility of such a man as Strafford ever joining forces with the Precisians. He was as far from the Puritans as Laud himself, sharing that reverence for the ark of God-protected State authority. At the same time, the Archbishop had a tactical advantage in dealing with an officer of State who was inclined to the more Protestant opinions in the Church of England. They could sail in company. Unlike Portland and Cottington and Windebank, the Lord-Deputy ran no danger of making shipwreck on the lee shore of Rome.

In their correspondence, the religious questions were seldom made explicit, but one of the Primate's references is worth recording. "But once for all," he wrote in the later years of their close friendship, "if you will but read over the short book of Ecclesiastes, while these thoughts [of disillusionment] are in you, you will see a better disposition of these things, and the vanity of all their shadows, than is to be found in any anagrams of Dr Donne's, or any designs of Vandyke; so to these lines there drawn I leave you."[2]

For the rest it was natural that the chief interest of their association should prove political. It was in this field that they exchanged opinions, the elder man constantly cautioning and warning and encouraging his younger colleague. Both men had a hatred of inefficiency, and Laud, at least, had always a keen relentless knowledge of their many enemies. The letters between them were written in a simple numeral cipher with a key to persons and sometimes to words and phrases. The situation was complicated by the fact that Strafford had enmities and friendships which the Archbishop did not share. Thus he had come into the Court on Lord-Treasurer Portland's invitation, and he always maintained a close personal relationship with Cottington. This must be remembered when Laud is seen labouring at the constructing of the influence of his new ally. "You must

[1] Another letter, dated 20 October 1634, contains an instance of Laud's punning in reference to the marriage between Sir Gerard Lowther and Sir William Parsons' daughter: "And I see you owe me much for that praise and commendations, which works upon the dullest capacities. And the more because it works not only on them, but on all *Parsons* and their children, and them that marry them, especially where praise is *Lowder* than ordinary, and hath it entailed" (*ibid.*, vol. vi, pt. i, p. 397).

[2] Letter from Archbishop Laud to Viscount Wentworth, dated 14 May 1638 (Laud's *Works*, vol. vi, pt. i, p. 524).

have daily use", he wrote from Lambeth to the Lord-Deputy in Dublin, "of his Lordship [of Portland] here, and I would not, both in regard of the King's service and your own good that this [difference of opinion] should occasion a breach between you. For myself I am not considerable, and can bear the jealousies that are upon me; but I would have your Lordship keep all your great friends entire."[1] It was a line both clear and generous, and leads on to a consideration of what Laud and Strafford meant when they expressed their hatred of the "Lady Mora".

A certain care is needed in disentangling the expressions in their correspondence, for they were accustomed to use certain phrases in order to conceal a further meaning. This practice is used in the case of the expression "the Lady Mora," which seems to have masked much that these friends loathed. "By the way," wrote the Archbishop to the Lord-Deputy in the summer of 1634, "as I was showing a passage of your letters to the King, he espied my marginal note 'the Lady Mora', and would needs know what we meant by it. I told him it was a common by-word between us when we meant to express any extreme delay, and so passed on."[2] But "Mora" had a different meaning for its authors. To them it seems to have implied the whole series of obstructions and delays which arose from the private mani-pulation, usually financial, of the King's servants. It thus denoted all that work for "private ends"; the customary unauthorised "rake off"; the unregulated, unavowed intrigue for money. It also included the whole wide mesh of courtiers who were accessible on their financial side. "For the Lady Mora is extreme potent in Court, and I would not give her Ladyship just cause for exception."

To Laud these aspects of the Court were in an especial manner linked with the Lord-Treasurer, and also with Cotting-ton, who held the posts of Chancellor of the Exchequer and Master of the Court of Wards. He was not, perhaps, exact in his appreciation of the factors; still it is beyond dispute that everything experienced and *rusé* came naturally to these public servants. At the same time each cheap and devious means invented to reward needed supporters found an opponent in

---

[1] Letter from Archbishop Laud to Viscount Wentworth, dated 11 March 1634 (Laud's *Works*, vol. vi, pt. i, p. 359).

[2] *Ibid.*, vol. vii, pt. i, p. 103.

the Primate and the Deputy. A few short passages will show the line thus taken. "But I will lay", wrote Dr Laud, "a 105 [Lord-Treasurer] to it [and let malice and jealousy go together] that they or Lady Mora is in fault if anything there or here go in too slow a pace. Here I am sure they do, and I cannot help it."[1] The following sentence refers to the same set of circumstances: "Certainly 100 [the King] hath a great opinion of 105 notwithstanding *mora ipsa* and somewhat more."[2]

The two final quotations date from some months later. "I do easily", declared the Archbishop, "believe that all which you writ to 102 [me] concerning 105 [the vacant Treasurership] and 110 [Cottington] is most true. And I have late seen more into the disposition of 110, since the death of his lady, the Lady Mora."[3] "If this hold," he concluded, "all will go on the same way it did, save that perchance the Lady Mora's waiting woman will pace a little faster than her mistress did, but the steps will be as foul."[4] The last sentence has a clear bitterness. It is a strange commentary on Laud's unworldliness and on Strafford's remoteness from his *confrères*.

There was something antique and Roman in this outlook. In addition, the Lord-Deputy possessed granite principles. He probably could not understand the temptations of his poorer colleagues. It is of interest to place his great phrases over against the record of an almost necessary chicanery which King Charles' other servants had inherited from their old Master's tired, insolvent Court. "Princes", declared Lord Wentworth, "are to be indulgent, nursing fathers to their people; their modest liberties, their sober rights ought to be precious in their eyes, the branches of their government be for shadow, for habitation, the comfort of life, repose, safe and still under the protection of their sceptres. Subjects on the other side ought with solicitous eyes of jealousy to watch over the prerogatives of the Crown; the authority of a King is the keystone which closeth up the arch of order and government, which contains each part in due relation to the whole and which once shaken, infirmed all the frame falls together into a confused heap of foundation and battlement, of strength and beauty."

[1] Laud's *Works*, vol. vii, pt. i, p. 101.   [2] *Ibid.*, vol. vii, pt. i p. 108.
[3] Letter from Archbishop Laud to Viscount Wentworth, dated 12 May 1635 (Laud's *Works*, vol. vii, pt. i, p. 129).
[4] Letter from the same to the same, dated 12 June 1635 (*ibid.*, vol. vii, pt. i, p. 145).

It was not "foundation and battlement", but the day-to-day struggle for existence and for the gathering of a fine, substantial family capital which occupied the minds of the other courtiers. They were concerned with income and not with doctrine. His ambition was self-dedicated and highly personal; theirs was dynastic. Again he came forward to roll his periods. "May the tent of this Court", Strafford exclaimed when taking over the Lord-Presidentship of the Council of the North, "be enlarged, the curtains drawn out, the stakes strengthened, yet no further than shall be for a covering to the common tranquillity and shelter to the poor and innocent from the proud and insolent."[1] From the chair of State his mind would sweep that great and ordered institute which he, in the first place, conceived as the chief pillar of the Stuart monarchy. "I not only profess", he then went on, "my entire filial obedience to the Church, but also covet a sound, a close conjunction with the grave, the reverend Clergy that they to us, we to them may as twins administer help to each other." Such views when put into operation were impracticable, and the very strength with which they were maintained would bring both ministers to their destruction. Seen from another angle, the picture which Laud and Strafford now presented looked very different.

For the Lord-Deputy was a portent, and it was necessary either to contrive to live with him or to destroy him. He had come not so much into favour as into power. The Archbishop was politically unapproachable, secure in the King's confidence, an inevitable adjunct to the State machinery; but Lord Wentworth was a different proposition. He could be gained, and Cottington thus meant to gain him.

There was much to be said for this endeavour. Francis Cottington kept to a line of policy which might be held to recommend him; he was resolutely opposed to France, and consequently to the Queen's influence. With all his rapid talent and his love for Spain, there was something very English, and even insular, in his approach to current problems. He had been an ally of Portland's, and had come into power with him when Buckingham was murdered. From the beginning he had made overtures to Strafford; for Portland was soon to die and he was

---

[1] These speeches, delivered in December 1628 and first printed in Browning's *Prose Life of Strafford*, Appendix II, pp. 291-6, were reprinted in Lady Burghclere's biography, vol. i, pp. 115-17.

urgently in need of some support. These offers of alliance were in great part successful, for Cottington appealed to that keen interest in sport and to that worldly courage which was not reflected in the Lord-Deputy's intercourse with the Archbishop.

It was in keeping with Strafford's simplicity that it was easy enough to gain his friendship. "He loved hawking", wrote his cousin and intimate, George Radcliffe, "and was a good falconer. He played excellently well at *Primero* and *Mayo*, and for company sake at Christmas, and after supper he would play sometimes. His chief recreation after supper [was] taking tobacco and telling stories with great pleasantness and free-dom."[1] Besides this, his private life, reflecting such a bright, hard standard of public virtue, must have been of curious interest to Cottington's rapier-like, fastidious mind. "He [Strafford] was never drunk in his life, as I have often heard him say." Further evidence of the Lord-Deputy's outlook is provided in the circumstances, first concealed and then acknowledged, of his third marriage with Elizabeth Rodes, his young, penurious, insipid bride. The simplest interpretation of the facts would seem to indicate his strong repugnance to involving a girl of some social standing in an equivocal relation-ship. There is so much about Strafford which suggests the central Victorian epoch, his high conscious rectitude, based on a private joviality, and that keen sense of obligation. He would have stood alone as an heroic figure in the English legend if the thought of the succeeding age had been conditioned not by the Whigs but by the Tories. As it is, his consciousness of his voca-tion as a ruler and of right dealing beckons across the crackling, cynical Walpole *jeux d'esprit* to the just land of the nineteenth century.

It was perhaps these characteristics among others which served to divide both Laud and Strafford from their sovereigns. Very naturally this prosy, cheerful and sedate hold upon government was highly distasteful to the Queen. From an early date Queen Henrietta had emerged as the Lord-Deputy's enemy. As far as he himself was concerned, the Archbishop arranged the situation with some skill, opposing a prelatical, stiff, court-eous manner to the consort's childish and brittle and sometimes offended suavity. Strafford, on the other hand, could not con-

[1] *Life of Strafford*, by Sir George Radcliffe, printed in Knowler's *Letters*, vol. ii, p. 433.

ceal his impatience and dislike for the Queen's managed alien frivolity, that light-minded and virtuous gaiety, quasi-political in its inspiration, which he had not the experience to parry.

There was a gulf between them which was past bridging. Keen, and at times reckless, she was inured to the idea of opposition between the minister and the royal consort, and even welcomed it. With Buckingham she had been at open enmity, nor did she care for Richelieu. It was natural for her to be swift and vehement, with her emotions tearing on the surface. A complaisant acquiescence formed no part of the inheritance of the Bourbons of Navarre. Her memories of Strafford, after all the disasters, were of his angers and his difficult character, and, as she told Madame de Motteville, his beautiful hands. For his part he underestimated the Queen, nor could he see that she and her supporters at the Court might ultimately ruin him.

He was, in fact, exposed to many dangers. The rule of Buckingham and Laud and Strafford had not, and could not have, that ruthless cutting edge which the great Cardinal relied on in his internecine conflicts. Where the Bourbons conquered, the Stuarts yielded. Seen against that class-dominance which was to prove victorious, both Laud and Strafford appear theocratic, sententious and provincial, rigid, unimaginative; above all else old-fashioned.

It was this high antique "virtue" which lay at the core of the tragedy of Strafford's relationship with Charles I. The minister was too rigid for a master who did not consider that his inalienable right required an ordered method, or an even hand, or balanced strict accountancy. In this, and in this alone, King Charles and his supporters and his enemies, the whole complex of the rich opposition gentry, thought as one. The slow development of perquisites, the quiet emergence of a pensions system by way of the sale of offices and of reversions; the joint stock companies and the monopolies, all formed part of that strengthening of the family system that would in time reveal an oligarchy which was well entrenched and singularly perfect.

Strafford, for all his insularity, was of the type of the great servants of the Bourbon monarchy. This temper of mind is exemplified in his instructions to the officers of the Court of the Council of the North, who were ordered to bear heavily upon "escheators, feodaries, under sheriffs, clerks of the market, attornies, registrars, bailiffs and such like, which snatch on the right hand and are hungry, eat on the left and are not satisfied".

With this there went a necessary zeal for the strengthening of his own position. He was somewhat remote from the interests of his own family, and constitutionally antipathetic to that long intake of land and grant and perquisite which was normally the very breath of life to politicians. He was insistent in his demands upon the King for a strong mark of recognition, while there was nothing which made Charles I so stiff and cold and formal as a tussle with an exacting subject. And Strafford had a withdrawn pride and self-assertion, was easily cast down, a prey to chagrin.

In 1634, and again in 1636, he had asked for an earldom to fortify him as a Lord-Deputy. "And as for that matter," the King replied to his first request, "I desire you not to think that I am displeased with the asking, though for the present I grant it not. For I acknowledge that noble minds are always accompanied with lawful ambitions."[1] It is a strange chill tone when we recall the warm affection which King Charles bestowed on Buckingham. The second reply was not dissimilar. "And believe it," the sovereign prosed along, "the marks of my Favours that stop malicious tongues are neither Places nor titles, but the little welcome I give to accusers, and the willing ear I give to my servants."[2] The second refusal went very deep, as a letter to the Archbishop shows. "I will serve His Majesty", the Lord-Deputy wrote in connection with this disappointment, "with the same diligence, labour, and faith as formerly; yet to confess a plain truth to your grace, with whom I neither must nor can ever dissemble, with less cheerfulness in myself hereafter."

Perhaps the King was on the defensive in face of his over-resolute viceroy. Those formal, meticulous and pricking lines seem to betray a conscious effort on the sovereign's part to maintain his courage and preserve his royal dignity. As his harshness to his equals in Ireland tends to show, the Lord-Deputy was only fit to serve a very powerful and ruthless master. One well-known passage indicates the difficulties which

[1] Letter from the King to Viscount Wentworth, dated 23 October 1634 (printed in Knowler's *Letters*, vol. i, pp. 331-2).

[2] Letter from the King to Viscount Wentworth, dated 3 September 1636 (*ibid.*, vol. ii, p. 32).

he was bound to meet. "You want not them", wrote the Archbishop, "which whisper, and perhaps speak louder where they think they may, against your proceedings in Ireland as being over-full of personal prosecutions against men of quality, and they stick not to instance in [Lord] St Albans, the Lord Wilmot and this Earl [of Cork]. And this is somewhat loudly spoken by some on the Queen's side. I know you have a great deal more resolution in you, than to decline any service due to the King, State or Church, for the barking of discontented persons; and God forbid but you should. And yet, my Lord, if you could find a way to do all these great services, and decline these storms."[1]

The King in time would be compelled to deal with a minister whose outlook had now hardened. He could not escape from the Lord-Deputy's northern sincerity and he was always aware of his independence. Even Laud was brought eventually to concur in his friend's estimate. One passage in a letter written in the early summer of 1638 can serve as an epitaph on their relations with their sovereign, who was so fastidious and so unregarding. "This done I shall not need", wrote the Primate to the Lord-Deputy, "to answer the next passage of your philosophy; but that he that serves shall see how to steer himself, whatever the governor do, or omit, that is over him, and make his best use of that, which is oftentimes worst done. But for your close, I agree wholly with you, that a Prince puts a great prejudice upon his own affairs, if he continue a servant longer in any great employment, than he will give him trust and power to execute."[2] This quotation may conclude the brief account of the nature of Strafford's influence.[3]

[1] Letter from Archbishop Laud to Viscount Wentworth, dated 16 November 1635 (Laud's *Works*, vol. vi, pt. i, p. 441).

[2] Letter from Archbishop Laud to Viscount Wentworth, dated 14 May 1638 (Laud's *Works*, vol. vii, pt. ii, p. 525).

[3] It must be borne in mind that much fresh information should be obtained when the manuscripts relating to Strafford in the Wentworth Woodhouse collection, and now at last accessible to the student, have been examined.

CHAPTER VII

PRIMATE AND SUFFRAGANS

A STUDY of the position of the Church of England in the years that followed the death of Buckingham gives rise to a not altogether delusive impression of peace and deep tranquillity. The atmosphere is that of summer weather. A quiet contentment, no less profound for being somewhat authoritative in its temper, wells up throughout the correspondences. It was an English calm relying on quite clear fixed values in politics and in theology. Two accounts of different aspects of Church life in the West of England will indicate the situation. They were both written in the autumn of 1633.

The first is a long letter written by the Bishop of Bath and Wells to the Archbishop of Canterbury. There had been certain unimportant complaints about the disorders on Revel days. "Throughout Somersetshire", he wrote, "there are not only feasts of Decication, but Church ales, Clerk ales and Bid ales. The feasts of Dedication are called Feast days or Revel days. When the constables told their neighbours that the judges would put down their feasts, they answered that it was very hard if they could not entertain their friends once a year to praise God for his blessings and pray for the King under whose happy government they enjoyed peace and quietness."[1] There is surely a conviction of security in this reference to peace and quietness and the happy government.

"Church ales", the Bishop continued, "have been most left off or put down, but by Church ales heretofore many poor parishes have cast their bells, repaired their towers, beautified their churches, and raised stocks for the poor, and not by the sins of the people (as some humourists have said), but by the benevolence of the people at their sports and pastimes. Clerk ales, for the better maintenance of parish clerks, have been used until of late, and since they have been put down, some ministers are afraid they shall have no parish clerks. A Bid ale is when an

[1] Letter from the Bishop of Bath and Wells to the Archbishop of Canterbury, dated from Wells, 5 November 1633 (State Papers, Dom. Charles I, ccl, 20).

honest man decayed in his estate is set up again by the benevolence of friends at a feast, but this is laid aside in almost every
place." The scene depicted is one of rooted custom maintained
through an unyielding social fabric. The very charges brought
against the practice of Revel days and Church ales show a
remoteness of spirit from the rural life.

"The chiefest cause of the dislike of these feasts among the
preciser sort", explained the Bishop, "is because they are kept
upon Sundays, which they never call but Sabbath days, upon
which they would have no manner of recreation, neither roast
nor sod." It is very understandable that the great prelates
should have felt that this last view was unlikely to gain much
hold upon the people.

The other account is likewise from the angle of the episcopate.
It is a familiar description sent to Sir John Coke, the Secretary
of State, by his younger brother, George, who had just been
promoted to the See of Bristol. Dr Coke, who here describes his
reception in his cathedral city, was a careful man of rather
limited capacity. The point of view is, however, all the more
characteristic in coming from a naïve and uncomplicated mind.
"Right Honourable and most loving Brother," he began, "as
I hold it fit to give you account of our coming to Bristoll, so
I will do it in few words. We came thither, especially in the
end of our journey, through much foul way and weather yet
I thank God we found good welcome there . . . . I preached the
first Sunday save one after my coming, where was the greatest
concourse of people that ever I saw: where were present the
Mayor with his Aldermen and Sheriffs, [and] the whole clergy
of the city, who, to increase the auditory, preached not one
sermon at their own churches in the forenoon."[1] So far this is
just the ordered progress of an Established Church, but the
second portion of this account has greater interest.

"It pleased God", the Bishop continued, "to give a fair and
lightsome day, and success to my comfort, and, as I perceived
by their patient and silent attention, their content. The clergy
I find both able and painful, and the city loving and friendly
to me, with a great desire, as I well perceive, of my answerable
aspect to them." There is an innocence in this satisfaction, and
a kind of happy and assured credulity. The benefits of royal

---

[1] Letter from the Bishop of Bristol to Sir John Coke, dated from Bristol, 4 September 1633 (Cal. Coke MSS., vol. ii, pp. 28-9).

sympathy were so apparent. In this dawn of the Church-and-State relationship Erastianism had not yet settled to its fatigue, nor had the Bishops eaten of the Tree of Knowledge.

"Mr Mayor", concluded Dr Coke, "hath already invited me with my family to a royal and sumptuous feast, as I have seen any. And we are going again to-morrow to Mr Sheriff Fitz Herbert's to another, I suppose the like. Amongst other I am acquainted with one Alderman Barker, whom I find an able and wise man, and very friendly to me: he hath sent me a present, as some others have done, and visited me himself, and hath given me some good light of the state both of the church and city. They deal with me very friendly in one thing, telling me plainly that they expect not the like answerableness of my inviting them, and that they did not expect it in my predecessor, neither did he do it to them: all they require is my friendly and loving acquaintance among them." It is pleasant that Bishop Coke should have felt that this was what the merchants in the great cities wanted, the friendly and loving acquaintance of their Fathers-in-God.

It is a sign of his stature that into this world of make-believe Archbishop Laud would never enter. It was alien to his whole nature, to that feeling for autocracy which marked his outlook and to the harsh edge of his self-confidence. A sense of Anglican security lapped about him, but it never served to blunt his iron purpose. He went on his way, to his great power and to his death, alone. Before considering the nature of Laud's influence, it would be as well to stress this aspect of his position; the authoritarian temper which owed more to Geneva than to Rome; the rather choleric confidence in his own mastery.

In the first place the Archbishop reacted violently against the habits of sycophancy which were often found grafted on to that respect for constituted authority which had already for so long characterised the established English world. The attitude of such a prelate as Theophilus Field, Bishop first of Llandaff, then of St David's and finally of Hereford, must have affected him most strongly. His matter-of-fact mind and his common sense alike combined to make him detest all urgent and obsequious flattery. In Laud's rule there were always present authority and isolation.

Among the churchmen of that generation he was unique. It was perhaps his vitality which first awakened Strafford's

for this project of a new chapel was for their own ease, and not that they should dispose of the Bishop's office. The Archbishop could never make a calm rejoinder.

This goes far to explain the spleen in Sir Simonds D'Ewes' oft-quoted comment—"A heavy loss also had our English Church by the death of Dr George Abbot, Archbishop of Canterbury. Dr William Laud, Bishop of London, a little, low, red-faced man, of mean parentage succeeded him. His own speech made in the Star Chamber, June 10th 1637, at the censure of some godly men being printed shews sufficiently his allowance and practice of the adoring or bowing to and towards the altar with other tenets, which made me even tremble when I read it."[1]

Sir Simonds D'Ewes has the rancour of one who writes about the chief enemy of his own party, but in a sense the Archbishop's asperity disguised his simple and profound love for the Church of England. He had a reverence for all her ordered life which could never have been shared by the Elizabethan Primates. His feeling for an English liturgy can hardly be dissociated from his pride in his country; it was bound up with England's temporal and spiritual supremacy. He belonged to the new age and was essentially a townsman; his mind rested gratefully on that work of the restoration of St Paul's Cathedral to which he dedicated so much energy. The reconstruction of the tower at the crossing, and the setting up of the new peel of bells assumed for him a symbolic value, the maintenance of the fabric of worship in town and country.[2] In the significance that Dr Laud attached to the manifestation of public worship, and in this only, he had some surely unconscious affinity with the prelates of the Counter-Reformation.

Thomas Fuller, never sympathetic to the character of this archbishop, and writing before his memory was in any respect rehabilitated, draws attention to certain qualities. "He was not partial in preferring his kindred, except some merit met in

---

[1] *Autobiography of Sir Simonds D'Ewes*, vol. ii, pp. 100-1.

[2] Thomas Fuller has a comment: "He [the Archbishop] communicated his project to some private persons, of taking down the great tower in the middle to the spurs, and rebuild it in the same fashion [but some yards higher] as before. He meant to hang as great and tuneable a ring of bells as any in the world, whose sound, advantaged with their height and vicinity of the Thames, must needs be loud and melodious" (*The Church History of Britain*, ed. Rev. J. S. Brewer, vol. vi, p. 304).

them with his alliance. Covetousness he perfectly hated."[1] It was an integral element in the situation that there was so very much in Archbishop Laud to earn his sovereign's approbation and grave respect.[2] Both men were conscious that they were in no way tempted towards extremes, and it seems likely that the æsthetic side of Dr Cosin's devotional approach made no appeal to either of them. It was order that Laud required and strict obedience. The Separatists were to his mind prejudicial to all discipline: they would prevent, were they not put down, the even progress of the Church of England.

Dr Laud was in some ways essentially the inevitably clerical head of a college, and his outlook altered little from the days of his disturbed Presidency of St John's. He was a maintainer of the statutes in Church and University. This point of view is manifest in one of his passages at arms with Dr Astley, the Warden of All Souls. "And this charge I require you, Mr Warden," the Archbishop wrote on that occasion, "to deliver to all the Fellows, but especially the officers, that they use not long, undecent hair, nor wear large falling bands, nor boots under their gowns, nor any other like unstatutable novelty in their apparel."[3] Thus on both sides he would cut and prune.

At Lambeth there was no one to restrain that tendency, which was native to him, to enlarge the bounds of his authority. In all Laud's dealings, there is a curious and complete absence of light and shade. In writing to his subordinates on every matter, his tone suffers but little alteration. His words come down to us, like the sun in a tropic country, as harsh and as unvarying.

Yet with his habitual roughness of expression, he had not been without a heavy element of self-pity. In his earlier years he

[1] *Ibid.*, vol. vi, p. 302. Fuller has this further comment: "I knew a kinsman of his in the university, scholar enough, but somewhat wild and lazy, on whom it was late before he reflected with favour, and that not before his amendment. And generally persons promoted by him were men of learning and abilities, though many of them Arminians in their judgments."

[2] It is worth noting that Laud was not a tall man and thus able to embarrass his sovereign. "Of stature he was low, but of strong composition: so short a trunk never contained so much excellent treasure; which therefore was to be the stronger by reason of the wealth which was hid within it. His countenance, cheerful and well bloodied, more fleshy, as I have often heard him say, than any other part of his body" (Heylin's *Life of Archbishop Laud*, p. 542).

[3] Letter from the Archbishop of Canterbury to the Warden of All Souls, dated at Croydon, 1 August 1634 (Laud's *Works*, vol. vi, pt. ii, pp. 387-9).

that note of devout reason and calm force—"But what stands with His wisdom, justice and goodness to do."

His religious convictions had a rock-like solidity. He was very English, sprung from that burgess class in which the religious changes had received their first and warmest welcome. He had not travelled, nor did he manifest desire to do so. All foreign countries lay beyond the horizon of his interests, and from England he drew a deep contentment. He could form no picture of the Cardinalate which was held out to him obscurely, and which meant so much to Con and to Panzani. Rome was without attractions for him. The idea of secession was a scourge in the hands of his opponents, but it offered the Primate no temptation. His attitude towards the Roman Church was cold and methodical and, above all, unconcerned. He knew but little of the English Catholics until he met them in the Court circle.

In dealing with the Court his manners acquired a certain patina, and he was never wholly at home with those who, unlike the King and Buckingham, in no way accepted his spiritual guidance. Yet in his Lambeth years he was impressive in the Anglican dignity that sustained him, and in his knowledge of his unquestioned rights. He was not unsuccessful with the Queen, and at sixty was too settled to be exacerbated by frivolity. From the circumstances of his college life he had remained a celibate. He was much occupied with his manuscripts, with the fostering of Arabic studies and with those Oxford buildings in which his practical sense had found its high expression. As he walked in meditation in his groves at Lambeth or knelt in his private chapel, quite remote from the trends of his own period, he gave himself in prayer to God. A certain austerity of approach and an utter honesty supported him. It was not his fault that he saw his path so clearly.

At the Court two factors contributed to increase Laud's isolation; the part that he was to play in politics, and the personal character of his predecessor who had always been so non-ecclesiastical and wide and companionable. The active life of Archbishop Abbot belonged wholly to the period of James I; he would not have received preferment at King Charles' hands; nothing in his life and outlook would commend itself to his younger sovereign. Even in Buckingham's time the idea of Laud's promotion had been settled, although it was not until the late summer of 1633 that the primacy at long last became vacant.

In one of Pory's newsletters there is a passage which recalls the elder Primate in each trivial detail. It is a description of a meeting between the Earl of Arundel and the old Archbishop, to whose safe keeping the Earl's son, Lord Maltravers, had been committed when he had offended King Charles by his secret marriage with Lady Elizabeth Stuart of Lennox. The air of the Jacobean world, with its ease and its heavy cheerfulness, is brought back in the very turn and structure of these sentences. That had been a *milieu* into which no man could ft who was at once so rigid in his notions and so stiff, so ever conscious of his state of prelacy.

"One day last week", thus runs the account compiled in September 1632,[1] "my Lord of Arundel and his son, my Lord Maltravers, having espied my Lord of Canterbury's coach on Banstead Downs coming towards theirs, before they came a butt's length short of it, both their lordships alighted, and went a great pace towards his grace's coach; who, when they approached, said, 'What! and must my lord marshal of England take so great pains to do me so much honour? Were my legs as good as my heart, I should have met your lordships the better half of the way.' Then my Lord of Arundel replied, 'It might well become an earl marshal to give so much respect to an Archbishop of Canterbury, besides the particular obligation from his lordship to his grace for his noble usage of his sons and daughter Maltravers, while they were his prisoners'. Whereupon my lord's grace took occasion to congratulate unto both my Lord Maltravers' brave and hopeful progeny of three sons and a daughter; and so they parted." That was how England had been ruled, the great bland ease at the coach window. It was in the tradition of Queen Elizabeth; it had nothing in common with Charles I.

"His grace [of Canterbury]," the newsletter continues, "by his diet hath so moderated his gout, as it is now rather an infirmity than a pain. He looks fresh, and enjoys his health, and hath his wits and intellectuals about him; so that if any other prelate do gape after his benefice, his grace, perhaps, according to that old and homely proverb, [may] eat of the goose which

[1] Letter from Mr Pory to Sir Thomas Puckering, dated at London, 20 September 1632 (printed in the *Court and Times of Charles I*, vol. ii, p. 177).

shall graze upon his grave." There was a scurrilous suggestion in this phrase of "gaping after benefice" that Laud would never tolerate.

The northern Primate, Archbishop Harsnett, was in certain respects but little more congenial to Laud's strict mind. He had been promoted from the See of Norwich in old age, and he was now in declining health, close to the officers of State and concerned in his last months with the promotion (which he could not effect) of Dean Hassall, "the honestest man in the world". In writing to Lord Dorchester,[1] the Archbishop describes himself as old in years, worn with infirmities, far distant from the sun, without preceding merits, and unable, within the little circle of his time, to express due thankfulness to the Secretary of State. It was against this Byzantinism that Laud reacted, against this Erastian framework and the ornate wording. He could not bear that prelates should place themselves beneath the yoke of the civil government so humbly and so willingly. Besides, he had a conception of the due order of the worship of God. If Laud had rigour, he had hardness too, and clarity.

It was these characteristics of his thought which brought the chief conflicts of the earlier period of his rule at Lambeth. Dry as were his sermons, his remarks had often a sharp common sense, salted and bitter. The very earnestness of his feeling produced a certain straining eloquence. Two phrases written in the Tower after his fall will show at once Laud's determination on unity, and that sense of a national Church which is inherent in the traditional thought of the Church of England. "My Lord Saye," he writes, for it was this peer who had attacked him, "it seems, 'knows not how far I will extend the word Sectary'. Truly, no further than the Church of Christ extended it, ever since sects and schisms broke in upon it, to help despoil it of peace and unity."[2] He was all his life, and surprisingly, a fighter. "And therefore", he wrote again, "certainly my comprehensions are not so narrow as theirs [the Sectaries], whose largest cannot, or will not, look upon an entire national Church; nay, a parochial is too big for them, and a conventicle big enough."[3]

Before him there lay the vision of the Church of England

---

[1] Letter from the Archbishop of York to Lord Dorchester, dated at Southwark, 30 January 1631 (State Papers, Dom. Charles I, clxxxiii, 42).

[2] Laud's *Works*, vol. vi, pt. i, p. 86.   [3] Laud's *Works*, vol. vi, pt. i, p. 88.

sober and righteous and God-fearing. His views on ceremonial were quiet and unemphatic. His chaplain and biographer, Peter Heylyn,[1] records that he "repaired the ruined windows in the chappel of his house in Croyden, where he spent the greatest part of his summers and whither he retired at other times for his ease and privacy". Again he describes[2] the communion table which the Archbishop set up in his own chapel "shadowed overhead with a very fair frieze, and framed with a decent and costly rail, the guilding of the one and the curious workmanship of the other, together with the table itself, amounting to thirty three pounds". It was no raising of the horn of popery, but his determination on conformity, that angered to the death "the railing Rabshekehs of the Puritan faction".[3] Laud was far too determined for the Puritans, and far too exact and simple for the Jacobean world. It was just this exactitude and a certain sharp simplicity which fastened the King to him and brought both into conflict with the chief of the Bishops who had survived from King James' reign.

There were other links which drew Laud and Charles I together. Both men shared a vexation at those conversions to Rome which occurred in the circle of the Court. It was in a sense wounding that they should take place at the very centre of the manifestation of Anglican kingship. They were, for the most part, sponsored by Endymion Porter's wife, Olivia, and were almost invariably feminine. The principal exception to this rule, Walter Montagu, had been immersed for several years in the intimate group of the Court ladies. For Laud's life these conversions had a two-fold consequence. They added a note of distaste to the indifference with which he had always regarded Roman Catholicism, and led him to underestimate the influence of the Catholic minority throughout the country. It is interesting to note that the Earl of Portland's conversion on his deathbed does not seem to have led the Archbishop to suspect the Catholic leanings of Cottington and Windebank. This ignorance on Laud's part was to some extent a result of the King's dislike for interference in the private concerns of gentlemen, although it must be admitted that the Court of High Commission bore hardly upon a limited number of men of standing. The informer of the Elizabethan type or the personal agent, such as those which Lord Burghley had maintained, are

[1] P. Heylyn, *Life of Laud*, p. 277.　　[2] *Ibid.*, p. 277.　　[3] *Ibid.*, p. 277.

hardly found in the years of King Charles' rule without a Parliament.

At the same time, these conversions had their effect on the Archbishop's relations with Queen Henrietta. To her they appear to have had a spice of that always decorous adventure which she sought through so many channels. Her own devotion had been fixed in childhood, and its manifestations were never congenial to Dr Laud: the attachment to the shrine of Our Lady of Liesse; the cult of relics. In a way this belonged to the hard and aristocratic side of her character. Their relations deteriorated in the later period of his rule at Lambeth, until eventually the Queen came to see him as an irritating factor in the English scene. It was a minor consequence of the Court conversions that, in the case of certain husbands, a personal bitterness was now added to their more general opposition to Catholicism. The conversion of the Countess of Newport, and that attempted in regard to the Marchioness of Hamilton, had a lasting effect upon the standpoint of these two peers.

Yet so many of the Bishops suffered, as did Laud himself, from a lack of the experience required for dealing successfully with the privileged circle. Apart from George Coke, the measure of whose capacity has been illustrated, only Richard Senhouse, who was promoted to the See of Carlisle in the last year of King James' reign, belonged to a family which was within the grouping of the new squirearchy.[1] None of them actually came from the Court circle, nor did any of them gain that early understanding of the ways of Courts which marked some of the prelates of the Church of France. On the other hand, they were in some respects too intellectual a body to win the confidence of the country lords and thus transmute an anti-papal feeling into Anglican attachment.[2]

There were of course certain exceptions, and the statement

[1] He was a son of John Senhouse, of Netherhall in Cumberland. "Dr Senhouse, bishop of Carlisle (chaplain to the king when prince) preached at the coronation; his text 'And I will give you a crown of life' " (Fuller, *The Church History of Britain*, vol. vi, p. 26).

[2] A comment made by Bishop Davenant, in regard to Richard Montague, who was perhaps the prelate who had most Court favour, bears on this point: "I could wish for his own good that he [Mr Mountague] had a more modest conceit of himself, and a less base opinion of all others who join not with him in his mongrel opinions. . . . He mightily deceives himself in taking it for granted that Dr Overall, or Bucer, or Luther, were ever of his mind in the point of Predestination" (Letter to Samuel Ward, Master of Sidney Sussex College, dated 10 October 1624, and printed *ibid.*, vol. vi, p. 22).

made by Thomas Fuller that the Marquess of Hertford and the Earls of Southampton, Bristol and Bath were "defenders of episcopacy" need not be questioned. The last-named did exhibit some traits which suggest a later Anglican tradition.[1] Still, even the defenders were inclined to adopt a standpoint which the Bishops must have felt incongruous. The speech that follows fails to mention either the Apostolic Succession or episcopal jurisdiction. "My Lords," declared Lord Newark in 1641 when speaking on the right of the spiritual peers to sit in the Upper House, "there is not any that sits here more for preaching than I am; I know it is the ordinary means to salvation; yet I likewise know there is not that full necessity of it as was in the primitive times. God defend that sixteen hundred years' acquaintance should make the gospel of Christ no better known unto us. Neither, my lords, doth their office merely and wholly consist in preaching; but partly in that, partly in praying and administering the blessed sacraments; in a godly and exemplary life; in wholesome admonitions; in exhortations to virtue, dehortations from vice; and partly in easing the burdened conscience. These, my lords, complete the office of a churchman."[2] In a later passage of the same speech he continued: "Indeed, my lords, I must needs say, that in charity it is a supposition not to be supposed; no, nor in reason, that they will go against the light of their understanding. The holiness of their calling, their knowledge, their freedom from passions and affections to which youth is very obnoxious, their vicinity to the gates of death which, though not shut to any, yet always stand wide open to old age: these, my lords, will surely make them steer aright."[3] Surely the prelates must have felt these words inadequate. This lack of interior sympathy may be in part explained by the weighted academic character which had for some decades marked the Bench of Bishops. It was, perhaps, reinforced by the mercantile origin of individual prelates.[4]

---

[1] "Henry Earl of Bath [was] a learned lord and lover of learning, oftentimes on occasion speaking for bishops; once publicly professing it one of the greatest honours which ever happily happened to his family, that one thereof [Thomas Bourchier by name] was once dignified with the archbishopric of Canterbury" (Fuller, *op. cit.*, vol. vi, p. 236).

[2] *Ibid.*, vol. vi, pp. 232-3.   [3] *Ibid.*, vol. vi, pp. 233-4.

[4] An exception must be made in regard to the members of the Welsh Bench. The will of the Rev. William Dolben, D.D., of Stanwicke in Northampton, Bishop-Designate of Bangor, dated 1 September 1631 and proved 25 October of the same year, throws an interesting light on the associations and sacramental

Such men represented, as had the Abbots in the previous generation, a new burgeoning power.[1]

Apart from such sons of the clergy as Bishop Henry King of Chichester, and Bishops Montagu and Goodman, the general tone was set by merchant stocks of greater or less significance. Among the elder prelates, Bishop Buckeridge of Ely had been educated at Merchant Taylors' School, as were his younger colleagues, William Juxon and Matthew Wren. Others, like Bishop Henchman and Archbishop Frewen, had close associations with the Skinners Company, while Bishop Potter was the son of a mercer in Kendal,[2] and John Cosin was sprung from a merchant family of some wealth in Norwich. The bond between the prelates can be defined as that of early university experience to which was, in many cases, added the holding of academic posts. Among the bishops of this period seven had been

standpoint of one prelate. "I appoint Richard Owen of Buckden, co. Hunts. gent. steward to the Bishop of Lincoln, supervisor of my will; my friend Henry Lorte of Stackpoole Court, co. Pembroke Esq is accountable to me for the profits of the rectory of Stackpoole. To my dear cousin his wife Judith Lorte I give one Jewell which is now in my deske at Stanwicke garnished with small pearles, having the holy lambe on the one side and the Crucifix on the other, which Jewell was my dear Mothers [Alice Middleton, wife of John Dolben of Haverfordwest]. To Nicholas Grey of Marchantailors' Schoole in London I give Casabane's and Montague's Exercitations against Baronius" (*Miscellanea Genealogica et Heraldica*, third series, vol. ii, pp. 49-50).

[1] A commentary upon this situation is provided by the data contained in "The anatomy of the Elizabethan Aristocracy", by Laurence Stone in the *Economic History Review*, vol. xviii (1949). Lords Abergavenny, Berkeley, Monteagle, Vaux and Windsor are cited as examples of peers who had become heavily embarrassed. "Lord Morley borrowed small sums during 1592-1600 from yeomen, blacksmiths and the like. Lord Darcy of Chiche was a retiring peer . . . living on a rent roll of £400 p.a. that had not risen in forty years of price revolution" (*ibid.*, pp. 51-2). Many country lords were thus at a disadvantage as compared with the new class.

[2] A passage in Fuller's *Church History* bears on this point. "About this time", he states in describing the events of 1641, "came forth the lord Brooke his booke against bishops, accusing them in respect of their parentage to be *de faece populi* 'of the dregs of the people', and in respect of their studies in no way fit for government, or to be barons of parliament. . . . Bishop Morton of Durham averred that his father had been lord mayor of York and borne all the offices of that city with credit and honour. . . . Bishop Curle his father was for many years auditor of the court of wards . . . Bishop Goodman of Gloucester, that though his very name seemed to point out his descent from yeomanry, yet [though the youngest son of the youngest brother] he had more left unto him than the lord Brooke his father had to maintain him and all his family. That his grandfather by his father's side purchased the whole estate of Sir Thomas Exmew, lord mayor of London 1517, and that by his mother's side he was descended from the best parentage of the city of London" (Fuller, *op. cit.*, pp. 212-14).

heads of Oxford colleges in addition to the three who had held
successively the deanery of Christ Church. Six had held the
mastership of Cambridge colleges. This shared experience had
a moulding force.

Very slowly the country was absorbing that Anglican
tradition which the prelates could only with difficulty put
persuasively. The great oak family pews were now constructed
with all their pinnacles and heraldic achievements. A remarkable
surviving example is that constructed by the Shirleys of
Stanton Harold in 1627, in Breedon church in Leicestershire.
The idea of the sitting, which each man of any position ought
to hold, was fast developing.[1] In this picture there is no doubt
that Bishop Williams would appear in some respects old-
fashioned. This, and a certain air of incongruity, is expressed
in a comment made about him: "One great prelate plainly
said in the presence of the King that 'the Bishop of Lincoln
lived in as much pomp and plenty as any Cardinal in Rome
for diet, music, and attendance'"[2]. Inevitably this churchman
was bound to rouse the active hostility[3] of Dr Laud as well as
deep uneasiness in his young sovereign.

Dr John Williams, Bishop of Lincoln, had come early to his
high place, and at thirty-nine had succeeded Bacon as Lord
Keeper. His heavy and flexible Byzantine phrasing had chimed
well with the old King's fancies, but was definitely distasteful to
his new master. Charles I was never easy when out-distanced,
and this prelate's swift talent aroused his disquiet. Any destruction of their peace of mind rendered each Stuart sovereign
harsh. A quarrel between the Bishop and his former protector,
Buckingham, settled the matter, and King Charles had relieved
himself abruptly of the most politically skilful member of his
episcopate. It was inevitable that Dr Williams should remain
a figure of much significance as he sat for the first fifteen years
of the new reign in the country-house of his diocese at Buckden,
a politician out of place. He was still Bishop of Lincoln and
Dean of Westminster.

[1] Cf. accounts of the churchwardens for the parish of Cheddar between 1631
and 1643. A typical entry runs as follows: "Received of Edward Crocker for a
seate upon the benche under the minister's pewe for his liffe 2/-" (Historical
Manuscripts Commission Reports, Appendix to Third Report, p. 330).

[2] Fuller, op. cit., vol. vi, p. 124.

[3] "Of all men Bishop Laud was the Party whose enmity was most tedious. . . .
He batter'd him with old and new Contrivances fifteen years" (Scrinia Reserata,
vol. ii, p. 65.)

Two contemporary accounts, which are both demonstrably accurate, one written by the Bishop of Gloucester and the other by Sir Symonds D'Ewes, will give some impression of the Bishop of Lincoln. "After Bacon", runs Dr Goodman's description of his fellow-countryman, "succeeded Williams, a man of as great wit and understanding as ever I knew any man. And whereas the knight [Sir Anthony Weldon] writes that he was of mean birth, truly he was as well descended and had as good kindred as any man in North Wales, none beyond him."[1] To these words Sir Symonds' statement forms a pleasant pendant.

"Much talk", he wrote in his autobiography, "there was of this divine's sudden rising, being a Welchman by birth, and, but a few years before, a poor subsizar in St John's College in Cambridge of little regard or learning. ... I heard it confidently reported that the old Lord Chancellor, Lord Ellesmere, prophesied of him, he being then his household chaplain, that he would prove another Wolsey, which was as strongly verified many years after by his fall, as now by his rising."[2]

There can be little doubt that the Bishop of Lincoln was difficult to deal with as he sat at Buckden on the great North Road with his gate open for the coaches of each peer or bishop. Hospitable and in speech most smooth, he allowed no openly expressed resentment to mar his careful homage. Laud, and in his measure Strafford, knew where they stood with him. It was the King who was to prove hesitant in face of this former minister, who was equally vigilant and unreassuring.

In *Scrinia Reserata*, the biography written by Bishop Hacket, his faithful chaplain, there is a passage on Dr Williams' life in his retirement which shows how remote were his preoccupations from those of Charles I and Bishop Laud. It is a glimpse in the new decorous reign of the ostentatious world of Lord St Albans. "I open the door now", begins this admirable account, "to let the Bishop in to his exchange."[3] He had been withdrawn from the office of Lord Keeper. "He came", Dr Hacket continues, "to his seat of *Bugden* [Buckden] in the Winter. And Winter cannot be more miry on any Coast of England, than it is round

---

[1] Goodman, *Court of James I*, vol. i, p. 287.

[2] *Autobiography of Sir Symonds D'Ewes*, vol. i, p. 204.

[3] *Scrinia Reserata. A Memoriall Offer'd to the Great Deservings of John Williams, D.D., who sometime held the Place of Lord Keeper of the Great Seal of England, Lord Bishop of Lincoln and Lord Archbishop of York*, by John Hacket, Lord Bishop of Lichfield and Coventry, vol. ii, p. 29.

SIR HENRY VANE, THE ELDER

From a painting in the National Portrait Gallery

about it. . . . From the time of his Predecessor [in the See of Lincoln] Dr *Russel*, that was Lord Chancellor of England and sat there in the days of *Edward* the Fourth, and laid out much upon that place, none that followed him, no not *Splendian Wolsey* did give it any new addition.

"This Bishop did wonders in a short time." He did indeed, but it was not in King Charles or Dr Laud to understand the charm of Splendian Wolsey and his tastes and his expediency and too-wide friendship. The account goes forward with the tale of his great building; the stables, barns, granaries and dairies, and the houses for doves and brewing. "And the outward courts, which were next to them, he [the Bishop]", we read, "cast into fair Allies and Grass-plats. Within doors, the Cloysters were the trimmest parts of his Reparations: the Windows of the Square beautified with stories of colour'd glass; the Pavement laid smooth and new: and the Walls on every side hung with pieces of exquisite Workmen[ship] in Limning, collected and provided long before." There was here no evidence of that ethical seriousness of outlook which alone would satisfy the Laudian school and reconcile the King's clear theories.

"The Bishop's Fancy", Hacket continues, "was marvellously charm'd with the Delight of Musick, both in the Chappel and in the Chamber: as *Solinus* says of *Alexander*, the Son of *Amyntas*, *Voluptati aurium indulgentissimi erat deditus*. Which was so well known that the best both for Song and Instrument and as well of the *French* that lodg'd in *London*, as of the *English*, resorted to him chiefly in the summer-quarter, to whom he was not trivial in his Gratifications.

"He loved", it is explained, "stirring and walking, which he used two hours or more, every day in the open Air, if the Weather serv'd: especially if he might go to and fro, where good Scents, and Works of well-form'd Shape were about him. But that this was his innocent Recreation, it would amount to an Error, that he should bury so much Money in Gardens, Arbors, Orchards, Pools of Water-fowls, and for Fish of all variety, with a Walk raised three Foot from the Ground, of about a Mile in compass, shaded and covered on each side with Trees and Pales."[1] The shadow of Verulam lies on this scene, and the spirit of that Jacobean world into which the King's strict mind would never probe.

[1] *Scrinia Reserata*, vol. i., p. 29.

A.C.—8

CHAPTER VIII

THE PURITAN ELEMENT

MR HOBBES, in his work *Behemoth*, raises a question which has often troubled more recent inquirers who find it difficult to define precisely the meaning and extension of the term Puritan. The late-nineteenth-century historians broadening down from precedent to precedent, seeking for signs of tolerance and liberty, were yet sufficiently familiar with a neo-Puritan temper of mind to be excused the necessity for explaining or defining it. Without interest in the theological aspect of the question, they tended to miss that profound accord on general values which Mr Hobbes stresses so unerringly; that great *corpus* of unanimous opinion held alike by the Church of England men and their opponents. "But what points do they disagree in?" he exclaims in *Behemoth*. "Is there any controversy between bishop and Presbyterian concerning the divinity or humanity of Christ? Do either of them deny the Trinity or any article of the creed? Does either party preach openly or write directly, against justice, charity, sobriety, or any other duty necessary to salvation, except only the duty to the King?"

This is, of course, an *ex parte* statement from one whose private mind stood far removed from these contentions. A form of Puritanism, whose dogmatic implications were Calvinist in character, had taken possession of many squires of the elder generation. It was a standpoint to which a great body of the mercantile class adhered. Parallel with this there ran an old-fashioned churchmanship, Puritan in temper, which had gained the loaves and fishes in the old Queen's time; the type of churchmanship which Leicester favoured.[1] Conviction of

---

[1] In this connection a comment made by Bishop Hall in *The Difference of the Condition of Foreign Churches and Divines from those of our Northern Neighbours* is interesting: "Yea, if the last Bishop of Geneva had become a Protestant, and consented in matter of doctrine to Calvin, Farel, Viret, have you or any man living just cause to think that the city would not gladly have retained his government still, and thought themselves happy under such protection? Would they have rejected him as an enemy, whom they might have enjoyed as a patron?" This passage is printed in *Anglicanism*, ed. Paul Elmer More and Frank Leslie Cross, p. 79.

Judgment bore heavily upon all men of the stricter school. The idea of their own Election came with force to those who had borne testimony to God's Word in the Pure Gospel. Those who adhered to this trend of thought were not necessarily in theory anti-episcopalian. A dislike for prelacy was, however, common to them and led to a half-sympathy with many Nonconformitants. It was likewise a bond with all those of a Protestant temper, for whom the climate of ecclesiastical authority was uncongenial. This attitude to what was termed "prelacy" was in essence political in character and very widespread. Under one aspect it was primarily an opposition to the machinery of Lambeth government, but it also possessed another quality: the clear animus of social doctrine. This applied to one section of the population, and was the approach of the unprivileged to the great primacy, the doctrine of those who might in time become the Fifth Monarchy Men and Levellers. Again, all sections were united by a profound but sometimes transient seriousness of outlook, which gave to them a bitter distaste for any levity. They sat over the Book, and in the light of that hastening Judgment they could not abide the maypole and the dancing and the wastrel pipers and the organs and the foolish songs.

Two quotations will give some indication. The first is from *Reliquiæ Baxterianæ*,[1] in which Richard Baxter described his Shropshire childhood at Eaton Constantine. "In the village where I lived", he wrote, "the Reader read the Common Prayer briefly, and the rest of the Day even till night almost except Eating time, was spent in Dancing under a Maypole and a great Tree, not far from my Father's Door, where all the Town did meet together: And though one of my Father's own Tenants was the Piper, he could not restrain him, nor break the Sport: so that we could not read the Scripture in our Family without the great disturbance of the Taber and Pipe."

The second quotation comes from the articles set out in 1628 against Dr Cosin by Peter Smart, a Prebendary of Durham. The latter had been chaplain to Bishop James of Durham, who in his turn was one of Leicester's chaplains; his was, therefore, the old tradition. "Nay the Sacrament itself is turned wel neare into a theatricall stage play," the Prebendary expostulated,

---

[1] *Reliquiæ Baxterianæ*, p. 2. This book was published in 1696 and edited by Matthew Sylvester, but the passage in question was written in 1664.

"and at that very season, very unseasonably [men's] eares are possest with pleasant tunes, and theire eyes fed with pompous spectacles of glittering pictures, and histrionicall gestures."[1]

Yet these well-stressed denunciations brought with them an obvious reaction. The temper of mind remains severe, but the values inevitably become stereotyped when once the ardour has cooled. "While I was in London, I fell into acquaintance with a sober, godly, understanding Apprentice of *Mr Philemon Stevens* the Bookseller . . . . Above a year after the death of my Mother, my Father married a Woman of great Sincerity in the Fear of God, *Mary* the daughter of *Sir Tho. Hunkes*: whose Holiness, Mortification, Contempt of the World and Fervent Prayer have been so Exemplary."[2] These are the wide phrases of a pietism in which each term would soon become a lapidary convention. By contrast, it was the focused animus that lent to the Puritans so much of their vitality. Guided by the impending Judgment, they would look out on the idolatries of Rome, and it was then that such a godly wife as Mrs Hutchinson would see in her exaltation the glorious flame that was destined quite to destroy "that bloody city".[3] Their ardour was marked by a noble carriage. "The former sort of these," wrote Mrs Hutchinson of what she termed the State Protestants, "in zeal to reduce the whole land from their idolatrous practices, procured laws and invented oaths to suppress popery, which they little thought, but we now sadly find, are the bitterest engines to batter down the pure worship and destroy the pure worshippers of God."[4]

From this passage it is clear that the strength of this movement lay in its final power to release enthusiasm. Such power could always lead to a temporary amalgam of many sections. This quality would feed upon attachment to the Scripture, and on an easy detestation for the horns of Rome and prelacy. At the same time the Puritans had the power to evoke a sympathy for suffering. Another quotation, again from Richard Baxter, indicates this aspect clearly. "At last," he wrote, "at about 20 years of age [in 1635], I became acquainted with Mr Simmonds, Mr Cradock, and other very zealous godly Nonconformists in Shrewsbury, and the adjoining parts, whose fervent Prayers

---

[1] *Bishop Cosin's Correspondence*, vol. i, p. 167. [2] *Reliquiæ Baxterianæ*, pp. 11-12.
[3] Described in *Memoirs of the Life of Colonel Hutchinson*, by Mrs Lucy Hutchinson, ed. Rev. Julius Hutchinson, p. 71. [4] *Ibid.*, pp. 70-71.

and savoury Conference and holy Lives did profit me much. And when I understood that they were People prosecuted by the Bishops, I found much prejudice arise in my heart against those that persecuted them, and thought those that silenced and troubled such Men could not be the genuine Followers of the Lord of Love."[1]

Among the factors in this situation that were now emerging, a certain confused compassionate sympathy was prominent, a drawing together of the Puritans among the common people which would later find expression in the Independents. The old Church and State Puritanism of the surviving Elizabethan dignitaries was of another character, desiccated and inflammatory, but without this element of compassion.

In the Puritan consciousness of the richer squires an attitude of patronage is manifested towards their poorer neighbours of strict principles. Thus Colonel Hutchinson is spoken of as "inclined to favour the oppressed saints and honest people of those times".[2] The mould of King Charles' Government bore down upon the diverse and contradictory elements among the Puritans. They were inevitably thwarted by the Laudian order, and it was only in New England that they could as yet go free.

At the same time it would be an error to regard the conflict between the Puritans and their opponents as arising in any marked degree from dogmatic cleavage. The men who were already in middle life belonged to the tired second generation in the religious struggle in which the theological interests lay close and dormant. Robert Browne, the separatist, who lived on at a great age as the incumbent at Achurch, was the last survivor of that ardent generation which had known John Penry's fire. It was now slack water. The Calvinistic doctrines had sunk into their place as part of a traditional set-up, and it was almost entirely with moral questions that the rising Puritan world would be preoccupied.

A hard clarity marked their unwavering and sure judgment of men's sinfulness. The Old Testament, long considered, had schooled them to a knowledge of their own perfection. Beneath this there lay a grim determination to root out "gauds and idolatries". All their strength of character was poured in to reinforce an assurance of the spirit, that was at once both molten

[1] *Reliquiæ Baxterianæ*, p. 13.   [2] *Life of Colonel Hutchinson*, p. 39.

and uncertain. This assurance had a *bourgeois* quality which well accorded with their clear integrity. It was no more suited to the landless man than palatable to king or bishop. A certain economic independence characterised the greater part of those in whom the Puritan values moved most strongly.

It is hard to trace English religious movements in those sections of the population whose lives were passed at an economic level below that of actual or potential prosperity. A description of Dudley in 1638 has therefore a value from one angle. "In this town of Dudley I lived", wrote Richard Baxter, "in much comfort, amongst a poor tractable People, lately famous for Drunkenness, but commonly more ready to hear God's Word with submission and reformation than most places where I have come: so that having since the Wars set up a Monthly Lecture there, the Church was usually as much crowded within, and at the Windows, as ever I saw any London congregations: (partly through the great willingness of the People, and partly by the exceeding populousness of the Country, where the Woods and Commons are planted with Nailers, Scithe-Smiths, and other Iron-Labourers like a continual Village)."[1]

Still, the idea of assurance was linked with the possession of a certain mundane status. Puritan values would mean little to that section of the population which was economically the least secure. It is difficult to see how such men could be affected by a Puritanism which was position-conscious, stringent and Sabbatarian.[2] The forerunners of Revivalism alone could move their hearts.

The Puritans stood for the untrammelled following of all that they might find in the Pure Gospel. It was approached as a volume possessing a religious and political and social character. It could be divorced wholly from a church atmosphere.

[1] *Reliquiæ Baxterianæ*, p. 14.

[2] The situation of the Heywoods as revealed in Oliver Heywood's *Diaries* is characteristic of a group which saw merit in labour and its rewards. The family settled at Little Leven, near Bolton, were of yeoman status, owning some freehold land and a fulling mill. Richard Heywood married at nineteen in 1617 and set up "trading in cottons". Further details are given in his son's diaries: "And my father being thrifty and carefull began to make fustians, which was then a very gainfull calling and, after a while, God opened a way for his trading in London, and raised up friends and brought him into acquaintance with one Mr Cotton in Milk-street, and Mr Cary who was Mr Cotton's servant and afterwards marryed his daughter. These he traded with many yeares and severall others" (Heywood, *op. cit.*, ed. Turner (1882), vol. i, pp. 18, 27, 76.

Using their new horn glasses, the countrymen would fumble with the Bible on the oak dresser. The interest aroused was in no way doctrinal. To the Puritan soldiery, the Old and New Testaments both appeared as lucid, integral, immediate and coherent. The minatory passages bit deep into their consciousness. They saw under a harsh light what must befall their enemies. In general, the Puritan generation was swept by conviction, a gale-force of conviction equally exhausting and impregnable.

This, in a way, accounts for the smooth or tired acceptance of the Restoration by those who had fought in that holy war. A considerable body of the younger men reacted against the biblical vigour which the Civil Wars had come to consecrate. There was so much food in scripture for those who sought in that rich soil. Thus, at the lower economic levels, men like Lilburne would come to concentrate on the designs of God in regard to property-holders and their influence. They were to come in time to Thomas Rainsborough in the Army discussions in Putney Church: "But I find nothing in the law of God that a lord shall choose twenty burgesses, and a gentleman only two, and a poor man none". And there was, too, the knowledge of those whom the sword of divine justice would strike down, the realisation of the King's preordained punishment "I think", cried Edward Sexby in these same discussions, "we have gone about to heal Babylon when she would not, we have gone about to wash a Blackamore, to wash him white, which he will not. I think we are going about to set up the power which God will destroy."

It is difficult to believe that this sentiment, which was so harsh and vigorous, found any echo in those circles in whose hands there lay the old privileged machinery of government. As one approaches the rank of the very rich and of those whose outlook was tempered by the Renaissance sophistication, it seems unlikely that one will find that Puritanism which could rouse enthusiasm. In such circles a high arid Presbyterianism or an Evangelical cast of thought (from which the line of the rich Low Churchmen was later to be derived) would seem to take the place of that ferment which was moving in the literal-minded sections of the people.

Yet if Puritanism can hardly be said to have moved the governing class, there is no doubt that a section of those great in politics gave an earnest consideration to the value and uses of Puritan feeling. The Puritan movement provided a singular opportunity for the manipulation of mass-opinion. The solidarity of this religious sentiment assisted such an operation. The patron of those who "scrupled" ceremonies could penetrate and gain support among politically valuable sections of the people, who were not normally accessible to a politician in high place. The old soiled leader would then see himself as the Angel who could move the waters of Bethesda. To the patron of the righteous there would come a rather stark, ungrudging gratitude.

The feudal nexus had broken down. The Northern Rising in 1569 had seen the last organised effort built upon an essentially feudal connection. Some new way of gathering support must be devised for those who no longer depended upon an hereditary system of friendship and alliance. Thomas Cromwell was, perhaps, the first of the wise men to reach down through the strata of the population. His thought had proceeded tranquilly in its fixed orbit. He had used with care, and had nourished, the iconoclastic sentiment which was to fortify the new religion.

After Cromwell had come Leicester. He was one of the earliest of public men to derive political benefit from that specifically Puritan feeling to which Burghley's Erastian mind was ill-attuned. It is unfortunate that there are such relatively scanty materials for the study of Leicester's policy and for the examination of his widespread and ramifying interest. The Puritan feeling was an engine which a political leader could employ to work fresh seams. In France that was well understood. A politician has to manœuvre political idealism where he can find it. In the early seventeenth century the religious mould into which political thought-forms ran left the Puritans exposed to such endeavours. Any line of affiliation which cut across existing class distinctions had great value.

It was easy to link up with other sections by showing compassion for the "oppressed saints". For men like Sir John Eliot or Lord Warwick it must have been encouraging to be able to fan this disaffection. Even those leaders who, like Pym, had a certain Puritan element native to them would use their wide political experience to foment discords and lead them into useful channels. The Puritan leaven had every quality which would recommend it to a great opposition party in the State. The Puritan reaction to public happenings was calculable and sincere and very durable. It was marked by courage. Yet one thing the Parliamentarian leaders could not foresee. They did not realise, for old, accustomed leaders seldom do realise, what spirits they were calling out of the vasty deep. It was beyond their power to imagine the Army and the Independents, who together would compass their destruction.

This said, one can examine the different manifestations of that Puritan way of life which was so deep in opposition to the Caroline spirit, and was in time to prove its solvent. The first question concerns the existence of a Puritan Royalism. Can it be said that there was a right wing of the movement which would range itself beside the King in time of conflict? Certainly there were many elements that were not Puritan which would throughout support the Parliament. The position of Bishop Bedell would seem to supply an example of the strict way of life which was at the same time bound up with the existing order in Church and State. Quotation at some length is required to give the savour of the attitude.

The Puritan outlook in its episcopalian form can hardly be better studied than in the case of Dr Bedell who, though he was Bishop of Kilmore from 1629 until 1641, was in some respects singularly representative of the Puritanism of East Anglia in its most moderate form. The true relation of his life and death, which was composed just before the Restoration, appears to have been the work of his son, another William Bedell, who was Rector of Rattlesden in Suffolk. The Bishop's general attitude is, perhaps, characteristic of those ministers who came from the pure House of Emmanuel.

"His Father and Grand-Father", so runs the introduction, "were both noted in their time for Love to true Religion. The Bishop's Father married a helper or yoke-fellow meet for him, Elizabeth Elliston. These two lived together to a great age in Black Notley [in Essex], much esteem'd and beloved; they were both very charitable and mercifull; their house was seldom without one or two poor children, which they kept upon alms. Mrs Elizabeth Bedell was very famous and expert in Chirurgery, which she continually practised upon multitudes that flock'd to her, and still *gratis*, without respect of persons, poor or rich. It hap'n'd occasionally that some would return like the heald Samaritan, with some token of thankfullness; though this was seldom."[1]

After describing his education at a good school "not above a mile off at a Market town called Braintry", and his entrance into Emmanuel College and his election as a Fellow of that foundation, an account is given of his ministerial call. "Mr Bedell being thus furnish'd," the Relation continues, " 'twas easy to perceive to what course of life God had destinated and his own inclinations led him; which was the ministry. His entrance into Holy Orders was before he had left the University: concerning which he would complain of the greedy gaping for money by the officers and servants of the Bishop, without heeding so much the sufficiency or insufficiency of the man, as of money. Yet his Orders he esteemed nevertheless religiously, tho' cumbred with some faults in the men that conferr'd them. His first call to the Ministerial work was to St Edmundsbury in Suffolk: where the great esteem he gan'd for his grave, humble, and diligent discharge of that employment is yet surviving in the mouths and memories of many."[2] This is an interesting comment on an attitude towards the episcopate which is somewhat reminiscent of that of the Scandinavian Churches.

"His sermons",[3] it is explained, "[were] such both for matter and method as gave no occasion of slighting, but alwaies affording even to the most knowing some farther information. . . . Yet he never affected tedious prolixity or needless verbosity; he allwaies avoided light expressions, and all words unbeseeming the spirituality and weightiness of the duty of prayer to God. No man less stinted in his gift of utterance, and yet no man more carefull in the government of his tongue.

"His voice was low, his action little; but the gravity of his aspect very great, and the reverence of his behaviour such as was more affecting to the hearers than the greater eloquence and more pompous pronunciation of others. In the handling of his text no man in his time was more exact, whether in opening the coherence, or the words themselves. His greatest excellency was in making plain the hardest texts of Scripture, wherin scarce any man was comparable to him."

---

[1] *A True Relation of the Life and Death of the Right Reverend Father in God William Bedell, Lord Bishop of Kilmore in Ireland*, Tanner MS., xxxvii, 147, Bodleian Library, ed. Thomas Wharton Jones, Camden Society, 1872, pp. 1-2.
[2] *Ibid.*, p. 4.   [3] *Life of Bishop Bedell*, pp. 5-6.

"Neither yet [for all this]",[1] it is explained, "was he ever the author or broacher of any novel opinion dissonant from the Doctrine of the Church of England; wherof no man was either a more able maintainer, or a more obedient observer. No, nor in the matter of Discipline was he any innovator; though privately, and to those of chiefest eminency in the Church, no man ever more bewaild or opposed the abuses therin. But the peace of the Church was that which he ever held precious; and therefore he was tender of uttering anything that might give occasion to turbulent spirits." It is curious to observe the limits of the criticism in the standpoint thus set out.

In a detailed account of his life at Horningsheath, there are two points in relation to Dr Bedell's attitude to his fellow clergy, and to the poor, which may be set down. "If", wrote William Bedell in an account of his father's visitors. "they were Ministers or Scholars he would tarry longer; but so as he would be sure their discourse should be profitable. And here it cannot be omitted what an admirable gift and grace God had given him in the command and ordering of his speech. For as he was well-stored with all kinds of knowledge; so he was of such sanctified wisdom, that still he would be communicating to others."

"There is yet further to be noted", the account goes on, "in his domestical course of conversation, his behaviour to the beggars, bedlams and travellours that use to come to men's doors. These he would not fail to examine, mixing both wholsome instructions and severe reproofs. Nor rested he there, but if they had any passes to travel by, he would be sure to scan them thoroughly, and finding them false or counterfeit, his way was to send for the Constable, and after correction given according to law, he would make a new pass, and send them to the place of their last settlement or birth."[2]

The passage on the "beggars, bedlams and travellours" is most revealing. The Puritans of Dr Bedell's pattern were sustained by the resources of their own piety based on the Scriptures. They were unperturbed and singularly calm, "compos'd and grave". Bedell, himself, was to go forward to the provost-ship of Trinity and the burden of the diocese of Kilmore and to the scrutiny of Laud and Strafford. Another phase of East Anglian Puritan life is reflected in the biography of John Angier by his son-in-law, Oliver Heywood. The subject of this study

[1] *Ibid.*, pp. 6-7.   [2] *Ibid.*, p. 19.

was born in 1603, the son and grandson of prosperous clothiers established at Dedham in Essex, where they had come under the influence of John Rogers, the preacher. "This Mr John Rogers", we are told, "was a mirror and miracle of zeal and success in his ministerial labours."[1] While still a boy John Angier lived for a time in the minister's house, "who sometimes put him upon praying in the family, which he performed with so much experience, humility and tenderness, that Mr Rogers would often commend him".[2] An interesting trait is preserved in regard to the minister's preaching. "Mr Rogers . . . his taking hold with both hands at one time of the supporters of the Canopy over the Pulpit, and roaring hideously, to represent the torments of the damned, had an awakening force attending it."

The development of Angier's studies is set out clearly: "She [Mrs Angier, his mother] resolved to send him to Mr John Cotton at Boston in Lincolnshire, where he was Tabled; he studied, and sometimes preached."[3] Mr Cotton of Emmanuel, who subsequently became minister at Boston, Massachusetts, was also the intermediary for the further step. "As for his investiture in his ministerial office, he had episcopal ordination, Mr Cotton having interest in Lewis Bayly a Bishop in Wales . . . and he did ordain him without subscription."[4] This represents the outlook of one wing of the barely Conformist clergy, though Angier would go out to join the Presbyterians.[5] One reference to James Lister, the Royalist vicar of Wakefield who was ejected in 1647, is rather appealing. "He [John Angier] often enquired after Mr Lister, to whom he bore a great respect, and indeed he had Catholick Principles and loved (*aliquid Christi*) any thing of Christ wherever he saw it, and continued this good old Puritan spirit to his dying day."[6] This is the more refreshing because it is surely a mark of the stricter sort that they were ready to declare their justice.

---

[1] *Life and Death of John Angier*, by Oliver Heywood, Chetham Society, ed. Ernest Axon, p. 50.

[2] *Ibid.*, p. 51.   [3] *Ibid.*, p. 52.   [4] *Ibid.*, pp. 56-7.

[5] Oliver Heywood gives details of John Angier's brothers: "Bizalid was a rich Clothier in Dedham, a gracious man; he died October 30, 1678. Samuel, the third son, being brought up a merchant, lived in good repute in Holland beyond seas, and there died in March 1666/7. Edmund the youngest being bound apprentice to a Grocer, went into New-England, and is [1685] the only survivor, hath many years kept a Grocer's shop in Cambridge there" (*ibid.*, p. 48).

[6] *Ibid.*, p. 61.

In the vicarage of Santon Downham, in that same East Anglian country-side which was fed from Emmanuel, John Rous, another minister of strict opinions from that college, made a collection of satiric verses. Those on the *New Churchman*[1] were aimed at the type of parson the preciser sort abhorred.

> "His gravity rides up and downe,
> In a long coate or a short govne;
> And swears by the halfe football on his pate,
> That no man is predestinate."

A consideration of these verses makes it plain that the vice of levity stood self-condemned. There is a passage in the auto-biography of that Puritan country gentleman Sir Symonds D'Ewes which bears directly upon this point. "I believe", wrote Sir Symonds in reference to his feud with Mr Danford, the parson of Stowlangtoft Church, "he found also the curses of the poor in town and country he should draw upon himself by driving me away, by whose hospitality and outward works of mercy many were refreshed."[2] In a later portion of his work the same author describes the attitude of men of his way of thinking towards the non-conformitants. "But this", he wrote, "I am confident, they do most of them in the main, aim sin-cerely at God's glory, and to reduce the public service of God to that power and purity which it enjoyed in the primitive times. Vices and sins are so severely punished amongst them, as in that respect it seems to be a true type of heaven itself."[3] There was in this approach a clear simplicity and a hatred of all sophistication. The Bible, and the Old Testament especially, was so close to them and quite unrelated to any history.

Still within the limits of the Church of England, but very much to the left of Dr Bedell, were those men who laid their every stress upon the gift of preaching. Among the more tem-perate exchanges in the celebrated proceedings taken at Dur-ham against Dr Cosin, was a declaration laid before Parliament which seems, in some respects, to have been most truly repre-sentative. "Your elder brother and a senior residentiary Peter Smart", so runs the accusation, "perceiving the simple people inveigled and beguiled, by Popish baits and all ornaments of

---

[1] Entry under 1635, *Diary of John Rous*, Camden Society, p. 79.
[2] *Autobiography of Sir Symonds D'Ewes*, ed. J. O. Halliwell, vol. ii, p. 65.
[3] *Ibid.*, vol. ii, p. 116.

glorious pictures, and Babalonish vestures, and excessive number of wax candles burning at one tyme, and especially the horrible profanations of both the sacraments with all manner of musick, both instrumentall, and vocall, so lowds that the Ministers could not be heard, what they saide."[1] This was the core of the objection beyond the brushwood of the verbal accusations.

It was, so the statement goes forward, "as if *Bacchanalia* the feasts of Bacchus, or the Ægyptian Isis, or the Phrygian Cybele, *cum multiforis tibiis, et crepitantibus sistris*; with fluits, and bag-pipes, with tymbrells and tabers; and not the Death and Passion of our Saviour Christ wer celebrated". They hated all complication and all infiltration, and in regard to Rome their animosity still burned implacable. The men of the real Puritan tradition were incapable of the folded processes of Court diplomacy. Their view of foreign politics was simple, and affected many who had not to deal with the complications of the actual situation. Sir Thomas Roe, the diplomatist, when out of place could write that "all leagues with any papist-blinded estate are Egyptian reeds". In this way they, in time, could gather in that mass of English anti-Catholic sentiment which had no other link with the preciser sort.

Yet it is an error to underestimate the force of the Puritans' contention from their own premise. "And is it not a base imploiment for you, John Cosin," so runs another passage with an authentic ring, "having two fatt benefices, and Arch-deaconrie, and a prebend, being Bachelaur of Divinitie, and more than a subdeacon, even a full priest, to leave all your charges of soules at 6 and 7, and sitt all day long eyther at home with a tobacco pipe in your mouth, or in the quire chaunting among singers."[2]

For the Puritan laymen of middling station it was a pleasurable duty to reduce the bishops' high pretensions. This comes out very clearly in the correspondence which Nathan Walworth, who was the Earl of Pembroke's steward at Baynard's Castle, carried on with his colleague Peter Seddon.[3] They were both

[1] *Bishop Cosin's Correspondence*, vol. i, p. 165.

[2] *Bishop Cosin's Correspondence*, vol. i, p. 185.

[3] Cf. letter of Peter Seddon to Nathan Walworth, dated at Pilkington, 14 December 1634. The BB referred to in this letter was Bishop Bridgman of Chester. "My advice is if you give Lord BB anie thanks let it be verbal not real but speare your money for better purposes and do not grass [grease] a fat sowe behind" (*Correspondence of Nathan Walworth*, Chetham Society (1880-, p. 33).

THE EARL OF PORTLAND
From a painting in the National Portrait Gallery

of North Country stock and given to forthright expression; John Angier was preacher at Ellis Walworth's house at Ringley. By contrast the men of strict opinions had a sharp declared respect for their own divines.[1] They were bound together and a certain sympathy linked them all; the master and mistress would know how to value a worthy virtuous man among their servants.[2] There was indeed an inchoate form of social solidarity. In that sense it was a difficult world for a stranger to penetrate. In a way this was concealed by the domestic and established side of the Puritan movement.[3] This last circumstance is emphasised by the nature of the judgments passed by all those who subscribed to the strict views. A note by Sir Symonds D'Ewes is typical. "My Lorde North and his Ladie", he wrote in a letter to his father, "did soe fill upp all the dinnertime with the needless and vaine discourse of a dogg they had which died a little before, as it showed them to be ill-catechized in the principles of religion."[4] We are returned to the atmosphere of savoury discourse and grave deportment. Still the emphasis upon preaching was radical, since by this means certain ministers could stir up in men that chief enemy of orderly government—Enthusiasm.

It is the raw material of Enthusiasm which keeps breaking

---

[1] Sentences from Heywood's life of Angier bear on this point. "Mr Anthony Tuckey . . . was a serious, settled good man before he went to Boston, afterwards Master of Immanuel and after that of St John in Cambridge Afterwards Dr Hill was Master of Trinity Colledge in Cambridge and Dr Winter, Master of Trinity College near Dublin in Ireland: all famous lights in the Church of God" (Heywood, *op. cit.* p. 51).

[2] In the Diary of Isabella, wife of Sir Roger Twysden, Baronet of Roydon Hall, there occurs the following entry: "Mr Johannes Hird a right good religious gentell man, he left this life the 15 Mar: 1650/51 at 9 a clock at night at Peckham, he was in his 73 yeare of his age: he had lived in this family [as major-domo to Sir William and Sir Roger Twysden] 32 [years] he was a German by birth, he never would let his writ name be known" (*Archæologia Cantiana*, vol. I, p. 132).

[3] The apprenticeship of Ambrose Barnes belongs to the years 646-55, but the record has a note of righteous prosperity: "In this town Mr Barnes was bound apprentice to that calling [merchant]. His mistress, who afterwards was the Lady Jennison, had an high value for him whilst she lived. His master entirely confided in him. . . . Trade then flourished mightily in all its branches. His master treated him like a partner, permitting him to venture on his own bottoms, whereby he cleared seven or eight hundred pounds to himself and this before the time of his apprenticeship was expired" (*Memoirs of the life of Mr Ambrose Barlow late merchant and sometime alderman of Newcastle upon Tyne*, ed. W. H. D. Longstaffe, Surtees Society, p. 37).

[4] From p. 16. Letter of Symonds D'Ewes to Paul D'Ewes dated at Islington, 17 August 1630 (*Correspondence of Sir Simonds D'Ewes*, vol. ii, p. 216).

A.C.—9

through in the description of Richard Baxter's early life. In spite of much that is formalised in the presentation, a picture of one aspect of rural England emerges from the carefully arranged pages of the *Reliquiæ Baxterianæ*: "We lived", he wrote in an account of his childhood at Eaton Constantine, a mile from Wrekin Hill, "in a country that had but little Preaching at all: in the village where I was born there were four Readers successively in six years time, ignorant Men and two of them immoral in their lives. Only three or four constant competent Preachers lived near us, and those [though conformable all save one] were the common mark of the People's Obloquy and Reproach, and any that had but gone to hear them, when he had no Preaching at Home, was made the derision of the Vulgar Rabble, under the odious name of *Puritane*".[1]

Side by side with the love of preaching there went a horror of the graven image. As long as no golden altars were set up there was no intrinsic repugnance to the idea of using a church for worldly purposes. It was not the Puritans who complained of the situation at St Paul's where "on Sundays and festival days the boys and maids and children of the adjoining parishes, after dinner, come into the church and play as children used to do till dark night, whence comes that inordinate noise, which many times suffers not the preachers to be heard."[2]

A more striking example is to be found in the autobiography of Thomas Raymond, a young man of Puritan antecedents then acting as secretary at the embassy at the Hague. "This place", he noted, "in summer is a very Paradis, wanting nothing for delight of the mynd or eyes. Organs in the Great Kirk . . . in winter evenings used to be played on in all times, the people in great numbers walking as in an exchange."[3] Here there was no bishop and no bishop's throne.

The question of jurisdiction loomed before the stricter men whenever they considered the episcopate. "It concerns", wrote Thomas Vicars, a Puritan, to his cousin, "your little *vituperium* of London [Dr Laud] and the great O'Neale of Winchester to foment and keep afoot the faction. They have learned their lesson: *Divide et impera*. They play the Rex. It was Barnevelt's

---

[1] *Reliquiæ Baxterianæ*, ed. Matthew Sylvester (1696), pp. 1-2.
[2] Report of Attorney-General Noy and Dr Thomas Rives, the King's Advocate, dated March 1632 (State Papers, Dom. Charles I, ccxiv, 94).
[3] *Autobiography of Thomas Raymond*, Camden Society (1917), pp. 31-2.

policy; they tread his ground."[1] Another letter from a different angle was written by the vicar of Braintree to Dr Duck. My Lord of London's displeasure had pierced deeply into him. "If he had suddenly fallen", the writer explained, "upon the strict practice of conformity he had undone himself and broken the town [of Braintree] to pieces. By his moderate and slow proceedings he had made stay of some [parishioners] and hoped to settle their judgments."[2] Upon the first notice of alteration many were resolving to go to New England. The concern thus manifested with jurisdiction and with rules was essentially characteristic of the middle class, a matter for the argumentative and propertied. It seems, in fact, that it was upon the middle class that the whole Puritan movement pivoted.

Granted that this was so, one can examine briefly the Puritanism that fell outside these limits, which could reasonably include the Cromwell family and Pym and Ireton. The case of Dr Bedell, and of the Anglican chaplains attached to the household of Parliamentarian lords, represents one extreme on account of the association with the Church and State position. In Bedell's *Life* one can see reflected the views held in those East Anglian rectories which were occupied by men of strict opinions. The Divine Right of Kings and the inalienable prerogatives of episcopacy would never be accepted there. Yet these doctrines were the lynch-pin of high royalism. The men of Dr Bedell's way of thinking were not sufficiently grounded in the necessity of episcopal rights to support them openly in the armed conflict. Those who would give the weight of doctrine to their episcopalian preferences would soon slough off their sympathy with the Precisians. Still one cannot underestimate that element in religious circles which was in the last resort aloof from the Civil Wars; but a moderate attachment to the monarchy, such as many of the stricter sort professed, would lead those who held these views into the detached conservative wing among the Parliamentarians. With groaning of spirit these "true professors" had accepted the gauds of the Court when the King's Government was in London. They could never have brought themselves to rally round such symbols.

---

[1] Letter from Thomas Vicars to John Vicars, dated from Cockfield, 22 April 1632 (State Papers, Dom. Charles I, cxli, 37).

[2] Letter from Dr Samuel Collins to Dr Duck, dated at Braintree, 18 January 1632 (State Papers, Dom. Charles I, cx, 41).

But if Puritan royalism can be said to have been liquidated by the outbreak of the war, it is all the more important to determine the degree of support which the devotion to the Pure Gospel aroused among the artisans and labourers. In the first place it seems clear that this support was very much greater than that aroused by the new doctrine in Tudor times. The whole layout of Fox's *Acts and Monuments*, with its enumeration of the Roman emperors and its citations from statutes and case-law, implied a considerable standard of education before the work could be mastered. The great volume which was early known as the *Book of Martyrs* had first appeared in 1563, and was useful for those households where a compendious universal history could be studied; it was unintelligible to the barely literate. The very term "the New Learning" has to be borne in mind when its extension is considered among the labouring class.

At the same time the seventy years since Queen Elizabeth's accession had witnessed a great increase of literacy, and this is a determining factor in the situation. It was a personal perusal, even if made haltingly and after studying the characters with some difficulty, that alone brought to men the deep conviction of that treasure of knowledge which God had given to their keeping and interpretation. It can be argued that this whole-hearted Puritanism could only take hold when the Bible was *read*. The "nailers and iron-labourers" of Dudley might be influenced by Mr Baxter's preaching; but they were unlettered men. It was seldom the unlettered man who was possessed of that exaltation which came to those who pondered on Jehovah's vengeance and that immediate logical history, the Book of Kings. The ungodly were a great multitude, and there were many swaths to be mown down. It was a mark of the "oppressed saints" that they should be profoundly conscious of their own integrity.

As to the general outlook of the poor, a distinction must be made between town and country. We have an interesting view of one element among the countrymen in the minute accounts of the escape of King Charles II after Worcester. In some parts of the country-side, for instance in the Fylde, Catholicism was maintained throughout the whole of the population. There were few districts without those Catholic "pockets" which were so characteristic of the West Midlands. In many counties there

was a widespread acceptance of that Anglican spirit which had
lately received such devotional expression. Throughout the
rural areas, and in the new industrial villages and in the towns,
the preaching element among the Puritans might gain adherents even among the very poorest. Yet surely the great majority
of the artisans were hardly affected by the doctrinal question.
The anti-Popish feeling of the London mob was in reality anti-
foreign in its inspiration.

Throughout England a concentration on their daily labour
seems to have marked the crowds of unapprenticed work-
people in the cloth trades, and among the colliers and those
who toiled in the iron and lead mines. This would equally apply
to that great mute London proletariat, the shifting masses of
unskilled workers in the building trades, the men who plied for
boat-hire on the Thames, the hackney coachmen, the horde of
grooms and servants and the linkmen, and all those hands in
industry or commerce who had no enduring status. There is
little evidence that these sections of the people had concern for
the religious topic.

Seen from this angle, it was the economic standing of the
Puritans and Separatists that brought them so constantly before
the mind of the authorities. No government could long be
unaware of their determination and conviction and their God-
sown knowledge.

CHAPTER IX

THE CATHOLIC MINORITY

THESE peaceful years of the reign of Charles I meant little in the history of the Catholic community. For them, in their increasing remoteness from political concerns, the reigns of the first Stuart sovereigns formed a unit. Ever since the death of Queen Elizabeth they had been at once solidifying and weakening. They had become weaker in the sense that defections among the landed families were frequent, and in most cases final; they were more solid in that the secret Catholics or Church papists of the Elizabethan era had often in the following generation rallied to the ancient faith. At least in the circles of the gentry, the position was clearer. There was now within that wide class which would form the squirearchy a definite and ascertainable Catholic *bloc* known with exactness.

Viewed from a certain angle, the Catholic body can be seen already to have acquired that self-contained and remote character which for two hundred years deepened continually. This was masked by the superficial cordiality which united the greater and the lesser gentry outside the ranks of the men of strict opinions. The Catholics of these groupings had an ease in their relationship with their neighbours of Anglican and Royalist convictions. At a deeper level the Recusants could often rely on the help of their Protestant kinsmen.[1] And, again within the same class framework, the act of conforming to the Established Church caused no breach with the members of the family who stood fast by their old allegiance.[2] Always recollecting that the Puritans stood aloof, the whole Catholic-Anglican relationship was very free from bitterness as far as laymen of

---

[1] As an example, the assistance given to William Blundell of Crosby by his cousins, the Bradshaighs of Haigh.

[2] In this period such secessions were often gradual. During their periods of education, the first Earl of Peterborough was under pressure from the Crown and the first Earl of Carnarvon from his guardian and future father-in-law, the Earl of Montgomery. Besides, Carnarvon returned to Catholicism on his death-bed. It was in the next generation, and especially under the Commonwealth, that changes in families of this character were induced by despair or tedium.

standing on both sides were concerned. In certain counties the Catholic phalanx was socially, if not politically, important. It was recognised as a profoundly conservative force, and as such would prove congenial to any instinctively Royalist body of opinion among the gentry. It seems likely that this approval was mixed with a feeling of pity for men who had given up their natural right to a place in the commission of the peace, men who had lost their share in county management through adherence to an unsympathetic scruple of conscience.

At the same time, at a level to which the surface acquaintanceships did not reach, the withdrawn life of the Catholic squires was now crystallising. In many parts of England their congregations could be likened to a series of "islands". The manor-house of a Recusant family would have its own religious climate; it would have its charitable preoccupations. It was a simple matter for members of such families to enter the English convents in France and the Low Countries. There was a recognised, if illegal, line of travel.[1] With this there went the formation of libraries of Catholic devotional works which themselves form a tribute to this new security. An example is the small collection of books at Mapledurham, which were either certainly or probably purchased as early as the reign of Charles I.[2] In other cases only a single volume has survived, perhaps representing the favourite book of devotion of some

[1] On 29 November 1634 William Rose of Queenborough was charged with carrying children into foreign parts to be bred in Popery (State Papers, Dom. Charles I, cclxxviii, 115). On 3 November 1634 John Phillpott, Somerset Herald, had reported that in September 1633 William Rose had carried to Dunkirk five English gentlewomen, who had arranged with Browne, an Irish merchant at Ostend, for wagons to convey them and their baggage to Louvain (ibid., cclxxxvii, 7). On 16 August 1633 details were set out of the case of William Benson of Halstow, Kent, fisherman, who was similarly accused (ibid., ccliv, p. 73).

[2] Among the books at Mapledurham, William Reynold's Treatise conteyning the True, Catholike and Apostolike Faith of the Holy Sacrifice, printed at Antwerp in 1593, and the English translation of Luis de Granada, printed as A Memoriall of a Christian Life at Rouen in 1586, contain the signature "Charles Blount". Sir Charles was killed at Oxford in 1644, and it seems probable that the Life of B. Aloysius Gonzaga, printed at Paris in 1627, The Life of the Blessed Virgin, Sainct Catherine of Siena, translated into English by John Fen and printed at Louvain in 1609, and the Lives and Singular Virtues of Saint Elzear Count of Sabran and of his wife the blessed Countess Delphina, printed by John Cousturier in 1638, were added to the library in his time. The Holy Bible, Doway version, printed in 1635, and The New Testament, Doway version, printed by John Cousturier in 1633, both bear Sir Charles Blount's signature.

member of the family.[1] In this connection the influence of the Jesuit confessor is often discernible.

The fact of the printing of these well-bound volumes, very different in style and format from the controversial pamphlets and broadsheets of an earlier generation, indicates a definite demand. The girls who went overseas to become nuns had been brought up on the Doway version of the Scriptures and on the lives of the saints, didactic in their quality, which were among the characteristic products of the Counter-Reformation. A study of Catholic libraries would be interesting.[2] It might produce valuable data in regard to the way of life of the Recusant families during these years.[3]

It seems likely that Sir Thomas More was now generally recognised by the Catholic community as the man who had given the great example of steadfastness. It is worth noting that Cresacre More's life and death of his ancestor was dedicated to the Queen on its publication in 1631.[4] Among the Catholic stocks, it was the daughters rather than the sons who studied this devotional literature; the convents in the Low Countries were slowly filling. It was the part of the men of the family to provide a regular supply of benefactions for the maintenance of these religious houses.[5] There was, in fact, an English world

[1] Mary, daughter of Edward Banester of Ilsworth, co. Southampton, and wife of Robert Dormer of Peterley in Great Missenden in Buckinghamshire, bequeathed to her daughter, Mrs George Eyston, her signed copy of *Meditations upon the Mysteries of Our Holy Faith with the practise of mental prayer*. The work, which was printed at St Omer in 1619, is described as being composed in Spanish by the Reverend Father Lewis of Puente of the Society of Jesus, native of Valladolid, and translated out of Spanish into English by John Heigham.

[2] It is clear that an Elizabethan house is likely to yield more useful information than one dating from that Georgian period, which saw the building or reconstruction of so many Catholic houses. In the latter case, many books which were at that time over a century old would probably not be considered worth removing to the new mansion.

[3] At the same time some books passed from one family to another by inheritance. The Mapledurham library contains some volumes which had come from Tichborne through the marriage of Michael Blount with one of the co-heiresses of Sir Henry Tichborne, who died in 1743. In this case, however, the seventeenth-century books were Anglican or general in character. It was the question of the survival of some handsome volumes.

[4] The dedication is unusual. "To the High and Mightie Princesse, Our Most Gratious Queene and Soveraigne, Marie Henriette, Queene of Great Britaine, France and Irland, Ladie of the Iles of the British Ocean."

[5] Thus, among the benefactors to the Benedictines at Brussels were "Lady Mary Percy, Lady Petre, Lady Digby, Mrs. Vaux, Lady Mary Neville and divers other ladies of Worcester House" (Catholic Records Society, *Miscellanea*, vol. v, p. 5).

within which the influence of Catholic ideas was unchallenged. To such an enclosed segment there belonged those who were touched by the influence of the devotional teaching of Fr Baker, during the years between June 1620 and July 1624, when he lived first in Devonshire with Philip Fursden and then in lodgings at Gray's Inn.[1] These private circles from which unfriendly criticism was thus excluded had something in common with those which were formed by the early Quakers. In each case there was a deliberate isolation from those who did not share their own tradition on the part of those who, broadly speaking, sought the City of God.

Yet it was the tragedy of the Catholics in the south of England that only the country gentry and their dependants and the townsmen, who possessed a certain status and freedom of movement, could benefit from such spiritual guidance. In this matter it is only fair to note that the servants who formed part of a large Catholic household were especially privileged.[2]

This was a transitional period in the development of the English Catholic body. The last generation of the Church papists was now dying out, and with it the idea of a doubtful or suspected allegiance to the Established Church.[3] A quiet acceptance of the Anglican tradition, usually with a strongly Protestant emphasis, was becoming the normal inheritance among those families whose economic status enabled them to

[1] Dom Augustine Baker returned from Douai in May 1638 and until his death on 9 August 1641 lived with the wife of Richard Watson, surgeon to King Charles, at her houses in Ampthill and London. A note on his earlier stay has interest. "Being arrived at London he took his lodging near Gray's Inn, partly because the place was more than ordinarily secure and partly for the convenience of the walks" (*Life of Father Augustine Baker*, by Fr Serenus Cressy, ed. Dom Justin McCann (1933), pp. 96 and 135).

[2] This is corroborated by the dying statement of Laurence Fitzpatrick at Tyburn on 6 July 1631. He had been page to Lord Castlehaven at Fonthill Giffard, in Wiltshire. "He had [declared Fitzpatrick] fallen into these sins by reason he had neglected, and not sodenly, as he should have done, repaired to his ghostly father, to make confession and take instructions from him" (*State Trials*, ed. W. Cobbett, vol. iii, p. 413).

[3] A list preserved among Sir John Conway's papers and dated 8 May 1628 gives a list of those with Recusant or non-Communicant wives, children or servants, who are therefore vehemently suspected to be ill-affected in religion. The list includes the names of the Earls of Banbury and Sunderland, Viscounts Savage and Newark, Lord Weston, Sir Henry Shirley, Sir Henry Compton and Sir John Shelley, both of Sussex, and Sir Richard Tichborne (Cal. Portland MSS., vol. i, pp. 1-2). Cf. *Diary of Walter Yonge 1604-1628*, Camden Society (1848), p. 117, for a list of Papists of eminence compiled in 1628.

aspire to public office. Yet the note of segregation which attached to the Catholic minority was only in part the consequence of their virtual exclusion from official life; it was also bound up with a certain indifference to questions of policy due to long residence in their own counties. The Catholic landed families were already manifesting those qualities of insularity, devotion to the reigning king, and sensitive aggressive patriotism, which by the end of the eighteenth century would be their special hall-mark.

They were firmly entrenched upon the right wing of the Royalists, and were thus outside that pull of interests that affected their richer neighbours, the great squires of what would soon become the Parliamentarian tradition. It was, however, obvious that they had no special sympathy for the Court. It is necessary here to make a reservation, because to Charles I himself they gave a well-considered gratitude.[1]

It is interesting to trace the stages of the King's goodwill and the ways in which he became their benefactor. As long as Parliament was sitting, the lists of Recusants continued to be compiled. Thus in December 1628 lists were sent in by the Lord Mayor and by the justices of the peace for Westminster.[2] It is worth setting out some of the more significant names obtained from these two sources. Those resident in London included Lords Brudenell, Montagu and Windsor, George Geldropp a picture drawer, Thomas Turner a physician, John Giffard, John More and Thomas Bardin doctors of physic, the Earl of Abercorn, Sir George Petre, and Mr Jaquinta an Italian doctor of physic.[3] Among the Recusants in Westminster

---

[1] For the favours granted, cf. a pardon issued on 27 February 1628 to Anthony second Viscount Montague for not repairing to the church and receiving the Sacrament of the Lord's Supper, and also for sending his children beyond the seas and harbouring Jesuits, seminary and other Popish priests, with licence to repair to any place within the kingdom (State Papers, Dom. Charles I).

[2] There was never any doubt as to the attitude of the Corporation towards Papists. A judgment on the political situation bears this out. "The evidence shows that delegates were returned to the Common Council in 1640 who had sat there the year before and for several years past, or at least had long held office in the precinct. The continuity of political opinion was unbroken, and if the City later aligned itself openly against the King the spirit of opposition had been growing over many years" ("The Disputed Election in London in 1641," by Melvin C. Wren, *E. H. R.*, vol. lxiv, p. 48).

[3] List of Recusants dated 16 December 1628 (State Papers, Dom. Charles I, cxxii, 48).

were the Earl of Nithsdale[1] and another physician, Dr Cadman.

The considerable number of Catholic doctors is accounted for by the fact that medicine was a profession which could be entered without tests. Padua was a great international centre for medical study. King Charles showed his sympathy with a relaxation of the penal laws by the ease with which he granted conditional release to priests in prison. In 1633 two Catholic doctors testified to the infirmity of Fr Francis Smith.[2] Later the same physicians gave evidence in favour of a layman.[3] Releases on medical grounds continued throughout the years during which the King ruled without a Parliament.[4] Peers and their widows benefited by explicit letters of grace and protection. In a list compiled by the Opposition at the beginning of the Long Parliament, it is asserted that such letters had been granted to nineteen peers and two peeresses.[5] A study of the list suggests that there were no Catholic lords who were refused this aid. Those whose names do not appear had probably not been indicted for recusancy.

Such prosecutions as took place were probably the work of local justices. They tend to occur in towns where the Anglican influence was powerful. In 1637 Richard Fielden, an innholder of Winchester, was ordered to be put out of his inn as a Recusant.[6] In 1640 when the troubles were already gathering a complaint was made by the Mayor and Aldermen of Oxford that the innholder of the *Mitre* was suspected of harbouring

---

[1] This Scottish peer was throughout protected by Charles I. On 27 March 1640 the King wrote to him from Whitehall. "It is now time to tell you to look to yourself" (Everingham Park MSS., printed in the First Report of the Historical Manuscripts Commission, p. 45).

[2] In a petition for the conditional release of Francis Smith, a priest near four score, John More and Thomas Turner, doctors of physic, testify on 19 July 1633 to the prisoner's infirmity (State Papers, Dom. Charles I, cclv, 35).

[3] A certificate dated 5 June 1637 was given by John More and Thomas Turner, physicians, in favour of Henry Morse a prisoner in Newgate "inclining to a consumptive indisposition" (*ibid.*, ccclxi, 20, 1).

[4] In an undated petition belonging apparently to 1639, Edward Maie, doctor of physic, and three others certify that they visited William Drury, gent., a prisoner in the Clink and have seen his arm and judge it to be a very dangerous fistula (*Ibid.*, ccccxxxvii, 61, 1).

[5] The beneficiaries were the Marquess of Winchester; the Earls of Shrewsbury, Worcester, St Albans, Rivers and Castlehaven; Viscounts Montagu, Dunbar and Cashel; Lords Abergavenny, Morley, Petre, Eure, Windsor, Vaux, Brudenell, Stourton and Teynham; Lord Herbert, son of the Earl of Worcester; the Dowager Countesses of Portland and Rutland. A note to the paper adds: "Lord W. Howard is now dead" (*ibid.*, ccccxxxvii, 67).

[6] Letter dated 10 May 1637 (*ibid.*, ccclv, 181).

papists.[1] Such cases would be beyond the scope of the royal action, but the King intervened to aid his servants.[2]

With the exception of the Marquesses of Winchester and Worcester, the peers of the Old Religion formed an inconspicuous grouping. Promotion in the peerage or service at the Court seemed hardly open to them.[3] They took a disproportionately trivial share in that work of the House of Lords which was not yet closed to them.[4] Already the poorer lords and more substantial gentry among the Recusants were settling down to those local attachments, which so swiftly earned them their neighbours' tolerance. As the Catholic estates consolidated, so also were their owners confined to a purely local consequence. While the Court and the great lords were for different reasons drawn towards that cosmopolitan outlook which the Whigs would never lose, the Catholic minority was digging itself into an ever-deepening county loyalty. It was in part a result of this concentration that small Catholic groups in the towns, and those in country areas remote from Catholic influence, tended to disintegrate. Again, the principal figures of the time, Eliot, Hampden and Strafford, for instance, were not only remote from the ancient faith, they were formed to a permanent antipathy.

It is not surprising that an air of unreality suffused the domestic politics of the Recusant gentry. This is evident in that internecine conflict which led to the retirement of the vicar apostolic. The community appears as deeply immersed in its

[1] Greene of the *Mitre* inn is described as a suspected Recusant and harbourer of Papists. It is explained that the *Mitre*, being an ancient inn of the inheritance of Lincoln College, came into the possession of Greene through his marriage with the late innholder's widow (*ibid.*, cccclvii, 21).

[2] Cf. petition of Henry Lord, "Your Majesty's servant and guide in the New Forest". The petitioner, a Recusant dwelling in the New Forest, had served as royal hunting guide for thirty years (*ibid.*, ccccxxxxvi, 66).

[3] On 11 March 1626 a Petition of the House of Commons was presented to the House of Lords alleging that Emmanuel Lord Scrope, Lord-Lieutenant of York and Lord-President of the North, is inclined to Popery and favouring Popish Recusants—rarely attends Divine Service at the Cathedral of York or receives the sacrament of the Lord's Supper. Omitted to disarm Lord Eure. Authorised Lord Viscount Dunbar and Sir Thomas Metham to be Deputy-Lieutenants (Cal. House of Lords MSS., Appendix to IVth Report, p. 6).

[4] Among the twenty-seven peers present at the trial of Mervyn, second Earl of Castlehaven, in 1631, only the Earl of Worcester and Lord Petre were Catholics. This trial throws another sidelight on the legal position of Catholics. Lord Audley objected that neither he [Laurence Fitzpatrick] nor any other might be allowed witnesses against him, until he had taken the oath of allegiance. The Judges resolved against him, [holding] that they might be witnesses, unless they were convicted recusants (*State Trials*, ed. Cobbett, vol. iii, pp. 404 and 413).

own affairs, while at the same time sectional opinion can be assessed in a way that was impossible with the looser texture of the Elizabethan grouping. The priests are seen as enclosed within a community which was itself already somewhat separated from the general body of the nation. To this busy priesthood, nurtured in the second wind of the Tridentine movement, the transient English political scene would seem of small significance.

For this reason, the quarrel between the secular and regular clergy, which led to the resignation of the Bishop of Chalcedon in 1631, appears hardly to belong to the Caroline period. It is difficult to relate it to the movement of English life in those easy years which followed the murder of the Duke of Buckingham, and it seems to bear only a slightly closer relation to the *milieu* of Con and Panzani, who successively headed the papal missions to King Charles' Court.

In a certain sense these quarrels were a legacy from the Archpriest controversy. They belong to the mood of James I and the royal interventions in theology. The matter concerned the six years' residence in England, from 1625 until 1631, of the second of the vicars apostolic, Richard Smith, Bishop of Chalcedon. Opposition to this prelate had come from many sides. It seems clear that there had been a disappointed hope that the Bishop of Chalcedon would prove amenable to the English Court. The tacit permission of entry into England presupposed a determination on the part of the Government to extract some benefit from the presence in England of a single ecclesiastical chief of the Catholic minority. The generation which had grown to manhood in the decade of the Gunpowder Plot was now in power. Dr Smith had a reputation as a solid opponent of the Jesuits, and this would have been welcomed by the civil authorities.

A Lincolnshire man, the new bishop had spent some time in Oxford, at Trinity College, many years previously.[1] He had lived in Rome and taught in Spain. Something professorial seems to have clung to him. He was rigid in the pressing of his points, very direct and unskilled in manœuvre. He had given satisfaction to his brethren of the secular clergy during the period of his agency in Rome, and he had since lectured in Paris at the College d'Arras. Father Robert Parsons, S.J., had declared of him that he had never dealt with any man in his

[1] Bishop Smith was born in 1568, and was at Oxford between 1583 and 1586.

life more heady and resolute in his opinions. He was a preacher of some power and a writer of merit, addicted to controversy phrased in cumbrous Latin.

Pastor maintains that Bishop Smith was a Gallican, but it seems more likely that he was a prelate attached to his own privileges and careless about protecting his position. His claims to ordinary jurisdiction, that is to say to the rights of a diocesan bishop, had been disavowed by the new Congregation *de Propaganda Fide*[1] and it was made clear to him that he had not been created *Episcopus Angliæ* but *Episcopus Calcedonen in Asia*, with faculties which were limited and revocable at the discretion of the Holy See. It was in this situation that the Remonstrance signed by the lay Catholics against the bishop's claims was introduced.[2]

This document requires a certain consideration. The prime movers were Sir Basil Brook and Sir Tobie Mathew, while the opposition was furnished by the secular clergy, who naturally supported their pastor against his enemies. It was said by his opponents that Dr Smith had asked that wills should be exhibited to him, and had wished for the payment of tithes. He was further stated to be determined to exercise his alleged rights of visitation. Such objections were bound to predispose the civil authorities in the complainants' favour. To the managers of this petition it may have seemed an ideal opportunity for gathering together both the Erastian Catholic laymen and the strong supporters of the Society of Jesus. The very act of signature was a manifestation of distaste for a foreign and illegal jurisdiction.

The Bishop of Chalcedon was, indeed, removed, but to no one's profit. As the long manœuvres reached their term, the civil authorities began to harass him. A spy, Benedicto Bellini, master gardener to the French Ambassador,[3] reported on his movements as he lay in the Embassy "in the chamber over Lady Falkland's". Finally, on the receipt of a Brief from

---

[1] Decree of the Congregation of the Holy Office, dated 16 December 1627.

[2] It is perhaps a mark of his isolation that the Congregation of the Holy Office communicated with the Bishop of Chalcedon *mediante confessore Reginæ Angliæ*.

(3) Cf. a paper apparently dated in 1630 (State Papers, Dom. Charles I, clxxviii). Dr Smith was naturally always under surveillance. A letter from John Cleare to Secretary Coke, dated at Sevenoaks, 5 February 1628, describes a conversation with the bishop and details of letters which he wished to send to France (*ibid.*, xcii, 27). Later a gentleman of the sword, styling himself the Chevalier de Bois Gaudry, sent in a memorial to the Secretary of State referring to his offers to seize the bishop (*ibid.*, clix, 5).

Pope Urban VIII in the summer of 1631, he crossed to Paris. Here he gave in his resignation to Cardinal Bichi, the Nuncio. The resignation was accepted, and the Bishop of Chalcedon never returned to his own country.

The whole episode shows the great weight attached to the signatures of peers. It was the contention of the parochial clergy that these men were pressed to sign the memorial by their chaplains.[1] It was part of the weakness of the situation that it was this circle which interested Rome during the pontificate of the Barberini. When Panzani came over on his mission in 1635, it was the motives and spontaneity of this action by the peers that he chose to analyse.[2] The papal envoy misunderstood the King's advisers, and beyond the precincts of the Court he did not go.

Nevertheless, throughout England there was already within the Catholic body a tendency to the enclosed group, to the form of expression and the habit of mind associated with the self-contained unit. It would be useful to make a study of the circle of which Mary Ward was the centre during the last seven years of her life in London and Yorkshire. She had spent a life-time on the Continent in endeavouring to establish a religious congregation, and after her many struggles came back to England in May 1638.[3] Her work can best be examined

[1] "For not to mention that all those Catholic lords who refuse to submit to me are penitents of the Regulars." Letter from the Bishop of Chalcedon, dated at London, 14 June 1631 (*Propaganda Archives*, Letters 100, ñ. 142, 143).

[2] In considering this analysis, it should be stressed that the act of signature was pleasing to the Government. The list is composed in unequal proportions of the indifferent, the timid and the zealous. According to a document from the *General Archives SJ*, Anglia, Historia IV, printed in Hughes, *History of the Society of Jesus in North America*, the following peers signed the Remonstrance against the Bishop: Earls Shrewsbury, Rutland, Rivers, Clanricarde; M. of Winchester; Viscounts Somerset, Savage; Barons Herbert, Abergavenny, Windsor, Morley, Mordaunt, Petre, Teynham, Wotton, Vaux, Stourton, Dunkellin and Baltimore. It is agreed that the Marquess of Worcester, Viscount Montagu and Lords Eure and Arundell of Wardour did not sign. Panzani maintained that Lords Herbert, Clanricarde and Dunkellin did not sign either, and that Lords Winchester, Rutland, Castle-haven and Brudenell were on cordial terms with the Bishop of Chalcedon. In this connection the second Earl of Castlehaven had rejoined the Church of England before the date of the Remonstrance. Morley and Vaux were hardly *pratiquant*; Teynham a child under Lord Petre's guardianship. Windsor is described by Panzani as devoted to the Benedictines.

[3] Mary Ward, the foundress of the Institute of the Blessed Virgin Mary, reached London on 20 May 1638 at the age of fifty-three, coming from Rouen. On 1 May 1642 she moved to Hutton Radby in Cleveland, to be near her relatives. She died at Heworth, in the East Riding, on 20 January 1645. Cf. *Life of Mary Ward*, by M. C. Chambers (1882), which uses the contemporary manuscript life by Winifred Wigmore.

within the general framework of the Jesuit effort, but it may be compared with the glimpses that Dame Gertrude More has left of her own outlook and that of her relatives.[1] In both cases one is conscious that such groups in England were working within narrow boundaries. The men and women of ardent principles were surrounded by a mass of relatively indifferent Catholics, the whole embedded in a culture which was by now profoundly hostile to them. It may be suggested that it was the restricted number of those engaged which gave an added point to the acerbity of the contest between the Bakerists and their opponents within the English Benedictine family. Throughout these years those Catholics who were deeply concerned about the implications of religious problems operated on a very small stage.

Their life was marked by an element of privacy rather than of concealment.[2] The adventurous quality which had charac-terised the period of the landing of the priests brought in from the colleges abroad during the Elizabethan persecution had given place to a caution which would soon become tradi-tional.[3] The custom by which priests used an alias survived, but the carefully constructed hiding-places were not required. It is probable that none had been devised since the last days of the old Queen's reign.

The question arises as to whether the Catholics of this time showed a hopeful spirit. Outside the convert-makers of the Court circle, this does not appear to have been the case. The young men would ride with the King and die for him, but it does not seem that in their hearts they were over-sanguine. They knew the strength of the forces that were opposed to them.

---

[1] For the life of Dame Gertrude and her childhood with her father Cresacre More at Gobions in Hertfordshire, cf. material quoted in the *Life*, by the Rev. Henry Collins. For her relations with Fr Augustine Baker, c.f. *Spiritual Exercises* of D. Gertrude More.

[2] Cf. a torn frament of the will of John Arismendy of the City of London, gent., dated 30 July 1634: "Tenne poundes to Mr Drury . . . Mr Lane of Riverparke for the maintenance of a good ma . . . to [admi]nister the sacraments to the poore Catholikes of Midhurst [wi]th obligation to say two masses every weeke for my soule [and] my lords [Montagu's] ancestors". Other manuscripts preserved at Midhurst (Historical Manuscripts Commission, Appendix to Third Report, p. 277).

[3] The Catholics had their own private language, their Lenten practices "The Earl", wrote John Arismendy to John Talbot of Cowdray in an undated letter, "goeth[soli] after the holy time to Wardour" (*ibid.*, p. 277). This seems to have referred to a journey undertaken by the Earl of Worcester when his religious exercises were completed.

With the Puritans as their bitter enemies, the Catholics gave to their sovereign a loyalty that was both necessary and based on doctrine. Still, they were never unaware of the coldness with which Charles I regarded the ancient faith.[1] The rigour of the law fell unevenly upon them, but with each decade the temper of their opponents was consistently hardening. At the moment, the Catholic peers had still their seats and votes in the Upper House. In Government circles the Catholics exercised a certain influence, but it was already clear that they would be totally excluded from the new political system which was emerging.

A letter from Wentworth, then Lord-President of the Council of the North, to the Attorney-General very well indicates their state and the opinion held about them at this period. In this communication[2] he complained that Mr Gascoigne of Barnbow (a man of £1,000 a year), Philip Anne (a gentleman of £800 a year) and Mr Cholmeley (a man of £800 a year) compounded for £60, £20 and £25 a year respectively: although Mr Gascoigne had formerly paid £100, Mr Anne's father £80 and Mr Cholmeley's brother £120. Here there is seen that social respect which bound the gentry to one another and enabled the Catholics to fight on equal terms with the Anglicans on the King's side in the Civil Wars. The very equality granted to name and blood was a constant temptation to secede. The heirs of Recusants who inherited estates in their minority could seldom be educated in their father's Faith. Altogether, the combined effects of the courtesy and the financial exploitation and the perpetual disquieting interest would have served to render many men uneasy. The Catholic gentry seem, however, to have been immune from such impressions. As a body they were protected by a certain determined self-possession, and by a curious, faithful realism which was not at the mercy of imagination.

Beneath their stubbornness there often lay a hardly conscious

---

[1] In some cases their offers of service were accepted grudgingly. The Royalist general, Lord Newcastle, gave as grounds for his undertaking, "the preservation of His Majesty's Person . . . and the defence of the Orthodox Church of England; where he also satisfied those that murmur'd for my Lords receiving into his Army such as were of the Catholic Religion" (*The Life of William Cavendish, Duke of Newcastle*, by Margaret, Duchess of Newcastle, ed. M. A. Lower, p. 23).

[2] Letter to Attorney-General Heath, dated 12 August 1629 (Cal. State Papers, Dom. Charles I, 1629-31, p. 35).

and deep contempt for the manipulations of a Civil Service. Their dogged imprudence was to be displayed at Marston Moor and Naseby. It was only those families whose members lived within the orbit of the Court or of the circle of the Lord-President of the North which came in time to be affected by the persistence of the hostile official world. It was likewise in this *milieu* that a loose adherence to Catholicism was most common. Certain of the more prominent laymen were entangled in moral difficulties, as in the case of Lady Banbury's lover, the fourth Lord Vaux of Harrowden. There was in other instances a tendency to a breaking extravagance. "I heard", wrote George Garrard sitting up by candlelight at Petworth at eleven at night, "my Lord Dunluce lost at the Wells at Tunbridge almost £2,000 at ninepins, most of it to Sir John Sutlin [Suckling]".[1]

But there was nothing to link Suckling's world with that of the northern Catholic gentry, whose lives had gone forward steadily since Elizabethan times. Two instances, contemporary in date, will give an impression of this divergence. The portrait of Sir John Suckling, now in the Frick Museum, has a stylised fantasy; the long, untrimmed hair and the fair beard, and the red-fringed cloak and the great negligent folio, and in the background the leaves and rocks and brambles. As a commentary on all such toys, there is an entry in Lord William Howard's household books at Naworth.[2] It is a charge for three carts to go to Carlisle to carry beer and bedding for the Assizes.

It is to this way of life across which the farm carts jolted heavily, as they had done for centuries, that there belonged the solid phalanx of the Catholic families in Northumberland and in the Bishopric—the Erringtons and Haggerstons and Widdringtons, the Grays of Spindleston, the Hodgsons of Hebborn with their coal-mines, the Smythes of Eshe, the Claverings, Fenwicks, Radcliffes, Swinburnes, Conyers, Tempests, Charltons, Jenisons and Leadbetters, the squires of a whole country-side.[3]

---

[1] Letter from George Garrard to Lord Conway, dated at Petworth, 18 September 1635 (State Papers, Dom. Charles I, ccxcviii, 10).

[2] *Household Books of Naworth Castle*, Surtees Society, p. 197.

[3] Abstract of a book of compositions for the lands, goods and arrearages of Recusants (Ushaw MSS.). With the exception of Sir John Clavering of Callaly, who was "no Recusant convict", the heads of all these other families paid their fines for Recusancy between the years 1629 and 1632.

Supporting the greater gentry there stood a numerous farming stock whose richer members were of yeoman standing. It was to this grouping of the yeoman farmers that the Lead-betters of Hexham belonged, a family from whom the eighteenth-century vicars apostolic of the northern district, Matthew and William Gibson, were descended. The Catholic populations in Northumberland and Durham, and throughout the greater part of Yorkshire, were singularly homogeneous, while they were also closely bound to the strong and separate tradition of Lancashire Catholicism.

There was about the Recusant families of this character a certain clear-sighted caution, and they were without a policy save for a resolution to support their sovereign. While the younger men among their leaders had a feeling for *pancche*, in the case of the countrymen of the Old Religion it took disaster to reveal their quality and their fathomless and stolid loyalty. It was by no accident that the Catholics were to find themselves so closely associated with the Royal Oak.

Still, in any case, the geographical area involved in these disturbances was circumscribed. The vicar apostolic does not seem to have gone farther north than Turvey, where he stayed with Lady Mordaunt. Sussex and Bedfordshire set the limits of the range of his coach journeys. It may be suggested that the whole matter under discussion, the activities of the chaplains and their protectors, the deposition of Bishop Smith and the inquiries of Panzani, was the concern only of a small segment of the Catholic community—the privileged grouping centred on London.

Information about the North is very scanty. The structure of Catholic life in Lancashire and the north-eastern counties would certainly repay a careful study.[1] The economic factor, for instance, has not been examined. It would be interesting to know how exactly the secular priests in the North Country maintained themselves through these years. We cannot as yet

[1] On 21 December 1641 the Governors of Blackburn Grammar School ordered that Richard Bradley, usher, "by reason of his Recusancie, shall be displaced from continuinge usher any longer in the said schole" (*Records of Blackburn School*, Chetham Society (1909-), ed. George Alfred Stocks, vol. ii, p. 207). It would be of interest to investigate how many other Catholics were placed in such schools, which served an area with a large Catholic population. The school accounts indicate that Bradley had held this post continuously for several years (*op. cit.*, vol. ii, pp. 186, 189, 195, 198 and 201).

form a picture of their circuits and Mass centres, or of the frequency of their visits to their outlying parishioners. It is the old-established farming and yeoman stock whose way of life is hidden from us.

Among printed sources relating to the northern Recusants, the volumes relating to William Blundell of Crosby have the most value. They deal, however, with that circle of the squire-archy which had affinities with London. It would be of more value if we could grasp the situation in the Fylde, where the dominant-family type of structure did not apply.[1] Keeping to the counties north of the Trent, very little light has hitherto been thrown on the matter of education. We do not know clearly where or how the children of the lesser gentry and sub-stantial yeomen found their schooling, except for those who went abroad to study for the priesthood. It is true that boys from the Home Counties were already being sent to St Omer, but this practice seems to have been confined to a great extent to those families who maintained permanently or offered occasional hospitality to Jesuit chaplains. The custom was slowly beginning to spread among the northern squirearchy.

This period is difficult to chart because in the years before the Civil War the Northern Catholics were less harried than in the old Queen's reign. Thus documents relating to actual or proposed prosecutions of Recusants are comparatively sparse. Among the wealthy Catholics, who had close links with the administration, the practice of sending sons to the University without taking a degree was well-established. Such youths would have been prepared by private study. One may speculate as to whether Catholics attended the Yorkshire and Northumbrian grammar schools.

[1] In the southern counties the Catholic squire would sometimes influence the Anglican incumbent. A note in the parish register of Pyrton runs as follows: "Whereas upon the entreatie of Mr Sheaphard Mr William Stonor's Curat, I did sett down the names of the said Mr Stonor his children in the Church book, and the time when they were christened, these are to give you notice that shall succeed me . . . that none of them were christened in the parish church of Pirton, neither do I know the time, place, nor person, where or by whom they were baptized". This is signed J. Barnard, Vicar of Pirton, and nine names are given christened at dates between 11 November 1622 and 17 March 1633, printed in *V.C.H.*, Oxford-shire, vol. ii, p. 46. It seems clear that they were baptised by a Catholic priest, and thus entered for legal security in questions of inheritance. An apparently similar case is the entry of the name of Edmund Plowden in the parish register of Aston-le-Walls in 1618—"because he is heir to the lordship of Aston-le-Walls" (*Records of the Plowden Family*, by Barbara Mary Plowden, p. 56).

CHAPTER X

THE ATTITUDE TO PROPERTY

A RELATIVELY circumscribed section of the nation was directly affected by the Puritan strain in English life, which has just been discussed. At the same time a general Protestant sympathy was much more widespread, while any circle influenced by the Court and Government was touched by that careful worldliness which tended to mark each expression of Caroline values. In the wills made by rich men, there was sometimes recognition of their parish duties[1] and much more often legacies to the poor of their birthplace,[2] but the emphasis was laid upon inheritance and property.

A clear distinction was made between lands which were inherited and those acquired by purchase. The fact that station should be so emphasised was, in fact, characteristic of a period of social change.[3] The new rich families stressed the fact that they were now armigerous. Relationships of one kind and another were readily acknowledged.[4] The sense of kinship between groups of families which came to mark the Georgian

---

[1] Cf. the will of Sir Hugh Middleton, Bart., Citizen and Goldsmith of London, dated 21 November 1631 and proved 21 December 1631: "To be buried in the church of St Mathewe in London where I was some time a parishioner" (printed in *Miscellanea Genealogica et Heraldica*, third series, vol. ii, p. 53).

[2] This practice was very common, and often gives information as to the birthplace of rich citizens. Thus Sir Hugh Middleton left "To the poor of Henllan where I was born £20"; while his younger son, Symon Middleton, made a similar bequest "To the poor of St Alban's, Wood Street where I was born £10" (*ibid.*, vol. ii, p. 53).

[3] These aspects of the rich merchant class in the reign of Charles I are illustrated by the will of Sir Thomas Middleton, Knt., Alderman of London, dated 20 November 1630 and proved 15 August 1631: "To be buried in the chapel of Chirk Castle or in the chapel at Stansted Montfichet, both being my late inheritance. . . . My late master, Mr Ferdinando Poyntz, Mrs Mary Ferrar, widow of Mr Nicholas Ferrar, my late partner" (*ibid.*, vol. ii, p. 49).

[4] The classic instance is, perhaps, the will of Roger Palmer, Earl of Castlemaine, who was born in 1634, and thus brought up during these years. "And my desire is as to the place of my buryall that if I dye in Wales I may be buried in the parish Church of Pole near my uncle Powis and others of my mother's family, if in England then I desire to be buryed in our own vault at Dorney, but if at my death I should be near to Wingham in Kent it is my desire to be buried there amongst my ancestors" (*ibid.*, first series, vol. i, p. 154).

polity was already emerging in the first Stuart generations. There was a conscious recognition of the bond created by the fact of the possession of landed interest. There had come into social relationships a quality of fluidity which was accompanied by a new freedom of movement. In some ways it is rather strange to find such a widespread stability on the eve of the outbreak of the Civil Wars. One of the first examples of the new attitude towards landed property is seen in the case of Lord Cottington, then Chancellor of the Exchequer. In 1637 he acquired the house and estate of Fonthill[1] for the sake of the amenities that they provided. Only the opportunities for the formalised sport of that period, a preference for Wiltshire and a desire not to be too far from the capital appear to have weighed with the purchaser.[2]

In contrast to this new practice, the Elizabethan courtier with prospects would seek out an heiress and make his country home on his wife's acres. There was now a certain tendency to return to earlier roots natural in a period of peace. Thus Sir Dudley Carleton repurchased his grandfather's small property in Oxfordshire. There were as yet few instances of the opposite practice—the purchase of a large estate as an investment without intention to reside. Amongst the richest families a large and celebrated house was sometimes bought for residential purposes with little or no consideration for the estate surrounding it. Thus the Duke of Buckingham had bought Newhall with the intention of rebuilding on a palatial scale. The second Earl of Antrim had bought Bramshill in 1637 in order to live in it unchanged. In the latter case the price paid for the house and property was £14,000, and the annual rental from the land was calculated at £400. The greater squires had, by this time, inherited the large houses which their fathers and grand-fathers had built in the reign of Queen Elizabeth.[3] To the sense

[1] Letter from George Garrard to Lord-Deputy Wentworth, dated 9 October 1637 and printed in *Strafford Letters*, ed. W. Knowler, vol. ii, p. 118. For a further consideration of this example, cf. *The Social Structure in Caroline England*, p. 9.

[2] As an example of entirely peaceful transfer, this example is, however, imperfect, since Fonthill had come into the market as a result of the execution of the second Earl of Castlehaven.

[3] In many cases the last touches had been put to the house in the previous generation. Thus the plaster work on the ceilings at Mapledurham was dated 1612, while the ornamental plaster ceiling on the first floor at Linstead Lodge was dated 1599 (*Archæologia Cantiana*, vol. xliv, p. 147). These were both large Elizabethan mansions, built respectively by Sir Richard Blount and Sir John Roper.

of possession there was added a new privacy. The wall spaces were ready for the Vandyck canvases. In some Recusant families religious emblems appear in contemporary portraiture.[1]

The rich landowners of the Old Religion could exercise their private choice in their own manors.[2]

The position of the widow was becoming stronger, as were her rights and claims on the estate.[3] The status of a dowager was slowly forming. The practice of the immediate remarriage of widows, which had been so prevalent in the landowning families of Tudor times, was now very gradually breaking down. There were cases where women kept considerable sums in their own houses.[4] They were sometimes the sole guardians, but more often the joint guardians of their children.[5] Yet it is important not to overstress these changes, for the old practices of the Court of Wards were still in force. There was much activity employed in the search for a grant of lucrative wardships, which had been a primary objective of King James' courtiers. The element of choice was now more clearly visible, choice of guardians and a wider range of selection in regard to

[1] These were for the most part associated with portraits of members of the family who had entered religion in France or the Low Countries. They are met with more frequently in the reign of Charles II, cf. the Wardour Castle collection. A picture at Mapledurham, with the emblems of the cross and thorns, appears to belong to the period of the Civil Wars.

[2] The extreme example of this private judgment against the tenor of the Statutes is the epitaph composed for the second Lord Teynham, and placed by his widow on the monument made for him by Epipanius Evesham. It is in Lynsted parish church. *D.O.M. Domino Christophoro Rooper, Baroni, filio Johanni Domini Teynham, Viro an infantia vitæ innocentiæ integerrimo. In fide ac religione Catholica constantissimo . . . piissime obiit Anno Domini MDCXXII Aetatis suæ lx. Die xvi Aprilis, Catharina uxor posuit* (printed in full in *Archæologia Cantiana*, vol. xliv, p. 156).

[3] Cf. details from the will of Sir Edmund Verney, dated 20 March 1639, his "fuell of wood, furze and cole at Claydon, the coach and four of the coach horses with their harness and furniture" (*Verney Memoirs*, 1907 ed., vol. i, p. 79).

[4] Thus after the death of Lady Verney, whose will was dated 2 May 1639, the following sums were discovered—"in a red velvet purse £5 : c : 9; in an old glove £1 : 15; in ye Black & White pocket £0 : 9 : 6; in ye Spanish pocket £7 : 3; in a white dish £1 : 1 : 4." This was in addition to £144 : 13 : 5 which was distributed between the Red Box, the Tufftaffaty purse and the blue paper (*Ibid.*, vol i, p. 224).

[5] The question of the religious upbringing of the Butler and Cary children turned upon the rights of guardianship possessed by their widowed and Catholic mothers, Viscountess Thurles and Viscountess Falkland. In 1628 an application made by Mary Lady Teynham, together with her father, Lord Petre, and Henry Earl of Worcester, for the joint guardianship of Christopher, fourth Lord Teynham, was refused on the ground that the applicants were Recusants (cf. *Archæologia Cantiana*, vol. liv, p. 156).

marriage. The idea of remote connections who might prove politically or financially useful now appears in English life.[1]

An outlook characteristic of later centuries can be traced in Lord Falkland's determination to move to Great Tew, and break away from those associations with Burford which his grandfather, Sir Laurence Tanfield, had built up so carefully. The Burford Priory estate was sold in 1636 to William Lenthall for £7,000, and it seems likely that already the great tomb set up for Sir Laurence and Lady Tanfield in 1618 appeared old-fashioned. The sentiment of the period had already moved away from the solemnity of the inscription incised into the black marble band on the canopy above the recumbent effigies in Burford Church—"Such honour have all his saints and plenteousness in all their pallaces".

The practice of a body of servants accompanying their master up from the country to his London house was dying out, but is still reflected in the will of the tenth Lord Stourton.[2] The cadets, especially when unmarried, would sometimes reside in the family mansion when in London, but this custom was now becoming rare.[3] On the other hand, an elderly gentleman might establish himself in lodgings. An examination of the section of the accounts of the ninth and tenth Earls of Northumberland relating to the affairs of William Percy gives an interesting view of the position of a younger son who does not seem to have been capable of the management of property.[4] From 1610 until his death in 1648 at the age of seventy-five,

[1] An example of this tendency is seen in Lady Fanshawe's comment on her family—"My father was born in Bemond, in Lancashire, the twelfth son of his father, whose mother was the daughter of Mr Heysham, cousin-german to the old Countess of Rivers" (*Memoirs of Ann Lady Fanshawe*, ed. H. C. Fanshawe, p. 21).

[2] By his will, dated 4 July 1632, Edward, tenth Lord Stourton, bequeathed one year's wages to "everie one of my servants, who does usually waite or attende upon my person at London or in the countrie". A codicil to this will runs as follows: "Alsoe I doe give unto my said sonne Sir William all my Parliament Robes and best velvett gowne with gold lace and my best black velvett cloak". This is a late example of the bequest of personal clothing to an heir. (Somerset House Wills, Russell 57, printed in *History of the House of Stourton*, by Charles Lord Mowbray, Segrave and Stourton, vol. i, pp. 59, 461.)

[3] Thomas Stourton, younger son of the tenth Lord, resided with his father and brother, first in Clerkenwell and later in Duke Street, Covent Garden. His property, which was sequestrated on account of his Recusancy in 1645, included at that date a tenement in Candle Marsh, Dorset, and houses in Warwick Lane and Paternoster Row (*ibid.*, vol. i, p. 455).

[4] Cf. "The financial affairs of a Jacobean gentleman", by Madeline Hope Dodge (*Archæologia Æliana* (1944), vol. xxxi, pp. 97-106).

William Percy boarded with Mr Nicholls in Pennyfarthing Street, St Ebbe's, Oxford. His income, which was paid to him through Mr Cartwright, who resided at the *Frying Pan* in Fleet Street and was solicitor to his brother the ninth Earl of Northumberland, amounted to £145 a year, and was made up of a rent of £65 from a manor left to him by his father, a sum of £50 being his share of rents from the Marches and an allowance of £30 from the head of his family.

The practice of making allowances not only to cadets but also to the direct heir was well established, so that work was constantly increasing in the estate offices. Thus Lord Herbert of Cherbury's heir, Richard Herbert, was allocated an income of £600 charged on the lands of the Herberts of St Julians.[1] It seems that Lord Herbert agreed to this arrangement in order to effect the marriage of his son with Lord Bridgewater's daughter. In the alliances now planned rather more weight was given to indirect political influence than had been the case in Tudor times. Marriages between landed and city stocks were placed upon a solid footing. The many different ways in which a mercantile association was of value to a country gentleman were already manifest. A letter among the Gawdy Papers addressed to Framlingham Gawdy by Mary, wife of Anthony Mingay, sets the note of that period. "I met", she wrote from Speldhurst on 1 August 1635, "a young widow in the street, Alderman Pears's widow. She hath a great voice; I heard her talk as she went. She is worth £11,000 and she hath four daughters and they have £5,000 a piece. She is child-bearing and tall and straight. She lives hard by the Old Exchange, near our lodging. Think of this."[2] The figures were doubtless exaggerated; the interesting point is the exact appraisal.

This same appraisal operated when the leaders of the new investing class examined the estates of those whom they were prepared to help in their embarrassments. A good example of this type of enterprise is seen in the disbursements made by

---

[1] The papers of the first Earl of Bridgewater, now in the Huntington Library, have provided material for a study of these negotiations. Lord Herbert undertook to make good any deficiency if the yield from the St Julians estates should fall below £600. Cf. *Huntington Library Quarterly*, vol. iv, "Lord Herbert of Cherbury and his son", pp. 317-32.

[2] Cal. Gawdy MSS., p. 154. As some indication of the relationship Anthony Mingay wrote to Framlingham Gawdy on 18 March 1636: "My wife hath lost £7 or £8 at gleeke lately, and it must be paid" (*ibid.*, p. 158).

Humphrey Chetham to landowners of standing who lived within reach of Manchester. The details are preserved in the manuscript collections left by this rich family of clothiers and linen-drapers, which had held an established position since the first years of the reign of Elizabeth. The earlier sums lent by Chetham were quite small.[1] In 1633 £100 was advanced to Sir William Brereton, who twelve years later paid £80 for the use of these moneys. In 1635 £300 was provided for Sir George Booth of Dunham at seven per cent. Two years later John Greenhalgh of Brandlesome paid £50 as interest on a loan. As the times became more troubled, the sums required grew larger. In 1641 £2,000 was borrowed by Sir Edward Mosley. A note under 1647 indicates that in that year Humphrey Chetham lent £2,500 to Robert Tatton of Wythenshawe on the security of his estates.

There is some reason to suppose that these transactions were not resented. Chetham had served as High Sheriff of Lancashire in 1625, and had perhaps gained status in 1621 when, together with his brother George, he purchased Clayton Hall from the Byrons for £4,700. An element of foreclosure had entered into Chetham's purchase of Turton Towers and a portion of the Ordsall estate. In this connection a judgment passed by historians of the cotton trade is valuable. "Often the [financial] transactions ran over many years and led in the end to forced sales. In his way Chetham and the moneylending nephew who succeeded him were the predecessors of the country banker."[2]

This reference to country bankers draws attention to the fact that in general the industrialists in the North of England did not establish themselves among the landed families. On the contrary, the more prosperous among them were usually attracted towards London. Thus the Chethams never attained the position among the Lancashire squires which their initial prosperity would have seemed to indicate. Throughout the North of England the townsmen and rich farmers had a marked independence in their attitude towards the armigerous landowning class. In Lancashire especially that mundane reverence for the squirearchy did not develop, and the distinction between town and country was lessened by the presence of

---

[1] *Life of Humphrey Chetham*, Chetham Society (1903), by F. R. Raines and C. W. Sutton, pp. 112-21. Details of the transactions are contained in Chetham MSS., vol. i, pp. 13, 15 and 37 and vol. v, p. 143.

[2] *The Cotton Trade and Industrial Lancashire, 1600-1780*, by Alfred P. Wadsworth and Julia de Lacy Mann, p. 34.

village industry. The Chethams had their own links with what can be called the rural population. Fustian makers in the Oldham district and weavers in other parts of Lancashire were supplied with raw cotton and linen yarn.[1] Here the same authors have a comment on the way in which this system was operated by the group under consideration. "In this way they were financed by Chetham to the extent of their raw materials, and were in that degree economically dependent on him."[2] It may well be that the maturity of such an economic relationship had its place among the factors which dissuaded the Chetham family from abandoning the world of trade.[3]

The rapid growth of industry in the North of England is reflected in the relatively elaborate transport system which was built up at this time. Special arrangements were made for the carriage of cloth, and there were efforts to improve the long-established river transport.[4] In the reign of Charles I the Severn was navigable as far as Shrewsbury. There was a small toll at Gloucester, but no charges were made for the use of towing paths. In 1636 William Sandys began to carry out the works on the Avon for which he had contracted, and by 1641 this river was navigable to within four miles of Warwick.[5]

The question of transport affected both the fine West

---

[1] It is explained that fustians were concentrated in the Oldham area, and that the linen industry predominated in the rest of Lancashire except in the parishes of "Lonsdale north of the Sands", which fell within the sphere of the woollen cloth-making in Westmorland (Wadsworth and Mann, *op. cit.*, p. 25).

[2] *Ibid.*, p. 33.

[3] The following details will serve to indicate the development of the interests of one rich commercial family. Humphrey Chetham and his brother James were both apprenticed to Samuel Tipping, a linen-draper whose father had come to Manchester from Preston. George Chetham, the third brother, was apprenticed to George Tipping, and by 1610 had bought a partnership in his business for £320 and settled in London. Henry, son of James Chetham, was apprenticed at the age of sixteen in 1611 for nine years to a citizen and haberdasher, paying £20. After the Restoration two grandsons of George Chetham were apprenticed to a London merchant, paying premiums of £300 each. They subsequently became merchants at Safi in Morocco and at Leghorn. The direct import of cotton was at that time controlled by the Levant Company. These details, scattered through the Chetham Society's publications, are assembled in Wadsworth and Mann, *op. cit.*, p. 33.

[4] In 1629 a contract was signed for the transport of cloth at fifteen shillings a pack from Brindle, Preston or Warrington to London or Cambridge. Each horse-pack weighed sixteen stone (*ibid.*, p. 46).

[5] Cf. *Economic History Review*, vol. viii, pp. 68-79. The Warwickshire Avon "never bore a boat of any burden before industrious Mr Sandys" (*Habington's Worcestershire*, ed. T. Amphlett, Worcester Historical Society, vol. ii, p. 468).

Country cloth, so much of which was used for home consumption, and the coarser northern material. In this connection Professor Lipson draws attention to the development of the export trade from the West Riding to the Baltic, which resulted from the needs of the sovereigns of Poland and Russia, who used coarse cloth for uniforms for their large armies. The statement that the North Country clothiers and linen-drapers seldom graduated into the ranks of the squirearchy also holds good to some extent in the parallel case of the Wiltshire clothiers.[1] In both regions the fortune was used in certain instances to endow an educational work or other charity. Thus Peter Blundell of Tiverton left the bulk of his property, estimated at £40,000, to found the school that bears his name.

In these years the shadow of trade depression hung over the West Country broadcloth industry. The situation was dominated by the operation of the Royal Commission on Clothing. Wage rates were proclaimed each year, and the Privy Council was prepared to intervene if the wages actually paid were insufficient.[2] A glimpse can be obtained of the difficulties of the small clothier. An inventory of the estate of John Francklin of Calne shows that at his death in 1631 his property included wool worth £150 and unsold cloth valued at £115.[3] The epitaph on the tomb of Thomas Hulbert of Corsham and placed in that parish church would have read strangely during these lean years:

"A master milde
Who never did the needy poor contemne
And God enrich'd him by the hands of them."

It is always necessary to stress the profoundly agricultural character of Caroline England. The impression given by the Gloucestershire occupational census, analysed by A. J. and

[1] In a letter written by Christopher Potticary to Edward Nicholas on 11 February 1631, it is claimed that in his trade as a clothier he has kept the most part of a thousand people at work (State Papers, Dom. Charles I, clxxxiv, 65). In spite of the large scale of his operations, it is most difficult to find further traces of this Wiltshire clothier.

[2] A study of this subject is contained in *The Wiltshire Woollen Industry*, by G. D. Ramsay, pp. 85-100.

[3] Salisbury Diocesan Registry, Inventory of Wills printed *ibid.*, p. 82.

R. H. Tawney,[1] certainly appears valid for this decade. "The picture", they write, "which emerges from these figures is confirmed by a good deal of other evidence. It is one of a system of family farms worked with the aid of relatives—more than half the sons and brothers in the returns are those of yeomen and husbandmen—and only to a small extent with hired labour. . . . The condition of large parts of seventeenth-century England was, in fact, still semi-colonial. The result was that it was easy for a small man to get a holding; that wage-labour, being scarce, was in a strong position; and that, since the largest group in rural society consisted not of wage-workers but of peasant farmers, the critical issues of the age were those not of wages but of land-tenure and credit."[2] This was the solid base upon which the wide group of the country gentry, and the much smaller body of landowners in contact with the Court, were in turn superimposed.

The remoteness of what may be termed the Court culture from the daily round of farmers and husbandmen was a feature common to all Western Europe. It was in no way peculiar to England, and it is indeed likely that the yeomen farmers in Gloucestershire or East Anglia had more in common with the great landowners of both the Royalist and the Parliamentarian traditions than had the peasantry in Champagne or Westphalia with their own leaders. There was much that unlettered men would take for granted, nor would they waste their thought on all those subsidiary occupations which were the fruit of mere book learning. For Englishmen a certain type of insular patriotism, and above all a love of sport, formed, as it had done for centuries, a common bond. Thus all countrymen would understand Lord Cottington's appreciation of his new estate at Fonthill—"the finest hawking-place in England and a wonderful store of partridge".

A line of division can be traced, but this comes not so much between town and country as between the agriculturists and those who gave themselves to the work of the counting-house or nascent industry. In "The Character of a Friend", William Habington puts this point clearly.[3] "He is not accustomed to any sordid way of gaine, for who is in any way mechanicke,

---

[1] "An occupational census of the seventeenth century," by A. J. and R. H. Tawney, *Economic History Review* (1934), vol. v, pp. 25-63.

[2] *Ibid.*, p. 53.   [3] *The Poems of William Habington*, ed. Kenneth Allott, p. 99.

will sell his friend upon more profitable terms." The note of contempt is also present in the same poet's verses "In Praise of the City Life":[1]

> "When the City Dame is gone
> T'her house at Brandford; for beyond that she
> Imagines there's no land, but Barbary,
> Where lies her husband's factor."

As set out, this is an expression of a point of view which is essentially Royalist.

The contrast with the mercantile world is further made explicit by Habington's insistence on a chain of pedigree and, indeed, on a multitude of high descents. This is displayed in an apostrophe to Castara, which is contained in a poem addressed to her mother, Lady Powis; it should be explained that Castara was the name assigned by Habington to his wife, Lucy Herbert:[2]

> "For when I wondring stand
> At th'intermingled beauty of her hand,
> (Higher I dare not gaze) to this bright veine
> I not ascribe the blood of Charlemaine
> Deriv'd by you to her. Or say there are
> In that and th'other Marmion, Rosse, and Parr
> Fitzhugh, Saint Quintin, and the rest of them
> That add such lustre to great Pembrokes stem."

This is a mood immediately reflected in the genealogical and heraldic work in Lydiard Tregoze church. There, in the stained-glass window erected in 1630, stands the olive tree hung with the escutcheons of the families which Sir John St John represented—Ewyas, Tregoz, Grandison, Pateshull and Beauchamp. Within the chancel and side chapels are placed the most elaborate series of monuments constructed in this period.[3] The tomb of Sir John St John, with its fine effigies, is notable for the portraits of the children, each small son carrying a prayer-book with marble ribbons. Sir Giles Mompesson kneels so that a similar effigy may be raised to his St John wife. The final triumph is the gilded statue of Sir John's youngest son.

---

[1] *Ibid.*, p. 77.

[2] The poem ' To the Right Honourable, the Lady, E. P.", is printed *ibid.*, pp. 41-2. Lady Powis was a daughter of the eighth Earl of Northumberland.

[3] The greater part of the work was carried out between 1630 and 1634, in which year Sir John St John describes himself as being "49 and mindful of mortality".

There is here a reminiscence of both Oxford and London.[1] The note is that of privacy. It was one man's work and no part of a grand design. The old rambling house at Lydiard was not improved, and it seems that the owner hardly lived there during the period of his constructions.[2] The St John monuments should be considered as the affirmation of a personal standpoint in regard to authority in Church and State, and ancient blood. They were the conceptions of an old rooted squire and had nothing in common with the rising aristocracy with its Venetian tendencies. Under one aspect they can be seen as the extension of a mode current in London and reflected in certain chapels in the universities. Deep as they lie in the Wiltshire country-side, the urban element is unescapable. They are one individual's reading of the Court's idea of almost regal privacy.

At this point some general comments may be attempted. The domestic and patrician character of the way of life of the English ruling class was now setting in a mould which would remain unbroken for at least two centuries. The notion of the picture gallery was emerging, not so much the collection of some magnifico like Lord Arundel, but rather the gathering together of portraits of kinsmen and friends done by painters of reputation. In 1637 Vandyck's portrait of Strafford in armour was already displayed in Lord Northumberland's gallery at Sion House.[3] The way was clear for Lely and Kneller, and then for Gainsborough and Reynolds. There was now present both the creation of a demand and the acceptance of the convention of one fashionable type.

Another characteristic of these quiet rich years of Charles I was the development of the hanger-on. One now meets for the first time the quasi-secretarial dependant (sometimes in Orders, sometimes not) who is the intimate of the women of the great households. He arranges the renting of London houses; con-

[1] In 1633 the chapel and chancel were thrown together by replacing the arcade by three columns carrying an entablature. The glass in the chancel resembles that in the chapel at Lincoln College, Oxford.

[2] In 1630 Sir John St John of Lydiard Tregoze, a Baronet of Nova Scotia, inherited the manors of Battersea and Wandsworth from his uncle, Lord Grandison. It seems that until the close of the seventeenth century the family lived mostly in the manor-house at Battersea, using Lydiard Park as a source of game and garden produce. This is an early instance of the relegation of a country-house whose owner has acquired a property in the immediate neighbourhood of London.

[3] Letter from George Garrard to Lord-Deputy Wentworth, dated 9 October 1637 (*Strafford Letters*, ed. W. Knowler, vol. ii, p. 118).

ducts the lesser interviews for his lord; retails the gossip. Leaving town in the dog-days, the supporter of the family would settle through the summer in the country, sitting beside the screen in the withdrawing-room and humouring his mistress with playfulness and flattery.

In Church as in State the element of patronage was ever increasing. The presentation to a living by the local patron was becoming, as it would remain, an element in the rural scene. The interest in church ornament and in the furniture of privilege was now apparent. Lord Dorchester, when Secretary of State, wrote to the Bishop of Oxford about the construction of a pew for his wife in Brightwell church.

"There was," he explained, "anciently one for the Mistress of Brightwell in the chapel where my father's and grandfather's tombs lie, but that is in decay and too much out of hearing. The place where a woman's pew already stands is the fittest for a divided pew, one for my wife and the other for her women, and it would be more convenient if the pulpit were removed to the other side."[1] The letter is worth pondering, so common sense and Erastian.

There was now no lack of candidates for the country benefice. The clients, lay and clerical, had come to press about the patron. The great clerical world of the Church of England was folding into its strata. The vocation was compelling and secure. Young clergymen poured out in these peaceful years from both the universities. The machinery of preferment was in process of construction. That corporate grouping of the cathedral close, which would ripen into the world of Barchester, could now be discerned. Such a group was already formed in the peaceful see cities of the south of England—at Wells and Salisbury and Winchester. It is true that it is in the reign of Charles II that the loyal Church of England received her golden shower. Yet, in the earlier portion of the century, she had entered into her high place and to her grave devotion.

George Herbert's approach, with its evangelical and sunlit peace, marks a point upon the Salisbury compass. "Wherefore", he wrote, "he [the Parson] hath one Comment at least upon every book of Scripture, and ploughing with this, and his own meditations, he enters into the secrets of God treasured in the

---

[1] Letter from Secretary Dorchester to Bishop Corbet, dated from the Court at Farnham, 9 August 1630 (State Papers, Dom. Charles I, clxxii, 40).

holy Scripture."[1] In the midst of his complex inheritance, there is found in Herbert a note which resumes all the spirit of the Evangelicals:

"But thou shalt answer, Lord, for me."[2]

This would meet with response as long as men turned for sustenance to the Bible, and rode or trudged each Sunday to the country churches across the breadth of the Anglican counties.

From the period of the Stuart reigns there also date certain changes in the general lines of the population. On the one hand, the more prosperous inn landlord emerges as the representative of a true *middle* class in the country towns. This calling tended to become hereditary, and soon the innkeeper was without roots in the ordinary rural unit of landowner and tenants. On the other hand, it becomes from this time possible to trace the outline of that great parasite trade of every oligarchy—the household servants of the rich. The oligarchic structure gave to them freedom of movement within its limits and their own place.

The organisation of travel was taking shape, the first signs of those facilities which were to mark the eighteenth century in England and on the Continent. The expression "Ordinary" is now first met with, as in the reference to "an Ordinary of six shillings a meal kept at the bowling place in the Spring garden".[3] The hiring of vehicles was becoming customary. "One thousand nine hundred", we read in a newsletter of 1634, "was the number of Hackney coaches of London, base lean jades, unworthy to be seen in so great a city".[4] Coaches could also be hired for journeys into the country.

At the same time the English hostelry was coming into its own. The trade carried more profit and the innkeeper more independence. The landlord could become a man of substance, and a class of licensee was gradually forming. The constant hospitality, which gentlemen had been accustomed to afford to one another, was fast going out of fashion. The Civil Wars were to give the *coup de grâce* to the miscellaneous entertainment of

---

[1] "The Parson's Life," Chapter IV, *Complete Works of George Herbert*, ed. Canon F. E. Hutchinson, p. 229.

[2] "The Quip," by George Herbert, *ibid.*, p. 111.

[3] Letter from George Garrard to Lord-Deputy Wentworth, dated 3 June 1634 (*Strafford Letters*, vol. i, p. 262).

[4] Letter from the same to the same, dated 20 June 1634 (*ibid.*, vol. i, p. 266).

strangers. Constant travel now meant the use of inns and not of private houses. Edward Nicholas, going down to the West as Secretary of the Admiralty, would always stay at Staines at the *Red Lion*. He would go to the *Maidenhead* at Basingstoke on journey after journey.

One of the consequences of greater independence and privacy in travel was the growth of the public fame of different inns. So many separate parties must converge to make their fortune. Landlords were no longer forced to rely on a narrow and linked circle of patrons, as had generally been the case in Tudor times. Travellers riding with their servants, great family coaches and new private chariots would throng the roads. From these the innkeeper made his profit, and the economic status of the whole body of inn servants became more tolerable. There was opened up a wide new livelihood.

The custom of "tipping" was well developed, and the sums paid were substantial considering the then value of money. The comparison of a series of accounts would seem to show that in regard to such gifts fixed rates were already established. A party journeying to London at the end of December 1638 gave a shilling to the chamberlains at Barnet where they stopped for dinner.[1] The next day at St Albans, where they stayed the night, 2s. were given to the chamberlains and 2s. to the ostlers. The latter seems the regulation gift to ostlers for a night's lodging. Chambermaids appear to have received rather less than the menservants. From other sets of accounts it is made clear that large sums were given to friends' servants.[2] One of Lord Worcester's grooms received a pound for guiding a party of gentlemen with a retinue of twelve attendants to London from South Wales; Sir Kenelm Digby's coachman got 10s.; the gardener at Hampton Court a florin; a sum of 5s. was given to a footman for engaging rooms in St Martin's Lane. Men thus favourably placed could add a calculable sum to their year's wages. This system of high customary remuneration would endure till it became established as the solid rake-off for the staffs controlling the great Victorian country-houses and the shooting and the Scottish moors.

---

[1] This particular detail comes from the Cal. *Hastings MSS.*, vol. i, pp. 384-5.

[2] A very comprehensive account of expenses of this nature is contained in an account of payments made by Mr Burgess, servant to Lord Conway, between 7 July 1634 and 19 March 1635 (State Papers, Dom. Charles I, cclxxv, 19).

It is more difficult to establish a standard for direct payment for occasional work. A chimney-sweeper was paid 2s. 9d. for sweeping 22 "tunnelles" at a house in Middlesex.[1] As a means of comparison, it can be noted that the current price for ale was 2d. the pint.[2]

These are, however, only indications. Yet they suggest that growth of custom, and the increase of an insular and English solidarity. London prices and southern ways were making headway. In another sphere the educational arrangements foreshadowed very dimly the coming dominance of the great schools. Sons were sometimes sent to Winchester, for instance, because their fathers had been at school there.[3] Very gradually the Inns of Court were being superseded by the Universities as a training-ground for the landed gentry. The naval service was still indeterminate in its character and undefined in its length of duty. Yet already the recommendation system had come into force, and the captain took responsibility for the acceptance of each young gentleman. This system of interlocked recommendation was of the very essence of the English polity. The character of entry into the Navy, as an example, was hardly to change until after the Crimean War. The domestic note predominated in a society which was never unaware of its initiative and its strength, and was very confident in its own security.

At the same time there could be traced a new temperate and diplomatic approach to general questions. There was a reaction against the imperious gestures and the flaring overt subtlety of the Elizabethans. The horse-play and the laborious cumbered jesting, which Strafford had brought with him out of Yorkshire, was beginning to look old-fashioned. A widespread courtesy was the new note at St James', and the custom of gentle flattery found favour far beyond the circle of the Court.

A remarkable development in the usages of politics was the birth of understatement. This can be found in the optimism of the official letters of Sir Henry Vane the elder. Even before the Civil Wars there was a recognition among the ruling class that their underlying accord was a possession that they must never

[1] From household expenses of the Countess of Derby from 15 May 1634 till 23 April 1635 (*Hastings MSS.*, vol. i, pp. 375-6).
[2] *Journal of Sir William Brereton*, Surtees Society, p. 3.
[3] State Papers, Dom. Charles I, ccclv, 143.

lose. This was a lesson taught them for all time by that bitter experience. In such circumstances Vane's statements and letters in the eighteen months before the outbreak of hostilities have an especial value on account of the form in which they are expressed. Understatement often has for its object the avoidance of embittered quarrel. It seems in this instance to have come from a recognition of the fundamental unity of the English polity. If we except for certain purposes the Catholic minority among the peers, there was so much that was held in common by all those who sat in either House of Parliament.

The life of the English privileged classes was becoming marked, not only by a certain composite solidarity, but still more by ease. A restricted circle had been influenced in the reign of Elizabeth by Giordano Bruno and by *Gli Eroici*, and the conception of the magnifico had obtained a wider currency. So much was required to maintain the grandiose display, consciously lavish and Italianate in inspiration, which had been the setting within which the whole life of the Earl of Essex was played out. The great house in its Elizabethan guise had embodied the magnificence of a single statesman.

On another plane there was a high-wrought quality about the Philip Sidney standards. These were individualistic and purely personal, the perfection of knighthood and the last flickers of Bayard. Now, after half a century, an entirely different mood, and one incomprehensible to earlier generations, was gradually coming to the fore. The fear of publicity, which was to mark the national character, came slowly creeping on.

The mould into which English life was now setting placed a half-spiritual and half-mundane value upon the state of marriage. Under the Stuarts a welcome had been given to the ministrations of the Church of England. The christening and the Anglican blessing upon men's marriages had come to be established as among the enduring values of the English polity. On the personal side the way was open to George Herbert's quiet religion, and high in the official hierarchy there sat the Bishops in their wide lawn sleeves. There they sat, so grave, and yet assailable.

The Puritan deeps were barely stirred by the thought-forms or the moods of the Stuart reigns. The men of the preciser sort remained aloof within the hard, clear lines of their oft-proclaimed integrity. Yet Puritanism, apart from its avowed adherents, appeared throughout the texture of the thought of the Church of England, as is shown by the documents which bear upon the life of the Ferrar family at Little Gidding. Regarded from a different angle, the Puritan section of the nation was to be found among the main supports of the new idea of more fluid capital. Still, beyond these closely related worlds there were other elements which would shiver the mirror of the seventeenth-century English life if that were possible. Apart from the men who would arise in the changes of the Civil Wars, there were those whose attitude could not be brought within a Cavalier or Parliamentarian synthesis. This can be best expressed by the comment of George Fox, made when he had first "espied the great steeple house in Nottingham". "When I came there", he noted down laboriously, "all the people looked like fallow-ground, and the priest, like a great lump of earth, stood in the pulpit above."[1]

[1] *Journal of George Fox*, ed. Norman Penny, p. 24.

CHAPTER XI

LIFE OF THE TOWNSMEN

IN this chapter certain impressions are gathered together. Possibly the data, when assembled, will serve to convey some idea of various ways of life among the town population under the Stuarts. The subject is difficult and has not yet been explored, nor have its implications been considered. It is very hard to present any valid account of the social scene, owing to the absence of manuscript sources comparable to that great mass of documentation which deals with the life of the privileged classes. Such correspondence as has survived is often remarkably valuable, free and spontaneous. It was the landed gentry and not the town middle class which prized the insipidity of the Stuart newsletter.

When the situation of the artisan class is examined, correspondence naturally fades out altogether, and another type of approach is required. It is only through a consideration of wage levels and trends, that a view of the life of the urban workers can be constructed. It is not surprising that these should have been the "forgotten men" of the nineteenth-century Stuart historians. Accounts and memoranda of expenses preserved in the big collections have their own value. They can contribute to the examination of wages and of casual payments. At the same time, apart from transport and inn charges, they tend to deal in great measure with the receipts of the satellites of the privileged class. It is only in the relatively integrated life of the country-side that detailed accounts of the lord of the manor throw any light on the whole community.

It is necessary to bear these facts in mind when considering the question of the town middle class. In London, in particular, this section of the population was buoyant as old trades prospered and new trades sprang up. Below the grouping of the great merchants who were associated with the Court, there was a considerable intercourse between families at different financial levels and, as always when a new class is being built up, sharp divergences of fortune in the same stock. The case of Richard Smyth, who, having been put as clerk to an attorney, afterwards held the legal post of secondary of the Poultry Compter, may be instanced here.[1] Smyth himself was sprung from minor gentry at Abingdon, but the varying trades and status of the London families into which his sisters married are worth examining.[2] Although Smyth had a steady professional income of £700 a year, he maintained contact with a former schoolfellow from Abingdon who was a warder at the Tower. One is left with a sense of urban solidarity. The streets in the City had not yet lost the quality of a neighbourhood.

The inquiry into the cause of the fire which destroyed the Six Clerks' Office brings this out clearly. "The plaintiff and his wife", it is explained, "lodged noe otherwise in his chamber than they had usually done for fifteen years."[3] The object of the statement was to prove that the fire had started in Sir Robert Rich's kitchen chimney. In the previous law term Mr Tothill had taken his meals with the Six Clerks and his wife had "dyeted" with her son-in-law. Such meals as Mr Tothill took in his chamber were prepared in the Six Clerks' kitchen.

Arrangements for the financial provision for the stranger come to town were now in force, and there were extensive city investments.[4] These were paralleled in certain cases by the

[1] Richard Smyth was born in 1590 in his grandfather's house at Lillingston Dayrell in Buckinghamshire. He always maintained contact with Sir Thomas Dayrell and the other members of his mother's family. As secondary, he was in effect undersheriff. Cf. Wood, *Athenæ Oxonienis*, ed. Bliss, vol. iii, col. 1031.

[2] There are references to "my brother Tho. Houlker", an attorney of Clifford's Inn, later living at King's Langley. Colonel Thomas Harrison, the regicide, "once my Brother Houlker's clerk". "Coz. Harby scrivener [in White Cross Street] husband to Mari Houlker." Sir George Tash "in whose house [near Uxbridge] my coz. Kath. Houlker once was servant". "Mr Cole, haberdasher once my cosen John Houlker's master" (Richard Smyth's *Obituary*, Camden Society (1849), ed Sir Henry Ellis, pp. 21, 36, 52, 60, 92 and 94). Then there were other connections with city tradesmen. "My cozen Tho. Houlker's wife, a chandler's daughter in Chancery Lane." "My cozen Coleman's brother, a grocer at ye corner house in Coleman Street, next Beach Lane." In this lane there also lived "Mrs Mynors, my sister Edney's cousin, wife to Mr Richard Mynors, beadle of the Drapers Company". "My coz. Coleman's wife, confit makers in Leadenhall Street" (*ibid.* pp. 36, 71, 73 and 78).

[3] The evidence relating to the responsibility of William Tothill (1557-1626) is printed in *Shardeloes Papers*, ed. G. Elan, pp. 4 and 7.

[4] In a letter dated 22 October 1633 and sent by H. Jenkyn and Dorothy Jenkyn to their son, Humphrey Fulwood, at his house in Westminster near the Broken Cross by the Gatehouse, it is explained that they have paid to his use to Mr Hodgson of York, mercer, £50 as part of the sum of £200 which he is to receive this year by their grant of an annuity out of Basly. It is made clear that Mr Hodgson will pay the money within one month and will send a bill of exchange which may be cashed with Mr Joseph Furness, clothier, at Mr Wild's house in Lothbury (State Papers, Dom. Charles I, ccxlvii, 45).

ownership of property abroad.[1] In the political circle there was a tendency to move close to the House of Commons. "And in regard", wrote Sir Heneage Finch in the winter of 1625-6,[2] "my house at St Bartholomew's was too farre from the Parliament house, I hired a howse in Cannon Row near Westminster of my Lord Viscount Grandison." Lawyers still retained their preference for Chancery Lane and Fleet Street. The most fashionable area was, perhaps, St Martin's Lane, where the new houses were of red brick with stone facings. As a novelty, the chief windows were protected by shutters, and there were locks on all the doors. Just before the outbreak of the Civil War, Covent Garden was being developed along similar lines. There was already an old-fashioned air about the palaces along both sides of the Strand.[3] An impression of the furnishing of the more expensive houses can be obtained from the Verney Papers and similar sources, but it is much more difficult to reconstruct a citizen's residence. In this connection an interesting view is given of the life of the urban middle class in an inventory of the goods of Roger Acton, a Master of the Company of Cooks, who died at 47 Broad Street, Oxford. The document was certified by William Davis, verger, and is dated 14 August 1626.[4] The kitchen contained a little table, four high stools, two low stools, a cupboard, a cupboard over the chimney, a pair of racks, four pairs of

---

[1] As an example, Jonah Goare, citizen and merchant tailor of London, left by his will, proved on 16 January 1608, houses, etc., in the country of Barbary. Ralph Gore, citizen and merchant of London, left by his will, proved on 15 November 1637, lands in the Somer Islands (*Miscellanea Genealogica et Heraldica*, vol. i, pp. 347 and 349).

[2] Notes by Sir Heneage Finch (Cal. Finch MSS., vol. i, p. 44).

[3] It would seem that a number of small houses in the neighbourhood were either bought or rented by the great families for the use of their dependants. Thus, in a letter dated 25 November 1634, it is mentioned that William King, a writer of reports, lodges in Little Drury Lane in the house of William Fleming, who is the Duke of Lennox's waterman (State Papers, Dom. Charles I, cclxxvii, 87).

[4] Oxford University Archives, Inventories, vol. i, printed as Appendix II to "The Development of Domestic Architecture in Oxford", by W. A. Pantin, *The Antiquaries Journal* (1947), vol. xxvii, pp. 149-50. Roger Acton left books, whose titles are unspecified, to the value of 16s. Some further details from the inventories preserved in the Oxford University Archives are given for purposes of comparison. In the inventory of the goods and chattels of John Banks, manciple of St John Baptist's College, Oxford, taken on 22 March 1635, there occurs this entry: "Item in the study some books, glasses, compasses and other lumber", valued at 13s. 4d. No details of books are given in the inventories relating to the goods of Roger Barnes, stationer, which was taken on 24 February 1630. Furnishings, strictly so called, are not mentioned in any of these documents. It is only with the inventory dealing with the property of Henry Aldworth, butler of Wadham College, and taken on 9 January 1699, that we find a walnut tree table and Kidderminster printed hangings.

hangers, four pairs of pothooks, three pairs of tongs, a fire shovel, two slices, seven spits, an iron in the chimney and an iron before the fire. The contents of the principal sitting-room on the first floor may be listed. It contained, in addition to certain beds complete with curtains, valance and rods, a table with six high stools, a chair, a turned chair, a low stool and three forms, a desk, a basin and ewer, a window curtain and rod, and a carpet. Presumably standing against the wall were a cupboard and a court cupboard; one of these was covered by a cupboard cloth. The objects in this room were valued at the considerable figure of £11 1s., and there appears to be substance in the suggestion that the house was probably used as an inn or for lodgings.[1]

It is worth noting that Roger Acton's wearing apparel was valued at £10, and that he left books to the value of 16s. The figure for the clothes is rather high, considering that he belonged to a section of the middle class which had not much prestige.[2] The question of the nature of his reading matter is difficult. The Bible, and to a lesser degree Foxe's *Book of Martyrs*, are perhaps the volumes which in the town middle class would be found almost everywhere.[3] Naturally the quantity of books possessed by resident members of the Universities was normally

[1] The house contained three standing beds, six feather beds, three flock beds, a truckle bed and an old bedstead. The silverware consisted of two bowls, six spoons and a double salt. Miscellaneous objects included a green rug, four pewter candlesticks, three brass candlesticks, a tin and an iron candlestick, "two flower pots with other lumber". The value of the whole amounted to the large total of £85 13s. 4d. (*ibid.*, pp. 149-50).

[2] The Rev. Richard Ashley, D.D., Warden of All Souls College, left a scarlet hood and habit and wearing apparel valued at £16, inventory taken on 26 March 1636. The Rev. George Bathurst, B.D., Fellow of Trinity College, left wearing apparel worth £1 15s. 4d., inventory taken on 7 August 1645. The Rev. Thomas Atkinson, B.D., Fellow of St John's College, left a surplice, a Bachelor of Divinity's hood, a tippet and a square cap worth £1 11s. 6d., inventory taken on 1 April 1639 (Oxford University Archives, Inventories, vol. ii.

[3] A typical example is the will of William Mordeboice of Hepworth in Suffolk, Blacksmith, dated 28 January 1644: "Unto Rose my daughter, my Byble" (*Wills from the Register of the Commissary of Bury St Edmunds*, ed. Samuel Tymms, Camden Society (1850), p. 186). In houses of greater consequence it was sometimes indicated where the Bible was kept. In the inventory of the goods of Richard Powell of Forest Hill, taken in 1646, it is noted as lying "in ye little chamber over ye pantry". Sometimes the reading of the Bible was enjoined. The following passage occurs in the will of John Sydenham of Combe Sydenham, dated 18 October 1626: "And if by lewde and wicked cownsalle myne heire shall at any time be insited to frustrate any of these estates my further desyre and direction is that before the same be put in practice he advisedly read and consider the two last verses of the five and thirtieth Chapter of the Prophet Jeremias" (Skynner 61, printed in the *History of Part of West Somerset*, by C. E. H. Chadwyck Healey).

quite exceptional.[1] The well-furnished clerical library, either in town or country, was a slow growth.

Sometimes a glimpse can be obtained of the homogeneous character of urban life. In the rather elaborate will made by Francis Pynner, gentleman, of Bury St Edmunds, on 3 May 1639, reference is made to two fellow citizens who had helped him in sickness—Francis Cotter, baker, a kinsman of his late wife, and John Newgate, maltster. Mr Pynner had put his son-in-law, Valentine Elsden, into an inn and tavern belonging to him called the *Greyhound*. He owned two houses fully furnished—the *Golden Bushel* and the *Bear*—as well as tenements in the Fishmarket and Whiting Street in Bury. He could not have been very strict, for he refers to "my inlaid playing tables". At the same time his will concludes as follows:[2] "I desire Mr Edmund Callamy that he wilbe pleased to preach at my funerall".

It would be interesting to speculate as to whether pictures and other ornaments were more sparse in the houses of men of Puritan tendencies, or whether they did not feel it necessary to mention such trifles in their wills.[3] The small town is still seen as a unit, where all men of any property were known to one another. It is probable that this applied to every town in England, except London. The capital alone seems to have had power to absorb men's life and interests; elsewhere the distinction between the town and country is a shade unreal.[4] It is

[1] The inventory of the Rev. John English, Fellow of St John's, who died in 1613, aged twenty-seven, gives some indication of the arrangement of his library, which was valued at £22 10s. 3d. Thirty-two books are described as standing on the shelf over the docr and one as in the south end of the study (*Oxoniensia* (1946), vol. xi, p. 102). Dr Ashley left books, maps and pictures worth £50. He had in his house as much as £395 15s. 8d. in ready money. Mr Bathurst's books were valued at £6 6s. 8d., which compares with his two pictures, oil colours and frames, worth 10s., and his seven maps in colours and frames set down at 4s. 8d. Mr Atkinson's accommodation is described. It consisted of a bed chamber, a little room, a dining-room and study. "In the Studdie. Imprimis his bookes that noe man layd claim to" (£21 2s. 6d.) (Oxford University Archives, Inventories, vol. i).

[2] *Bury St Edmunds Wills*, p. 183.

[3] An example is seen in the will of Thomas Bacon, the elder, of Bungay in Suffolk, gent., dated 3 November 1638: "Item I give and bequeathe unto Thomas Bacon my sonne after the decease of Elizabeth my wyffe all my tables, formes, buffett stooles, chaires, bedsteades, brewinge vessles, copper pump and sisterne now standinge and remaynine in the new house I dwell in" (*Miscellanea Genealogica et Heraldica*, vol. v, p. 38).

[4] There is sometimes a nostalgic quality in the contact of a Londoner with his birthplace. Ellis Crispe, citizen and alderman and founder of a great City family, left by his will, proved on 17 November 1626, a legacy to "the poor of the town of Marshefield in the Countie of Gloucester where I was born" (*ibid.*, vol. v, p. 93).

only in London that one must consider the citizens of the same economic standing group by group.

Certain trades were still grouped in their localities, as in the case of the booksellers in Duck Lane and Little Britain.[1] The vintners and apothecaries and other men of property had their special standing,[2] while within this grouping there was already developing a tendency to retire from business in old age, and to go to live in the country towns of Hertfordshire and Essex.[3] It appears to have been the custom in this circle to give a measure of support to the City churches. An adherence to the Church of England with a strongly Protestant emphasis was characteristic. It was not among the vintners that one would find those precise men who would in time become the King's opponents. References to Catholic Recusants are very sparse.[4] It would be interesting to investigate the proportion of the children of this prosperous City world who found their way to the schools which led to the universities, to Merchant Taylors' or to St Paul's. The influence of the clergy in the case of their own children and in those of their friends or patrons would prove important here. It seems likely that very many boys were soon taken into their fathers' counting-houses. Thus in 1626 Sir Marmaduke Rawdon, a merchant, freighting ships for the Bordeaux wine trade, brought his nephew down from St Peter's School at York and placed him first in his office and then on one of his vessels as a supercargo.[5] But

---

[1] During the reign of Charles I the following booksellers of these two streets figure in Smyth's *Obituary*—Richard Wase, Francis Hill, Lancelot Toppyn, Daniel Fryer and Laurence Sadler, all of Little Britain, and Mr Nealand and Richard Cartwright of Duck Lane (pp. 9, 10, 17, 21, 23, 27 and 28). Lancelot Toppyn was brother-in-law to Cornelius Bee, who was for many years a bookseller in Little Britain. Mr Bee's eldest daughter was married to James Flesher or Fletcher, printer, of Clerkenwell, and the youngest to Nathaniel Hooke, her father's servant who eventually took over the shop (pp. 23, 35, 89, 93 and 99).

[2] Thus George Chamberlayne, vintner at the *Mitre* in Wood Street, Mr Phillips, vintner at the *Flying Horse* in Wood Street, together with Laurence Hill, grocer, Christopher Coleman, oilman, Robert Warner, chandler, and Mr Beaumond, attorney, all residents of Wood Street, would appear to have formed a group apart (*ibid.*, pp. 12, 14, 21 and 28).

[3] At unspecified dates Oliver Markland, innkeeper at the *Castle* in Wood street, moved to Stratford Bow; Humphrey Mitchell, pewterer in Wood Street, and his wife moved to Baldock, and John Hamond, "a spruce taylor in St Martin's L'Grand", moved to Romford (*ibid.*, pp. 47, 50 and 75).

[4] Cf. *ibid.*, pp. 10, 26.

[5] His father being dead, Marmaduke Rawdon the younger rode down from York to Hoddesdon in the company of Mr Sutton, draper. He was then aged sixteen. He spent 1628 and part of 1629 "in London as his unckle's cash keeper" (*The Life of Marmaduke Rawdon of York*, Camden Society (1863), ed. Robert Davies, pp. 5, 6).

Rawdon's family was too closely allied to the squirearchy to be typical.[1] It is from the long series of documents known as the Wellingham Letters that we can obtain a much clearer picture of the London merchant world.

These letters, which are scattered through the Domestic State Papers, deal not so much with the London house as with the life of the English factor overseas. They exhibit a happy combination of close detail and unselfconsciousness; they were not remotely intended for preservation. They were written by a young English factor established at San Sebastian through the years of peace. Their especial value lies in the glimpse that they provide of the true middle class, remote from every aspect of privilege and unaffected either by attraction or by repulsion by the Court and its *habitués*.

The letters in question are part of a continuous correspondence maintained between Mr Prestwick Eaton, then acting as representative for various London trading-houses, and his sister's husband, George Wellingham, who carried on business at the sign of the *Golden Anchor* in St Swithin's Lane. Only the letters from Eaton were collected, and the replies do not appear to have been preserved. They cover a period of eleven years, and the series opens with a letter written in the Downs in January 1631 as the *Nathaniel* was beating down the Channel on her voyage to Spain.[2]

Eaton was a young man and apparently unmarried, homesick for London and oppressed by the difficulty of securing business. In the heats of his first Spanish summer he suffered considerably from the colic, and wrote to England for a prescription since he could find no sure remedy among those suggested by the doctors at San Sebastian. Both his isolation and his insularity come out in all his letters.[3] There is a strong presumption that he did not know the Spanish language as he tried to do business on that unfriendly coast. He found it hard to secure purchasers for the goods consigned to him from London. After a year matters eased a little and Eaton formed the hope that the arrival of the next Plate Fleet at Cadiz was

---

[1] Sir Marmaduke Rawdon lived during the summer at Hoddesdon, rebuilding the manor-house which he had acquired on his marriage in 1611. In the late autumn he was accustomed to move to his London house in the parish of All Hallows, Barking. He died in 1646 at the age of sixty-four (*ibid.*, pp. xlii and 5).

[2] State Papers, Dom. Charles I, clxxxiii, 48.

[3] Cf. *ibid.*, cci, 67; cciii, 6; cciv, 102; ccxiv, 14.

bound to stimulate the flow of trade.[1] When he was disappointed
in this, he wrote home that it would be better to be a turnspit
than a factor.

His lodgings at San Sebastian were fairly comfortable, and
he asked his sister to send him a woven Norwich petticoat of
some civil colour which he could give as a present to his land-
lady. At the beginning of his second winter he lost his friend,
William Bowyer, another Englishman in business, who died
suddenly at Bilbao. He made the journey of about sixty miles
to attend the funeral.[2] With the exception of an occasional
visit to Bayonne, Eaton seems to have travelled little and he
did not return home for several years. He settled down for a
smoke each evening, and he got his pipes from England. In one
of his letters he asked his brother-in-law to send him a couple
of pounds of good tobacco packed in glasses.[3] He also ordered
some Bristol hangings for his chamber. His tastes were very
insular, and he asked that a small barrel of oatmeal should be
despatched to him "for here they know not what it meaneth".
On another occasion he sent a case of bottles home to be
replenished with the best liquor.[4] At different times he ordered
a couple of bulldogs and a spaniel, and recommended that they
should be procured at the Bear Garden.

Although trade was bad, his personal circumstances appear
to have been easy, and at one time he sent back a remittance of
a thousand rials which, he pointed out, was worth £25 at the
then rate of exchange. Eaton was careful about money, and
complained that a beaver hat and rapier, which he had ordered,
were more expensive than he liked. Most of his personal effects
came out from England: a rough, broad-brimmed beaver hat
sharp in the crown, a gold hatband, two black embroidered
girdles, the black nightcaps. He bought for his rooms two close
stools, a dozen good rich knives, a dozen Venice glasses and
pewter trenchers.[5] For decoration he ordered two globes in
frames, and his sealing-wax was sent to him from London with

[1] Letter dated 22 April 1632 (*ibid.*, ccxv, 71).
[2] Letter dated 9 November 1632 (*ibid.*, ccxxv, 17).
[3] Letter dated 17 September 1632 (*ibid.*, ccxxiii, 33).
[4] Letter dated 28 May 1632 (*ibid.*, ccxvi, 93).
[5] In this connection Eaton ordered on 6 April 1633: "two cwt of wrought
pewter, of which 150 lbs to be in trenchers and the rest in dishes of sundry sizes;
eight yards of cloth for a suit; another gold cap, with coloured flowers" (*ibid.*,
ccxxxvi, 28).

his barrels of ink.[1] He was accustomed to order a keg of sturgeon and a barrel of neats' tongues for Lent. There is very little evidence of contact with the Spaniards. On one occasion, after he had been nearly three years in San Sebastian, Eaton wrote asking for some satin lace as present for the mayor of the province, and for some carnation silk stockings for the mayor's lady.[2]

The correspondence with Wellingham is private and does not deal, except incidentally, with Prestwick Eaton's business ventures. In one letter he mentions that he had freighted the *Hopewell* of Yarmouth, a ship of 150 tons, and he seems to have dealt principally in stuffs for the London merchants.[3] There are two or three orders of quantities of white "Cordovall" gloves from London, presumably for retail purposes, and in one letter he mentions that he will give them the Spanish perfume. Once he inquired from Mrs Wellingham how gold caps should be washed to preserve the gold.[4]

By 1636 he had a companion, for in September of that year Wellingham gave to James Duncan of Dundee, then command-ing the *Gift of God*, a sum of £65 18s., which was due to the master of that vessel from Prestwick Eaton and Timothy Alsopp, merchants resident in San Sebastian.[5] Possibly Alsopp was a junior partner. In only one letter does Eaton express his views of the market. In this note he complains of the peculiar fickleness of the estate of merchandise, and declares that the world was never more gallant and had never less cause. Early in 1637 he wrote home to say that he was tired of San Sebastian. After outlining the mercantile doings of that poor place, he announced his intention of removing to Bilbao unless the situation altered for the better. It was about this time that he had written requiring that his goods should be insured against the Turks.

In this later portion of the correspondence there is one interesting reference. In December 1636 he thanked his young

[1] *Ibid.*, ccxiv, 8.

[2] Letter dated 14 July 1635 asking for twenty-six yards of satin lace (*ibid.*, ccxciii, 109).

[3] Letter dated 3 December 1635 (*ibid.*, ccciii, 41).

[4] Letter dated 5 June 1634. He also asked for two ounces each of coloured silks, carnation, watchet and other good colours chosen by his sister (*ibid.*, cclxix, 35).

[5] Letter dated 17 September 1636 (*ibid.*, cccxxxi, 59).

cousin for sending him a copy of Dr Hall's *Contemplations*.[1] He remarked that it was dangerous to keep the Bishop of Exeter's works in Spanish territory, and that he would not for his bishopric be taken with his letter to the Pope. This solitary reference makes it clear that Eaton shared the attitude of the London merchant world towards the Papacy. About the end of 1637 he asked his sister to take charge of certain articles that he was sending home by Robert Sergeant.[2] These included a silver basin and ewer, a rich salt-cellar, a case of pictures and a trunk of books. Shortly afterwards Prestwick Eaton removed to Bilbao. Here he was closer to the official world, and occasionally took charge of correspondence sent out by sea from England for the King's ambassador in Spain. His last letter to George Wellingham was sent from Bilbao in the autumn of 1642.

It is not easy to convey the impression which this correspondence gives of the young Englishman abroad; the bulldogs and the tobacco; the boredom with politics; the isolation. It is difficult to overstress the insularity. The young men carried with them the memory of the London playhouses and the Bear Garden, the meeting-places and the prices. With certain exceptions, they were not in the strict sense Puritan. There was too much preoccupation with their rapiers and scarlet waistcoats.

At the same time, the social groupings of France and Spain meant nothing to them. They lived within a circle which was both intimate and of slight influence. Thus Prestwick Eaton looked back to St Swithin's Lane, to his sister Wellingham, and to Uncle Watson and his wife, and to Aunt Lewis and her husband. It seems reasonable to suggest that in general young English factors of this type were inured to residence on the Continent. They would be unaffected by the streaming life of the great monarchies. In their business dealings they trusted nearly always to interpreters; the Tridentine idiom passed them by. It was in the city of London that their inarticulate sympathies were anchored. Very naturally they remained equally remote from Catholicism and from the Cavaliers.

It is seldom realised how far the ramifications of the town

---

[1] Letter dated 2 December 1636 (*ibid.*, cccxxxvii, 3). It appears from the letter dated 9 February 1637 that Eaton later ordered a second copy (*ibid.*, cccxlvi).

[2] Letter dated 12 December 1637 (*ibid.*, ccclxxiii, 19). Eaton also inquired after a damask bed that he had sent to be dyed.

middle class extended. It included, for instance, a large body of clergy who were neither Laudian nor Puritan. As a particular example, there is the case of Mr Faggard, the naval chaplain who makes several appearances in Lord Conway's letters. He was a careful observer of the Book of Common Prayer, and as such linked to the Government outlook. At the same time, he was mocked and treated as a butt by the gentlemen in the King's service.[1] To him, too, may be attributed the middle-class quality of isolation. Men such as Mr Faggard had no contact with Lambeth or the great Laudian prelacy. In their poor town parishes, the Court surely must have seemed unreal and the Puritans both near and unappealing. They were concerned with neither quarrel.

A particular difficulty recurs in any attempt to study the question of the opinion of the townsmen by means of an examination of the private literary sources. So often the correspondence is one-sided, and is only complete from the angle of privilege. Very naturally Mr Faggard did not commit to paper his outraged and humiliated feelings. In general, the doings of the burgess class are seen from the outside, and only a certain aspect of their daily life is manifest. The surviving documents are most often about them and not by them; they are seen in their relation to men possessed of an economic status which is stronger than their own.

The life of the lower middle class, that of the small independent shopman, passes unrecorded. Very often the private documents which have survived are linked with great houses, as in the case of the Walworth Letters. It seems that this correspondence, which is Puritan in its tone, had been preserved because Nathan Walworth was Lord Pembroke's steward at Baynard's Castle, the London headquarters of the Herbert estate.[2] There

---

[1] The second Viscount Conway, writing on 28 June and 10 July 1636 to George Garrard, has the following allusions to the chaplain: "A secret antipathy makes him and gunshot irreconciliable. Mr Faggard durst not be slung into a boate, nor goe in with the ketch. He hath travailed into France, and that he might goe free from boyes or the Inquisition, he put himself into a scarlet suite, a night raile band, a sugarloafe hat with a galan in the hat band, a frentch belt, a sword with a hilte à la occasion, bootes à la mode, a cane in his hand. We called him Captaine Faggard" (Cal. Portland MSS., vol. iii, pp. 35 and 44).

It is interesting to contrast Faggard's experiences with those of Henry Teonge. The latter was born in 1621, although he did not become a naval chaplain until he reached the age of fifty-seven. Cf. The Diary of Henry Teonge, ed. Charles Knight (1825).

[2] Correspondence of Nathan Walworth and Peter Seddon, Chetham Society.

are records of the young men of fashion fighting the watch and molesting the quiet citizens. Writers of a religious tone sometimes refer to the evil courses that they have abandoned, as in the notes of William Ayshecombe—"A.D. 1619. Then did I shake of[f] my sharkinge comrades."[1] So, little is known of what passed in the small wainscoted rooms behind the shop with its closed shutter.

It is, naturally, particularly difficult to trace the outline of the lives of the servants who waited on these quiet, middle-class families. Richard Smyth has certain references. It is true that these cover a wider period than the decade under consideration, but it seems that the secondary retained his servants long and always continued to keep in touch with them.[2] Among the maids employed were two pairs of sisters.[3] From the nature of these lists there is no indication of the wages paid. There appear to have been none of those casual perquisites on which the servants of the Court world depended.

It is important not to exaggerate, but there is a sense in which those who lived to the East of Temple Bar formed a closed community. A distinction was now becoming clear between those merchants and professional men who still resided within the confines of the City and those few possessors of great mercantile fortunes who had attached themselves not only to the Court, but to the landed interest.[4] It was the men of what may be termed the second rank who still lived in the old town houses. They were at the summit of their own hierarchy, and in consequence by nature conservative. Their names are prominent in the benefactions to the city parishes.

[1] Notes by William Ayshecombe, attributed formerly to John Pym and printed in Cal. Bouverie MSS., p. 83.

[2] On leaving Mr Smyth's service his maid Katherin married a plumber of the name of Day. His man George Whitcher was a Londoner whose father lived in Middle Row, Holborn. His maid Alice Comins married a man named Hodkins, employed at the Rose and Crown alehouse in Cursitor's Alley. His maid Margaret Large was the wife of Thomas Large and lived at the Spittle, near Shoreditch. Her widower died in Half Moon Alley in Bishopsgate Street—"a very poor alms man" (Smyth, Obituary, pp. 24, 36, 81, 89, 101).

[3] Nell Hutchins and her sister, whose home was in Tenter Alley, and Jane Harris and Anne Vize, whose uncle, Mr Stanton, lived in Shoe Lane (ibid., pp. 63, 65, 89).

[4] Sir William Cokayne had moved from Cokayne House in Broad Street to Combe Neville in Surrey before his death in 1626. He had also purchased estates at Elmethorpe and Rushton. Lord Bayning had purchased the estate of Bentley Parva in Essex.

It was with their help that the extensive church work of the years between 1628 and 1634 was carried forward; the construction of the new church of St Katharine Cree; the restoration of St Helen, Bishopgate and St Olave, Hart Street; the rebuilding of St Alban, Wood Street. Such assistance went with a taste for the dignity of armorial bearings cut in marble and a feeling for wall monuments.[1] It was a support for the established order whose implications were social rather than religious or political.

The impression left is of a state of deep peace, and this, curiously enough, is only enhanced by a study of the criminal records. It is, of course, not the criminals themselves who are of primary interest in a consideration of opinion or of detailed custom. The value of such records lies in the glimpses of ordinary life which are afforded incidentally and almost inadvertently. Here again the more celebrated State Trials, such as that of the murderers of Sir Thomas Overbury in the previous reign, are almost useless. They deal with an underworld created by the parasites of the circle of privilege. At no point in the retailing of these potions, spells and "clysters" does one touch the normal prosaic life of England's capital.

Sometimes, however, a single phrase serves to light up a whole neighbourhood, as in the case of the confession of Andrew Humphrey, an enthusiast who lived by the practice of geomancy and the setting of figures for the recovery of things lost and stolen.[2] He declared that he dwelt in a garden in Finsbury Fields, over against the six windmills westward, and close by Bunhill. One can almost see the man working at his "paterns for the darkening of the sun" sitting in the March evenings in his wooden shanty in those bare, mist-laden fields.

Similarly, details of the ordinary town life of the time can be discovered in the material relating to a very different legal

---

[1] As examples, Sir Chrisopher Clitherow, who was lord mayor in 1635, is commemorated by a wall monument placed in the church of St Andrew, Undershaft, in 1642. Sir John Gayer, who was lord mayor in 1646, gave a font adorned with marble armorial cartouches to St Katharine Cree at some date before 1640. Both men were presidents of Christ's Hospital, and considerable benefactors. Clitherow was a governor and Gayer a director of the East India Company. Sir Nicholas Crisp, who was granted by the King a monopoly of the Guinea trade, gave two silver flagons in 1631 to St Mildred, Bread Street. Cf. *Royal Commission on Historical Monuments, London*, vol. iv, "The City", pp. xxv, 6, 10, 26.

[2] Confession of Andrew Humphrey, dated 19 March 1632 (State Papers, Dom. Charles I, ccxxiii, 17).

problem—the depositions concerning an impostor. These depositions acquire significance from the everyday facts which they record and the impression of domestic interiors that they convey. The case in question concerns an impostor of some pretensions, Lodowyck Bowyer, who claimed to be the son of Sir John Bowyer, of Herefordshire. Early in September 1633 Bowyer was committed to the charge of the constables at Reading in consequence of certain wild assertions. These related to the alleged death of Sir Tobie Mathew and to Dr Laud's supposed communications with Rome.[1] He claimed to have received his information at the *Blackmoor*, in Kingston-on-Thames, from Francis Smith, the son of a clothier at Newbury.

Inquiries were set on foot by the Council and it was learned that there was no inn at Kingston with the sign of the *Blackmoor*, nor could Francis Smith of Newbury be traced.[2] Notes made by Secretary Windebank attach a certain credence to the following account of the prisoner. It was affirmed that Bowyer had been six years beyond the seas, a year and three-quarters prisoner at Sallee in Barbary, and then for a year and a half living with a Hamburgher who had redeemed him. He claimed to have taught this merchant's son the English language and how to play upon the orfarian. On returning from Germany to England, he had stayed at Faversham with Lady Roper, who had given him a suit of apparel.[3]

As a result of the inquiries made into this case, Dr Thomas Some came forward with an interesting deposition. He said that about three weeks since "that prodigious liar and villain who calls himself Bowyer" had come to Dr Horne's lodgings at Windsor with a petition signifying that he had been a prisoner in Turkey for three or four years past. He had then explained that he was travelling towards the Bishop of Oxford, who was his uncle; that he had been a scholar of Trinity College, Cambridge, and a pupil to Dr Topham, Dean of Lincoln, and that he was so well known to the Dean of Windsor that, had he been present, he would have relieved his wants. Upon these motives Dr Horne sent him to the College Treasurer to receive 10s.

[1] Letters and enclosures sent to Secretary Windebank by William Kendrick, Mayor of Reading, on 13 September 1633 (State Papers, Dom. Charles I, ccxlvi, 28).

[2] Cf. notes by Secretary Windebank, dated 23 September 1633 (*ibid.*, 63).

[3] Lady Roper was a young Catholic widow, the daughter of the second Lord Petre and the mother of Lord Teynham, then a child. The charity of Catholics opened the eyes of many scoundrels to opportunities of preying on them.

He then came to Dr Some's house, saying that he was well acquainted with Dr Turner, the Master of Peterhouse (Dr Some's college) and had seen Dr Some in his company. He inquired also concerning divers fellows of Trinity College, but the deponent had no private speech with him. In Dr Some's absence he came again to the house and told his servants he had been bidden to dinner, where dining with the family, he after dinner stole a Bible, and going to Dr Horne's he stole thence two Venice glasses; getting forth out of the town he was pursued by the innkeeper for 17s., and his cloak taken from him to satisfy that debt.[1]

Bowyer's case owed the wide publicity which it received to the attack on Laud; but the episode serves to emphasise the tranquillity of the prosperous Anglican clerical grouping. It is a mark of a stable way of life that it is wide open to the rogue. In this connection further light is thrown upon the customs of that day in a letter written to Edward Nicholas, then Secretary of the Admiralty, by the steward in charge of his London house at the sign of the *Golden Wheatsheaf*, in King Street, Westminster.

"Your house", he wrote to his master, "is well and safe, but Mr Gritten's house was broken open and, as he says, he lost £300. On Sunday night there were thieves found untiling a house in Duffield's Alley, but got nothing, yet escaped. For your house I have begun to burn a candle for half an hour in your uppermost dining-room every night at ten o'clock, and the like in one of the chambers towards the street."[2] An almost Victorian peace is suggested by this picture of the window, and in it the flickering light which brought security.

Another impression of town life is obtained from a study of the examinations in the Court of High Commission, but these, in general, relate rather to the lower middle class and the artisans than to those prosperous groupings whose lives we have been considering. A typical example is the case of William Trendall, who was brought before the mayor and jurats of Dover in July 1639 on a charge of holding conventicles in that town.[3] He was a freemason about fifty years of age, a Londoner

---

[1] Deposition dated 26 September 1633 (State Papers, Dom. Charles I, ccxlvi, 82).

[2] Letter from William Bell to Edward Nicholas, dated at Westminster, 15 August 1637 (*ibid.*, ccclxv, 69).

[3] These examinations were taken on 27 July 1639 (State Papers, Dom. Charles I, ccccxxxii, 27, i, ii and iii). Cf. *The Social Structure of Caroline England*, pp. 93-4, for a more detailed account of this matter.

normally resident at Battle Bridge, St Olave's, who had come to Dover in the previous autumn, hired to work on Archcliffe Bulwark. He had brought his wife and two young children with him, as also his servant Humphrey Watts, who was probably in fact his assistant. Such evidence is valuable for the light thrown on religious and sometimes on political opinion. On the social side we learn little. The economic pull of London is underlined, and the ease of movement as the artisans went out from the capital to the towns where their trades led them.

There still remained a very marked simplicity of intercourse. It was, perhaps, mainly the new industries which tended to become hierarchical. Certainly it is only through them that some view may be gained of the mass of unskilled town labour. In this connection the coal industry is the easiest to study.[1] At the summit of the London coal trade there stood the wood-mongers, who sold in bulk to the dyers and brewers, and later to the great private households. At a lower economic level the chandler retailed coal by the sack. Coal traders managed the landing of coal from the hoys anchored below Tower Wharf. Carmen, licensed by the Woodmongers Company, drove the carts from the wharves to the new coal-yards. The loading was done by the coal-heavers.

During the early seventeenth century the London River witnessed the development of the sailing collier, which would survive until the age of steam. These ships were differentiated from the vessels which had brought in coal as ballast in the Tudor times. They bore no resemblance to the beer boats, or those engaged in carrying on the coastal traffic in corn and cloth and wine. The situation was governed by the great increase in the coal imports, amounting in a poor year to nearly one hundred and fifty thousand tons brought ashore at the Port of London.[2] To meet this large demand, Newcastle colliers, manned by a crew of ten and with a cargo-carrying space of between 200 and 300 tons, had been put into service. They would come into the Thames in fleets through the spring

[1] This is a result of Professor John U. Nef's pioneer work. All students are indebted to his masterly analysis in *The Rise of the British Coal Industry*, 2 vols. (1932).

[2] After assessing the figure of coal imports at London from Christmas 1637 to Christmas 1638 at 142,579 tons, Professor Nef gives it as his opinion that these imports in the 'thirties amounted in a normal year to nearly 200,000 tons (*op. cit.*, vol. i, p. 21).

and summer averaging annually between five and nine round trips from the Tyne before they were laid up for the winter.

The lighters used to unload the colliers were of a type long familiar on the London River and now adapted to the handling of "sea coal". Their general lines were similar to those of the barges used for this work on the Tyne, and there known as keels. With this background, some facts as to the lives of the men employed can be discovered. The men unloading colliers in the Port of London worked in gangs of sixteen. They were singularly unprotected. In the booths of the Exchange at Billingsgate the coal traders, who hired the lighters, bargained with the shipmasters, who had just landed from the hoys. Outside in Roomland the coal-heavers waited leaning on their shovels, smoking their pipes; men who had drifted into this work, disunited and unlettered. Even much later, gangs of heavers paid by piece-work only earned between one and three shillings per London chaldron.[1] In the result the traders had to accept such "poor labourers as they could get to unlade the shipps".[2] When this seasonal employment was interrupted, the inevitably unorganised workers came within the reach of the vagrancy laws. Omitting the members of the criminal underworld, those who offered themselves as heavers seem to have been at the base of the urban economic pyramid. They were caught up in the "great wen", cut off from their roots. There was nothing to bind them together, no sense of locality. Like all submerged elements, they tended towards disintegration. They were part of the wastage of Vandyck London.

During this period, efforts to reduce the number of the vagabonds were continual. This comes out clearly in a report of the Lord Mayor and Court of Aldermen sent to the Council, in which it is treated among other matters.[3] After certifying that ten thousand quarters (of corn) would be a sufficient store in the City magazine if restraint were had of the newly erected buildings and the brewers were restrained from using such great quantities, the Court of Aldermen turned to this subject. They drew attention to the fact that great sums of money had been raised the previous year for the relief of the poor and the setting them to work. Four thousand-odd vagrants had been

---

[1] Eight Newcastle chaldrons were the equivalent of twenty-one tons.
[2] Dale, *Fellowship of Woodmongers*, p. 136.
[3] Letter dated October 1632 (State Papers, Dom. Charles I, ccxxiv, 65).

conveyed according to the Statute. Seventy vagrants had been taken as apprentices into Bridewell, and seven hundred and seventy-three poor children (forty of whom had been put as apprentices to trades since Easter last) were maintained by Christ's Hospital. They reported that fifty vagrants had been bound apprentices to merchants to serve in the Islands of Barbados and Virginia.

CHAPTER XII

LIFE IN THE COUNTRY

NO very sharp distinctions can be drawn between the parallel and mingled urban and rural groupings in what was ultimately a composite society. It is true, however, that the actual farm life and the details of farm management can be envisaged much more clearly than the data relating to the small-town business man and his employees. On the other hand, the immense mass of documentation dealing with the squirearchy leads to a tendency to neglect other, and in some ways more significant, rural classes. The families whose lives are best known—and the Verneys are perhaps a good example—are in no way typical. They were much richer than the average, even among their own section of the squires; they were much more closely associated, by antipathy as well as sympathy, with the Stuart Court.

As a general rule, it is the more prosperous groupings in any class which leave the most elaborate memoranda. The writings of the greater squires tend to screen us from an understanding of the outlook of the middle gentry. Thus so much of the accessible material deals with families, like the Gawdys, who had a direct interest in parliamentary representation. Inevitably only a small proportion of country gentry were polarised to the House of Commons. The limit of their attainment and their natural sphere of influence was the commission of the peace.

If it is difficult to penetrate to the ideas held by the gentry of medium fortune, this is still harder in the case of the lesser gentry. This relatively impoverished grouping is very scantily represented in any continuous series of documents until after the Restoration, and it is perhaps only in Hanoverian times that their background and opinions can be really understood. It is rare to find any detailed exchange of letters emanating from the yeoman farmers. They had not the habit of letter writing, and business was conducted by word of mouth. At lower economic levels the manuscript material, apart from wage-sheets, tends to disappear completely.

As far as the rural employees are concerned, it is only in the highest rank of estate servants, the factors and stewards, that we find detailed memoranda preserved. Even these papers nearly always relate to the official, and not to the private, life of their writers. Such papers have, as records, various merits. They are business-like and explicit, and quite unselfconscious. On the other hand, they seldom extend the area of our knowledge, since they tend to reflect not the way of life of the stewards themselves but that of the wealthy privileged class which employed them.

In fact, one of the rare impressions of the state of the agricultural working class which emerges from any literary sources is that conveyed by religious journals. For the rest, this subject is best approached through a study of legal proceedings and economic enactments, and an examination of wage levels. In addition to the *Reliquiæ Baxterianæ*, already quoted, the well-known opening of George Fox's Journal bears on this point. "I was born", wrote the founder of the Society of Friends, "in the month called July, 1624, at Drayton-in-the-Clay, in Leicestershire. My father's name was Christopher Fox: he was by profession a weaver, an honest man; and there was a seed of God in him. The neighbours called him Righteous Christer. My mother was an upright woman; her maiden name was Mary Lago, of the family of the Lagos, and of the stock of the martyrs."[1]

Very occasionally, the detailed life of the English village stands out clearly in the account of some disaster, as in the various descriptions in the Nicholas Papers of the Winterbourne fire. Here is one of the many reasons for concentrating upon this series of documents, which mirror with unstrained fidelity the homely and prosaic customs of the lesser gentry. So much of the outlook of the country squires, which was to remain unchanged for centuries, took shape in the quiet first period of the reign of Charles I. From the great storehouse of the Nicholas Papers an impression can be built up of one such family. It has the additional interest that it centres upon the career of Edward Nicholas, who was to become a Secretary of State to Charles I, and one of the chief advisers of the royal house in exile.

In 1633, when the material first assumes a massive character, the head of this family of small squires was Mr John Nicholas,

[1] *Journal of George Fox*, ed. Norman Penney, p. 1.

then sixty-seven years of age. He had lived through all his
manhood at Winterbourne Earls, which lay to the north-east
of Salisbury. Here he appears to have rented the parsonage
house. At an earlier period he had moved for some years into
the county town in order to have at hand a teacher for his
sons. He belonged to the type of lawyer with local connections
who had always resided in his own county. With old age he
had become prosperous above the average; he had a liking for
the company of churchmen.[1]

Mr Nicholas busied himself with various employments,
partly of a legal and partly of an administrative character. He
kept through life the chambers in the Middle Temple, which
he had obtained at the time of his association with the Six
Clerks' office. He was steward for Lord Pembroke's Wiltshire
land, escheator of Clarendon, a post in the gift of the Herbert
family. His tastes were conservative, and he very seldom left
Wiltshire. He was particularly interested in the breeding of
Persian and Muscovy ducks. His younger son, Matthew, later
Dean of Bristol, was of a somewhat bustling disposition and
impatient of his father's simplicity. Mr Nicholas was deeply
attached to his grandchildren, and persuaded his son, Edward,
to let them come to Winterbourne. He was happy when their
return to London was delayed "because of the snow along the
hollow ways". His wife, who was the daughter of a local squire,
Mr Hunton of Knoyle, was likewise devoted to the family, and
in her old age suffered severely from rheumatism in the face.
The old couple spent a good deal on apothecaries' remedies,
and among the items in Mr Thomas Hickes' bill was a sum of
five shillings for ingredients for making China broth.[2] Mr

---

[1] The standpoint of the family in religious matters is indicated in the "advice
from a father to his son on going abroad written by Sir Edward Nicholas at
Oxford on 15 February 1643". This was printed by Sir R. Colt Hoare in *The
Modern History of Wiltshire*, vol. v, p. 92. "Read diligently every day certain
Chapters of ye Bible, either in French or in some other tongue. . . . Be diligent in
goeing duely to the Protestant Church in France upon all ye dayes and times of
their assembly and preaching, as well on the week days as on Sundays."

[2] The whole family were served by this fashionable apothecary whose charges
one winter amounted to the considerable figure of £6 7s. 6d., two bills sent in to
Edward Nicholas in December 1631 (State Papers, Dom. Charles I, cciv, 119, 120).
It is worth noting other charges. A bill for making a cloth suit amounted to
£2 11s. 6d. Nicholas paid £10 3s. 5d. to Richard Allport, upholsterer, for hangings
for two chambers at Richmond and gave £18 13s. for a bed supplied by another
upholsterer, George Webbe. A draper's bill came to £15 19s. 11d. A bill for beer
supplied over an unspecified period by Job and Abraham Bradshaw amounted to
£1 2s. (*ibid.*, cciv, 20; ccxliii, 7; and ccxlviii, 24 and 41).

Nicholas' son, Edward, procured with some trouble "my Lord Treasurer [Portland's] receipt of a physic drink to prevent the stone in the kidney".

Three letters give the atmosphere of the place and time. In the first Mr Nicholas declared that he was at his old employment of Court-keeping, which he found very unprofitable. He would rest with his cousin, Sir William Calley, that day sennight and the next day would keep court at Ramsbury. After a little gossip, he explained that in Wiltshire men began to fear the great preparations of the French.[1]

There then follow those plans for the preservation of local offices which were so characteristic a preoccupation of the families dependent upon a great estate. Mr Nicholas had approached Mr William Herbert, who had undertaken to speak to "my Lord" in favour of a grant of the escheator's place at Clarendon to Edward Nicholas. A grant to both of them and to the survivor was proposed, since Lord Pembroke did not care to grant reversions. It was suggested that the name of Mr Nicholas' young grandson should be inserted into the bond relating to the parsonage of Winterbourne.

Meanwhile, arrangements were made for Edward Nicholas' visit, and he was asked to give the exact date of his arrival, since his sister, Mrs Butterworth, would return in the hired coach which brought him from London.[2] A letter from Edward reached Mr Nicholas as he was taking horse for Drayton to see his daughter's lease sealed. The old gentleman wrote that he had sent Edward's dog to his brother, as instructed. This is a hasty note, and Mr Nicholas explains that he cannot write more "for fear of being benighted this dark night".

An idea was mooted that the living of Winterbourne, which would yield £40 per annum, might be purchased for £800 from Mr Barnes (his son being dead). Cousin Young was reported as being in treaty with Sherfield, the Recorder, about a farm at Amesbury, and the owner was ready to accept £2,000, "but Mr Young was fearful to deal with him".[3] Matthew Nicholas,

[1] As an example, Mr Nicholas referred to the distraction in the worthy family of the Sherfields, the arrest of Mr Prowett senior, the debt of his son Squire Prowett, and the journey made by Sir Haslewood Gorges to take his mother's body back into her own county for burial (*ibid.*, ccxiv, 92.)

[2] Letter dated 19 July 1631 (*ibid.*, cxcvi, 93).

[3] These matters are set out in three letters written between 9 September and 7 October 1633 (*ibid.*, ccxlvi, 28 and 58, and ccxlvii, 35).

the parson, wrote censoriously of his father's visitors. Edward's two sons and their master had dined with Mr Upton when he kept court at Dinton. The master and his usher were in great hopes to make them scholars. It was these quiet happenings that were disturbed by the fire at Winterbourne.

On 21 March 1634 Mr Nicholas wrote an account of this occurrence to his son Edward.[1] The court at Chalk had risen some hours before nightfall, and he had suddenly determined to ride home. On reaching the Two Barrows, while it was still twilight, he saw his parsonage and barn, with a rick of nearly thirty loads of wheat, with two mows of barley, all in a flaming fire and twenty houses besides. His own loss must have amounted to at least £1,000, for his very carts were burned and all provision of beer and malt and above twenty quarters of pure seed barley.

In a more prosaic fashion, Matthew Nicholas took up the tale.[2] The fire had started at Kidgell's house through his wife carrying a firebrand over the straw-yard. The wind had carried the flames to Mr Webb's house, and from thence to Mr Sherfield's and so to their father's parsonage. Mr Sherfield had a house plentifully furnished with good furniture, both his own and his eldest son's. He saved nothing but his money, about six score pounds, his plate and the apparel on his back. Their father had lost his farm buildings and corn in ricks and barns. His dwelling-house at the farm was saved, but the greater part of the parsonage was burned. The total loss at Winterbourne was estimated at £10,000.

And then, after this vivid impression, the correspondence settles down again to quiet domestic detail and altercation. A rather earlier letter is characteristic. Matthew Nicholas is found writing to his brother that he has heard no speech of any husband or sweetheart "towards his sister Betty or any of the rest".[3] He gave it as his opinion that their father must either make a public profession of greater portions or else bring his unmarried daughters down to a lower rank in their habit and fashions. Otherwise they would be likely to remain a good while

---

[1] Letter from John Nicholas to Edward Nicholas, dated 21 March 1634 (State Papers, Dom. Charles I, cclxiii, 44).

[2] Letter from Matthew Nicholas to Edward Nicholas, dated 31 March 1633 (this is placed a year out in the collection) (ibid., ccxxxiv, 78).

[3] Letter from Matthew Nicholas to Edward Nicholas, dated at St Nicholas Warnham, 29 July 1633 (ibid., ccvliii, 45).

upon his hands. In conclusion he referred to their sister Lettice's journey between Sister Eliot's and Mr Kenn's in order to preserve a pound of cherries.

An interesting section of the correspondence deals with the education of the young grandsons. For several years the possibility of Winchester was borne in mind, Mr Nicholas asserting that he had no doubt of the boys' scholarship "if they be not harshly treated withal".[1] He suggested that Edward should call to mind his own fearfulness at Winchester, which had nearly cost him his life. For the time being the lads returned to Mr Pinckney, their grandfather hoping that they were nearly cured of the itch.[2]

Finally, in May 1637, the educational question was settled. In that month Matthew Nicholas wrote to acquaint his brother with the outcome of his visit to Winchester, where the schoolmaster had undertaken to board his nephew John at an annual cost of £20.[3] The Rector of West Dean made two final points. He had found that in any quarters near the college the rate of tabling was very high unless the boy should lodge in mean houses. The master had further promised that John should be in the fifth book so that he might be altogether under his teaching.

This plan was carried out, and in the following November old Mr Nicholas sent an account to his son Edward. "He likes the school well. He was very brag that in an exercise of twenty verses his master would not find one fault or would not seem to find it. Indeed, Mr Pinckney has taken pains with him."[4] At Christmas Mr Nicholas' man Will Gauntlett was sent to bring Jack and Ned home to Winterbourne. The younger boy had also been sent to Winchester, for Mr John Ashburnham had reported that after Jack's departure from Dinton "he had lighted on a very ill schoolmaster". By July 1638 they were both well established, and their grandfather wrote that the

---

[1] Letter from John Nicholas to Edward Nicholas, dated at Winterbourne, 20 January 1635 (ibid., cclxxxii, 66).

[2] In a letter to Edward Nicholas, dated 4 January 1636, John Nicholas mentions that he had given ten shillings to Mrs Pinckney and five shillings each to Mrs Pinckney and the usher. At that date the balance of moneys owed to Mr Pinckney for the last quarter ending at Christmas 1635 amounted to £8 (ibid., cccxi, 49).

[3] Letter from Matthew Nicholas to Edward Nicholas, dated from West Dean, 8 May 1637 (ibid., ccclv, 143).

[4] Letter from John Nicholas to Edward Nicholas, dated from Winterbourne, 13 November 1637 (ibid., ccclxxi, 96).

brothers were in need of new shirts and more bands.[1] They had
but three apiece, and at Winchester the soiled clothes were sent
to the wash once in each month. A pleasant note concludes the
detail of this education. With the passing years Edward
Nicholas had come to gain some influence at Oxford. His
friend the Vice-Chancellor, Dr Frewen, had recommended to
him Mr Thomas Smith, a Fellow of Queen's College. "I thank
God", he wrote in the opening months of 1641 to his son's new
tutor, "he [Jack] is endowed with convenient natural parts,
and I hope you will find him reasonably well grounded in
Latin and Greek."[2]

The picture here presented reflects that more expensive
form of education for the English countryman of means which
was now coming into fashion. It was an alternation of term
time and country life, which was to change very little until a
new and urban class came to invade the schools later modelled
upon Arnold's Rugby. In the case in question, Edward Nicholas' official position, which was constantly increasing in responsibility until he became Secretary of State in the last months
before the Civil Wars, gave his children a special opportunity
which was still rare among those with his father's background.[3]
In these respects the boyhood of John Evelyn and William
Dugdale was more representative than that of Jack Nicholas.
It was not a question of riches, but of immediate London
contacts. Winchester was already favoured by the bureaucratic
world.

The detail provided in the Nicholas letters indicates customs
which would develop. The house system is foreshadowed, and
the relation of the parent with the housemaster. The old
retainer sent to take charge of the boys' journey to and from
school was a feature which would survive until the Napoleonic
War and the days of the fast stage coaches. The independent

---

[1] Letter from the same to the same, dated 9 July 1638 (*ibid.*, cccxcv, 28).

[2] Letter from Edward Nicholas to Thomas Smith, dated 24 February 1641
(*ibid.*, cccclxxvii, 49).

[3] Edward Nicholas had two houses in or close to London. One was leased from
William Caldwell, together with stables and a garden fronting Axe Court and
King Street, Westminster, at a quarterly rent of £40 (*ibid.*, ccxxxvi, 8, and similar
entries). The other was a tenement situated on the Green, Richmond, and
leased from 1634 onwards at a rent of £3 10s. a quarter (*ibid.*, cclxiii, 73). On the
back of the receipt note just mentioned Nicholas wrote: "I also this day gave him
[George Pierce, his landlord] ten shillings for the minister of Richmond for the
whole year".

schoolmaster is still seen as a survivor from Tudor times. The resident, and often clerical, tutor of the Hanoverian period had not yet come among the landed gentry. To this last general rule there are two exceptions. In certain cases a resident chaplain was maintained, usually among very wealthy families of the preciser sort. In such circumstances he would normally act as tutor to the sons of the house. Among Catholic families the chaplain would almost invariably act in this capacity. The attachment of the more devout Recusant families to the Benedictine and Jesuit traditions was reinforced by this practice. Again, Catholic chaplains were found in the households of the middling squires, whose Protestant counterparts would never need them. The priest or clergyman who undertook tuition was as a type quite distinct from the professional tutor, although it might be to the latter's advantage to seek Orders. In one sphere this new type was already making an appearance. The travelling tutor engaged for a period in some great peer's household can be traced to the second quarter of the seventeenth century. No serious work has yet been undertaken on the status, attainments and emoluments of the independent schoolmaster. Up and down the country there were gentlemen's sons at work learning with a master and his usher. It would be of the greatest interest to recover the receipt books of Mr Pinckney.

A view of another aspect of rural life, that of the factor and the small tradesman, is given in another correspondence preserved among the State Papers.[1] The greater part consists of letters written by Richard Harvey, which are mainly concerned with the affairs of the Calley family, who also belonged to Wiltshire and were related to Mr Nicholas. Incidental glimpses are afforded of a family engaged in weaving at Taunton, whose brother was in the confidential service of men of property.[2] There were associations with different parts of the West Country, while the Harveys appear originally to have been tenants on one of Lord Pembroke's estates in Somerset.[3] In the country, at any rate, confidential servants seem usually to

---

[1] Contained in the volumes of the State Papers, Dom. Charles I, covering the years 1635-40.

[2] Cf. letter from Roger Harvey to Richard Harvey (ibid., ccclxiii, 15, and ccccxiv, 127).

[3] For this point and Harvey's London associates, cf. ibid., ccccxviii, 12, and cccxciii, 10.

have been chosen, and promoted on a system of recommendation from members of the employing class living within a well-defined neighbourhood. Given their status and locality, it is not surprising to note that the Harveys' background was Puritan.[1] A brief impression of the family life is given in a letter from Roger Harvey the weaver to his brother Richard.[2] "My mother", he wrote, "has been very dangerously sick and doth yet so remain. She has devised all the goods [which by the inventory came to £7] to her daughter and her husband so secretly that I only obtained knowledge of it through our minister, Mr Godwin." This scene, grim in its tone with its faint anticipation of the Ironsides, can act as a foil to that quick prudent service which Roger's brother gave first to the Calleys and later to Endymion Porter.

These first employers are known to us almost entirely through their needs; but the luxury purchases which they obtained through Richard Harvey provide a curious commentary upon the way of life of a prosperous county *milieu*, which was careful to reflect the London fashions. They were four in family, Sir William and Lady Calley, and their son and daughter-in-law. There was, in the first place, the Christmas shopping; the ten leaves of wafer in a pasteboard; the box of pistachios; the grains of musk. Young Mr Calley wrote asking that twelve packs of the best cards should be sent down with his father's Christmas provisions. A certain amount of wine was laid in. Sir William Calley ordered a tierce of the best claret, pointing out that Mr Foster had greatly abused them about the previous consignment. Some cutlery was ordered, including six good table knives without a case.

One letter suggests the way in which these purchases were financed. "I have written", explains Sir William, "to Long to call in £200. The reason is I must buy three hundred sheep extraordinary. Send me by the carrier two good brass locks and twenty or thirty pounds of good lump sugar or Motville sugar. I have given the bearer Edward Harrison £10 in gold to pay you for the well rope and these things."[3] Foodstuffs ordered include a barrel of oysters and a Danzig sturgeon, also carroway comfits and a pound of the best and clearest brown

---

[1] *Ibid.*, ccccxxvi., 70.   [2] Letter dated 2 September 1639 (*ibid.*, ccccxxviii, 12).
[3] Letter from Sir William Calley to Richard Harvey, dated from Burderop, 16 October 1637 (*ibid.*, ccclxix, 87).

sugar candy. Five or six dozen cork stopples were required, "without them we cannot draw our wine".

There were considerable purchases of clothes. Lady Calley asked that Mr Davison's advice should be taken and that he should make up a rich flowered satin gown after the fashion most used.[1] By the same post young Mr Calley ordered a black satin dress and a white satin waistcoat for his wife, and a pair of gold-colour silk stockings for himself. On another occasion William Calley asked for a piece of kersey of a crimson and liver colour or of a marble grey or rat colour. It is pleasant to come across these homely names. Sir William ordered quantities of holland, some of it for handkerchiefs, linen boot-hose, linen socks, white gloves, a black tiffany hood. His wife copied out on a fly-leaf five patterns of lace.

It is difficult to know whether the interest in books was serious. The ordering of a "book of occurrents" to give the foreign news seems in accordance with the normal practice of a country gentleman. The reference to the volume containing the arguments set out by the divines of the university of Aberdeen against the Presbyterians suggests a desire to know what arguments might be adduced on the King's side.[2]

The life of the family had for its circumference Wells and Marlborough, where the groceries were purchased and the Calleys saw a bloody battle between cocks. In the course of years Richard Harvey's status changed, and he passed over to the service of Endymion Porter still ready to assist his former masters. In this connection the presents destined for the tables of the Court, which were sent up from Burderop, recall the largesse of Tudor times.[3] "I sent", explained Sir William, "a man on purpose to St Andrew's fair at Wells for a boar. He bought one that seemed to be good for £4, but being killed it proves very bad, being lean and old, yet a great body."[4]

[1] As an instance of the straining after effect Mr Calley wished Mr Harvey to search for a new coloured felt hat, but not with so steeple-like a crown as the last one sent down, and he asked for a fan of black feathers with a handle of either silver or otherwise as most used (*ibid.*, ccclxxiv, 18).

[2] Letter from Sir William Calley to Richard Harvey, dated from Burderop, 26 January 1639 (*ibid.*, cccx, 46).

[3] Thus six collars of brawn went to Lord Cottington, presents of game to Endymion Porter and a fat young swan and two dozen of hog's puddings (half black, half white) to Endymion's wife.

[4] Letter to Richard Harvey, dated from Burderop, 8 December 1638 (*ibid.*, cccciv, 431).

There was also some attempt to make polite profit. Young Mr Calley authorised Harvey to sell a gelding for him at any price in excess of £20. There were negotiations with a view to assisting Sir Tobie Mathew to find coach-horses. Richard Harvey sat in his office in Mr Endymion Porter's lodging beside Durham House in the Strand, attending to those instructions which came up to him from Wiltshire. Sums were deposited for him with Mr Weaskate, a scrivener working at the *Naked Boy* in Fetter Lane.

The picture here built up specifically excludes that range of life which was linked closely with the Court and was merely an extension into rural England of the mannered ways and that carefully arranged sentiment which found favour at St James'. It is therefore all the more necessary to insist upon the ordinary preoccupations of the gentry, the local administration and the purchase of land and mortgage, the marrying and educating of children, the hunting and hawking, and the fighting cocks. It was a far cry from Queen Henrietta's ladies to the sober country wives, who sat at home with simples and receipt books.[1] The still-room maids were busy, and upon the dresser there stood in rows the basins which contained the black hog's pudding.

This was not a period of ostentatious building. Very few great houses date from these years. It was rather a time of refacings and additions and rearrangement. The economic position of the country gentry was confused, for some sections

---

[1] By the reign of Charles I the receipts, which would be handed down for generations, were being systematised. The name attached to them is normally that of the lady of the house where they were first propounded. Among the Arundell of Wardour MSS. there is a receipt book with the early pages missing. Internal evidence suggests that it belongs to the latter part of the seventeenth century. Receipt books of this character would make an interesting study both from the sociological and the medical angle. In the Wardour Castle volume the *provenance* of the receipts is worth noting. They seem to have come from a certain range of Catholic and Anglican houses in the southern and eastern counties. "A cordiall powder of my Lady North and my Lady Paget. My Lo: of Dorset's spirits of carrowaies. Mrs Jeffreys receipt to order neat's tongues. Sir Wm. Paston's meade. Mrs Sherwood's way to pickel pidgeons. Dr Stephens' rare water, a rare cordiall palsey water of ye same vertues as Dr Matthewes' water but of less price. A surfit water of my Lady Anne Howard's. To make white marmalade of quinces my Lady Lewkner's way. To make quince paste Mrs Roper's way. Syrup of snailes my Lady Heron's way." There is reference to a "dyet drink for many diseases out of my Lady Compton's book". After a note of my Lady Mohun's way of making syrup of violets, a way to preserve damsons is given. Against this entry occur the words, "I had it of my Lady Mohun".

were sinking in status while others were buoyant. The feature most in evidence was probably establishment and consolidation.[1] Curiously enough, in these years before the Civil War, life in the country-side was more peaceful than it had been for generations. The litigation between neighbours, so characteristic a feature of the Elizabethan landed families, had decreased in recent reigns, and the relaxing of the penal laws had made for easier relations between the squires of different faiths.

The Church of England ploughed through its heavy summer. As the memory of the pre-Reformation centuries grew faint, tradition gathered round the Anglican observances which were held to embody the ancestral customs. There was the old peaceful and musty struggle between the parson and the churchwardens. Thus, even the sentences of the Archbishop's High Commission Court serve to bring out those quiet ways of life which bore so little hint of future trouble. A light is thrown upon this scene by the preamble to a sentence in that court in a cause promoted by Peter Woodcock, grazier, against Robert Rudd, clerk, vicar of Liddington-cum-Caldecott in Rutland.[2] It is an example of the type of conflict which could arise in a distant parish where the squire-parson relationship was not yet formed. It was alleged that for some years Mr Rudd had neglected to read divine service in Caldecott, and had also "neglected prayers on divers holidays, especially St Thomas' Day, St Stephen's Day, Innocents' Day and Twelfth Day". The list is interesting, for it would seem to show some popular attachment to the devotional aspect of old Christmas custom.

And then there are set forth the ways in which Mr Rudd "abused the pulpit". "Especially", we read, "about the twentieth of February 1637 he preached at Caldecott that Nebuchadnezzar was a great grazier, and died like an ass, and

---

[1] The practice of purchase for the purpose of resale was now developing. Thus, on 27 October 1632 the manor of Glympton, two miles from Woodstock, was sold by John Cupper to Sir John Sedley, baronet of Aylesford in Kent, for £5,386, including the standing corn. On 17 July 1637 Sedley sold the same property to William Wheate of Coventry for £5,000 and £516 for the farm stock and sundry effects. The yearly revenue of the estate is given as £309 18s. 7d., and there were "two cottages att £3 per annum". The two valuations from manuscripts at Glympton Park are printed in Glympton: The History of an Oxfordshire Manor, ed. by the Rev. Herbert Barnett for the Oxfordshire Records Society (1923), pp. 24-7.

[2] Sentence of the Court of High Commission, dated 2 May 1639 (State Papers, Dom. Charles I, ccccxx, 16).

that divers such graziers did live in these days, whereby, as witnesses conceive, he meant Peter Woodcock, of this parish, who useth grazing. He also preached that whosoever forsook the trade into which he was bound apprentice was absolutely damned, intending thereby, as was conceived, the said Woodcock who from being a butcher lately turned grazier."

This episode raises the question of the distribution of armigerous families in the parish units. Quarrels of such a character were naturally more liable to arise where there was no landowner of position in residence. In such cases there was no one individual whose family formed the apex of the social grouping. The sermon in its social, rather than its doctrinal, implications harks backs to the more rigid gradations of the later Middle Ages, but by the reign of Charles I the agricultural classes passed over easily into many trades, and into certain occupations like that of innholder, which needed no apprenticeship. It is, perhaps, useful here to make some comment on the situation of the yeomen and the extension and meaning of that term. The old-fashioned legal definition of a yeoman as a forty-shilling freeholder gives only a vague impression of the wide agricultural class immediately below the gentry.[1] It was a class including, in addition to freeholders, a proportion of those whose lands were copyhold. Throughout the seventeenth century its numbers diminished through a double process of elimination. For more than a century its prosperous members had felt the lure of an armigerous status and the designation of "gentleman". This last factor also affected those who entered the professional and clerical *milieu* by way of the grammar schools and the universities. On the other hand, the drift to the towns and the development of apprenticeships drew away a much larger number.[2] As Professor Campbell well observes,

[1] The yeoman can be defined as predominantly agricultural, but Professor Campbell has collected evidence in regard to subsidiary trades practised by those so described. Thus, yeomen are found operating grist-mills, water corn-mills and fulling mills, while inns were occasionally leased. In one instance, that of Thomas Ford, yeoman, the *George Inn* at Sherborne was his own property, having been acquired by purchase from a Somerset gentleman (*The English Yeoman*, by Mildred Campbell, Yale Historical Publications, 1947, p. 157).

[2] In this connection the list of apprentices admitted by the Skinners' Company during the first seventeen years of the reign of Charles I is interesting. The sons of yeomen came, for the most part, from the Home Counties: "Thomas Ashe from Weston Turvill in Bedfordshire, Thomas Dymoke from Bekinfield in Buckinghamshire and Thomas Joyner from Milton in Berkshire, Edward Plomer from Ashwell in Hertfordshire and Kellam Fitzhugh from Newhall in Essex." Three came

the son of a yeoman only retained this designation if he succeeded to his father's agricultural interest or during the period of his unemployment. By the mid-seventeenth century many of those of yeoman stock had joined the ranks of the small-town tradesmen.

In this connection some figures for Worcestershire are arresting. "In the Worcestershire quarter sessions papers for 1591-1664", remarks Professor Campbell, "approximately 14000 names with status identification are mentioned in the recognisances alone: of this number there were 1810 yeomen, 1303 husbandmen and 667 labourers."[1] The proportion of yeomen is very high. It seems reasonable to suggest that it was from this source, where initiative was often linked with a little capital, that the burgess stocks in all the country towns in England were replenished. In the South and Midlands the bulk of those who remained upon the land joined the ranks of what in the eighteenth century would become the tenant farmers. In the North of England, where the township development in the pre-industrial age was so much less marked, the status and position of the yeoman as an independent farmer owning his own freehold remained in many districts quite unimpaired. In this connection it would be of interest to study the drift towards a position of tenantship, which was implicit in the growth of such great estates as those of the Lowthers and the Carlisle Howards.

Under another aspect a mark of the yeoman grouping was potential mobility. They can, perhaps, essentially be considered as that rural class which possessed skill, and in many cases initiative and inventive power without the aid of formal education. In certain circumstances the sons of men of yeoman status were sent far afield for their apprenticeships. The yeoman had the initial capital for such a venture, resources which were lacking to the groups of labourers and husbandmen.[2]

At the same time it would be a mistake to attribute too much

from the Midlands: "Jonathan Paley from Newark, Thomas Mackarnes from Northampton and Simon Berry from Whichford in Worcestershire." List printed in *Miscellanea Heraldica et Genalogica*, third series, vol. i, pp. 41-6, 104, 172, 177, 195 and 246.

[1] Campbell, *op. cit.*, p. 27.

[2] Among the apprentices to the Skinners' Company three are described as sons of husbandmen and one as the son of a labourer. John Standish, who was bound apprentice in 1635, was the son of William Standish of the Isle of Man, husbandman. In these cases the influence of the schoolmasters may perhaps be detected.

significance to terms denoting groupings when these were
neither occupational, as in the case of trades or professions,
nor certified by the Heralds' College, as was the case with the
rank of gentleman and esquire. It seems, in general, accurate to
suggest that the progress of purely rural families to armigerous
status was a fairly gradual process. It was a matter of increasing
a holding until its substantial nature justified the change, and
this again occurred more often in the South of England, where
the influence of the very numerous and graded gentry exercised
an especial appeal upon the rural and urban classes placed
below them. In the cases where large properties changed hands
owing to impoverishment, the purchasers were most often the
attorneys in the county towns or merchants seeking to establish
themselves as the possessors of landed estate. These years
before the Civil Wars have a particular interest, since there
were no extraneous political factors to hasten the social changes.

In this time of peace, the trend of changes was hardly per-
ceptible. It was the ending of generations of tranquillity, which
had not been seriously disturbed except in the summer of the
Armada. In this quiet decade the trained bands were not
called out. Order was maintained by the justices and constables.
Husbandmen worked undisturbed in their villages, and the
soldiers of the expedition to the Isle of Rhé were long disbanded.
For these reasons it can be understood that there was no campaign on which the countrymen would engage with more
reluctance than that short and abortive soldiering upon the
Scottish border which came to herald the Civil Wars. A letter
dealing with a country parish suggests an aspect of the life of
the shires which the impressment of soldiers came to harass.

"The honest constable of Burton, George Plowright, who has
done His Majesty so much service gainst the English Puritans
for ship-money," so runs the letter from Dr Robert Sibthorpe,
Rector of Burton Latimer,[1] "has had press-money given him
and must to the Scottish service. . . . Our town is now burthened
more than any other in the country, three soldiers being sent
from us and but two from the next town Thingdon [Finedon],
which is bigger than ours by a fourth part and richer by half,
one from Harrowden Magna and two from Harrowden Parva,
both towns very near as big as ours and richer, none from

[1] Letter from Dr Robert Sibthorpe to Richard Kilvert, dated from Burton
Latimer, 6 April 1639 (*ibid.*) ccccxvii, 47).

Barton Seagrave, a common receptacle of disorderly persons, and at this proportion is all this side of the country carried, only Burton Latimer must be at three and the constable one of them.

Besides the warrant from the high constable came to him third hand and open, so that all idle and young fellows, who most feared or were fittest for the service, had notice beforehand to convey themselves out of the way."

The use of the expression "town" to denote these little villages in Northamptonshire to the south-east of Kettering is very pleasant. The names suggest a way of living which was rooted in custom and quite unperturbed. The constable had brought in two villagers of Burton to go for service with the Army and then found that he was impressed with them. A later document seems to suggest that Mr Plowright suffered at the hands of those who did not like his "honest service".[1]

The tension, more religious than economic in its open expression, is always close beneath the surface in these last years. The term Puritan, intended in an offensive sense, is thus used to mark a form of opposition which was singularly confident and self-assertive. At this time John Bunyan was passing through his boyhood, the son of a tinsmith in Bedfordshire, growing up and learning his father's trade.[2] The towns, particularly the little country towns, would soon attract the countrymen; it was there that a man might find apocalyptic religious thought for his mind to feed upon. The antithesis between the country parts and the small townships should not be overstressed, and the artisans, especially the masons and weavers and smiths of different kinds, had a freedom of interchange between the town and the village unit.

A study of the class of travelling journeymen would prove of interest. They were among the elements which made for strength in the New Model Army, and the confidence which

---

[1] There was also the question of alleged unjust impressment. On 30 June 1627 a petition was delivered at Whitehall by Ferdinando Trigg of Anthony in the county of Cornwall "wherein he showed that he is and hath been a merchant adventurer beyond the seas for thirty or forty yeares past and that he is owner of three of four shipps. That he is rated at five pounds to the subsidie which he hath still paid. That he is a constable and hath been for many yeares. That he is aged sixty yeares and upwards and hath not bin at sea theise twenty yeares and more, and never as captine, master or marriner. Yet nevertheless he is now prest to goe n a small shipp for his Majestie's service" (*Acts of the Privy Council*, 1627, p. 384).

[2] To give the date, John Bunyan was born at Elstow in 1628.

they would display arose as much from a consciousness of their social worth as from their military victory. As a body they had an assurance of the quality of their labour, whether on a farm or in the workshop, and a certain protected status.[1] They were free from the hazards and the insecurity which characterised the situation of the depressed agricultural workers. The men who had been drawn into the new industries were in some ways still more unfortunate, for they were without the support of an integrated social grouping. A quotation from Professor Nef's work bears on this point. He is considering the lot of those who had been brought from the country-side into the now enlarged coal-mining industry.[2] "Every descent", he wrote, "into the mine was hazardous, and many colliers lost their lives either because the rope broke or because the winding machinery got out of the control of the horses or men whose business it was to prevent the rope from unwinding too rapidly from the axle of the drum. . . . Once down the workman was confronted with a series of dangers against which his candles and work tools could not afford him protection. He might be struck down or buried alive by sudden 'thrusts', or falls of earth, which were constantly occurring because of a failure to leave supports for the roof. These accidents were seldom thought worth recording."[3]

In any account of the country life, these men and the agricultural labourers who shared their economic insecurity cannot be forgotten. They were far from a struggle which concerned them but very little. Even their link with the landowners and their agents was quite slender. Far remote from them there went forward the King, the Court, the Universities.

---

[1] It would seem that William Weston, who was carter at Robert Loder's farm at Harwell in Berkshire, would come within this category. "In Anno 1617. Money payd my servants for their wages in Anno Supradicto. Imprimis William Weston my carter, I hired to board wages; & Soe he had in money xjl: & iiijb. of wheat worth xvjs: and iiij wekes borde in ye harvest worth also I judge xvjs: & a hogs keping all the yeare which was worth I judge xiijs.iiijd: & he was not to worke a nightes in the winter which was worth I reckon iiijs" (Robert Loder's *Farm Accounts,* Camden Society (1936), pp. 136-7).

[2] Professor John U. Nef (*op. cit.*, ii, p. 169).

[3] In well-managed collieries, like those of Mr Bradshaigh at Haigh near Wigan, such accidents were usually the result of miscalculation. In 1632 there was a fatal accident in one of the pits at Haigh due to the pillars of coal left to support the roof being wrought too slender. Cf. Haigh Colliery Orders, the Earl of Crawford's MSS.

CHAPTER XIII

THE UNIVERSITIES

IT can be maintained that the name and influence of Archbishop Laud lent an especial character to the University life of the last years before the Civil War. This was, perhaps, in particular the case in regard to Cambridge, where the effect was produced by the Laudian movement in the Church of England rather than by the direct intervention of the prelate himself. In this matter it was not the numbers that adhered to the movement which counted, but rather its impact upon a cloistered academic life which was inevitably so closely linked with a nascent governing class.

The high tables of the University were in some respects more securely anchored in the general ecclesiastical traditions of Europe than is now recognised, or was then admitted. A worldly celibacy fitted easily with one of the moods of the seventeenth century. It was not without its parallel in that carefully arranged and technically monastic life which the Abbé de Rancé was to shatter. The more Erastian elements of the Cambridge scene needed no explanation to those who were familiar with the world in which the *Maximes* of La Rochefoucauld came into being.

The members of the senior common room had now their established order in the framework of the State. It was not only that the high places of the Church of England lay open to those who attained to the government of colleges, it was rather that all except the stricter Puritans saw their status in an ordered society which was envisaged as God-given and recognised by the clergy as peculiarly beneficent. The rich livings and the "golden stalls" of Durham lay before them; the Fellows had only in their middle life to move into their place. The Aristotelian setting of the studies, so long immovable, had given to the tutors an unembarrassed confidence. The status of the clerical don had risen with the buoyant fortunes of the Church. These were the days of Laud and Juxon. There was less division between the standing of master and pupil than was to exist again for many years. It was the great, mellow century for the Universities.

Never before, and not again, were the ancient Universities to be brought so close within the orbit of the Government. The ideas of Laud were found reflected. Both at Oxford and at Cambridge the methods of the dominant faction were acceptable to the bulk of the clerical Fellows. The Primate's scheme of values was designed to provide for the seats of learning with such ample care. It was cogent and all-embracing with the twin vine of Church and Sovereign. The Stuart-Anglican position was sober and majestic and not to be denied; in fact, it was grateful to the academic mind. It was only the destruction of the grand ecclesiasticism of the later Carolines and the rise to power of a philistine oligarchy which was to drive the Universities out into the desert of the eighteenth century. They were to go out in bondage into the land of patronage.

In the reign of Charles I the spirit of the Laudian movement ran through Cambridge. It was pastoral and evangelical. There was the example of the tranquillity of Little Gidding; but before examining these facets in some detail, we might consider the general life of the University, the background against which the play of personalities developed. It is simplest to begin in 1630 with an account of how the plague of that year came to Cambridge. The alehouse keepers and the bookbinders and the college bakers are placed in the setting of this catastrophe, the town and all the colleges are seen as embedded in East Anglia. The description gives an interesting view of social levels, and one can sense the independence of that country-side which would produce the Ironsides. There is something fresh and unexaggerated about all Stuart Cambridge.

Such an occasional outbreak of the plague, described in this instance in the Mead Newsletters, was in fact the chief dislocation in the quiet life of the Universities. "We have had",[1] wrote the Rev. Joseph Mead from Christ's College on 17 April 1630 in a conscientious chronicle of this event, "some seven died; the first, the last week [suspected, but not searched], a boy. On Tuesday a man, one Homes, dwelling in the midst between the two former houses [first affected]. All three stand together at Magdalen College End. It began at the farther

[1] Letter from the Rev. Joseph Mead to Sir Martin Stuteville (*Court and Times of Charles I*, vol. ii, p. 72).

house, Forster's, a shoemaker, supposed by lodging a soldier, who had a sore upon him. The other two houses, the one is a smith, the hithermost, and the middlemost Homes', a tap-house, all [stand] beyond the bridge.

"But the worst of all told me this morning by one of the searchers is, that this last night died a child of Pembroke Hall baker's, next the *Cardinal's Cap*, with all the signs of the plague, both spots and swelling, which discovers the town to be in very great danger. For there died some fortnight since one Disher, a bookbinder, suddenly, and another [one] or two, one being a soldier, whom this Disher, keeping an alehouse, lodged, and was comrade to the soldier that was supposed to have infected the shoemaker's house at St Giles'. Nothing would be confessed till now this happened upon this child, whose mother is that Disher's wife's sister, and was with her both at and since the death of her husband. We hear the plague, by some relation to these houses, is broken out at Histon and Gurton. Besides, that it is begun in Northampton and other places. God have mercy upon us, and deliver us."

A week later the infection was still beyond the bridge and in Trumpington Street, although one victim had died in a lodging at the back of Peterhouse. "In the mean time", Mr Mead continued, "our University is in a manner wholly dissolved, all meetings and exercises ceasing. In many colleges, almost none left. In ours of twenty-seven messes, we have not five; our gates strictly kept; none but Fellows to go forth, or any to be let in without the consent of the major part of our society, of which we have but seven at home at this instant. Only a sizar may go, with his tutor's ticket, upon an errand. Our butcher, baker and chandler, bring their provisions to the college gates, where the steward and cook receive them. We have taken all our officers we need into the college, and none may stir out. If he doth, he is to come in no more. Yea, we have taken three women into our college, and appointed them a chamber to lie in together; two are bedmakers, one a laundress. Thus we live as close prisoners, and I hope without danger."[1]

By the next post Mead could write[2] that "all our parish, all the petticurie, all the market-hill and round about it, are yet

[1] Letter from the Rev. Joseph Mead to Sir Martin Stuteville, dated 24 April 1630 (*ibid.*, vol. ii, pp. 75-6).
[2] Letter from the same to the same (*ibid.*, vol. ii, p. 78).

(God be thanked) absolutely clear and unsuspected". The plague continued through the summer, although by this time the sick were gathered into the pest-houses. The Michaelmas term was well begun before the disease had quite abated. "There died this last week", wrote Mr Mead from Balsham on 20 October, "but three, all in the pest-houses: but a suspicion is of a house in Jesus Lane, where some are said to have died of the purples. This morning one died at a house by the Tolbooth, who had returned from the Green, and was thought to have been clear. All acts and assemblies of the University are adjourned until the 20th of the next month; by which time the sophisters must return to keep their acts, though but privately in their colleges."[1]

There is something singularly unpretending in this account. It would seem accurate to state that Cambridge had a place in the wide structure of East Anglian life that Oxford was never called upon to fill in relation to the southern Midlands. During the reign of Charles I there was already a sense in which Oxford could be described as fashionable. The fact that both Archbishop Laud and Bishop Juxon had held the presidentship of St John's brought their University within the stream of current politics. Laud was active as chancellor throughout his years as Primate. At Cambridge one can detect a workmanlike sobriety.

The men who would fill East Anglian parsonages sat side by side on the benches of the grammar and free schools in Norwich, Yarmouth and Ipswich with those would-be doctors, apothecaries and merchants. It was at the conclusion of these studies that those destined for the learned professions would gravitate towards the East Anglian University.[2] A certain air of purposeful repose lay over Cambridge. It was not that the religious antagonisms were not present; they were in no way muted, but they remained within the limits of the tolerable.[3]

These dissensions had been a long time growing. Thus the Puritans had controlled "the Pure House of Emmanuel" for

---

[1] Letter from the Rev. Joseph Mead to Sir Martin Stuteville, dated 24 April 1630 (ibid., vol. ii, p. 79.)

[2] Cf., for an analysis of this development, The Social Structure in Caroline England, pp. 59-66.

[3] Cf., for the Puritan point of view, a brief reference to opinion at Christ's College in the Life of Master John Shaw, Surtees Society (1877), pp. 125-6, and references to St John's College in the Autobiography of Sir Simonds D'Ewes, vol. i, pp. 109-27.

many years. It is in keeping with this atmosphere that a certain quietness may be observed in the development of Peterhouse as a Laudian centre.

Erastianism here had an effect both on the Puritans and on the Laudians. There was a balanced determination not to cavil at the claims of the avowedly Christian state. An unexpectedly wide degree of contact with literary sources on the Continent tended to breed a certain indifference in disputed matters, which was, however, kept within its bounds by a creed of patriotism that was ultimately Protestant. Henry More, the leader of the Cambridge Platonists, was elected to a fellowship at Christ's College in 1639. The spirit was abroad which would make Cambridge the Latitudinarians' true home.

The question as to the degree of religious indifference among the body of the undergraduates is difficult to resolve. The crypto-Catholics and the children of those of immediate Recusant ancestry were probably very few in number. Certain colleges, St John's and Gonville and Caius for instance, would be favoured only by the more Protestant gentry.[1] An important element in the latter college came up from the school at Norwich kept by the Rev. Matthew Stonham and arrived well-grounded in the Reformation principles. The children of the richer followers of the Flemish church in that city had been educated with them. This was, perhaps, a typical cross-section. It is not hard to detect a clear anti-Roman animus.

Under these circumstances, it is plain that it was the royal preference and example which led to the establishment of a Laudian form of worship in certain colleges. Some chapels adopted a high sacramental practice through the decision of those strong heads of houses in which the University abounded. In this way the ornamenting of Peterhouse Chapel was the work of Dr John Cosin, whose way had been made easier for

[1] This had been a characteristic of Strafford's college. James Oxinden at St John's and Anthony Gawdy at Caius came from Kentish and East Anglian stocks, which were easily exacerbated at the thought of Popery. Cf. *The Oxinden Letters* and Cal. Gawdy MSS., *passim*. The responsibilities of the tutors should not be exaggerated. Cf. a letter dated 6 April 1635 from Henry Fallowfield to Henry Oxinden: "Yow may justly doubt both of my honesty and care, being tutor soe long to your brother and never yett accountable to yow . . . it would much weaken and undervalue his discretion if I should; for the first I am only ingaged to the Coll. for his commons and sizing, of which I show him monthly a bill; for the bed-maker, landresse and the rest of that rable I medle not at all; for the second he is now noe child" (*The Oxinden Letters*, ed. Dorothy Gardiner, pp 103-4).

him by his authoritarian predecessor, Matthew Wren, who was promoted to the See of Hereford and translated successively to Norwich and Ely.

Cosin's portrait in the hall of Gonville and Caius College seems a good likeness. He is shown as a grave, tall, reverend divine in the Elizabethan fashion, his white parted collar turned down over a rochet, with a black and red chimere over it. The face is sober, a little puritanical perhaps beneath the square black cap, the nose long and rather narrow, the brown eyes firm and questioning. In Cosin's case it would seem to have been a love of seemly ordering and due discipline that most prevailed with him. He shared with his archbishop a determination to attain to decent order in matters scholastic and ecclesiastical. A note dealing with the chapel at Christ's College and apparently drawn up by Dr Cosin makes this point clear. "Their service", we read, "reformed of late. Of their organ nothing left but a broken case. Scholars lodge out at the *Brazen George*."[1]

Men of a like mind had been promoted to other college headships—Edward Martin at Queens', Richard Love at Corpus and William Beale at St John's. These changes had all come about within the three years between 1631 and 1634. It was natural that men of a Puritan complexion should be seldom found in the high places of the official world as long as King Charles reigned. Besides, John Preston, the strong Master of Emmanuel whom Buckingham had favoured, had died young. Still, Benjamin Whichcote had lately joined the foundation of the same college. At this time Whichcote was a Sunday afternoon lecturer at Trinity Church, a man "more given to meditation and invention than to reading. What he read most in was the Bible".[2] In such an atmosphere, where opposition was not pushed to extremes, the particular character of Laudian Cambridge came to a full development.

The enemies, of course, seized on externals.[3] "In Peterhouse

---

[1] Notes on a visitation made on 23 September 1636, printed by F. J. Varley, *In Cambridge during the Civil War*, p. 25.

[2] A comment printed by F. J. Powicke, in *The Cambridge Platonists*, p. 7.

[3] Cf. the comment of Sir Simonds D'Ewes: "One Doctor Beale [being made master of St John's College in Cambridge] caused such a general adoration to and towards the altar and sacraments to be practised, that many godly fellows and scholars of the house left their places to avoid the abomination" (*op. cit.*, vol. i, p. 112).

Chapel", wrote William Prynne, "there was a glorious new Altar set up to which the Masters, Fellows and Scholars bowed and were enjoined to bow by Dr Cosins the Master, who set it up: there were Basons, Candlesticks, Tapers standing on it."[1] Exception was also taken to the hanging crucifix.

Viewed from another angle, this chapel denoted the yielding to an æsthetic impulse from "beyond the seas". The arcading of the new chapel, the cherubs over the entrance door, the cornucopia and the weather vane reflected the Court style in a fashion which was not original. Many would describe this as "popish" as a simple term of abuse, but it seems more accurate to suggest that any liking for such work presupposed an awareness of continental values. The Laudians were those who, in architecture, did not react against the Baroque spirit. In this they were at one with all those of the Court who were indifferent in religious matters but appreciated the civilisation and the style of France. By this means the anti-Puritans were linked together; they were charged with a defect in insularity. Now that we are considering the group at Peterhouse, it may be noted how far this defect in insularity led Richard Crashaw. He was to die as a minor canon at Loreto.

In this connection it would be of interest to disentangle the motive of a desire for order from that which would lead men to ornament a church on foreign lines. Laud himself had not the least sympathy with anything continental. Clear-sighted as he was in many ways, his own sharp dislike for Rome may have seemed protection to him. There was, too, in the world of Peterhouse a quality which Laud did not possess—the note of gentleness.

Men of strict opinions, like the young John Hutchinson, still came up to the college. There is an element of quietness and an absence of compulsion. "He was constant", we read of Hutchinson in the well-known *Memoirs*, "at their chapel [at Peterhouse], where he began to take notice of their stretching superstition to idolatry; and was courted much into a more solemn practice of it than he would admit."[2] Reasons may be brought forward to explain this strange amenity. It is, however, worth remembering that while on the æsthetic side there might be continental sympathies, this was hardly true of the religious

[1] *Canterbury's Doom*, p. 73.
[2] *Memoirs of Colonel Hutchinson*, by Lucy Hutchinson, p. 51.

background. In so many cases the men of sacramental outlook could recall their own strict childhood. The Ferrars of Little Gidding are a case in point. In general, the clergy came from those sections of the people who had held to a strong Protestant opinion. Much as the Puritans might abhor a sacramental doctrine, it cannot be said that a necessary cleavage existed between the Laudians and Puritans in matters of private devotion. They could understand one another well enough until politico-religious questions entered in.

Tolerance and comprehension are expressions which it would be anachronistic to apply to the thought of divines at Cambridge in the reign of Charles I. Still, the men who joined the high tables at this time formed the first generation of those on whom the Authorised Version had set its stamp in childhood. There was already present this uniting bond between all Englishmen of the Reformed tradition who belonged to the literate classes. A world of metaphor was common to them.

Linking each group there was a Messianic piety. "After all this, it is no great Thing", declared Chillingworth in his fourth sermon, "if the Lord should require our whole selves, Souls and Bodies, for a whole burnt-offering, a Sacrifice of Praise and Thanksgiving; if He should require from us our whole Substance, whole Rivers of Oil, and all the Cattle feeding on a thousand Hills."[1] Here was the novel stiff scenery of the Old Law, which passed so quickly into English life; none need be excluded from this comity except the Papist.

It may be hazarded that much of the dislike shown by men of the preciser sort for those of Anglican opinions turned on the refusal of the latter positively to outlaw the Church of Rome. The mildness and tranquillity of those who worshipped at Peterhouse would, in themselves, be deemed offensive qualities; it was indifference that proved most suspect. The cleavage was at this point rather political than social. Bastwick and Prynne came from, and remained within, the same social grouping as the clergymen whom they denounced so fiercely.

It was the pull of the Court, the idea of a foreign Queen and the sense that Popery was entrenched in the high circles that served to concentrate the attack. To this was added in certain cases the hard dislike of the embittered for smooth distasteful practices which now led to preferment. Another factor also

[1] Chillingworth, *Works*, p. 49.

THE ABBATE SCAGLIA

From a painting by Vandyck formerly in the collection at
Dorchester House

aroused dislike—the element of privacy. This feeling was particularly widespread, since men of strict opinions favoured a religious approach that was exemplary and public. For this reason the private character of the liturgy, developing from the usages in the chapel of the late Bishop Andrewes' palace, aroused a disproportionate antagonism. It seems reasonable to suppose that it was not so much the moderate, careful ceremonies themselves, the alms basin and the two lighted candles that caused heart-burning. It was rather jealousy that any man could rise in the Church by such soft means.

Behind it all was xenophobia and a sense of imported and continental mystery. There was also present a conviction that men who did not hate the Church of Rome must needs be triflers. Many saw the ancient faith as Burton[1] saw it, "the habiliments of the great whore, and the ensigns of anti-Christ with his church malignant". To such men there were few phenomena more unacceptable than Peterhouse with its eirenic peace.[2]

It is important not to overstress either the Laudian element in the college, or the degree of separation, from the other foundations. At the same time, there is a sense in which Peterhouse in the seventeenth century was still affected by the traditions associated with the long mastership of Andrew Perne, which had lasted for thirty-five years. Dr Perne had been appointed in the reign of Queen Mary, and died in office in 1589. During that period and since, not only Anglicans of many schools but crypto-Catholics, like Henry Walpole and Sir Kenelm Digby, and Puritans of the temper of John Penry and William Brewster of the *Mayflower*, had studied side by side. There was a wide commerce in ideas. And in this connection the Perne Library had an especial significance.

The question of the cultural relationship between England and the countries beyond the Narrow Seas during the early Stuart period has not yet been made the subject of expert study, but there is some reason to suppose that the Anglican divines of the first Caroline Age had a familiarity with continental writings which their successors in the reign of Charles II

---

[1] Henry Burton, *Replie to a Relation*.

[2] This is borne out by a comment in Prynne's *Breviate*, referring to a member of Peterhouse who was imbued with the spirit of that college. "Master Shelford hath of late affirmed in print that the Pope was never yet defined to be the AntiChrist by any Synode" (*op. cit.*, p. 308).

often lacked. In this connection it may be noted that High Church principles, as such, were only attacked with violence in the days of Laud. His second successor, Archbishop Sheldon, was certainly no whit less high and authoritarian. The difference was not so much in the Primates as in their colleagues and supporters, and indeed in the character of the times. It was linked with the fact that the churchmen of the Restoration had proved themselves impervious to Popery. The divines of 1662 were patriotic, satisfied, regalian in a mode which was intrinsically English; they were calm, glorious and self-sufficient. The episcopate, and with them the whole Church order, had entered on its mundane heritage. There was to be no return to the quiet of Peterhouse and Little Gidding. Meanwhile another factor, which in the days of Charles I contributed to the development of cultural contacts, was the importance still attached to Aristotle in the university curriculum. It may be suggested that without the Aristotelian tradition the library which Dr Perne had founded would not have been likely to keep its close links with the Continent. It was the continuing prestige of this school which ensured contact with the commentaries brought forth in Tridentine universities. On the other hand, it is more remarkable that the products of the Douai printing presses, which were studied by the Catholic priests in exile, should likewise have been purchased for Peterhouse. This will be clear from an examination of some gifts made to the library about this time.

Thus Richard Drake, a friend of the house, gave Banes' commentaries on St Thomas.[1] Estius' commentaries formed part of a gift from Dr Rayment.[2] Commoners on going down from Cambridge would follow their tutors' example. Traianus' edition of the *opera omnia* of William of Auvergne was presented to Peterhouse by young Tom Apleton.[3] Catholic commentaries

---

[1] The volumes are described as follows: *Scholastica Commentaria* on *S. Thomas Aq. usque ad lxiiii Quæstionum* and a continuation from *Quæstio lxv usque ad cxix et ultimum Scholastica Commentaria in secundam secundæ, Decisiones de Jure et Justitia*. The first three books were printed at Douai in 1614 and 1615. Their author is termed *Dominicus Banes Mondragonensis, Ordinis Prædicatorum Theologiæ Salmaticæ Primam Cathedram Regens*. They are inscribed *ex dono Domini Domini Ricardi Draki, Socii Aulæ Pembroki*.

[2] This commentary on the *Sententia* and on the *Summa Theologica* by Chancelor of Douai was printed in two volumes in that town in 1626, and presented to Peterhouse in the same year by Dr Thomas Rayment, a senior Fellow.

[3] They are inscribed *ex dono clarissimi iuvenis Thomas Apleton huius Collegii quandam alumni*.

on the Scriptures were much in use. Dr Rayment gave a whole set of Cornelius a Lapide.[1] Dr Catcher gave a copy of Baronius' *Annales Ecclesiastici*. A modern edition of Guicciardini's *History* was a gift from Algernon Peyton,[2] whose father gave the organ for the new chapel.

Books of a similar character were in private possession. Thus Joseph Beaumont, who was one of the first two chapel clerks under the new dispensation, had a copy of a recent Dominican commentary on Aristotle.[3] One gift to the library is perhaps especially significant. In 1637 John Taylor, who does not appear to have been a member of the college, gave a modern edition of the *Missale Romanum*.[4] The library was particularly rich in histories and chronicles. Some medical books had come from Mrs Gulston,[5] whose husband had been long at work upon an edition of Galen. Books of Protestant continental *provenance* are rare. Simon Simoni's commentary presents a Genevan approach to Aristotle. One volume of Isaac Casaubon's *Animadversiones* was given in 1636; the works of Melanchthon had been in the library from its beginning. This analysis will give some impression of a line of interests which could be pursued at Peterhouse at the time when Richard Crashaw, then a Bachelor of Arts at Pembroke College, was elected to a Fellowship.

His period at Peterhouse exactly covers the brief years of Laudian control. He was twenty-two at his election; he was ejected in 1644 at the age of thirty-one. He died in Italy just five years later. Coming from the centre of the clerical middle class and strongly Puritan in his upbringing, Crashaw responded quickly to this life with the contact with the Latin world that it opened for him. On one side he was influenced, but perhaps transiently, by Little Gidding. His connection with Nicholas

[1] These books were clearly collected from different sources and purchased as they appeared. The commentary on the Pentateuch was printed at Antwerp in 1616, those on the four major prophets and on Jeremias and Baruch at Paris in 1621, and the commentary on St Paul's Epistles at Antwerp in 1622. All were presented to Peterhouse Library in 1626.

[2] This was the Venetian edition of 1599, but the accession date is not given. Peyton became a Fellow Commoner in 1637.

[3] This commentary by Didacus Maius Valentinus, O.P., was printed in 1618. Joseph Beaumont was Master of Peterhouse from 1663 until 1699 and a protégé of Bishop Matthew Wren, whose stepdaughter he married.

[4] The Missal was a Plantin edition, printed at Antwerp in 1654.

[5] For details of the Gulston Bequest, which was of a varied character, cf. *The Social Structure of Caroline England*, p. 85.

Ferrar was of some standing,[1] and Ferrar Collet came up to Peterhouse *sub titulo Dmni. Crashaw* in March 1636. In the society of this small college we can trace some of Crashaw's pupils and certain of his friendships. Samuel Booth came up in the same month as Collet, but to the inferior grade of sizar;[2] George Calveley had arrived a few months previously. In 1638 John Belasyse, a North-country Catholic of position, later the Royalist Lord Belasyse of Worlaby,[3] was received at Peterhouse with that distinction which his father's rank exacted. A deep security marked that whole world. Meanwhile Crashaw's ideas were in evolution. He was moving away from the mood in which he had written his series of verses on "Gunpowder Treason".

It is necessary to avoid exaggeration in the matter of the influence of Crashaw and his contemporaries. The Civil War broke on them when they were still immature.[4] The main factor was the character of the heads of colleges, Dr Cosin and his companions. Peterhouse was united by close ties with other colleges, and perhaps especially with Caius, where the Master had once been an undergraduate. At Caius there was at this time a junior Fellow exactly Crashaw's age, Jeremy Taylor. He was a local boy, the son of a Cambridge barber, at school for ten years under Mr Liveridge. He had first joined Caius

---

[1] Richard Crashaw was the only child of the Rev. William Crashaw, who held the living of St Mary, Whitechapel, from 1618 until his death in 1626. His sermon before the Lord Governor of Virginia and the rest of the Adventurers in that Plantation was preached on 21 February 1609. The Ferrars were closely associated with church life in the city of London and with the Virginia Company. "The Bishop of Lincoln ... having for many years known Nicholas Ferrar & his Brother, in the publick affairs of Virginia Plantation" (*A Life of Nicholas Ferrar*, by John Ferrar, ed. Bernard Blackstone, p. 68). Mr. Ferrar, sen., by his will gave £300 towards erecting a School or College in Virginia for the better education of such Infidel children as should be there converted to the Christian Religion (*ibid.*, p. 22).

[2] The contrast is seen between the entries. On 1 March 1636 Samuel Booth *admissus est sizator sub Domino Crashaw*. On 16 March 1636 Ferrar Collet *admissus est sub titulo Domini Crashaw*.

[3] He was the second son of the first Viscount Fauconberg, and his arrival is noted in these terms—*annos natus septemdecim admissus est pensionarius ad primam mensam scholarium sub tutela Mgri. Beaumont*. It is worth noting that Thomas Crashawe was witness to the will made by Lord Fauconberg's father, Sir Henry Belasyse, of Newborough, on 25 February 1622 (Cal. Wombwell MSS., p. 111).

[4] The Civil War broke out in 1642. To take the members of the senior common rooms—John Cleveland of St John's was the same age as Crashaw and born in 1613; Henry More of Christ's was born in 1614; Abraham Cowley who was born in 1618 and Andrew Marvell who was born in 1621 were both scholars of Trinity.

as a sizar to his surety. Here the new Primate had noticed him,
and in 1635 he had transferred to All Souls. Crashaw was at
that time curate of Little St Mary's.[1] Jeremy Taylor was thus
a link between the members of the young Anglican generations
in the two universities.

In Oxford, of course, the effect of Dr Laud's influence was
outwardly more considerable. A singularly perfect impression
of the state of the college buildings will serve to emphasise this
point. The description occurs in one of Garrard's letters to
Lord Conway in which he deals with the visit of the King and
Queen to the University during August 1636. "The churches
or chappells", he wrote,[2] "of all the colledges are much beauti-
fyed, extraordinary cost bestowed on them; most of them newe
glazed, richer glasse for figures and painting I have not seen,
which they had most from beiond the Seas; excellently paved
thyre quires with black and whyte stone; where the East end
admitts not glasse, excellent pictures, large and greate worke
of the best hands they cold get from the other side, of the
Birth, Passion, Resurrection & Ascension of our blessed Saviour.
All theyre Communion Tables [are] fayrely covered with rich
carpetts, hung some of them with specyall good hangings. I am
sure Merton Colledge is soe, and rayld about with costly rayles.
But that chappell of Lincoln Colledge, built by the present
Bishop of Lincolne now under a cloude, deserves a particular
commendation, which is raised with cedar; the Communion
Table, pulpitt, and an excellent fayre skreene all of cedar.
which gives such an odoriferous smell, that holy water in the
Romish Church doth not exceed yt."

"I went", continues Garrard in a description of St John's,
"to view his [Grace of Canterbury's] new Quadrangle, built
wholly by himselfe, a noble building, for soe Sir Tobye Mathewe
and Mr Gage wold stile yt, which is caryed up with pillars of
a fine marble on two sides, a grayish culler interlaced with
vaynes of blewe, founde out nere Woodstocke, by the Lord

---

[1] There seem to be little data as to the contacts of Crashaw with his contemporaries. With Cowley there was some acquaintance. In regard to his later life,
it is not clear when Crashaw first met his patroness, Susan, Countess of Denbigh.
It was certainly when she was still an Anglican. Her husband and eldest son had
been up at Emmanuel, which perhaps accounts for the Puritan preferences of the
second Earl of Denbigh.

[2] Letter dated from Hatfield, 4 September 1636, preserved in State Papers,
Dom., and printed in *Oxoniensia*, 1937.

Treasurer [Juxon] when he hunted in those parts; in the two gate houses whereof stands one against the other, the figures of the King and Queene in brasse."

The interest in certain forms of architectural detail and the resolute concentration upon symbolism are reflected very clearly. George Garrard was himself a clergyman, and this is sufficient to account for the emphasis placed upon the seemliness of the church order. It is now worth considering some papers which give a view of the life of Fellows and undergraduates as distinct from the mannered Caroline setting. A series of documents, wholly official in their character, deals with Merton College during these years. They give an account of a visitation made by order of the Chancellor and provide a glimpse of the house customs. The matter is introduced in a letter [1] written by Dr Richard Baylie, then Vice-Chancellor, to the Archbishop of Canterbury to explain how he and his fellow commissioners had sat in the hall at Merton "taking examinations and answers by candle till eight o'clock at night".

The subjects of complaint [2] both throw light upon the ordinary college life and at the same time indicate the nature of the old tight discipline that was expected. It was alleged that diet was not kept in the college hall and that certain lectures were not read. Money for the college library was not collected. It was asserted that twenty copies of Chrysostom's works, given to the college, were still retained in the Warden's hands. It was in accordance with the spirit of the time that ceremonial religious observances should receive their meed of comment. Attention was directed to the fact that the liturgy had been curtailed.[3] The reading of the Bible was neglected at meals in hall and the custom of speaking Latin had fallen into disuse.

Returning to more secular complaints, it was asserted that postmasters went in need of chambers, while the rooms required were given to battellers and clerks. It was remarked with disapproval that the college was served wholly with double beer. Undergraduates were accused of lying out of college. These charges in turn led to accusations made against the Fellows. "The greatest corruption of our discipline", con-

---

[1] State Papers, Dom. Charles I, ccclxxxvii, 8.

[2] Cf. paper dated 1 April 1638 (ibid., ccclxxxvii, 7).

[3] It was stated that the *Te Deum, Benedictus* and *Magnificat* were omitted as well as the *Gloria Patri* at the conclusion of the psalm. The undergraduates did not bow with due reverence when coming in and going out of chapel.

fessed the Warden, Sir Nathaniel Brent, "proceeds from two or three of our masters who have lately frequented the company of bachelors and scholars, making them their bedfellows in their chambers and in the town in inns and alehouses".[1] He then went on to provide examples. "Within these last few days a master and a bachelor, Fellows of the College, were by the Pro-Proctor taken together in a drinking school on a Sunday morning in sermon-time, and some young women have lately been begotten with child, where two of our masters frequently resort and sometimes lodge." These details certainly fit into place in the accustomed picture of the loyal city.

In another set of charges two or three members of the high table of Merton were accused of receiving bribes at the admission of postmasters, and the Sub-Warden was said to have sold college woods near Maidstone to a friend for £200 less than their market value. This last item suggests those local contacts, the closed scholarships and the county connections which were so marked a feature of Oxford life throughout the seventeenth and eighteenth centuries.[2]

In this connection it may be suggested that the action of regional opinion on university ideas has not yet been examined, but it would be a mistake to allow the view of Oxford under Charles I to be dominated by the picture of the Royalist high tables of 1644. It is true that the clergy of the Established Church and the undergraduates of Cavalier opinions were principally in evidence during these years. At the same time behind the façade of Oxford life, with its markedly Royalist implications, there was at least in certain colleges the constant pull of what, for want of a better term, may be described as the Parliamentarian counties.[3]

---

[1] Letter dated 6 August 1638 (ibid., ccxcviii, 18). Sir Nathaniel Brent was a layman and commissary of the diocese of Canterbury and Vicar-General in the time of Archbishop Abbot, whose niece he had married. He was an opponent of and a witness against Dr Laud. Later he was a Presbyterian supporter of the Parliament.

[2] James Oxinden, when already a scholar of St John's College, Cambridge, was one of the nine candidates for a closed Kentish scholarship to Corpus Christi College, Oxford, in June 1631 (The Oxinden Letters 1607-1642, ed. Dorothy Gardiner, pp. 65-74).

[3] This position is manifest in the case of Magdalen Hall and New Inn Hall. At the time of the Visitation after the King's defeat, all the fifty-five members of Magdalen Hall and all the forty members of New Inn Hall acknowledged the authority of the Parliament (The Register of the Visiters of the University of Oxford from 1647 to 1658, Camden Society, 1881, ed. Montagu Burrows, pp. 564-70).

Within the college the status of the butler, cook and porter was clearly recognised.[1] Their position was in some respects analogous to that of the battellers who acted as servitors to their tutors' wealthier pupils.[2] It is perhaps permissible to trace a relatively egalitarian spirit which would vanish with succeeding generations. The high tables were recruited to a considerable extent from the ranks of the sizars and battellers, while on the other hand the tutors had to struggle against the parsimonious outlook of some wealthy parents.[3] There was a curiously old-fashioned air about some of the colleges, for the Laudian emphasis was superficial. The effect of the rich London burgess stocks had long been noticeable in the promotions to the episcopate, but at Oxford it was the yeoman stocks, often from some particular county, which tended to dominate the high tables of this period.[4] As far as Fellowships were concerned, the sons of country gentry of property were, perhaps, most strongly entrenched at All Souls,[5] and also in consequence of

---

[1] The reports of the Visitation throw some light on the political outlook of the long-term college servants. Thus, William Harding, cook at Exeter College, declared that the power of the Visitation was a matter too high for him (*ibid.*, p. 152). Nicholas Jay, basket-bearer, and John Brown, cook to the students at Christ Church, stated that they would do their service (*ibid.*, p. 155). Richard Pepper, under-butler of New College, stated that he could not submit without perjury, as did William Clunn, one of the college clerks (*ibid.*, p. 156). The college staff of Corpus agreed to answer that they would acknowledge Dr Staunton as President put in by the authority of both Houses of Parliament, but cannot acknowledge him as President according to the Statutes of the College since they are altogether ignorant of them. The cook and under-cook, butler, manciple-porter and groom of Corpus Christi College subscribed this form of statement (*ibid.*, pp. 147-9). The cook and under-cook of New College and the cook of St John's agreed to another and similar wording (*ibid.*, p. 157). These cases give an interesting impression of scrupulous Royalism.

[2] Cf. "History of Brasenose College, 1603-1660," by G. H. Wakeling in *Brasenose Quatercentenary Monographs*, vol. ii, pt. xi, p. 17.

[3] Cf. undated letter written between 1608-12 by Richard Taylor, of Brasenose, tutor to Francis, elder son of Sir Peter Legh: "I am sorye", he explained to Sir Peter, "I should be inforced so often to mediate in a matter wherein I do so little prevaile. Your sonne Mr Francis (height: 6 ft, 2 inches) must needs have a gowne, a civill hood, a cappe and a habit, a suite of apparell, and divers other things which he wants, or els he will not be thought fitt by many, to become a suiter for a fellow-shippe in All Soules" (*ibid.*, vol. ii, pt. xi, p. 15).

[4] Thus the Visitation list for Queen's College, in so far as it relates to those who joined the foundation not later than 1643, gives the names of twelve Fellows all of whom came up from Westmorland and Cumberland. Eleven are described as the sons of *plebei* and in the twelfth case a question mark is added to the entry. The only sons of *generosi* in the list are commoners (*Register of the Visitors*, pp. 542-5).

[5] At All Souls, out of a total of thirty-one Fellows listed, one (Henry Coventry) is entered as the son of a peer; eight, including Thomas Culpepper, Thomas Gorges,

the successive masterships of Sir Eubule Thelwall and Francis Mansell at the Welsh college, Jesus.[1] Although there was always a certain measure of support for Puritan opinions in the University, the main impression conveyed is that of a deep-rooted conviviality. A phrase from one of the Primate's letters bears immediately upon this point. "And farther," wrote Dr Laud to the Vice-Chancellor, "I would have you speak with the Principal of Brazen-nose, that he would command their Cellar to be better looked to, that no strong and unruly argument be drawn from that Topick-place."[2] It seems that the country values, the prejudices and the heavy drinking of the shires were reflected in an Oxford which Dr Laud could not amend.[3]

The Elizabethan influence which had come down unmodified by any changes was very strong in both the universities. It appears to be reasonable to suggest that the Puritan ways of thought, which had been so strong in the colleges in the old Queen's time, had greatly weakened. The Elizabethan character that is visible behind the superficial emphasis which Charles I

Nathaniel Napier and George Stradling, as sons of knights; six as the sons of *armigeri* and six as the sons of *generosi*. Two are described as sons of *clerici*, one of a doctor and two of *plebei*. The parentage of four Fellows, including that of Gilbert Sheldon and Oliver Lloyd, is not given. Only Thomas Prestwich came from the North of England. Four came from Wales and five from Middlesex, four from Oxfordshire and Berkshire. With the exception of Culpepper, they had all been elected to Fellowships between 1611 and 1643. Dr Martin Ayleworth, the eldest, had been born in 1591-2, and Francis Talbot, the youngest, in 1623-4. None of the Fellows of All Souls are entered as founder's kin, but this note is appended in the case of five Fellows of New College (*ibid.*, pp. 473-5 and 527-31).

[1] Sir Eubule Thelwall, Master from 1621 until 1630, and Dr Mansell, Master from 1630 until 1648, were linked respectively with the rich squires in Flintshire and Carmarthen. Sir Leoline Jenkins entered Jesus College in 1641. His *Life of Francis Mansell*, printed in 1854, and Dr William Wynne's *Life of Sir Leoline Jenkins*, contain information which underlines the strong Royalism of Jesus. There are very few contemporary biographies dealing with the heads of Oxford and Cambridge colleges at this period.

[2] Letter printed in *History of Brasenose*, by G. H. Wakeling, p. 29.

[3] The colleges in which the local affiliations of the senior common room are set down most completely are Exeter and Corpus. They provide an interesting contrast. Corpus had three Fellows each from Somerset, Gloucestershire, Bedfordshire and Lincolnshire, two each from Devon, Hampshire and Lincolnshire, and one each from Surrey, Kent, Sussex, Wiltshire and Durham. In Exeter, out of a total of twenty Fellows, fourteen came from Devon and four from Cornwall. These West Country affiliations were shared with Wadham. Four Fellows came from Somerset and four from Dorset, including Lionel Pine and Tristram Sugge from Yeovil, and Thomas Manning and Nicholas Strangways from Abbotsbury (*Register of the Visitors*, pp. 494-6, 499-501 and 559-61).

had imposed was the secular variant of that great age, robust and confident and authoritarian.[1]

The same impression is conveyed by the interesting details in the Crosfield Diary. The journal is rather sketchy, but in some respects it gives a unique view of life in the university. Thus an entry made by the Rev. Thomas Crosfield in December 1633 includes a note of "some books I see in Mr Langbaine's chamber".[2] Both men were Fellows of Queen's College. The fourteen titles would seem to represent a haphazard collection and private taste. They show a familiarity with French, and include the Le Maçon translation of the *Decameron*, the *Œuvres de Rabelais* and Commines' *Memoirs*. These indicate a spirit which must issue in Royalism, and in fact Dr Langbaine would be known for his attachment to his sovereign.[3]

It is a difficulty in assessing the influence exerted by the universities that nearly all the vocal opinion emanated from groups within the Anglican clerical body. There is criticism, especially of Cambridge, from the Puritan side, but it is rare to find the voice of the Royalist layman.[4] There appears to be a contrast between the influence of the university leaders over the members of the senior common rooms and the small effect produced on their pupils except those who proposed to take holy orders.[5] An undergraduate mass is traditionally impervious.

[1] Details relating to Brasenose in 1635 confirm this impression of an old-fashioned regimen. A catalogue for the college library had been transcribed in that year at a cost of 10s. The Bible Clerk was the custodian of the chapel books, and Roger Porter's receipt for 1632 describes these volumes as consisting of a Bible, book of martyres and "three old Latin bookes". The most recent common prayer book was purchased in 1627. There was a carpet for the communion table and three copes. An entry for Christmas 1635 reads, "hollye and ivy for the Chappell 10/-" (*History of Brasenose*, pp. 21-2).

[2] *The Diary of Thomas Crosfield*, ed. F. S. Boas, p. 68.

[3] The succession to the provostship of Queen's provides an interesting view of an academic family. Gerard Langbaine, who became provost in 1646, was born at Barton in Westmorland in 1609, and educated at a free school at Blencow in Cumberland. He entered Queen's as a batteller in 1625. He married Elizabeth Potter, *née* Sonnibanke, who had been the young wife of his predecessor as provost. Christopher Potter was a pluralist of the Laudian political alliance, who held the provostship from 1626 until 1646, together with the deanery of Worcester and other preferment. He in turn was the nephew of Barnaby Potter, who was provost from 1616 until promotion to the See of Carlisle in 1626. Bishop Potter belonged to the Puritan academic tradition in its Elizabethan form, and survived until 1642.

[4] Cf. Sir Simonds D'Ewes and Colonel Hutchinson.

[5] A considerable undergraduate section was composed of those sons of the lesser gentry who intended to study law or to obtain some post in London. An example of modest expenses at Oxford is provided in the letters of John Willoughby, son of

In this connection it is worth turning attention to the studies. For many undergraduates these were as ever unexacting. It is perhaps appropriate to consider the influence of Henry Peacham's *Compleat Gentleman*. It may be held that this well-known book is chiefly valuable as conveying an incidental record of the educational customs of the age.

In spirit it is wholly Jacobean. The late President of Magdalen, in an introduction to a reprint of the edition of 1634, states that "the double motive of the Cavalier and the Schoolmaster is evident in the opening chapters"; but, in fact, Peacham is very far removed from the freshness and simplicity of the Caroline approach or from the forthrightness of the Royalists. Importance should be attached to the fact that it was not difficult reading. It was a book whose chapter headings so many young men skimmed. Perhaps within its pages can be found the residue of knowledge of the unlearned. It does not seem to have become widely known until the middle period of King Charles' reign.[1] The very dullness of Henry Peacham only serves to make his book more representative.

"Imitate Tully", we read, "for his phrase and stile."[2] "After Cicero", the advice goes on, "I bring you Cæsar, whom Tully himselfe confesseth of all Orators to have spoken the most eloquent and purest Latin. To read him as you ought you must bring with you an able judgment, beside your Dictionary: by reason of the diversity of countries, tracts, people: then strange names and formes of warlike Engines and weapons then in use: sundry formes of fortifications, waterworkes, and the like, which notwithstanding since, have beene made known and familiar unto us, by the painefull labours of those all-searching wits, Lipsius, Ramus, Giovanni de Ramellis, and others." Here the Elizabethan pomp is seen reflected.

Yet from other sections one obtains a view of those solidified judgments in which the seventeenth century was so rich. It is the spirit of Bacon easing down towards the Hanoverians.

John Willoughby (1571-1658), of Peyhembury, near Honiton, who was an undergraduate at Wadham in December 1630. His brother-in-law, Bampfield, had given him £8 for the current quarter. "5s. I was enjoined to bestow in apples and sugar for my admittance to the fires, which has always been a custom in the house." He asked his father to meet a mercer's bill for £1 11s. 5d. (*Trevelyan Papers*, pt. iii, Camden Society (1872), p. 178).

[1] Peacham had been tutor to Lord Arundel's sons in 1613-14. Editions had been brought out in 1622, 1626 and 1627, besides the enlarged edition of 1634.

[2] *Compleat Gentleman*, ed. G. S. Gordon, p. 45.

"Now offereth himself Cornelius Tacitus, the Prince of Historians. The next Titus Livius, whom like a milky Fountaine you shall everywhere find flowing with such an elegant sweetnesse, such banquet-like varietie." "Be you acquainted", the exhortation runs, "with Quintus Curtius . . . after him followeth Salust. For morality and rules of well living entertain Plutarch. After him the vertuous and divine Seneca."[1] One can see already the busts and the gentlemen's libraries.

By contrast a certain lightness of touch is apparent in the author's discourse on poetry and music. After references to "our phœnix Sir Philip Sidney" and to "our phœnix Mr William Byrd", there comes this note: "Nor must I forget our rare countryman Peter Philips, organist to their Altezzas at Bruxels, now one of the greatest Masters of Musicke in Europe. He hath sent us over many excellent Songs, as well Motets as Madrigals: he affecteth altogether the Italian Veine".

There is also some practical advice. "To avoyde", explains Peacham, "the inconveniences of moethes and moldinesse let your study be placed and your windows open, if it may be, towards the East." It is pointed out that with a south or west aspect the air is subject to moisture "whereby your maps and pictures will quickly become pale, loosing their life and colours, or rotting upon their cloath, or paper". As these passages indicate, science as understood by men of leisure was still bound up with the military art; it was in middle life that men came to such concerns as they pored over the great books which set out the plans of model fortresses with each nice implication of mathematics.

At Oxford further studies were certainly sketched out. Medicine is in a class apart. There was, perhaps, more planning than achievement. The Botanical Garden had been laid down in these years, and the Savilian chair of geometry and astronomy had been founded.[2] The mathematical library was well

---

[1] *Compleat Gentleman* ed. G. S. Gordon p. 49.

[2] The Oxford Physic Garden was founded in 1621 and the stone gateway was erected in 1632. John Tradescant formed the physic garden at South Lambeth about 1630, and at his death in 1637 left his cabinet of rarities to his son, from whom it passed to the Ashmolean. The Tradescants introduced lilac and acacia into England. As a comparison, it may be noted that Le Nôtre was born in 1613 and completed Vaux-le-Vicomte for Fouquet in 1657.

An early instance of the transfer of gardeners, conceived perhaps as architects, from one great employer to another is seen in the following comment on John Tradescant: "that painfull industrious searcher and lover of all natures varieties

housed, and fine astronomical instruments, which still survive, were acquired in 1636. Sir William Sedley's legacy for the establishment of a lecture in natural philosophy had been received in 1621, and in the last years of the reign of James I a lectureship in astronomy had been annexed to the professorship of physics. Provision had been made for the body of an executed person to be prepared and dissected by a "skilfull chirurgeon". For the purposes of the University it was convenient that the body should be delivered immediately after the Lent Assizes.

It was a prosaic development and not a rapid one. Copernicus was the only text-book prescribed for those who followed the Savilian professor's courses which was not derived from the classical astronomy. The old courses familiar in Elizabethan times went forward and men received[1] or neglected[2] them. This Oxford era singularly lacks the charm of the corresponding Cambridge decade. Little as the undergraduates may have cared, it was a time of husbandry under the stern Chancellor.

... sometime belonging to the right honourable Lord Robert Earle of Salisbury, Lord Treasurer of England in his time, and then unto the right honourable the Lord Wotton at Canterbury in Kent, and lastly unto the last Duke of Buckingham" (*Paradisus Terrestris*, by John Parkinson (1629), p. 152).

[1] For an example of a late comer to university studies, cf. the case of Elias Ashmole, who was born in 1617, the son of a saddler in Lichfield, and entered Brasenose College in 1644 to study physics and mathematics there. He was then with the Royalist forces at Oxford.

[2] For the expenses of Ralph Verney at Magdalen Hall in 1631, cf. *Verney Memoirs*, vol. i, p. 119.

CHAPTER XIV

FALKLAND AND CHILLINGWORTH

IT is necessary in any discussion of the Caroline Age to consider the over-written episode of Lord Falkland's influence. Various circumstances have contributed to the significance which now for some eighty years has been attributed to his life, work and character. In the first place, he was eulogised by Clarendon in terms which chimed in well with the habit of nineteenth-century thought. His character was gentle, and gentleness was considered an attractive quality when found in a man of birth and feeling. Moreover, his outlook was based upon those ethical conservative conceptions of the privileged English life which, in the event, proved so enduring. He displayed a combination of propriety and sentiment which made a deep appeal to the Victorians. In this connection a comment by Dr S. R. Gardiner is most revealing. "Falkland", he wrote, "was unable to conceive that anything could be true which was not pure and of good report."[1] At the same time, his reputation was bound to gain in all those circles where Latitudinarian views were popular because of his close links with Chillingworth.

In his own day he possessed certain advantages. In particular, he had a form of attachment to the Church of England which bore a marked resemblance to the King's. It was an adherence at once quiet and unshakable. Falkland apparently did not possess Charles I's preoccupation with the devotional elements in his faith; but both men had a desire to prevent the spread of Catholicism in their own families. A certain stubborn resoluteness united them on this one point. Both were affectionate towards the wife and mother whose religious wishes they opposed so consistently and with such an absence of all bitterness. One is struck by the singularly positive approach which Falkland and his sovereign brought to their consideration of the Church of England and its structure and all its facets. Both sensitive and hasty, it was there they placed their peace.

Lucius Cary, second Viscount Falkland, had come as a young

[1] S. R. Gardiner, *History*, vol. viii, p. 257.

man into his great estates. The title had been purchased by his father, an angry, unsuccessful Lord-Deputy of Ireland, but the landed property and the rents came from his maternal grandfather, Sir Laurence Tanfield, chief baron of the Exchequer, who had amassed a heavy legal fortune. Through his father's side, Falkland was a cousin of the Suffolk Howards, and his kinsmen, the Hunsdon Careys, had an unimportant court-led phalanx in the upper house—Lords Dover and Monmouth and their heirs Rochford and Leppington. The University of Oxford, such men as Dr Sheldon of All Souls, came very willingly to Falkland's house at Great Tew, where that hospitality was maintained which Clarendon was to celebrate. Yet for all his serious effort to play his part in the debate, the host's rôle was surely that of the young, the noble patron.

His childhood had been unhappy. It was, perhaps, this that gave him another affinity with his royal master. His father had little feeling for his eldest son, and quarrelled with him bitterly over his marriage. The first Lord Falkland was a disappointed man in his last years, and died in 1633 from an accident in falling from a stand when shooting with the King at Theobalds. His broken leg was cut off by the King's surgeon, but not before gangrene had set in. He died unreconciled with Lucius Cary.

Lady Falkland, who had become a Catholic in 1624, had been deserted by her husband. Except for her eldest daughter, Lady Home, and her son Lucius, then aged fourteen, all the children, five more daughters and two sons, were brought up as Catholics by their mother, who was constantly threatened, embarrassed and in penury. She was protected by Lady Carlisle, aided by Lady Banbury, dunned by her creditors and every day in trouble.[1] A letter to Lord Conway shows the relations between Falkland's parents. "For she [my wife]", wrote the Lord-Deputy, "being replete with serpentine subtelty and that conjoined with Romish hypocrisy, what semblance can she not put on, and what oblique ways will she not walk in hardly discoverable."[2] This is an *ex parte* statement. She was

[1] Cf. petition of Margaret Williams to the Council, dated 1631. The petitioner stated that about six years since she kept the *Maidenhead* inn in St Giles in the Fields and there entertained many of the horses of Lady Falkland, then inhabiting Drury House. The charges amounted to £13, whereof she had been paid £5 (State Papers, Dom. Charles I, ccv, 44).

[2] Letter in Cal. State Papers, Ireland, dated 5 July 1627.

harassed, "very low and for a long time very fat".[1] It is agreed that her wit was lively, her learning on the massive side, her will determined.

It is clear how Lucius Falkland, a little lacking in vitality, would seek for peace. He can be imagined sitting in the high chairs in the parlour at Great Tew or pacing through the groves in that damp Oxfordshire valley. He was determined not to be driven by court-ambitions or by Roman zeal. With his choice companions he would put forth all his talent, playing with the adumbrations of some philosophic problem, seeking and finding an Anglican tranquillity.

It was under such circumstances that Falkland, small, unimpressive, and in some ways unprepossessing, set out to create the first conscious oasis of learning since the break-up of the circle of Sir Thomas More. He had exorcised, as the privileged eighteenth century was also to exorcise, the Elizabethan love of action.

The passages from Clarendon dealing with the circle at Great Tew are over-familiar, but there are one or two aspects which are worth stressing. "Truly", we read in the *History of the Rebellion*, "his whole conversation was one continued *convivium philosophicum* or *convivium theologicum* enlivened and refreshed with all the facetiousness of wit, and good humour, and pleasantness of discourse, which made the gravity of the argument itself [whatever it was] delectable. His house where he usually resided . . . looked like the University itself by the company that was always found there. There were Dr Sheldon, Dr Morley, Dr Hammond, Dr Earles, Mr Chillingworth, and indeed all men of eminent parts and faculties in Oxford, beside those who resorted thither from London; who all found their lodgings as ready as in the colleges." Here is an impression of that collegiate life which was under different aspects to continue through the Restoration-Hanoverian world, past Barchester to the All Souls common room; a first stirring of those secular amenities which have meant so much in the development of the English politically controlling class. It was the great Anglican churchmen entering into their spacious heritage.

If one side of the life of the *convivia* looked towards the world of patrons, another was turned towards those colleges which

---

[1] *The Lady Falkland, her Life*, p. 86.

were to be at once so independent and restrained, both opulent and celibate. The strata jostle one another, and one comes past the arranged Chesterfieldian atmosphere to the conception of a college immune from patronage. "Many come thither", the account goes on, "to study in a better air, finding all the books they could desire in his [Lord Falkland's] library, and all the persons together whose company they could wish."

One sentence here should give us pause: "finding all the books they could desire". It would be unwise to look too narrowly at Clarendon's sweeping antitheses or to try to pin down his clear self-righteous and nostalgic memory. At the same time this is, perhaps, the place to consider the actual content of such a library, and the amount of information that these gatherings presupposed.

The classical equipment, borne less self-consciously than in the previous century, has been examined in the last chapter. Theology had been affected by the changed controversial fashions. There were still the massed quotations, but the argument now rose and sank as heavy as an Atlantic swell, the run of the water slow and expected, monotonous and soporific. The lengthy paragraphs from Fr Knott in the *Religion of Protestants* (a work written at Great Tew) are given detailed copious rebuttal. There are no longer the bitter quips, like steep cross-waves, of the controversy of the Tudor period. The long rollers break on what George Herbert called "the American strand".

A passage from Fr Edward Knott's *Mercy and Truth, or Charity maintained by Catholiques*, which was printed in 1634, and four years later was incorporated and refuted by Chillingworth, will serve to indicate the form of thought and expression which was the background from which Great Tew made its own specific contribution. "Our joy", so runs the long, encumbered sentence, "riseth not from their trouble or grief, but as that of the apostles did from the fountain of Charity, *because they are contristated to repentance*, that so, after impartial examination, they, finding themselves to be what they say, may, by God's holy Grace, begin to dislike what themselves are. For our part, we must remember that our obligation is, to keep within the mean, betwixt uncharitable bitterness and pernicious flattery, not yielding to worldly respects, nor offending Christian Modesty, but uttering the Substance of Truth in so *Charitable* a manner, that not so much we, as Truth and Charity, may seem to speak."[1]

If this was the foundation from which the ordinary workman of controversy approached his subject, it is of interest to consider the contribution of St Francis of Sales, whose *Treatise on the Love of God* had only recently appeared in English. Among those moving in the circle of Great Tew were Sir Kenelm Digby and Wat Montagu, who had both Parisian and Catholic interests. Ætherealised and remote as was the whole Salesian tradition, there is some reason to suppose that Chillingworth was familiar with St Francis' writings, of which there appears a distant echo not in the *Religion of Protestants* but in the *Sermons*.

The point at which the work of St Francis of Sales impinged upon the English seventeenth-century divines and on the writers of the Anglican tradition has not hitherto been determined with any accuracy; but it is clearly relevant to this discussion. After the warmth and daring of the Italians, and after the piled verbal conceits, we come to this work of the Bishop of Geneva, which has in its style the character of delicate and moulded furniture, the perfection of cloisonnerie.

The first English edition of the *Treatise on the Love of God* was printed at Douai in 1630,[2] from the translation of Miles Car, priest of the English College there, and based upon the eighteenth French edition. A passage from the preface will convey accurately the nature of the approach. "The stage", wrote St Francis in reference to the Duke of Savoy's re-establishment of Catholicism in the Chablais, "was small, but the action great. And as that ancient craftsman was never so much esteemed for his great pieces as he was admired for making a ship of ivory fitted with all its gear, in so tiny a volume that the wings of a bee covered all, so I esteem more that which this great Prince did at that time in this small corner of his dominions than many more brilliant actions which others extol to the heavens."[3]

With these examples there would go a bestiary in no way mediæval, but suited to the great Tridentine pulpits of the late French Renaissance with their canopies and the florid oak and the beadwork and the vine leaves. It was an influence at once

---

[1] Quoted in the *Religion of Protestants*, chap. vi, p. 231.

[2] It is worth noting that this was the year of Chillingworth's stay at Douai.

[3] Preface, p. 12. These quotations are taken from Dom Benedict Mackey's translation.

gentle and hierarchic. "Even as harts," explained the Bishop in the later portions of his first book, "upon whom princes have had collars put with their arms, though afterwards they cause them to be let loose and run at liberty in the forest, do not fail to be recognised by any one who meets them not only as having been once taken by the prince whose arms they bear, but also as being still reserved for him. And in this way was known the extreme old age of a hart which, according to some historians, was taken three hundred years after the death of Cæsar; because there was found on him a collar with Cæsar's device upon it, and these words: *Cæsar let me go.*"[1]

St Francis' sentences were all placed within the convention of the conference chair, and it was now for the first time that this *pulpitum* had come to England. As the Bishop sat at his clean parchment one can imagine him entrusting his thought to a setting which he had made deliberately fragile. "Wine, Theotimus," he has written in a famous passage, "is the milk of grapes, and milk is the wine of the breasts, and the sacred spouse says that her well-beloved is to her a cluster of grapes, but of Cyprian grapes, that is of an excellent odour."[2]

Then he would parallel the Cyprian grapes by the gentle care with which he posed his *flora*. "Meditation", explains St Francis, "reminds of one who smells a pink, a rose, rosemary, thyme, jessamine, orange-flower, separately one after the other; but contemplation is like to one smelling the perfumed water distilled from all those flowers."[3] Soon, he would settle again to such analogy. "All yellow flowers," we read, "and especially that which the Greeks call *Heliotropium*, and we sunflower, not only receive gladness and pleasure from his [the sun's] presence, but by an affectionate turning movement follow the attractions of his rays, keeping him in sight, and turning themselves towards him, from his rising to his setting."[4]

The courtesy of the whole approach suggested that the reader was assumed to be of generous standing. The mannered examples fell lightly from his pen, touched with the sweetness of that honey of Narbonne of which he wrote. It is the same with every subject, as witness the Bishop's words upon detachment and the states of prayer. "It is", he sets out with that careful etching, "God that they love; not only above all things,

[1] *Treatise of the Love of God*, bk. i, chap. xviii.   [2] *Ibid.*, bk. v, chap. ii.
[3] *Ibid.*, bk. vi, chap. v.   [4] *Ibid.*, bk. xi. chap. iii.

but even in all things, and all things in God, resembling the phœnix when perfectly renewed in youth and strength, which is never seen but in the air, or upon the tops of mountains that are in high air."[1] Thus we are led on to the commentary on cicalas and master-nightingales, and to the vermilion of the pomegranate as a symbol of holy charity.

One final passage is of a considerable significance. "Pearls", wrote St Francis,[2] "in sooth (as we have said often enough) are nothing but drops of dew, which the freshness of night rains, over the face of the sea, receive into the shells of oysters or pearl-mothers. Open thy heart towards me as the pearl-mothers open their shells towards the sky."

The date when St Francis of Sales' writings first came before the Anglican divines would be of interest. There appears little evidence to show that they were known in the Ferrar household, and there is hardly a sufficient margin of time to have allowed the *Treatise* to reach Bemerton before George Herbert died. A translation of the *Introduction to the Devout Life* had been issued at Rouen in 1613, but there does not seem much reason to suppose that this had penetrated into England. Until the Restoration period, with its feeling for the French approach, the idiom of both works and especially that of the *Treatise of the Love of God* must have appeared too novel.

The Salesian spirit, with its conscious classicism and its careful fragrance, was in marked contrast to the solid built-up writing of Laud and Cosin, which was aimed at the convinced and sober churchmen. Yet in the Anglican strata it was, perhaps, in the circle of Great Tew that the Bishop of Geneva's work was most likely to receive, not acceptance certainly but recognition.

A Savoyard of noble birth, St Francis was without that nationalistic feeling which came to reinforce the breastwork of the Anglicans. On the other hand, the whole *corpus* of Salesian writings was characterised by an assurance, supranational in its quality, which was the accompaniment of the Bishop's trained simplicity. The mundane triumph of the Tridentine world was present in their quiet overtones. It is worth recalling that St Francis' deliberate metaphor was intended to appeal both to the ladies of the Catholic tradition and also to the religious man of sensibility. He existed within a temperate zone, and it

---

[1] *Treatise of the Love of God*, bk. x, chap. v.   [2] *Ibid.*, bk. v, chap. v.

was this fact which brought a certain link with Falkland and
with Chillingworth.

If we prescind from the dogmatic basis, a possible line of
descent becomes apparent. Thus a passage in the *Introduction to
the Devout Life* has in its mannered perfection a certain foretaste
of Chillingworth's marked quietness. A quotation of some
length is needed to illustrate the parallel. "When charity
requires it', we read, "we must freely and gently impart to
our neighbour not only what is necessary for his instruction, but
also what is useful for his consolation; for humility, which
hides and covers virtues in order to preserve them, causes them
nevertheless to appear at charity's command, in order to
develop, increase and perfect them. Wherein it resembles that
tree in the island of Tylus, which at night shuts up its beautiful
red flowers and keeps them closed and only opens them again
at sunrise, so that the inhabitants of the country say that these
flowers sleep at night. For so humility covers and hides all our
virtues and human perfections, and never allows them to
appear except for the sake of charity, which, being a virtue
not human but celestial, not natural but supernatural, is the
true sun of the virtues."[1] In his second sermon Chillingworth
has these sentences which in their nature-metaphor may reflect
his stay at Douai. "Now", we find him writing, "how well does
this express the nature of charity? For what else is love but a
sweet breathing of the Holy Spirit upon our passions, whereby
the Holy Ghost does, as it did in the beginning of Genesis,
incubare aquis, move by a cherishing, quieting virtue upon the
sea of passions."[2]

This is seemingly found again in the eighth sermon, in which
Chillingworth refers to "those twinkling, cloudy Stars of Jewish
Ordinances, and that once glorious, but eclipsed Light, the
Law of Works".[3] The parallel recurs more strikingly in the
sermon which he preached, towards the end of his short life,
before the King. "These heat-drops," we read in a metaphor
which is so close to St Francis, "this morning dew of sorrow,
though it presently vanish and they return to their sin again
upon the next temptation."[4] There is here, as in so much of

[1] *Introduction to the Devout Life*, pt. iii, chap. v
[2] "Second Sermon", printed in Chillingworth's *Works*, ed. 1663, p. 21.
[3] "Eighth Sermon", printed in Chillingworth's *Works*, p. 93.
[4] "First Sermon", *ibid.*, p. 9.

Chillingworth's writing, a quality which was cool and rational, and would in time link Great Tew with the school of Locke.

Chillingworth's temperament was as attuned to the universities as was the general circumstance of his life. It was later generations that would value his quiet implicit scepticism as to the authenticity of human institutions. He was attached to the existing order and was in a sense a martyr to it. Yet his hesitations fell like gentle rain. Like all Latitudinarians, he was an opponent of top-hamper. He had no real feeling for the towering scaffolding in Church and State. For these reasons, he was a tranquilly dissolvent element. His style at its best was pure and bare, and his thought was welcome to the eighteenth century. He was thus to survive the pulpits and the moulded oaken columns and all the stone work of Gilbert Sheldon. The later Tudor period had known the flamboyant scepticism of the Renaissance, but in England William Chillingworth was, perhaps, the first to manifest a very peaceful scepticism devoid of all pretension.

Three final quotations will serve to indicate the quality of his thought. "Ninthly", he wrote in his "Letter relating to the Infallibility of the Roman Church," "Remember the Roman Church claims no notes of the Church, but what agrees with the Grecian too (as Antiquity, Succession, Miracles, etc.), but only Communion with the Pope and Splendor; both of which made for the Arians in Liberius his time."[1] Here one comes past the wrist-turn of controversy to an appeal, unusual in that day, to the merits of antique simplicity.

"*Hoc Ithacus velit et magno mercentur Atridae*", Chillingworth again begins, the easy-driven Latin tag suggesting the ripened eighteenth century. "They will never be unfurnished of matter to write books to the World's End, if this shall be the method of stating controversies. Oh what an impregnable cause should we have against the Church of Rome if we ourselves did not help to weaken and betray it."[2] And then a passage brings to mind the quiet, low-toned decorum of the tradition that was ushered in by Tillotson at Lambeth. "It may be", he wrote in the sixth sermon, "God has suffered the antient, superstitious, histrionical Adorning of his Temples to be converted into the late slovenly Prophaneness (commonly called Worshipping in Spirit, but intended to be Worship without Cost) that you may

[1] Chillingworth's *Works*, p. 177   [2] "Seventh Sermon", *ibid.*, p. 83.

find a happy occasion to restore those sacred Places, dedicated
to his Honour, to that Majesty and Reverence, as may become
Houses wherein God delights that his Name should dwell."[1]
When read carefully, this is revealing. It has that reverence
which is native to the mind of the Church of England, and it
will serve to explain how the Latitudinarians could not, even
if they would, exclude the Deists. It is not difficult to understand how Laud was hesitant in regard to Chillingworth, and
how the Puritans were unrelenting.

It is on this quiet and academic figure that the significance of
Great Tew turns, though Falkland was destined to go out to
play a part in politics. For Sheldon or for Hammond this house
was as other houses, to which they came in their dignity, which
was at once abiding and prelatical; for Chillingworth it proved
a harbour. One final quotation will indicate a most attractive
element in his thought. "Suppose", he declared in his third
sermon, "our garments should be presented to God with the
same question that Jacob's sons sent their brother Joseph, 'Is
this thy son's coat?' Would they not rather be taken for the
skins of Savage Beasts, so unlike are they to that garment of
Humility and Patience, which our Saviour wore, and which he
bequeathed us in his Legacy?"[2] Chillingworth in his simplicity
was very far both from the Court and from the Civil Wars.

[1] "Sixth Sermon", Chillingworth's *Works*, p. 77.   [2] *Ibid.*, p. 38.

CHAPTER XV

THE SCIENTISTS

AGAINST this background there was set, in science as in other matters, that wide encyclopædic approach which Falkland's generation still appreciated. The Elizabethan taste for the universal, a taste somewhat refined by Francis Bacon, was present in them. The pursuit of general learning could still be followed in compendia. The mastery of a Body of Knowledge seemed attainable; it was only with the Restoration that science would begin to be atomised and dissected in the experiments of the Royal Society. Now, in the sixteen-thirties, Falkland and his companions would turn to study the works of Robert Fludd, Censor of the College of Physicians and doctor of medicine of Christ Church, whose titles clearly indicate the scope and nature of his erudition—*Utriusque Cosmi Maioris scilicet et Minoris Metaphysica, Physica atque technica Historia.*

The reader is led by slow degrees right through those fields of knowledge which could give such satisfaction to the exact minds of the Post-Renaissance. The seventeenth-century mind was not yet tired of those concepts of universal history to which Sir Walter Raleigh's age had been addicted. *De Macrocosmi Principiis* begins Dr Fludd's great treatise. A map of the original chaos is appended. The titles of the chapters give a cool and precise confidence. *De musica mundana* they would come to as the second section, and then *de creaturis cœli empyrei* and *cœli ætherei*. From *cœli elementaris* the author turned to *Arithmetica* with its sub-headings *arithmetica geometrica, arithmetica militari, arithmetica musiaca* ; here come the detailed plans and branching categories, *arithmetica pythagorica* and *arithmetica memoriali*.

The element of mathematics, set out in a form very easily apprehended, naturally dominates the military section. The mind is led on to this after a consideration of music by the treatment of such matters as *de praxi geometrica, de optica scientia, de radiis directis* and *de usu geometrica in arte pictoria*. The lessons are imparted through simple geographical examples, each strengthened by a thick plain woodcut. The chapters *de munimentis & propugnaculis* begin with the three perfect fortresses *Tridentum*; *Orivetum Thusciæ*, with an illustration of Orvieto; and Aden, described as *emporium Arabiæ Fœlicis in summis verticibus scopulorum eminentes.*

An examination is then conducted into the simply planned type of fortress with six bastions. In each case the natural strength of the position, the cliffs and rivers, and the marshy soil, is first examined. There are pictures of the new citadel at Amiens, and of the walls of Gravelines, and of the star-shaped fortress of Castel Sant' Elmo. The more complex examples are set out. A map shows the chain across the waterway which divides the works at Pischiera on Lake Garda—*Habet septem, ne fallor, bastiones.* A most elaborate plan of Milan carries with it this annotation—"*Mediolanum, Lumbardiæ metropolis, potentia & dignitate eximia, munitur propugnaculo 9; bastionibus & semibastionibus 7*".

As a further elaboration, the nine bastions of Gorkum are described, while another map sets out to show the tree-lined walls of Lucca with unequal bastions, and yet another the city of Brescia in the pride of her four rows of fortifications. There is a strange drawing of *Radiocofani castellum seu munimentum in territorio Sienæ*, and then we come to the plan of the ideal fortress. This is provided with a six-sided outer wall with projecting works at each apex; then a complete inner moat with another six-sided wall and an inner citadel of the same shape. There are six drawbridges, and the outer works are in their turn surrounded by water.

It was from such drawings and their meagre texts that the squires of both sides learned the art of war. Falkland was to die in the fight at Newbury, and this knowledge was a gentleman's equipment which must normally be presupposed whether or not he went on to discuss philosophical or literary speculations. An understanding of the principles of modern war, as exemplified by Spinola's sieges, was the birthright alike of the Court and of the country party.

Experimental science was closely associated with military developments in this period, as the career of Sir Kenelm Digby shows. In Dr Fludd's treatise the reader moves from a discussion of siege warfare, past a *schema* of the Italian and Spanish orders of battle, to the ground-plan of inventions. Among the constructions of battering rams, cannon measured for the angle of elevation, chain-shot of different kinds, and *variæ globulorum tormentariorum effigies*, there are other less-expected subjects. After the account of an invention for listening with greater accuracy for subterranean tunnelling, there is a really interesting illustration. It is described as a method to enable a man to cross a river unseen. The soldier is depicted wearing a sealed helmet with a flexible tubing, the mouthpiece of which, opening from a float, is thus above the water-level. He has a stick to help him in walking along the river-bed.

This has something of the inventiveness and the lightness and the lack of technical experience of that questing age. It is in contrast to the disquisition on the *Artis Magnæ Artilleriæ*, with the great munition carts and horse-drawn cannon. Yet it leads on directly to accounts of the construction of clocks and combinations of levers and pulleys. There is the engine used at the metal works at Markirch, and a high-built curious affair with twisted pipes for pumping running water. Each gentleman of philosophic tastes could study to reinforce his knowledge of the mechanical laws. He would probe at these mysteries as he sat at his great folio. Before him on the page there lay the view of Helvetius' machine to procure perpetual motion. It would be known in the circles interested in such matters that this subject of the quintessence of motion had engaged the attention of Lord Herbert, whose ingenious artisan, Caspar Kaltoff, had been employed for some years in carrying out his master's plans for constructing such a machine as would ensure motion perpetually and usefully.

There are several angles from which this question of the scientific equipment of the men of the seventeenth century can be studied. For the most part, it was the fruit of military interests. It was the possession of gentlemen who had examined works dealing with the art of war, like Captain A. Ramelli's writings or Cyprian Lucar's *Lucar solace*. For certain spirits an attention to the minor engineering feats of water-works led on to the making of mechanical contrivances designed to play at masques and festivals. Falkland's concern was on a different level. At Great Tew it was not the scientific phenomena which aroused interest but rather the laws which ruled their transformations. The point is worth a brief examination.

It was an axiom held in that circle that mysteries were providentially reduced to ordered reason. In time man would pierce through to every secret, including that of alchemy. The laws of mechanics, when fully apprehended, would serve to form a basis for a general discussion of ideas.

In this connection, too, much attention should not be concentrated on the details of the actual working plan which lay so well upon the heavy page. Such designs for seventeenth-century "engines" as were set before the men of quality of Lord Falkland's time were not scale drawings, but rather illustrations of the assured principles which bound the elemental forces. The mechanical expressions had in the terminology of that age a wide extension. Thus reference is found to "engines of sympathy and antipathy", and much of the research seems to be guided by primitive views of magnetic effluvia.

The crude question, so often asked in the nineteenth century, as to whether the machines could work does not appear to have posed itself in that form to the Stuart mind. Thus, in the *Century of Inventions*, which was written in 1655 and published in 1663,[1] the "devices" apparently could all be operated, but that was hardly the intention of some of the elucidations of general principles which depended upon the harnessing of elements. After all these plans, those in Dr Fludd's treatise for instance, would be found printed in the same volume as a map of the original chaos. The scientific knowledge of that time was drawn from deep, and sometimes unexpected, wells, and was seldom without its philosophic bearing; but it was not precise, nor were its approaches technical.

This last quality is especially notable in the case of the scientific and quasi-scientific writings of the clergy. At the same time, it was in these less technical forms that knowledge was absorbed most easily. All books then required their own pretensions; but those treatises exercised the greatest influence which, beyond the brave façade of erudition, were diffuse and inexact, and readily assimilable. As an illustration of this type of work, it is worth examining the earlier publications of Dr Wilkins, the author of the well-known *Mathematical Magic*.

John Wilkins had not the temper of mind associated with the

[1] The author of the *Century of Inventions*, Edward Lord Herbert, who succeeded in 1646 as Marquess of Worcester, was born in 1601 and died in 1667. Caspar Kaltoff had entered his employment as early as 1629. A consideration of Lord Worcester's published work really belongs to the era of the foundation of the Royal Society.

Caroline approach, neither was he in strong opposition to it.[1] Chaplain to the Prince Palatine Charles Louis, Warden of Wadham under the Parliament, Master of Trinity under the Commonwealth, Bishop of Chester in King Charles II's reign, he had the pliant wisdom and the sympathies, curious and wide and markedly unethical, which were to be found in a type of churchman in that cool and later day. The best, if somewhat hostile, impression of his attitude is that which Anthony à Wood has left us. "He was", that great repository of Oxford lore insisted, "a person endowed with rare gifts; he was a noted theologist and preacher, a curious critic in several matters, an excellent mathematician and experimentist, and one as well seen in mechanisms and new philosophy as any man of his time. He also highly advanced the study and perfection of astronomy both at Oxford and London; and I cannot say that there was anything deficient in him, but a constant mind and settled principles." He was certainly very far from the high, gnarled Regalian conceptions of the author of *Athenæ Oxonienses*.

Dr Wilkins' more serious work did not begin to appear until 1648, but occasional writings often throw more light on the state of knowledge of a generation than do those books which are the fruit of hard study and prolonged gestation. Certainly the small volumes on the *Discovery of a New World*, the *Discourse concerning a new Planet* and *Mercury or the Secret Messenger* seem to reflect the last years of tranquillity, and the diverse and easy learning which their young author had mastered while he studied at Magdalen Hall or tutored in the University. The first two books were published anonymously, in 1638 and 1640 respectively, and the third under Mr Wilkins' name and style as chaplain to the Electoral Prince in 1641. The *Discovery of a New World*, a somewhat diffident treatise on the moon, which resumed in a haphazard way the work of previous seleno-graphers, ran through three editions within two years of publication. The references to the subject in the Old Testament are annotated copiously, and for all its simplicity (perhaps on account of it) this exercise well reflects the current knowledge.

One passage throws a pleasant light upon the country

---

[1] "Mr Francis Potter knew him [Bishop Wilkins] very well, and was wont to say that he was a very ingeniose man, and had a very mechanicall head. He was much for trying of experiments, and his head ran much upon the perpetuall motion" (Aubrey, *op. cit.*, ed. Powell, p. 308).

gentleman's geography. A rather long quotation is required to give the impression of the outlook. "From whence it must necessarily follow", writes Mr Wilkins, "that there may be some mountains in the Moon so high that they are able to cast a shadow an hundred miles off. . . . You must consider that the height of the mountains is but very little if you compare them to the length of their shadows. Sir Walter Rawleigh observes that the Mount Athos, now called Lacas, casts its shadow above thirty-seven miles. Nay Solinus affirms that this mountain gives his shadow quite over the sea from Macedon to the Isle of Lemnos, which is eighty-four miles, and yet according to the common reckoning doth scarce reach four miles upwards in its perpendicular height."[1]

As the disquisition winds forward, the map of the continents unfolds before us with all its predetermined and imprecise geography. "I affirm", continues Mr Wilkins, "that there are very high mountains in the Moon. 'Tis the common opinion and found true enough by observation that Olympus, Atlas, Taurus and Emus with many others are much above this height (a mile perpendicular). Teneriffa in the Canary Islands is commonly related to be above eight miles perpendicular, and about this height (say some) is the Mount Perjacaca in America. Sir Walter Rawleigh seems to think that the highest of these is near thirty miles upright."[2]

The author then goes forward, carefully quoting his authorities, with speculation as to the existence of life on the moon. "Wherefore", he concludes, "notwithstanding this doubt [as to the too great heat] that place may remain habitable. And this was the opinion of the Cardinal de Cusa. When speaking of this planet he says, *Hic locus Mundi est habitatio hominum & animalium atque vegetabilium.* 'This part of the World is inhabited by Men and Beasts and Plants.' To him assented Campanella."[3]

Upon this there breaks the idea of invention. For the edition of 1640 contains an appendix entitled: "The Moon, a discourse on the possibility of a passage thither". "I do seriously and upon good grounds", declares Mr Wilkins, "affirm it possible to make a Flying Chariot; in which a man may sit, and give such a motion unto it as shall convey him through the Air. And this perhaps might be made large enough to carry divers men at the same time, together with food for their *Viaticum*, and

[1] *Discovery of a New World*, 1684 ed., p. 87. [2] *Ibid.*, p. 88. [3] *Ibid.*, p. 127

commodities for Traffick. It is not the bigness of anything in
this kind that can hinder its motion, if the motive Faculty be
answerable thereunto. This Engine may be contrived from the
same principles by which Architas made a wooden Dove and
Regiomontanus a wooden Eagle."[1]

The names of Copernicus, Kepler and Galileo are furnished
forth. In his *Discourse concerning a new Planet*, Mr Wilkins argues
that the sun and not the earth is the centre of the universe. His
book *Mercury*, on the other hand, deals with ciphers, and is in
some ways highly technical. It gains in seriousness because it is
linked with the art of war. Even here, we find the massed
quotations from earlier writers. "That which is written", we
read in an inquiry into sympathetic inks, "with the water of
putrified willow, or the distilled juice of glow-worms, will not
be visible but in the dark as Porta affirms from his own
experience."[2]

These books that we have been considering, and especially
the first two, were easily compiled, but they were read. They
had those attributes which a man of leisure would require who
was minded to pass a curious hour. Certainly they required but
little concentration, and their acute hypotheses excited interest.
The gentlemen would scan them lazily and seek out beneath
the verbiage the idea of the flying chariot, just as in a later
work they would follow this same author in his speculations
concerning a universal character that may be legible to men of
every nation.

It was still the custom to refer to all the commentators on
Pliny's *Natural History*. These years before the Civil Wars
witnessed, in fact, the last expression of that easily constructed
erudition which jostled each recondite quotation as evidence of
the truth of scientific theories. Already the fashion had set in
for simpler and more austere approaches. Thus, the two sections
into which Dr Wilkins' chief work is subdivided are described as
Archimedes or Mechanical Powers and Dædalus or Mechanical
Motions.

To the ordinary reader there was much in *Mathematical Magic*
which would prove convincing. Already there was stirring a
tendency to disentangle the element of fact and to cut loose

---

[1] *Discovery of a New World*, 1684 ed., p. 159.
[2] "Mercury or the Secret Messenger", Bishop Wilkins' *Works*, ed. 1802, vol. ii,
p. 21.

from the clouding word play. Van Helmont had completed his life's work, and the age of the "great experimentists" was at hand. Men were to move rapidly away from the Baconian conceptions, and from the whole ground plan of the *Novum Organum* by which Lord Verulam had sought "to bring in estimation Philosophy or Universality name and thing". They could no more survive the coming of the Civil Wars than could the wide and genial and antique notions of Sir Walter Raleigh.

While emphasis shifted, the scientific background was seen in an advanced circle like Great Tew as primarily a question of mathematics. Work done already lent a foretaste of that verified accumulated data which would give to the Hanoverian world their unimpassioned certitudes. The elements of unimpeachable factual knowledge were gradually established; the circulation of the blood set forth by Harvey in 1628, Boyle's Law in 1662 and then in 1687 Isaac Newton's *Principia*. It was inevitable that the men of this new phase should welcome Chillingworth's hesitation about the thirty-nine articles and his decision to interpret them in the widest sense. His aversion to the Schoolmen made his work acceptable to those who felt the full effect of the Cartesian temper.

The influences from France and Italy were by no means confined to, nor indeed for the most part centred upon, the universities. Men of learning coming to England, and English travellers abroad would alike add to the store of curious and polite knowledge. The experimenters among the upper classes became well-known upon the Continent: Sir Kenelm Digby attracted quasi-scientific data like a magnet. In his autobiography, Lord Herbert of Cherbury sets out his view upon the desirability of obtaining an understanding of medicine, "It will", he wrote, "become a gentleman to have some knowledge in medicine, especially the diagnostic part. . . . Besides, I would have a gentleman know how to make . . . medicines himself, and afterwards prepare them with his own hands; it being the manner of apothecaries so frequently to put in the succedanea, that no man is sure to find with them medicines made with the true drugs which ought to enter into the composition when it is exotic or rare."[1] The idea of the acquisition of unusual and useful skills seems to belong naturally to this period. It is a part of Lord Verulam's heritage. "In the mean-

[1] *The Autobiography of Edward, Lord Herbert of Cherbury*, ed. Sidney Lee, p. 28.

while", goes on Lord Herbert, "I conceive it is a fine study, and worthy a gentleman to be a good botanic, that so he may know the nature of all herbs and plants, being our fellow-creatures, and made for the use of man."[1]

A rather similar outlook, directed however to mathematical studies, is found reflected in Aubrey's[2] note on Sir Charles Cavendish, who was the younger brother of Lord Newcastle. "He was a little, weake, crooked man, and nature having not adapted him for the court nor campe, he betook himself to the study of the mathematiques, wherin he became a great master. His father left him a good estate, the revenue whereof he expended on bookes and on learned men. He had collected in Italie, France, & with no small chardge, as many manuscript mathmaticall bookes as filled a hoggeshead." This interest was shared by William Gascoigne,[3] who served in Newcastle's army and was killed in the wars. "I remember", Aubrey continues,[4] "Sir Jonas told us that a Jesuite (I think 'twas Grenbergerus of the Roman College) found out a way of flying, and that he made a youth performe it. Mr Gascoigne taught an Irish boy the way, and he flew over a river in Lancashire (or therabout) but when he was up in the ayre, the people gave a shoute, wherat the boy being frighted, he fell downe on the other side of the river, and broke his legges. This was *anno* 1635."[5] From many quarters the frame of mind was being built up which would in time produce the Royal Society.

In a world remote from the universities, there existed the private teacher and those who came to him for knowledge. It seems reasonable to consider him as the ancestor of the eighteenth-century mathematician or scientist or antiquary. A teacher of this type was often, but not invariably, in holy orders. Such a clergyman, giving much time to his particular studies, was seldom in the line of controversy or preferment. In the years after the Restoration men of this character were sometimes sought out and offered promotion or a livelihood by

[1] *The Autobiography of Edward, Lord Herbert of Cherbury*, ed. Sidney Lee p. 31.

[2] John Aubrey, *Brief Lives*, ed. by Anthony Powell, p. 138.

[3] Aubrey has this note: "Mr Edmund Flamsted, who sayes he [Gascoinge] found out the way of improveing telescopes before Des Cartes" (*ibid.*, p. 138).

[4] *Ibid.*, p. 148. The Sir Jonas referred to was Sir Jonas Moore.

[5] Although the date of the experiment is given as 1635, it is also stated by Aubrey that William Gascoigne "bred up by the Jesuites . . . was killed at the battaile of Marston-mooore, about the age of 24 or 25 at most [1644]" (*ibid.*, p. 138).

some lay patron. They would thus enter into that network of patronage which the great families extended unceasingly. Before the Civil Wars, however, this was infrequent. In the case of the Rev. William Oughtred, who was rector of Albury in Surrey throughout this period, the Earl of Arundel appears in some sense as a protector. It is worth noting down the facts which Aubrey has preserved for us.

"Mr William Oughtred, B.D.,"[1] he begins, "was born at Eaton in Buckinghamshire, near Windsor, *Anno Domini* 1574, March 5th. His father taught him to write at Eaton, and was a scrivener;[2] and understood common arithmetique, and 'twas no small helpe and furtherance to his son to be instructed in it when a schoole-boy. . . . He was chosen to be one of the King's scholars at Eaton Colledge. He went to King's Colledge, in Cambridge. *Anno ætatis* 23, he writt there his *Horologiographia Geometrica*, as appeares by the title. He was instituted and inducted into the rectory or parsonage of Albury, *in com.* Surrey, lett for a hundred pounds *per annum*: he was pastor of this place fifty yeares."

There then follows a description of his day. "His oldest son Benjamin . . . told me that his father did use to lye a bed till eleaven or twelve a clock, with his doublet on, ever since he can remember. Studyed late at night; went not to bed till 11 a clock; had his tinder box by him; and on the top of his bed-staffe, he had his inke-horne fix't. He slept but little. Sometimes he went not to bed in two or three nights, and would not come downe to meales till he had found out the *quæsitum*. He was more famous abroad for his learning, and more esteemed, than at home. Severall great mathematicians came over into England on purpose to converse with him."[3]

Seth Ward lived for half a year with him at Albury, and Sir Charles Scarborough and Sir Jonas More both studied under him. Mr Oughtred was hospitable and there is a note of his appearance. "He . . . dressed himselfe, thus, an old red russet cloath-cassock that had been black in dayes of yore, girt with an old leather girdle, an old fashion russet hatt, that had been

[1] *Brief Lives*, p. 139.
[2] Aubrey has two notes on this subject. "Mr Sloper tells me that his [Mr Oughtred's] father was butler at Eaton Colledge: he remembers him, a very old man. Mr John Sloper . . . tells me that Mr Oughtred's father was the pantler of Eaton College" (*ibid.*, pp. 139 and 145).
[3] *Ibid.*, p. 140.

a bever, *tempore Reginæ Elizabethæ.*"[1] There are further details of his studious inquiries. "Ben Oughtred told me", explains Aubrey, "that he had heard his father say to Mr Allen [the famous mathematical instrument-maker] in his shop, that he had found out the Longitude; *sed vix credo.* . . . He was a great lover of chymistry, which he studyed before his son Ben can remember, and continued it; and told John Evelyn of Detford, esq. R.S.S., not above a yeare before he dyed, that if he were but five yeares (or three yeares) younger, he doubted not to find out the philosopher's stone. He used to talke much of the mayden-earth for the philosopher's stone. It was made of the harshest cleare water that he could gett, which he lett stand to putrify, and evaporated by cimmering."[2] It is interesting to examine this careful phrasing. "He was", it is explained, "a good Latinist and Græcian, as appears in a little treatise of his against one Delamaine, a joyner, who was so sawcy to write against him (I thinke about his circles of proportion)."[3] In a sense it was a life of unrequited labour. "Before he dyed", wrote Aubrey of Mr Oughtred, "he burned a world of papers, and sayd that the world was not worthy of them: he was so superb. He burned also severall printed bookes, and would not stirre, till they were consumed."[4]

A final reference deals with Thomas Hobbes' attitude to Oughtred. "I have heard Mr Hobbes say, and very truly, that with all his great skill in Algebra, he did never adde one proposition to Geometrie: he could bind up a bundle well."[5] A comment on Hobbes' attitude to these studies may be added here. "I have", wrote Aubrey, "heard Sir Jonas Moore say that 'twas a great pity he had not began the study of the mathematics sooner, for such a working head would have made great advancement in it. So had he donne, he would not have layn so open to his learned mathematicall antagonists. But one may say of him, as one sayes of Jos. Scaliger, that where he erres, he erres so ingeniously, that one had rather err with him then hitt the mark with Clavius. I have heard Mr Hobbes say that he was wont to draw lines on his thigh and on the sheetes, abed, and also multiply and divide."[6]

---

[1] *Brief Lives*, p. 140.   [2] *Ibid.*, p. 142.   [3] *Ibid.*, p. 143.
[4] *Ibid.*, p. 143.   [5] *Ibid.*, pp. 144-5.
[6] *Ibid.*, pp. 242-3. It is explained that he did not begin to study mathematics until he was forty years old.

The impression left by the mathematical studies of this period is that of a new-found and almost light-hearted animation. It was marked by the gradual incursion of the amateur into a subject which had for generations been considered as primarily military or architectural in its implications. In these years before the Civil War the work of a speculative mathematician had begun to appeal to the civilian mind, while at the same time the disciplines of Sir Isaac Newton's day had not yet formed themselves.

The obscurity of any contemporary experimenters should not be over-stressed, for in a sense all serious students were comprised within a circle of correspondents, and were to that extent well-known. Thus Oughtred had been assisted by Sir Kenelm Digby[1] and was familiar with Lord Arundel's clients in their different groupings. It was, perhaps, in this way that he was brought in contact with William Harvey, who was physician to his patron's embassy to Germany. "He", it is explained in regard to Dr Harvey, "was pretty well versed in the Mathematiques, and had made himselfe master of Mr Oughtred's *Clavis Math.* in his old age; and I have seen him perusing it, and working problems, not long before he dyed, and that book was alwayes in his meditating apartment."[2]

Harvey was in a very different position from other workers, a rich and famous man and King Charles' own physician.[3] Aubrey sums up what was the current view of him.[4] "All his profession would allowe him to be an excellent anatomist, but I never heard of any that admired his therapeutique way. I knew severall practisers in London that would not have given 3d for one of his bills; and that a man could hardly tell by one of his bills what he did aime at. He did not care for chymistrey, and was wont to speake against them with an undervalue." His attitude to Lord Verulam has a certain interest. "He had been physitian to the Lord Chancellor Bacon, whom he esteemed much for his witt and style, but would not allow him to be a great philosopher. 'He writes philosophy like a Lord Chancellor,' he said to me, speaking in derision; 'I have cured

[1] "His first edition of his Circles of Proportion was in quarto, and dedicated to Sir Kenelem Digby" (Aubrey, *Brief Lives, op. cit.,* p. 144).

[2] *Ibid.,* p. 229.

[3] "He dyed worth 20,000 *li.* which he left to his brother Eliab. In his will he left his old friend Mr Thomas Hobbes 10 *li.* as a token of his love" (*ibid.,* p. 229).

[4] *Ibid.,* p. 232.

him.'"[1] Another comment is interesting. "He was far from bigotry." Harvey had, indeed, imbibed very much of that Baconian mannerism and method of expression with which his sovereign was to be so ill at ease. "He [Dr Harvey] did delight to be in the darke, and told me he could then best contemplate. He had a house heretofore at Combe, in Surrey, a good aire and prospect, where he had caves made in the earth, in which in summer time he delighted to meditate. . . . He was wont to say that man was but a great mischievous baboon."[2]

This sceptical strand could be discerned as an element in both medical and astrological opinion in the previous century. Harvey's comment has a resemblance to the ideas thrown out by Thomas Hariot, who was Sir Walter Raleigh's mathematician and physician. Viewed from another angle, there was a fairly widespread desire to find a basis for the Authoritarian State that was not theological. The talk and generalised discussion of two or three generations of men of science lay behind the construction of Thomas Hobbes' *Leviathan*. It was, perhaps, natural to find the intellectual scepticism linked with one wing of the Royalists. It had always formed an alternative in Elizabethan thought, and was consistent with a pragmatic acceptance of authoritarian monarchy. Many thus supported an autocratic royal administration who would reject the divine right of any king.

[1] *Brief Lives*, pp. 229-330.   [2] *Ibid.*, p. 229.

CHAPTER XVI

AN ANTIQUARIAN

LINKED with these scientific preoccupations and bringing at least the shadow of an Elizabethan vigour into the delicate reservations of this later age, there stood the still surviving figure of a great antiquary, who was in some ways reminiscent of such mediæval patrons as Duke Humphrey of Gloucester or the Duc de Berri. Lord William Howard was the youngest son of that Duke of Norfolk who had perished on the scaffold in 1572. He carried into a later period ideas, and indeed a manner of life, which were in certain respects pre-Tudor, and it is precisely for this reason that the detailed account of his expenses and of his library that have come down to us possess so sharp an interest. It is not that the great families on the Scottish Border could ever escape the influence of the capital. It is rather that the London fashions of an earlier age still lingered. An examination of the daily life at Naworth Castle will serve to illuminate that Caroline world which it by-passed.

Lord William was now old, and a hard life had increased through the years that self-sufficiency which had always marked him. He had been born to the share of a great heritage, and a keen appreciation of the qualities of generous blood had only been emphasised by the misfortunes of his house. His father and grandfather had been sacrificed by the English sovereigns, victims of their own unskilfulness in the face of the Renaissance monarchy. His mother had died at his birth, and his father on the scaffold some nine years later. It is not surprising that there was a vein of hardness in Lord William Howard, and that his antiquarian tastes served as a foil to a character which was at once courteous, watchful and ungentle. To an extent very rare in his own day, he maintained a resolute privateness of life carried through on a scale of some magnificence and marked by a curiously complete detachment.

Towards his successive sovereigns Lord William's attitude was very clear and cold. Yet he was rightly trusted, and he had an unbiased loyalty on which the Stuart kings could place a calm reliance. Hot views were most distasteful to him, whether they were those of Sir Walter Raleigh or of Father Parsons. The dignity of his order and the qualities of a *grand seigneur* meant very much to him. He was a collector rather than a patron; very conscious of his obligations. The rôle of a great landowner came to him easily, and there is some reason to suppose that he had a justified and a hard confidence in the political future of the landed families. It is less easy to determine whether he was convinced that Catholicism would be maintained in his own country.

He was by choice a Catholic, and there was added to his conviction an interest in religious things which deepened with the years. He was attached in a measured fashion to the Benedictines; attracted by the mystical writers; independent; a trace self-conscious. It is obvious that he viewed the Anglican Church order without prejudice or the least trace of hostility. As a young man he had endeavoured to make good his right of presentation to Greystock parsonage. He supported the oath of allegiance in King James' reign, and he provided the bread and wine for the communion service at Cumwhitton Church. The impression is conveyed that he saw the Established Church move forward as an appanage of that new State which was to him both irresistible and welcome.

He cherished his Catholic faith in privacy, and in the accounts of the great household[1] which he ruled in his later years there are hardly any entries which refer to the proscribed worship with any certainty. There are purchases of candles and silver bells, and a curious entry of "xxvijs. jd." received in exchange for an old chalice. A considerable sum was paid for garnishing a picture in crystal of St Ignatius. But it is clear that Lord William and his steward both intended that it should not be possible to distinguish the devotional from the artistic uses. The outline of his slight public service alike reflects the same fixed caution and security. Cornelis Jansen has left an interesting portrait of Lord William Howard, in which the long and bearded face, with the high forehead and the nose with its coarse modelling, is rendered remarkable by the dark eyes at once commanding and very watchful.

His only published work was his translation of Florence of

---

[1] *The Household Books of the Lord William Howard of Naworth Castle,* ed. Rev. George Ornsby, Surtees Society, 1878.

Worcester, and he was jealous of his Latinity. There was, in fact, one aspect from which he could be regarded as over-educated in the sense of Castiglione's *Il Cortegiano*. His phrasing in English was very forceful and marked by an almost Pre-destinarian bias. It did not appear to him that there was need to expect that God should show much mercy. For twenty years he had had to struggle against first the Dacres and then the Lowthers, who tried in vain to bar his way to his wife's inheri-tance as co-heiress of the great Border family of the Lords Dacres of the North. In this connection a sentence from his narrative of this conflict, which is written in the third person, will throw light upon Lord William's views. "The former fire-brand Gerard Lowther", he wrote, "did again stir up the coales, for now to his former ambitious and covetous humour he had also united and added infinite malice, being taught by his Master Machevyll to stryke home, and synck deep enough under the water, the Earl of Arundel and Lord William Howard, whom before he had wounded and made bleed but not mortally."[1] His conceptions were large and touched by an Elizabethan rhetoric.

Towards the end of the same narrative there are two further passages which reveal his standpoint still more clearly. "I cannot in better sort conclude this discourse", he wrote, "than shew, by auncient evidences and authenticke recordes, how the sayd possessions have descended in elder ages, and how often they have heartofore, by heires generall, been transferred into severall surnames; the which, noe question, was then the handy-worke of God, and He being whear He was, it is past the power of any Lowther or human creature, to alter His desynes or to oppose against His determination."[2] "And therefore", he concluded, "LET GOD MAKE HEIRES, for *in vanum laborant* that endeavour the contrary, and it is directly *contra consilium Domini*, as allsoe, noe question, great presump-tion in the frayle creature to oppose against, and to crosse the designment of the omnipotent Creator."[3] These sentences will serve to indicate the stiff, almost Castilian, sense of pure descent which is set against the Augustinian background of Lord William's thought. He and his wife, Elizabeth Dacres,

---

[1] *Lord Dacre's Possessions*, a manuscript composed by Lord William Howard, *Household Accounts*, p. 372.

[2] *Household Accounts*, p. 391.   [3] *Ibid.*, p. 393.

lived at Naworth on their wide estates from the time of King James' accession until they died in 1639 and 1640.

A study of the household books gives some impression of the life led at Naworth Castle on the Scottish Border in the stronghold of the Dacres, which looked across the Irthing to the Waste of Bewcastle. It was an isolated way of living with a rather primitive and cumbered dignity, and it is always surprising that such a library, the fruit of twenty years of antiquarian and religious reading, should have been brought up in the carts which carried the pictures and the household stuffs from Newburn to Naworth across the fells. In return for further books, which were sent from London, Lord William would send to the antiquaries in the South such stones with Roman inscriptions as he could find. "Till haie tyme was past", he wrote on one occasion in this connection to Sir Robert Cotton, "I could get no draughts to undertake to carrie them."[1]

The patriarchial element had a binding force in the routine at Naworth, and it is interesting to observe the way in which the lord's personal interest in genealogy and antiquities and herbals is reflected in the list of casual sums disbursed at the castle door.[2]

"To widow Hetherton for finding honey vi^d.
To W. Bowman's son for finding an earthen pot v^s.
To ij boyes for getting yvie for the deer iv^d.
To Mr Lowden's man bringing saxifrage vj^d.
To Jo. Lambert bringing cherries xij^d.
For drawing a pedigre, to Mr Pryce i^s.
To iij musicians at the gate xij^d."

Journeys to London took place from time to time, and in his later years Lord William had a set of lodgings in Arundel House. His principal servants were put up at the Angel[3] behind St Clement Dane's, and he used the stables of this inn during his visits to the capital. But he would very soon be back in the

---

[1] Letter from Lord William Howard to Sir Robert Cotton, dated from Naworth Castle, 13 August 1608, printed in Household Accounts, appendix, p. 412.

[2] Nearly all the following items appear in October accounts under the heading "Rewards, and given to the Pore" (Household Accounts, pp. 88-9).

[3] Under the heading "Riding Charges and Errands" for November 1633, there are interesting details of the various charges at the Angel, and of the sums given to ostlers and chamberlains (ibid., p. 333).

North again. There is record of a single journey to the Spa in the Low Countries, made for the sake of the waters in 1623.

The state of his health seems to have occasioned several of the London visits, for there are notes of consultations with the Catholic physicians of this period, Mr Dr Moore and Mr Hickes, the latter an apothecary whose nostrums were at that time greatly valued. Compared to the small sums spent on books and the very slight expenditure on boat hire from Arundel House steps,[1] the payments to the doctors seem considerable. Among the charges met were £10 to Dr Moore, a bill of four guineas from Mr Hickes, and one of ten shillings from Mr Clarke, the tooth drawer. Lord William's life was not without a certain valetudinarian background.

In the fine weather he would sometimes ride down to Lady Wyntour's house at Lydney, staying on the way at Shiffnal Manor with his sister-in-law, Lady Arundel, for whom he entertained a deep respect. Journeys into Lancashire were more frequent, and there is evidence that he would occasionally, in the house of some Catholic gentleman, obtain a book which he could not have purchased in the open market. Thus a copy of the office de Beata[2] had belonged to Mr Thomas Talbot of Lancaster before Lord William acquired it in his Naworth period. It was possibly his association with these Lancashire Recusants that led him to make a journey to St Winifred's shrine at Holywell in 1629, in company with his friends Sir Cuthbert Clifton of Lytham and Mr Preston of the Manor Furness.

At Naworth a certain formal hospitality was practised, and visits were exchanged with the Bishop of Carlisle at Rose Castle. The coach, which appears frequently in these accounts, with its curtains and leather hangings, was sent on occasion as far as Appleby to meet distinguished travellers. It is also clear that, as he grew old, Lord William's interest in mechanical contrivances developed. There were constant repairs to the clock which he had installed in a wainscot case, and he busied

---

[1] A pair of oars bringing Lord William from the Temple Stairs to the *Old Swan* or from Arundel House to the *Old Swan* cost "xij^d", which was likewise the cost of a pair of oars from Arundel House to Westminster. The charge for two pairs of oars from Arundel House to Westminster was "xviij^d" (*Household Accounts*, pp. 262-3, 333).

[2] This copy of the *Horæ in laudem Beatissimæ Virginis Mariæ, ad usum Romanum*, published at Paris in 1531, has the following entry written on the fly-leaf: "Liber Thomas Talbotti, Lancastr., qui obiit 10 die Julii, 1598. Willm Howard, Naward".

himself with an astrolabe and dials and compasses. It will be seen that his literary interests were likewise marked by this same concern for the description of physical phenomena. He can be imagined bending over his instruments or examining the well-tricked arms in his heraldic manuscripts. His green spectacles would be exchanged for the multiplying glasses with which he was used to scan each detail. Beside him would stand his diet drink of oat malt, and on his head his satin cap to save him from the draughts of winter.

Lord William's numerous sons remain somewhat indistinct in these household records, and his wife's personality emerges less clearly than his own. She was obviously very fond of cards, and spent a considerable sum on this diversion. This is perhaps sufficient detail to introduce a consideration of the library itself.

The information about the books and manuscripts then at Naworth can be checked from three sources. In the first place there is the *Catalogus Librorum Manuscriptorum Honoratissimi D. Caroli Howard, Comitis Carlioli, in Bibliotheca apud Castrum suum de Naworth in Comitatu Cumbriæ; quos collegerunt Abavus ejus Domini Wilhelmus Howard*. In a certain number of cases the printed books contain Lord William's signature or his motto, *volo non valeo*. The rare occasions on which a date is entered in the volume would seem to indicate the times of purchase. It seems to be only certain of the books, which he bought when he was forming his collection as a young man in the years before the Armada, that are thus dated. In other instances the purchase of the books is mentioned in the household accounts, although unfortunately their titles are seldom given. All the printed books in this catalogue can be checked by their date of publication. In one or two cases, and notably in that of Sir Nathaniel Brent's translation of Soano's *History of the Council of Trent*, there is some doubt as to whether the volume actually arrived before the founder of the library had died. This book, which was published in the year of his death, was probably, at any rate, on order. The greater part of the library was in Latin, with many English books and a good deal in French. There were occasional volumes in Greek. Lord William's notes in a copy of Casa-Galateo's *Trattato de Costumi* suggest that he prided himself upon a knowledge of Italian. Although he survived so long, he had been born three years before the Earl of Essex and thus belonged to that Elizabethan generation which regarded some playing with Italian as the necessary and supreme accomplishment.

More interesting than the *Trattato de Costumi* and the two modish volumes of the *cinquecento* is the series of volumes which dealt from different angles with the English Catholic tradition. He had, of course, the *Chronicles*, Berners' *Froissart*, the *Polychronicon*, the *History of Sir John Mandeville*, Hardyng's *Chronicle* and the *Chronicle of Fabian*. But the special nature of his interests is shown by the religious writings. There is John Gwinneth's *Declaration of an heretique*, and with it two other tracts by Thomas Berthelet, both dating from Queen Mary's reign, *A manifest Detection of the notable falsehood of John Frithe's book* and *A playne Demonstration of John Frithe's lack of witte and learninge*. He had a fifteenth-century metrical life in English of St Cuthbert, a life of Thomas à Becket, and the Wynkyn de Worde edition of the *Orcharde of Syon*, "in the which is conteyned the revelacyon of Seynt Katheryne of Sene, with ghostly frujtes and precjous plantes for the helthe of mannes soul".

These were supported by manuscripts of the lives of English saints, John Lidgate's *Vita S. Edmundi Regis & Martyris*, and accounts of St Guthlac of Ely, St Botolph and St Anselm. There were also codices of the works of St Aldhelm and of the venerable Bede.

The religious works in Latin which were of English *provenance* are very numerous. Two of these are Marian editions, the *Exetasis Testimoniorum quæ Martinus Bucer ex S. Patribus non sancte edidit* of Stephen Gardiner, Bishop of Winchester; and the *De Veritate Corporis et Sanguinis Domini* of Cuthbert Tunstall, Bishop of Durham. The library possessed a manuscript volume containing several treatises of Richard Rolle of Hampole, including the *De Amore Dei et contemptu mundi*. There were Thomas Netter of Walden's book against the heresy of Wycliffe, and one of the controversial works of Thomas Stapleton. In the case of this last book, which was published at Antwerp in 1592, there is a note in the accounts stating that it was bought by Lord William Howard on 6 August 1623 at Dunkirk for two shillings, while he was waiting in that port for a ship for Newcastle on his return journey from the Spa.

In this connection it is worth noting that in many cases Lord William appears to have bought modern books on publication. An unusually large number of the works in his library were published at Cologne, Louvain and Antwerp; but it seems probable that the actual arrangements for their purchase were made through London booksellers. At the same time, this would raise an interesting problem, since the volumes dealt for the most part with Catholic theology and controversy. Technically they were liable to seizure, since they were Popish books imported from the dominions of the Archdukes and of the Spiritual Electors.

By contrast, almost the only Anglican book in the whole library was William Page's *A further Justification of Bowing at the name of Jesus*, which had been published at Oxford in 1631, and had come into his possession in his last years. There was also a copy of the Jacobean controversial work, *Tortura Torti*. Two volumes advocating the principles of the Reformation contain warning notes. On the fly-leaf of a copy of Calvin's *Institutio* there is written in Lord William's handwriting the text "*Qui sibi videtur stare, videat ne cadat*", while the cover of *Antisanderus* has the words "*Parce nobis Domine*" cut right across it. Such a sentiment would have been echoed in any Catholic house in regard to that attack on Dr Sanders, the defender of the Papacy.

On the other hand, one entry in a Catholic sense has a special interest. It is not easy to determine which of the printed books and manuscripts at Naworth had belonged to the house in the days of the Lords Dacres, although the Register of Lanercost had descended from that time. But there was in the library an Antwerp edition of an *Hymnorum cum notis opusculum ad usum Sarum* printed just before the religious changes in 1528. The back of the title page has an inscription stating that on 3 September 1553 Mass was again said in St Cuthbert's Church in the city of Carlisle.

The general spiritual and mystical writers are well represented. There was a Cologne edition of Rupert of Deutz' *de Divinis officiis*, a *Martyrologium Romanum* printed at Antwerp which appears to have been purchased after Lord William came to Naworth, and Richard of St Victor's *in Trinitate*. There were, of course, the eight volumes of Mosander's edition of Surius' *Vitæ Sanctorum*. In addition to a work in praise of Sancta Brigida Thaumaturga, the library contained copies of St Bonaventure's *de Vita S. Francisci*, and of the *Consuetudines* of Dom Guigo, Prior of the Grande Chartreuse. Some of the

books were modern editions of spiritual classics, as in the case
of Ludolph of Saxony's *Vita Jesu Christi*, which was purchased
in the Antwerp variant of 1612. Towards the Carthusians, as to
the Benedictines, Lord William showed himself most generous.
According to a manuscript formerly at Corby, he left one
quarter of a sum of £200, set aside for Masses, to the Carthusians, "particularly desiring these might have a share in what he
intended for such uses".[1] It is possible that he may have visited
the English charterhouse at Nieuport on his journey to the
Low Countries, but the dispersal of the archives of that
monastery in 1782 makes it impossible to determine whether
Lord William Howard was among the rare patrons of Sheen
Anglorum.

Naturally the works of the sixteenth-century defenders of
Catholicism were not neglected[2] in the formation of the
Naworth library. Ribadeneira's *Les Fleurs des Vies Saincts*,
Martin Becanus' *Manuale Controversiarum*, Canisius' *in Evangelicas
Lectiones* and Suarez' *Opuscula Theologica* give an indication of
the titles. There were books by Possevino and Hosius and
Gregory of Valencia, and several works of Bellarmine and a
Latin edition of the letters of St Francis Xavier.

In the more general section, St Augustine was represented
by an imperfect copy of the *De Civitate Dei*. There is no reference
to the Confessions. The situation in regard to St Thomas was
rather curious. There was a fifteenth-century edition of a
Textus Sententiarum, a copy of the *Summa contra Gentiles*, printed
at Lyons in 1586, in which was inscribed the name "Charles
Howard, Naward", and a copy of the *prima pars* of the *Summa
Theologica*. In the library there was also a copy of the *tertia pars*
in a late-sixteenth-century Venetian edition. This had the
words "Sr. Willm Howarde of Thornthwaite" on the fly-leaf.
The two inscribed volumes clearly belonged to Lord William's
younger sons, and this raises the question as to whether they
may have been put through a prescribed course of reading with
the chaplain.

---

[1] This paper is quoted in the introduction to the *Household Books of Lord William
Howard of Naworth*, p. xl, and was at Corby in 1878. It is naturally not explicitly
stated that the pious uses in question were in fact Mass stipends.

[2] Lord William's interest in the field of spiritual writing was maintained, and
one of the last of his purchases was the *Lilia Cistercii* of Chrysostom Henriquez.
He also possessed an abridged French version of pieces from the *Thesaurarium* of
Luis of Granada.

It seems certain that Fr Augustine Hungate, O.S.B.,[1] must have had a definite influence on the formation of, at any rate, a portion of the library. From 1633 entries of sums given to him "by my Lord's command" appear in the Accounts, and he was obviously on a most intimate footing with the family. He came of the old Yorkshire stock of the Hungates of Saxton, and his sister Mary was married to Lord William's son, Sir William Howard.

One section of the library, the school books, must have lain very definitely within the chaplain's province. Among the sums expended in March 1621 there figured: "A grammar xij[d], Terence xij[d] and Vives vj[d] for Mr Thomas".[2] The last entry presumably refers to the *Epistola de ratione studii puerilis, cum rudimentis Grammatices*, composed in 1523. The education of children in the North still went forward in the Tudor fashion. Among the school books was a Cicero and a Horace, and in 1619 a Latin primer was procured for Lord William's daughter Mary, who later married Sir John Wyntour. There is not enough evidence to determine whether this book was a manual of devotion or whether her father bestowed especial pains upon the education of his favourite daughter.[3]

The whole question of the price paid for books is full of interest. Eighteen-pence would be given for binding a volume, and two shillings and sixpence for such work in parchment. The sums laid out were strictly moderate. A bill of £2, sent in by Mr Lownes, the London bookseller, would appear to be among the larger items, but the prices were seldom recorded except in the case of the current heraldic and antiquarian works like Camden's *Remains* (half a crown). Very occasionally a book of a doctrinal character is included in the orders sent to London through the steward. A couple of shillings was paid for one of Bishop Fisher's treatises.

[1] The various entries relating to the chaplain are invariably headed "Mr Hungate", and the editor of the *Household Accounts* could not determine whether the priest in question was Dom Augustine Hungate or his brother Dom Robert. It was, however, Fr Augustine who retired in his old age to the house of Viscountess Fairfax, who figures in the Accounts as Lord William's granddaughter Alathea. He seems to have been the priest who was so closely linked with the Howards throughout his long career.

[2] *Household Books*, p. 179, under the heading "Utensiles or Necessaries".

[3] This entry comes under the heading of "Payments for Necessaries and Extraordinaries since the viij October 1619" and the price paid for the volume was six shillings and sixpence. This figure rather suggests a present than a school book.

Almanacs, costing a few pence each, were sent for regularly, and the numbers of *Mercurius Gailo-Belgicus*, published half-yearly, would enable the family at Naworth to keep up with a somewhat inefficient presentation of fairly recent world events. This periodical was well supplied with maps, in which Lord William clearly took a curious pleasure. In this same field the *Book of the Duchy of Cornwall* and the *Doomsday Bock* "with picktures" must have made a real appeal. It is necessary to stress in regard to any library of this period the element of serious perusal. Past all those volumes which were kept for show or courtesy, there lay that range of study in which a man of generous blood would find support. In this, as in so many similar cases, it was surely the great heraldic manuscripts which gave the mind its characteristic and most solid nutriment.

To explain this more plainly, a single instance can be taken from among those *schemata* which the owner of Naworth Castle had ordered to be prepared for his own use. In one manuscript the arms which depicted the quarterings of his house were found blazoned in the margin in their crude, exact colours, while down the centre of the parchment ran the brief, sustaining narrative. There Lord William could study carefully the lineage of the Dacre ancestors. "Thomas VI", he would read, "married Elizabeth Graystocke, reigned xxx yeares. Further at God's pleasure."[1]

By unsuspected ways the religious conception was always entering. There lay the Dacres in the tombs at Lanercost, and a new line had entered into their inheritance. But Lord William held to this conception of a Divine protection guarding over the destinies of the established order. Justice and right descent: LET GOD MAKE HEIRES. Among the doctrines one was by now of almost universal acceptation, that of the unrestricted nature of the Rights of Property. It was hedged about by dignity, and lucid and incontestable. There is a certain uniformity about the history of those families who passed through the Civil Wars as Cavaliers, but holding great possessions. Already at Naworth Castle there could be discerned a central calm and a possessive quality, assured and most enduring. Such a family was carried forward to its own destiny. As in the cases of

[1] This is taken from a Record at Naworth Castle, made by Lord William Howard of the lineage of the Dacres, as given in an armorial window at Kirkoswald.

the Paulets and the Lumleys, their adherence to Catholicism would drop away before the pressure of a caste opinion. Very smoothly these families would come into their place, thus the Carlisle Howards entered the haven of the Whigs.

Under another aspect, the library at Naworth would foreshadow that of the country-houses of the future, with their reasoned and ample furnishing. There stood the editions of the *Statutes at Large*, those tall and calf-bound volumes which, behind the glass of the locked bookcases, would form a background for the gentlemen of England in their chosen leisure. Already that character of magnificence which was to mark the English library could be discerned. Beyond the *Statutes* there stretched forward a line of dignified and handsome folios, the Annals of Baronius and Gratian, Hakluyt's edition of the *Navigacions*, the Universal Histories and the Lexicographers. The *Acts of Parliament*, and books of these two last categories, ministered to a clear distinctive need as the dust settled on the fine thick calf. They were among the earlier experiments in the arranged background.

This idea was only just emerging. In the North, pictures were still conceived as casual decoration, like fitted panels which could as well be used for any other ornament. Among the payments made at Naworth is one which throws a clear light upon this way of life. "June 10. To Mr Heskett for mending my Lord's closett, gilding a bedstead, drawing Mrs Elizabeth and Mrs Marye's pictures, and Mr Thomas', x^{li}."[1] In keeping with this entry is a note under November 1633 which mentions the large sum of £44 8s., given "for one sute of lanskipp hanginges, containinge 148 ells, at 6s. an ell". This was an approach very remote from that of the Mortlake tapestries and Buckingham and his expert advisers. Landscape work ordered in this fashion resembled the Elizabethan tapestry which was primarily a seemly and uninteresting covering for the rough wall spaces. In some respects these accounts of Naworth resemble those of Wardour some thirty years before. The fashions of the earlier reign still lingered in these northern parts, which were so far removed from the capital and its new influence.

It was not the detail of the house furnishing but Lord William's personal effects which suggested a more modern spirit, the quadrant and dial, "the needle for one Austrolobb",

[1] "Extraordinary Paiments", *Household Accounts*, p. 182.

the drills and pliers. And on another side he had those anti-quarian interests in Roman inscriptions and in the markings on the Cross of Bewcastle which were to characterise the Stuart century. With this there went a genuine concern for natural history. Thus the Cornish diamonds, which Thomas Roscarrock, Lord William's old friend and quasi-pensioner, had brought to Naworth, were the quiet precursors of those curious objects of nature which the Restoration world and the eighteenth century would soon collect. In time they would be set out and classified in the specimen cases between the pilasters in the noblemen's seats under the Hanoverians.

Though there was much at Naworth to suggest the general lines of reading in the Stuart period, there was little which reflects the constitutional troubles of the time or the approaching conflict. Among the manuscripts there was a single folio volume comprising Arguments for Ship money—*Pro & Con.* A copy of Jean Bodin's *Methodus* is an example of a kind of writing which was likewise ill-represented. In really modern controversy, there was a book by Marco Antonio de Dominis, printed by the Jesuit Press at Dillingen and written after his return from England. But it was the calmer writing that was more character-istic of this library, the quiet description of events recorded within the framework of established values; the volumes of the *Concilia Generalia*; the genealogies of sixty-seven noble houses by Estienne de Cypre—the *Annales Sultanorum Othmanidarum.* A complement to this world view was a work much favoured throughout this century—Philemon Holland's translation of Suetonius. Perhaps the keynote of the patron of letters in Lord William's youth had been the desire to be versatile. At Naworth in his later years we can perceive this versatility reduced to serried order.

In the summer of 1639 Lady William Howard died. The eldest son was dead for many years, and the way of life at Naworth did not survive Lord William's time. His grandson and heir, Sir William Howard, was already a widower, and only survived till 1644. The first Earl of Carlisle was brought up with a very different set of values from those of his great-grandfather. In the summer of 1640 Lord William's health was clearly failing. In the accounts there is a payment to Lord Fairfax's man for bringing conserve of primrose for my Lord, and for coals which were carried up to the Carlisle Tower. He

was past dragon water and mithridates, and Dr Steven's potion
and clove water. In the early autumn there was a payment of
"12^d" to the brewer for bags for putting in herbs for my Lord's
beer. The disbursal of £15 paid at Michaelmas for the printing
of "St Marie of Egipt her life in Vearse" attests Lord William's
interest as a patron. On 7 October there occurs a final entry
"for a coffin for my Lord".

CHAPTER XVII

THE NAVAL SERVICE

IN any study of aspects of official life during the years before the Civil Wars, a special place must be given to a survey of conditions within the naval service. It cannot be maintained that naval life in the decade following Buckingham's assassination was specifically different from the general *régime* in the first quarter of the century. Nevertheless, precedents were being established, and there was a certain close connection with the Court, which foreshadowed the naval life of the periods of those Dutch Wars which developed after the Restoration. In these years of peace the practice of summer cruises was established. Warships were used to convey ambassadors. From one angle the peace-time navy was then seen as a royal appurtenance and an adjunct to the sovereign's policy.

On the administrative side the years of the independent rule of Charles I mark an especial phase in the history of the Royal Navy. On the death of the Duke of Buckingham the office of Lord High Admiral was placed in commission. One of the motives for this course of action appears to have been the intention to provide the widowed duchess with such perquisites of her husband's office as the King could grant to her.

Too much emphasis need not be placed on the names of the commissioners now appointed. The first place was granted to Lord-Treasurer Weston, who was succeeded at the Admiralty as at the Treasury by Bishop Juxon. There were manifest advantages in such close financial control. The two Secretaries of State became permanent commissioners. Lords Pembroke and Dorset were added, and on the former's death, Lord Cottington. Sir Henry Vane became an extra member. Up to this point the commissioners could hardly have been less professional, or with less knowledge of naval, or indeed maritime, affairs. To them was added one name belonging to a different category, the Earl of Lindsey, who had commanded the expedition sent in 1628 to La Rochelle. The collective title of the Lords of the Admiralty now appears for the first time.

Inevitably this new Board gave enhanced importance to the secretary. Edward Nicholas, who had graduated through the secretaryship to the Warden of the Cinque Ports to become Secretary of the Admiralty under Buckingham, is the key figure through this run of years. The duties later carried out by the naval constructor's department were at this time fulfilled by the corporation of Trinity House. A great deal of the administrative work devolved on the officials known as the Principal Officers of the Navy. This committee at first consisted of the Treasurer of the Navy, the Surveyor and Controller and two Clerks of the Acts.[1] The Officers of the Navy met in a house in St Martin's Lane, for which they paid an annual rental of £30. The Lords of the Admiralty met in Whitehall, but a great part of their work was carried through by the Secretary in person.

A study of the conditions of the naval service in 1632 will serve to give an impression of the duties and spirit of the fleet of Charles I. There was present from the first a hampering lack of funds and a consequent irregularity in payment. It is worth noting that there was, however, a marked reluctance to press home the blame for such deficiency. As a result of slipshod financial methods the different officers, and indeed departments, had to some extent delivered themselves into each other's hands. It is difficult to examine the evidence without concluding that Nicholas' administration was marked by competence and an unsurpassed honesty of purpose. This is brought out the more clearly since at that period there was an absence of any close surveillance.

Before attempting a detailed picture, it should be mentioned that the principal vessels then sent to sea were second rates of between five and six hundred tons burthen. A comment should be made on the *Lion's Whelps*. These, originally ten in number, were small, three-masted, square-rigged ships of about one hundred and eighty-five tons. They had been built at the beginning of the reign and carried twelve guns each.

A consideration of the state of the Navy during the summer of

---

[1] To these were added three extra Principal Officers: William Burrell and Phineas Pett in 1629, and Sir Kenelm Digby in 1630. The two first-named were practising shipwrights. This was liable to cause difficulty when the placing of contracts was in question. Sir Thomas Aylesbury, who died as Surveyor of the Navy in 1632, was Clarendon's father-in-law. Sir Henry Palmer, Controller of the Navy, Dennis Fleming, one of the Clerks of the Acts, and Phineas Pett were suspended from their functions in 1634 for malversation of stores.

1632 can perhaps be best opened with the notice of appointment sent by the Lords of the Admiralty from Whitehall to Captain John Pennington on 5 March.[1] By this warrant he was named captain of the *Convertine* and admiral of the fleet to be employed in guarding the Narrow Seas.[2] At this date the term admiral still implied an office and not a rank. On the previous day it had been settled that the *Convertine*, the *Assurance* and the *Second* and *Tenth Whelps* were to be employed in the Narrow Seas, and that the command of these ships was to be given to the officers who had held command the previous year.[3] It would be interesting to study such elements of permanence as can be traced in such seasonal employment. Without any set rules it would still appear that the prescriptive right to re-employment was at this period recognised.

Captain Pennington was informed that he could, if he preferred, transfer his flag to the *Assurance*, or indeed to the *Happy Entrance* or the *Garland*, should these vessels be fit to go to sea. It was also made clear that the first ship which could be made ready was to be sent to Margate to embark the Abbot of Scaglia, ambassador from the Duke of Savoy, and transport him to Dunkirk or to some other port in Flanders.[4]

The next letter throws further light upon the uses of the fleet.[5] The officers of the Ordnance wrote recommending that the *Assurance* should become the flagship. They stated that brass ordnance had been shipped in the *Convertine* in place of iron on the occasion of her going into Spain to fetch Lord Cottington. Later her former iron ordnance had been replaced. The Ordnance officers explained that the *Assurance*, being furnished with none but brass ordnance, should carry the admiral for this time. They added as a rider that this borrowing and transporting of ordnance was very chargeable to His Majesty.

At this stage the general object of the summer's voyages was defined as the protection of the King's subjects from the

[1] Letter from the Lords of the Admiralty to Captain Pennington, 5 March 1632 (State Papers, Dom. Charles I, ccxiv, 10).

[2] The name of this vessel usually appears as *Convertine*, but sometimes as *Convertive*.

[3] Letter from Secretary Coke to Edward Nicholas, dated 4 March 1632 (State Papers, Dom. Charles I, ccxiv, 6).

[4] Letter from the Lords of the Admiralty to Captain Pennington, dated 5 March 1632 (*ibid.*, ccxiv, 11).

[5] Letter from the Lords of the Admiralty to Secretary Coke, dated 6 March 1632 (*ibid.*, ccxiv, 12).

Algerine corsairs.[1] The attack on Baltimore had taken place in the previous summer, and the Privy Council required an estimate of the ships needed to perform this service.[2]

The naval vessels were now to leave their winter harbours. The number of ships employed was much inferior to that comprised in the ship-money fleets set forth after the new taxation. Still, in some respects it is easier to examine the working of the naval administration when there are fewer ships and captains and a quiet programme.

With the commissioning of the fleet for the summer voyage there began those efforts to obtain the naval posts which the absence of any regular system of promotion rendered inevitable. The position was complicated by the fact that there seem to have been few offices which could not be performed by deputy. Thus in a statement from the Officers of the Navy it is explained that Henry Playce, boatswain of the *Nonsuch*, had been for many years incapacitated, "being one hundred years as the writers are informed".[3] Subject to Captain Pennington's concurrence, it was recommended that Thomas Wilson, boatswain of the *Red Lion*, and Samuel Story, boatswain of the *Dreadnought*, should be employed as masters of the *Second* and *Tenth Lion's Whelps*.[4] This raises the interesting question as to what officers and petty officers were maintained on the pay-roll of ships laid up during the winter guard.

Meanwhile, information came through from Bristol of the preparations in that port. On 22 March Robert Kitchen, who was in charge of the dockyard arrangements in that harbour,

---

[1] In this connection a letter from the Masters and others of the Trinity House to the Council, dated at Trinity House, Ratcliff, on 7 March 1632, has some interesting detail. The Brethren explain that they have refused to pay to some person unnamed the whole sum for the redemption of captives in Barbary. It had been agreed that the sum collected should be applied for the freeing of forty-one named individuals, twenty-two being natives of Poole and nineteen natives of London (State Papers, Dom. Charles I, ccxiv, 15).

[2] Order of Council, dated at Whitehall, 9 March 1632 (*ibid.*, 19).

[3] Recommendation of the Officers of the Navy to the Lords of the Admiralty, dated 9 March 1632 (*ibid.*, 23). Proposals for appointments at any rate of a subordinate character issued from the office of the Navy in Mincing Lane. Among the employees of this office was a messenger whose status is indicated in a letter in which it is requested that Robert Whentnall, late purser in the *St George*, lent to the Earl of Carlisle, should be appointed as ordinary messenger in place of Richard Woodward incapacitated by sickness (*ibid.*, 36).

[4] Recommendation of the Officers of the Navy to the Lords of the Admiralty, dated 7 March 1632 (*ibid.*, 16).

reported that the *Ninth Lion's Whelp* and the *Fifth Whelp* had come into the anchorage.[1] He also mentioned that Captain Hooke, in command of the latter vessel, had brought a letter from the Lords Justices of Ireland with detailed instructions for the fitting out of both these ships. He asked that a carpenter might be sent down to see the ships careened, and he enclosed a schedule of the prices of sail cloth, belt rope, hemp, tar, oakum and resin in Bristol at that date. A covering letter was sent to Edward Nicholas asking him to expedite affairs.[2]

An effort was now made to straighten out some difficulties which had lain over from the previous year. In the common jail at Bristol there were six mariners who had been brought in by Captain William Thomas, lieutenant to Sir Thomas Button in the *Ninth Whelp*, an officer who was himself in trouble with the Admiralty. These seamen had been charged with piracy, but there was a disposition to deal leniently with them.[3] At the same time, it was decided to pardon Captain Robert Nutt and his associates, who had committed various acts of piracy off the coast of Ireland.[4] Captains Thomas Ketelby and John Nutt were made responsible for the latter's brother, who was to be apprehended if he proved "so wedded to his lewd courses as to refuse to come in within the time limited".

After such preliminary instructions documents were prepared which defined the nature of the Admiral's duties for the current year.[5] In addition to the voyage of the Savoyard ambassador, large naval vessels would be required for the diplomatic journeys which Mr Weston and Lord Leicester would undertake. Other distinguished passengers were conveyed after direct negotiations with the captain. Thus, in April of this year, Lady Strange, with her brother the Comte de Laval and a large

[1] Letter from Robert Kitchen to the Lords of the Admiralty, dated at Bristol, 22 March 1632 (State Papers, Dom. Charles I, ccxiv, 57).

[2] Letter from Robert Kitchen to Secretary Nicholas, same date (*ibid.*, 58).

[3] Letter from James Dyer to Secretary Nicholas, dated at Bristol, 23 March 1632 (*ibid.*, 63).

[4] Letter from the King to Captains Ketelby and Nutt, March 1632 (*ibid.*, 84).

[5] Thus he was instructed by the Lords of the Admiralty to secure that no nets called trawls were used from the Long Sand Head northward or southward as far as Beachy Head, and to see that no French vessels were permitted to fish upon that coast without licence from the Lord Warden of the Cinque Ports. Captain William Cooke, in command at Tilbury, sent in the examinations of owners of trawls to the Judge of the Admiralty in London, letters dated 7 and 8 April 1632 (State Papers, Dom. Charles I, ccxv, 15 and 22).

train, was carried in the *Convertine* from Tilbury Hope to Brill.[1]
It was very much to Captain Pennington's advantage to secure
the favourable interest of Lord Derby and his son. Sitting in
his stern cabin, with the gold leaf about the doorway and the
caryatides on the quarter-gallery, the prudent officer would
scan the Court. Relationships were formed by mutual service.

While the Admiral was engaged upon this journey, Captain
Richard Plumleigh of the *Assurance* sought leave to sail beyond
the circuit from the Downs to Beachy Head, which his senior
officer had allotted to him. He asserted that a Biscay pirate was
operating in the approaches to the Channel.[2] Four days later
Captain Pennington reported that he was himself setting sail
to the westward to deal with ten Turkish men-of-war said to be
lying off the Cornish coast.[3] From Plymouth this officer
wrote again in the middle of the next month, explaining that
he had ranged the coast as high as the Land's End and had
found it free of pirates.[4] He had sent away the *Second Lion's
Whelp*, commanded by Captain Simon Digby, to the Channel
Islands to clear those parts of pirates, and intended to direct
Captain Plumleigh to ply to and fro about these western
parts. He himself would return with the *Tenth Whelp* to the
Downs. In conclusion he reported that the French had six
ships and pinnaces in the Bay of Biscay (a somewhat loose
definition) and five more making ready at Morbihan to go to
the river of Canada.

It is worth noting that Captain Plumleigh corresponded with
Sir John Coke instead of with the Secretary of the Admiralty.
He appears as a discontented officer determined to underline
his special claims. He explained that the effort to bring Nutt
to submission had proved ineffective, and that that freebooter
had shipped in a poor vessel with but three pieces of ordnance

---

[1] Captain Pennington wrote letters on this subject to the Lords of the Admiralty,
dated 10 and 22 April 1632 (*ibid.*, 28 and 68). The ship was weather-bound in the
Thames for several days, and the journey took nine days from the time that the
party set out from Derby House. In this connection Lord Strange describes himself as "an affectionate friend to do (Pennington) service" (*ibid.*, 83). Charlotte
de la Trèmouille, Lady Strange, was a friend of Queen Henrietta, and later
celebrated as the Countess of Derby of the siege of Lathom House.
[2] Letter from Captain Plumleigh to Secretary Coke, dated 22 April 1632
(State Papers, Dom. Charles I, ccxv, 69).
[3] Letter from Captain Pennington to the Lords of the Admiralty, dated 26 April
1632 (*ibid.*, 79).
[4] Letter from the same to the same, dated 10 May 1632 (*ibid.*, ccxvi, 37).

and had gone for the Flemish islands.[1] A personal difficulty
had developed when the ships were returning to the Downs
and Captains Pennington and Plumleigh were at a distance.[2]

A further complication was now added by the competition
to transport the Earl of Leicester into Denmark. It was not long
before Captain Plumleigh had set out his case. He was in hopes,
he wrote to Edward Nicholas on 4 June, to have heard from him
about Lord Leicester's voyage.[3] He continued by saying that
he understood that the Admiral was ambitious of this service.
"Where anything may be gotten", he explained, "he will be
sure to put himself forward, except it be knocks, and there his
humility is such that he cares not much who takes the place of
him." In conclusion he said that he was weary of his senior
officer's peevishness and punctilios, and that he would sooner
serve the King in a jail than under Captain Pennington's
command.

This string of letters must produce a cumulative effect. The
uneasy fatigue is very striking. The sea-officers were without
those shared traditions which might have served to abate their
rivalries. They had come to their captains' posts by different
channels. The objectives of their present service were ill-
defined, and they lacked the prospect of secure employment.
Harassing cares oppressed them, for their ships were under-
manned and badly victualled.[4]

A note sent by the Admiral on 16 June describes one form of
breach of discipline.[5] Captain Henry Stradling, in command of
the *Tenth Lion's Whelp*, wrote stating that Rice Thomas, gunner
of that vessel, had given no attendance on board for six weeks
past. Mr Thomas had served in the Navy since the voyage to
Cadiz in 1625, and had been master-gunner of the *Tenth Whelp*

[1] Cf. letters from Captain Plumleigh to Secretary Coke, dated 15 and 18 May
(*ibid.*, 50 and 60).

[2] Cf. letter from Captain Pennington to the Admiralty, dated from the Downs
24 May 1632 (*ibid.*, 73).

[3] Letter from Captain Plumleigh to Secretary Nicholas (State Papers, Dom.
Charles I, ccxviii, 14).

[4] Cf., for the question of the complement of the flagship, a letter from Sir Robert
Mansell, Sir Sackville Trevor, Sir Henry Palmer, Sir Henry Mervyn and Captain
Phineas Pett to Secretary Nicholas, dated from Whitehall, 11 May 1632, and
Captain Pennington's reply dated from the Downs, 6 June 1632 (*ibid.*, ccxvi, 39,
and ccxviii, 16).

[5] On 16 June 1632, Captain Pennington wrote to the Lords of the Admiralty
that at least one hundred seamen had deserted from the fleet since the beginning
of the voyage (*ibid.*, 58).

since she was built. In this case there was more than a suspicion of peculation. On a survey being taken of the gunner's stores seven barrels of powder and three hundredweight of small shot were found wanting.[1]

In many directions the shortage of money was apparent. The following letter of the same date gives[2] an impression of the damage caused to the King's service as a result of the amassed arrears of payment. In this document the Officers of the Ordnance begin by acknowledging warrants for the supply of the two *Lion's Whelps* at Bristol, and for His Majesty's ships at Portsmouth and Chatham, and for the forts of Tilbury and Gravesend. They then set out the nature of their difficulties. The Officers explain that they require provisions of cordage and materials, but that these had been refused by the Carpenter and Smith. These latter officials had alleged that there were great sums of money owing to them as a result of the departure from the ancient practice of paying their accounts upon the ordinary. The Carpenter and Smith further complained that there had been too great questioning of their prices. But in any case matters were difficult at Bristol, where Captain Hooke, who had been in that port since March, was engaged in a dispute with his *Whelp's* master.

Under these circumstances it is not surprising that the office of the surveyor of victualling for the Royal Navy was likewise in some confusion. From his headquarters on Tower Hill, Sir Sampson Darrell endeavoured to extend the limits of a charge from which he could only with difficulty wring a profit. Some eighteen months previously he had applied for a warrant for commissions to buy corn for the King's service, and had asked urgently for £1,000, without which he was sure he could not procure delivery of the victuals.[3] Sir Sampson was an official of somewhat timorous approach, and he had cast about for quiet dealings with the pursers.[4] His hope (in which he was frustrated) lay in the chance of arranging matters behind the backs of

---

[1] The various papers dealing with Rice Thomas' case are to be found in the State Papers, Dom. Charles I, ccxxviii, 17, 44 and 58, and ccxxxiii, 33.

[2] Letter from the Officers of the Ordnance to the Lords of the Admiralty, dated 4 June 1632 (*ibid.*, ccxviii, 13).

[3] Letter from Sir Sampson Darrell to Secretary Nicholas, dated at Tower Hill, 2 April 1631 (*ibid.*, clxxxviii, 12).

[4] Sir Sampson Darrell depended ultimately upon the Treasury, and he assured Lord-Treasurer Weston that he hoped to behave himself so carefully as to hear his Lordship speak mildly and not in thunder as he had done hitherto (*ibid.*, 12).

those naval captains who had hitherto made their profit by taking the victualling of ships into their hands.[1]

To this distracted man a letter came from the Lords of the Admiralty early in June requiring him to complete speedily the victualling of the four ships in the Narrow Seas. Sir Sampson represented that he was quite without funds. There was a stoppage in the Treasury, and he asked the Secretary of the Admiralty to help him. "One word from my Lord [Treasurer] to Mr Dawes", he explained, "would open this obstruction."[2] Thus slowly the fitting out of the fleet went forward.

On 22 June Pennington reported from the Downs that he had but sixteen days' victuals remaining and still heard of no supply.[3] He had sent over the *Tenth Whelp* to Calais to bring word as to when the body of Sir Isaac Wake, who had died as ambassador in Paris, would reach the coast. Captain Plumleigh had been ordered to hold the *Assurance* ready to stand over to the French coast for the remains. He then asked as to whether the Earl of Leicester was to be transported to the Elbe or to the Sound so that he could make arrangements about a pilot.[4]

With such preoccupations in the Downs, life went forward quietly in the other naval centres. Portsmouth had become sleepy now that the Duke of Buckingham was dead. In this time of calm the mayor and corporation of that town were able to evade the demand made to them by the Privy Council for the removal of all hedges, rails and fences within forty feet of the ramparts, and for the taking down of buildings which had been put up against the wall between the Quay Gate and the Square Tower. The mayor claimed that the approach to the

[1] Cf. for an account of a particularly sharp exchange with Sir Thomas Button who claimed to have had the charge of victualling his own ships "these 17 years" (*ibid.*, cxciv, 15).

[2] Letter from Sir Sampson Darrell to Secretary Nicholas, dated 14 June 1632 (*ibid.*, ccxviii, 52).

[3] Letter to Secretary Coke, dated 22 June 1632 (*ibid.*, ccxix, 2).

[4] A letter from Captain Simon Digby commanding the *Second Lion's Whelp*, addressed to the Lords of the Admiralty, and dated 15 September 1632, indicates to what an extent gentlemen of some official standing could claim the services of a *Whelp* for their own transport (*ibid.*, ccxxiii, 26). During the summer Captain Digby had carried Sir Peter Osborne, Sir Francis Rainsford and Sir Philip Carteret to the Channel Islands. In this connection Edward Nicholas had written to Captain Pennington that Sir Peter Osborne and the rest of the gentlemen that go for Guernsey had hoped that the Admiral would send them Captain Stradling, for the other "Rhodomathe" (as they termed Simon Digby) was already very infamous on that coast for having taken French friars and queanes aboard the King's pinnace (*ibid.*, ccxxi, 24).

fortifications was as clear as it had ever been in the time of the Earls of Sussex and Devonshire and of Sir Francis Vere and the late Lord Steward.[1] He admitted that some fences had been erected for preserving gardens. This recital of the list of the late governors of Portsmouth, and indeed the whole tone of the correspondence, suggests the repose which had settled on the harbour fortress.

Down in Bristol there was some confusion. The mayor had sent for Mr Kitchin, the clerk of the cheque, and for the master of the *Ninth Whelp*, beseeching that the ships be sent to sea. Some men had come to him who had been taken about Lundy by an English pirate and robbed of all they had. Kitchin in his turn wrote to the Admiralty to say that his ships still required three months' provisions and part of their cordage.[2] He asked that their captains might come to Bristol. At the same time the Lords Justices of Ireland pressed for the naval protection which they had already been promised some four months earlier.

In consequence, Captain Hooke was brought from London and immediately reported that the master of the *Ninth Whelp* was perpetually drunk ashore.[3] He had not once been on board the vessel, either when she lay in King's Road or when she was brought in to be careened. The commanding officer expressed his readiness to set sail for Waterford as soon as he had a new master; but there was small comfort to the Justices of Ireland to be gained and little danger to the pirates to be apprehended from the coming of Captain Hooke. It is not to be wondered at that he had a distaste for this employment, since he had been the officer upon these coasts at the time of the sack of Baltimore.

The movements of this summer of 1632 have to be set against the memory of that tragic accident. Just after nightfall on a calm June evening in the previous year, two Algerine corsairs had reached Baltimore, a small fishing port on the Illen River, a few miles to the north-eastward of Cape Clear.[4] The larger

---

[1] Letter from the mayor and others of Portsmouth to the Council, dated 28 June 1632 (*ibid.*, ccxix, 44).

[2] Letter from Robert Kitchin to Secretary Nicholas, dated at Bristol 4 July 1632 (*ibid.*, ccxx, 11).

[3] Letter from Captain Hooke, at King's Road, Bristol, to Secretary Nicholas, dated 15 July 1632 (State Papers, Ireland, Charles I, n. 2146).

[4] The following account was sent by the Lords Justices to the English Privy Council, and was certified by the sovereign and burgesses of Baltimore. Four of the captives were released and the information culled from their depositions (State Papers, Ireland, Charles I, n. 1973).

vessel was a ship of 300 tons, armed with twenty-four iron pieces, and carrying a crew of two hundred men. She had in company a smaller ship of 100 tons burthen which carried a crew of about eighty. On their way up from the south they had been sighted off the coast of Cornwall, and it is said that their captain had been warned to avoid Kinsale by the master of a fishing smack from Dungarvan which he had captured.

The captain, who was a Dutch "renegado", had been rowed ashore by ten Turks, their oars wrapped in oakum to muffle sound. They had brought with them a Christian captive, who had explained the lie of the town and had told them where the ablest men had their abode. They then returned to their ships and cheered their comrades, saying "we are in a good place and shall make a boon voyage".[1] About two o'clock in the early hours of that same night they had silently landed two hundred and thirty musketeers, who bore firebrands to burn the houses and iron bars to break them open. They divided into parties, and had surprised twenty-six houses in the Cove of Baltimore, carrying one hundred persons of all ages out of their beds. They had then pushed forward to the upper levels of the town, but the drums were beaten and the townsmen roused. Before dawn they had sailed away with one hundred and seven captives from Baltimore, some men and quite a number of women, and very many young and healthy children.

It was this event which had placed Captain Hooke, who was at that time lying in Kinsale harbour and corresponding with Sir Thomas Button about the bad quality of the meat, in such a difficult predicament. The Earl of Cork had written[2] to England about his misconduct in lying idle in Kinsale, and it was not a complete answer to assert[3] that the *Ninth Whelp* was without victuals as a result of Sir T. Button's corruption. The latter officer, who was at his home in Wales and admiral of the Irish Seas, had hastened to disown his subordinate.[4] It is not

---

[1] Presumably a captive's memory of some expression "bon boyage" or "buono" or "bueno" from the *lingua franca* of the corsairs and "renegados".

[2] Letter from the Earl of Cork at Dublin to Lord Dorchester, dated 28 June 1631 (State Papers, Ireland, Charles I, n. 1975).

[3] Letter from Captain Hooke at Kinsale to Secretary Nicholas, dated 19 July 1631 (*ibid.*, n. 1998).

[4] "How dishonourable and how unchristianlike a thing it is that these Turks should dare to do these outrages and unheard-of villainies upon his Majesty's coasts." Sir Thomas Button to Secretary Nicholas on 5 July 1631 (State Papers, Dom. Charles I cxcvi. 24).

surprising that the Lords Justices of Ireland showed no wish for the return of Captain Hooke.[1]

Meanwhile there had been a division of the fleet, and Captain Plumleigh had received a new command as admiral of the ships on the coast of Ireland. His instructions laid down that he was to take his own ship, the *Assurance*, and the *Ninth* and *Fifth Whelps*, and so dispose his vessels as to guard St George's Channel and the Severn, plying between Scilly, Cape Clear and Milford Haven, with Kinsale as his place of rendezvous. He was to escort the Irish vessels on their journeys to and from Bristol for St James' Fair. By the same post he was ordered to haste away for Ireland and the Severn "where pirates swarm".[2]

There were difficulties over victualling and with his captains, and a doubt as to the naval authority in Ireland.[3] On 22 July he went to sea. At Plymouth Captain Plumleigh learned that the pirate Nutt was on the coast of Spain, but that his "vice admiral" was off Lundy, expecting the return of the Irish merchants from St James' Fair. On 5 August he arrived off Lundy to find that Nutt's "vice admiral" had sailed away. A certain malaise had settled down upon the expedition.

By the 18th he had beaten up into Pwllheli Roads and was now in company with both the *Whelps*. He complained to Nicholas of the captains with whom he was matched; the one

---

[1] In a letter to the English Privy Council, dated 23 July 1632, they asked for an officer resident in Ireland (State Papers, Ireland, Charles I, n. 2148).

[2] Referred to in a letter from Nicholas (State Papers, Dom. Charles I, ccxx, 44).

[3] Captain Fogg of the *Ninth Whelp* had resigned, explaining that his fortune was insufficient to enable him to fit himself for an employment so remote and whereof he had already experienced that the charge exceeded the benefit (*ibid.*, 56). Captain Hooke had been transferred into the *Ninth Whelp*, and in spite of Captain Plumleigh's efforts, Captain Dawtry Cooper was appointed to the *Fifth Whelp*. He was accused of a "contentious disposition and sharking ways", cf. letters from Captain Plumleigh to Secretary Coke on 19 July, and to Edward Nicholas on 19 and 22 July (*ibid.*, ccxxi, 4, 5 and 20).

Captain Cooper had seen much service and had lost his son and all that he possessed in the wreck of the *Seventh Whelp*. He was an enemy of Sir Thomas Button, cf. for details of claim his petition to the Admiralty (*ibid.*, ccxx, 6). One point is interesting. There had been some religious affiliation which was damaging. Captain Cooper put in a statement from the Rev. John Bourchier, incumbent of St Botolph's without Aldgate, to certify that he had received the sacrament on Low Sunday last past and had been born and bred a Protestant. It is stated that for the last four or five years he had been strangely misled, and this must indicate that he had been a Catholic or one of the straiter sort of non-conformitants. Cf. certificate dated 16 July 1632 (*ibid.*, ccxx, 78).

a notorious drunkard and enured to laziness; the other refractory and contentious.[1] In some respects he considered it an achievement that he had got the *Whelps* to sea. They were only victualled for another ten days, and Sir Sampson Darrell had farmed them for the future to the purser of the *Ninth Whelp* at an under rate of sixpence per man. The mathematics of insufficiency were very obvious. Plumleigh explained that he had been assured that he would find these men for the most part in harbour with a bag and bottle.

He reached Dublin on 20 August, and some days later claimed to have met Nutt and his company in Dublin Bay.[2] He made it clear that after he had bestowed some thirty great shots upon them they trusted to their heels, and being light and clean ships wrought the *Assurance* out of sight. Making a sweep southward he went to examine Lundy and Caldey, which were described as the pirates' dens. He remained in the Irish Seas till late October. When he left Kinsale he claimed that the coast was in peace both from Turks and pirates, and that it would now be secured by the winter season.[3] On 24 October Captain Plumleigh in the *Assurance* dropped anchor in the Downs.[4] Meanwhile Captain Pennington had performed his duties: Lord Leicester had embarked in Margate Roads on 15 November, returning from Denmark two months later.[5] The last words of Simon Digby's letter seem to resume the situation.[6] "There are many ships in the Downs from the Straits and Spain, most of them laden with salt, the rest with wool and wine. The coast is clear of pirates."

[1] Letter dated at Pwllheli Roads, 18 August 1632 (*ibid.*, ccxxii, 42).

[2] Letter from Captain Plumleigh to the Lords of the Admiralty, dated at Stidwales Bay, 4 September 1632 (*ibid.*, ccxxiii, 5).

[3] It is only fair to Plumleigh to quote the testimony given in his favour by John Griffith, vice-admiral of North Wales, who, writing to the Secretary of the Admiralty, describes his great industry, daring, vigilancy and diligence (*ibid.*, 32).

[4] Letter from Captain Plumleigh to the Lords of the Admiralty, dated 29 October 1632 (*ibid.*, ccxxiv, 55).

[5] Details are given in a letter sent by Captain Pennington to Secretary Nicholas from Margate Roads on 30 November 1632 (*ibid.*, ccxxv, 76). The ambassador's table in the *Convertine* numbered some eight or nine persons of rank, besides ten gentlemen attendants and twenty serving men, footmen and cooks. There was a hoy to carry Lord Leicester's furniture and baggage. It is noted that among the provisions were bucks baked in pies.

[6] Letter from Captain Digby to Secretary Nicholas, dated from the *Second Lion's Whelp* in the Downs, 28 October 1632 (*ibid.*, ccxxiv, 54).

CHAPTER XVIII

THE SHIP-MONEY FLEETS

SIR HENRY MAINWARING, who was himself a reclaimed rover, had set out very clearly the methods that he deemed necessary for the suppression of piracy in the Irish Seas. "Lastly," he wrote in his *Discourse of Pirates*, which he offered to King James I in 1615, "for the disappointing of them in Ireland, which I hold to be the most material of all; being that is the great earth for foxes, which being stopped, they are easily hunted to death . . . so I verily think that if they were once debarred Ireland, they might easily be confounded, and without further trouble end *Per simplicem desinentiam*."[1] It is all explained in the language of the school of Raleigh. "To this purpose your Highness must allow", continues Mainwaring, approaching the point of his discourse, "a good ship for the South Coast, that must continually keep the Sea, not coming into Harbour, but to trim and victual; which must lie South of Cape Clear, betwixt twenty and fifty leagues, for they that come from the South do ever make that Cape for their landfall if they can."

Yet the situation was not so simple as Mainwaring would represent it. This powerful man-of-war was only one of a number which would be required for such close guarding of the coasts. And in dealing with the Algerines there was always a great fear of reprisals. Their hostages were valuable. A few years earlier there had been some "1,500 poor captive souls now under the miserable oppression of the Turks in Argier, Tunis, Sally and Tituane".[2] This number was only gradually reduced by the ransoms paid through the Levant Company. It seems that the object which the Admiralty had in mind was not so much to secure the destruction of the Turkish galleys as their avoidance of the English coast. To a lesser degree the

[1] *Discourse on Pirates*, by Sir Henry Mainwaring, Navy Records Society, pp. 46-7.
[2] Details from a petition presented to the House of Lords in 1624, *Lords' Journals*, vol. iii, pp. 41-3.

Admiralty was willing to take the Irish coasts within the orbit of some vague protection.

As the English captives lay in the summer nights on the terraced roofs of the prison by the harbour in Algiers, they must have regarded this policy with mixed feelings. For those who were to labour at the oar there was little danger of death in battle, but also a very slender hope of rescue. For their part, the Moors were always anxious that their slaves, acquired at so much trouble and expense, should find a ransomer. An envoy was, in fact, sent from Algiers to King Charles with a present of lions and Arab horses to hasten on negotiations. Behind all the measures taken in England lay a determination to avoid reprisals and an entangling war. The safety of the Mediterranean was a problem for the Spaniards and the French, and there were few attacks made by the Algerines upon the Levant Company's well-armed vessels. The only expedition in this period, that under Rainsborough against Sallee, had a clearly limited objective.[1] There was no question of any action by the Western Powers to drive the corsairs from their strongholds in Africa.[2] The galleys built on that coast, lined with timber from the woods of Bougia, slipped out of the harbour at Algiers and past the round castle and the battery at the Gate of the Sea. Behind them lay the terraced arcades beneath the Kasbah, and the mosques with their white rough plaster and the thick crude minarets. If the pirates constituted a naval problem, it was one which was not thoroughly examined. It was determined to concentrate upon the policing of the Channel.

"One league off the Lizard", wrote Nathaniel Boteler in his *Dialogues*, "the depth is forty fathoms, coarse sand, but clear; and the more to the westwards the deeper water and the finer sand. Then again for the depth: the deepest water betwixt Scilly and Ushant is sixty-four fathom, so unless there be sixty-four fathom when you ground the channel is not yet entered."[3] It is here that the English naval ships began their

---

[1] In the two years prior to 1637, two thousand captives had been taken by the Sallee pirates, while the town itself had revolted from the Sultan of Morocco. It was, in a sense, a strictly localised attack and negotiation.

[2] Some of the captives were passed from Algiers to the Eastern Mediterranean. Thus Richard Blundell was at Nauplia. Cf. ' An humble petition by Marie, wife of Richard Blundill, now a captive in Napoly de Romaine" (*Acts of the Privy Council*, 1627, p. 251).

[3] Boteler's *Dialogues*, Navy Records Society, p. 31.

real duties.[1] A draft of instructions for the Fleet issued by Sir John Coke in 1635 set out these duties very clearly. "Our intentions", this document begins, "is not to offend or incommodate our neighbours or allies, or in any sort to break that peace which, by God's great blessing, we enjoy with all Princes and States. Our Seas, commonly called the four English Seas, are much infested by men-of-war and others tending to the denial and impeachment of that sovereignty, peculiar interest, and property, which we and our progenitors, time out of mind, have had and enjoyed in the said seas. We have therefore put our navy in order for the maintenance of this right. And that in the due execution of these [rights] our sovereignty may be acknowledged and maintained, we require you to let none pass by you of what quality soever without veiling bonnet and performing the due homage of the sea." The naval history of the reign can be barely understood unless full stress is laid upon this duty of "preserving His Majesty's regality in the Narrow Seas". In this sense the Navy was a buttress of the monarchy and symbol of the King's external power. Corsairs off the coast of Ireland, or the doings of some privateer turned pirate, were relatively trivial episodes. What mattered was the control of the English Channel.

Viewed from this angle, one can understand the appeal of the service for those who would join the Cavaliers. Among the letters addressed to Secretary Coke is one of great freshness written by young Ralph Conway, who was then serving in the *Garland* in the Downs.[2] He had joined the fleet between Falmouth and Fowey, coming out from Plymouth in Captain Stradling's *Whelp*. He had been received by Captain Ketelby of the *Garland* with extraordinary kindness. At the time of writing,

---

[1] In this connection the attitude to English pirates is worth examining. Here a similar moderation was displayed. In a petition from the Mayor of Dublin and other merchants of that city to the Lords Justices of Ireland it is requested that "if these pirates [Nutt and his companions] are pardoned they may be first compelled to give some compensation" (State Papers, Dom. Ireland, Charles I, n. 2151). It is clear that John Nutt had possessed letters of marque, which he had misused. These were granted to him as master and part-owner of the *Swan* of Lyme Regis on 11 September 1630. Finally it was reported on 27 November 1632, by a ship coming from Bilbao, that "Nut and most of his company are hanged at the Groyne" (State Papers, Dom. Charles I, ccxxv, 65). Several of the pirates who operated in English waters met their deserts in France or Spain.

[2] Letter from Ralph Conway to Secretary Coke, dated from the *Garland* in the Downs, 5 October 1634 (State Papers, Dom. Charles I, ccxxiv, 17).

he had served for several months, and there was as yet no sign of the approach of winter. "These ships," he concludes, "as they have enjoyed the felicity of a whole summer, so has the weather continued since their coming to the Downs."

This was the fleet as seen by old Lord Conway's son as he sat a privileged volunteer at the captain's table. Against it there may be set the report sent in to the Admiralty by Sir Henry Mainwaring, who had commanded the *Unicorn* in a summer fleet. "Concerning the victuals", he began, "I have had many complaints this voyage and much with my company. There was in the *Unicorn* much bad victuals . . . all the dry salted beef proved very bad . . . for it was white and blue mouldy, not fitting to be spent but in necessity. The pickled beef was very faulty, because it was not re-pickled from the bloody pickle except for ten hogsheads, which being re-pickled proved well. Two or three hogsheads of pease were faulty. One hogshead of pork stank. Both the ling and the haberdine [sun-dried cod] was very bad."[1] It must be remembered that Mainwaring was in some respects a disappointed officer. His rank was not commensurate with his experience, and he had a certain prejudice against the surveyor of victualling for the Navy.

If this strong contrast existed between letters from the fleet, it is not surprising that there should be a difference in tone in regard to the ship's company. "I never saw", wrote Mainwaring in this connection after his voyage, "a ship so meanly manned as the *Unicorn* was when she came from Chatham to the Hope . . . men of poor and wretched person, without clothes or ability of body."

As an opposite view a quotation may be given from *The Honour of Bristol*, which was composed about this time.[2] This marks a deeper cleavage between ballad and fact than was to exist in the eighteenth century. The verses in question deal with the engagement between the Bristol ship *Angel Gabriel* and three Spanish vessels.

"Our captain to our master said, 'Take courage, master bold'.
The master to the seamen said, 'Stand fast, my hearts of gold'.
The gunner unto all the rest, 'Brave hearts, be valiant still'.
Let us fight in defence of our *Angel Gabriel*.'"

[1] Sir Henry Mainwaring's *Works*, vol. ii, Navy Record Society.
[2] Printed in *Naval Songs and Ballads*, Navy Records Society, p. 35.

This is delightful in its closed remoteness from actuality. It is as unreal as that other fantasy from the same period. "You gentlemen of England . . . Give ear unto the mariners and they will plainly show." Viewed from the side of literary expression these last years before the Civil Wars gave so tranquil an acceptance to the Golden Legend.

As a counterpart to any impression of life at sea, it is worth taking a glance at some developments in the Office of the Navy. In the summer of 1632, when Plumleigh was off the Irish coast and Pennington waiting to embark the ambassador for Denmark, Sir Kenelm Digby settled down to write to Secretary Coke. Digby, who had been appointed an extra Principal Officer of the Navy in 1630, was at this time a young man of twenty-nine, with a military reputation won at Scanderoon and considerable influence at Court. His ingenious mind had not yet earned that reputation for eccentricity which came to mark him. He was for the moment unconcerned about religion and in the last year of his marriage to Venetia Stanley. In the discussion which he now undertook, his position was strengthened by the fact that he was financially uninterested in the building of ships.

Briefly he accused Captain Pett of using his authority as a principal officer to forward his own work to the prejudice of that of Mr Goddard, another shipbuilder.[1] Two royal ships, the *Henrietta Maria* and the *Charles*, were under construction at Woolwich by these rivals. The chief difficulty lay in the inadequate supply of timber.[2] Mr Edisbury, who was Digby's candidate for the surveyorship of the Navy, stated that Mr Goddard feared that he would not have enough beams to lay his main orlop deck.[3] Pett for his part was attempting to obtain the necessary wood from the forest of Redbridge in Hampshire, from East and West Beere and the New Forest.[4] He had also

---

[1] Letter from Sir Kenelm Digby, dated at Deptford, 12 September 1632 (State Papers, Dom. Charles I, ccxxiii, 21).

[2] Goddard, in addition to complaints of ill-usage, stated that there was insufficient timber in the yard to enable him to build a King's ship at Deptford. At the same time he undertook to continue his work, and would not say, as Andrew Burrell did, that he would as soon build a ship in hell as in Deptford Yard. Letter to Secretary Coke, dated at Deptford, 29 August 1632 (*ibid.*, ccxxii, 57).

[3] Letter from Kenrick Edisbury to Secretary Coke, dated at Deptford, 30 August 1632 (*ibid.*, 60).

[4] In regard to the first project, Edisbury remarked that the owners of the barges would not fit them out since they had not been paid for their former

found a supply at Alice Holt in Surrey.[1] Both shipbuilders were in negotiation for felling rights on Shotover. In the course of correspondence with the Navy Office, Pett made the valuable suggestion that, provided designs for the ships were first passed, timbers could be moulded in the woods, which would save nearly one-third of the cost of carriage.[2]

From a study of these letters there emerges an impression of relative efficiency. The hoys with ordnance were stopped at Gillingham. The moulded timber was brought down in carts into the dockyard before the onset of the miry season. The officials of the Trinity House surveyed the hulls of Captain Pett's and Mr Goddard's ships, and gave their opinion on the contriving of the ports for the gun carriages. A great boom swung across the Medway below Upnor, composed of masts and iron and cordage and the hulls of ships and pinnaces.

In Mainwaring's Journal there is an account of the trials of the *Unicorn* in the Thames estuary, which gives an impression of naval routine and idiom. She was a large but unsatisfactory vessel, constructed in 1633 by Edward Boate. "May 1," so runs this entry, "we weighed and stood to and again in the River to try our ship, and found her so tender-sided that all our company affirmed she was not fit to go to sea, for she laid the ports of her lower tier under water. Yet Captain Pett and Mr Austin were of opinion that if she took in more ballast she might serve to lie in the Narrow Seas the summer season."[3] The stress on the

services. He considered that Flemish bottoms would be too long to turn in the narrow creeks near Redbridge (*ibid.*, 60). In the previous April Pett had sent his nephew, Peter Pett, to mark two thousand trees in the New Forest. Four hundred trees making the same number of loads were procured in East and West Beere and the balance of sixteen hundred was made up by felling in the Forest and at Alice Holt. Statement of the Officers of the Navy, dated 13 April 1632 (*ibid.*, ccxv, 39).

[1] The negotiations were carried through with Mr Melsam, who seems to have acted as agent for Lord Lindsey. He reckoned that the forest was worth £20,000 less than when Sir Timothy Tyrrell had come to be lieutenant five years previously. He offered to replant Shotover woods so that his Majesty should see them £60,000 better than their present state, letter from George Melsam to Phineas Pett, dated at Garsington, 12 December 1632 (*ibid.*, ccxxvi, 35). A memorandum on the preservation of timber for building and repairing his Majesty's ships, apparently written in 1632, states that owing to the decay of timber in Waltham Forest and the Forest of Dean, Shotover and Stow Wood remain the best sources of supply (*ibid.*, ccxxix, 112).

[2] *Ibid.*, ccxv, 39.

[3] Sir Henry Mainwaring's *Journal* under 1 May 1633.

summer season is interesting, as is the way in which the shipwrights were prepared in the last resort to stand together.

In these papers the interplay of forces comes out clearly, the
shipwrights against the Trinity House surveyors, the Ordnance
against the Principal Officers of the Navy, the Secretary of the
Navy (at times) against the Principal Officers, and the victualling department against the rest. It is important not to exaggerate these jealousies, which were professional in character
and bound up with authority and profit and obligation.

They were very different from that acute resentment which
was engendered by the promotion of certain commanders who
were without sea experience. In this matter, too, there is a
further division. The granting of posts to peers was regarded as
inevitable and under some aspects even welcome. Thus such
appointments as those of the Earls of Lindsey and Northumberland to sea commands provided no difficulty. It was the introduction of impoverished landsmen to posts for which experienced
candidates existed that gave rise to such bitter feeling.

Still, this jealousy had another side. The men who had
entered the naval service through what can very accurately be
called the merchant navy had a social solidarity, and in many
cases a certain wealth; they were often part-owners of the
merchant ships which they commanded. On the other hand,
the captains who had obtained their posts through influence at
Court were generally young and without resources. They were
gentlemen of the sword with all the economic insecurity which
that term implied. A comment made by Captain Stradling
illuminates the lack of ease between the groupings which would
be further separated by the circumstances of the Navy during
the Civil Wars.[1]

"No ships", wrote Captain Stradling, "[are] more stubborn
and unwilling to give his Majesty's ships respect than our own
merchants. They [the merchant captains] hate all gentlemen,
especially such as serve his Majesty at sea."[2] It was not uncom-

[1] Henry Stradling was the fourth son of Sir John Stradling of St Donat's, and
was given command of the *Tenth Whelp* in 1631, when he appears to have been
just over twenty-one. He was related to Sir Thomas Button, who was himself a
younger son of Miles Button of Worlton, in Glamorgan. Stradling was entrusted
with the task of bringing over the Duchesse de Chevreuse. He was knighted about
1642 and fought for the King in the land campaigns.

[2] Letter to Secretary Nicholas, dated at Plymouth, 7 September 1632 (State
Papers, Dom. Charles I, ccxxiii, 13).

mon to find this strain developing when the two types of commanding officer were joined together in one employment. This appears as a contributory element in the difficulties between Captain Rainsborough and his vice-admiral, George Carteret, on the voyage in 1637 to attack Sallee.

A factor in the situation is the fairly close Court connections[1] of the naval officers who had entered the service through quasi-political influence.[2] It might be suggested that at this time practically every naval appointment was made in London. Consequently it was for the most part those young gentlemen who had contact with the capital who obtained the nominations. In regard to the other channel of entry, it was very natural that naval commands should be offered to captains who had long sailed from the port of London. Their absorption into the naval service was often a gradual process, as can be seen in the case of Captain William Rainsborough, whose career has been made the subject of a special study.[3]

The voyage made to Sallee under Rainsborough and Carteret proved successful and a large number of captives in Morocco were released, but the point of especial interest is the tension engendered between the two commanders. This may have been due to the fact that George Carteret, a young courtier of

[1] Sir George Carteret, who was later governor of Jersey, was about the same age and belonged to the same type of family grouping as Henry Stradling. His first command was in the *Eighth Whelp* in 1633. There is very little information as to the schooling of these officers, and Pepys, in later life, used to complain of Carteret's "ill education" (*Pepys' Diary*, 4 July 1663). Among the senior officers, Sir Robert Mansell (b. 1573) was a cousin and protégé of Lord Howard of Effingham. For the relationship between Mansell, Button and Stradling, cf. G. T. Clark, *Limbus Patrum Morganniæ*. Sir William Monson (b. 1569) was younger brother to Sir Thomas Monson, master of the armoury at the Tower, and was doubly connected by marriage with Lord Howard of Effingham. Sir John Pennington (b. 1568?) came from a Yorkshire family with city connections, his cousin, Sir Isaac Pennington, was lord mayor of London in 1642. Sir Henry Mervyn was a son-in-law of the first Earl of Castlehaven.

[2] A letter from Sir Kenelm Digby to Secretary Coke, dated at London, 6 August 1632, gives an excellent idea of the exercise of influence in naval promotions. If, explained Digby, Captain Plumleigh's lieutenant has that ship (the *Ninth Whelp*), Captain Plumleigh would make his cousin, Kenelm Digby, his lieutenant in the other's room. He gives his cousin the character of a discreet and well-tempered gentleman. Sir Kenelm then concludes that he is sorry that he cannot so much commend his other kinsman, Captain Simon Digby, and after this voyage will no more be a suitor on his behalf (State Papers, Dom. Charles I, cxxxi, 22).

[3] "William Rainsborough and his associates of the Trinity House", by Captain W. R. Chaplin, *The Mariner's Mirror* (1945), vol. xxxi, pp. 178-97.

Royalist instincts who was not more than twenty-eight and formerly lieutenant in the *Convertine*, found himself surrounded by merchant captains. In this particular service it was natural that officers should be chosen who had long experience of the Levant trade. Captain Rainsborough, himself a man of some fifty years of age, had been part-owner of the *Sampson* since his father's death in 1622, and had commanded her since 1625.[1] In the summer of 1635 this ship, which had been armed for the Levant trade, joined the fleet under the Earl of Lindsey, being provided and maintained by the City of London. It is worth noting that Captain Rainsborough had held letters of marque since 1627. Serving continuously up the Straits, he had a detailed knowledge of the methods of the Algerine pirates. He did not retain command of his own ship, but was appointed to the *Merhonour*, wearing the flag of the vice-admiral, Sir William Monson. At the time that he set out for Sallee, he had had two summer cruises in the King's service.[2]

The officers who were appointed to commands in the expedition against Sallee were for the most part residents of Wapping, where Rainsborough had lived since his marriage.[3] It is probable that they were nominated on his recommendation. Brian Harrison, the captain of the *Hercules*, seems to have commanded one of the merchant ships in which Rainsborough had an interest,[4] while George Hatch, captain of the *Mary*, had commanded the *Barbara Constance* in which the family had cer-

---

[1] William Rainsborough was the son of Thomas Rainsborough, merchant and mariner, residing at Whitechapel and latterly in East Greenwich. William's younger brother, Thomas, was an armourer, while his brother-in-law, Thomas Lee, followed the same trade. The Rainsboroughs, father and son, were part-owners of the ships *Exchange*, *Charity*, *Rainbow* and *Barbara Constance*. On his father's death William Rainsborough inherited his father's share in the *Royal Exchange*, *Rainbow* and *Lily*, all registered in London. Mrs Thomas Rainsborough, who survived until 1631, inherited her husband's share in the *Barbara Constance* (*ibid.*, pp. 178-9).

[2] In the summer service of 1636 he was captain of the Earl of Northumberland's flagship, the *Triumph*.

[3] It would be interesting to trace the connection between these merchant captains and other groups of London capitalists. William Rainsborough married as his first wife a daughter of Captain Rowland Coytmore of Wapping, who had been one of the early adventurers to Virginia, and later a member of the East India Company commanding the *Royal James* on a voyage to Surat. In 1617 Captain Coytmore was one of the founders of St John's, Wapping.

[4] Brian Harrison came from Sedgfields, in Durham, although he lived all his life in Wapping. In 1620 he married Elizabeth, widow of William Harris, who died on a voyage to the East Indies, and was a son of Mrs Rowland Coytmore by her first husband.

tain shares.[1] These officers were both senior captains and men of substance. Edmund Seaman of the *Providence,* and Thomas White of the *Expedition* were younger men from the same background.[2] Rainsborough does not seem to have gone to sea again after the Sallee voyage. In addition to his shipping interests, he was linked with the Wapping shipyards and had landed property in Essex.[3] His house property included cottages in Gun Alley, Wapping. The connection of this group of officers with the chapel of St John's, Wapping, was rather close. Without an exception, they gave their support to the Parliament. Carteret went out, and equally inevitably, to join the Cavaliers. It is not surprising that the merchant captains, with their minds focused on the trade position, should have felt that the gentlemen in the King's ships had failed to grasp the situation. The fashion in which the courtiers overflowed into the fleet was uncongenial, as was the privileged way of life reflected in the summer flagships.

Partly for this reason, the King's interest in the Navy never served to render him popular with the sailors. His private mind was as ever dominated by the element of ceremonial. He had an æsthetic interest in the gold-leaf, the scroll work and the carving of the royal vessels. He attended the launching of the principal ships built in the Thames dockyards, and he had a certain general interest in the practice of shipbuilding. One reference will throw some light upon the quality of his concern. In March 1633, Charles I came down to see the two new ships set sail from Woolwich. "His Majesty", wrote Kenrick Edisbury, "continued [aboard the *Charles*] about an hour, and then went in his royal barge and rowed about a mile in the ship's way and then returned to London to save the tide."[5] It must have

---

[1] George Hatch had commanded the *Barbara Constance* in 1625, when Mrs Rainsborough had a share in her. In 1626 he appears as part-owner, with William Rainsborough, of the *Royal Exchange.*

[2] Edmund Seaman was a native of Harwich, resident in Wapping, and Thomas White seems to have lived at Deptford.

[3] William Rainsborough's second wife was Judith (d. 1658), daughter of Reynold Hoxton, master shipwright of Wapping. Her brother, John Hoxton, married Martha, sister of Nehemiah Bourne, the Cromwellian admiral, and daughter of Robert Bourne, shipwright, whose family shipyard at Wapping was leased by his widow in 1625 to John Hoxton and John Taylor. Cf. for these various points Captain W. R. Chaplain, *The Mariner's Mirror,* vol. xxxi, pp. 189-97.

[5] Letter from Kenrick Edisbury to Secretary Coke, dated at Chatham, 4 March 1633 (State Papers, Dom. Charles I, ccxxxiii, 24).

been a source of pleasure to the sovereign to view the great ships, alike seaworthy and so dignified, which would preserve his regality in the Narrow Seas.

The verses in *Neptune to England*,[1] which appear to have been composed in connection with a masque at Court, have an especial interest:

> "If Little Venice brings alone
> Such waves to her subjection,
> As in the Gulfe doe stirre,
> What then should great Britannia please,
> But rule as ladie ore all seas,
> And them as Queen of her?"

It was not the mariners who would be touched by the play upon *Maria* in this delicate and complicated tribute to Queen Henrietta.

Besides, in the King's attitude there was blended a precise interest in mechanical contrivance with a serious appreciation of both line and splendour. Surely this was not lost upon that courtier who built the *Royal Sovereign*. And this masterpiece of Phineas Pett came at the climax of the reign; laid down in 1635 and finished two years later. She had three tiers of ordnance, and ten persons could stand upright in her great lanthorn. The lines *Upon the Great Ship*[2] hit off one aspect of the impression created by this vessel most exactly.

> "I meane the ship so lately built,
> Without, within soe richly gilt;
> O never man saw rapier hilt
> Soe shine."

It is this that explains an otherwise rather surprising letter[3] sent by the second Viscount Conway, then serving as volunteer in the *Triumph*, to his secretary George Rawdon. It is, in effect, a series of instructions. He reminds Mr Rawdon that if the velvet for the coach is tawny the fringe should be of the same colour. He states that he had ordered an edition printed on the best paper of *Theophylacti Epistolæ*, Greek and Latin, set out

---

[1] Printed in *Naval Songs and Ballads*, Navy Records Society, p. 36.

[2] *Naval Songs and Ballads*, Navy Records Society, p. 37.

[3] Letter from Viscount Conway to George Rawdon, dated from the Downs, 18 May 1636 (State Papers, Dom. Charles I, cccxxi, 47). Lord Conway was an elder brother of Ralph Conway. He was an exquisite of the period, and one of the King's generals against the Scots.

by the late Bishop of Hereford. He then bids him to send by the vice-admiral, Sir John Pennington, some gilt paper in large quarto to write to women.

Conway was serving in the Ship-Money Fleet, which had swelled since the days of Pennington and Plumleigh. In 1635 there were three flagships, the *Merhonour*, wearing the flag of the Earl of Lindsey, and the *James* and *Swiftsure*, wearing those of Monson and Sir John Pennington. Fifteen large vessels assembled in the Downs in addition to four *Lion's Whelps*.[1] And the fleets of later years were larger still. It is natural that the courtier element among the officers was soon increasing. "This day", wrote Lord Conway from the *Triumph* on 28 June 1636, "Sir Robert Howard and my Lord of Suffolk's second sonne came aboard and dined here. Sir Robert will goe along with us the rest of this summer, and I shall be very glad of his company."[2]

Further details of life on board the *Triumph* which wore the flag of the Earl of Northumberland during the following summer cruise, that of 1636, will serve to reinforce the same impression. In September the fiddlers who had played for the admiral throughout the voyage were dismissed, and the private physician also left the ship. There was a sense of decorous and seemly pleasure. On one occasion Conway ends a note with this phrase,[4] "I am called upon for my letter, Mr Smith I heare knocking, sealing my Lord's letters." Nor did they suffer unduly from the ship's company. Only one unpleasant incident is recorded. "Captain Hoste", wrote Lord Conway, "had the other night a disastrous adventure, three shillings was stolen out of his pocket, and a bande out of his trunke; the theafe was found and dukt at the maine yard."[5]

A letter written on board the *Triumph* in Yarmouth Roads at the close of the first summer's voyaging gives an idea of the degree to which the interests of these new officers were bound

---

[1] Sir William Monson's *Tracts*, vol. ii, pp. 223-4.

[2] Letter from Viscount Conway to George Garrard, dated from the *Triumph* in the Downs, 28 June 1636 (Harley Papers in Portland MSS., vol. iii, pp. 34-5).

[3] The series of letters among the Harley Papers dealing with Lord Conway's two voyages in the *Triumph* were written at various dates between 28 June 1636 and 25 August 1637.

[4] Letter from Viscount Conway to George Garrard, dated from the Downs, 18 July 1636 (Portland MSS., vol. iii, p. 37).

[5] Letter from the same to the same, dated from the *Triumph* in the Downs, 13 September 1636 (*ibid.*, vol. iii, p. 39).

up with the Court. "Although", declared Conway, "we have lived long in this place of honour where our patience hath brought us through stormes [and] our diligence hath taken many a herring busse [fishing vessel]; yet as all things under the moone have an end soe our stay here will not now be long.

"We are in Yarmouth roade and expect every hower we shall receive dismission, I believe we shall see the King at New-market . . . You may come in my Lord's [the admiral's] coatch or if have noe coatch take your bootes from the pinne where you intended they should hang untill next yeare, send for a horse from grasse, and meete us, or if you please send for my coatch and come in that."[1]

Two final extracts, both dealing with the cruise of 1637, have their own interest. The first is a description which has the ease of manner and the carefree quality that marked one school of thought among the Cavaliers. "When the winde was faire", so runs this passage,[2] "we set saile and passing along the river on the sandes; on either hand saw the remains of ships that had made more haste than good speede. There is a mariner in this fleete that being this yeare, immediately before he came hither, in a ship that traded to the Canaries, in that wide ocean, the ship being over set, all were drowned but he that got upon the bottome of the ship as she lay overturned in the sea, and by another ship was by strange accident taken up. . . .

"If I stay by the way in my relation it is but as we did in our voyage; the winde was contrary, whitch made us often cast anchor, and our slow comming into the Downes gave leave to the people of Dover and the country to assemble on the shoare side to see my Lord of Northumberland comme in. The ships that were here with Sir John Pennington when my Lord came to them bid him wellcome according to the curtesy of the sea with theire guns; he, when the captaines came to him bid them wellcome with excellent good cheare."

This is a delightful picture of the ships beating up against the wind and the loyal crowds and all that careful spectacle. At Canterbury lay the young Prince Elector waiting to be conveyed

---

[1] Letter from the same to the same, dated from the *Triumph* in Yarmouth Roads, 6 October 1636 (*ibid.*, vol. iii, p. 41).

[2] Letter from the same to the same, dated from the *Triumph* in the Downs, 22 June 1637 (*ibid.*, vol. iii, p. 43).

across to Holland.[1] It was an essay in Royalism and breathed the preservation of the King's regality; it was far from the world of Robert Blake. The way of life at the admiral's table was a prolongation of the movement of Whitehall, even down to one of Conway's last requests: "I pray send hither Sir John Suckling's play".

The second extract is singularly expressive. "I would then allso have told you", wrote Conway to his friend, "that my Lord of Carnarvon comming from supper where meate and drinke was noething scarce, as sayth the songe, goeinge into the cabbin whitch was as good a roome and wherein was as good a bed in whitch he was to lye as any he could have one shoare, from thence into the gallery where he had the prospect of a great fleete, a cleare skye and a calm sea, he swore that there was noe soe happy life as to live in sutch a ship and reade romances, but by God's blood he would have three whoores."[2] This is surely the mood of the later Carolines and of the courtiers of Charles II in the Medway and at Solebay.

The world of the merchant seamen and of those who made their way to North America was quite remote, uncomprehended and uncomprehending. Among the means of escape from harsh reality was the use of the ballad. In "Sailors for my Mony", a work of Martin Parker's which was sung to the tune of the "Jovial Cobbler", there occur the following lines.

"Those who could live in England and nourish vice with ease,
When hee that is in povertie may riches get o' th' seas?
Let's saile unto the Indies, where golden grass doth grow,
    To sea, to sea; *how ere the wind doth blow.*"

Given all the circumstances of that time, there is a simplicity, unbelievable and most pathetic, in this whole conception. "Let's saile unto the Indies, where golden grass doth grow."

---

[1] In an account of the actual journey Conway wrote: "Much good company came to my Lord of Northumberland, where was all the good cheere that England France and Flanders could affoord. What was wanting at dinner was taken out at supper, and it is a greater and a truer miracle how soe mutch meate should be dresst in one ship than any the Papists bragge of. The next day we set saile and my Lord of Northumberland dined with the Prince; what entertainment he had you may guesse if you please. He dined with a Prince that was feasted by a King" (Portland MSS., vol. iii, p. 44).

[2] Letter from Viscount Conway to George Garrard, dated from the *Triumph* in the Downs, 10 July 1637 (*ibid.*, vol. iii, p. 44).

CHAPTER XIX

THE COUNTRY ROYALISTS

IT is always difficult to define such terms as town and country when considering the characteristic background of the landed stocks in these last quiet years under Charles I. It was rather a question as to which of the country families came either by attraction or repulsion within the orbit of the Court. There were at this time, in addition to the squires who would go out with the Opposition and the considerable body who contrived a precarious neutrality, three sections of what may be roughly called Royalist opinion: that connected with the Court, that which the Court would succeed in winning over to itself, and finally the large and scattered groupings which would form the core of the instinctive Royalists.

It would be a matter of minor interest to consider how far the Court, accepted as being in the nature of a coterie, could penetrate to the middle landed class. At Saxham Hall, the house long since pulled down, in the parish of Saxham Parva in Suffolk, there lived a family which may serve as an example of this first type. Sir Henry Crofts and his wife both came from the middle ranks of the gentry but with Court connections. The younger daughter had been taken into the Queen's household, apparently soon after Buckingham's murder; the son also held a post about her person. The elder Crofts remained in the country, although not too far from Newmarket. They did not purchase or rent a house in London or Middlesex like the true courtiers.

Cicely Crofts had been to some extent but mildly a favourite of the Queen's, and there had even been a certain difficulty with Lady Carlisle about this matter.[1] In 1636 Cicely Crofts married

[1] Letter of Sir Tobie Mathew to Sir Henry Vane, dated at London, 25 March 1632: "All the world came good friends from Newmarket, only Lords Carlisle and Holland are at the old distance, and Mrs Crofts is not so great a courtier at Lady Carlisle's" (State Papers, Dom. Charles I, ccxiv, 64). Letter of Thomas Lermy to the same dated at Whitehall, 1 May 1632, "Between her [Lady Carlisle] and Mrs Crofts there is a great coolness in friendship, but they were both so wise as they would rather have it thought *desuetudo* than *malitia*" (*ibid.*, ccxvi, 5).

Thomas Killigrew, the dramatist, who was at that time one of
the royal pages. A little later her brother, Will, came to some
prominence; there was a duel[1] and his conversion to Catholicism
was reported.[2] The Crofts have this interest that Thomas Carew
centred upon them. He and Killigrew had something in common
as the younger sons of old King James' Cornish courtiers.[3]
Later there would be links between Killigrew and Will Crofts
in the Royal Family's intimate service.[4] Saxham was one of the
very few houses to be chosen as the subject of Caroline verse.
Thomas Carew's "To Saxham" has the formalism and the
similes marked in the same poet's "To G.N. from Wrest", but
the words given to Master John Crofts in the poem "To the
King, at his entrance into Saxham" have a more individual
quality:

> "Sir,
> Ere you pass this threshold, stay,
> And give your creature leave to pay
> Those pious rites, which unto you,
> As to our household gods are due.
> Instead of sacrifice, each breast
> Is like a flaming altar drest
> With zealous fire, which from pure hearts
> Love mix'd with loyalty imparts."

Carefully considered, this does, perhaps, add to our understanding of one very restricted aspect of country-house life in
the seventeenth century.

Claims made upon them, and accepted as a consequence of
the King's personal service, set such families as the Crofts and
Killigrews in a group apart. They were bound not only to the
King but to the Queen. Thomas Killigrew's father had been

[1] In the Garrard correspondence under 10 May 1638, a duel is recorded between
Lord Elgin and Sir William Crofts "in the fields over against Hyde Park near my
Lord Goring's garden wall" (*Letters and Dispatches of Thomas Earl of Strafford*, ed.
William Knowler, vol. ii, p. 166).

[2] Under 3 July 1638: "Will Crofts also is become a Papist" (*ibid.*, vol. ii, p. 181).
If this change ever took place, Lord Crofts of Saxham had reverted to the Church
of England before 1657.

[3] Carew was born about 1598, the younger son of Sir Matthew Carew, master in
chancery, a cadet of Carew of Antony. Killigrew was born in 1612, his father
being a cadet of Killigrew of Arwennack.

[4] Lord Crofts was the first guardian of the Duke of Monmouth, who was known
by his name. Killigrew was the elder brother of Lady Shannon, a mistress of
Charles II in exile.

her vice-chamberlain, while his stepfather, Sir Thomas Stafford, was her gentleman-usher.[1] John Ashburnham, groom of the bedchamber to the King, was another landowner within the circle of this close royal friendship. Saxham Hall and Ashburnham Place were houses dedicated to the support of all the King's intentions; such houses were few and far between among those owned by the prudent East Anglian and Sussex gentry.

To every section of the squires the Court was in some ways incomprehensible, and to every section except the Catholics it was also inevitably a little suspect. It was held that literary figures and artistic characters were very likely to lack staying power. And there was this to be said for such an outlook that in 1644, the hard year of Marston Moor, young men of the Court atmosphere like Andrew Marvell and John Evelyn, and an old connoisseur like Arundel, were not in Yorkshire but in Italy.

There was also the element of impatience, which is always engendered in a case of government by coterie. And to this was added the quite special animus that was aroused by intellectual or artistic Catholicism. The country gentry knew that the Court, as opposed to the King, could never be held to be proof against Popery. They were ready within certain limits to tolerate their Catholic neighbours, it was the presentation of that religion by the Court and anything that savoured of "overseas" that they detested. It was here that the squires were separated from the Laudians, for they disliked the cultural pattern of the Tridentine world quite as much as the doctrinal. Marvell, in spite of all his later dealings with the Protector, was constitutionally unfitted to acquire that case-hardened and instinctive anti-Popery which was a mark of the Parliamentarians.[2] If

---

[1] In this connection Lady Warwick, admittedly a prejudiced witness, makes a comment on Killigrew's mother: "She [Lady Stafford] was a cunning old woman who had been herself too much, and was too long versed in amours" (*Autobiography of the Countess of Warwick*, Percy Society (1848), p. 9). In dealing with the circle of Henrietta Maria, one can never forget either her delicate virtue or the tolerance of her friends' shortcomings. There was always the influence of the Duchesse de Chevreuse.

[2] When Marvell was living with Lord Fairfax as tutor to his daughter, he wrote the familiar lines in "Upon Appleton House to my Lord Fairfax xlii", suggested by the Swiss Guard at the Vatican.

> "Tulips in several Colours barr'd
> Were then the *Switzers* of our *Guard*."

Poems and Letters of Andrew Marvell, ed. H. M. Margoliouth, vol. ii, p. 69.

PRINCE RUPERT

From a painting by Vandyck formerly in the Imperial Collection
at Vienna

Chillingworth was Latitudinarian, so also, in a general sense, was the Royal Court. It was not only that the Queen was easy towards any frailty which was consonant with the notion of a man of honour. She also did not inquire into the actions or the beliefs of those about her. It is obvious that this attitude was anathema to the Puritans. It was likewise extremely uncongenial to those squires who stood for the high party in Church and State.

Perhaps in that generation which was born at the turn of the century, and was thus contemporary with Charles I, we can for the first time see how strong was the hold that a calm and Erastian Anglican position had obtained among the new squirearchy. It is true that in a section of this body there was a Puritan tradition less strong, however, among the men than among the women. The term Puritan covers a wide variety of opinions and habits of thought. It is impossible to avoid noticing the class emphasis with which this standpoint was maintained by ladies of position.[1] Nevertheless, there was a sense in which the Puritanism of the landed families resembled the extreme Evangelical opinions which were prevalent in the early nineteenth century in the same grouping.

Thus, squires of the Puritan fashion still remained within the frontiers of the Church of England, either as these frontiers existed or as they imagined them. Such men possessed a social solidarity with all those who shared their economic background and educational experience. They were far removed from those who would in time become the nonconformist separatists. On the other hand, a type of churchmanship which was at once Erastian and sacramental would seem to have been fairly widely held. It was, perhaps, not very far removed from the more Protestant preferences which we find set out so clearly in Wentworth's writings.

The core of a deep social uniformity is manifest in all the wide and varied groupings of the greater Yorkshire gentry. Thus, there does not seem to have been a marked divergence in the matter of the purely religious approach between the ideas of the squire of Wentworth Woodhouse and those of such a Parliamentarian Yorkshire leader as the third Lord Fairfax of

---

[1] Cf. the correspondence of Lady Brilliana Harley covering the years 1625-33 and 1638-40 and edited for the Camden Society by the Rev. T. T. Lewis. *Letters of the Lady Brilliana Harley* (1854).

Cameron. The term Presbyterian in its English as opposed to its Scottish sense can hardly be said to appear before the Civil Wars. At the same time it is worth noting that the English Presbyterians were essentially Erastian and anti-nonconformist. It was not their intention to leave the Church of England, but to achieve a modification in her character and discipline. In some cases the expression Presbyterian, when applied to peers and to the greater gentry, must be held to bear a connotation which was almost purely political. It was largely a question of a sharper or less sharp insistence upon Protestant as opposed to Anglican values among the members of a privileged class, whose economic interests were inseparable.

On the other hand, it must be admitted that in the North, Anglicanism conceived in a Protestant setting would, in fact, prove a lever for bringing men from political indifference over openly to the King's side. It has already been suggested that the Jacobean and Caroline decades have little meaning in a North Country background; they were, in fact, contemporaneous with a deepening of Elizabethan values. The old Queen had scorned the Brownists, and northern gentlemen would for the most part give short shrift to any sectary. To them the Church of England stood for all the stable things, for lineage and for patriotism. A section of this world was still steeped in the ideas of the late Tudor period. To such men the constitutional problems must have seemed at once remote and very unusual.

The diary of a wealthy Yorkshire squire covering the crucial years 1640-41 suggests a way of life which would, in fact, prove indestructible. And this particular example is all the more interesting because it takes for granted a static High Church position which the writer does not regard as threatened and which owed nothing to foreign influence.[1] Sir Henry Slingsby's self-conscious entries are modelled on the work of Michel de Montaigne;[2] his improvements are described for effect; his moralising is set within a frame. A very great mass of detail is required to build up his careful picture.

[1] It would be interesting to trace the genesis of his opinions. There is no reason to suppose that he was affected by his studies at Queens' College, Cambridge. It is more likely that he was influenced by the Rev. Phatuell Otby, then parson of Foston, who taught him between the ages of six and fifteen. It is worth noting that in 1640 Slingsby supported the Bill for removing the bishops from the House of Lords. Cf. *Diary of Sir Henry Slingsby*, ed. Rev. D. Parsons, *passim*.

[2] *Ibid.*, p. 55.

It was during the rough northern winter of 1638 that the accident occurred which led Sir Henry Slingsby to take up his pen. He was at that time a very wealthy Yorkshire squire and thirty-six years of age. He had become a baronet of Nova Scotia at the last creation. His wife's nephew, the eldest son of Sir Edward Osborne, vice-president of the Council of the North, had been killed, aged seventeen, while reading with his French tutor. "About 10 of ye clock", so runs Slingsby's first entry, "ye wind blew down with great violence seven chimneys shafts upon the roof of that chamber in ye manor house where he was at study."[1]

The effects of this disaster throw a light on the architecture of this period, and on the fear inspired by the great old buildings, the rotting legacy of the overladen ornament of Tudor days. News of this tragedy was brought to Archbishop Laud at Lambeth by Wentworth, upon whom both Slingsby and Osborne in some measure depended. "Truly I am so sorry also", wrote the Primate to the Lord-Deputy,[2] "for the Vice President's loss of his son by the fall of the chimneys at York Manor, and cannot blame the women and children which are with you if they be fearful of such old rotten and yet high-built chimneys, which you say are in the Dublin Castle." With this mood Sir Henry Slingsby chimes. "Having been warned by this accident", he writes of his wife's reactions, "she would not let me rest till I had pull'd down a chimney that stood on ye garden side at ye Red House which was high built & shaken with ye wind."

He adds of his wife, the first of many touches in regard to Barbara Belasyse, that "she is by nature timorous and compassionate which makes her full of prayer in ye behalf of others." This vein of piety was strong in him, and comes out in the account of the devotional setting of the family life.

A description of his private chapel built at the Red House by his father, Sir Henry Slingsby the elder, is revealing. Here are set down the reverent embellishments which to Laud's mind would seem congruous. "This chappell", he explains, "is built in ye form of a colledge chappell; in ye east end of ye chapple upon ye glass is painted a Crucifix not as ordinary crucifixes

---

[1] *Diary of Sir Henry Slingsby*, p. 1.
[2] Letter from Laud to Wentworth, dated 29 December 1638 (Laud's *Works* vol. vi, pt. ii, p. 556).

are made but with a transverse piece of wood at ye feet as there
is for ye hands; at ye feet of ye crucifix is set ye Virgin Mary; &
on ye one hand ye picture of ye Apostle St John: and on ye
other Elizabeth and underneath St Peter, St Andrew, St Paul.

"In ye north corner is an handsome Pulpit, a table altar-wise
under ye east window, with a cloath of purple colour wrought
with stripes of worstett, which was my wife's own Handiwork."[1]
Already there is foreshadowed that quiet and dominant
association of the squire and his lady with the parish church in
an enclosed rural unit freed from the Papist and the Nonconformist.

In this particular instance the establishment was too large
to be typical. The family numbered six and was attended at
Red House by a staff of twenty-four; there were sixteen men
and eight women servants.[2] In the reference to the withdrawing-
room to the new parlour there comes an echo of the newer
fashions. The painting was carried out by a York tradesman,
the hangings were purchased from Bethnal Green. In the parlour hung designs of the Nine Muses. "Those in ye Lodging
chamber", explains Slingsby, "are calfe skins silver'd, & wrought
upon with a large flower in blew worstett: they came short of
ye ground having ye breadth of a pannell of wainscott below
them & a frieze & cornish above them. The chimney piece is
paint'd answerable in blew and sylver. There is above ye door
that goes into ye minor chamber a head carv'd in wood like a
Roman head, which I caus'd to be made for him that keeps ye
chambers & hath charge of ye Wardrope, as a remembrance
of him that hath so long & faithfully serv'd."[3]

These sentences are interesting, for the picture that they
conjure up in no way suggests the Caroline Age. The last words
bear a reminder of the squire's duty to his dependants, but for
the rest the whole tone is Elizabethan. It is decoration on the

---

[1] Slingsby's *Diary*, p. 2.

[2] Sir Henry Slingsby, in describing the household, also states that each year "I
spende £500, if ye demesne ground which I keep in my own hands be reckoned
according to ye Rent it would give & ye charge in getting it" (*Diary*, pp. 26-7).
As late as 1660 the total number of women servants employed at Woburn Abbey
did not exceed eight in number, and there were eleven or twelve footmen. No
women were employed in the kitchen. Cf. Woburn Abbey accounts described in
Life in a Noble Household, 1641-1700, by Gladys Scott Thomson, pp. 113-25. No
comparison can be established, for it is not clear how many of Slingsby's men
were in effect employed on the farm.

[3] Slingsby's *Diary*, p. 5.

Tudor pattern, the idea of magnificence and of display. The note about the staircase brings back the Elizabethan devices like those which Sir Thomas Tresham worked out at Rushton. "The staircase", so the entry runs, "that leads to ye great chamber . . . there sits a blackamoor cast in led by Andrew Carne a Dutchman, who also cut in stone ye statue of ye horse in ye garden."[1] In the North Country these fancies were not yet outmoded. There is no doubt that Sir Henry's mind was slow, but this picture is very far away from Ship Money and its intricacies.

Throughout this earlier portion of the diary Sir Henry was preoccupied by his wife's health. During two years her heart gave constant trouble, and in the winter of 1641 she died of what was termed a consumption, in the lodgings that her husband had taken in Monsieur Sebastian's house in Covent Garden. "The night before she dy'd she said by heart some part of ye 103 psalm."[2] This phrase will bring us back to Slingsby's theological preoccupations.

Although there was in his own family and in his wife's an admixture of religious affiliations, Sir Henry Slingsby himself was a resolute Anglican churchman. His opinions were generally in accord with those of Mr Thurscross, a prebendary of York who introduced to the household "a book call'd ye hundred & ten considerations of John Valdesco a Spaniard".[3] This volume had recently been translated by Nicholas Ferrar, and it is of interest to date its arrival in Anglican circles in Yorkshire. Sir Henry's attitude to the prebendary is set out tersely.[4] "He is a man of most holy life, only he is conformable to ye Church discipline that now is used & to those late impos'd ceremonies of bowing & adoring towards ye altar."

It is at this point that an inquiry made by the layman as to

[1] Slingsby's *Diary*, p. 6.

[2] *Ibid.*, entry under 31 December 1641, p. 75.

[3] *Ibid.*, entry under 19 December 1638, p. 57. There is no reason to suppose that either the Rev. Timothy Thurscross or Sir Henry Slingsby was aware of the identity of the translator. There is one reference in the *Life of Nicholas Ferrar* printed as a composite of the surviving manuscript accounts, each of which derives ultimately from the original *Life* by John, whose principal manuscript is lost: "And as N. F. communicated his heart to him [George Herbert], so he made him the Peruser, & desired the approbation of what he did, as in those three Translations of Valdezzo, Lessius & Cardo. To the first Mr Herbert made an Epistel" (*The Ferrar Papers*, ed. B. Blackstone, p. 59).

[4] *Ibid.*, p. 61.

Laudian practices throws a light on the explanations which were offered to them.[1] "When I ask'd him his opinion concerning this or that", we read of an exchange with Mr Thurscross, "I thought it came too near idolatry to adorn a place with rich cloathes & other furniture & to command to use towards it bodily worship: to which he answer'd that his bowing was not to the altar but to God especially in that place; which gesture he said was frequently used in Primitive times & every one may do as he is persuad'd in mind."

A little later Sir Henry returned to another aspect of this question in a discussion on the consecration of his private chapel. His view is set out with all his pursed self-confidence. "It is not amiss", he writes, "to have a place consecrat'd for Devotion, as our Churches are, therby to separate them for that use: but we cannot stay our self here, but must attribute a sanctity to ye very walls and stones of ye Church: & herein we of late draw near to ye Superstition of ye Church of Rome, who do suffer such external devotion to efface & wear out ye inward devotion of ye heart."[2]

At the same time it is of interest to note as characteristic of the period that such repugnances went side by side with a moderate sacramental approach not far removed from the devotions practised at Bemerton or Little Gidding.[3] "My wife", Slingsby explains, "this christmas [of 1638] intending to receive ye holy sacrament, & being also great with child, did send for Mr Ascough, a preacher in York, that she might receive from his mouth ye absolution of ye church & some whoolesome council for her soul, he being a man very eloquent both for his ordinary preaching, & private discourse. It is a doctrine but of late practis'd, tho it hath been taught always in our church, ye benefit of confession in some cases."[4]

---

[1] It may be said that they belonged to the first generation so to inquire, since for their ancestors had been more Catholic or more Protestant. Through the maternal lines there was a lingering Catholic influence in nearly all the families of the greater Yorkshire gentry. Thus, Sir Henry Slingsby the elder had married Frances, daughter of William Vavasour of Weston, and Thomas, first Lord Fairfax of Cameron, married Ellen, daughter of Robert Aske of Aughton.

[2] Slingsby's *Diary*, p. 25.

[3] Lady Slingsby belonged to a family predominantly Catholic, her father, Lord Fauconberg, adhering loosely to that Faith. Some sisters were married to Anglicans and one to a Recusant, Sir Walter Vavasour of Haslewood. Her younger brother, Lord Belasyse of Worlaby, was an ardent Catholic. She herself was firmly Anglican.

[4] Slingsby's *Diary*, p. 19.

The term auricular confession has indeed a Tridentine implication, and it is worth noting that Sir Henry gives a form of approval of this practice as useful for his womenfolk rather than for the head of the household. At the same time there had come in with this reign the notion of the clergyman as a counsellor. This seems in sharp contrast to the ideas prevalent in the old Queen's reign. It is, in general, a fair statement that such advice as the "painful preachers" of Elizabethan times saw fit to offer to men of quality was almost always proffered from the pulpit. The private consultations which Dr Laud held, both with the Duke of Buckingham and Lord Scudamore, belonged psychologically to this new age.[1]

It may be said that there was now initiated a relationship between the layman and his counsellor which was a novelty in the Church of England.[2] The widespread fear that this development would result in secessions to Rome on a wide scale was never warranted. No prominent divine, even of the second rank, abandoned the Anglican Communion, except Serenus Cressy and Thomas Bayly; nor in these two cases is there any record of their devotional practice during the years of their Anglican ministry.[3]

Viewed from another angle, there is little doubt that the

[1] This is especially evident in the letter written on 18 January 1627 by Dr Laud, then Bishop of Bath and Wells, to Sir John, later first Viscount, Scudamore. The latter had inquired as to the lawfulness of the holding of impropriations. Laud's phrase, "I pray fear not my exposing your conscientiousness to any man—God bless you in the tenderness of it, and I hope he will", is perfectly in character. Cf. Laud's correspondence with Lord Scudamore, preserved in Chancery Masters' Documents, Duchess of Norfolk's Deeds, and printed by H. R. Trevor-Roper in an appendix to his life of Archbishop Laud, pp. 437-56.

[2] It is worth noting the influence of the ideas behind Sir Henry Spelman's famous work, *The History and Fate of Sacrilege*. The book was not actually published until 1698, but the materials seem to have been assembled before 1633. The subject seems to have appeared in Spelman's conversation during his residence in London, first in Tothill Street and then in the Barbican, between 1612 and 1641. His treatise, *De non temerandis Ecclesiis, a tracte of the rights and respect due unto Churches,* was printed in 1613. Lord Scudamore was among those who sought Spelman's advice as to the restoration to the Anglican authorities of lay impropriations consisting of tithe, cf. *Reliquiæ Spelmanniæ,* ed. Edmund Gibson, p. 64.

[3] Hugh, later Serenus, Cressy was born in Yorkshire, either at Thorpe Salvin or Wakefield, in 1605. He was chaplain to Lord Wentworth, both in York and Ireland, and from 1642 a protégé of Lord Falkland. He was Dean of Leighlin from 1637. Thomas Bayly was born when his father was rector of St Matthew's, Friday Street, about 1607, and was made Sub-Dean of Wells in 1638. Bishop Goodman is in a different category. His adherence to Rome was only made manifest in his will.

parson's increased authority reflected the growth of a corporate spirit in the clerical body. The Anglican succession in the parishes had endured for nearly eighty years, and a balanced relationship had emerged between the rector and his chief parishioner. It was a relation which can be described as in most cases tolerable to both parties. The clergy gave respect which they now exacted in their turn.

It is a mistake to confuse the demonstrations of extreme respect with subservience; but in the Caroline polity the conception of the secular and spiritual arms with their respective spheres had taken shape.[1] The Church of England called forth and expressed a loyalty to the Crown which was traditional, insular and, above all, patriotic. There was a religious duty to respect the office of those who were placed in the commission of the peace by their sovereign.

In consequence of these and other factors, it is not so much the divergence as the solidarity within the Church of England which is the note of the nascent squirearchy. Leaving aside the minority of the Old Faith, a class feeling bound men to the King's mode of worship. Sir Henry Slingsby's generation was contemporary with Charles I. Scepticism and indifference were forms of expression which at that time were little regarded. Men of that age had been brought up from boyhood with the Authorised Version; the primacy was invested with dignity by both Charles I and his father; theology preoccupied both these sovereigns. And with this, the Church of England was manifested as profoundly and tenaciously conservative, and, in consequence, as respectful to constituted and legitimate authority as the Lutheran Consistories in the German States. Anglicanism had by now become, as it was for so long to remain, the religion of the gentlemen of England.

---

[1] As an example, Mr Crowther, an elderly clergyman who was Ralph Verney's tutor at Magdalen Hall, wrote to his pupil, then aged nineteen: "I have not initiated you into the science of geography. If you cannot have leisure to come over hither, I will attend you for a week or soe at Claydon till I have shewed you the principall grounds" (*Memoirs of the Verney Family*, ed. Frances Parthenope Verney, vol. i, p. 119).

CHAPTER XX

THE CHURCH ORDER

THERE are certain aspects of the ecclesiastical situation which can only with difficulty be reconciled. Over against the widespread anti-clerical feeling there must be set the fact that the position of the clergy was much stronger in the estimation of the governing class than is generally admitted. In this connection a sentence in Lady Fanshawe's *Memoirs* is most illuminating. "My father and mother", she writes of Sir John and Lady Harrison of Balls, "were both great lovers and honourers of clergymen, but all of Cambridge, and chiefly Doctor Bainbridge, Doctor Holdsworth, Brownrigg, Whalley, Micklethwaite, and Sanderson, with many others."[1] It is true that the Harrisons had strong civic connections,[2] and that the London merchants had had their favourite preachers since the turn of the century, but the idea of a university-trained parochial clergy has something of novelty.[3] It was a development which both repelled and attracted; but already we can detect the outlines of that strong corporate body which the Anglican clergy would prove themselves to be at the Restoration.

The idea of the family living was as yet hardly formulated, but already the value of the advowson as a seemly property, and a sometimes useful piece of patronage, was gaining ground. In this matter the Crown set an example. When the rich parsonage of Stanford Rivers in Essex became vacant through Bishop Montague's preferment, it was bestowed on Mr Mainwaring, who had likewise shown attachment to the King's ecclesiastical prerogative. At the same time, the position was

---

[1] *The Memoirs of Ann Lady Fanshawe*, 1907 ed., p. 23.

[2] Sir John Harrison had an estate at Balls in Hertfordshire, but from 1625 until 1640 lived in the parish of St Olave's, Hart Street, and in 1642 at Montague House in Bishopsgate Street (*ibid.*, pp. 17-18 and 24).

[3] As a contrast, there is Aubrey's comment on the Rev. Thomas Hobbes, vicar of Westport juxta Malmesbury, the father of the philosopher. "Thomas, the father, was one of the ignorant 'Sir Johns' of queen Elizabeth's times; could only read the prayers of the church and the homilies; and disesteemed learning as not knowing the sweetness of it" (Aubrey, *op. cit.*, ed. Powell, p. 237).

complicated by the fact that peers of strict opinions maintained chaplains or ministers who were only nominally conformist[1] or had been silenced.[2] They would also, and in this they were joined by the great city families, give protection to preachers who had not received the bishop's licence.

It is not very easy to disentangle the complex strands of the religious opposition. There were, for instance, two wholly distinct sections among those who favoured Presbyterianism. A link may perhaps be found in the Genevan idea of a counter-church. As opposed to the insularity of the Laudian position, there was a widespread sentiment favourable to the notion of a Protestant Faith, which would transcend national boundaries and manifest external union. It is this that is found reflected in the preamble to the Solemn League and Covenant, which would be tendered to the House of Commons in 1643. The desire, nostalgic in quality, lies behind the words "the true religion and professors thereof in all places".[3] The same idea is phrased in the Grand Remonstrance presented by the Commons to the King in December 1641. "We desire there may be a general synod of the most . . . judicious divines of this island: assisted with some from foreign parts, professing the same religion with us."[4]

These sentences indicate a wish, perhaps especially strong among one section of the gentry, for the political strength that could come from a union of all Protestants. This view was shared by influential circles within the Church of England, who held that such hopes were threatened with failure in view of

---

[1] Fuller has a comment on the attitude of Archbishop Harsnet of York (d. 1632) towards this question: "He was a zealous assertor of ceremonies, using to complain of (the first I believe who used the expression) conformable puritans, who practised it out of policy, yet dissented from it in their judgments" (*Church History*, ed. J. S. Brewer, vol. vi, p. 88).

[2] Arthur Hildersham, a protégé of successive Earls of Huntingdon, died in 1631, having served as minister of Ashby-de-la-Zouch for forty-three years. He had been silenced for the first time by the High Commission in 1590 and had been educated as a Catholic. In this connection Bastwick, who was sentenced with Prynne and Burton, had Catholic associations and his father was a tenant of Lord Petre. "Dr John Bastwick was born at Writtle in Essex, bred a short time in Emmanuel College, then travelled nine years beyond the seas, made doctor of physic at Padua. Returning home he practised it at Padua" (Fuller, *op. cit.*, vol. vi, pp. 83-5 and 113).

[3] Easily accessible in *The Constitutional Documents of the Puritan Revolution*, ed. S. R. Gardiner, 1947 ed., p. 268.

[4] *Ibid.*, p. 229.

a particular doctrine of the episcopate. In this connection it is worth noting that the Presbyterian peers and gentlemen were either themselves, or in the person of their sons, ready to accept the ecclesiastical provisions of the Restoration Settlement. The line of division would seem to come between those who desired Presbyterianism-by-law-Established and those to whom the concept of a State Church was in some cases unappealing and in others repellent. In the first place, a wide grouping desired that the National Church should be both Protestant and Established, other considerations being secondary to these two factors. For reasons which have already been examined, the Reformed Faith abroad was thought of as primarily Calvinist. In spite of the difficulties between the Scottish lords and the Presbytery during the reign of James VI, it could be maintained that in general both in Scotland and in France the Protestant landowning class was in accord with the existing Calvinist system. In any case, a non-episcopal Church order was at that date the norm of the continental Protestant structure. The English Parliamentarian peers and squires were drawn to the Scottish covenanting lords by the fact that both looked on episcopacy with a jealous eye. The latter grouping was determined to sweep away the Scottish episcopate which the Stuarts had fostered. In England the opposition in both houses was moving gradually towards the same conclusion in regard to Dr Laud and his associates. The wealthy element which was becoming Presbyterian had found the episcopal apparatus increasingly distasteful. They were determined to eliminate the Court of High Commission. There were various reasons for this hostility.

In the first place, the relationship between the temporal and spiritual peers was distant at the beginning of King Charles' reign, and grew progressively more tenuous. There was still less contact between the bishops and the greater squires. Such acquaintanceship as existed with either grouping was very seldom marked by any cordiality. They had neither common tastes nor a common background, nor had they shared social and administrative experiences. At the same time, the bishops had a strong and clearly self-conscious independence.

Many reached the bench after holding the headship of a college. Such men came usually from a city childhood to pass their maturity as tutors in the universities. The relationship of patron and client, which so often marked the link between the Whig peer and the Whig bishop, was not yet forged. The promoted bear-leader or private tutor, who had served respectfully in a nobleman's household, would not be found until the eighteenth century. As a rule, it may be said that the Caroline bishops had little experience of the life of the peers or the greater squires before their promotion to the bench or to a deanery.

Much has been made of the degree to which the leaders of the country party must have found the attitude of the Jacobean and Caroline prelates uncongenial. This can be overstressed, but it is true that each manifestation of the bishop's power was galling to the peer or greater squire of strict opinions. In these circles it was not so much their harshness and their pretensions which were criticised. The crux of the matter was the incursion of the bishops into the sphere of statesmanship, the political influence of Archbishop Laud and the office of Lord-Treasurer now held by Bishop Juxon. In a sense this was no new development, for Bishop Williams had been Lord Keeper during the last years of James I. Dr Williams, however, was pliable and an individualist; he showed no sense of his own order. Dr Laud and Dr Juxon, on the other hand, acted as members of a corporate body; they were always consciously prelates and churchmen. This development was aided by King Charles' outlook on the Anglican episcopate. The leaders of both Houses of Parliament could see what might in time become the second estate of the higher clergy.

The impression left by the Caroline Episcopate is the relative isolation of its leading members. The peers, who would in time form the Presbyterian grouping, looked on with jealousy as Laud's power grew. Such accretion of influence was an unwelcome novelty. For this reason, it seems just to suggest that it was primarily a diminution of the political influence of the bishops for which the Parliamentarian leaders sought. This was their motive as they considered plans for a primitive episcopacy or even for a Presbyterian model. To all the privileged circle, what was then termed a moderate episcopacy implied a political, rather than a doctrinal, change. On this reading there is little inconsistency in the return to Anglicanism after 1660 of all those wealthy men who had formed the Presbyterian *bloc* in the Civil Wars. For the Restoration Settlement, in effect, curtailed the power of the Crown and left the influence of the episcopate very sensibly diminished. Such development would not be unacceptable to those supporters of the Parliament in both houses who had been bitterly disillusioned by the Protectorate, and had never lost their feeling for a monarchical constitution and some form of Church establishment.

The Presbyterian ministers and the bulk of the Presbyterian middle class were in a very different case. They were outside the governing circles, and had little care for political balances. It was the actual institution of episcopacy, not its presentation and not its power in politics, which was distasteful to them. These matters were secondary to their doctrinal opposition. There were, of course, cross-influences. Thus peers, who would in time become amenable, often maintained as chaplains Presbyterian preachers who were addicted to the stiff opinions. But in the reign of Charles I such ministers were harried, while the laymen from the poorer sections of the Presbyterian grouping stood marshalled behind their wealthy leaders, whose real ideas were different from their own. Further, within the Houses of Parliament the form of Presbyterianism that existed was masked at least until 1641. The line between the Protestant Church of England men who accepted episcopacy and those who wished to modify that institution could not yet be drawn precisely. The whole was seen within a real but unacknowledged political setting. In this matter the development of the Scottish situation cannot be neglected, for it was this factor, acting in the Opposition in the Lower House, that would bring about the acceptance of the Solemn League and Covenant.

On the other hand, there does not seem to have been any close association between the bishops and those of the peers who would always be Royalist. Lord Scudamore, the intimate and perhaps the penitent of Dr Laud, stands quite alone. There were many reasons for this lack of any sustained or intimate contact. The apparatus of episcopal visitation as insisted on by the Primate would necessarily grate on the Erastians, who could recall that in Elizabethan times the bishop was so often represented as the Queen's servant. The King was very solitary in the nature of the understanding that he gave to their labours. Again the note of moral earnestness which marked the great majority of the prelates made small appeal to those who were accustomed to the circle of the Court.

There was also a natural coldness between the bishops and the relatively numerous body of Recusant peers. Both prudence and inclination led the Anglican episcopate to avoid the society of those who maintained priests of the Old Faith as their private chaplains. In this connection, it is a little surprising that the bishops should have been so widely charged with Roman sympathies. This is a point which deserves some consideration.

With the exception of Goodman of Gloucester and possibly Montagu of Norwich, all the members of the Caroline Bench were deeply opposed both to the Tridentine Church order and doctrine. Even Bishop Goodman was careful of his Catholic contacts when in the country, and his sophisticated questing personality roused suspicion rather than liking in the heredi- tary Recusant circles. As for Bishop Montagu, he was a proficient in anti-papalist controversy,[1] and the celebrated *Apello Cæsarem*, which was so bitterly attacked by his opponents, was a vindication of his teaching from any Roman tendencies. There is, however, some reason to suppose that he had a certain sympathy with the Tridentine Church order. If this is so, he and Dr Goodman were alone, since the rest of the episcopate were resolutely insular.[2] Neither the fabric nor the presentation of the Church of Rome made any more appeal to them than it did to their royal master. A study of the period leaves the impression that the bishops were quite unprepared for the bitterness of the attack made upon them as Romanisers in the House of Commons. Laud could detect the gathering of his political opponents, but it is doubtful if he realised the character of the religious note which they would sound.

Several factors account for the situation. Hooker's *Ecclesiastical Polity* had helped to mould the clerical body. At the same time, the opinions based on that work, which were crystallising among the churchmen, seem to have been hardly reflected in the lay world. It is true that the episcopal attitude in the matter of the Divine Right of Kings did, indeed, find support among

---

[1] Cf. letter from Richard Montagu: "To stand in the gapp against puritanisme and popery, the Scilla and Charybdis of Ancient Piety" (*Cosin Correspondence*, Surtees Society, vol. i, p. 21).

[2] Panzani, whose unsupported judgments were notably unreliable, described Robert Wright, Bishop of Lichfield and Coventry, as *quasi Cattolico*. This may have resulted from some smooth phrases of the old prelate who had had some contact with Catholics when he was a protégé of Dorothy Wadham (*P.R.O. Roman Transcripts*, under 27 April 1636, printed in Albion, *op. cit.*, p. 413).

the High Royalists. It was, however, a point to which more attention was drawn during the time of their master's misfortunes. It would be interesting to study the degree of support accorded to sacramental teaching among the laity.[1] What is not in doubt is the uniformly cold reception given to the teaching on Church order as set out by the Caroline divines. This was a case of projects and conceptions worked over within the clerical body with the minimum of lay co-operation. In any consideration of Church order it is not easy to distinguish at all clearly between the sacramental and sacerdotal aspects, but the latter was most strongly opposed by the mass of lay opinion. It is, indeed, the key word in the struggle. The great body of members of the House of Commons was resolutely hostile, not only to Rome but also to any increase or strengthening of the ecclesiastical structure. In contentious matters for two generations, in the question of the cross in Baptism, the surplice, the place of the communion table, the emphasis was placed on the elimination of the sacerdotal element. On this reading it was a sharp dislike for the growing political power of individual bishops, an inchoate desire for a Protestant foreign policy and a rooted dislike for sacerdotalism that concentrated so much opposition against the Caroline Episcopate. In this sense the Grand Remonstrance may be held to sum up the standpoint of the bishops' enemies in the Lower House. "And", we read in the one hundred and eighty-fourth article of the petition presented by the House of Commons,[2] "we do here declare that it is far from our purpose or desire to let loose the golden reins of discipline and government in the Church, to leave private persons or particular congregations to take up what form of Divine Service they please, for we hold it requisite that there should be throughout the whole realm a conformity to that

---

[1] The account of her upbringing given by Anne Murray, later Lady Halkett, bears on this point. "But my mother's greatest care, and for which I shall ever owe to her memory the highest gratitude, was the great care she took that, even from our infancy, we were instructed never to neglect to begin and end the day with prayer, and orderly every morning to read the Bible, and ever to keep the church as often as there was occasion to meet there, either for prayers or preaching. So that for many yeares together I was seldom or never absent from divine service, at five a'clocke in the morning in the summer, and sixe a'clocke in the winter, till the usurped power putt a restraint to that publicke worship so long owned and continued in the Church of England" (*The Autobiography of Anne Lady Halkett*, Camden Society (1875), ed. John Gough Nichols, pp. 2-3).

[2] Printed in Gardiner *Constitutional Documents*, 1947 ed., p. 229.

order which the laws enjoin according to the Word of God. And we desire to unburden the consciences of men of needless and superstitious ceremonies, suppress innovations and take away the monuments of idolatry."[1]

If this is carefully considered, it will be found to lead back to the aspirations of some among the Marian exiles. It was not Calvinist theology that was denied to Laud's opponents, for this was still held by certain bishops; it was a Church order Genevan in its simplicity that was their aim. It was to this end that they would remove the "monuments of idolatry".

At a first glance it would appear that there were members of the episcopate who were not without sympathy for a certain portion of these aims. Still, it is by no means easy to assess the different trends of opinion within the episcopal body. In the first place the Primate had an admiration for secular efficiency. Prelates of Calvinist tendencies were congenial to him when they brought forward anti-Roman controversy. High teaching on the respect due to the King's person was given by bishops of every school of thought. Finally it was what may be termed the opposition bishops who were most attached to their prerogatives as lords spiritual. It was part of Dr Laud's character that, except in certain cases, he gave sympathy to his colleagues in the measure that they inspired respect in him. His own position with his sovereign was unique; the view that he took of his rôle was grand; there is no evidence that he considered his supporters as a party. As a consequence, he never lost a distant cordiality towards the bishops whose ideas were most remote from his own.

These, until they were joined by Prideaux before the end, were Morton of Durham and Hall of Exeter. They had both travelled on the Continent, and had a feeling for the foreign Churches. They were both attracted by a world-wide union or at least alliance against Rome. Dr Morton went so far as to regard ordination by presbyters as valid in case of necessity. By this time he was an old man, consecrated as far back as 1616, and in his outlook a survivor of the Elizabethan episcopal Puritan tradition. A glimpse of his approach is given in the

[1] In *The Architectural Setting of Anglican Worship*, by C. W. D. Addleshaw and Frederick Etchells, the authors draw attention to the statement of Pocklington in *Altare Christianum* that in the services held for the Order of the Garter in the reign of Charles I the knights bowed towards the altar (*op. cit.*, p. 138).

CHARLES I AND SIR EDWARD WALKER
From the painting by an unknown artist in the National Portrait Gallery

Journal of Sir William Brereton, later the Parliamentarian commander, who visited him on 20 June 1635 at Bishop Auckland. "I demaunded from him", explains Sir William in describing his interview with the bishop, "whether bowing to the altar was injoyned, and commanded by any canon, or left free and arbitrarie. Hee annswered: Itt was left free and arbitrarie. Itt was not bowing to the altar now in use, but towards the East, as Daniell pray'd: and it was not to bee accounted an altar, butt the communion table."[1]

Regarding Bishop Morton as the relic of another age, wholly alien to the Queen's Vandyck world, it may be wondered that the opposition in the House of Commons did not try to separate the bishops of the more Puritan tradition from their colleagues. The answer seems to lie in the predominantly political aims which moved the leaders in the Parliament. With this motive brought into play the situation is seen in a different light, for the prelates whose training harked back to the Elizabethan universities had an Erastian outlook on their own office. The less that they magnified its intrinsic powers and privileges, the more closely did they associate it with a royal gift. The King seems to have been conscious of this intense loyalty to the royal office and of the manner in which the prelates of Calvinistic sympathies held themselves to be the Crown's intimate instruments. Considered from the political angle, there was a certain similarity in the view that all the bishops took in regard to their legislative functions.

An element in the opposition aroused against the bishops in the House of Commons would seem to have arisen from their political cohesion. They were ready to act together and cherished their independence. The subservient Hanoverian Bench could never have been the object of such sharp dislike. To most of the Stuart prelates the opposition which developed may well have seemed incredible. They had their own high place and that peculiar respect which their sovereign gave to their spiritual office; they were conscious of their anti-Roman rectitude. Among themselves they are seen as possessing a cool

---

[1] *Journal of Sir William Brereton*, Surtees Society (1915), p. 11. A markedly sympathetic attitude towards the foreign Calvinist traditions was not inconsistent with a certain measure of episcopal ceremonial. Thus Sir William noted that at the administration of Communion in Durham Cathedral ' the Bishopp useth the new red embroidered cope which is wrought full of starres: like one, I have seene worne in St Dennis in France" (Brereton, *op. cit.*, p. 13).

and unintimate solidarity. It is interesting to note the influence
which Bishop Williams now at last exerted on his brethren.
During the opening stages of the Long Parliament eleven other
prelates followed his leadership. It seems likely that even to the
end they never gave their trust to a lay peer.

They were, perhaps, most deeply wounded, not by the King's
open enemies, but by his lukewarm friends. "Mr Speaker,"
said Lord Falkland in the Lower House on 8 February 1641,
"I do not believe them [the bishops] to be *Jure divino*, nay I
believe them not to be *Jure divino*, but neither do I believe them to
be *Injuria humana*: I neither consider them as necessary, nor as
unlawful, but as convenient or inconvenient."[1] It is not hard to
see why the prelates of the Restoration world could not abide
the Latitudinarians.

[1] Rushworth, *op. cit.*, vol. iv, p. 184. This speech is printed in full in the *Life and
Times of Viscount Falkland*, by J. A. R. Marriott, pp. 181-90.

CHAPTER XXI

THE BREAKDOWN

VARIOUS factors brought about the destruction of the particular mood which the Court had inspired. The Caroline period could not survive the outbreak of the Civil Wars and the impairment of the royal authority. The tension leading to the conflict and the alignment and realignment of forces was conditioned, to a considerable extent, by economic factors. The causes of the conflict recognised by contemporaries were diverse. The situation in Ireland and in Scotland, and the calculated manœuvres of the parliamentary opposition, all lie outside the scope of the present study. Only the last factor was likely to have been envisaged early in the reign, and in a sense it dominated the run of years during which Charles I attempted to rule without recourse to Parliament.

At the same time, it is difficult to believe that the outbreak of actual war could have been imagined during the tension of 1637. It was the calling together of armed forces to deal with the Scottish opposition that first turned men's minds towards the possibility of a military conflict. A precedent was likewise created when forces were levied by the Scottish Assembly. Yet there was already in 1637 an ominous note of harshness, the nature of the punishment of Mr Prynne, which involved the mutilation of a gentleman, and the imprisonment of the Bishop of Lincoln. It was imprudent of Dr Laud to assent to the arrest of any member of the Episcopal Bench. The precedents were thus established for the prosecution of the Archbishop as well as that of the Lord-Deputy. In this respect, it was remarkable the degree to which these two great men showed to their many enemies the methods by which their own destruction could be compassed.

One factor was present throughout the later part of the peaceful portion of the reign—the steady power of the Archbishop. These last years were, in fact, dominated by a personality which was both very vigorous and quite unhopeful. Granted that he was without experience of the Scottish temper and had a disdainful ignorance of Irish matters, it remains that Laud's knowledge of the English scene had a certain unimaginative precision. Within the limits of his interests, few men have had so clear an insight into the forces massed against them and have at the same time taken so few precautions. It was, perhaps, the vein of apprehension in Laud's character and the sense of foreboding that served to numb him.

Moreover, the success that had attended him had always had the quality of the unexpected. The fulfilment of his matured ideas had borne the marks of the period of their gestation. He had long pondered, and had then set to work in many fields almost simultaneously. The ecclesiastical opposition had been always present, but it was rather Laud's financial policy that gained for him the new effective enemies. It was his attitude upon financial questions that led men to change from apathy to a determination to destroy him.

The fact that he was a churchman combined with his unyielding temper to sharpen the opposition. He was not only incorrupt but peculiarly inaccessible. The enemies of his policy grouped together—the monopolists; the peers with mercantile affiliations; the colonisers. The Primate detested all private financial combinations. He was in some ways out of date, he did not fear to make Bishop Juxon Lord-Treasurer. His rule was given to the building up of the church fabric, and to restoring to the Crown and to the great ecclesiastical corporations each parcel of the alienated lands. Archbishop Laud had an ingrained distrust of all monopolies and of the method of their operation. It was at this point that he and the Lord-Deputy drew away from all the other royal ministers.

The politicians did not heed the pamphleteering attack which Prynne initiated and to which Milton later lent himself. "What relish", wrote Milton in a famous sentence, "it would give to his Canary-sucking and swan-eating palate let old Bishop Mountain judge for me." These words have very little meaning, and Laud himself was almost abstemious. The conflict raged on a more crucial level. It was not the luxury that roused the opposition of men of substance, it was rather the moulding power of the Archbishop's conceptions, the vision of the governed ordered State allied to a theocracy.

Discontent had been growing during the years without a Parliament as the possessing classes studied the new sources of revenue, the insistence on fines in the case of landowners who neglected to apply for knighthood, the application of the forest laws and the enforcement of the statutes against enclosures. It is, perhaps, anachronistic to lay much stress on the archaic character of certain measures. In that closed society it was of more consequence that each new project for increasing the revenue should have had its spectacular victim or series of victims. Partly because a rebellion on the scale that occurred was unimaginable, little thought appears to have been given to those who were mulcted by these new expedients. It was, however, just these men who formed a silent chorus of approval when the avowed Opposition moved against the King's great ministers. Among the prosperous classes there were many heads of families who were not actually hostile to the Crown but who can best be described as alienated from it. The exactions of the Court of Wards, for instance, as applied in these last years served little by little to destroy the old attachment to the Crown among a section of the wealthier and more cautious gentry. The King's position during the first four years of the Civil War would have been very different but for the group of the alienated peers and the body of the alienated greater squires.

It would be interesting to examine the incidence of these financial expedients in the South and Midlands as compared to the position in the counties which comprised the lord-presidentship of the North. It would be found that in the North Country the exactions were for various reasons much less severe. As a generalisation, it seems fair to state that the northern squires were relatively poor, in a particular sense attached to the royal standard and in financial matters much less molested.

The question of ship money, which has already been touched upon, was on a different footing from the other measures. The decision to contest the right to levy this charge on inland counties was a considered move by what may be called the official Opposition. It seems to have been judged to be the most effective method of concentrating opinion against the practice of governing without Parliament. The ship-money plan was not without its subtlety, for it appears that it was intended to evoke from the judges expressions favourable to the royal prerogative. Such judgments given in an issue of this nature would serve to range together the episcopal bench, the judiciary and the rest of the King's immediate councillors as opponents of a responsible parliamentary system. Only to this extent does Hampden's action in contesting the legality of the third ship-money writ enter into the development of that volume of hostility which was piling up against the Primate and Lord-Deputy.

Yet the suggestion that King Charles was barricaded behind the supporters of his royal prerogative would be wide of the mark. In fact, it was his difficulty that he was always so accessible to his concealed enemies and ill-wishers. This was another quarter from which his ministers were under fire. It was their misfortune that their sovereign did not care to whom he turned at moments when he was actually in need of money. The whole range of public activities was open to the adventurer, and there were few who might not hope to minister to their King's necessities.

The last factor was grievous to authoritarians like Laud and Strafford. The political arena has seldom been examined from this angle, and a note of moneys lent to Charles I by special warrant has interest in this connection. It throws light upon a complex situation, since the King, although he never recognised the fact, surrendered a portion of his liberty to those who very willingly became his creditors. The document was compiled in the mid years of the extra-parliamentary *régime*, and at that date the sums outstanding amounted to rather over eighty-three thousand pounds.[1] It does not appear that it was intended that any debt should be liquidated by a grant of honour. No sale of a peerage was involved in this transaction.[2] Short of repayment, the persons mentioned would remain His Majesty's creditors. It is not the figure involved which is significant, but rather the list of parties to whom His Majesty had agreed to incur an obligation. The names read as follows:

Lord Goring	£15,000
The Soapmakers . .	£10,973
Sir James Bagg . . .	£16,500
Sir Cornelius Vermuyden	£10,000

[1] State Papers, Dom. Charles I, cclxxxvi, 43.

[2] It should, perhaps, be noted that Edward, second Viscount Campden, and at that date Lord Noel of Ridlington, had, on 5 May 1628, obtained a reversion to himself and his heirs males of the peerages conferred on that day upon his father-in-law, the celebrated moneylender, Sir Baptist Hicks.

Charles Harbord	.	.	£8,000
Philip Burlamachi	.	.	£6,000
Sir John Winter .	.	.	£4,000
Viscount Campden .	.	.	£2,500

An analysis of these items has a certain value.

There were, in the first place, the old straightforward money-lenders of King James' time to whom the Crown had time out of memory been so indebted—Mr Burlamachi and Sir Baptist Hicks. The latter's commitments had been taken over by Lord Campden, his son-in-law and heir. It was now more than thirty years since Burlamachi had come to England, by religion a Protestant, by temperament both suave and patient, by birth a native of Sedan in the Duke of Bouillon's territory. He was at this date almost out of business and come to the winding-up of his affairs, living retired at Putney with his wife and family. Certain rooms were still retained at Mr Gould's establishment in Fenchurch Street "for the necessary occasions of writing there".[1]

The Soapmakers' Company was an unpopular monopoly and running into storms. It had long been clear to the promoters that their proceedings would soon be questioned. Sir James Bagg, who dealt in the victualling of the fleet, had found it prudent to provide large sums. His character had been aspersed severely. All was grist that came to the sovereign's mill. It is worth remembering that the King's sense that his subjects should meet the royal necessities freed him from any consciousness of obligation. He never felt that he could be bound down by any staining contract; in this sense he understood his royal prerogative. He would accept help from almost any quarter and, when dealing with the most mercenary and the least reputable, King Charles' mind went free.

To return to the list. Sir Cornelius Vermuyden was the great engineer of the Bedford Level, and his loan was a form of reinsurance. Sir John Winter had interests in coal mines, and his relatively small sums were lent against grants from Crown lands in the Forest of Dean, where he worked his enterprises. He was the only Catholic among these donors. Lord Goring was deep in many matters, and it would be interesting to know

[1] Details from a letter from the Lord Mayor to the Council, describing the strangers inhabiting the city of London, 23 December 1623 (State Papers, Dom. Charles I, ccv, 11).

whence he gained the sums to relend to His Majesty. Goring and Winter were both attached to the Queen's household. With them there was the gesture of the intimate relief of the King's necessities by those whose privilege it was to protect His Majesty from inconvenience. Such an attitude would be reflected by the new sophisticated moneylenders. It was this that made the situation so very different from the previous reign. King Charles' dignity did not impair his Stuart gift of asking. No prince could ask more easily and heedlessly and gracefully.

In another direction a difficulty was caused by the King's disinclination to assist old pensioners, and the survivors among the older Scotsmen who had been at Court since his father's time. It was a misfortune for Charles I that he alienated those whom his new measures mulcted, and at the same time embittered men whose projects he refused to further. He could not manipulate the astute petitioner. Sir John Meldrum's application is a case in point. The position is set out with an almost painful clarity. The question at issue related to a patent for the erection of lighthouses. The lights at Winterton, so the petitioner explained, had been intended by the late King for Dr Welwood and Sir William Erskine. In the event Meldrum had purchased the interests of these gentlemen and was still £7,000 in debt on that account. He went on to assert that he maintained the light at Orfordness at his own charge, and that the lights to be erected at the two Forelands were "all his livelihood".

It was contended that the Master of Trinity House opposed any private man who attempted to perform this service. Meldrum explained that, although he would have to erect three lighthouses, it was his intention to charge the same figure as that paid by vessels for the single light at Dungeness. The just charge, he concluded, was a toll of one penny per *ton* levied on shipping.[1] Behind him, and hardly distinguishable, there stood the men who had the technical knowledge to set him on his enterprise.

The episode just set out is significant. The King had not the capacity to deal, and Laud and Strafford were not prepared to deal, with the more outrageous of the petitioners. These had piled up their hopes in the easy reign of their old master. Their

[1] State Papers, Dom. Charles I, cclxxxvi, 28.

patience and their loyalty did not survive this non-fulfilment. In Gervase Holles' straightforward memorials of his family, there is an account of the siege of Newark at which he was present. "The rebelles", we read without surprise, "sett downe before the towne on the south side of the Trent commanded by that perfidious and ungratefull Scot Sir John Meldrum."[1] He was not the only one among such men who had gone out to serve the Parliament.

It is worth stressing the many quarters from which the royal cause was now recruiting enemies. There were shades of disapprobation and of unfriendly neutrality. There was perhaps, above all, a very real determination among the leaders of the Commons that they would not permit Parliament to be dissolved. Once the Long Parliament had met it was soon manifest that it proposed to remain in being. It was at this point that the Protestant temper became significant, enabling Parliament, and especially the Lower House, to stand forth as the champion of threatened religious liberties. In all this matter it is difficult to disentangle the complex elements, the financial concern of all the wealthier taxpayers, the specific merchant groupings, the constitutional-political solidarity and that touch of mass hysteria which affect the whole amalgam. The last factor was given rein because the King was so incomprehensible to his opponents. Even his enemies were brought to realise that he would never give up what he believed to be his influence upon them.

In general it may be said that, while certain class and sectional interests brought wide groups into the Royalist or Parliamentarian camps, the reactions of individuals seems unpredictable. There were surely those who went with the Parliament because Laud had compelled them. Sir Nathaniel Brent, Warden of Merton, is an example. On the other hand, Sir Henry Marten died before it could become clear that his quarrel with Laud would develop into a quarrel with the King. In the circumstances of the time, it must have been difficult to imagine that men would actually oppose their sovereign in arms. It was particularly hard for those who had been brought up in the new bureaucratic class and under the Tudor discipline.

The oscillation in public events in the period between the first campaign against the Scots and the Battle of Marston

[1] *Memorials of the Holles Family*, Camden Society, p. 182.

all his choleric impatience, had a strange sense of detachment from the trend of political events. His wits were sharpened by the knowledge that he would be sacrificed. It was, perhaps, in the summer of 1637, after Prynne's second prosecution for aspersions on Their Majesties, that the danger signals became evident. This was the year of the riots in Edinburgh occasioned by the King's attempt to enforce the liturgy drawn up under the Primate's guidance.

In August the Archbishop was at Croydon in his country palace, and two letters give a view of his high outlook. "My Lord," he wrote to the Earl of Traquair in regard to the affairs of Scotland, "I think you know my opinion how I would have Church business carried, were I as great a master of men as I thank God, I am of things."[1] A letter to the Lord-Deputy bears on this point. Dr Laud recurs to his fear of the weakness of the instrument. "Once again", he explained, "you return to Prynne and his fellows, and observe most rightly, that these men do but begin with the Church, that they might after have the freer access to the State; and I would to God other men were more of your Lordship's opinion, or if they be so already, I would they had some of your zeal too for timely prevention; but for all that we are too secure, and will not believe there's any foul weather towards us till the storm breaks upon us."[2]

Laud's strength of purpose presses through the long, coiled sentences. He had always tried to moderate the courage with which Lord Wentworth gathered adversaries. For all his authoritarian temperament, there was in the Archbishop's character something of the bureaucrat as opposed to the pure dictator. His mind built up the combinations in which he was predominant; he would plough on through this intractable material. The Lord-Deputy's great gift for firm, high-handed solitude had never come to him. "My last advice", he wrote, "is that whosoever your enemies be, and whatsoever they attempt, you would offer at no defence, till they shall dare to appear openly."[3] Laud worked upon a doctrine which in some ways foreshadowed ministerial responsibility in embryo. This can best be described as advisory collective action tempered by theocracy. It was the kernel of the Archbishop's view

---

[1] Letter dated 7 August 1637 (Laud's *Works*, vol. vi, pt. ii, p. 494).
[2] Letter dated 28 August 1637 (*ibid.*, p. 500).
[3] Letter dated 24 October 1637 (*ibid.*, p. 511).

that he alone had an approach to the conscience of the sovereign beyond the serried ranks of the King's advisers. Such an outlook was impracticable, for it required from his royal master a sustained inflexible docility which was never found in the members of the House of Stuart. There was in Laud a quality which was at once direct and simple. He had none of that wisdom born of tired knowledge which was the heritage of the Tridentine world.

These varying elements in his character are all revealed in his letters, whose crystal honesty illuminates the heavy phrasing. As autumn changed to winter he formulated now for the last time his royalist beliefs. "For there is no reason in the world", he wrote to the Lord-Deputy from Lambeth, "that the sourness of every negative should be put upon you on that side. Great reason there is, that it should be kept off from the King as much as may be, and as great that it should be divided among the Ministers with some indifferency, and not lodged upon one or few."[1] And then the disillusion broke upon him. "But this is not the way, for every man saves himself as well as he can, let the burden light where it will. And now I am grown almost as proud as you; for whereas you write that his Majesty must not always look to be served upon such terms, I shall say so too; and perhaps when I am gone my saying shall be found true."

Two other passages are worth noting in this long letter. "Your Lordship apprehends right the ill consequences of the liberty of these times. Nor have I any great hope to see these things settle till reward and punishment have their full course." And then there comes the first reference to a new ally which seems to set the stage for all the final tragedy. "I shall thank your Lordship", so the phrase runs, "for writing according as you speak to the *Countess of Carlisle*. For that was true which I wrote to you in my last letters, and I must needs say I am beholden to her."[2]

It is a strange contrast, Laud turning to men like Hyde and Selden, showing friendship to those who were powerless to help him, and Strafford coming within range of Lady Carlisle's influence. The earlier associations were breaking up. It was an official nexus rather than a personal relationship which bound Laud to the prelates of his creation, and his old relationship

[1] Letter dated 11 November 1637 (Laud's Works, vol. vi, pt. ii, p. 512).
[2] *Ibid.*, p. 513.

the secretary's place consequent upon the forced withdrawal of
Sir John Coke, now eighty years of age. The motives which led
Lord Leicester to desire this post are still obscure. He was at this
time ambassador extraordinary in Paris, and much of the
detailed bureaucratic work would seem to have been uncongenial to the owner of Penshurst. The King himself explained
that the post was not suited to a man of Leicester's rank. The
secretaries were, in fact, always chosen from the civil-service
world, considering that term in its wide extension; it was an
office that would come in time to Edward Nicholas.

In this test of strength, Lord Northumberland was the
spokesman for his brother-in-law, Leicester. It is interesting to
consider Northumberland's standpoint and what can be
gathered of that of his sister, Lady Carlisle. In their different
ways each set of letters leaves the impression of the indestructible
quality of Strafford's power if annexed to that of the Archbishop.
Thus, as late as December 1639 Lady Carlisle subscribes to this
judgment. "I am glad", she wrote to her sister, Lady Leicester,
"that you wish a friendship betwixt Leicester and the Lord
Deputy for I am confident it will be ane easy Worke. Northumberland is better with the Lord Deputy than he has beene . . .
and is now cal'd to all the greatest secrets of the King, which
are now only in the trust of the Archbishop, Lord Deputy,
Northumberland and Hamilton."[1]

In the matter of the succession to the secretaryship, Strafford
was represented as standing Leicester's friend. Northumberland,
writing to his brother-in-law, set out this view. "If possible", he
wrote on 16 January 1640, "that can be done I have better
hopes than ever that it will be obtained for you for I do assure
you of the Lord Deputy's using the uttermost of his Power."[2]
In fact the post was given to the Queen's Treasurer, Sir Henry
Vane, and the Archbishop had shown himself reluctant to
permit Leicester's appointment, since in Paris he had treated
Lord Scudamore with some coldness; the latter was one of
Laud's few special protégés. The question is mainly of interest
as showing how late the two great ministers held their undi-

[1] Letter dated 19 December 1639, preserved among the Penshurst MSS. and
transcribed by Arthur Collins. A simple numeral cipher was used, 65 representing
the King, 80 the Archbishop, 82 Northumberland, 85 Leicester, 93 the Lord-
Deputy and 98 Hamilton (*Letters and Memorials of State*, p. 626).

[2] Letter dated 9 January 1640. In this letter 115 represents the Lord-Deputy,
135 Northumberland and 137 Leicester (*ibid.*, p. 631).

minished influence. Within a year both the Primate and Lord Strafford were impeached and imprisoned.

What can be conceived as the real purpose of these manœuvres? Behind this chain of events can be detected the intention to substitute one theory of government for another. The first idea would seem to have involved the establishment of a simple cabal—the sharing of power among a small body of advisers to the sovereign. The Scottish troubles had brought the Marquess of Hamilton into that sphere where the Archbishop and Lord-Deputy guided their master. Into the inner group, consisting for a period of Strafford, Laud and Hamilton, it was perhaps intended to insert a representative of the Penshurst-Petworth circle. This would result in the invasion of the authoritarian position by the oligarchic idea. The possibility of this change had been foreshadowed by the emergence of Hamilton, who was a representative of the Scottish peers rather than an individual leader. This is at least a reasonable explanation of why a rich landowner like Lord Leicester should be ready to accept, and indeed to press for, all the tedious almost subordinate work which must fall to a secretary. The office would provide the vantage point from which to bring his personal weight to bear. Nevertheless, the whole conception rested on a fallacy which would soon be disproved. The manœuvre was only useful provided that King Charles was quite resolved to sustain his great ministers. Even those with some access to their sovereign did not realise the extent to which the fire had gone out of the King since his defence of Buckingham.

The next stage is in sharp contrast. Once it was clear that Laud and Strafford were to be sacrificed, the hopes of what may be termed an oligarchic *régime* took concrete form. Working along these lines, the preparation for the Civil War, and indeed its early stages, can be seen to be affected by the Venetian ideals of the circle which comprised the Earls of Northumberland, Leicester and Essex. One line of thought led forward to the Whig doctrine of kingship, but it was Penshurst that gave birth to the republicanism of Algernon Sidney. At the same time, this little world was not without its influence in moulding the thought of James Harington, which found expression in the *Commonwealth of Oceana*.

The rejection of Leicester's service and Strafford's impeachment marked the gulf that was opening. An authoritarian monarchy, such as Richelieu and Strafford were constructing, was inevitably repugnant to those whose private hopes were always centred on class government. In Venice a man of education could observe the pattern of a sovereignty in which the Doge was, in fact, the servant of the Seigniory.

It was in part a consequence of these ideas that the opposition peers were so often found to be men of substance. There were occasional fanatics like Lord Saye and Sele, but the fourth Earl of Bedford, with his mercantile preoccupations, was much more typical. Beginning with Northumberland and Essex, for Leicester never actually separated himself from the King, it may be said that certain notes marked those lords who by degrees came to oppose their sovereign. There was an element of high-minded responsibility that foreshadowed the Whigs, an insular concern that was Protestant in its emphasis, a nostalgia for what were wrongly conceived to be Elizabethan values. There was, as these ideas have indicated, much confusion of thought. It was rare to find that cool, innate and mercenary capacity which would mark their descendants in 1688. The attachment to the King-in-Parliament had its Venetian element. There was the sharp class consciousness of those who are the arbiters of their own divisions. With this there went a note of seriousness. The opposition lords were very far from what was under certain aspects the egalitarian humanism of the King's Court.

Nevertheless, this last statement needs to be qualified. It is true that the permanent opposition, represented by such men as Lords Essex, Manchester and Warwick, had viewed the Queen's friends with overt disapproval on religious grounds, but the new category of disobliged noblemen included the Mæcenas equally with the philistine. Philip, Earl of Pembroke, is an example of a Parliamentarian of the former type. The whole Penshurst family and Edmund Waller, who was Lady Dorothy Sidney's *prétendant* had entered into the spirit of the Caroline æsthetic manner, while Lady Carlisle and Lord Holland came from the inner circle of the Court itself.

Bearing these facts in mind, it appears accurate to state that the Caroline world in its political connotations came to an end with the fall of Laud and Strafford. Both men were uninterested in that Caroline emphasis which their fall destroyed. Still, their political ascendancy was the sustaining force which made

possible the way of life which the King and Queen maintained.
The privacy, modernity and elegance were swept away.

The presence of a faction alienated from the Court, and at
the same time enjoying first freedom and then power, was
wholly novel. Pym has his part in this, as the minister and
inspirer of the opposition. The Parliamentarian lords resembled
the King in that they also needed to discover men who would
do the work of governing on their behalf.

Lady Carlisle may be conceived as the searcher out of
instruments. She seems to have been the pure *intrigante* remote
from sex. She brought the men of her family and acquaintance to Lord Strafford; it may have been because the King
sacrificed his minister that later she did what she could to bring
the same phalanx to Mr Pym. This Fronde-like atmosphere
assisted King Charles in his delusion that none of his subjects
could ever prove implacable. He was convinced that he could
manœuvre and outwit them, and separate and purchase them.

Meanwhile the Royalists themselves had no concern with
those civilised values which their sovereigns hoped to extract
from a Court at peace. The Royalists drew their strength from
circles where the Court was not just a name but a rooted conservative powerful kingship. The Tudor conception of monarchy
and the Elizabethan ideal of implicit loyalty drew men to King
Charles; it was what he had inherited and not what he had done.
The royal cause gained the support of all old-fashioned men and
all the Catholics.

The great body of the neutrals can never be forgotten, but in
so far as men ranged themselves consciously on either side, it
was those who looked to the future, such as the capitalists, using
that term very widely; the lawyers; the modern squires; the
hopeful yeomanry; who tended to support the Parliament.
With them there went the old, hard Puritans. In general, the
men who are remembered as fighting reluctantly for their
sovereign and hoping for a compromise died like Lord Falkland
and Sir Edmund Verney in the Fronde period of the conflict.
The King had all the archaic forces; he had the adventurers
and the younger sons, and all those who, like the Elizabethans,
felt branded by the accusation of disloyalty. But the Caroline
spirit, which was essentially sophisticated, sensitive and contemporary, had nothing in common with this conflict. It is true
that certain aspects of the Court life were revived when the

King and Queen were both at Oxford in 1643-4. Still, in effect
the Caroline Age ended before the Civil War; it had no
meeting-place with the age of Cromwell, which would so soon
obliterate the accommodating policies. In essence, the earlier
Caroline period had a peaceful and in some respects a pastoral
spirit—Herrick at Dean Prior, Little Gidding, the Laudian
colleges. With its rather mannered simplicity there went a
freshness, which once gone was not recaptured. On the religious
side it can best be expressed as George Herbert's quiet after-
math. In letters, in certain aspects of social custom, in rural
traditions and in Anglican religious life, this was a time of ease,
both quiet and simple. This spring-like quality was shattered by
the Civil War, nor did it reappear in the bruised world of the
Restoration.

BIBLIOGRAPHICAL NOTE

THE following list contains certain primary printed authorities used in composing this study. Full titles will be found in notes to the text. The sources mentioned are chosen for the sidelights that they throw on the life of the period. The various collections of State Papers, not here referred to, were used throughout.

I. HISTORICAL MANUSCRIPTS' COMMISSION REPORTS

Calendar of Coke MSS. (sometimes known as Lord Cowper's MSS.).
Calendar of Finch MSS.
Calendar of Gawdy MSS.
Calendar of Harford MSS.
Calendar of Hastings MSS.
Calendar of Pepys MSS.
Calendar of Portland MSS.
Calendar of Rutland MSS.
Calendar of Talbot MSS.
Calendar of Wombwell MSS.

II. DIARIES, JOURNALS, CORRESPONDENCE, ETC.

Autobiography of Sir John Bramston, ed. Lord Braybrooke (Camden Society, 1845).
Autobiography of Sir Symonds D'Ewes, ed. J. O. Halliwell.
Autobiography of Anne Lady Halket, ed. J. Gough Nicholls (Camden Society, 1875).
Autobiography of Edward Lord Herbert of Cherbury, ed. Sidney Lee.
Autobiography of Joseph Lister, ed. Thomas Wright.
Autobiography of Phineas Pett, ed. W. G. Perrin (Navy Records Society, 1918).
Autobiography of Thomas Raymond (Camden Society, 1917).
Autobiography of Mrs Alice Thornton (Surtees Society, 1875).
Autobiography of the Countess of Warwick, ed. T. C. Croker (Percy Society, 1848).
Commonplace Book of Sir John Oglander, ed. Francis Bamford.
Correspondence of Bishop Cosin (Surtees Society, 1868 and 1870).
Correspondence of Dr Matthew Hutton (Surtees Society, 1843).
Correspondence of Sir George Radcliffe, ed. T. D. Whitaker.
Correspondence of Nathan Walworth and Peter Seddon (Chetham Society, 1880).
Diary of Thomas Crosfield, ed. F. S. Boas.
Diary and Correspondence of John Evelyn, ed. William Bray.
Diary of Rev. Ralph Josselin, ed. E. Hockliffe (Camden Society, 1908).

Diary of Archbishop Laud, ed. Rev. Henry Wharton.
Diary of John Rous, ed. Mrs Everett Green (Camden Society, 1856).
Diary of Sir Henry Slingsby, ed. Rev. D. Parsons.
Diary and Correspondence of Dr John Worthington (Chetham Society, 1847).
Household Books of Naworth Castle, ed. Rev. George Ornsby (Surtees Society, 1878).
Journal of John Aston (Surtees Society, 1910).
Journal of Sir William Brereton (Surtees Society, 1915).
Journal of George Fox, ed. Norman Penney.
Journal of Sir Roger Wilbraham (Camden Misc., x, 1902).
Life of John Angier, by Oliver Heywood, ed. Ernest Axon (Chetham Society).
Life of Bishop Bedell, by Rev. W. Bedell, ed. Thomas Wharton Jones (Camden Society, 1872).
Life of Humphrey Chetham, a compendium of notes and documents, by R. R. Raines and C. W. Sutton (Chetham Society, 1903).
Life of Sir John Digby (Camden Misc., xii, 1910).
Life of Dr Henry Hammond, by Dr John Fell.
Life of Colonel John Hutchinson by Mrs Lucy Hutchinson, ed. Rev. Julius Hutchinson.
Life of Archbishop Laud, by Peter Heylyn.
Life of William, Duke of Newcastle, by his wife, ed. C. H. Firth.
Life of Marmaduke Rawdon, ed. Robert Davies (Camden Society, 1853).
Life of Master John Shaw (Surtees Society, 1877).
Life of the Earl of Strafford, by Sir George Radcliffe, printed in W. Knowler *Letters*, ii.
Memoirs of Lady Fanshawe, ed. C. R. Fanshawe.
Memoirs of Cyprien de Gamache, printed in Birch's *Court and Times of Charles I*, ii.
Memoirs of Edmund Ludlow, ed. C. H. Firth.
Memoirs of Gregorio Panzani, ed. Joseph Berington.
Memoirs of the Reign of Charles I, by Sir Philip Warwick.
Memoirs of Sir John Reresby, ed. Andrew Browning.
Memoirs of the Verney Family, by Frances Parthenope Verney.
Memorials of the Holles Family, by Gervase Holles, ed. A. C. Wood (Camden Society, 1937).
Records of Blackburn School, ed. G. A. Stocks (Chetham Society, 1909).
Register of Visitors of the University of Oxford, ed. Montagu Burrows (Camden Society, 1881).
Relation of Sydnam Poyntz, ed. Rev. A. T. S. Goodrick (Camden Society, 1908).
Reliquiæ Baxterianæ, by Richard Baxter, ed. Matthew Sylvester.
Scrinia Reserata, a life of Archbishop Williams, by John Hacket.
Travels of the Earl of Arundel, by William Crowne.
Travels of Peter Mundy, ed. Sir R. C. Temple.

III.   MISCELLANEOUS

Brief Lives, by John Aubrey, ed. Andrew Clark, also ed. Anthony Powell.

Century of Inventions, by the Marquess of Worcester, ed. Henry Dircks.

Discovery of a New World, by John Wilkins.

Expedition with the Scots Regiment, by Robert Monro.

Fairfax Correspondence, ed. G. W. Johnson.

Ferrar Papers, ed. B. Blackstone, containing a Life of Nicholas Ferrar from the Baker MS.

Fortescue Papers (Camden Society, 1871).

Letters of Lady Brillicna Harley, ed T. T. Lewis (Camden Society, 1854).

Archbishop Laud's *Works*.

Shardeloes Papers, ed. G. Elan.

Strafford Letters, ed. William Knowler.

Sydney Papers, ed. R. W. Blencowe.

Sydney State Papers, ed. Arthur Collins.

Tixall Papers, ed. Arthur Clifford.

Trevelyan Papers (Camden Society, 1872-3).

INDEX

And God took a handful of southerly wind,

blew His breath over it and created the horse.

Bedouin Legend

FOREWORD BY
JAMES A. MICHENER

William Morrow and Company, Inc.
New York   1977

ROBERT VAVRA
EQUUS
the creation of a horse

In memory of Bernardo González Real, friend, dedicated photographer, naturalist and horse lover, who if he hadn't died so young, might have created this book.

Drawings and design for this book were done by John Fulton

DURING my lifetime I have met dozens of writers and photographers in dozens of different countries, but I have encountered none who could both write and photograph with the artistry of Robert Vavra. The fact that he is also a devoted naturalist makes him the only person I know capable of producing this gracious tribute to the horse.

Though equus has fired the imaginations of painters from the prehistoric hunter-artists of Altamira to Leonardo da Vinci, Velázquez, Goya and Picasso, still, in the history of photography no cameraman has recorded the horse with such excitement and personal style as are shown in these pages—pictures so exquisite they are of universal appeal.

I met Robert Vavra almost twenty years ago, shortly after he had arrived in Spain, when he was still more boy than man. Few of us who knew him in those days, including creative men like Ernest Hemingway, David Lean and Tom Lea, made his acquaintance without being impressed by his enthusiasm, his natural manner, his feeling for animals, and his personal style as a photographer. While others who admired his work left Sevilla, I was so impressed by his distinct style and his sensitivity to people and places that, one afternoon while I sat in his studio studying a batch of his recent photographs, it occurred to me that he might be just the person I had been looking for to help me with a book I had long planned but never written: a philosophical appreciation of the Spanish experience. To accomplish this I would need both words and photographs, and it seemed highly probable that Vavra could supply the latter. However, at that time I did not raise the question of our working together, because I was entwined with another subject which would absorb my attention for some years: a novel on the Holy Land.

In the spring of that year 1959, I often accompanied Vavra to the wild marshes of the Guadalquivir where he was photographing and taking notes on the Spanish fighting bull, an animal he felt to be in danger of eventual extinction and about which he was preparing a book. During those delightful outings, I had the opportunity to appreciate his naturalist's eye as he pointed out creatures and told me of their ways, among them the Bee-eater and the Hoopoe, birds which would later become important in my own work.

It was not until 1966 that I managed to get back to Sevilla for Holy Week and its ensuing feria; now I was ready to devote uninterrupted time to the book on Spain, and I proposed to Vavra that he cooperate with me in an unusual way: 'I want photographs, but not the ordinary kind presented in the ordinary way. If I write about the cathedral at Toledo, I don't want the reader to see on the facing page a faithful shot of the cathedral's facade. I want you to roam Spain at the same time I do, you going your way, I going mine. When we're finished, we'll put the text and photographs together in some haphazard way, so that your portrait of a fighting bull might possibly face my words about the cathedral.' Because of Vavra's special intuitions I never doubted that his photographs and my words would unite to form the impression I sought. When *Iberia* was published half my correspondents said, 'I liked the pictures better than the text.' The other half said, 'When a man writes about Toledo cathedral in an illustrated book, I expect to see a photograph of the cathedral.' But all agreed that it was a happy union.

While I was finishing my text on *Iberia* Vavra started an interesting new project. He had seen, been inspired by and begun to write a book around paintings by Fleur Cowles. He was now working in reverse; in my book he had supplied the graphics to accompany my words, in *Tiger Flower* he was producing the words to accompany someone else's graphics. As he organized unrelated paintings into an artistic sequence and wrote a story around them his poetic insight and sense of direction appeared. When I saw *Tiger Flower* I was re-assured in my early conviction that Vavra was destined for fine things in the field of nature writing and the photography of wild life.

As I first turned the pages of this book with each photograph as exquisite as the one before, I expected to come across one or two that weren't quite up to the rest, but I am sure the reader will agree that each of the pictures in this book has its own lovely unity; each is not only a revealing study of the horse, but also an example of the author's unmistakable style. Last spring when Vavra and I stood together in the darkness of the Denver Museum, admiring the millions of years old remains of the ancestral horse, and he told me of his plan to do this book on horses, I would not have believed that in less than forty full working days he could take all the photographs reproduced here. But in the fall of that same year I received the Spanish edition of this book. Those amazingly short days of work seem a special feat when one considers that all of the horses were photographed at liberty in situations where Vavra had little or no control of his subjects. Other fine books of photographs I have seen, regardless of their themes, were taken over periods that ranged from two to ten years.

The photographs here are a feast for the eye, but Vavra's sensitive combination of them with quotations from all ages and peoples makes this book a special experience—one in which the eternal beauty of the horse is revealed again and again. Vavra has also provided us with more than fifty pages of notes on his personal observation of the social behavior of equines which laymen as well as students of animal behavior will find intriguing.

Some years ago the enterprising curators of the Amon Carter Museum in Fort Worth came up with a great idea for an art exhibition: gather from all over the world examples of great art depicting the Appaloosa horse, and what they were able to assemble was astounding. They had paintings from Persia, from China, from Africa and especially from Europe. Rubens, Titian, Delacroix had all depicted these majestic animals in their works, and had done so in a manner which proved they loved horses.

Robert Vavra, with his camera and pen, has now produced a worthy successor to that exhibition. For these photographs are works of art; they are interpretations of the horse as perceptive as those done by Stubbs and Remington. They are a joy to see, because they evoke the inner nature of the horse, and the words which Vavra will later quote from things I've written will indicate my love for this splendid animal.

James A. Michener
St. Michaels, Maryland

February 24, 1977

6

EQUUS

the creation of a horse

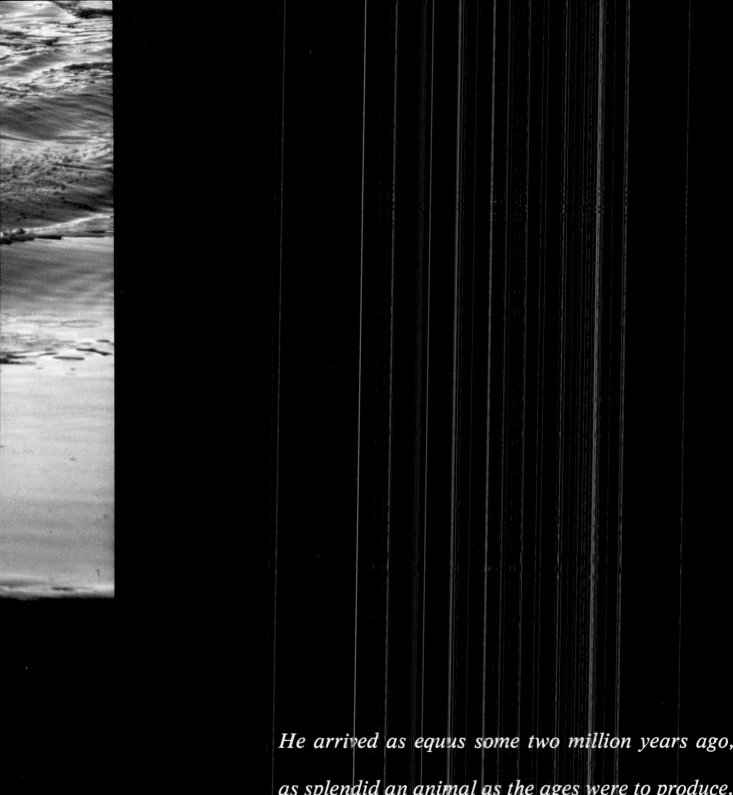

He arrived as equus some two million years ago,

as splendid an animal as the ages were to produce

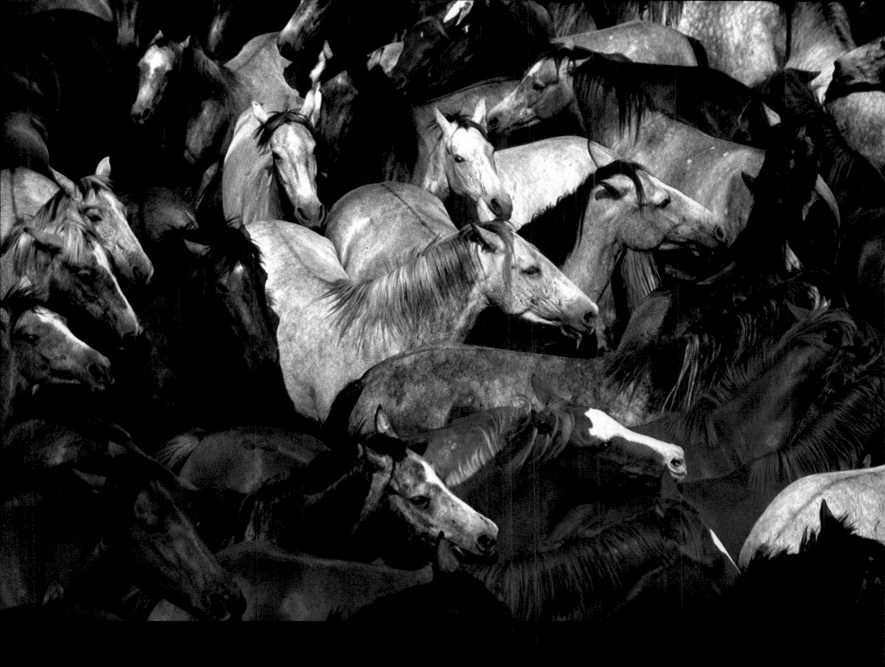

the four winds are blowing

some horses

are coming

Teton Sioux — Song of the Horse Society

. . . they move in herds, assemble for the pleasure of being together, and become quite attached to each other.

Buffon

13

When pleased, they rub their necks together.

When angry, they turn round and kick up their heels at

each other.   Such is the real nature of horses.

A strange stilln[ess]

dwells in the eye[s of]

the horse,

a composure tha[t]

appears to rega[rd]

the world from [a]

measured

distance . . .

It is a gaze from

the depths of a

dream . . .

Hans-Heinrich Isenbart

Far back, far back in our dark soul the

horse prances . . .   The horse,

the horse!   The symbol of surging

potency and power of movement,

of action . . .

D. H. Lawrence

The rigid curved neck, such as ancient sculptors

modeled . . . the interplay of muscle . . . in each of

his poses he was . . . the composite of all the equestrian

statues of history.

Felix Salten

By reason of his elegance,

he resembles an image

painted in a palace,

though he is as majestic

as the palace itself.

Emir Abd-el-Kader

Hast thou given the horse strength?

Hast thou clothed his neck with thunder?

He swalloweth the ground with fierceness and rage . . .

Book of Job. Old Testament

Horse of the sun, who slowly crosses the surface of the earth,

turquoise horse, I have made a sacrifice to you!

Navajo Prayer

Or was it cold wind in the leaves of the shadow tree

That made such grievous music?

Stephen Vincent Benét

. . . this pageant of proud horses, grey and bay, sorrel and black . . .

with blazing eyes and glistening flanks, recalled a procession of gladiators

marching to some circus, hidden from view, but near at hand . . .

Peter Shiraeff

I watched the great stallions rake the air with their forefeet,

High in the air they rose on their hind legs,

their forelegs pawing, striking madly at each other.

Walter Farley

Even what Gros and Rubens conjured up to depict the Furies was nothing compared to these stallions.

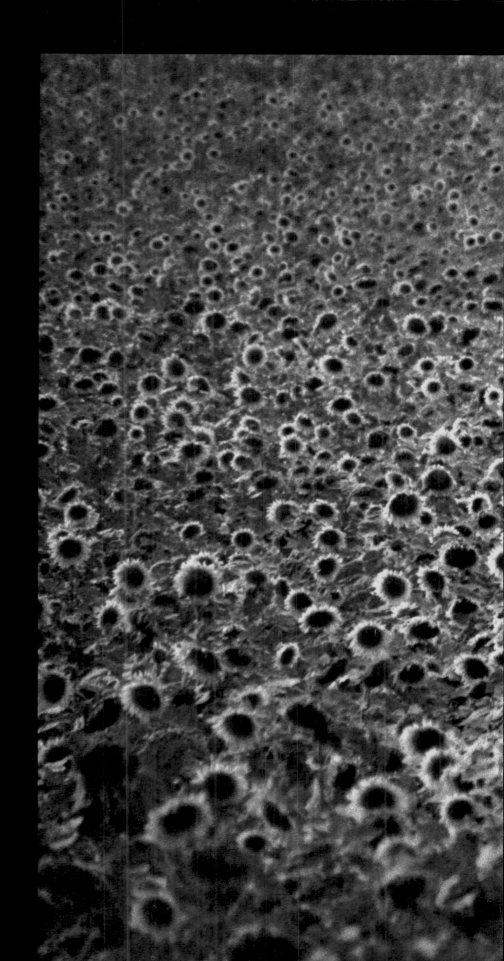

There on tips of fair fresh flowers

feedeth he;

How joyous is his neigh,

There in midst of sacred pollen

hidden, all hidden he;

How joyous is his neigh . . .

Navajo Song

. . . through his mane and tail the high wind sings,

Fanning the hairs, who wave like feather'd wings.

William Shakespeare

the animals rising and falling mysteriously along the rocky

surface is to see . . . drawings done by men who studied

animals and who loved them.

James A. Michener

He is swift and strong among the swift ones, but it is that flowing mane and tail that mark him chiefly from afar.

Ernest Thompson Seton

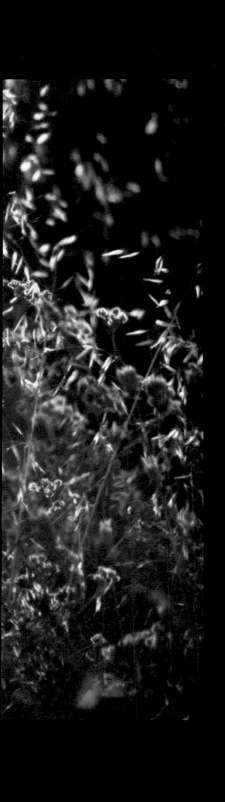

Seeds spring from seeds, beauty breedeth beauty . . .

By law of Nature thou art bound to breed,

That thine may live, when thou thyself art dead;

And so in spite of death thou dost survive,

In that thy likeness still is left alive.

William Shakespeare

From the West comes a red mare . . .

She comes to me.

Navajo Chant

From the North comes a white mare . . .

She comes to me.

Navajo Chant

. . . all shining beautiful and gentle of herself,

she seemed a darling life upon that savage

soil not worthy of her gracious pasterns:

the strutting tail flowed down even

to the ground, and the mane was shed by the

loving nurture of her mother Nature.

His ears up-prick'd; his braided hanging mane

Upon his compass'd crest now stands on end . . .

His eye, which scornfully glisters like fire,

Shows his hot courage and his high desire.

William Shakespeare

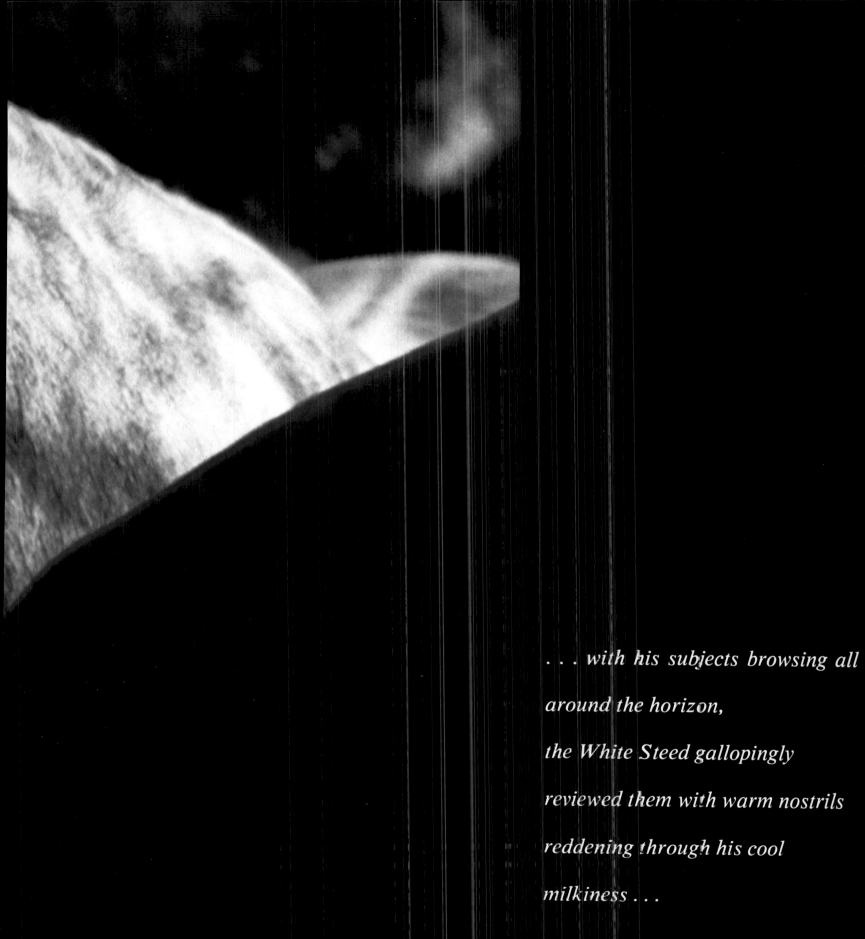

. . . with his subjects browsing all around the horizon, the White Steed gallopingly reviewed them with warm nostrils reddening through his cool milkiness . . .

Herman Melville

See how the stallions shake

in every limb,

If they but catch the scent

of love upon the breeze.

Virgil

The stallion caressed the mare's lips

with his warm, velvety muzzle,

and she lowered her head, seemingly entranced

by his sensual nuzzling.

Robert Vavra

. . . gigantic beauty of a stallion . . . eyes full of sparkling wickedness . . . nostrils dilate . . . well-built limbs tremble with pleasure . . .

Walt Whitman

scenting the mare, the stallion began to paw the ground,

Wheeling after her, neighing, and plunging,

he arched his splendid neck and pushed against her.

Her bright coat shone in the sunlight, and little shivers

and wrinkles passed up and down its satin because of

the flies.   Then for a moment she stood still . . .

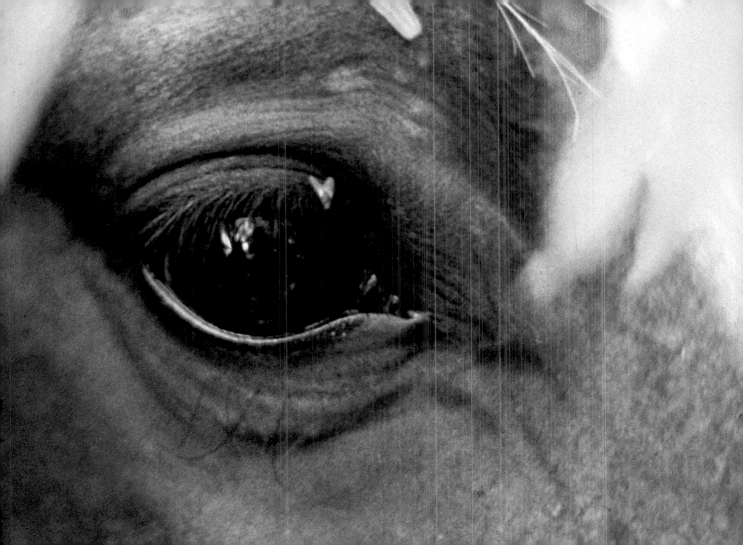

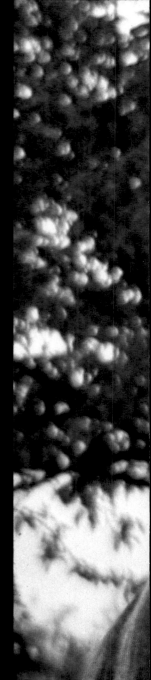

The horse stood on its hind legs . . . I could

smell it, so lovely . . . I could hear it breathing,

so exciting . . .

William Saroyan

Right into the stars he reared aloft,

his red eye rolling . . .

Flung back on his haunches,

he loomed . . . then leapt—

and the dim void lightened.

William Rose Benét

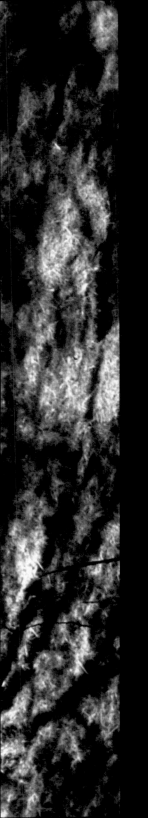

The sun was high and there was no sound

but the calling of a hawk and the stallion's heavy breathing,

as the shadows of the mating horses slid slowly

across the earth like a prehistoric cave painting brought to life

Robert Vavra

And God blessed them,

and God said unto them,

Be fruitful,

and multiply . . .

Book of Genesis

The sun rises through a break in the clouds .

flowers unfold through a crack in Mother Earth

prayers are recited for the blossoming mare . . .

Henceforth the mares

demand the greater care.

When in the course

of months they are

in foal,

Allow them not to gallop

in swirling floods.

But let them graze in

glades by brimming

streams.

Virgil

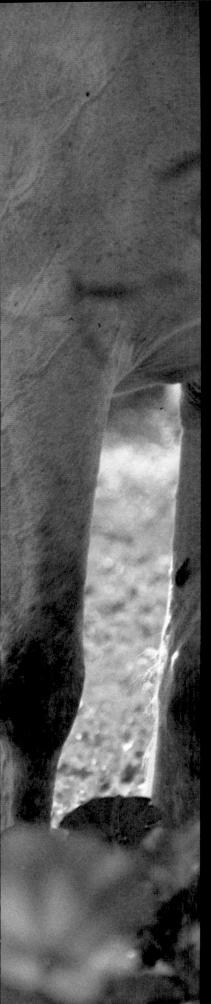

The laboring mare lay down on the ground.

The foal, impose his will as he might, was helpless.

The violent surges continued, coming at regular intervals,

and he was being turned this way and that . . .

until he took the position of a diver,

front hoofs stretched out and his little muzzle

resting on them . . .   There was the sensation

of movement through a passage and suddenly a jar

as he slid out to the earth.

Mary O'Hara

There was life in that silver

shroud.   Through its

beautiful transparency,

a pair of black, shiny hoofs

tore...

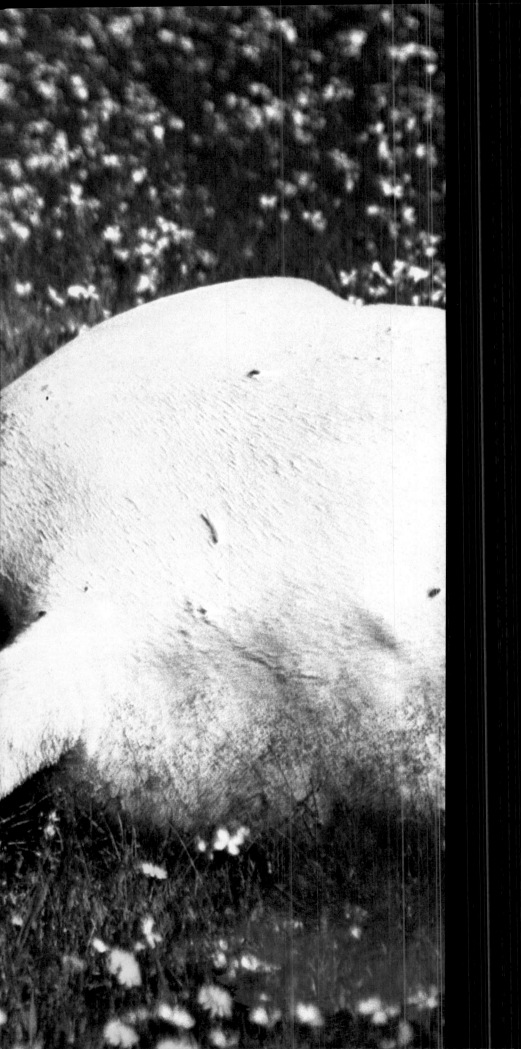

He kicked the covering off

himself . . . abalone shell foal . . .

black onyx foal . . .

Navajo Legend

And God took a handful

of southerly wind,

blew His breath over it and

created the horse.

Bedouin Legend

The foal tried to get up.

He thrust out his forefeet,

but they splayed

and he seemed to get all

tangled up with himself.

Marguerite Henry

It seemed that Mother Nature

was sure agreeable that day

when the little black colt

came to the range world,

and tried to get a footing

with his long wobbly legs . . .

Taking in all that could be seen,

felt, and inhaled, there was no day,

time nor place that could beat

that spring morning . . .

Will James

The butterflies there

in the brush were

romancing,

The smell of the grass

caught your soul

in a trance,

So why be a- fearing

the spurs and the traces,

Oh broncho that would not

be broken of dancing?

Vachel Lindsay

. . . there was a faint sound

of neighing of steeds . . .

no louder than the hum

of the bee or the summer-fly

in the drowsy ear of him

who lies at noontide

in the shade.

Washington Irving

115

Around and around

he galloped, and sometimes

he jumped forward

and landed on stiff legs . . .

quivering . . . ears forward,

eyes rolling so that

the whites showed,

pretending to be afraid.

John Steinbeck

Nature is more beautiful than art; and in a living creature freedom of movement makes nature more beautiful.

Buffon

. . . virtue shall be bound into the hair

of thy forelock . . .   I have given thee

the power of flight without wings.

The Koran

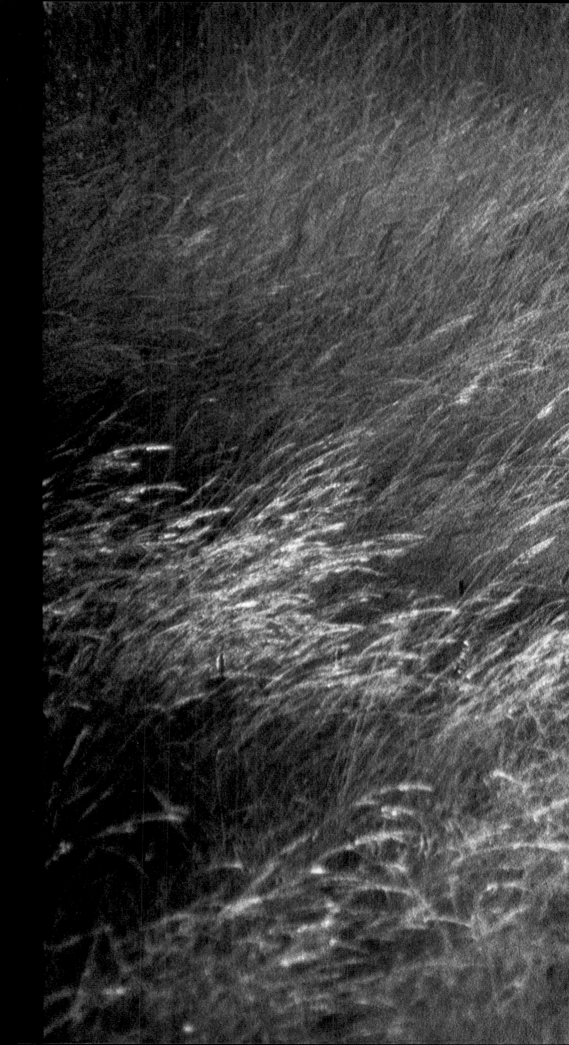

. . . presently he would

wheel around and stare

in another direction,

pointing his ears forward

to listen to some faint far

sound which had touched

his senses.

William Henry Hudson

His neigh is like the

bidding of a monarch,

and his countenance

enforces homage.

He is indeed a horse . . .

William Shakespeare

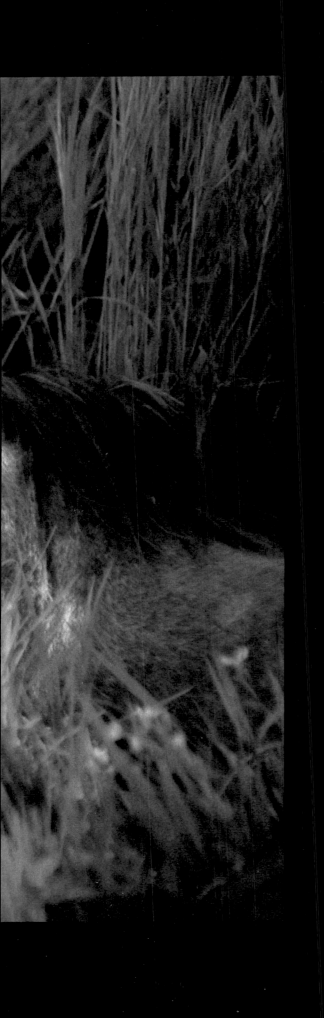

Before the gods that made the gods

Had seen their sunrise pass,

The White Horse of the White Horse Vale

Was cut out of the grass.

G. K. Chesterton

Movement is the primeval element of his being, joyous movement in the wide spaciousness of freedom.

He dipped his head

And snorted at us.   And then he had to bolt.

We heard the miniature thunder where he fled,

And we saw him, or thought we saw him, dim and gray,

Like a shadow . . .

Robert Frost

134

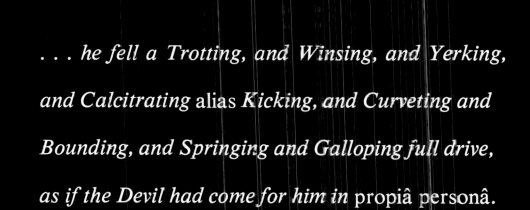

. . . *he fell a Trotting, and Winsing, and Yerking, and Calcitrating alias Kicking, and Curveting and Bounding, and Springing and Galloping full drive, as if the Devil had come for him in propiâ personâ.*

François Rabelais

. . . a horse is a thing of such beauty . . .

none will tire of looking at him

as long as he displays himself in his splendor.

Xenophon

takes a jump, anticipating, he

h almost as if he could fly . . .

Hans-Heinrich Isenbart

. . . Pegasus was a snow-white steed . . .

as wild, and as swift, and as buoyant,

in his flight through the air, as any eagle

that ever soared into the clouds.

Nathaniel Hawthorne

Now the wild white horses play,

Champ and chafe and toss in the spray.

Matthew Arnold

Fillies as lovely, stallions thrice as strong.

Returned that day to join their tribal throng . . .

The Conches sounded for the tide to flow

And reddened by the evening afterglow . . .

Roy Campbell

I heard a sudden harmony of hooves . . .

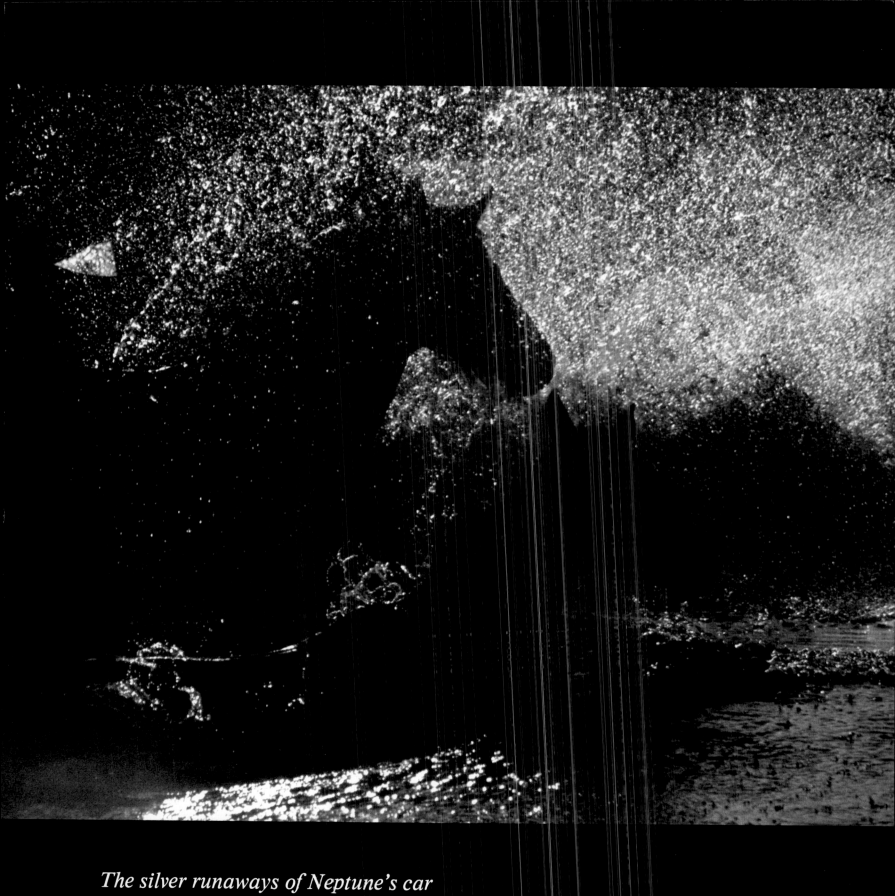

The silver runaways of Neptune's car

. . . stampeding horse that raves

. . . when it meets the sea at last

is swallowed outright by the waves!

Federico Garcia Lorca

Under the last golden rays grazed the Sun's hor

Instead of grass they ate ambrosia;

Browsing quietly while resting tired legs,

In readiness to stampede the skies of dawn.

s the stallion rose . . .

e moonlight poured over him,

eaching his hide . . .

white horse dappled with shadows.

Mary Stewart

A shape in the moonlight, a bulk in the dark,

And beneath, from the pebbles, in passing, a spark

Struck out by a steed flying fearless and fleet;

That was all!

Henry W. Longfellow

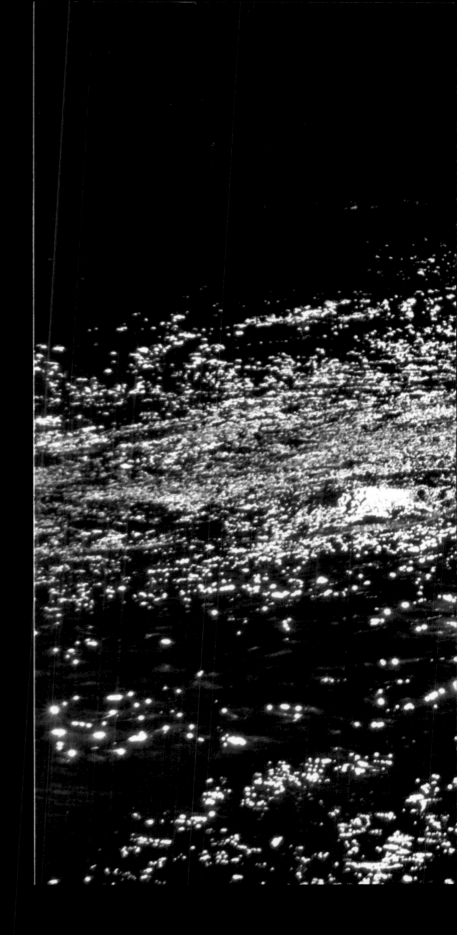

All the moon long I heard . . . the nightjars

Flying with the ricks, and the horses

Flashing in the dark.

Dylan Thomas

A blue stallion, a black stallion;

The sun's horse has come out to us.

Apache Ceremonial Song

AUTHOR'S NOTE ON THE PHOTOGRAPHS AND A COMMENT ON THE SOCIAL BEHAVIOR OF HORSES

THE seed for this book was planted more than thirty years ago, long before I had a chance to observe at first hand the stallions of North Africa, Mexico, the Western United States, and of more than half a dozen European countries. When the colt Silver was given to me, Casablanca, Newmarket, Lisbon, Jerez de la Frontera, Paris and Querétero were merely romantic names in a geography book full of pale maps.

Silver, the only horse I ever owned, had just three legs, but oh, how we loved him! I was ten years old and my stallion was two inches high and cast in lead. On rainy days my twin, Ron, and I would play with our toy horses; to us they were as wild as any mustangs galloping free in the backlands of Wyoming or Montana. And though Silver was a cripple, for us he would run as fast as Man o' War.

Then there were the herds of horses at Columbus Grammar School. Ron and I and all our friends would split into two bands, tossing our heads and voicing shrill whinnies and, since each troop had a lead stallion, fights were inevitable. Often these combats became so violent that a stallion's war cries turned into the sobs of a small boy.

However, there were also real horses in our lives during those years of the Second World War. They belonged to my great uncle Charlie Jankovsky, a wizened, brown Czech who had come to America sometime at the end of the last century, where he had worked like crazy in Wyoming as a tailor, saving almost every cent he ever made until he could retire in Long Beach, California. Uncle Charlie's dream was to own a ranch and to have some horses, and happily for him—and us!—he was able to make his dream come true. After purchasing six hundred acres near Hemet, California, the first thing he did was to go to an auction and buy "livestock"; Polly was an old chestnut mare and Appaloosie was a sharp-looking Appaloosa. Uncle Charlie knew a lot about tailoring and saving money, but he always got taken at those auctions (even though my brothers and I were convinced he was a gypsy).

Our great uncle had bought Polly in foal with the promise that she had been bred to a prize Quarter Horse. This excited Ron and me so much that toward the end of the mare's pregnancy we talked our folks into spending as much time as possible at that old Last Gate Ranch that didn't have electricity or running water, and whose outhouse spider webs made us cautious about sitting on the seats. I can remember running down to the lower meadow the morning Polly had given birth. Her offspring, we were sure, would be as handsome a foal as the one in the film *Thunderhead* (which we had seen four times at the Alex Theater in Glendale). God, how sick we were when out of the sage brush stepped a baby mule! Polly died a year later. Appaloosie was another problem. She shied so much that only my father could ride her, so Uncle Charlie went back to the auction and bought Gypsy, a coal black Morgan with a white star on her forehead. Soon enough, however, we found that not a fence on the ranch could hold that mare.

Once I remember Uncle Charlie got so mad at Gypsy that his brown face turned the color of split-pea soup. The mare leapt the barbed-wire right in front of the cabin and messed up the new pond and destroyed the water lilies that our great uncle had so carefully hauled in milk cans from Long Beach to Hemet. (Bringing those precious plants to the ranch the car had heated up twice and boiled over, but Uncle Charlie had refused to use water from his lovely lilies; he had preferred to walk a mile to the nearest farm.) I was scared and stood in the background when he tied Gypsy—our "Black Beauty"—to a tree and then beat her in the face with a bridle. It was an awful thing to see and it ruined the mare forever.

Chick was a small bay mare that also came from one of the auctions. How many owners she had had, and how many of them it had taken to spoil her, I don't know, but I never will forget sitting on Lizard Rock, above the outhouse, loading a B-B gun, talking with my mother who was currying Chick in the meadow, when the horse—for who knows what reason—whirled around, grabbed Mother by the shoulder, threw her on the ground and tried to trample her. If Dad hadn't raced up

from the cabin to scare the mare away, I don't know what would have happened.

Later, as we drove Mother to the hospital, Dad said we shouldn't let Uncle Charlie's auction misfits ruin our love for horses. They really could be noble and beautiful animals, he told us, and to prove this, a few weeks later he took us to what was then the Kellogg Arabian Horse Farm near Pomona, California. To our twelve-year-old eyes, what could have been more beautiful than the Arab stallions and mares that were paraded before us in the golden light of that late California afternoon—certainly not Veronica Lake or even a Buick convertible. "How could anything be lovelier?" Ron and I wondered, "except maybe wild mustang stallions galloping free across the mesas of Colorado."

Not much later we had the chance to prove in person what we had heard so many times: that stallions were wild demons, couldn't be trusted and had to be kept under lock and key. Ten miles from the Last Gate Ranch was a farm dedicated to the raising of Hereford cattle and Quarter Horses, where our uncle asked Dad to have a look at a Palomino stallion and to find out what kind of stud fee would be charged for covering either Chick or Gypsy. So early one morning we left the raw wilderness of the old Last Gate Ranch; my brothers Bill and Ron on one mare, and Dad and I on the other, we rode down the canyon, valley quail calling from the sage on either side of us, doves and jays taking off from dead branches of

cottonwood trees that twisted silver against the sky. Finally, the dusty trail ended and we entered the neat white fences and lush green fields of the farm of the Palomino stallion.

While we boys stood outside with the mares, Dad went into the stable with a cowboy. All of a sudden we heard the banging of hoofs against wood and the battle screams of a horse. Bill ducked inside the building to have a look, returned shaking his head in respect, and then held the mares while Ron and I entered the cool darkness that housed not only the stallion, but the smells of fresh hay and horse sweat and manure—all lovely to our noses. "He's a real son-of-a-gun," the cowboy was saying to our dad. "Meaner than cat pee and twice as nasty." Then we knew why so few people in America had stallions for pleasure riding; it was like keeping a wild animal! Eyes rolled back, ears flat to his head, teeth bared, forelock tossing, the Palomino, like a dragon, thrust his head out of the box. "Stand back, fellas," warned the cowboy.

Later that night at the Last Gate Ranch, I couldn't get the stallion off my mind until I started for the outhouse and then stopped halfway along the path to unzip my pants; the nights in those mountains were so dark and the picture of the cougars trying to kill Flicka in the movie were still so vivid in my mind and imagination, that every movement or owl's hoot from the oak trees sent chills up my back. After midnight, when the kerosene lamps had been turned off and everyone was in bed, when my father was snoring and the white-footed mice were scampering across the tin roof of the cabin, I remember thinking how sad it was that a stallion, except maybe in the movies or in a book, had to be such a wild beast, a savage to whom neither I nor any boy could be a friend. And yet, at the same time, I delighted in the thought of the Palomino's fiery display, for in truth, it was what I had always been told stallions were.

In the years that followed, I never lost my love for horses. Even today, in Sevilla, if I close my eyes and concentrate for a few minutes, I can brew up strong recollections of experiences with them from years ago. There was a rickety maze of corrals and loading ramps at a livestock auction near Downey, California, and we never passed it in our old Model T Ford without my father yielding to Ron's and my pleas to stop alongside the road.

Then we boys would climb up on the fences and stare down at the nags nobody wanted and who, if they weren't sold for a few dollars at one of the auctions, would end up next door in billows of stinking smoke that rose from a glue factory. But we didn't see bony nags or notice those odors much, we just saw horses—horses! And how we loved that sight.

Mixed with those same childhood memories are scenes from Taft, California, a hick oil town on the edge of Steinbeck country, where my wonderful old grandmother Hamilton lived; where on hot summer nights there was nothing to do but go to the rollerskating rink and whirl around the warm cement to phonograph records of someone playing Strauss waltzes on a Hammond organ. In the daytime, however, even though the sun beat down with such intensity that the blacktop roads became soft underfoot, we would wander over to some nearby corrals and do nothing but look at the mares and geldings. Ron, my cousin Gary and I would have liked to ride those animals, but, like the grey lizards that basked in the sun out of reach of our hands, we were satisfied just to hang on the splintery fences and stare at the horses; to watch them and listen to them and smell them.

Not all those recollections, though, are as seemingly unexciting as were the inhabitants of those slipshod board corrals. I wouldn't trade anything for an experience at Uncle Charlie's ranch that flashes as dramatically before me today as it did in real life thirty years ago.

Dusk was settling as Ron and I left the North Forty where we had been twigging doves with a .22. Happy with having shot enough birds for supper, we walked in tired silence; the only sounds were our boots through the dry grass, the distant yapping of a coyote, and the chatter of a covey of quail going to roost in the surrounding oak trees. Then it came, like the cry of another child, from the canyon behind us— the scream of a mountain lion. We whirled around, shaking, white-faced, each knowing that there never was a recorded case of an unprovoked attack on man by a puma in the wild (but still fresh in our minds were those two big cats in the film *Thunderhead*, clinging like shadows to a tree, heads turning weasel-like, yellow eyes and fangs gleaming, ready to pounce on Flicka and her foal).

Suddenly, from the far side of the meadow, muffled sounds of hoofs thudded madly from the weeds and soft earth. "God!" I thought as I looked at the panicked expression on Ron's face. "A big cat's after the horses!"

Gypsy burst first through the shoulder-high sage at the clearing's edge, head high in fear, ears laid back, her mane rising and falling like a black wave as she galloped in violent surges, closer and closer. Behind came old Polly, then heavy in foal, and just as she passed us— "Boom!"—into the air overhead burst a covey of what must have been almost a hundred quail. Ron and I exchanged glances; were we really at the Last Gate Ranch or were we slouched deeply into the cheap seats and darkness of the Alex Theater? But here the horses

166 ago.

didn't whinny in fear, they just ran like crazy, flying towards the cabin as if the puma's claws were touching their flanks. "What shall we do?" Ron's voice was trembling.

"Mountain lions won't attack people," I answered. My hands were shaking so that one of the doves dropped to the ground, but I was too frightened to stoop over and pick it up, sure the puma was crouching right then on one of the twisted limbs overhead. "But . . . but anyway," I whispered, "it might be a good idea to try to keep him from going after the horses." To which Ron emptied half his gun's magazine into the air, the shots ringing in lonely echoes off the granite boulders around the meadow.

Not many months after that experience, my uncle Jim introduced us to a new kind of horse. That chestnut filly, coming out onto the Santa Anita Race Track, sleek and gazelle-like, with large, lovely, dark doe eyes, and coils of charged-up muscle under her smooth coat—the beauty of that sight touched the deepest places of my soul. The infield grass was so green, the flowers so bright, and the silks of the jockeys so dazzling, that I grinned up at my handsome, silver-haired uncle and he smiled back because he knew that I then understood why he so loved the races. The horses were at the gate, they were inside while the world stood still for a moment, and then they were on the dirt, with the announcer's voice booming out to the purple haze beyond the track. Around the curve they glided, blossoms of color in the distance, swinging into the home stretch, coming so fast. Could horses move that fast? Each

spread out in great strides, full drive, the jockeys pressed tightly to their mounts, the roar of the crowd suffocating the announcer's voice.

Strangely enough, in those early years I never learned to ride well; I was content just to look at horses. The explanation is simple, I suppose; those misfits of Uncle Charlie's either had too many problems for us boys, or, like old Polly, they were nags. The other horses we rode were from one of the rental stables across from Griffith Park. Those plugs had long since been turned into walking robots and the only time they showed any life was when we turned them back towards the stables, and then there was no stopping their mad, homeward gallops.

Soon sports, girls and studies just about crowded horses out of our lives. At college, however, some new stallions—Bucephalus, Alborak, Rocinante, Marengo—did gallop from history into my imagination. To be honest, though, until shortly before coming to Spain, horses had been replaced in my world by other interests.

I was in Mexico one Sunday for a corrida when some friends introduced me to Carlos Arruza, a famous matador who, once he had retired from fighting bulls on foot in the ring, had turned to killing them from horseback in the classical tradition. The Andalusian mounts that Arruza used that afternoon were some of the most magnificent animals I had ever seen. They weren't large, though they did have full chests, exceptionally long manes and tails, well-formed heads, and body conformations that, although I knew little technically about

such things, seemed close to artistic perfection in their beauty. Two of Arruza's horses had unusually high and showy (but untrained, I was told) leg action. However, what most impressed me about those stallions was their gentle dispositions. At that time in America few stallions were kept for pleasure riding because they were generally considered dangerous. Thus, I assumed Arruza's horses were simply exceptionally beautiful and tame animals, and gave them little more thought. Also, this was the period in life when I was completely taken with what seemed to be the most impressive animals I had ever seen—fighting bulls—and I spent many free hours in Mexico studying their behavior and photographing them in the ring.

It was the fighting bull, in fact, that in 1958, when I was twenty-three years old, brought me to Spain, where I spent six years working on a naturalistic study of brave cattle. Not equipped with formal education for animal observation, I had to rely on the first lessons my father had given us in the ways of wild creatures which, along with an intense interest in nature, helped partly to overcome my lack of technical training by sometimes offering an open and fresh point of view.

During those wonderfully happy years in Andalusia, far from Uncle Charlie's Last Gate Ranch and the stockyards of Downy, I once again came in close contact with horses, spending day after day with the bulls, and it then became obvious that Arruza's mounts had been no exceptions in their extreme beauty and their noble dispositions—Spanish horses were normally that way. It was also exciting to realize that most of the horses in America were in one way or another related to Andalusian stock taken to the New World by the conquistadors. Even the race horses we had watched with Uncle Jim at Santa Anita, Hollywood Park and Bay Meadows, as well as those I had seen in England and France, had backgrounds that could be traced in part to Spain and North Africa. The Wyoming mustangs my father had told us about, and the Quarter Horses I had known in Texas and Mexico all had some Spanish blood. So it seemed that most of the horses in my life were suddenly tied together in an intriguing manner.

During those first years in Spain, I had the good fortune to enjoy the friendship of a number of men who not only loved fighting bulls, but felt just as strongly for their horses. Of these, the one I recall with most affection is the late Juan Belmonte (the matador who half a century ago revolutionized bullfighting). Though seventeen years have passed, I can still almost taste those cold bowls of *gazpacho* that were served to us by Asunción in the dining room of Belmonte's country house, Gómez Cardeña, followed by afternoons of open-field testings of young bulls. In my mind, as well preserved as a fresh photograph, is the picture of Belmonte on a white gelding, far off in the distance, a white speck against a sea of grey-green olive trees, the portrait of happiness in the union of man and horse.

Those mornings and afternoons of *acoso y*

derribo presented the opportunity to renew my interest in horses. Not content to photograph the testing from the edge of the field in the normal fashion, I asked Belmonte if there wasn't a new angle that could be used, a problem which he pondered on a number of occasions over coffee at the Café Los Corales in Sevilla. The first solution he suggested—with a slight smile on his rugged face—was to dig a hole a couple of meters deep at the edge of the field so that the action could be photographed from ground level. But I convinced him that the horses and cattle would flash by so fast there would barely be time to photograph them; those were the days before zoom lenses and motor drives were available to beginning photographers like me.

Then I remembered some pictures of an ox cart race in India that had been taken by the famous Hungarian woman photographer, Ylla, from the hood of a moving Land Rover. So one morning at Los Corales, with much enthusiasm, I suggested the use of a Land Rover to Belmonte who, after he listened attentively to the plan, thought for a moment and then in his stutter asked, "B-b-but, won't that be dangerous? The field isn't as smooth as the Palmera Avenue, you know." It was then that I had to admit that Ylla had been killed during the cart race in India, thrown from the hood of the Land Rover when it hit a hole. "And you still want to do this?" he questioned. I smiled and nodded yes.

So arrived the opportunity of not only being able to photograph bulls from the hood of a 169 fast moving vehicle, but also to observe at close range the brilliant action of Spanish horses at work. Never had I seen such noble heads, curved necks, flowing manes, and natural gaits on animals anywhere. It was as though the stallions of the Prado had come to life before us.

In those years of the late fifties and through the sixties, while photographing in the fields and bullrings of Spain, Mexico, Portugal and North Africa, I was each day brought closer to horses. Many of the animals were used by rejoneadors, mounted bullfighters, and of these, perhaps the finest horsemen were the Alvaro Domecqs, father and son (what a magnificent evening they gave when they appeared together in El Puerto de Santa María), the Peralta brothers, and Josechu Pérez de Mendoza. They were as serious in their somber formal country dress as the Portuguese rejoneadors, that I saw in provincial rings as well as in Lisbon's Campo Pequenho, were colorful. And what master horsemen they were—Conde, Nuncio, Lupi, and Ribeiro Teles—as was the Mexican, Gastón Santos, who performed splendidly not only in his own country but also in Spain.

It was while photographing in the Latin countries that it occurred to me that the preservation of the Andalusian horse was no accident. Famed as outstanding mounts for both war and parades, favored by the Romans, praised by the Arabs, used by Iberian knights and noblemen hundreds of years ago, these stallions have never become obsolete despite the advent of the car and a society whose values have shifted from the romance of the past to

the utility and comfort of a world that is moving towards universal conformity. Watching those Spanish and Portuguese gentlemen and cowboys carrying long lances, racing up and down hot fields while mounted on "Velázquez" stallions, or while performing in the bullring, made it clear to me that horses today are almost as useful and important to some Iberians as they had been to El Cid. And it is this usefulness, the need for working cattle with horses on the ranches and in the *plazas de toros*, as well as the Spaniards' appreciation of beauty and love of showing off on fiesta days (the Sevilla Fair is unquestionably the most spectacular display of horseflesh in the world), that has preserved living Andalusians as much as those rearing, galloping, parading, posing stallions have been preserved in the Prado.

In this way my childhood interest in horses was renewed in Spain, and it was thrilling to remember that wild Palomino stallion near Uncle Charlie's ranch and to imagine that hundreds of years ago his distant ancestors had maybe grazed the same pastures and marshes through which I trudged while photographing fighting bulls. Eighteen years ago those *marismas*, or marshes, were still untouched and wild, and frequently there was the opportunity to observe, hour after hour, semi-wild horses in games not completely unlike those of Ron and me and our fourth grade friends on the dusty grounds of Columbus Grammar School in Glendale, California.

It was not until the early 1970's, however, that my interest in equines leapt the barrier of silent admiration to possible subject matter for a book. This came about because of a friendship with Bernardo González Real, a fine photographer and horse lover in his early twenties, who lived in Jerez de la Frontera, the undisputed equestrian capital of Spain. In the few short years of our friendship, until he was killed in an automobile accident in 1974, Bernardo often said that he dreamed of doing some kind of book on horses, a plan that I tried to encourage with as much enthusiasm as he had shown for my projects.

Some years following my friend's death, when a publisher offered a contract for a photographic study on horses, how I wished that Bernardo had been around to do his book. In late April I did sign the contract, but with some reluctance, for it stated that the book would have to be finished in August and ready to print in the fall, an incredibly short time when compared with the years I had spent on the bull book. Without the assistance given by some two dozen people—friends, owners and trainers—it would have been impossible to complete the photographs in the contracted time.

A great deal of enthusiasm for this project had been accumulating over the years, passed on by friends from all parts of the world who shared their love and knowledge of horses. In England Nora McAlpine not only took me on my first hunt, but also was able to communicate sensitively her love of Thoroughbreds. I learned something of polo ponies from one of the kindest men I've ever met, the Maharaja of

Cooch Behar. Colonel Tom Nickalls and his wife, Tigre, took me along on delightful afternoons at both flat racing and steeplechasing in Britain. In Texas, Tom Lea expressed a love for American horses that left a profound impression, and it was inspiring to see how often and successfully he had contributed both the graphics and texts for his fine books. Another Texan, the late Robert Kleberg, Jr., who has a living tribute in the Quarter Horse, provided generous encouragement for my animal studies. South American Criollos were made more meaningful because of the hours spent with Bob Adams and Michael Hughes, long-time residents of the Argentine and Paraguay. In France, Françoise Courriere not only showed me the beauty of her country, but of its horses. Casey Tibbs and Spike Van Cleve both brought into sharper focus the world of the rodeo and the livestock used for it. Arab horses and the American show world were carefully explained by Tish Hewitt and Father Robert Q. Kennaugh. Australian Neil Dougall offered new insights into stud management. A pride in Morgan horses was transmitted to me by Steve and Aline Reeves. Jeff Ramsey shared his experience with stunt horses in Hollywood. The American saddlebred was made more important by a friendship with Gwen Harrison. Christiane Cutter, a German, helped me to see better the relationship of horses to art. And Budd and Mary Boetticher, Carolyn Moyer, Marilyn Tennent, Chuck Nuanes and Floyd Scrivens were examples of just how much joy horses can bring into people's lives.

In retrospect, some two years ago a decisive moment occurred that led to the doing of this book, but not until several months ago, on a flight from Denver to New York, did I fully realize its importance. James Michener and I were discussing moments of artistic expression in the performing arts which had most moved us, limiting ourselves to five performances each. At the head of my list, next to a magnificent *faena* by Curro Romero in Sevilla, Alicia Alonso dancing the dying swan, a dazzling trapeze performance by a troupe of Mexican flyers, Bjorling and Nillson singing Act Three from *Turandot*, I selected, without question, a performance by the Spanish Riding School of Vienna during which a horse doing the extended trot had seemed to glide across the ring. The movements of that Lipizzaner—a direct descendant of the stallions of Andalusia—caused the kind of awe that touched emotions deeply enough to give me goosepimples.

The idea of using photographs with quotations from a wide range of literary sources came first when I was doing the bull book, in which, at the last moment, I substituted my own captions for the descriptive phrases of other authors. However, it seemed the ideal marriage for this book, in that the combination of pictures with quotations from all over the world and from all ages, would show the eternal beauty of and man's fascination with horses. All the photographs were taken before the quotations were selected. Also, I tried to photograph as many breeds as possible—Andalusians, Arabs, Quarter Horses, Thoroughbreds, Lipizzaners—so that the book would be about the horse in general, and more important, the horse at liberty.

The photographic equipment used included two 35 mm cameras, one mounted with a motor drive, together with a 50-300 mm zoom lens and a 28 mm wide-angle lens. Film shot was Ektachrome X force—developed to 160 ASA.

The notes that follow were usually jotted down while scouting locations or while waiting for changes in light during actual photography. A good part of the material was drawn from observations of semi-wild horses during the past eighteen years, along with animals living at liberty in the marshes of the Guadalquivir. At various times horse observations were also made in the United States (mainly in California, Arizona, Texas and New Mexico), as well as in North Africa, Mexico, England, Portugal, and France.

It is hoped that these brief notes on behavior will encourage young naturalists to do further studies on free-living horses.

P. 2 At sunset a herd of Arab, Thoroughbred and Andalusian mares crosses a ridge at the Spanish Army farm, Vicos, located between Jerez de la Frontera and Arcos. In groups of horses like this, living in liberty or semi-liberty, there is a strong hierarchy. Distinguishable to even the most casual observer, this pecking order serves a vital need by giving the animals hard and fast rules for social interaction. Each horse knows his role and, as long as his station is well-defined, feels relatively secure, even

though he is at the bottom of the totem pole. In contrast to animals like the tiger, which come together just once a year during the breeding season, horses have had to develop a mode of living together which allows them to perform their life functions while united and with a minimum of difficulties. Only because each animal carries within itself the instinct for applying and functioning under this code of social behavior have equines been able to survive. Though domesticated for millennia, the horse's prime patterns of social behavior seem to have undergone mimimal changes. When freed today in the marshes of the Guadalquivir, a Spanish stallion probably behaves not too differently from his primeval ancestor who galloped through the steppes two million years ago.

P. 8 At daybreak a Quarter Horse mare emerges from a lagoon at the King Ranch España property of Los Millares near Huelva. By numbers the world's most popular breed, the Quarter Horse is a descendant of Andalusian stock taken to the New World by the conquistadors. Most modern horses boast some Spanish blood.

P. 10 Over one hundred and fifty Arab, Thoroughbred and Andalusian mares swirl together at Vicos. Fortunately for these breeds, the Spanish Army maintains stud farms throughout the country, a military tradition sadly lost in most of the modern world. Herds such as those of mares at Vicos, and of stallions and geldings at Ecija, provided the chance not only to photograph large numbers of horses together, but also to observe their behavior while living in semi-liberty. In the strict sense of the word, these groups of animals cannot be considered true herds, since they are controlled by man. The legitimate herd, today almost extinct, except for the zebra and the feral horse, is generally formed by several family groups living in fairly close proximity, each headed by a lead stallion. Outside these highly guarded family units roam groups of young bachelors not yet psychologically ready to challenge an established stallion or take on the responsibility of a harem of mares. Herd living not only offers the collective warning system but is especially important to breeding. In these pages of captions, however, the word "herd" will be used to describe not only combined units of several family groups, but also will be applied to all groups of animals living together whether of the same or of opposite sexes.

P. 13 At the ranch of the Conde de Odiel near Sevilla, I observed horses like these form strong friendships and show obvious affection for one another. This old gelding's ears, pointed forward and slightly relaxed in a lateral position, together with his relaxed facial muscles, show him to be content. Between horses, much more important than vocal communication are visual signals and of these, ear positions are a virtual barometer for reading a fellow herd member's moods, and are essential in animal-to-animal communication. Positions can range from the forward, slightly lateral attitude of the animal in this photograph, expressing tranquility and well-being, to more and more backward positions, until the ears are virtually pressed flat against the mane—in a threat warning—to show massive aggression. Between extreme forward and backward positions are a whole range of subtle signals, all easily understood by equines. If the ears are flapped out completely laterally, they most often signal tiredness or inferiority. There are also combinations of positions, as well as an even finer means of communication in which one animal receives a message about the location of sound stimuli by glancing at the aperture position of a fellow horse's ears. After days of observation it also became apparent that horses determine the wind's direction mostly with their ears—by sound—and not by smell with their noses.

P. 15 Probably one of the most important means of social and physical interaction among horses is mutual grooming, as shown by these Arab and Andalusian mares at the Vicos Army farm. The Spanish mare on the right was standing moping on this hill when she was approached by the Arab mare, who was searching for a grooming partner. When such contact is sought, the passive animal is usually approached from the half front by the horse which desires to initiate grooming. This animal, with a subtle facial expression which can clearly be read by the other as "let's scratch backs," advances or retreats depending upon

the facial response of the horse it is propositioning. If, as in the case of the mares in this photograph, a proposition has been accepted, the animals will usually stand together for a few minutes moping or grazing, after which they will position themselves next to one another, head to tail, and start biting in short, firm nibbles at each other's necks. If the action is intense, the sound of their teeth is clearly audible as they start on the mane crest, pulling at loose hair and dead skin. Slowly working along necks, shoulders and backs, they usually stop at each other's tail roots—one of the most delicious places to be scratched if you're a horse. When grooming is finished, horses generally stand next to one another for a short while in the head-to-tail position, moping or grazing, before they wander off or change sides to resume grooming. Not only does this activity allow animals to scratch parts of their bodies that are unreachable by their own mouths, but it also probably serves to form friendships and strengthen the social contact that was once so important to the wild herd. Although most grooming takes place between just two horses, on several occasions I saw three mares at Vicos and three stallions at Ecija scratching each other's backs.

P. 17 During the hot noon hours this nine-year-old mare of the Conde de Odiel mopes under an olive tree. Since she is an old animal, wise in the ways of searching out food and familiar with the geography of the ranch, a bell has been tied around her neck which will not

only attract the other brood mares to her, but aid man in locating the herd. The mare stands in the typical moping position, ears relaxed and laterally drooping, neck straight out (or down), front legs together, croup down, and one back leg cocked at an angle with only the tip of the hoof touching the ground. Equines spend more time moping than they do in either of their other two forms of sleep: resting, in which the animal drops to the ground with its legs positioned partly beneath its body, or deep sleeping, in which the horse lies flat out on its side. In fact, after eating, more of a horse's life is spent moping than doing anything else. It is the one activity during which the animal appears least attractive to the human eye—even a fine stallion, when he is moping, will look like a nag to most people.

Among the horses I observed, moping generally took place during the hot midday hours, lengthening in its duration as the Andalusian heat became more intense, or after eating (on a number of days at Ecija the temperature reached 114°F). At noon the Vicos mares and the stallions at Ecija divided themselves into groups of from five to twenty animals, and stood heads together, in circles, rear ends out, tails swishing in an attempt to protect themselves from flies and other insects, and moped silently for hours. Primitive instinct manifested itself not only in this effective cooperative attempt to deal with insects, but also in the moping position which in the wild is the safest form of relaxation for a horse. If threat presents itself to the moping horse he is not in too

deep a sleep to react and, being on his feet, can either flee or kick. The only effort that moping requires is to change fairly often the position of the back legs, which must be relaxed or moved to relieve a muscle tension that, because of the construction of the tendons, does not affect the front legs. Apart from hot weather, horses will also mope longer on cold or wet days with their tails to the rain or wind.

P. 19 At Vicos even though this Spanish mare was in close daily contact with man, because she was alone and grazing out of sight of the herd, my appearance was enough to put her to flight. Horses are timid animals, regardless of their size and strength, and can be put into blind panic by even the most harmless stimulus if it is unknown or comes as a surprise. Animals observed in the herd followed the same escape patterns, whether they were family groups like those at the Coto Doñana, the King Ranch or the ranch of Paco Lazo, or if they were exclusively mare herds or herds of stallions. If the surprise or threat was overwhelming to them, the entire group fled in blind panic, temporarily dissolving the hierarchy of the herd. However, if the threat was not considered great, the horses would react in the same manner and would escape with the high ranking mares and foals in the lead, followed by the rest of the mares with the stallion always bringing up the rear. When the group was made up only of mares, the stallion's position was taken by one of the more aggressive females, who snapped at the flanks of the animals in front of

her. Each herd of males at Ecija also had a high-ranking stallion. It appeared to me that when family groups were involved, the direction of flight was always set by the lead female, usually a wise old mare, while the stallion's duty was primarily to hurry on lagging animals which might become prey for pursuing predators.

P. 21 This sixteen-year-old Spanish stallion, Majestad, owned by John Fulton, has a face considered too long by many breeders, yet he is one of the most photogenic horses I have ever photographed. His head length, once typical of all Spanish horses, has the kind of artistic balance that attracted painters like Velázquez. Unfortunately this noble element is lacking in the shorter faces of some modern Spanish purebreds.

The lateral position of Majestad's closest ear here shows his attraction to some sound stimulus. Next to ear positions, facial expressions are the most important optical signals in animal-to-animal communication. So subtle that they were often hardly distinguishable, nostril flaring, muzzle wrinkling and jaw flexing played an important part in the expression of the horses photographed. The sticking out or tightening of the lips, the angle of curve at the edges of the mouth, and the amount of teeth shown were everyday means of silent communication utilized by herd members in Andalusia. Obviously, equines must be in fairly close proximity in order to use these forms of visual language. Mares use their eyes in expressing

feelings to a much lesser degree than ear and muzzle signals. Blinking or closing the eye, depending on the degree of opening, can serve as a show of passiveness to an outside stimulus. Most stallions, however, use their eyes constantly during display rituals.

P. 22 Majestad grazes in a field of spring poppies at the ranch of Rocío de la Cámara. Eating, in terms of time spent, is the most important activity in the life of the horse. At pastures where I was working, the animals often grazed between eleven and thirteen hours a day. Unlike carnivores, who can subsist on relatively small amounts of food because of the high nutritive value of meat, horses must eat immense quantities of vegetation in order to maintain enough weight and strength for normal activity. Because of the low nutritive value of their diet, equines have relatively long digestive tracts, requiring an extended digestive period in order to get the most out of every blade of grass.

Since their food-to-stomach process is a one-act operation, horses, unlike camels, cows and antelope, must mill vegetation and grain in their mouths more slowly and thoroughly than do their cousins.

P. 24 This five-year-old stallion, Jerezano, of Romero Benítez, is caught up in the excitement of having just been turned to a herd of mares. He rolls his eyes, arches his neck, and flexes the muscles of his cheek and muzzle in a fine display of strength and masculinity. During this initial introduction-confrontation, some of the younger mares jealously guarded an older sister in heat, and when the stallion tried to get too close they kicked out viciously at him.

A pasturing herd of animals is generally peaceful until a strange horse, whether it be a stallion or a mare, arrives. Then, because of the rigidly defined hierarchy, each herd member must reestablish its position in the group either by challenging the newcomer or by reacting submissively. Even in the exclusively female herd at El Hornillo, quarrels for supremacy often lasted several days—depending on the ambition of the participants.

P. 26 A herd of Andalusian, Arab and Thoroughbred mares moves to higher ground as the wind that often thrashes the southern coast of Spain begins to subside. Since horses are extremely weather-conscious, weather fluctuations have a remarkable effect on their behavior. Apart from the temperature and air movement, the degree of humidity is also important to equines. On sultry days, the animals I observed were far less active than they were during milder weather. Just before a storm, when there was great atmospheric tension and the air was filled with ions, almost all the horses were nervous, restless and aggressive. Years before, when I was doing a study of the fighting bull, the effect of thunder storms on animals was even more apparent as I watched in single pastures perhaps five or six sets of bulls

concurrently engaged in combats triggered by atmospheric tensions—combats that sometimes ended in death. During similar weather there was also increased fighting among the stallions at Ecija; and horses of both sexes showed inner tension by hyperactive eating, which slowed down markedly once the storm had broken. Strong winds also stimulated activity—running and fight games—among the stallions at Ecija, to the extent that, before leaving home on such a day, I knew good camera material would always be waiting in the country.

P. 28 A herd of seventy-five mares rushes along a trail at Vicos. Later in the day some of these same animals returned to this dry basin for dust baths, which they usually preferred to take at noontime when the earth was hot and dry. A surprisingly large number of horse hours are spent engaged in grooming and care of the hair and skin. Some animals in the marismas seemed to prefer mud to dust for baths, probably not only because mud served as protection against insects, but because dislodged dried earth was effective in the removal of dead hair and skin.

Practically all the horses observed had favorite dusting spots like the dry basin in this photograph. Rolling on dry ground not only feels good to a horse, but it is essential in removing excess oil from the skin, thereby helping to order hair in its natural direction. When mares arrived at this basin, they would lower their heads, ears forward, smell the ground

and paw at it slightly, after which, with short steps, they would circle several times the chosen spot before lying down. It is not easy for horses to lower themselves to the ground, for unlike meat eaters, they do not have very flexible vertebral columns. To be able to get to the ground for a bath, a horse normally collects his four legs under his body, then bends at an angle so sharp that the muscles vibrate with tension until they will no longer hold his weight, at which time he drops down onto his forelegs and rolls over on his side. Clumsy, old or pregnant mares sometimes practically let themselves fall to the ground.

Once on the ground, the head and neck are pressed to the earth to scratch the flat sides of both, especially the cheek region. After having dusted and scratched one side of their bodies, most horses will roll to the ungroomed side. Active animals repeat this process several times. At the ranch of Francisco Lazo, one stallion would rise from the flat-out position to the huddling or sitting position, hind legs partly under his body, forelegs extended to dig at the soil with one of his front hooves, loosing the earth in preparation for another roll over. At the ranch of Juan Manuel Urquijo some of the heavily pregnant or old mares, which could not or did not want to roll completely, would get to their feet after having dusted one side, to lower themselves back to the ground to dust their other side.

Dusting is highly contagious, and once other animals have watched one horse start to roll, they follow suit. If the dusting area is large, such as the one shown in this photograph, several animals may be seen involved in self-grooming at the same time. If the area is only big enough for one or two horses, herd hierarchy is once again clearly seen, as dominant animals dust first, followed by the more passive members of the herd. The instinctive need for an animal to satisfy itself, by either dusting or taking a mud bath, is so great that within minutes after a stabled horse is freed into a corral where there is mud or dry earth, the first thing he does, once he feels secure in those surroundings, is to drop to the ground and roll.

P. 30-31 The herds of bachelor stallions at the Army ranch near Ecija, some of which appear in these two photographs, provided an excellent opportunity to observe the social structure of the all-male herd. The animals in the photograph on page 30 have just arrived at the crest of a hill and are on the run. The ear positions of the two horses at the left of the photograph, slightly pointed forward, show curiosity. The third animal from the left, with his ears flat against his mane, expresses aggression. The grey next to him has his ears in the lateral position, which indicates that he may be shifting his ear apertures in search of sound. The bay next to him has its ears back, as do the running horses on page 31. Horses moving at fast speed usually lay their ears flat in an attempt to keep dust and insects from entering the ear apertures.

The grey stallion biting the neck of the darker horse was one of the few animals at Ecija who, before he arrived at the Army farm as a two year old, had covered a mare. The behavior of such a stallion was completely different from that of the calmer male virgins around him. On a number of occasions I observed such animals among the young bachelors, and each of them, not long after having been turned to the herd, picked a companion who was possibly the same color as the mare that such a sexually experienced stallion had covered for the first time—most probably by accident. As in the case of the two animals in this photograph, the sexually practised stallion jealously guarded his virgin friend. This companionship, on one hand, had in part become real torture for the virgin, for he was never left alone, always being nipped at, hurried on and herded this way and that by his suitor; on the other hand, however, it meant that he enjoyed a high place in herd hierarchy. Since sexually experienced stallions are hyperaggressive and active animals, they are nearly always the lead males in bachelor herds. This means that their partners, like foals of dominant mares, can do as they want, having the security that the animal which loves them will always be there to protect them; prime spots are thus assured at dusting, feeding and watering places.

At Ecija there was one hyperactive half-Arab stallion who became such a pest to his virgin companion that on a number of occasions the virgin rebelled against his suitor with flurries

of kicks that several times brought blood to the

Arab's chest. In these partnerships at Ecija, though animals would often have erections while grooming one another, only once in many hours did I see an experienced stallion try to mount his virgin friend. Once the pairs of stallions at Ecija were gelded, the relationship between them remained just as close, or closer, but what did change was the aggressive behavior of the dominant stallion. Gone was the continual biting and driving, replaced by what appeared to be tender affection.

P. 32 In battle games when young stallions finally do rise up against one another, they do so as if in slow motion, which is delightful to watch in contrast to a serious, fast combat between mature horses. Shown here are two Conde de Odiel animals, Divertido aged four and Barquillero aged five. Often, I saw young stallions rear against one another and, as if in a slow dance, one would clasp the other's shoulders with his forelegs, both staying on their hind legs for a half minute or more. When the animals were in this position, the more aggressive one would take playful bites at the other's face. The "attacked" horse would raise his head high, trying to keep from being nipped, at the same time opening his eyes very wide. Facial muscles of both stallions would be relatively relaxed and their ears would generally remain pointed forward. Sliding away from each other to drop their forefeet once more to the ground, the horses might continue their fight or begin grazing or grooming one another.

Often, what started out with playful sparring would begin to look like a carbon copy of a serious fight, if one of the partners lost his temper or would not quit when the other signaled "I give." In my first days of observation, it appeared that when this happened the horse that had had enough would turn tail and, chased by the other, dash off for maybe fifty yards, where sparring would be resumed. However, after several days it became apparent that what I had often interpreted as flight response was not that at all, but merely a part of the play ritual of young stallions. It was all a game to them; spar, bash necks, nip at faces and shoulders, circle to bite hind legs, rear up, drop back to the ground—and then turn tail and run to a new spot to repeat the activity, making the game more interesting. If one animal did, however, really lose his temper, wanting to end the game but failing to get this message across to his opponent, he would finally whirl around, screeching, and kick out violently, often thudding his hoofs against the molester's side or chest.

P. 34 These three-year-old stallions at the Army's Ecija farm are not involved in serious combat. Perhaps the most interesting hours of observation spent during the short work on this book were those with herds of young bachelors at Ecija and at the ranch of Romero Benítez near Jerez.

The play fights between young animals had none of the air of urgency and threat of violence that accompanied several battles that I witnessed between mature stallions. Fight games were the primary source of exercise for most members of the bachelor herd. Often one animal with a mischievous expression on its face, ears pricked, facial muscles relaxed, would approach another and begin playfully to bite at the passive stallion's head and neck. When both animals were looking for a fight, they would gallop towards one another, stop face to face, and with neck muscles high and using imposing body movements they would position themselves side to side, smell each other's flanks and genitals, and start turning in circles, at the same time voicing shrill war cries. Sometimes, before this circling started, the animals would push at one another with their necks, taking only half-serious nips, shoving, feinting and dodging, each trying to bite the other's forelegs, shoulders and flanks. Often, face to face, they would both drop to their knees and continue snapping and knocking their heads and necks together. Almost without fail, when they got to their feet from this position, they would again circle around and around, head to tail, each trying to bite the enemy on the hind legs. The number of circles usually ranged from four to ten, but once I counted twenty-four turns as two bays whirled in the dust, and I was surprised when they stopped this part of their battle to find that both were not only able to keep their balance, but that they renewed circling for a further ten turns in the opposite direction.

P. 36 At Ecija, a three-year-old stallion, screaming, lunges at an enemy's neck. Most fights are ended really before they start because of the elaborate pre-combat display ritual which manifests itself when two older animals meet—that is, under natural circumstances. If the animals in question are not free-running stallions, but corralled or enclosed in the presence of mares, then violent combat is almost sure to explode. Only on a few occasions did I see stallions involved in serious battles that, although exciting, were disagreeable to anyone who loves horses. Animals that under normal circumstances probably would not have been pressed into such bloody combat, bashed at each other with their hoofs, slashed with their teeth and whirled to kick with blows that could break a leg or destroy a horse's face.

When stallions meet in serious battle they voice war cries, and rear up trying to thud their heavy, sharp-edged, fast-flying hoofs against the enemy's chest or face. Ears laid flat, they bite at each other's necks and heads. Even the most furious fight, though, cannot destroy a certain pattern of combat that is innate in horses. Because rearing up is exhausting for them, stallions soon have to come down on all fours, when they continue biting, circling around, throwing their weight against one another, before rearing up once more. When the loser has been determined, this animal will usually drop to the ground, whirl and kick out frantically just before fleeing. Violent fights are most often the result of an attempt to steal a mare from a family unit. Death or serious injury from such battles is not usual, and more than likely accidental. If the two animals involved in such a combat are very different

from each other in physique and temperament, then the rules for normal battle may no longer apply, and the faster and stronger stallion may surprise his enemy and seriously wound him before escape is possible.

P. 38 At Vicos a lovely Spanish mare stands in a field of sunflowers. Although the leaves of these plants were green and seemed appealing in contrast to the July-burnt fields where this mare was accustomed to graze, she would not touch the sunflowers. At the Urquijo ranch, the first time I really paid any close attention to the way the mares ate, I was amazed at how adept they were in selecting and plucking individual grasses. Although springtime had filled the pastures with all sorts of plants, the animals I watched were quite choosey in what they ate; some, however, were more selective than others. Even very hungry horses (at liberty) won't eat everything green in sight, something cattle will do and which often has fatal consequences.

P. 40-41 Owned by Eduardo Tuya, this Andalusian stallion shows the breed's tendency to have thick, long manes and tails. A horse's primary means of defense against insects, especially flies which seek the moist facial and body areas, are his forelock, mane and tail. When I was in the marshes of the Coto Doñana, working on another book with the stallion Majestad, he had to contend with everything from small gnat-like insects that clustered around his eyes, mouth and genitals, to large, green flies that left pea-sized spots of blood every

185

time they bit him, mostly on the stomach. Even these bites, however, did not seem to bother Majestad much. (I'm sure they "hurt" the humans who were working with him much more.) A horse's pain threshold numbs him against degrees of hurt that would cause a human to scream.

P. 42 This picture was shot near Ecija. All the photographs of herds of young stallions were taken either at the Army farm there or near Jerez at the ranch of Romero Benítez.

One daybreak I arrived at the latter ranch shortly before half a dozen two year olds, which had spent a week at the Jerez Fair, were returned to the herd. Aware that each of the eight animals pasturing calmly before me would have to re-establish his position in the hierarchy, as would the six young stallions who had been absent, I expected some good material for my camera, but what started out as a photographic venture finished with the importance shifting from film to the rough notes on horse behavior that I was able to take.

As soon as the six newcomers were turned into the pasture, all fourteen animals raced around, galloping together, the lead stallion and two males which ranked below him posturing, crests arched and swollen, tossing their heads and nipping the necks and flanks of the younger horses. Finally, when this exuberant stampede stopped on the far side of the field, I picked up my cameras and took off in that direction.

Then, in no certain order, the lead stallion and the other three year olds would gather around one of the recently arrived horses and, lifting their feet in high, stamping steps, they smelled the younger animal's lower flanks, genitals and anus, at the same time voicing the high shriek of a male horse in close contact with another stallion. This sniffing was similar to that done by male dogs and other animals with *one* exception: when the herd members reached the lower flank of a recently arrived horse, sniffing became highly intense and breathing was exaggerated. At this point they seemed more like dogs at a rabbit hole. What were they trying to learn? What message could be received from the odor emitted by another horses's *lower* flank? It is said that horses can smell fear in humans. Can they also detect it in each other? Can dominance be determined without battle, by merely a war of nerves that results in a submissive animal signaling defeat through his odor?

Through a series of posturing and imposing their importance on one another or, on the other hand, communication by submissive gestures, and possibly odors, the hierarchy of the herd began to re-establish itself. Some of the animals, probably old friends, would suddenly dash off together in pairs, stop a short distance away and slowly rear up against one another, forelegs clutching shoulders, while one would nip at the high-held face of the other.

When this initial excitement was over, though things were not completely back to normal in the herd for another day and a half,

I noticed a form of behavior that was completely strange to me—one that I had never heard mentioned. While packing up the cameras I saw a handsome bay two year old approach and present his rump to the grey lead stallion. The grey smelled the younger bay's lower flank, genitals and tail root, at which time the bay playfully kicked out his back legs, seeming to try to capture more of the stallion's attention and excite him, before running off a short distance with the dominant animal in pursuit. The stallions stopped fifty yards from the grazing herd, where the bay once more deliberately presented his rear to the grey in exactly the same manner as I had often seen young baboons present themselves to the highest-ranking baboon male, gesturing submission in a clear definition of dominance hierarchy.

Distracted by the neighing of a horse in another pasture, the grey had his head lifted in that direction when the young bay backed his rump right up against the older horse's chest. Then followed more smelling by the lead stallion, during which time he had a half erection. Finally the bay again kicked out playfully and weakly at the top-ranking stallion before returning to the herd after a performance which clearly seemed to say, "I'm back in the herd and I've shown you by the most submissive behavior I can that you're still the leader I respect. So don't worry about me, I'm no threat." That day two of the other young horses presented themselves in exactly the same manner to the grey, as well as to the second-ranking stallion. The action I had seen was too clear to have been a product of imagination; however, I was left with the desire to see a group of male horses under similar circumstances so that I could verify this—new to me—ritual of submission of stallions.

A few afternoons later, upon returning to Jerez, I asked my friend Antonio Romero Girón if he could take a three-year-old stallion, one that had been dominant, but who had been moved from the pasture to the stable for training, and release him with the herd of animals I had observed several days before. Because Antonio has an adventurous spirit, because he was a close friend of Bernardo González Real, and because his great love in life is horses, he agreed to help with this experiment.

When the stallion was returned to the herd he postured, swung his head and rolled his eyes, finally standing still next to the highest-ranking animals in the group, at which time the flank-sniffing ceremony commenced. In two cases, because superiority may not have been determined by odor, there followed a series of brief skirmishes, first with the lead stallion, in which no blood was drawn and which, at its most serious point, was fought on their knees by both horses. After the newcomer clearly proved his superiority to the former leader, confrontations continued with other animals, consisting mostly of flank sniffing and posturing, in which the new and dominant animal imposed his presence on each of the other bachelors.

187

It was then time for my previous day's observation to be verified: that young stallions will make known their inferiority and submissiveness to a lead stallion by presenting their rumps to him, baboon fashion. The more serious confrontations over, the dark grey began to gather all the animals into a herd as, head held about eight inches from the ground and swinging laterally from side to side in fish-like movements, he nipped at flanks and legs to bunch the other stallions tightly, guiding them to a far corner of the pasture. Once there, he engaged in two or three brief confrontations with several high-ranking animals, after which all the horses began to graze. It was at this time that a black two year old emerged from the herd, trotted to the new leader, and presented his rump. The dark grey sniffed the younger animal's flank and genitals and when he reached the anus the submissive horse began to move forward, but only fast enough to keep the leader coming after him and interested. Fifty feet from the herd, the black stopped and again backed into the dominant horse. The smelling ritual followed, in which even from a fair distance the intense sniffing could be heard, after which the leader with a half erection tried to mount the younger animal, who kicked out playfully and rejoined the herd. That same afternoon I watched three other two year olds submissively present themselves to the new leader in the same manner. This behavior was initiated each time by a young animal, generally two years of age; never by any of the older,

higher-ranking bachelors.

Just before I left the pasture, the leader was once again involved in gathering the other bachelors into a group, herding them exactly the way a stallion drives mares. When he had accomplished this and was circling with his head held high, a two-and-a-half-year-old roan stallion lashed out so forcefully that his hind hoofs thudded against the leader's ribs, to knock him completely down and over onto his side. Before the leader could get to his feet—and I was truly worried about his well-being, since he had been knocked down with such force—the roan slipped back deep into the cover of the herd, like an assassin trying to hide in a crowd. The leader painfully got up, his dignity seemingly more hurt than his ribs, and again, head down, began circling the herd, moving them along the fence toward the other corner of the pasture. Reflecting on what had occurred, it was obvious that the young roan had stood in wait, his forequarters partly concealed by other horses, for the leader to pass, so that unidentified and at close range he could throw his blows with terrific force. This behavior was especially interesting in that the roan was both the chosen friend of the former herd leader, though their association was not as close as between the sexually experienced stallions and the virgins at Ecija, and also one of the few young horses who that afternoon had not presented his rump to the new leader.

P. 44 This is the Cárdenas stallion Vasallo.

P. 46 Grasses, dried by July heat, are back-lit by the setting sun in a field near Ecija. The amount of vegetation available to animals living in semi-liberty has a pronounced effect on their social life. When food is abundant, horses graze in close contact with one another, narrowing the distance from animal to animal, which escalates social interaction. High-ranking animals, ears laid back, teeth bared, necks outstretched, occasionally threaten other horses who pasture too close. When food is scarce, they must spread out in their search for it, with dominant animals monopolizing the choice spots.

P. 48 Paco Lazo's six-year-old stallion, Nostálgico, prances, arching his neck, before a mare. The mare, with forward-pointing ears and relaxed eyes, shows the stallion that he may approach without the danger of being kicked. In the top photograph on page 49, the stallion assumes the typical "smiling" position (called flehmen), head held high in the air, nostrils flared, lips peeled back, after having just lowered his head to smell the ground where the mare had urinated. Flehmen is an olfactory process used by most hoofed males to test a female's excrement to establish if she is sexually receptive. In the lower photograph on page 49, the mare's ears are still pointed forward, her eyes remain relaxed, as do the edges of her mouth, reassuring the stallion of her good intentions. The chests of most free-living males are marked with half-rounded

scars from the hoofs of mares. Although a stallion often harasses his mares, driving them and biting at their flanks and hind legs, most ranchers agree that a male horse receives much more punishment from his harem than he inflicts on them. Nostálgico's ears, held slightly back and in a lateral position, along with his flexed eye muscles, flared nostrils and tightened mouth that curves decidedly down at the edges, shows that because he is still not sure of the mare he is posturing in an attempt to impose his importance and strength on her.

P. 50 At Los Millares this Spanish stallion follows a mare in heat. The horse's tightly pursed lips, his extended neck, exaggerated eye rolling and the lateral snake- or fish-like wobbling of his head show him to be in an excited state and serves as a warning to females that they had better hold to his prescribed course of direction. This posturing, apart from signaling intentions to mares, also warns other horses to stay away. Most free-living stallions try to add as many females as possible to their family units. Even a strong animal, however, has far fewer mares than do the wild males written about in fiction or shown in most motion pictures. Of family units observed during the last eighteen years in the marshes of the Guadalquivir, none had more than eight mares, the average number of female members being five. No marsh stallion was lucky enough to rule over a dozen mares, as did the Concha y Sierra stallion at Los Millares, or to be pastured with

thirty females such as those enjoyed by Paco Lazo's stallion.

In the photograph on page 51, the mare has stopped and is not only showing the stallion by urinating that she is ready to be mounted, but is using two additional visual signs to indicate her receptiveness. Apart from use of ears and face, horses also employ several body signals in animal-to-animal communication. First the mare spreads her legs slightly, in a sawhorse position, and next she lifts her tail. Previous to having been approached by the stallion, and while at quite some distance from him, she had also lifted her tail and begun flashing, which consists of opening and closing the vulva lips, often to expose the clitoris. Besides flashing when in heat, mares generally do so following urination.

P. 52 Salerosa, an eight-year-old mare who has just come into heat, grazes at the ranch of Juan Manuel Urquijo. While watching horses eat, I was continually amazed at how selectively they seemed to take the blades of grass with their lips, before biting with their cutting teeth and slightly raising their heads. It was impressive to see how skillful they were, in spite of their broad mouths, in avoiding the less tasty vegetation.

At other ranches I visited in Andalusia, where fields were heavily grazed, mares often pulled roots up with the grass. This not only destroyed pastures, but where soil was sandy, quartz taken in with roots noticeably caused premature wearing down of teeth. One twenty-year-old mare who had passed most of her life feeding on such fields near Córdoba, showed teeth that had been sanded down practically to stumps.

During the spring, when there was such a paradise of greenery everywhere, most mares seemed almost to suffer from a food mania as they chomped away, bulging their bellies to immense proportions, putting on fat that would help them survive the harsh, barren, baking summer months when temperatures in the shade often reached 111°F. During the winter, when the marshes of the Guadalquivir were flooded, I was fascinated to watch horses grazing with their muzzles below water, something I would have thought impossible for them to do. On a number of occasions when grass was scarce, food envy manifested itself as one mare threatened another—gesturing or lunging at her. Distance from animal to animal, however, never became so great as to dissolve the herd.

P. 54 Justiciero, a three-year-old stallion of Romero Benítez, opens his eyes wide and postures, threatening an intruder. Eye rolling, in which the eyeball rolls back in the head until only the white and the very red edges of the eye show, is an elemental part of a stallion's repertoire of display gestures. This action of the eye, accompanied by head swinging and exaggerated and impressive body posturing, has been accorded little importance by most human observers, probably because it occurs quite rapidly and because of the more obvious and distracting gestures that accompany it. Some stallions use their eyes more than others. One family leader at the King Ranch was so exaggerated in his gestures, that the first time I saw him driving mares—when another stallion was in close proximity—he rolled his eyes to such a degree that I had the feeling we were not watching a real horse at all, but rather some mythical creature sent to earth by Zeus.

Because of the rapidity of this action, the amount of eye rolling done by most of the stallions I photographed was not apparent until I received the developed film. Having to use a fast shutter speed to minimize the movement of a large telephoto lens on the motorized camera, I was amazed to see those images, frozen at a two-thousandth of a second, which showed very exaggerated and constant eye rolling of excited stallions, whether the stimulus had been another male or a mare. In bachelor herds, for some reason, I found that stallions who had covered mares rolled their eyes more than did virgin males, probably because they had sampled sex and were thus constantly in an excited state, desiring more.

P. 57 Barquillero, a five-year-old Conde de Odiel stallion, arches his neck impressively as he smells a mare's rear. In 1959, while photographing cattle on the ranches, I spent long hours in the marshes of the Guadalquivir, and often when the bulls' behavior wasn't interesting I turned my attention to the other inhabitants of that then-wild area: birds, horses and even camels. Those observations, together 191

with later, briefer periods spent casually watching several units of semi-wild horses in the Coto Doñana Wildlife Reserve, gave me my only contact with animals living under fairly natural conditions. In some ways, no doubt, their behavior differed from that of wild horses in other parts of the world, but still I'm sure that most ritual patterns were basically the same.

The stallions observed in the marismas did not seem to guard strict boundaries as I would have expected them to do. Family groups used their own paths and each had its own sleeping area, but on several occasions I saw families meet, and it was then that I witnessed a ritual strange to me, used by lead stallions, apparently to avoid bloody combat. One morning I had been sitting in a cork oak since two hours before sunrise, waiting to photograph bulls and cattle egrets, when from my left came the sounds of a group of horses which soon appeared with an old pinto stallion bringing up the rear. Just before they reached the oak, the herd stopped and the black and white stallion, head held high and ears cocked forward, posturing slightly, walked in front of the mares. Then from the right, from out of the scrub, appeared another group of mares and colts, followed by a handsome chestnut stallion who, when he sighted the pinto, also walked forward, posturing. As both harems stood still the stallions, who were then about seventy-five yards apart, approached one another, necks highly arched, ears pricked, and faces blessed

with the most noble of equestrian statue expressions.

When the horses met they stood forehead to forehead, muzzle to muzzle, smelling one another. It was then that their ears, which had remained straight forward, suddenly tilted back and forth, to remain pressed tightly against their manes in signals of massive aggression. This I read as a kind of symbolic fight action, which was accompanied by stamping and striking out with the forefeet and legs, along with the stallion-to-stallion high-pitched squealing, which grew in intensity but did not explode in violence. Head to tail they circled one another, smelling each other's flanks, genitals and anuses. Smelling of the lower flank lasted relatively long and sniffing was intense enough to be clearly heard. During this display ritual, in which superiority was determined or verified as clearly as if the animals had engaged in violent combat, the head-to-tail position was maintained seemingly as a symbol of peaceful intentions. Finally, one of the stallions stepped aside and defecated. The other leader then smelled the dung and urinated over it. Next, both horses lowered their heads to sniff the urine before they rejoined their respective family units.

On several occasions during those years in the marshes I saw symbolic battle rituals repeated in almost exactly the same form as described here. Perhaps this ceremony makes one stallion's mares taboo to the other, in which case certain distance restrictions, from unit to

unit, can be dropped, allowing relatively peaceful co-existence which makes possible the sharing of vital food and water supplies. A stallion respecting the rules will generally not pursue a mare from another family unit. During the encounters witnessed in the marshes between heads of families and young bachelors, the excrement-marking ritual was seldom practiced. These examples of fight posturing in which real battle is avoided through a ritual composed of symbolic attitudes and perhaps flank sniffing, were for me fascinating evidence of the horses' ability to coexist sensibly and peacefully by following a set of basic rules that were probably laid down hundreds of thousands of years ago.

P. 58 In this photograph, Barquillero has just smelled a mare's urine and is testing it to determine if she is in heat. Even before a mare comes into season, however, a stallion is generally aware of her condition by continually sniffing her excrement. When urine deposits carry signs of approaching fertility, the stallion starts watching the mare more carefully.

P. 60 One of Paco Lazo's stallions nuzzles a mare in heat. Does love exist between horses? Displays of undeniable affection are often seen between a stallion and his favorite mare, between mares, between bachelors, and between mares and foals. Individual horses, however, seem to differ in temperament and sexual appetite as much as do humans. A few stallions clearly favor one mare, treating her with attentive tenderness. Other studs are rough and unaffectionate with all females. Some mares seem to hate stallions, while others have sexual thirsts that are barely quenchable. Though a good many purebred, stabled stallions are sexually cold, to the point of being a problem at breeding time, most pastured males are always ready to mate. Mares, on the other hand, are sexually receptive only once every three weeks; their periods of fertility can last a couple of hours or, most usually, two to three days. Female horses who have not conceived come into heat approximately every twenty-one days during late winter and spring—a few, however, repeat their periods during the entire year. Mares who get especially "hot" while in heat rub their rumps against poles or any hard object, and often in moments of sexual frenzy mount other females. A rancher friend from Montana, Spike Van Cleve, says he keeps mares from getting "rank" during estrus by either putting copper in their water or in their mouths (a bit ring, etc.), a trick he learned in Mexico. Mares who have given birth usually come into season and are bred on the ninth, tenth and eleventh days after they have foaled.

P. 63 Shown here is Antonio Romero's splendid young stallion, Justiciero. A stallion's courtship behavior often depends upon the personal appeal of the mare in heat. If she is a young female that he hasn't covered, he will prance up to her, crest arched, forelegs lifted

high, body muscles flexed, to try and impress her as much as possible. If she is an old mare or former "girl friend," he won't waste time posing and showing off. Since experienced males know that mares at the beginning of their estrus are often not ready for coitus, a stallion will not approach such a female directly from behind, but from an angle, carefully measuring with his eye the reach of her hind hoofs. At this time unready females threaten with outstretched necks and ears laid back in the three-fifteen position. If a stallion doesn't respond to these warnings, most mares lash out with their hind hoofs, at the same time screeching and urinating. Seasoned males, however, know how to avoid this punishment by quickly stepping aside, at the same time swinging their heads in a high arc.

P. 65 The mare that Divertido, the Conde de Odiel's stallion, has just smelled is clearly in heat and ready to be mounted. The stallion's excitement is triggered not only by the mare's lack of resistance, but by her use of the sawhorse position—legs spread, tail slightly lifted, head immobile, facing straight forward— and by the urine she has just poured onto the ground, and by her flashings. The visual signals used by receptive mares seem much more important in attracting a mate than are the sexual odors that their bodies emit.

P. 66 Here Barquillero strikes a handsome pose, frozen at a one-thousandth of a second, to remind one of the noble horses captured in action so well by Leonardo and other artists, who drew before the camera could provide reference images. "What eyes those men had!" I often thought when I looked at a roll of developed film for the first time and saw stallion attitudes and expressions that had hardly been noticeable in the field.

P. 69 When this lovely young Arab mare was photographed at Vicos, one of the soldiers with me remarked, "How could any stallion help but fall in love with her?" Some of the pasture-bred mares I observed while doing these photographs differed as much in their use of or abstinence from sexual foreplay as do humans. It seemed that sex to some mares was just a duty and they would never nuzzle a stallion. Other mares, however, if they were particularly fond of a certain stallion, would nibble sensually at his face and flanks or sniff at his genitals. The lovemaking of horses, especially if it takes place naturally in a pasture, can be erotic and exciting. One Army colonel, a retired veterinarian, laughingly said that during breeding time at the stud farms, city recruits were detectable because most of them got erections the first time they watched a stallion cover a mare.

P. 70 Pinturero, the Conde de Odiel's four-year-old stallion, in his excitement tries unsuccessfully to mount this mare from the side. The range of breeding techniques used by stallions, which vary as much as their individual temperaments, is best observed in pastures. Because of the risk of damage from kicking and biting, most mating of purebreds is done under controlled conditions in which the stallion is haltered and kept on a lead rein and the mare is not only held but restrained from kicking by hobbles that run from front to rear legs—unnatural elements that are necessary, but that remove most of the beauty, passion and display of individual personality from an act that, under natural circumstances, can be full of violence and tenderness.

One of the most interesting personal observations I was able to make while taking these photographs was to verify some stallions' preference for mares of a certain color (I had read of wild stallions in America limiting their harems to females of a single color). Of the stallions I saw bred, most had no color preference; however, some did prefer either light or dark mares. A few studs' color prejudice caused them to be so slow in achieving an erection with, for example, white mares (when they were excited by brown ones), that a dark mare would be presented and, once the stallion was sexually excited, she would quickly be replaced by the light-colored female who was scheduled to be covered. When color prejudice does occur, it usually stems from a stallion's memory of the first mare he covered. With the exception of one or two animals, all the stallions studied showed much more interest in young virgin mares than they did in the eighteen year olds they were frequently chosen to mate.

P. 73 Here the Conde de Odiel's stallion, Divertido, though he has not achieved a full erection, tries to cover a mare he has just mounted. The stallion's half-aroused state shows he is either young and inexperienced or that he has already copulated with this mare—no wise stallion would attempt to mount a female unless he were positive she was in heat and few stallions, having proved to themselves the receptiveness of a mare, would not, at this moment, have a

full erection. If the stallion were not absolutely certain that the mare was ready for him and still tried to mount her, he would risk having a back leg broken if she decided to kick.

P. 75 Paco Lazo's Nostálgico covering a mare in the field was photographed on one of the most beautiful early summer days I spent while doing this book. Before gentle but spirited Nostálgico was turned into this pasture with two mares in heat, a bay and a chestnut, his stable mate, the larger, rougher, more aggressive stallion, Dichoso, was placed with them. For their first few minutes together this excited trio galloped around the pasture, the stallion posturing, until finally the mares slowed down and he, head low to the ground, began to try to direct their course of movement. At last, when the mares stopped, Dichoso began smelling the bay's flank and, just as he had positioned himself behind her, she lashed out with both rear hoofs to thump him on the chest, blows that he was unable to avoid.

Within minutes the stallion turned his attention to the chestnut mare who started flashing, urinated, and assumed the sawhorse position. With a complete absence of foreplay, Dichoso smelled the urine, raised his head to "smile," and then mounted the mare. When a stallion throws himself on top of a mare he is often unable to find her vagina with his penis, which means that he shoves and pushes, positions and re-positions his hind quarters, while

clutching the mare's sides with his forelegs. Frequently, in their attempts at mounting, excited studs do not rear up directly behind the mare, which foils the possibility of entry. Most stallions when they have made entry, lay their straining heads against the mare's neck or shoulder. Other, more passionate, males bite their partner's mane, ear or shoulder skin, or sink their teeth into her neck, lustfully drawing blood. Coitus usually lasts about one minute, though after ejaculation some stallions will, with a completely spent look on their faces, remain relaxed on top of a mare for another half minute.

Dichoso's thrusts were especially vigorous once he was on top of the mare, but he refrained from biting her neck. When copulation was over, the two horses started grazing together, at which time the ranch foreman entered the pasture and haltered both of them. After twenty minutes had passed, the stallion was freed, although the mare was held on a rein, for a second mating. It was then that Dichoso, once he had smelled the chestnut who had her legs spread and tail lifted, must have remembered the bruises on his chest from the bay mare's kick, for suddenly—by biting—he vented his hostility on the nearest female: the chestnut mare he had just covered and who at that moment stood waiting to be mounted. Naturally surprised, the mare screamed, lashed out with her hind hoofs, and from that moment it was impossible to hold her still as long as the stallion was near.

This seemed like the ideal time to test a mare's preference for or reactions to a stallion according to his reputation as a gentle or rough "lover," so I asked Paco Lazo if they could remove Dichoso and bring the "charming and suave" Nostálgico to the pasture.

When the chestnut mare heard the new stallion's distant neigh, she swung her head around to stare, with an obviously interested expression on her face. Whereas minutes before she had been fidgety, nervous and defensive, ears laid back at the three-fifteen position, the mare now stood completely still with her ears directed sharply forward.

As Nostálgico was led around to the mare's head and began to sniff at her muzzle, she assumed the sawhorse position, grinding her teeth and flashing. When the stallion nibbled at her shoulder and started to get an erection, the mare, who had previously been covered by Dichoso, was led from the pasture, for she had proven that she, at least, was partial to a particular sexual partner. Just as both horses were leaving the field, I asked Paco if we might continue the experiment with the other mare, the bay who earlier in the morning had kicked Dichoso and who had been taken to another enclosure.

As the bay was being caught, I wondered if she had lashed out at Dichoso because she had not been completely in heat; because she was with the chestnut mare and felt some kind of jealousy of her; or because on a previous occasion she had also been roughly treated by the big stallion.

Once the bay mare had been brought to the pasture and was quietly grazing beneath a cork oak that served as my perch, Paco released the stallion. As Nostálgico approached the stationary mare, he raised his legs higher than even the unusually high natural Spanish lift, arched his splendid neck and came towards us fast enough for the wind to lift his black mane. Five yards from the mare his pace turned to a walk which led him slowly to within inches of her face. The stallion caressed the mare's lips with his warm, velvety muzzle, and she lowered her head, seemingly entranced by his sensual nuzzling. Already she was in the sawhorse position as Nostálgico nibbled at her neck and shoulder in gentle bites that left silver threads of saliva on her deep red coat. How different was this scene from that we had so shortly before witnessed between Dichoso and this same mare, or even with the chestnut he had covered.

As the stallion rubbed his muzzle against the mare's flank she turned her head to sniff at his genitals, softly nudging them with her muzzle. The stallion began to get an erection as he gently bit the elbows of the mare's hind legs. The horses were directly under my tree when Nostálgico, having smelled the mare's urine, lifted his muzzle, lips peeled back. Then his head flew up into the air, towards me, as he reared, mounting the mare. What a moment that was. The sun was high and there was no sound but the calling of a hawk and the stallion's heavy breathing, as the shadows of the mating horses moved slowly across the earth like a prehistoric cave-painting brought to life.

P. 76 In this photograph two horses mate in the marshes, under a tree full of cattle egret, night heron, little egret, purple heron and spoonbill nests. When a mare is in heat, a stallion will mount her several times a day. If a number of females come into season at the same time, not all of them will be covered. Witnessing courting and copulation in the free-living herd is an important part of a foal's or colt's formation. Horses who have not grown up in a family unit, like captive animals in zoos, are sometimes not effective breeders partly because, while young, they were deprived of the learning process of seeing their own kind mate.

Members of free-living herds watch with interest when a stallion covers one of the family mares. Foals in their excitement even get underneath the mating horses or jump around them. Occasionally a domestic stallion will turn colt killer, and, during breeding, nine- to eleven-day-old foals must be carefully guarded when their mothers are mated. This danger, however, is rare among free-living horses, though wild stallions have been known to kill very young foals who were slowing down the escaping herd. Fillies show an open curiosity toward pairs of mating horses, as do young 199 stallions, who often become so excited that they masturbate.

Settings, like the one in this photograph, provided the most pleasure during my hours of horse observation. To see animals living in semi-freedom such as in the Coto Doñana National Park or in the marshes—still wild and primitive as I knew them nineteen years ago—made the observer feel almost as though he were in paradise. Watching stallions and mares, curtained in diamond beads of spray, gallop through shallow water over which circled hundreds of egrets and spoonbills, their white wings flushed by the setting sun, I enjoyed priceless moments, seeing horses at home with nature and—thus—at their best.

P. 78 Being surrounded by spring flowers like these at El Hornillo, the Conde de Odiel's ranch, made doing this book even more enjoyable. California has magnificent fields carpeted solidly with golden poppies or Indian paintbrush—but nowhere in the world have I seen anything that could compare with the lush, wildly mixed varieties of flowers found in Southern Spain. Sometimes the colors seemed almost too intense, to the point that at any moment I expected an animated butterfly or sparkling Disney dewdrop to light on one of the blossoms that appeared in the camera's viewfinder. In scouting floral backgrounds for the photographs in this book, I imagined some of the excitement that Monet must have experienced when he discovered his red poppies, or that Van Gogh might have felt when his eye

zeroed in on a field of sunflowers. It is into this glorious setting that Andalusian foals are born.

P. 80 Eighteen-year-old Divertida, the mother of fourteen Conde de Odiel horses and of the stallion who appears on page 136, grazes, heavily pregnant, in a field of wild mustard. The gestation period of horses is from 320 to 355 days.

P. 82 During her fifteen years at El Hornillo, the mare in this photograph, Ibérica, has given birth to ten foals. Unusually youthful for her age, always ready to play or run, Ibérica, like most female horses, became quiet and serious during pregnancy. Even four-year-old mares, once they are in foal, behave in a more mature manner. As the fetuses grew inside them, all the mares at El Hornillo showed marked appetite increases. During the last three or four months of pregnancy, when embryos grow most, changes in the mares' drinking behavior could also sometimes be noted. It seemed that the very heavy mares drank less early in the morning. Perhaps especially cold water, if taken in large quantities, causes cramps and stimulates movement of the embryo. Some two months before birth, when the embryo seems to change position, mares appear not only to experience discomfort, but also sometimes discharge small quantities of blood or mucous. Especially important to free-living mares is their ability to delay birth a few hours. At least ninety-eight percent of the more than two hundred pregnant mares that I observed foaled at night, usually in the hours shortly before dawn.

P. 84-86 The series of birth photographs on the following pages is the product of a small amount of patience and a great deal of good luck. When work on this book was begun, I didn't have the slightest hope of being able to include the birth of a foal in its pages. Experience from work on the bull book, when six weeks were spent before I was able adequately to photograph a fighting cow giving birth, convinced me of the impossibility of harboring such a hope, especially since the actual full working days of photography on this book would be limited to less than forty. "Horsey" friends were unanimous in their advice: "Concentrate on all phases of horse life, but completely dismiss the idea of including a birth in your book, an effort which will not only be a great waste of time, considering the almost impossibly short period allowed for photography, but which can only end in disappointment."

One spring morning, after watching the breeding of a mare at El Hornillo, I decided to wander down to one of the lower pastures where the foals and their mothers were almost sure to be found. Just before leaving the dirt road to enter an olive grove, I met the *yegüero,* Alfonso, who was complaining that one of the ranch's nicest mares, Noticiera, was several days overdue in foaling. "I don't know what's wrong with her," he grumbled as he left me

and plodded through the wildflowers that were still heavy with dew.

The clouds that had greyed the past week's skies had been blown from Andalusia. Somewhere ahead in the olive grove a nightingale was singing, accompanied by the faint, alluring sound of the mares' bells.

After reaching the herd, most of which were grazing in a field of mustard, the better part of an hour was spent photographing new foals at play. At about ten-thirty I decided to leave the yellow field; somewhere not far away the nightingale was still singing, and I wanted to try to get a close look at him. Of all the spring mornings spent on the book, this was perhaps the loveliest; the sky was so freshly blue, and dew was sparkling on the thousands of brilliant blossoms that spread out around the olive trees.

Locating the nightingale was not difficult, but staying with him as he tried to lure me from his nearby mate, who was sitting on a carefully woven, cone-shaped nest, was not easy. However, because there was nothing else to do—the sun was almost too high for good photography—I followed him.

After I wandered about a quarter of a mile, the bird's singing suddenly stopped and, as I swung around hoping to see his rust-colored body bursting in flight from one tree to another, I noticed a white horse spread out on the ground, almost hidden from view by low-hanging olive branches. At first, this sight did not rouse my curiosity; often mares could be seen stretched out in deep sleep, but usually somewhat earlier in the morning and closer to the herd. Approaching the white mare, I noticed that she was breathing heavily and that her eyes were not shut—she was also obviously pregnant, but so were a number of other females in the herd.

When Noticiera heard footsteps she lifted her head and swung it around to stare with large limpid eyes. Fourteen years old, the mother of nine foals, she was handsome for her age and, washed clean by the recent rain, looked beautifully white against the thousands of flowers that blossomed around her. As I walked towards her tail she stood up, and it was then the thought flashed: "She's giving birth!" But, as the mare turned around and started to graze, no secretion could be detected coming from below her tail. Still, I was terribly excited. Then, seeing Noticiera on her feet, I began to worry that if she were really in the process of giving birth my presence might disturb her. Mares, I knew, could postpone foaling for hours. Off somewhere in the grove the nightingale had resumed singing and, trying to remember every landmark in sight—the grove was so extensive and each tree looked alike—I began walking in what seemed to be the bird's direction. I also checked my watch; I would give the mare fifteen minutes before returning to her.

I could barely contain the urge to turn back, as the nightingale's song grew louder. Reflecting on the existing birth photographs I had seen, before me appeared pictures of mares foaling at night, taken in boxes where the camera's flash gave a ghoulish cast to what should be a beautiful scene; the blood and placenta always seemed like something out of front-page photographs of a car accident. I thought of another set of photographs where the photographer had been lucky enough to find a mare foaling during the daytime, but the morning had been so grey and the mare's sides had been so dirtied with mud that the pictures, though they were fine shots, somehow seemed tainted, and had none of the freshness and poetry of creation that vibrated from the animal and setting that waited so close to my lens.

When eight minutes had passed I turned around and rapidly but cautiously retraced my steps to one of the larger olive trees that stood not more than twenty feet from where I had left the mare. Through the leaves Noticiera could be seen stretched out on the ground, a pair of small, blue hoof tips just emerging from below her tail! Obviously, before lying down she had expelled the birth water, and was now on her side, which would help to press out the foal. The mare sighed and her sides rocked with heavy breathing as she lifted her rear top leg into the air, straining to force out the baby horse that her belly had carried for nearly a year. Almost ten minutes passed before the foal, except for its hind legs, slid from its mother.

P. 89 The foal, who had been sleeping inside his mother, was not only suddenly bumped awake as he slipped onto the ground, but was also shaken into consciousness by the terribly bright light around him. Front-lit, the scene 203 was beautiful, but it became even more poetic when I moved around cautiously to the other side of the mare to photograph the back-lit foal. Noticiera, breathing hard, was still in too much of a trance from the birth to notice me. When the foal became more awake, he lifted his head and a front hoof to break the sac, which hung over his head like an Arab hood.

P. 91 In this photograph the foal's hind legs are still inside his mother. The sac membrane was strong and not easy for him to break. After about ten minutes, Noticiera raised her head, glanced back at the foal and then, with a great effort, got to her feet as the foal's back legs slid free from her body. The mare turned around and looked curiously at the foal, as if to say, "Where did you come from?" before she briefly licked his muzzle, probably instinctively trying to remove any remaining birth fluid from his nose.

P. 93 When the foal felt his mother's tongue he made a soft, bleating sound, which she answered. Seemingly stimulated by the brief licking, he feebly attempted to get up, which freed him from the sac. At this point, I was so caught up in experiencing the scene in front of me and enjoying photographing it, that I didn't have time really to reflect on my extraordinary luck.

P. 94 After another few minutes had passed, the foal again tried to get up. Watching him and his mother, who had started to graze, it

was suddenly obvious how completely exhausted the birth had left both of them. Occasionally mares who give birth for the first time are frightened by the foal, an apprehension which disappears as soon as the new baby gets to its feet and takes on the appearance of a horse, though a very miniature one. At times the foal's completely wide-eyed look fully expressed his reaction to the newness of absolutely everything around him. Each time he tried to get to his feet, to make work the legs that had never been used before, he rose slowly and then wavered before tumbling back to the ground, limbs spread in all directions.

P. 96 Three-quarters of an hour had passed before the foal was able to stand and maintain his balance. Taking a few wobbly steps this way and that, his long, slim legs seemed not at all sure of their course. It was a great effort for such a new-born animal, and each time he fell to the ground he had to stay there and rest, before making another attempt to stand. Shortly after he was able to keep his balance, one of the younger mares appeared through the trees and came curiously toward the foal. Noticiera, who had seemed to pay abnormally little attention to her new offspring (from the time she had licked his muzzle she had continued to graze), lifted her head in threat, ears flat back, neck outstretched, teeth showing, to discourage the young mare from approaching any closer. The foal's sense of balance was still so delicate that it seemed if the slightest breath of wind

swept through the grove he was sure to capsize.

P. 98 In this photograph the mare grazes, the torn sac still hanging from under her tail. A few minutes later the afterbirth was cast out (horses, unlike other animals, rarely eat their afterbirth). Then, the foal, who had been nosing around his mother's forelegs, sides and tail, knowing instinctively that somewhere there was something to be found and sucked, discovered one of Noticiera's bulging teats. In those moments the foal appeared to be in a vegetative state, barely able to make out forms, his muzzle testing rough and smooth surfaces, his ears, eyes and nose taking in stimuli that were all then unidentifiable to him. The mare, however, at precisely the wrong moment, took a step forward toward taller grass, and the foal lost contact with the udder. Those were anxious moments—I wanted to put down the camera, take hold of Noticiera's bell strap, grab the foal and press his muzzle to the mare's udder. Finally, though, he found the teat again and fastened on. A few minutes later he stopped drinking and lifted his tail to expel a thick, bad-smelling excrement, the digested product of the metabolism of eleven months as an embryo. I released the camera and let it swing from the shoulder strap. My watch showed just before noon. I had been with the mare for little more than an hour, and now she was moving off into the olive grove with the foal behind her, and what a handsome *potro* he was. It was then I named him—Potri—though Noticiero would be written on his pedigree. Walking back through the olive trees, I felt completely but joyfully spent as the nightingale sang somewhere ahead. Every minute of that walk through the grove I tried to enjoy, knowing that shortly my happiness would be blemished with the worry that the undeveloped film of the birth would be lost in the post or damaged in developing.

P. 100 At El Hornillo, the two-day-old daughter of Revoltosa fills her stomach. The foals spent their first few days nursing, exercising their legs and becoming acquainted with everything around them. However, it seemed that most of their time was spent sleeping, periods of rest that lasted from twenty minutes to an hour. Once they were on their feet they nursed every ten to fifteen minutes; short feeding periods that prevented their stomachs from becoming too full.

P. 102 For the first week after Potri was born I returned to El Hornillo as often as I could to see him. The photo on this page shows him walking along behind his mother. Because I was the first living thing the foal had seen after being born, and because his mother knew I presented no threat, I had little trouble getting as close as I wanted to both of them. Noticiera only threatened me once or twice, and then it was because I had approached her from down wind in the pasture and she had been startled by sudden, nearby movement before she recognized my form. None of the mares was allowed to approach the colt, and once Noticiera attacked a burro who in curiosity was sniffing at Potri. Most of the mares at the ranches where I worked, those with new foals, would start walking away if I got too close to them or their young. Some were very touchy about my presence, as were their foals. Because of this,

it was a real joy to have established a close relationship with Noticiera and Potri, for when the light in the grove was too white for the kind of photographs I wanted I would seek out the mare and her black offspring, and spend those afternoon hours, until the sun was lower and the light was warming up, playing with the colt or lying in the flowers near him and his mother.

P. 103 A Quarter Horse mare and her foal emerge from a lake at Los Millares. Horses are natural swimmers and foals can take to water, if the distances are short, when they are surprisingly young. Upon emerging from water, equines spread their legs, sawhorse fashion, for stability, and then what first starts as a head shake travels all along the animal's body to the root of its tail.

P. 104 These spring flowers filled the fields at El Hornillo, where I spent most time working with mares and foals. It was here that I first observed that foals, almost without fail, inherit hierarchical positions from their mothers. Inevitably, the offspring of high-ranking mares were privileged with their mothers' positions in the herd, just as the young of low-ranking mares were generally low on the social totem pole in relation to their contemporaries. Obviously, there are certain genetically inherited characteristics that are essential to achieving high rank, such as the physical ability to be extremely active and aggressive.

At El Hornillo, each member of the herd respected Potri as much as they did his top-rank mother. The black colt could afford to be mischievous, teasing the other foals and some of the older mares, because he was always able to run to Noticiera. He could be seen growing up with a feeling of self-confidence, something that was lacking in the offspring of most submissive mares. Even though the foals of insecure mares might be bigger and stronger than their contemporaries, it seemed almost impossible for them to obtain a higher rank than that of their parent.

P. 106 This filly foal stands beside her mother in a field of poppies, daisies and wild mustard at El Hornillo. When vegetation is abundant foals, toward the end of their first month, nurse less and nibble more at grass. This nibbling, however, begins shortly after birth, for in their curious explorations of the world, baby horses test all sorts of objects with their mouths, chewing and sucking branches as well as the hair of other horses. Now and then some animals experience a hair mania, and as adults are a serious threat to the good looks of horses with long manes and tails. In arid regions, because foals need to obtain nourishment by drinking more milk, which extends the period of suckling, some mares are reported to conceive every other year, so that their foals can nurse longer and have a better chance of survival.

P. 108 These foals meeting one another at El Hornillo are both moulting, as can be seen from their mottled coats (most Andalusian foals are born with dark hair which later turns grey and eventually becomes white). Friendships usually develop between horses of similar temperament, and practically always between young animals of the same sex. Apart from engaging in running games, filly foals are more subdued than are young males, who quite early begin to form their own "gangs."

P. 110 At Vicos two Arab foals engage in mutual grooming, a pastime young females prefer to the rougher games of colt foals. Grooming among young horses usually terminates with running contests or playful fighting. Foals, until they are well over a year old, show little interest in mud and dust baths, probably because they spend much time on the ground where they can rub and scratch themselves. Stallions rarely groom their foals.

P. 112 At El Hornillo this foal dozes in the late afternoon, lulled by the singing of goldfinches and nightingales and the call of cuckoos. While their mothers moped at El Hornillo and Vicos, most of the foals I watched dozed. To doze—the horse's second and more intense way of sleeping—the animal lowers itself to the

ground to rest in a huddling position, legs half positioned under the body, and the head either raised or stretched out on the ground. A few of the mares at El Hornillo, as far as I could tell, never stretched flat out on the grass in the deepest form of sleep, but seemed to prefer the huddling position. They were generally animals that were either heavily pregnant or of uneasy temperament. When horses get up from this position, they first straighten both forelegs, pull their back legs under their bodies, hunch, and with a strong push of the hind legs, stand up.

P. 115 Here Potri is sleeping so deeply that I could touch him and he would not awaken. To prepare for this third and deepest form of sleep, horses roll from the huddling position completely onto their sides, with head, neck and body relaxed flat on the ground. During deep sleep, which usually takes place more often at night than in the daytime (unless the ground is very wet), they are almost completely unconscious. I always enjoyed watching Potri when, having woken from deep sleep, he got to his feet to stretch, arching his neck and back like a cat, rising up on the tips of his hoofs to stretch his hind legs one after the other. When he was less than a week old, he would become so tired from any activity that often I had to laugh as he literally threw himself into tall grass, to fall deeply asleep immediately, with Noticiera moping or grazing nearby. Since mares feel most responsible for their

youngest offspring, several times I saw Noticiera chase off—in a real show of temper—her
two-year-old daughter when the filly became
too rough with Potri.

In the weeks that followed, the white mare's
concern for the whereabouts of her foal lessened, and on more than one occasion Noticiera
followed the grazing herd, leaving a sleeping
Potri behind. When the black colt awoke and
couldn't find his mother, terrified he began
neighing and galloping up and down until he
heard either Noticiera's bell or her short, gut-
tural call. Of the young foals at El Hornillo,
the only one I ever saw mope was a sick filly.
Sick adult horses rarely lie down—they seem
to fear being unable to get up if danger presents
itself.

The horses I watched would never rest just
anywhere. They had special places, and while
the mares at El Hornillo often had favorite
trees for moping, deep sleep always took place
with the animals stretched out in the open
where the wind's messages could easily reach
them. Apart from choosing areas that offered
more security by being open to the wind, the
mares' only other bedding preference seemed
to be that of dry ground.

The normal distance horses keep from each
other while grazing was generally respected at
rest time. For example, one ancient white mare
at El Hornillo, who seemed to enjoy her solitary
life, grazed far from the herd and also stayed
away from the others when she slept. However, family members, especially young foals,

could often be seen sleeping in close proximity, occasionally even touching one another.

P. 116 Three days after Potri was born, I was in the grove watching him and his mother when suddenly he stopped nibbling at a fallen olive branch, looked about with wide eyes and then stretched out his long, thin legs to gallop in tight circles around Noticiera. It was one of the most delightful displays of freedom I've ever witnessed. Around and around he ran, like the brown filly in this photograph, galloping full out until even his mother had to lift her head from the grass and stare. Obstacles that lay in his path he leapt with complete confidence.

In the weeks that followed, Potri often repeated his running games; the gallop became faster and the circles larger as he grew older. It was fascinating to watch him learn about himself and the world around him. At first it wasn't easy for him to keep his balance when he tried to scratch behind an ear with a rear hoof tip; and he was forever licking, tasting and gnawing at almost everything he encountered. When he tried to imitate Noticiera grazing, his neck was so short that he had to spread his legs out, giraffe-fashion, to reach the grass. Potri had great ability to learn, something that is imperative to the survival of horses in the wild. He was curious about everything, and ever ready to play, even if he could only find some tall flowers to run back and forth through or a butterfly to chase.

P. 118 This is the same filly as on the previous page, shot at one-sixteenth of a second as I panned the camera after her while she practically flew through a field of poppies. Often a foal would start circling its mother and then dash off to race through the grove with a "school" of friends. The raising of the tail root was a sure sign of the wish to run, and once the colts were rushing through the flowers, even some of the old mares would join them. Running is so contagious to horses that if one starts, most nearby herd members join in.

P. 120 At the age of about two months, male foals, like the one in this photograph, running through a field of wild mustard, are forever engaged in vigorous play, pushing and nipping at each other, while laying down the rough framework for future fight games. When one foal, wishing to play, approaches another, he not only approaches with both ears pointed forward, but also wears an expression that can only be described as mischievous!

Potri not only had a stronger play instinct than the filly foals around him, but unlike them showed an interest in sex when only several days old. Often while smelling his mother's genitals, he would spring an erection, and not much time passed before he began to mark excrement with his own urine. The older he became, the more clearly could be seen the stallion in him.

P. 122 Early summer has already dried this field at El Hornillo. The foal stands, his ears pointed forward; no visual stimulus is present, so he cocks his ears in search of sound. To watch a horse's ears working independently of each other, the right one pointed forward while the left is turned toward the back of the head with the aperture in a lateral position, is like watching two radar antennae rotating at the same time but scanning in opposite directions. If a colt's mother is out of sight, he relies on his ears and nose to locate her.

P. 125 Red poppies like these photographed at El Hornillo blanket expanses of cultivated land in Southern Spain. A photograph that I really wanted for this book was one of a white horse in a poppy field. Rainy weather, the threat that upon the first hot day the flowers would lose their petals, the difficulty of finding a handsome white stallion who would stand still for the photograph, had me uptight, but finally the skies did clear, the petals didn't fall, and the stallion didn't run away until the last roll of film was in the camera.

P. 126 Here Majestad "poses" for the poppy field photograph. His sharply pointed ears show him to be alert to some sound, in this case the neighing of another horse. When facial and body signals can't be seen, horses use their voices. At El Hornillo, for example, with its fairly dense olive groves, there was more vocal 211 communication among herd members than at Vicos, where there were few trees to obstruct vision—and where repeated calling was unnecessary to keep the herd together. Potri only used his voice if he suddenly found himself alone, separated from his mother. Noticiera, because she was an older mare who had foaled many times, didn't seem as concerned with her son's cry as were new mothers, and often was fairly late in giving him a reassuring answer. As the black foal grew older, Noticiera's vocal response to him changed from a reassuring neigh to the contact call normally used by herd members. All the horses I observed seemed to recognize each other not only by sight but also by their different voices. The high voices of the colts begin to change at puberty (roughly at one and a half) and reach their full depth at the age of two to three.

P. 129 In the early morning at El Hornillo, upon finding the sleeping herd, I felt as though I had come across some bloodless battlefield, with horses' bodies flung out flat and still in all directions.

This seven-year-old Conde de Odiel mare, Tamborilera, was sleeping so soundly that minutes after the photograph was taken, I touched her lightly and still she didn't wake. Breathing loudly, something most horses do in deep sleep, she was probably dreaming—moaning and groaning, as well as twitching her eyelids, ears, and now and then a leg. Patrick

Duncan told me he's not only sure that horses dream but also that males sometimes have erotic dreams. Several times he's observed his Camargue stallion in deep sleep, breathing loudly while voicing courtship sounds, only to wake in a flash, spring to his feet and mount the closest mare.

When finally I touched one of Tamborilera's hoofs she gradually began waking in various stages of consciousness. First her breathing changed, becoming forceful and louder. A couple of minutes passed before her ears showed more pronounced movement, her eyes opened and a few seconds later she lifted her head, stared at me through half-opened lids, then put her head back to the ground. In less than a minute, however, the message that something was not right reached her mind and she raised her neck, bent back her head, straightened her forelegs and jumped to her feet.

Many horses live their entire lives without being able to stretch out on the ground to enjoy deep sleep—their only form of rest is moping. At El Hornillo I rarely saw a mare sleeping deeply for more than an hour. The combined resting period for adult horses observed—moping, resting and deep sleep—averaged about six to eight hours a day. At the Andalusian ranches, not only did most births take place between midnight and sunrise, but horses also slept deeply during those hours. A possible explanation for these time preferences: since

most predators hunt and kill between dusk and midnight, the safest hours of darkness for a horse are those from midnight until dawn.

P. 130 In this series of photographs, together with the photograph on page 131, the four-year-old stallion Farruco, owned by the Marqués de Salvatierra, gestures, postures and plays, assuming attitudes that are not only obvious expressions of joy, but which also spell "stallion." When the photograph on page 131 was taken, Farruco was also neighing. His imperious call differed from the voices of the Salvatierra mares around him, being clearer and more penetrating, and having a metallic tone distinct from the tonal quality of females. As soon as Farruco saw or heard a mare he gave the stallion's high neigh. I often wished I had recorded on tape some of those rolling and impressive sounds that seem to come from a stallion's very depths and that are heard most often during the spring. The shrill, abrupt war cry that males emit when in close contact with one another, lifting their legs stiffly to strike at the ground, is fascinating.

During love games, mares have their own forms of vocal expression. Females (such as the one at Paco Lazo's ranch) who are not ready to be mated but are bothered by a stallion, use a scream that starts out almost normally but can build to a real war cry. Mares also screech when squabbling and kicking at each other, but seem to avoid serious battles by arguing, something they do quite often. I almost never saw one female rear up against another in battle. In most fights the mares used their back legs to kick out violently. A sexually "hot" female will occasionally grind her teeth while she is flashing, as well as use subtle neighs to encourage a stallion.

Often, if I surprised an animal of either sex in the open field, I was greeted with yet another vocal signal, a warning snort which seemed a breath of apprehension issued almost unconsciously, but which served as a warning to herd members.

132 At Vicos, a young Arab stands on his favorite ridge, which overlooks a meadow where the herd grazed most afternoons. Some animals seem to become quite attached to certain areas. Most hot summer afternoons this same horse could be found either on the ridge or walking toward it, shaking his forelock and mane up and down or from side to side in a continual effort to shoo away the flies. Horses also have the ability literally to vibrate their skin in order to flush insects.

When equines are in the herd or alone, like this Arab, they often groom themselves, using their teeth to scratch their shoulders, backs, legs, stomachs and flanks. Scratching is also done with the fore edge of a back hoof, which allows a horse to reach areas that are inaccessible to his teeth—behind the ears and parts of the head and neck. When a horse is scratching 213

himself, generally done slowly, seemingly to savor every second, his satisfaction can be read in the look of complete ecstasy on his face. Low-hanging olive branches were used as back or rump scratchers by all the mares at El Hornillo.

P. 134-5 Shown on these pages are some young Ecija bachelors at play. Much play time was spent practicing posturing and threat displays. The young males were far more active than the fillies at Vicos and gave the impression that they were cleverer, being more interested in everything new around them. On several occasions I also saw them mark each other's excrement. When this book was started I wondered if family stallions marked territories with excrement, something I was never really able to prove. The freest animals observed (those with almost unrestricted territories) were the marsh horses that I had casually watched years ago, and I had not then cared about or been aware of this kind of equine behavior.

The family stallions at Paco Lazo's ranch and at Los Millares seemed to mark certain places in their pastures with dung and urine. What was clear, however, especially at Paco's, was that the stallion, when he came to fresh mare excrement, would smell it, "smile," and then usually mark the spot with his own urine. In the marshes I observed that one group of horses, when they came to a road that had to be crossed daily, would frequently defecate, seemingly from nervousness.

Last spring, when I started visiting the horse ranches of Andalusia, I asked country people if they had noticed horses in the pasture marking boundaries with excrement. Though the answer to this question was generally "no," most of the grooms said that stallions quite clearly marked their boxes—which can be considered territories—each time the straw was changed. After a summer of observation, however, I concluded that in fact these stabled stallions were not marking territory, but simply waiting until the box floors were covered by clean straw to prevent their hocks being splattered with urine. On a number of occasions in the field I did see both stallions and mares seem to choose ground that was soft or covered with grass before urinating.

P. 136 Divertido, like most of the horses I got to know, had a strong personality. Aggressive, determined horses—regardless of size and strength—usually get their own way. It was easy to rank animals in the dominance hierarchy, observing how each was punished or respected by the rest of the herd. Superior animals were always the first to eat and drink or to use prized dusting and scratching areas. Once an animal had achieved a high rank he jealously guarded his position and when not given proper respect he laid back his ears and started swishing his tail. If he was ignored, he extended his neck, showed his teeth and, if necessary, either bit or kicked.

The respect shown a couple of the stallions at Vicos was such that the other bachelors seemed too overwhelmed even to think "challenge."

P. 138 At Vicos, I watched horses like this young Arab mare gallop, jump and leap in what to the horse, apart from sex and eating, is undoubtedly the ultimate pleasure—running. Often young animals would race off half a mile across a field, one chasing the other, until they were just specks in the distance, where they would stop to rear up against one another. During those late summer afternoons in Andalusia, I felt privileged to be the only witness to equestrian spectacles that included variations of the curvet, cabriole and levade, performed by horses living in semi-liberty against backgrounds of summer-yellowed fields or the purple mountains of Ronda.

P. 140 Vasallo, the ten-year-old Cárdenas stallion, performed so beautifully when set free that I wished the camera in my hands could be used for motion pictures instead of still photographs. Working with Spanish stallions all summer, each day I was more impressed by their nobility. While we were resting between photographs I often went into the enclosure with free-running Vasallo, who not many days before had been covering mares, put my arm around him and brushed his long mane. He was such a splendid subject that, upon receiving the developed film I had taken of him, and finding that the camera had malfunctioned, and that roll after roll was black, I returned to Ecija in 114°F heat to work again with the white stallion—and every second of that time with Vasallo was a pleasure.

P. 142-3 In these photographs appears one of the "grand old men" of Spanish horses, the Terry stallion Nevado. Without exaggeration, when working with horses like Nevado I felt as privileged as if I had been photographing Goya's in the Prado. The men, like Sebastián Gómez of Terry, whose jobs and lives were these horses, made the afternoons in Southern Spain doubly enjoyable. Jerezano, Divertido, Nevado, Vasallo, Farruco, Nostálgico and Majestad are names I'll never forget, and the memory of them will always stir up recollections of the most profound beauty.

P. 144 A summer evening at the Puerto de Santa María beach with the Terry stallions Hosco and Nevado, was the perfect way to finish work on this book. When Nevado was close to his son, he often postured, neck arched, and once reared up against him. The neck is not only one of the key forms of communication among horses, but tail lifting is also used by both mares and stallions. The degree of raising or tucking of the tail and, most important, the 215 elevation of the neck, as a prelude to the arching of the crest or extending or lowering it, are codes in the "reading" of a stallion's aggressiveness or temper. When one stallion is trying to impress another, he arches his neck to the most imposing attitude possible, ears are cocked forward, nostrils half-flared, and the tail is raised. The lateral swinging of head and neck increases the sense of superiority. Again, however, the most common threat warning is signaled by the ears.

P. 146 A herd of Spanish mares at Los Millares bursts across a lake in late afternoon. In moments of panic like this, all signs of herd hierarchy are dissolved.

P. 148 At two thousandths of a second, the camera freezes Nevado's mane in the air and his ears in a lateral position. The appearance of a horse in photographs can vary drastically from one frame to another. Some stallions are beautiful but not photogenic, others are not so beautiful but very photogenic. Nevado was both.

P. 151 These grazing mares at Vicos may spend the next twenty years of their lives at this same ranch, being bred year after year to some of Spain's finest stallions. Often it appeared that the brood mares were overworked mothers; bred one spring, in foal for the next eleven months, and just nine days after giving birth, mated once more. However, on second thought it seemed that the greatest pleasure in life for most mares was sex and taking care of their young.

P. 152 The Marqués de Salvatierra's Orgulloso rears up in a grove of poplars. As I photographed stallions in scenes like this, I couldn't help but imagine the excitement horses have stirred in artists since the beginning of time, an excitement that is the best testimonial to the animal's beauty.

P. 154 A group of mares gallops under the tree where I was waiting at Vicos. Even though moving rapidly, there still appears to be some unity to the herd. At most ranches, animals could be seen day after day walking in single file from food to water or from dust bath to moping tree. Trails etched into the earth were proof of their habitual use, whether on the side of one of the hills at Vicos or scored across the flat marshes. Well-worn paths were found even in small pastures. Horses are such animals of habit that they not only eat and drink at approximately the same time each day, but also may be found under a moping tree at close to an established hour.

P. 156 This Quarter Horse mare at Los Millares swam a few circles before returning to shore. Several times when I watched herds of mares wade into water, which was soon over their heads, they were always led, as in the pasture, by one of the older females, not necessarily the highest-ranking horse.

P. 158 At Vicos a Spanish horse crosses the crest of a hill at sunset. Scenes like this made me feel close to Arizona and California.

P. 160 This photograph of Nevado was the last picture taken for the book, and as the horses were led from the beach and I was packing up my cameras, I felt some sadness, knowing that soon I would be leaving Spain for a stay in California where I would miss the beauty and gentleness of Andalusian stallions. However, a few days later I was surprised to hear that in my home state not all that far from Uncle Charlie's Last Gate Ranch and the stock yards of Downy, there was an established breeding herd of Andalusians said to be related to Nevado and in number larger than all but two of the herds I had been working with in Spain.

Until I phoned Jesús Terry, I doubted this could be true. Before 1963, by government regulation, Andalusians were not allowed to leave Spain, and even since the lifting of this embargo, the U.S. Department of Agriculture's health tests make importation of Spanish horses just about impossible. Also, I had always been under the impression that the Terry ranch (which has the most sought after of Andalusian blood lines) had never sold mares.

Greg Garrison, a Hollywood television producer, by his unwavering determination and dedication is responsible not only for the first serious introduction of Andalusians into North America, but for establishing a breeding farm that is the largest in the Western Hemisphere. Garrison's horses, which are as fine as anything to be seen in Spain, are mostly the progeny of Spanish Grand Champion Legionario III (of Terry), and of a number of Terry mares that were sent to America in foal. The story of how Garrison was able to obtain these "unavailable" animals and get them to his ranch in Thousand Oaks (where his herd now numbers over 50), is material for a book in itself.

Legionario III, shown on this page in John Fulton's drawing, is an animal splendid enough looking to make me regret he had not been in Spain when I took the photographs for this book. Seeing at first hand Garrison's dedication and search for perfection as I later accompanied him to Spanish ranches, and considering the beauty and noble disposition of Andalusians, it doesn't surprise me that his Thousand Oaks farm has for its clients Orson Welles, Dean Martin, Jimmy Stewart and other celebrities. Happily, the Andalusian in its purest form, after an absence of nearly five hundred years, has returned to North America.

217

POSTSCRIPT

While the Spanish edition of this book was being printed, I had the good fortune (thanks to Laura Castroviejo of the Coto Doñana) to meet the ecologist Dr. Patrick Duncan and his wife, Clare. Our introduction was especially happy, considering the hope expressed in this book that further studies of equine social behavior will soon be done.

Patrick, who has spent years of field study in the Serengeti, is now working on such a project in the Camargue. I thus had the opportunity, often feeling remote in Southern Spain with few sounding-boards for my work, to show him the manuscript of this book.

Not many days after our visit (which had lasted into the early morning hours), I received from Patrick the following letter, which seems a fitting end to these pages:

Station Biologique
de la Tour du Valat
Le Sambuc, Arles, France
November 1st 1976

Dear Robert,

Of all that Seville has to offer, meeting you was the most rewarding. It was exciting to see the photographs, illustrations and text for your remarkable book, and to have the opportunity of discussing them with you. As a student of horses over the last two years, I was able to learn from your own acute observations of horses' behavior, which are illustrated so well by your photographs: these are of considerable scientific value in addition to their beauty. The reader is moved by, and will also learn much from this book. Communication between horses, as you show, is subtle: for example, it may rely on nuances of facial expression (fleeting signs such as the configuration of a stallion's lips or the flaring of his nostrils), and olfactory signals that the human nose cannot detect. While in the text, you rightly stress the intensity and frequency of ritualized sniffing (particularly between stallions), your photographs are a unique record of the less obvious means of visual communication.

Why has the horse, inspiration of so much creative art over millennia, been so little studied except in captivity or for breeding purposes? This lack of scientific attention is particularly striking when contrasted with the abundance of excellent new work on the behavior and ecology of exotic and distant species, such as gorilla and lion (George Schaller), elephant (Iain and Oria Douglas-Hamilton) and chimpanzee (Jane Goodall). As for the genus *Equus*, the best behavioral study is that of the plains, Grevy's and mountain zebra in South and East Africa by Hans and Ute Klingel. Zebra live in ecosystems not yet dominated by man and where, we presume, conditions are similar to those under which they evolved. But the results of studies of free-living horses (such as mustangs in the U.S.A., or the New Forest ponies of England) are hard to interpret, since man has altered not only their genetic make-up (by artificial selection) but also the conditions under which they

live (most obviously, by reducing the numbers of predators or even eliminating them). This difficulty may largely explain the paucity of scientific studies of the horse.

However, I thought you would be interested to hear more about the research in which I am involved. In the Camargue, a study of horses' behavior and ecology was begun three years ago as part of the program of the Foundation Tour du Valat, an organization created by Dr. Luc Hoffmann to promote conservation in the Camargue and similar Mediterranean environments. In spite of industrialization, intensive agriculture and tourism, the Camargue retains extraordinary numbers of water fowl (particularly in winter), important breeding colonies of herons and egrets, and the only European breeding colony of flamingoes. For over twenty-five years studies of the ecology, numbers and migration of certain bird species have been conducted at Tour du Valat; in the early 1970's the program was broadened to include studies of aquatic communities and of the commonest mammalian herbivores, namely horses, rabbits and coypu. Though herbivores are, in a sense, the product of their environment, they in turn modify it, and thus affect the plants and other animals. In the short term, horses may make trails and bare patches of earth (used as rolling places), open up reedbeds and keep down grass height; in the long term, their presence alters the biological cycles of matter and energy (by consuming and excreting large quantities of plant material).

The horse study involves several people and

has two aims: one is to describe the social organization which Camargue horses develop when human interference is kept to a minimum, and the other is to discover the ways in which the environment affects the horses and *vice versa.* A breeding herd of fourteen horses (one stallion, seven mares, six juveniles) was released in an area of 300 hectares containing plant communities as diverse as deep-water reedbeds, coarse grasslands and desolate salt flats. Various studies have been completed or are in progress—on social structure, stallion behavior, the mare-foal relationship, feeding behavior and diet, activity patterns, movement and choice of habitat—and we are beginning to get some exciting insights into questions which have interested you and which you raise in your book.

To work with horses which are not exploited by people, either for riding or for breeding (nor indeed for meat) is a moving experience. The first consequence of this lack of human interference is that there are in the herd (now totaling 33) animals of both sexes and all ages, and it is thus possible to watch the maturation of foals in a social environment which is richer than the standard artificial herd of brood mares. We have found (as you have seen) that after the stage in which foals' relationships with their mothers exclude almost all others they develop not only links with other foals but also strong bonds with their immature siblings. Within the herd, the horses live in matriarchal families. Females preserve weak family bonds, even after integration into the hierarchy of

breeding mares, at two or three years old; young males, however, are closely associated with their mothers until sometime in their third year of life. Between 15 and 40 months of age, nine young males had left the herd and formed a bachelor herd; some of these were seen to be driven out by the herd stallion, and the evidence strongly suggests that they all were. Their mothers appear to have acted as a partial barrier against the stallion's aggression; nonetheless, for those which remained in the herd until their third year, these maternal links disappeared and the young males usually attached themselves closely to particular mares, selecting those who spent little time close to the herd stallion. In one three-year-old, behavior patterns typical of an adult stallion appeared: he drove mares, attacked young horses and became involved in conflicts with the herd stallion—with the full ritual of imposing postures, sniffing and defecation which you have described—and even combat.

After the exclusion of all the young (weaned) males, the herd stallion has recently driven a yearling female from the herd. Her arrival in the bachelor herd had a much greater effect on it than had that of the males, whose advent was marked by rituals and play fights resembling closely those you describe—*except* that we have not observed the presenting and leading behavior shown by submissives towards a dominant stallion in Spanish herds. The female and her two-year-old brother, who had not been members of the same herd for five months, immediately renewed their strong attachment

to each other; and the older members of the bachelor herd spent a day in intense conflicts over the new arrival which resulted indirectly in the death of the dominant one. At the time of writing, the "bachelor herd" consists of eight males and one female, living as a single group which has consistently displayed the kind of close attachments between individuals that you describe.

However, in their grooming behavior, Andalusian and Camargue horses differ; you interpret grooming as a major factor contributing to group unity, but in our herd grooming is rare—and never shown by the dominant mares. Obviously our study is young; group composition is changing rapidly and our breeding herd is very large compared to zebras and mustangs; we hope to continue for long enough to come to some firm, general conclusions.

Much of our effort has gone into studies of feeding, by which the horses modify their environment most. Observation throughout the year is showing us some of the ways in which selection of habitat and diet, and the time of grazing, are modified in response to the sharp seasonal changes which occur; experimental exclosures provide quantitative data on how the vegetation would be were there no horses. You have pointed out that Andalusian horses can feed very selectively; in the Camargue, we have found not only that horses feed very selectively, but also their selectivity changes dramatically from one season to another. For example, they feed intensively on reeds in spring

and summer, but ignore them completely in winter.

Feeding behavior is thus flexible; social behavior is also subject to variation both within and between herds. And it is certain that social behavior can be understood only with a knowledge of environmental constraints, as you yourself point out. It is striking that the eye of the artist can see in a very short time what takes scientists years to discover and describe. Most impressive of all, to me, are your unprecedented observations of eye-rolling in experienced stallions—a facet of behavior which will no doubt occupy students for years to come!

Clare and I look forward greatly to a visit from you, and this brings our very best wishes,

Patrick

PS: A suggested bibliography for your book: 1) J. D. Feist (1974), *Behavior of Feral Horses in the Prior Mountain Wild Horse Range,* M.Sc. Thesis, University of Michigan, USA; 2) H. Klingel (1969), *The Social Organization and Population Ecology of the Plains Zebra* (Equus Quagga) and Zoologica Africana (pp. 249-63), and 3) M. Tyler (1972), *The Behaviour and Social Organization of the New Forest Ponies,* Ph.D. Thesis, University of Cambridge, UK.

ACKNOWLEDGMENTS

FOR the time, help and encouragement given me while doing this book, first thanks go to friend, publisher and printer Rudolf Blanckenstein, who kept my spirits up with his enthusiasm and advice for this project.

Patricia Luisa Serrano not only helped during the photographing of foals on a ranch near Sevilla, but upon her return to America she spent many hours supplying page after page of quotations from which most of the material used with the photographs was drawn. Without Patricia and her sensitive selections and long hours spent, it would have been impossible to finish the book within the four month deadline. Mary Boetticher, Carolyn Moyer and Marilyn Tennent also supplied quotations.

While working with mares and foals, I enjoyed the company and assistance of Jim Ray and Federico Fulton.

To John Fulton I am grateful for the splendid design and drawings he supplied.

Juan Manuel Urquijo Novales, the Conde de Odiel, was the first rancher to give me complete freedom of his breeding farm. During the hours spent at El Hornillo, I enjoyed the company and help, especially at breeding time, of foreman Antonio Garamendi Márquez.

For work in and around Jerez de la Frontera, I counted on the friendship of veterinarian Francisco Abad Alfaro. It was Paco who provided the introduction to a young rancher who is not only completely dedicated to his horses, and whose company and sense of humor I looked forward to enjoying during visits to La Ducha, but who often carried out personally requests for arranged situations with his horses. Antonio Romero Girón, who was a special friend of Bernardo González Real, will always have my deepest gratitude, as does his foreman, Juan Aguilar Herrera.

Quite by accident I met General Pedro Merry Gordon, the Captain General of the Second Military Region, and his charming wife, and once the horse book idea had been explained to him, the General took immediate interest in the project and generously arranged for visits to two of the Army farms in Andalusia.

At the Army farm at Vicos, near Jerez de la Frontera, I spent a number of days with the hundreds of mares and colts that are kept there, thanks to the wonderful gentleman who is in charge of that operation, Colonel Eduardo Pérez Ceresal. For work in the field at Vicos, I was assisted and given advice by Captain Antonio Ribarda González, and NCO Alfonso Cañero Muñoz. During those trudges around the rolling hills of the Army farm, I enjoyed the company and conversation of several recruits: "El Sevillano," "El Granadino," and "El Rubio."

Arrangements at the Army's farm near Ecija were kindly made by Colonel Antonio Doce López. At La Isla, I profited from the help and suggestions of one of the most charming and dedicated men I met during my work, NCO Antonio Sola Castillo.

It was Antonio Méndez Benegassi, a Sevillan veterinarian friend, who supplied some important introductions in this area. Through Antonio I met Francisco Lazo Díaz and his wife Mari Tere, who not only offered their assistance, but also perhaps the most open hospitality I have received anywhere. Paco even helped carry the cameras and umbrella. The umbrella was used to shade lenses from the sun, and on each of the occasions that we used it at Lerena it brought rain to the countryside. I am also appreciative of the assistance given by Paco's foreman, Antonio Sánchez Carrasco.

For observations of marsh horses and work done at the Coto Doñana, I thank its director, Javier Castroviejo, and his wife Laura. During the past few years Javier has been an example of friendliness and cooperation on each visit to Doñana.

This book would have been incomplete had it not contained photographs of perhaps the most famous of all Spanish horses, the Terry stallions of Puerto de Santa María. I wish especially to thank Jesús Terry Merello and his wonderful old foreman, Sebastián García Nieto, for the time and interest they devoted to this project.

Though I had a short time in Ecija at the ranch of Miguel Angel Cárdenas Llavaneras, the owner's son, Miguel Angel Cárdenas Osuna, in his willingness to help, provided the opportunity to try for some photographs that I very much wanted to include in this book.

In Sevilla at the ranch of the Marqués de Salvatierra, one of the five most important breeders of Andalusians in this country, I was assisted by the owner's son, Rafael Atienza Medina, and by the ranch director, Francisco Montaño Galán, and had the pleasure of working several afternoons with foreman Manuel Cervera Camarero and his brother, Diego.

Michael Hughes of King Ranch España was the key figure in helping me through the last stages to publication of *Bulls of Iberia.* Once again, with this book, he demonstrated his great love for livestock, his generosity and his friendship, as he and a wonderful gentleman and cattleman, Bob Adams, actively helped to photograph the Quarter Horses and Spanish stock at Los Millares.

Some of the photographs in this book were in part made possible by the Club Pineda of Sevilla, most especially by José Calvo Dorca, Antonio Espigares Molinero, and Ricardo Jurado Castillo.

The fields of red poppies were photographed through the kindness of the Señora Viuda de Fernando de la Cámera, and with the assistance of her foreman, Antonio Cortez.

Félix Moreno de la Cova, Agricultural Delegate for Andalusia, provided sound advice, as he had warmly done for many of my previous projects.

For help with certain photographic problems, I thank my long-time friend and fellow photographer, Emilio Sáenz Cembrano, along with Santiago Saavedra Ligne.

Carolyn Murphy, friend and secretary, has my thanks, as does Perdita Hordern, Matthew Robinson, Jim and Abby Werlock, and Gerald Guidera for their help with the manuscript.

Time, advice, and various forms of assistance were generously given by old friends, John and Cecilia Culverwell, Guillermo and Virginia Benvenuty Díaz, as well as by Jacobo Delgado López, José María Conde Muñoz, and Ramón Guerrera and his sons.

For care and concern with book production, the staffs of Imprenta Sevillana, Folies and Fotomecánica Castellana have my deepest gratitude.

And for having such tremendous patience I thank all the mares who appeared in my camera viewfinder, especially Noticiera and her son Potri, as well as Nevado, Divertido, Vasallo, Majestad, Farruco, Nostálgico, Jerezano and Justiciero, the stallions who turned the spring and summer of this year into one of the most beautiful memories of my life.

Color reproduction by Folies. Composition of text by Castellana, Madrid. Paper Estucado Limoges 2/c Sarrió Cia. Papelera de Leiza S.A.

American

MILITARY UNIFORMS

1639~1968

A COLORING BOOK
BY PETER F. COPELAND

DOVER PUBLICATIONS, INC.
New York

To Ingrid Lorrain Jonsson

INTRODUCTION

Modern military uniforms can be traced back to ancient times. Originally one of the reasons for clothing soldiers in uniforms was to help distinguish friend from foe in the heat of battle. In addition to insuring that soldiers were appropriately dressed and equipped for action, uniforms were also thought to contribute to esprit de corps. Elegant uniform dress was also effective as an inducement for recruiting purposes.

Military uniforms have existed in the United States since colonial times. Troops were raised in the American colonies in the early seventeenth century. Some attempt was made to establish a form of uniform dress, or symbol of recognition, for the troops to wear, even though this was before the time when all soldiers wore uniforms. Early in the eighteenth century companies of soldiers were raised in various colonies, some in uniform but most without. Many of these troops fought alongside the British forces in the colonial wars.

During the American Revolution, the desperate efforts of George Washington and the Continental Congress to clothe the soldiers of the patriot army in proper military dress were only partially successful. Many soldiers never received a real uniform at all. It was not until after the Revolution that most of the forces of the United States were properly uniformed. Sailors in the United States Navy were not authorized uniforms until 1841.

This book shows some of the military uniforms—both dress, for formal occasions, and combat, for the battlefield—worn by the American armed forces from 1639 to 1968. These uniforms have varied in cut and color in accordance with the military fashions of the times. For example, at the time of the Civil War, many of the armies of Europe had adopted uniforms cut in the French fashion, so both the Union and Confederate armies fought the war in uniforms patterned, more or less, on those of the army of Napoleon III.

With the advent of the rifled musket, the machine gun, and the high explosive shell, soldiers the world over gradually went into drab, functional, earth-colored combat dress—brilliant uniforms made easy targets on the battlefield. Much of the color and pageantry of the military uniform passed away under the murderous conditions of modern warfare. The uniforms of today retain little to remind us of the gaudy era of scarlet coats, sparkling buttons, and fluttering plumes.

Published in Canada by General Publishing Company, Ltd., 30 Lesmill Road, Don Mills, Toronto, Ontario.

American Military Uniforms, 1639-1968, A Coloring Book is a new work, first published by Dover Publications, Inc., in 1976.

DOVER *Pictorial Archive* SERIES

This book belongs to the Dover Pictorial Archive Series. You may use the designs and illustrations for graphics and crafts applications, free and without special permission, provided that you include no more than four in the same publication or project. (For permission for additional use, please write to Dover Publications, Inc., 31 East 2nd Street, Mineola, N.Y. 11501.)
However, republication or reproduction of any illustration by any other graphic service, whether it be in a book or in any other design resource, is strictly prohibited.

International Standard Book Number: 0-486-23239-5

Manufactured in the United States of America. Dover Publications, Inc., 31 East 2nd Street, Mineola, N.Y. 11501.

1. OFFICER OF THE MILITARY COMPANY OF MASSACHUSETTS, 1639.

The company was composed of pikemen in half armor and musketeers carrying matchlock muskets. Like the officer shown here, both wore red feathers in their hats and buff coats (worn by the pikemen under their armor). The officer's breeches, breast ribbons, and shoulder knots are scarlet, his stockings white and his boots and hat light brown. His iron-hilted rapier hangs from a light brown belt bordered with gold. His lace collar and cuffs are white. His coat is leather with gold trim.

**2. OFFICER OF
NEW YORK MILITIA
TROOP OF HORSE, 1725.**
New York raised a number of militia
units early in the 18th century,
among them artillery and cavalry
units and two companies of
cadets. The officer wears a
white wig, a scarlet coat and vest,
both trimmed with silver lace,
buff leather breeches, and black
leather boots with steel spurs.
His neckcloth is white and his waist
belt is of buff leather edged with
silver lace. His sword has a steel
hilt, a silver sword knot, and
a black leather scabbard. His hat
is of black felt edged with
silver lace.

3. OFFICER, SOUTH CAROLINA PROVINCIAL REGIMENT, 1757. The men in Colonel Howarth's Regiment, raised in 1757, were known as "the Buffs," after the color of their facings, and served in what is now Tennessee during one of the Cherokee wars. The officer wears the English-made uniform adopted by the regiment: a dark blue coat cuffed and lined with buff cloth, a buff vest edged with silver lace, and dark blue breeches. His buttonholes are edged with silver lace, as is his black cocked hat. The sash over his shoulder is of crimson silk and his stockings are white. His shoes are of black leather with silver buckles. His wig is white, and his shirt and neckcloth are white linen.

**4. OFFICER,
11TH NEW HAMPSHIRE
PROVINCIAL REGIMENT, 1774.**
Only the officers in this brief-lived
regiment were authorized uniforms.
This one wears a scarlet coat, trimmed
with silver lace. The lapels of
his coat (turned back at the top), his
cuffs, vest, and breeches are sky
blue. His stockings, shirt ruffles, and
neckcloth are white. His hat is of black
felt. His buttons, the lace edging on
his waistcoat, shoulder knot and
crescent-shape gorget are silver. His shoes
are of black leather with silver buckles.

5. SAILOR, CONNECTICUT STATE NAVY, 1776.
States' navies only weakened the efforts of the Continental Navy in the Revolution. Instead of a uniform, this gunner aboard the *Oliver Cromwell* wears clothing issued to him and the other crew members of the vessel. He wears a dark blue jacket with black leather buttons, a red vest, and blue and white striped trousers. His neckerchief is green with white spots. His hat is black with a white edging on the brim, and his stockings are striped red and white. His iron-hilted cutlass hangs from a black leather belt and rests in a black leather scabbard. In his left hand he holds a rammer.

6. COMPANY OFFICER, BUTLER'S RANGERS, 1779. Basically a unit of frontier raiders, this Loyalist regiment waged a bloody fight against the patriot forces. The officer wears a black cockade, black felt cocked hat with a gold edging, a white ruffled shirt, and a dark green vest and coat with scarlet collar, lapels, cuffs and lining. His buttons are brass, and his epaulette gold. His breeches are of buff leather. His stockings are gray worsted, and his short leggings and shoes are black. Around his waist he wears a crimson silk sash, and over his shoulder he wears a yellow, white, red, and blue Indian beaded belt with ermine's tails, supporting a haversack slung behind his left hip. His sword has a brass hilt and fittings with white grips and a black scabbard. His firearm is a frontiersman's rifle, with steel fittings and a brass trigger-guard.

7. INFANTRY OFFICER, WAYNE'S LEGION, 1794.

The Legion, which defeated the Indians at the battle of Fallen Timbers in 1794, was composed of 4 sub legions, each a miniature army within itself, with companies of infantry, riflemen, cavalry, and artillery. This officer wears the colors of the 2nd Sub Legion: dark blue breeches and coat with red collar, cuffs, and lapels, lined with white; a black hat, and boots. His buttons, belt plate and spurs are of white metal, as is his epaulette. His vest is white. His sword has a brass hilt, and the scabbard is of black leather. His sword belt is of white leather.

8. ARTILLERY CADET, WEST POINT, 1805.

The first cadets at the Academy were destined
for the Artillery and the Corps of Engineers.
This cadet wears a uniform which is partly that
of a commissioned officer, and partly
that of a non-commissioned officer. His coat
is dark blue, with red collar, lapels,
cuffs and lining. The wings on his coat (at
the shoulder below the epaulette)
are dark blue with a red edging. His buttons
are brass, as is his sword hilt and sword
belt plate. His vest and breeches are white, and
his boots are black with red edging, and
tassel. His hat is of black felt, with
a red feather. His sword belt is of white
leather and his cartridge pouch, worn at his
waist, is of black leather. His musket
has steel fittings.

9. ARTILLERY DRUMMER, U.S. ARMY, 1812.

Drummers, fifers, and musicians commonly wore "reverse clothing"; if the regiment wore blue uniforms faced with red, the musicians wore red coats faced with blue. As most musicians of U.S. regiments wore red coats, captured British uniforms were often used to clothe them during the War of 1812. The drummer wears a scarlet coat with brass buttons, and dark blue collar and cuffs. His gaiters (short leggings) are black, as are his shoes and hat (called a *chapeau bras*) with gold tassels, a small gold eagle on the cockade, and a white feather. The braid on his collar is of gold, as is his sword hilt. His breeches are white. His drum has a gold and white eagle on a dark blue field with gold stars. The hoops, at the top and bottom of the drum are red, and the carrying sling and sword belt are of white leather. The braid on his coat front and cuffs is black.

10. SERGEANT, 32ND INFANTRY REGIMENT, U.S. ARMY, 1813.

A member of one of the hastily raised regiments in the War of 1812, he is dressed in a fatigue uniform, and never received a proper dress uniform. His cap is of black leather with a pewter metal plate in front, and a white braided cord and plume at the side. His "roundabout" jacket and his trousers are light blue-gray. His rank is shown by his white epaulette and crimson sash. His canteen is bright red with "U.S." in white. The gaiters he wears beneath his trousers are dark gray, and his shoes are black. The haversack worn beneath his canteen is of white duck, and his knapsack is dark blue. His blanket is green, and his cross belts are of white leather with a white metal or pewter plate. His musket has iron fittings and a white leather strap. His black leather scabbard has a steel tip.

11. FIELD OFFICER,
U.S. MARINE CORPS, 1826.

The green coat worn by the Continental Marines during
the Revolution (and worn by Marines today as part of
the winter field uniform) gave way to the dark
blue worn by the Army and Navy of the nineteenth
century. This officer wears a black hat with gold cord;
a dark blue coat with gold braid and scarlet
cuffs, collar, and lapel; and white trousers and gloves.
His sash is of crimson silk. His sword has a white
ivory hilt; the sword knot, fittings and scabbard are
brass. His waist belt is of white leather with a
brass plate. His epaulettes are gold, his
boots are of black leather.

12. ARTILLERY OFFICER, U.S. ARMY, 1827.
In peacetime this captain wears a black leather cap
with a gold eagle on the front, gold cords and band,
and a yellow pompom. His coat is dark blue.
The wings, shoulder straps, collar braid, buttons,
and the chevrons on his arms are gold.
His waist belt is of white leather with a brass
plate. His trousers are light blue, his gloves are
white, and his sword is in a brass scabbard.
The sash around his waist is of crimson silk. The
braid on the front of his coat is black.

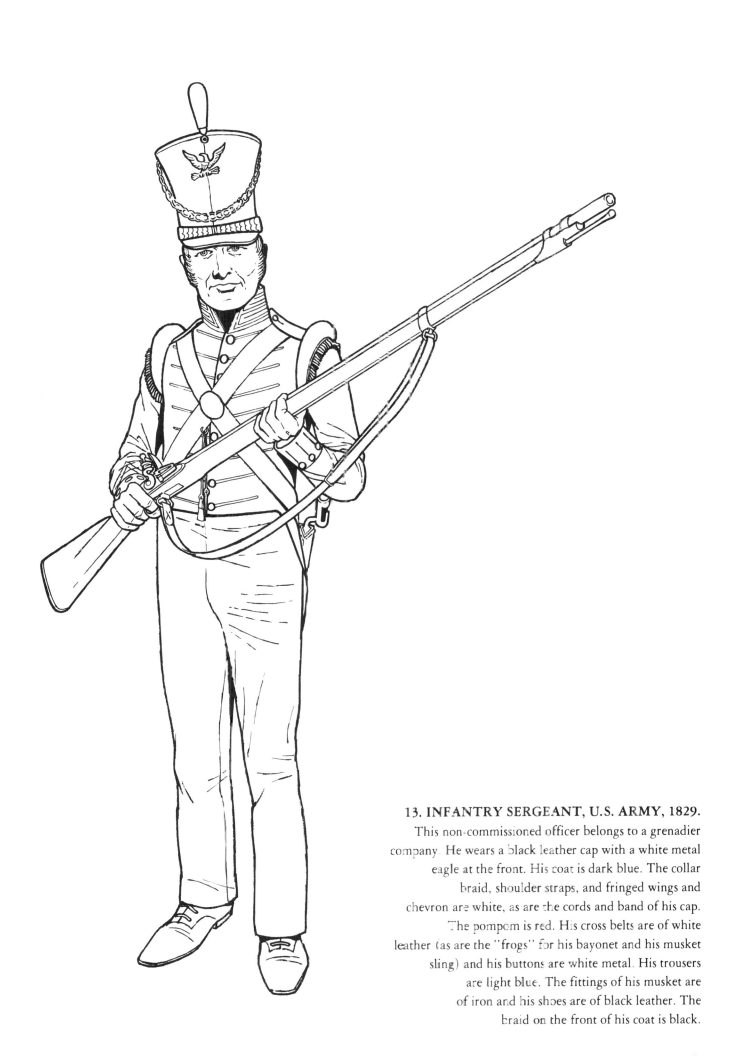

13. INFANTRY SERGEANT, U.S. ARMY, 1829.

This non-commissioned officer belongs to a grenadier company. He wears a black leather cap with a white metal eagle at the front. His coat is dark blue. The collar braid, shoulder straps, and fringed wings and chevron are white, as are the cords and band of his cap. The pompom is red. His cross belts are of white leather (as are the "frogs" for his bayonet and his musket sling) and his buttons are white metal. His trousers are light blue. The fittings of his musket are of iron and his shoes are of black leather. The braid on the front of his coat is black.

14. MEDICAL OFFICER, U.S. NAVY, 1830.
This assistant surgeon is in the undress uniform of
1830–1841. While the dress uniforms of the military
services of this time were elaborate, the
undress uniform often tended to approximate the
civilian dress of the day. He wears a black hat, with
black cockade and gold cord, and a dark blue
coat with brass buttons. His waist belt and sword
slings are of white leather and his trousers are white.
His shoes are of black leather, as is his sword
scabbard with brass fittings. His sword has
white grips, brass hilt. and gold sword knot.

15. BOATSWAIN, U.S. REVENUE CUTTER SERVICE, 1834.

The U.S. Revenue Cutter Service became the U.S. Coast Guard in 1915. This is uniform dress prescribed for seamen and petty officers. The jacket is dark blue with brass buttons. The neckerchief, shoes, hat, and ribbon are black. The shirt, or frock, is white with a light blue front enclosed within the stripes. The trousers are white. The boatswain wears a silver whistle around his neck as a symbol of his rank. The collar of his shirt is light blue with white stripes and stars.

16. SERGEANT, BRISBANE'S REGIMENT, SOUTH CAROLINA MILITIA, 1836.

Members of this regiment, raised for the Seminole War, wore different uniforms; some had none at all. The sergeant wears a brown civilian felt hat with a red, white. and blue cockade. His green-fringed hunting shirt and trousers are of brown homespun. His under shirt is of a pale yellow unbleached linen. His belts and scabbard are of black leather, and his sash, worn under his waist belt, is red. His canteen is light blue with white initials, and his sword has a brass hilt. His leggings are of light brown and his shoes are black. His powder horn, slung at his right side by a leather thong, is light yellow-brown. He wears a small rifleman's knife in a sheath on the shoulder belt which supports his shot pouch behind his right hip. His long rifle has a steel lock and brass trigger guard and patch box on the lower end of the butt. The outfit resembles a woodsman's.

**17. ORDNANCE SERGEANT,
U.S. ARMY, 1836.**
This non-commissioned officer took care of
weapons, ammunition, and stores at
military posts. He wears a dark blue coat with
brass buttons, and yellow braid on the
collar, cuffs, and epaulettes. His cap is of
black leather, with a brass eagle and
crossed cannons on the front, and a red plume.
His sword belt is of white leather with a
brass plate. His sash is red, and his trousers are
of light blue with a dark blue stripe down
the side. His sword, in a black leather scabbard,
has a black leather hilt and iron metal fittings.

18. CORPORAL, 3RD INFANTRY REGIMENT, U.S. ARMY, 1846.
This NCO (non-commissioned officer) wears the winter field uniform worn by the infantry during the war with Mexico. His cap is of dark blue cloth with black leather strap and visor. His jacket and trousers are of light blue, the collar of the jacket is worked with white braid, which also edges the shoulder straps. His corporal's stripes are white, as are his waist belt, shoulder belt, and haversack (worn under his canteen, which is red with white lettering). His waist belt has a brass plate. His knapsack is black, and his blanket, rolled on top, is red. His buttons are of white metal. His musket has steel fittings and a wooden stock.

19. SERGEANT, FIRST DRAGOON REGIMENT, U.S. ARMY, 1849.

The regiment was first raised in 1833 to fight the Indians and protect the caravans of covered wagons. On frontier service the troopers wore a simpler uniform than the dress uniform shown here. The sergeant wears a leather cap on the front of which is a silver eagle in a brass sunburst. Its cords are yellow; the plumes are white. His coat is dark blue with yellow collar, chevrons, and cuffs trimmed with gold braid, which also edges the tails of his coat. His belts are of white leather. His black leather cartridge box, worn in the middle of his back, has a brass plate. His trousers are light blue with yellow stripes up the sides. His sword is in a steel scabbard, and his carbine, slung from the shoulder by a white leather belt, is of iron with a wooden stock. His shoes are of black leather; his spurs are of brass, as are the metal scales on his shoulders and his buckles. His gloves are white.

20. MIDSHIPMAN, U.S. NAVY, 1852.
This undress uniform was established by a regulation
of 1852, and was worn throughout the Civil War. His
cap is dark blue with a gold band about the
bottom of the crown; the visor and chin strap are
of black leather. The device on the front
of the cap is a silver anchor in a gold wreath.
His coat and trousers are dark blue with
brass buttons. His shoulder strap and trouser stripes
are gold. His shoes and belt are of black leather,
and his belt buckle is brass. His sword has
a white leather grip and brass fittings. The scabbard
is of black leather with brass fittings, and
his sword knot is of gold.

21. FIRST SERGEANT, LIGHT ARTILLERY, U.S. ARMY, 1855.

The jacket is dark blue, with red piping on the edges, cuffs and collar, the color of the artillery. His sergeant's stripes and his sash are also red, as is the peaked welt of cloth around the crown of his cap and the pompom. The cap has a dark blue top, black leather visor and a brass insignia on the front. His trousers are sky blue, and his shoes, waist belt, and sword knot are of black leather. The belt buckle is of brass, as is the hilt of his sword, which has a steel scabbard.

**22. PRIVATE, 83RD PENNSYLVANIA
VOLUNTEER INFANTRY REGIMENT,
U.S. ARMY, 1861.**
The regiment is reported to have fought in more
battles and lost more men in the Civil War than
any other Pennsylvania regiment. This
uniform was modeled on that of the French
Chasseurs. The cap and coat are dark
blue, both edged in yellow braid, with white
metal buttons and gold epaulettes. His
shoes and belts are of black leather. The
trousers are light blue-gray, and the
gaiters have light brown tops and are white at
the lower parts around the ankles. The
overcoat, rolled atop the knapsack behind
the soldier's shoulders, is medium gray.
The musket has steel fittings, its
sling is of brown leather.

23. PRIVATE, 4TH TEXAS VOLUNTEER INFANTRY REGIMENT, C.S. ARMY, 1861.

The private is in the uniform worn by the regiment when the famed Hood's Texas Brigade first arrived in Virginia in 1861. He wears a black felt hat with a silver star. His uniform coat and trousers are of Confederate gray, with black trim. His canteen has a light brown cloth cover, and his belts and cartridge box are of black leather. The cartridge box has a brass plate upon it with a Texas star. His blanket roll is green. His Bowie knife has a wooden handle and a brown leather sheath. His shoes are of brown leather. His Enfield musket, with a sling of white duck cloth, has iron fittings.

24. VIVANDIERE, 114TH PENNSYLVANIA VOLUNTEER INFANTRY REGIMENT ("COLLIS ZOUAVES"), U.S. ARMY, 1862.

A number of regiments raised at the beginning of the Civil War were patterned on the French colonial Zouave Regiments from North Africa. The vivandière traveled with the regiment, tending the soldiers in battle, and serving drinks from her small keg. She wears a straw hat with a black ribbon and ostrich plume. Her jacket and skirt, both trimmed in scarlet, are dark blue. Her buttons are brass, as are the metal fittings on the keg. Her blouse is white, and her sash is crimson. Her waist belt and pistol holster are of black leather, as are her shoes. Her trousers are scarlet. Both the vivandieres and the colorful (but impractical) Zouave uniforms disappeared after the first months of the war.

25. MAJOR, VIRGINIA CAVALRY, C.S. ARMY, 1863.

Jeb Stuart and the officers of his famous cavalry unit wore their own distinctive variation of regulation uniform. This officer wears a broad-brimmed, black-plumed, gray felt hat caught up on one side with a silver star. His short cavalry jacket (with yellow lining), the lapels turned back at the top, is Confederate gray, as is his vest. His collar is yellow, the cavalry color, and his Major's star is embroidered in gold. He wears a red checked shirt and a yellow silk sash. His buttons and belt clasp are of brass, and the braid on the sleeves of his jacket is gold. His gauntlets are pale buff leather. His trousers are a light brown corduroy. His boots are of black leather as are his belt and pistol holster, the tip of which can be seen beneath his right arm. His sword has a black leather grip, brass metal fittings and a steel scabbard, and his spurs are brass.

26. CORPORAL OF HEAVY ARTILLERY, CORPS D'AFRIQUE, U.S. ARMY, 1863.

The Corps d'Afrique, composed of black soldiers, was
raised in 1862. Its heavy artillery unit defended
New Orleans after its capture by Federal forces.
This soldier wears a dark blue coat edged
and trimmed with red. His hat is black with a brass
insignia at the side. His waist belt, the
scabbard of his short artillery sword, and his
shoes are of black leather. His buttons, belt plate,
shoulder scales, and the hilt and fittings of
his sword are of brass. His trousers are sky blue
with red stripes down the sides. His corporal's
stripes are red. His musket sling is of
brown leather. His gloves are white.

27. PRIVATE FIRST CLASS, 7TH CAVALRY REGIMENT, U.S. ARMY, 1876.

This is the field uniform of the troopers of the 7th cavalry, five troops of which perished with General George A. Custer at the battle of the Little Big Horn in 1876. This soldier wears a dark gray slouch hat with yellow cord. His kerchief is either red or yellow, and his jacket is dark blue. His private's stripe is yellow, and his cartridge belt, with a brass buckle, is of black leather as are his pistol holster, carbine sling, slings on his saber, and boots. His gloves are pale buff, and his trousers are sky blue. His saber (none were worn at Little Big Horn) has brass fittings and a steel scabbard. His carbine has iron fittings and his spurs are of brass.

28. PRIVATE,
71ST NEW YORK REGIMENT, 1898.

The 71st fought in Cuba during the Spanish-
American war. The soldier wears a light brown felt
hat and leggings, a dark blue jacket with brass
buttons, and light blue pack, canteen with dark blue
initials, and trousers with dark blue stripes. His
shoes are dark brown. His shelter tent,
half rolled above the knapsack, is dark gray. His
valise, slung below the canteen, is black.
His haversack, at the bottom of his pack, is light
blue with dark blue initials. His bayonet scabbard,
projecting from beneath the valise, is
steel. His drinking cup is of unpainted tin. He
carries a Krag Jorgensen magazine rifle, though
most of the militia carried the old
single-shot Springfield.

29. CORPORAL, 1ST VOLUNTEER CAVALRY, U.S. ARMY, 1898.

The "Rough Riders," led by Col. Leonard Wood and Theodore Roosevelt, became famous for their charge up San Juan Hill in the Spanish-American War. This non-commissioned officer wears stable dress—a light brown slouch hat with brass cavalry insignia, a khaki jacket and trousers, and a brown leather pistol belt, holster and shoulder strap. His corporal's stripes are in cavalry yellow. His boots are of black leather with steel spurs. His undershirt is red, and his gauntlets are of pale buff.

30. CAPTAIN OF INFANTRY, U.S. ARMY, 1907.

This full-dress uniform consists of a cap with a dark blue top, a light Infantry blue band around the crown (which is edged with gold) and a gold chin strap and insignia at the front. The coat is dark blue, with a light blue collar edged with gold, brass buttons, and gold sleeve insignia and shoulder straps. The belt is of gold with a brass buckle; the sword (with black grip) and scabbard are steel. His trousers are sky blue with a white stripe and his boots are of polished black leather with steel spurs.

**31. MACHINIST'S MATE SECOND CLASS,
U.S. NAVY, 1908.**
This uniform was worn by enlisted men of the Navy
from the late 19th century through World War I.
The blue uniform was the winter uniform; the
summer uniform, of similar cut, was white. The sailor
wears a flat-top cap with the name of his vessel
embroidered on a black silk band around the crown.
His jumper, worn tucked into his trousers, is
dark blue, the collar and cuffs having three white
stripes bordering them, as did the uniforms
worn by Petty Officers and Seamen First Class. His
trousers are dark blue with black buttons.
His shoes are of black leather, and the rating
badge on his sleeve shows a white eagle
and stripes, and a red propeller.

32. ENSIGN,
U.S. NAVY AVIATION SERVICE, 1917.

The aviator seen here is wearing an unofficial uniform adopted in 1914, a combination of Navy and Marine Corps dress. The cap has a khaki top, a gold chin strap, and silver Navy insignia in front. The coat is khaki, with brass buttons. The pilot's wings over the left pocket are gold, as are the shoulder star and stripe. The khaki breeches and brown wraparound leggings are Marine Corps issue. His shoes are black leather Navy issue. The uniform became the official summer uniform of flying officers of the Navy in 1917.

33. CAPTAIN OF ARTILLERY, AMERICAN EXPEDITIONARY FORCE, U.S. ARMY, 1918.

This field service uniform was adopted in the first years of the 20th century, and was worn by the Army and Marine Corps in France during World War I. The captain wears a steel helmet painted drab brown or green. His jacket and breeches are olive drab, with buttons and collar insignia of dull bronze. His rank is indicated by the silver bars on his shoulder straps and the brown strip of braid on his sleeve. His waist belt, boots and pistol holster are of brown leather, while his pistol belt and the wide belt over his right shoulder are tan web.

**34. LIEUTENANT,
U.S. ARMY SIGNAL CORPS
(AVIATION SERVICE), 1918.**
The pilot is wearing one style of dress worn in
the air in combat over France in World War I.
His flying helmet and Sam Brown belt are
of brown leather and his flying coat is tan,
with a brown fur collar. His uniform tunic,
worn beneath the flying coat, is of olive drab,
as are his breeches. His buttons are a
dull bronze. His flying boots are dark brown.
He leans against a fighter plane that
would be camouflaged green and brown.

**35. LIEUTENANT, U.S. ARMY TANK
CORPS, ARMORED FORCES, 1938.**
This officer in field uniform is wearing a brown
reinforced leather crash helmet with fleece-lined
goggles. His shirt, breeches, and web waist belt are
khaki. His web pistol belt is brown. His map
case, worn on his left side, is brown canvas. His
binocular case, slung behind his right arm,
is of brown leather, as are the straps crossing over
his chest, his boots, and his pistol holster.
The collar insignia are of brass.

36. PRIVATE, INFANTRY, U.S. ARMY, 1943.

This infantryman wears a uniform typical of the
European Theater of Operations of World War
II. His steel helmet, painted olive drab, is
covered with a camouflage netting. His field
jacket is khaki; his cartridge belt is brown.
His haversack, slung at his side, and his
knapsack and leggings, worn over brown
shoes, are tan. His bayonet has a black handle
and a gray scabbard. His trousers are
olive drab. His private's chevron is light
brown with a dark brown border.

37. MACHINIST'S MATE FIRST CLASS, U.S. NAVY, 1945.

This Petty Officer is wearing "dress blues," the winter dress uniform of the Naval enlisted man. His cap is white, and his jumper and trousers (with black buttons) are dark blue. His collar and cuffs are bordered with three white stripes. His shoes are of black leather, and his sea bag is white. On his left arm he wears his Petty Officer's rating badge. The eagle is white and stripes, or inverted chevrons, and the machinist's propeller are red. Below this he wears three red "hash marks" signifying three enlistments in the Navy. His neckerchief is black, and his campaign ribbons, worn above his breast pocket, are of various bright colors.

38. SERGEANT, U.S. MARINE CORPS, 1945.
This is the winter service uniform. The cap, coat, and
trousers are of forest green, with black buttons and lapel
insignia. His leather waist belt is black, as are his
shoes. The sergeant's stripes are yellow, edged in
red, as are his "hash marks." His shirt is tan, as is his
tie. His campaign, or service, ribbons, worn above
his left breast pocket, are of various bright colors.

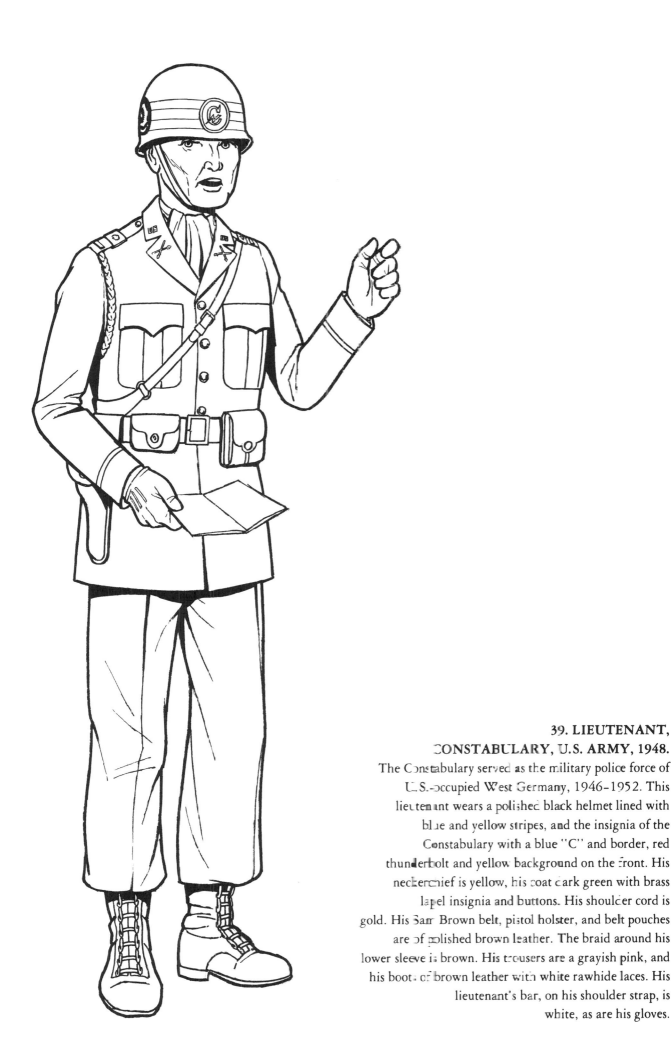

39. LIEUTENANT, CONSTABULARY, U.S. ARMY, 1948.
The Constabulary served as the military police force of U.S.-occupied West Germany, 1946–1952. This lieutenant wears a polished black helmet lined with blue and yellow stripes, and the insignia of the Constabulary with a blue "C" and border, red thunderbolt and yellow background on the front. His neckerchief is yellow, his coat dark green with brass lapel insignia and buttons. His shoulder cord is gold. His Sam Brown belt, pistol holster, and belt pouches are of polished brown leather. The braid around his lower sleeve is brown. His trousers are a grayish pink, and his boots of brown leather with white rawhide laces. His lieutenant's bar, on his shoulder strap, is white, as are his gloves.

**40. PRIVATE, FIRST CAVALRY DIVISION,
U.S. ARMY, 1950.**
This soldier is in field dress worn in Korea. His cap is
of brown fur, and his neckerchief is cavalry yellow.
His field jacket and trousers are olive drab. His
cartridge belt and suspender belts are tan. His gloves
are yellow leather. His boots are of brown
leather. In his hand he holds a Browning automatic
rifle with all steel metal fittings.

41. DRUM MAJOR, U.S. ARMY, 1954.
Bandsmen have always been the most colorfully dressed soldiers in the army. This one is in winter full dress uniform. His cap has a dark blue top and a yellow band around the crown. The chin strap and visor are of black leather. His coat is yellow, with dark blue collar, cuffs, and braid trimmings. His collar, cap insignia, buttons, and belt plate are of brass. His belt is of white leather. His trousers are dark blue with a yellow stripe. His shoes are of black leather and his staff is of natural wood color with a silver knob at the top, and white cords around it. His shoulder straps are dark blue.

**42. LIEUTENANT,
U.S. MARINE CORPS, 1954.**
This company-grade officer is wearing the blue
undress uniform with a boat cloak over it. His
cap is dark blue. The chin strap and Marine
Corps device are gold. His coat is navy blue
with gold buttons, insignia and belt buckle.
His trousers, with a scarlet stripe,
are also blue, somewhat darker than sky blue,
but not as dark as the blue of the coat.
His shoes and visor are of black leather. His
boat cloak is of dark blue, with a scarlet
lining, a black velvet collar, and a black
cord fastening at the top.

43. CORPORAL, WOMEN'S ARMY CORPS, 1955.
The Corps was raised in 1942. Its uniform in the 1950s
was the same as that of the Army Nurse Corps, but with
different insignia. This corporal wears the summer
service uniform. Her cap, dress, and belt are tan. Her
buttons and collar and cap insignia are brass,
and the chevrons on her sleeve are yellow. Over her
shoulder she carries a white handbag with brass
clasp. Her stockings are flesh colored, and
her shoes are light brown.

44. CAPTAIN, U.S. AIR FORCE, 1961.
The Air Force has tried to keep the uniform plain, yet
distinctive. This officer is wearing the winter service
uniform, which is of a color described by the Air
Force as "Blue, Shade 84"—a medium blue,
with a touch of gray in it. His cap, coat, trousers,
and tie are of this color. The visor of his cap,
the chinstrap, and his shoes are of black leather.
The captain's bars on his shoulder straps are
of silver, as are his Air Force wings, worn over his
service ribbons above the left breast pocket.
His cap device buttons and lapel insignia are
white metal. His shirt is sky blue.

45. PRIVATE, 101ST AIRBORNE DIVISION, U.S. ARMY, 1968.

The paratrooper wears the typical field service uniform worn by airborne and infantry units in Vietnam. His soft hat is camouflaged in patches of green and brown. His jacket, trousers and backpack are olive drab, which soon faded under the tropical sun and monsoon rains to a pale gray-green. His canteen covers are buff-colored web material. The groundsheet and air mattress enclosed within his backpack are a medium gray. His M-16 rifle is black, and his jungle boots are light brown with dark brown heels and toes. On his right sleeve he wears the shoulder patch of the division—a white eagle's head with yellow beak within a black shield. His machete has a steel blade and a black handle.

ACCLAIM FOR

SWIMSUIT

"Many clever twists...Patterson fans will devour this one in a single sitting."
—*Publishers Weekly*

"Warning: this juicy thriller might cause nightmares."
—*Cosmopolitan*

"An emotional wringer of egotism, fear, and ultimately triumph...The novel is a powerhouse."
—*AudioFile*

"Once again James Patterson has created a masterful tale of cat and mouse."
—lorisreadingcorner.blogspot.com

"A thrilling tale where the pursuit of the *why* is more important than the pursuit of the whodunit."
—Examiner.com

"This is a riveting tale that you'll want to read from cover to cover...Patterson and Paetro have created a frightening scenario and a brilliantly deranged villain who will not soon be forgotten...*Swimsuit* sets a new standard for their joint efforts, one that by turns will heat up and chill the beach this year."
—BookReporter.com

RAVES FOR JAMES PATTERSON

"James Patterson writes his thrillers as if he were building roller coasters. He grounds the stories with a bare-bones plot, then builds them over the top and tries to throw readers for a loop a few times along the way."

—Associated Press

"A must-read author...A master of the craft."

—*Providence Sunday Journal*

"The page-turningest author in the game right now."

—*San Francisco Chronicle*

"James Patterson always delivers a fascinating, action-packed thriller."

—*Midwest Book Review*

"One of the bestselling writers in history."

—*New York Sun*

"Patterson is a master."

—*Toronto Globe and Mail*

A complete list of James Patterson's books is on pages 356–358.
For previews of upcoming books by James Patterson
and more information about the author, visit
www.jamespatterson.com.

JAMES PATTERSON
& MAXINE PAETRO

SWIMSUIT

GRAND CENTRAL
PUBLISHING

NEW YORK BOSTON

This book is a work of fiction. Names, characters, places, and incidents are the product of the author's imagination or are used fictitiously. Any resemblance to actual events, locales, or persons, living or dead, is coincidental.

Copyright © 2009 by James Patterson
Excerpt from *Toys* copyright © 2011 by James Patterson
All rights reserved. Except as permitted under the U.S. Copyright Act of 1976, no part of this publication may be reproduced, distributed, or transmitted in any form or by any means, or stored in a database or retrieval system, without the prior written permission of the publisher.

Toys illustrations by Danny O'Leary New York City

Grand Central Publishing
Hachette Book Group
237 Park Avenue
New York, NY 10017
Visit our website at www.HachetteBookGroup.com

Grand Central Publishing is a division of Hachette Book Group, Inc.
The Grand Central Publishing name and logo is a trademark of Hachette Book Group, Inc.

Printed in the United States of America

The publisher is not responsible for websites (or their content) that are not owned by the publisher.

Originally published in hardcover by Little, Brown and Company
First International mass market edition, May 2010
First United States mass market edition, February 2011

10 9 8 7 6 5 4 3 2 1

ATTENTION CORPORATIONS AND ORGANIZATIONS: Most HACHETTE BOOK GROUP books are available at quantity discounts with bulk purchase for educational, business, or sales promotional use. For information, please call or write:
Special Markets Department, Hachette Book Group
237 Park Avenue, New York, NY 10017
Telephone: 1-800-222-6747 Fax: 1-800-477-5925

To the home team:
Suzie and John, Brendan and Jack

Prologue

JUST THE FACTS

I KNOW THINGS I don't want to know.

A true psychopathic killer is nothing like your everyday garden-variety murderer. Not like a holdup guy who panics and unloads his gun into a hapless liquor store clerk, or a man who bursts into his stockbroker's office and blows his head off, and he's not like a husband who strangles his wife over a real or imagined affair.

Psychopaths aren't motivated by love or fear or rage or hatred. They don't feel those emotions.

They don't feel anything at all. Trust me on that one.

Gacy, Bundy, Dahmer, BTK, and the other all-stars in the twisted-killer league were detached, driven by sexual pleasure and the thrill of the kill. If you thought you saw remorse in Ted Bundy's eyes after he'd confessed to killing thirty young women, it was in your own mind, because what distinguishes psychopaths from all other killers is that they don't care at all. Not about their victims' lives. Not about their deaths.

But psychopaths can *pretend* to care. They mimic

human emotion to pass among us and to lure their prey. Closer and closer. And after they've killed, it's on to the next new and better thrill, with no boundaries, no taboos, no holds barred.

I've been told that it's "distracting" to be so consumed by appetite, and so psychopaths screw up.

Sometimes they make a mistake.

You may remember back to the spring of 2008 when the swimsuit model Kim McDaniels was abducted from a sandy beach in Hawaii. No ransom demand was ever made. The local cops were slow, arrogant, and clueless, and there were no witnesses or informants who had any idea who had kidnapped that beautiful and talented young woman.

At that time, I was an ex-cop turned mystery writer, but since my last book had gone almost straight from the shipping carton to the remainder racks, I was a third-strike novelist doing the next best thing to writing pulp fiction.

I was reporting crime for the *L.A. Times,* which, on the upside, was how the highly successful novelist Michael Connelly got his start.

I was at my desk twenty-four hours after Kim went missing. I was filing yet another routinely tragic story of a drive-by fatality when my editor, Daniel Aronstein, leaned into my cube, said "Catch," and tossed me a ticket to Maui.

I was almost forty then, going numb from crime scene fatigue, still telling myself that I was perfectly positioned to hook a book idea that would turn my life around one more time. It was a lie I *believed* because it anchored my fraying hope for a better future.

The weird thing is, when the big idea called me out—I never saw it coming.

Aronstein's ticket to Hawaii gave me a much-needed hit. I sensed a five-star boondoggle, featuring oceanfront bars and half-naked girls. And I saw myself jousting with the competition—all that, and the *L.A. Times* was picking up the tab.

I grabbed that airline ticket and flew off to the biggest story of my career.

Kim McDaniels's abduction was a flash fire, a white-hot tale with an unknown shelf life. Every news outlet on the planet was already on the story when I joined the gaggle of reporters at the police cordon outside the Wailea Princess.

At first, I thought what all the journos thought, that Kim had probably been drinking, got picked up by some bad boys, that they'd raped her, silenced her, dumped her. That the "Missing Beauty" would be top o' the news for a week, or a month, until some celebrity bigot or the Department of Homeland Security grabbed back the front page.

But, still, I had my self-delusion to support and an expense account to justify, so I bulled my way into the black heart of a vile and compelling crime spree.

In so doing, and not by my own devising, I became *part* of the story, selected by a profoundly psychotic killer with a cherished self-delusion of his own.

The book you hold in your hands is the true story of a skillful, elusive, and, most would say, first-rate monster who called himself Henri Benoit. As Henri told me himself, *"Jack the Ripper never dreamed of killing like this."*

For months now, I've been living in a remote location getting "Henri's" story down. There are frequent electrical brownouts in this place, so I've gotten handy with a manual typewriter.

Turns out I didn't need Google because what isn't in my tapes and notes and clippings is permanently imprinted on my brain.

Swimsuit is about an unprecedented pattern killer who upped the ante to new heights, an assassin like no other before or since. I've taken some literary license in telling his story because I can't know what Henri or his victims were thinking in a given moment.

Don't worry about that, not even for a second, because what Henri told me in his own words was proven by the facts.

And the facts tell the truth.

And the truth will blow your mind, as it did mine.

—*Benjamin L. Hawkins*
May 2009

Part One

THE CAMERA LOVES HER

Chapter 1

KIM McDANIELS WAS BAREFOOT and wearing a blue-and-white-striped Juicy Couture minidress when she was awoken by a thump against her hip, a *bruising* thump. She opened her eyes in the blackness, as questions broke the surface of her mind.

Where was she? What the hell was going on?

She wrestled with the blanket draped over her head, finally got her face free, realized a couple of new things. Her hands and feet were *bound*. And she was in some kind of cramped compartment.

Another thump jolted her, and Kim yelled this time, "*Hey!*"

Her shout went nowhere, muffled by the confined space, the vibration of an engine. She realized she was inside the trunk of a car. But that made no freaking sense! She told herself to *wake up!*

But she *was* awake, feeling the bumps for real, and so she fought, twisting her wrists against a knotted nylon rope that didn't give. She rolled onto her back, tucking her knees to her chest, then *bam!* She kicked up at the lid of the trunk, not budging it a fraction of an inch.

She did it again, again, *again,* and now pain was shooting from her soles to her hips, but she was still locked up, and now she was hurting. Panic seized her and shook her hard.

She was *caught.* She was *trapped.* She didn't know how this had happened or why, but she wasn't dead and she wasn't injured. She *would* get away.

Using her bound hands as a claw, Kim felt around for a toolbox, a jack or a crowbar, but she found nothing, and the air was getting thin and foul as she panted alone in the dark.

Why was she here?

Kim searched for her last memory, but her mind was sluggish, as if a blanket had been thrown over her brain, too. She could only guess that she'd been drugged. Someone had slipped her a roofie, but who? When?

"Hellllllllpppp! Let me out!" she yelled, kicking out at the trunk lid, banging her head against a hard metal ridge. Her eyes were filling with tears and she was getting mad now on top of being scared out of her mind.

Through her tears, Kim felt a five-inch-long bar just above her. It had to be the interior trunk release lever, and she whispered, *"Thank you, God."*

Chapter 2

KIM'S CLAW-HANDS TREMBLED as she reached up, hooked her fingertips over the lever, and pulled down. The bar moved—too easily—and it didn't pop the lid.

She tried again, pulling repeatedly, frantically working against her certain knowledge that the release bar had been disabled, that the cable had been cut—when Kim felt the car wheels leave the asphalt. The ride smoothed out, and that made her think the car might be rolling over sand.

Was it going into the ocean?

Was she going to drown in this trunk?

She screamed again, a loud, wordless shriek of terror that turned into a gibbering prayer, *Dear God, let me out of this alive, and I promise you*—and when her scream ran out, she heard music coming from behind her head. It was a female vocalist, something bluesy, a song she didn't know.

Who was driving the car? Who had done this to her? For what possible reason?

And now her mind was clearing, running back, flipping through the images of the past hours.

She started to remember. She'd been up at three. Makeup at four. On the beach at five. She and Julia and Darla and Monique and that other gorgeous but weird girl, Ayla. Gils, the photographer, had been drinking coffee with the crew, and men had been hanging around the edges, towel boys and early morning joggers agog at the girls in their little bikinis, at the wonder of stumbling onto a *Sporting Life* swimsuit shoot right *there*.

Kim pictured the moments, posing with Julia, Gils saying, *"Less smile, Julia. That's great. Beautiful, Kim, beautiful, that's the girl. Eyes to me. That's perfect."*

She remembered that the phone calls had come after that, during breakfast and throughout the whole day.

Ten freaking calls until she turned off her phone.

Douglas had been calling her, paging her, stalking her, driving her crazy. It was Doug!

And she thought about earlier that night, after dinner, how she'd been in the hotel bar with the art director, Del Swann. It was his job to oversee the shoot and be her chaperone afterward. But Del had gone to the men's room, and somehow he and Gils, both of them as gay as birds, disappeared.

And she remembered that Julia was talking with a guy at the bar, and she'd *tried* to get Julia's attention but Julia wouldn't make eye contact . . . so Kim had gone for a walk on the beach. . . . *And that was all she remembered.*

Her cell phone had been clipped to her belt but switched off. And now she was thinking that Doug had flipped out, rage-aholic that he was—stalker that he'd become. Maybe he'd paid someone to put something into her drink.

She was getting it together now. Brain working fine.

She shouted, *"Douglas? Dougie?"*

And then, as though God Himself had finally heard her calling, *a cell phone rang inside the trunk.*

Chapter 3

KIM HELD HER breath and listened.

A phone rang, *but it wasn't her ringtone.* This was a low-pitched burr, not four bars of Weezer's "Beverly Hills," but if it was like most phones, it was programmed to send calls to voice mail after three rings.

She couldn't let that happen!

Where was the damned phone?

She fumbled with the blanket, ropes chafing her wrists. She reached down, pawed at the flooring, felt the lump under a flap of carpet near the edge, bumped it farther away with her clumsy... *oh no!*

The second ring ended, the third ring was starting, and her frenzy was sending her heart rate out of control when she grasped the phone, a thick, old-fashioned thing, clutched it with her shaking fingers, sweat slicking her wrists.

She saw the illuminated caller ID number, but there was no name, and she didn't recognize the number.

But it didn't matter *who* it was. Anyone would do.

Kim pushed the Send button, pressed the phone to her ear, called out hoarsely, "Hello? *Hello? Who's there?*"

But instead of an answer, Kim heard singing, this time Whitney Houston, "I'll al-ways love you-ou-ou" coming from the car stereo, only louder and more clearly.

He was calling her from the front seat of the car! She shouted over Whitney's voice, "Dougie? Dougie, what the hell? *Answer me.*"

But he didn't answer, and Kim was quaking in the cramped trunk, tied up like a chicken, sweating like a pig, Whitney's voice seeming to taunt her.

"Doug! What do you think you're doing?"

And then she knew. He was showing her what it was like to be ignored, teaching her a lesson, but *he wouldn't win.* They were on an island, right? How far could they go?

So Kim used her anger to fuel the brain that had gotten her into Columbia premed, thinking now about how to turn Doug around. She'd have to play him, say how sorry she was, and explain sweetly that he had to understand *it wasn't her fault.* She tried it out in her mind.

See, Dougie, I'm not allowed to take calls. My contract strictly forbids me to tell anyone where we're shooting. I could get fired. You understand, don't you?

She'd make him see that even though they'd broken up, that even though he was *crazy* for what he was doing to her, *criminal* for God's sake, he was still her darling.

But—and this was her plan—once he gave her an opportunity, she'd knee him in the balls or kick in his kneecaps. She knew enough judo to disable him—as big as he was. Then she'd run for her life. And then the cops would bury him!

"Dougie?" she yelled into the phone. "Will you please answer me? Please. This really isn't funny."

Suddenly the music volume went down.

Once again, she held her breath in the dark and listened over the pulse booming in her ears. And this time, a voice spoke to her, a *man's voice*, and it was warm, almost loving.

"Actually, Kim, it *is* kind of funny, and it's kind of wonderfully romantic, too."

Kim didn't recognize the voice.

Because it wasn't Doug's.

Chapter 4

A NEW KIND of fear swept through Kim like a cold fire, and she started to pass out. But she got a grip on herself, squeezed her knees together hard, bit her hand, and kept herself awake. And she replayed the voice in her head again.

"It is *kind of funny, and it's kind of wonderfully romantic, too.*"

She didn't know that voice, didn't know it at all.

Everything she'd envisioned a moment ago, Doug's *face*, his *weakness* for her, her learning how to win him over when he got out of control—that was all *gone.*

Here was the new truth.

A complete stranger had tied her up and thrown her into the trunk of his car. She'd been *kidnapped*—but why? Her parents weren't rich! What was he going to do to her? How was she going to escape? She was—but how?

Kim listened in silence before asking, "Who is this?"

The voice was mellow and calm when he spoke again.

"Sorry to be so rude, Kim. I'll introduce myself in a minute or two. It won't be very long now. And don't worry. Everything's going to be fine."

The line went dead.

Kim blanked when the phone call cut off. It was as if her mind had been disconnected, too. Then the thoughts tumbled in. She found hope in the stranger's reassurance. So she clung to it. He was acting... nice. He'd said, *"Everything's going to be fine."*

The car took a hard left, and Kim rolled against the side of the trunk, braced her feet against the wall of the compartment. And she realized that she was still gripping the phone!

She held the keypad close to her face. She could barely read the numbers by the pale light of the faceplate, but she still managed to punch in 911.

She listened to the three rings, then four, and then the operator's voice. "Nine-one-one. What's your emergency?"

"My name is Kim McDaniels. I've been—"

"I didn't get that. Please spell your name."

Kim rolled forward as the car came to a stop. Then the driver's side door slammed—and she heard the key turning in the trunk lock.

Kim gripped the phone tighter, scared that the operator's voice would be loud enough to give her away, but more scared that if she hung up she'd lose the GPS connection between herself and the police, her best hope of rescue.

The phone call could be traced. That was correct, wasn't it?

"I've been kidnapped," she spat.

The key was turned, left and right, the lock not

quite unlatching, and in that fraction of a minute Kim desperately revisited her plan. It was still good. Say her kidnapper wanted to have sex with her. She could survive that, obviously, but she had to be smart, make him her friend, remember everything so she could tell the police.

The trunk lid lifted, and moonlight spilled over her feet.

And Kim's plan to seduce her abductor flew out of her mind. She hauled back her knees and kicked hard at the man's thighs. He jumped back, avoiding her feet, and before she could see his face, the blanket was thrown over hers, the cell phone ripped from her hands.

Then—there was the prick of a needle in her thigh.

Kim heard his voice as her head rolled back and the light faded.

"Fighting me is pointless, Kim. This isn't about you and me. It's a whole lot bigger than that, trust me. But, then, why should you trust me?"

Chapter 5

KIM CAME TO consciousness.

She was lying faceup on a bed inside a glowing, yellow-painted room. Her arms were tied and anchored behind her head. Her legs, a long way away, were roped to the metal frame of a bed. A white satin sheet was tucked under her chin, draped between her legs. She couldn't be a hundred percent sure, but she thought she was naked under the sheet.

She pulled at the rope holding her arms behind her, and she got terrifying glimmers of what might happen to her next, nothing that matched the man's promise that "everything's going to be fine." Then she heard grunts and squeals coming from her throat, sounds she'd never made before.

She got nowhere with the ropes, so she lifted her head and as best she could, looked around the room. It seemed unreal, like a stage set.

To the right side of the bed were two closed windows, hung with gauzy curtains. There was a table beneath the windows loaded with lit candles of all heights and colors, and there were tropical flowers.

Birds-of-paradise and ginger—very masculine to her eyes, sexual really—stood erect in a vase beside the bed.

Another look around, and she took in cameras, two of them. Professional grade, mounted on tripods on either side of her.

She saw lights on stands and a sound boom she hadn't noticed at first, positioned above her head.

She became aware of the roar of surf, loud, as if the waves were crashing against the walls. And there she was, pinned like a butterfly at the center of it all.

Kim took in a deep breath, and screamed, "HELP MEEEEEE."

When her scream faded, a man's voice came from behind her head. "Hey, hey. Kim. No one can *hear* you."

Kim turned her head harder to the left, stretched her neck with tremendous effort, and saw a man sitting in a chair. He was wearing earphones, and he pulled them down from his head so that they were resting on his collarbones.

Her first look at the man who'd taken her.

She didn't know him.

He had medium-length hair, was maybe in his late thirties. He had regular features that could almost be called handsome. He was muscular, wearing form-fitting, expensive-looking clothes, a gold watch she'd seen in *Vanity Fair*. Patek Philippe. The man in the chair looked to her like the actor who played the lead in the latest James Bond movie, Daniel Craig.

He put the earphones back on and closed his eyes as he listened. He was *ignoring* her.

"Hey! Mister! *I'm talking to you!*" Kim shouted.

"You should hear this," the man said. He named the music, told her that he knew the artist, that this was a first studio cut.

He stood, brought the headphones over to her, and put one of the earpieces against her ear.

"Isn't that great?"

Kim's escape plan evaporated. She'd missed her big chance at seduction. She thought, *Whatever he wants to do, he's going to do*. But she could still beg for her life. Tell him it will be more fun if she participated—but her mind was scrambled from the injection he gave her and she felt woozy, too weak to move.

She looked into the man's light gray eyes, and he looked back as though he felt affection for her. Maybe she could use that. She said, "Listen to me. People know I'm missing. Important people. Life Incorporated. You've heard of them? I have a curfew. All the models do. The police are already looking for me . . ."

"James Blond," as she suddenly thought of him, said to her, "I wouldn't worry about the police, Kim. I was very careful." He sat beside her on the bed, placed his hand on her cheek admiringly. Then he put on blue latex gloves.

He lifted something from a nail in the wall, a mask of some sort, and when he put it on, his features became distorted. And *very* scary.

"*What are you doing? What are you doing?*"

Kim's screams ricocheted around the small room. The man said, "That was *great*. Could you do that again? Are you ready, Kim?"

He walked around to each of the cameras,

checked the angle through the lenses, turned them on. The bright lights blazed.

Kim followed the blue gloves as they whisked the satin sheet away from her body. It was cool in the room, but the sweat immediately beaded up on her skin. She knew.

He was going to rape her.

"You don't have to do this," she said.

"I *do*."

Kim started keening, a whimper that rose to a cry. She turned her face away, stared toward the closed windows, heard the nameless stranger's belt buckle hit the floor. She began sobbing without reservation as she felt the drag of latex running over her breasts, the feeling in her groin as he opened her with his mouth, the blunt feel of him pushing his way in, her muscles tightening to stop him from entering her.

His breath was soft against her face as he spoke into her ear.

"Just go along with this, Kim. Just go along. I'm sorry, but it's a job I'm doing for a lot of money. These people watching are big fans of yours. Try to understand."

"I want you to *die*," she said. She bit down on his wrist, drawing blood, and then he hit her, slapped her hard on each of her cheeks. Tears made her skin sting.

She wanted to pass out, but she was still conscious, very much under the blond stranger's body, hearing him grunting, feeling—too much. So she did her best to block out everything but the sound of the waves and thoughts about what she would do to him when she got away.

Chapter 6

WHEN KIM WOKE UP she was sitting in a bathtub of warm water, leaning with her back against the sloping rim, her hands tied under the suds.

The blond stranger was on a stool beside her, washing her with a sea sponge as naturally as though he'd bathed her many times before.

Kim's stomach heaved, and she vomited bile into the tub. The stranger stood her up in one powerful swoop, saying "Alley Oops," and she noticed again how strong he was. This time she heard a hint of an accent but couldn't place it. Maybe Russian. Or Czech. Or German. Then he pulled the bathtub plug and turned on the shower.

Kim swayed under the spray, and he held her up, supported her body as she cried out and hit at him, trying to kick but losing her footing. She started to go down, and he caught her again, laughing, saying, "You're a little something special, aren't you?"

Then he wrapped her in very plush white towels, swaddled her like a baby. When he settled her on the closed toilet seat, he held out a glass of something for her to drink.

"Take this," he said. "It will help you. Honestly it will."

Kim shook her head, said, "Who are you? Why are you doing this to me?"

"Do you want to remember this evening, Kim?"

"You've got to be kidding, you effing pervert."

"This drink will help you forget. And I want you to be asleep when I take you home."

"When are you taking me home?"

"It's almost over," he said.

Kim raised her hands toward him, noticing that the rope binding her wrists together was different now. It was dark blue, possibly silk, and the pattern of knots was intricate, almost beautiful. She took the glass from him and emptied it down.

Next the stranger asked her to bend her head forward. She did, and he towel-dried her hair. Then he brushed it, making tendrils and curls with his fingers, and he brought bottles and brushes out of the long drawer of the vanity surrounding the sink.

He applied makeup to her cheeks and lips and eyes with a deft hand, dabbing a little concealer at a raw place near her left eye, wetting the brush with his tongue, blending the foundation in, saying, "I'm very good at this, don't worry."

He finished his work, then reached his arms around and under her, lifted her towel-wrapped body, and carried her into the other room.

Kim's head lolled back as he placed her on the bed. She was aware that he was dressing her, but she didn't assist him at all as he pulled a bikini bottom up her thighs. Then he tied the strap of the swimsuit top behind her back.

The suit looked to Kim a lot like the Perry Ellis she'd been wearing toward the end of the shoot. Red with a silver sheen. She must have mumbled, "Perry Ellis," because James Blond said, "It's even better. I picked this out myself when I was in Saint-Tropez. I got it just for you."

"You don't know me," she said, the words pouring sideways out of her mouth.

"Everyone knows you, honey. Kimberly McDaniels. What a beautiful name, too." He moved her hair to one side and knotted a second swimsuit tie behind her neck, tied a bow, apologized if he'd pulled at her hair.

Kim wanted to make a remark, but she forgot what she was going to say. She couldn't move. She couldn't scream. She could barely keep her eyes open. She looked into the pale gray eyes that caressed her.

He said, "Stunning. You look so beautiful for your close-up."

She tried to say, "Screw you," but the words blended together and came out as a long, tired sigh. "Scoooooooo."

Part Two

FLY BY NIGHT

Chapter 7

A MAN STOOD at the edge of a lava-rock seawall staring out at the dark water and at the clouds turning pink as dawn stormed Maui's eastern shore.

His name was Henri Benoit, not his real name, but the name he was using now. He was in his thirties with medium-length blondish hair and light gray eyes, and he stood at about six feet tall in his bare feet. He was shoeless now, his toes half-buried in the sand.

His white linen shirt hung loosely over his gray cotton pants, and he watched the seabirds calling out as they skimmed the waves.

Henri thought those birdcalls could have been the opening notes of another flawless day in paradise. But before the day had even begun, it was down the crapper.

Henri turned away from the ocean and jammed his PDA into a trouser pocket. Then, as the wind at his back blew his shirt into a kind of spinnaker, he strode up the sloping lawn to his private bungalow.

He swung open the screened door, crossed the lanai and the pale hardwood floors to the kitchen, poured himself a cup of Kona java. Then out again to the lanai, where he sank down into the chaise beside the hot tub and settled in to think.

This place, the Hana Beach Hotel, was at the top of his A-list: exclusive, comfortable, no TV or even a telephone. Surrounded by a few thousand acres of rain forest, perched on the coast of the island, the unobtrusive cluster of buildings made a perfect haven for the very rich.

Being here gave a man a chance to relax fully, to be whoever he truly was, to realize his essence as a human.

The cell phone call from Europe had shot his relaxation all to hell. The conversation had been brief and essentially one-way. Horst had delivered both the good and bad news in a tone of voice that attacked Henri's sense of free agency with the finesse of a shiv through a vital organ.

Horst had told Henri that the job he had done had been well received, but there were *issues*.

Horst's buddies weren't quite happy enough. They wanted *more*. More twists. More action. More clapping at the end of the movie.

"Use your imagination, Henri. Surprise us."

They would pay more, of course, for additional contracted services, and after a while the prospect of more *money* softened the edges of Henri's bad mood.

They wanted more?

So be it.

By the time his second cup of coffee was finished, he had mapped out a new plan. He dug a wireless phone out of his pocket and began making calls.

Chapter 8

THAT NIGHT SNOW FELL LIGHTLY on Levon and Barbara McDaniels's house in Cascade Township, a wooded suburb of Grand Rapids, Michigan. Inside their efficient but cozy three-bedroom brick home, the two boys slept deeply under their quilts.

Down the hall, Levon and Barbara lay back-to-back, soles touching across the invisible divide of their Sleep Number bed, their twenty-five-year connection seemingly unbroken even in sleep.

Barbara's night table was stacked with magazines and half-read paperbacks, folders of tests and memos, a crowd of vitamin supplements around her bottle of green tea. *Don't worry about it, Levon, and please don't touch anything. I know where everything is.*

Levon's nightstand favored his left brain to Barb's right: his neat stack of annual reports, annotated copy of *Against All Reason*, pen and notepad, and a platoon of electronics—phones, laptop, weather clock—all lined up four inches from the table's edge, plugged into a power strip behind the lamp.

The snowfall had wrapped the house in a white silence—and then a ringing phone jarred Levon awake. His heartbeat boomed, and his mind reeled in instant panic. *What was happening?*

Again the phone rang, and this time Levon made a grab for the landline.

He glanced at the clock, which read 3:14 a.m., and wondered who the hell would be calling at this hour. And then he knew. It was Kim. She was five hours behind them. He figured she'd gotten that mixed up somehow.

"Kim? Honey?" Levon said into the mouth-piece.

"Kim is gone," said the male voice in Levon's ear.

Levon's chest tightened, and he couldn't catch his breath. Was he having a heart attack? "Sorry? What did you say?"

Barb sat up in bed, turned on the light.

"Levon?" she said. "What is it?"

Levon held up a hand. *Give me a second.* "Who is this?" he asked, rubbing his chest to ease the pain.

"I only have a minute, so listen carefully. I'm calling from Hawaii. Kim's disappeared. She's fallen into bad hands."

Levon's fear filled him from scalp to toes with a cold terror. He clung to the phone, hearing the echo of the man's voice: *"She's fallen into bad hands."*

It made no sense.

"I don't get you. Is she hurt?"

No answer.

"Hello?"

"Are you listening to what I'm saying, Mr. McDaniels?"

"Yes. Who is this speaking, please?"

"I can only tell you once."

Levon pulled at the neck of his T-shirt, trying to decide what to think. Was the man a liar, or telling the truth? He knew his name, phone number, that Kim was in Hawaii. How did he know all that?

Barb was asking him, *"What's happening? Levon, is this about Kim?"*

"Kim didn't show up at the shoot yesterday morning," said the caller. "The magazine is keeping it quiet. Crossing their fingers. Hoping she'll come back."

"Have the police been called? Has someone called the police?"

"I'm hanging up now," said the caller. "But if I were you, I'd get on the next plane to Maui. You and Barbara."

"Wait! Please, wait. How do you know she's missing?"

"Because I did it, sir. I saw her. I liked her. I took her. Have a nice day."

Chapter 9

"WHAT DO YOU WANT? Tell me what you *want!*"

There was a *click* in Levon's ear followed by a dial tone. He toggled the directory button, read "Unknown" where there should have been a caller ID.

Barb was pulling at his arm. "Levon! *Tell me! What's happened?*"

Barb liked to say that she was the flamethrower in the family and that he was the fireman—and those roles had become fixed over time. So Levon began to tell Barb what the caller had said, strained the fear out of his voice, kept to the facts.

Barb's face reflected the terror leaping inside his own mind like a bonfire. Her voice came through to him as if from a far distance. "Did you *believe* him? Did he say where she *was?* Did he say what happened? My God, what are we talking about?"

"All he said is she's gone…"

"She never goes anywhere without her cell," Barb said, starting now to gasp for breath, her asthma kicking in.

Levon bolted out of bed, knocked things off Barb's night table, spilling pills and papers all over the carpet. He picked the inhaler out of the jumble, handed it to Barb, watched her take in a long pull.

Tears ran down her face.

He reached out his arms for her, and she went to him, cried into his chest, "Please…just call her."

Levon snatched the phone off the blanket, punched in Kim's number, counted out the interminable rings, two, then three, looking at the clock, doing the math. It was just after ten at night in Hawaii.

Then Kim's voice was in his ear.

"Kim!" he shouted.

Barb clapped her hands over her face in relief—but Levon realized his mistake.

"It's only a message," he said to Barb, hearing Kim's recorded voice. "Leave your name and number and I'll call you back. Byeeee."

"Kim, it's *Dad*. Are you okay? We'd like to hear from you. Don't worry about the time. Just call. Everybody here is fine. Love you, honey. Dad."

Barb was crying. "Oh, my God. Oh, my God," she repeated as she balled up the comforter, pressing it to her face.

"We don't know anything, Barb," he said. "He could be some moron with a sick sense of humor—"

"Oh, God, Levon. Try her hotel room."

Sitting at the edge of the bed, staring down at the nubby carpet between his feet, Levon called information. He jotted down the number, disconnected the line, then dialed the Wailea Princess in Maui.

When the operator came on, he asked for Kim McDaniels, got five distant rings in a room four thousand miles away, and then a machine answered. "Please leave a message for the occupant of Room Three-fourteen. Or press zero for the operator."

Levon's chest pains were back and he was short of breath. He said into the mouthpiece, "Kim, call Mom and Dad. It's important." He stabbed the 0 button until the lilting voice of the hotel operator came back on the line.

He asked the operator to ring Carol Sweeney's room, the booker from the modeling agency, who'd accompanied Kim to Hawaii and was supposed to be there as her chaperone.

There was no answer in Carol's room, either. Levon left a message: "Carol, this is Levon McDaniels, Kim's dad. Please call when you get this. Don't worry about the time. We're up. Here's my cell phone number…"

Then he got the operator again.

"We need help," he said. "Please connect me to the manager. This is an emergency."

Chapter 10

LEVON McDANIELS WAS SQUARE-JAWED, just over six feet, a muscular 165 pounds. He had always been known as a straight shooter, decisive, thoughtful, a good leader, but sitting in his red boxers, holding a dinky cordless phone that didn't connect to Kim—he felt nauseated and powerless.

As he waited for hotel security to go to Kim's room and report back to the manager, Levon's imagination fired off images of his daughter, hurt, or the captive of some freaking maniac who was planning God only knew what.

Time passed, probably only a few minutes, but Levon imagined himself rocketing across the Pacific Ocean, bounding up the stairs of the hotel, and kicking open Kim's door. Seeing her peacefully asleep, her phone switched off.

"Mr. McDaniels, Security is on the other line. The bed is still made up. Your daughter's belongings look undisturbed. Would you like us to notify the police?"

"Yes. Right away. Thank you. Could you say and spell your name for me?"

Levon booked a room, then phoned United Airlines, kept pressing zeros until he got a human voice.

Beside him, Barb's breathing was wet, her cheeks shining with tears. Her graying braid was coming undone as she repeatedly pushed her fingers through it. Barb's suffering was right out in the open, and she didn't know any other way. You always knew how she felt and where you stood with Barb.

"The more I think about it," she said, her voice coming between jerky sobs, "the more I think it's a lie. If he took her ... he'd want money, and he didn't ask for that, Levon. So ... *why would he call us?*"

"I just don't know, Barb. It doesn't make sense to me either."

"What time is it there?"

"Ten thirty p.m."

"She probably went for a ride with some cute guy. Got a flat tire. Couldn't get a cell phone signal, something like that. She's probably all worked up about missing the shoot. You *know* how she is. She's probably stuck somewhere and *furious* with herself."

Levon had held back the truly terrifying part of the phone call. He hadn't told Barb that the caller had said that Kim had fallen into "bad hands." How would that help Barb? He couldn't bring himself to say it.

"We have to keep our heads on straight," he said.

Barb nodded. "Absolutely. Oh, we're going over there, Levon. But Kim is going to be as mad as *bees* that you told the hotel to call the police. Watch out when Kim's mad."

Levon smiled.

"I'll shower after you," Barb said.

Levon came out of the bathroom five minutes later, shaven, his damp brown hair standing up around the bald spot at the back. He tried to picture the Wailea Princess as he dressed, saw frozen postcard images of honeymooners walking the beach at sunset. He thought of never seeing Kim again, and a knifing terror cut through him.

Please, God, oh, please, don't let anything happen to Kim.

Barb showered quickly, dressed n a blue sweater, gray slacks, flat shoes. Her expression was wide-eyed shock, but she was past the hysteria, her excellent mind in gear.

"I packed underwear and toothbrushes and that's all, Levon. We'll get what we need in Maui."

It was 3:45 in Cascade Township. Less than an hour had passed since the anonymous phone call had cracked open the night and spilled the McDanielses out into a terrifying unknown.

"You call Cissy," Barb said. "I'll wake the kids."

Chapter 11

BARBARA SIGHED UNDER HER BREATH, then turned up the dimmer, gradually lighting the boys' room. Greg groaned, pulled the Spider-Man quilt over his head, but Johnny sat straight up, his fourteen-year-old face alert to something different, new, and maybe exciting.

Barb shook Greg's shoulder gently. "Sweetie, wake up now."

"Mommmmm, nooooo."

Barb peeled down her younger son's blanket, explained to both boys a version of the story that she halfway believed. That she and Dad were going to Hawaii to visit Kim.

Her sons became attentive immediately, bombarding Barb with questions until Levon walked in, his face taut, and Greg, seeing that, shouted, "Dad! What's goin' on?"

Barb swooped Greg into her arms, said that everything was fine, that Aunt Cissy and Uncle Dave were waiting for them, that they could be asleep again in fifteen minutes. They could stay in their pj's but they had to put on shoes and coats.

Johnny pleaded to come with them to Hawaii, made a case involving Jet Skis and snorkeling, but Barb, holding back tears, said "not this time" and busied herself with socks and shoes and tooth-brushes and Game Boys.

"You're not telling us something, Mom. It's still dark!"

"There's no time to go into it, Johnny. Every-thing's okay. We've just—gotta catch a plane."

Ten minutes later, five blocks away, Christine and David waited outside their front door as the arctic air sweeping across Lake Michigan put down a fine white powder over their lawn.

Levon watched Cissy run down the steps to meet their car as it turned in at the driveway. Cissy was two years younger than Barb, with the same heart-shaped face, and Levon saw Kim in her fea-tures, too.

Cissy reached out and enfolded the kids as they dashed toward her. She lifted her arms and took in Barb and Levon, as Barb said, "I forwarded our phone to yours, Cis. In case you get a *call*." Barb didn't want to spell it out in front of the boys. She wasn't sure Cis got it yet either.

"Call me between planes," Cis said.

Dave held out an envelope to Levon. "Here's some cash, about a thousand. No, no, take it. You could need it when you get there. Cabs and what-ever. Levon, take it."

Fierce hugs were exchanged and wishes for a safe flight and love-you's rang out loudly in the morn-ing stillness. When Cissy and David's front door closed, Levon told Barb to strap in.

He backed the Suburban out of the drive, then

turned onto Burkett Road, heading toward Gerald R. Ford International Airport, ramping the car up to ninety on the straightaway.

"Slow down, Levon."

"Okay."

But he kept his foot on the gas, driving fast into the star field of snow that somehow kept his mind balanced on the brink of terror rather than letting it topple into the abyss.

"I'll call the bank when we change planes in L.A.," Levon said. "Talk to Bill Macchio, get a loan started against the house in case we need cash."

He saw tears dropping from Barb's face into her lap, heard the click of her fingernails tapping on her BlackBerry, sending text messages to everyone in the family, to her friends, to her job. To Kim.

Barb called Kim's cell phone again as Levon parked the car, held up the phone so Levon could hear the mechanical voice saying, "The mailbox belonging to—*Kim McDaniels*—is full. No messages can be left at this time."

Chapter 12

THE McDANIELSES HOPSCOTCHED by air from Grand Rapids to Chicago and from there to their wait-listed flight to Los Angeles, which connected just in time to their flight to Honolulu. Once in Honolulu, they ran through the airport, tickets and IDs in their hands, making Island Air's turbo prop plane. They were the last people on, settling into their bulkhead seats before the doors to the puddle jumper closed with a startling bang.

They were now only forty minutes from Maui.

Only forty minutes from Kim.

Since leaving Grand Rapids, Barbara and Levon had slept in snatches. So much time had elapsed since the phone call that it was starting to feel unreal.

They now spun the idea that after Kim had given them hell for coming there, they'd be laughing about all of this, showing off a snapshot of Kim with that "oh, please" look on her face and standing between her parents, all of them wearing leis, typical happy tourists in Hawaii.

And then they'd swing back to their fear.

Where was Kim? Why couldn't they reach her? Why was there no return call from her on their home phone or Levon's cell?

As the airplane sailed above the clouds, Barb said, "I've been thinking about the bike."

Levon nodded, took her hand.

What they called "the bike" had started with another terrible phone call, seven years ago, this time from the police. Kim had been fourteen. She'd been riding her bike after school, wearing a muffler around her neck. The end of the scarf, whipping back behind her, got wrapped around the rear wheel, choking Kim, pulling her off the bike and hurling her onto the roadside.

A woman driving along saw the bike in the road, pulled up, and found Kim lying up against a tree, unconscious. That woman, Anne Clohessy, had called 911, and when the ambulance came, the EMTs couldn't get Kim to come back to consciousness.

Her brain had been deprived of oxygen, the doctors said. She was in a coma. The hospital's posturing told Barb that it might be irreversible.

By the time Levon had been reached at the office, Kim had been medevaced to a trauma unit in Chicago. He and Barb had driven three hours, got to the hospital, and found their daughter in intensive care, groggy but awake, a terrible bruise around her neck, as blue as the scarf that nearly killed her.

But she was alive. She wasn't back to a hundred percent yet, but she'd be fine.

"It was weird inside my head," Kimmy had said then. "It was like dreaming, only much more real. I heard Father Marty talking to me like he was sitting on the end of the bed."

"What did he say, sweetheart?" Barb had asked.

"He said, 'I'm glad you were baptized, Kim.'"

Now Levon took off his glasses, dried his eyes with the back of his hand. Barb passed him a tissue, saying, "I know, sweetie. I know."

This is how they wanted to find Kim now. *Fine.* Levon gave Barb a crooked smile, both of them thinking how the story in the *Chicago Trib* had called her "Miracle Girl," and sometimes they still called her that.

Miracle Girl who got onto the varsity basketball team as a freshman. Miracle Girl who was accepted into Columbia premed. Miracle Girl who'd been picked for the *Sporting Life* swimsuit shoot, the odds a million to one against her.

Levon thought, *What kind of miracle was that?*

Chapter 13

BARB TWISTED A tissue into a knot, and she said to Levon, "I should never have made such a fuss about that modeling agency."

"She wanted to do it, Barb. It's no one's fault. She's always been her own person."

Barb took Kimmy's picture from her purse, a five-by-seven headshot of eighteen-year-old Kim, taken for that agency in Chicago. Levon looked at the picture of Kim wearing a low-cut black sweater, her blond hair falling below her shoulders, the kind of radiant beauty that gave men ideas.

"No modeling after this," Levon said now.

"She's twenty-one, Levon."

"She's going to be a *doctor*. Barb, there's no good reason for her to be modeling anymore. This is the end of it. I'll make her understand."

The flight attendant announced that the plane would be landing momentarily.

Barb raised the shade and Levon looked out at the clouds flowing under the window, the peaks of them looking like they'd been hit with pink spotlights.

As the tiny houses and roads of Maui came into view, Levon turned to his wife, his best pal, his sweetheart.

"How're you doin', hon? Okay?"

"Never better," Barb chirped, attempting a joke. "And you?"

Levon smiled, brought Barb close, and pressed his cheek to hers, smelled the stuff she put in her hair. *What Barb smelled like.* He kissed her, squeezed her hand.

"Hang on," Levon said, as the airplane began its steep, sickening descent. And he sent out a thought to Kim. *We're coming for you, honey. Mom and Dad are coming.*

Chapter 14

THE McDANIELSES STEPPED from the plane's exit door to a wobbly staircase and from there down to the tarmac, the heat suffocating after the chilled air on the plane.

Levon looked around at the volcanic landscape, an astounding difference from Michigan in the black of night, with the snow falling down the back of his shirt collar as he'd hugged his sons good-bye.

He took off his jacket, patted the inside pocket to make sure that their return plane tickets were safe—including the ticket he'd bought for Kim.

The terminal was full of people, the waiting room in the same open-air section as the baggage claim. He and Barb turned cards over to an official in blue, swearing they were not bringing in any fruit, and then they looked for taxi signs.

Levon was walking fast, feeling a heightened need to get to the hotel and not watching his feet when he sidestepped a luggage trolley and just about stumbled over a young girl with yellow braids. She was clutching a fuzzy toy, standing in the middle of everything, just taking it all in. The child looked so self-assured that she reminded Levon again of Kim, and a wave of panic rose in him, making him feel dizzy and sick to his stomach.

Levon swept blindly forward, asking himself if Kim had used up her quota of miracles. Was her borrowed time up? Had the whole family made a tremendous mistake buying into a headline written by a reporter in Chicago, giving all of them a belief that Kim was so miraculous that nothing could ever hurt her?

Levon silently begged God again to please let Kim be safe at the hotel, make her be glad to see her parents, have her say, *I'm so sorry. I didn't mean to make you worry.*

With his arm around Barb, the two headed out of the terminal, but before they reached the taxi rank, they saw a man approaching—a driver holding up a sign with their name.

The driver was taller than Levon. He had dark hair streaked with gray, a mustache, and he wore a chauffeur's cap and livery jacket and alligator cowboy boots with three-inch heels.

He said, "Mr. and Mrs. McDaniels? I'm Marco. The hotel hired me to be your driver. Do you have claim tickets for your luggage?"

"We didn't bring any bags."

"Okay. The car's right outside."

Chapter 15

THE McDANIELSES WALKED behind Marco as Levon noted the driver's odd rolling gait in those cowboy boots and the man's accent, a trace of something—maybe New York or New Jersey.

They crossed the arrival lane to a traffic island where Levon saw a newspaper lying faceup on a bench.

In a heart-stopping double take, he realized that Kim was looking up at him from under the headline.

This was the *Maui News,* and the large black type spelled out, "Missing Beauty."

Levon's thoughts scattered, taking him a few stunned moments to understand that during the eleven or so hours he and Barb had been in transit, Kim had officially gone missing.

She wasn't waiting at the hotel.

Like the caller said, *she was gone.*

Levon grabbed the paper with a trembling hand, his heart bucking as he looked into Kim's smiling eyes, took in the swimsuit she was wearing in this picture, probably taken just a couple of days ago.

Levon folded the newspaper lengthwise, caught up to Marco and Barbara at the car, asked Marco, "Will it take long to get to the hotel?"

"About a half hour, and there's no charge, Mr. McDaniels. The Wailea Princess is paying for as long as you need me."

"Why are they doing that?"

Marco's voice turned soft. "Well, in light of the situation, sir."

He opened the car doors, and Levon and Barbara climbed in, Barb's face crumpling when she took the paper, crying while she read the story as the sedan slipped into the traffic stream.

The car sped onto the highway, and Marco spoke to them, his eyes in the rearview mirror, gently asking if they were comfortable, if they wanted more air or music. Levon thought ahead to checking in at the hotel, then going straight to the police, the whole time feeling as though he'd suffered a battlefield amputation, that a part of him had been brutally severed and that he might not survive.

Eventually, the sedan crawled down what looked like a private road, both sides massed in purple flowering vines. They drove by an artificial waterfall, slowed to a stop in front of the grand porte cochere entryway of the Wailea Princess Hotel.

Levon saw tiled fountains on both sides of the car, bronze statues of Polynesian warriors rising out of the water with spears in their hands on one side, outriggers filled with orchids on the other.

Bellhops in white shirts and short red pants hurried toward the car. Marco opened his door, and as Levon walked around the sedan to help

Barb, he heard his name coming at him from all directions.

People were running toward the hotel entrance — reporters with cameras and microphones.

Racing toward *them*.

Chapter 16

TEN MINUTES LATER, Barb was dazed and jet-lagged as she entered a suite that on another day, and in different circumstances, she would have thought "magnificent." If she had peeked at the rate card behind the door, she would have seen that the charge for the suite was over three thousand dollars a day.

She walked into the heart of the main room, as good as sleepwalking, seeing but not taking in the hand-knotted silk carpet, a pattern of orchids on a pale peach ground; the tapestry-upholstered furnishings; the huge flat-panel television.

She went to the window, looked out at the beauty without really seeing it, *just looking for Kim.*

There was a gorgeous swimming pool below, a complicated shape, like a square laid over a rectangle, with circular Jacuzzis at the shallow end. A fountain, like a champagne glass, in the middle spilled water over the children playing.

She scanned the rows of pure white cabanas around the pool, looking for a young woman in a chaise sipping a drink, Kim sitting at the poolside.

Barb saw several girls, some slimmer or heavier or older or shorter, but none of them Kim.

She looked out beyond the pool, saw a covered walk, wooden steps going down to the beach dotted with palm trees, fronted by the sapphire blue ocean, nothing but water between the edge of the beach and the coast of Japan.

Where was Kim?

Barb wanted to say to Levon, "I feel Kim's presence here," but when she turned, Levon wasn't there.

She noticed an ornate basket of fruit on the table near the window and went to it, heard the toilet flush as she lifted out the note that was in fact a business card with a message written on the back.

Levon, her poor dear husband, his eyes unblinking and pained behind his glasses, came toward her, asking, "What's that, Barb?"

She read out loud, "Dear Mr. and Mrs. McDaniels, please call me. We're here to help in any way we can."

The card was signed, "Susan Gruber, *SL*," and under her name was a room number.

Levon said, "Susan Gruber. She's the editor in chief. I'll call her now."

Barb felt hope. Gruber was in charge. She'd know something.

Fifteen, maybe twenty minutes later, the McDanielses' hotel room was full. Standing room only.

Chapter 17

BARB SAT ON one of the sofas, her hands clasped on her lap, waiting for Susan Gruber, this take-charge New York executive, with her bright white teeth and face as sharp as a blade, to tell them that Kim had had a fight with the photographer, or that she hadn't photographed well enough and so she'd been given the time off — or something, *anything* that would clear it all up, make it so that Kim was simply absent, not missing, not abducted, not in danger.

Gruber was wearing an aquamarine pantsuit and a lot of gold bracelets, and her fingers were cold when she reached out to shake hands with Barbara.

Del Swann, the art director, had dark skin, platinum hair, jewelry in one ear, and he was dressed in fashionably worn-out jeans and a tight black T-shirt. He looked like he was about to have a mental collapse, making Barbara think maybe he knew more than he was saying — or maybe he felt guilty because he was the last one to see Kim.

There were two other men. The senior one was

forty-something, in a gray suit, had corporation written all over him. Barb had met men like this at Levon's Merrill Lynch conventions and business cocktail parties. She thought it was a pretty safe bet that he, and the junior clone standing to his right, were both New York lawyers who'd been overnighted to Maui like a FedEx package in order to cover the magazine's ass.

And Barb looked at Carol Sweeney, a big woman wearing an expensive, if shapeless, black dress. As the booker from the modeling agency who'd landed this job for Kim and had gone on the shoot as Kim's chaperone, Carol looked like she'd swallowed a dog, that's how choked up she was.

Barb couldn't stand to be in the same room with Carol.

The senior suit, Barb forgot his name as soon as she heard it, told Levon, "We have a security team working to find out where Kim may have gone."

He didn't even look at Barb. Directed his attention to Levon. Pretty much, they *all* did. She knew she looked emotional, fragile. And who could say she didn't have good reason.

"What more can you tell us?" Barb asked the lawyer.

"There's no sign that anything happened to her. The police assume she's sightseeing."

Barb thought, *Levon, tell them,* but Levon had said to her before the magazine people arrived, "We'll take information in. We'll listen. But we've got to keep in mind that we don't know these people." Meaning, anyone attached to the magazine could have had something to do with Kim's disappearance.

hotel bar on her own, and no one's heard from her, and she's been gone for a day and a half, and that means to you that Kim ditched the shoot and went sightseeing? Am I getting that right?"

"She's an adult, Mr. McDaniels," Gruber said. "It wouldn't be the first time a girl dumped a job. I remember this girl, Gretchen, took off in Cannes last year, showed up in Monte Carlo six days later."

Gruber was talking like this was her office, and she was patiently explaining her job to Levon. "We've got eight girls on this shoot." She went on to say how many people she had to supervise and all the things she had to cover, and how she had to be on the set every minute or looking at the day's shots...

Barbara felt the pressure building inside her head. All that gold on Susan Gruber, but no wedding ring. Did she have a child? Did she even know one? *Susan Gruber didn't get it.*

"We love Kim," Carol Sweeney blurted to Barb. "I...I felt that Kim was safe here. I was having dinner with one of the other models. I mean, Kim is such a good girl and so responsible, I never thought we had reason to worry."

"I only turned my back for a minute," said Del Swann. And then he started to cry.

It all became clear to Barb, why Gruber had brought her people to see them. Barbara had been

No one met her gaze.

"We've told the police everything we know," said Gruber.

Levon stood up, put his hand on Barb's shoulder, and said to the magazine people, "Please call if you learn anything. Right now, we'd like to be alone. Thanks."

Gruber stood, slung the strap of her handbag across her narrow chest, said, "Kim will be back. Don't worry."

"You mean, you *hope and pray with every miserable breath you take*," said Barbara.

Chapter 18

A MAN STOOD in the thick of the media gaggle outside the Wailea Princess main entrance, waiting for the press conference to start.

He blended in well, appeared to be a guy living out of a duffel bag, maybe sleeping on the beach. He had on sports sunglasses wrapped around his face like a windshield, even though the sun was going down. Dodgers cap over his rusty brown hair, vintage Adidas, rumpled cargo pants, and hanging down in front of his cheap Hawaiian shirt was a perfect replica of a press pass identifying him as a photographer, Charles Rollins of *Talk Weekly*, a publication that didn't exist.

His video camera was expensive, though, a state-of-the-art Panasonic, HD-compatible with a stereo microphone boom and a Leica lens, costing over six thousand bucks.

He pointed the lens at the grand front entrance of the Wailea Princess, where the McDanielses were taking up their positions behind a lectern.

As Levon adjusted the mic, Rollins whistled a few notes through his teeth. He was enjoying himself now, thinking that even Kim wouldn't recognize him if she were alive. He lifted his vid cam over his head and recorded Levon greeting the press, thinking he'd like the McDanielses if he got to know them. Well, fuck it anyway, he already liked them. What was not to like about the McDanielses?

Look at them.

Sweet, feisty Barbara. Levon, with the heart of a five-star general. Both of them, salt of the fucking earth.

They were grief-wracked and terrified, but still comporting themselves with dignity, answering insensitive questions, even the de rigueur "What would you say to Kim if she were listening to you now?"

"I'd say, 'We love you, darling. Please be *strong*,'" Barbara said with a quavering voice. "And to everyone hearing us, please, we're offering twenty-five thousand dollars for information leading to the return of our daughter. If we had a million, we'd offer that..."

And then Barbara's air seemed to run out. She turned, and Rollins saw her take a hit off an inhaler. And still, questions were fired at the supermodel's parents: *Levon, Levon! Have you gotten a ransom demand? What was the last thing Kim said to you?*

Levon leaned toward the microphones, answered the questions very patiently, finally saying, "The hotel management has set up a hotline number," and he read it to the crowd.

Rollins watched the journalists jumping up like flying fish, calling out more questions even as the McDanielses were stepping down, moving toward the embrace of the hotel lobby.

Rollins looked through his lens, zoomed in on the back of the McDanielses' heads, saw someone coming through the crowd, a semicelebrity he'd seen on C-Span hawking his books.

The subject of Rollins's interest was a good-looking guy of about forty, a journalist and best-selling detective novelist, dressed in Dockers and a pink button-down shirt, sleeves rolled up. Kind of reminded him of Brian Williams reporting from Baghdad. Maybe a little more rough-and-ready.

As Rollins watched, the writer reached out and touched Barbara McDaniels's arm, and Barbara stopped to speak with him.

Charlie Rollins saw an interview with the legitimate press in the making. He thought, *Kim McDaniels is going big-time. This is turning into a very big event, indeed.*

Chapter 19

THE JOURNALIST IN the Dockers and pink shirt? That was me.

I saw an opening as Levon and Barbara McDaniels stepped away from the lectern, the crowd closing in, circling them like a twister.

I lunged forward, touched Barbara McDaniels's arm, catching her attention before she disappeared into the lobby.

I wanted the interview, but no matter how many times you see parents of lost or abducted children begging for their son or daughter's safe return, you cannot fail to be moved.

Barbara and Levon McDaniels had gotten to me as soon as I saw their faces. It killed me to see them in such pain.

Now I had my hand gently on Barbara McDaniels's arm. She turned, and I introduced myself, handed her my card, and lucky for me, she knew my name. "Are you the Ben Hawkins who wrote *Red*?"

"*Put It All on Red*, yes, that's mine."

She said she liked the book, her mouth smiling, although her face was rigid with anguish. Right then, hotel security made a cordon with their arms, a path through the crowd, and I walked into the lobby with Barbara, who introduced me to Levon.

"Ben's a best-selling author, Levon. You remember, we read him for our book club last fall."

"I'm covering Kim's story for the L.A. Times," I told Mr. McDaniels.

Levon said, "If you want an interview, I'm sorry. We're out of steam, and it's probably best that we don't talk further until we meet with the police."

"You haven't spoken with them yet?"

Levon sighed, shook his head. "Ever talk to an answering machine?"

"I might be able to help," I said. "The L.A. Times has clout, even here. And I used to be a cop."

"Is that right?" Levon McDaniels's eyelids were sagging, his voice ragged and raw. He walked like a man who'd just run his feet off in a marathon, but he was suddenly interested in me. He stopped walking and asked me to tell him more.

"I was with the Portland PD. I was a detective, an investigator. Right now I cover the crime desk for the Times."

McDaniels winced at the word "crime," said, "Okay, Ben. You think you can give us a hand with the police? We're going out of our minds."

I walked with the McDanielses through the cool marble lobby with its high ceilings and ocean views until we found a semisecluded spot overlooking the pool. Palm trees rustled in the island breeze. Wet kids in bathing suits ran past us, laughing, not a care in the world.

Levon said, "I called the police several times and got a menu. 'Parking tickets, press one. Night court, press two.' I had to leave a message. Can you believe that?

"Barb and I went over to the station for this district. Hours were posted on the door. Monday to Friday, eight to five, Saturday, ten to four. I didn't know police stations had closing hours. Did you?"

The look in Levon's eyes was heartbreaking. His daughter was missing. The police station was *closed* for business. How could this place look the way it did—vacation heaven—when they were slogging through seven kinds of hell?

"The police here mostly do traffic work, DWIs, stuff like that," I said. "Domestic violence, burglary."

I thought, but didn't say, that a few years ago a twenty-five-year-old female tourist was attacked on the Big Island by three local hoods who beat her and raped her and killed her.

She'd been tall, blond, sweet-looking, not unlike Kim.

There was another case, more famous, a cheerleader for the University of Illinois who'd fallen off the balcony of her hotel room and died instantly. She'd been partying with a couple of boys who were found not guilty of anything. And there was another girl, a local teenager, who called her friends after a concert on the island, and was never seen again.

"Your press conference was a good thing. The police will have to take Kim seriously," I said.

"If I don't get a call back, I'm going over there again in the morning," Levon McDaniels said. "Right now we want to go to the bar, see where Kim was hanging out before she vanished. You're welcome to join us."

Chapter 20

THE TYPHOON BAR was on the mezzanine floor, open to the trade winds, wonderfully scented by plumeria. Café tables and chairs were lined up at the balustrade, overlooking the pool and beyond, a queue of palm trees down to the sands. To my left was a grand piano, still covered, and there was a long bar behind us. A bartender was setting up, slicing lemon peel, putting out dishes of nuts.

Barbara spoke. "The night manager told us that Kim was sitting at this table, the one nearest the piano," Barbara said, tenderly patting the table's marble surface.

Then she pointed to an alcove fifteen yards away. "That would be the famous men's room over there. Where the art director went, to ah, just turn his back for a minute..."

I imagined the bar as it must have been that night. People drinking. A lot of men. I had plenty of questions. Hundreds of them.

I was starting to look at this story as if I were still a cop. If this were *my* case, I'd start with the security tapes. I'd want to see who was in the bar when Kim was there. I'd want to know if anybody had been watching her when she'd gotten up from this table, and who might have paid the check after she left.

Had Kim departed with someone? Maybe gone to his room?

Or had she walked to the lobby, eyes following her as she made her way down the stairs, her blond hair swinging.

What then? Had she walked outside, past the pool and the cabanas? Had any of those cabanas been occupied late that night? Had someone followed her out to the beach?

Levon carefully polished his glasses, one lens, then the other, and held them out to see if he'd done a good job. When he put them back on, he saw me looking out at the covered walkway beyond the pool area that led to the beach.

"What do you think, Ben?"

"All of the beaches in Hawaii are public property, so there won't be any video surveillance out there."

I was wondering if the simplest explanation fit. Had Kim gone for a swim? Had she waded out into the water and gotten sucked under by a wave? Had someone found her shoes on the beach and taken them?

"What can we tell you about Kim?" Barbara asked me.

"I want to know everything," I said. "If you don't mind, I'd like to tape our conversation."

Barbara nodded, and Levon ordered G and Ts for them both. I was working, so I declined alcohol, asked for club soda instead.

I had already started shaping the Kim McDaniels story in my mind, thinking about this beautiful girl from the heartland, with brains and beauty, on the verge of national fame, and about how she had come to one of the most beautiful spots on earth and disappeared without trace or reason. An exclusive with the McDanielses was more than I'd hoped for, and while I still couldn't know if Kim's story was a book, it was definitely a journalistic whopper.

And more than that, I'd been won over by the McDanielses. They were nice people.

I wanted to help them, and I would.

Right now, they were exhausted, but they weren't leaving the table. The interview was on.

My tape recorder was new, the tape just unwrapped and the batteries fresh. I pushed Record, but, as the machine whirred softly on the table, Barbara McDaniels surprised me.

It was *she* who started asking questions.

Chapter 21

BARBARA RESTED HER chin on her hands, and asked, "What happened with you and the Portland police department—and please don't tell me what it says in your book jacket bio. That's just PR, isn't it?"

Barbara let me know by her focus and determination that if I didn't answer her questions, she had no reason to answer mine. I wanted to cooperate because I thought she was right to check me out, and I wanted the McDanielses to trust me.

I smiled at Barbara's direct interrogatory style, but there was nothing amusing about the story she was asking me to tell. Once I sent my mind back to that place and time, the memories rolled in, unstoppable, none of them glorifying, none of them very pleasant, either.

As the still-vivid images flashed on the wide screen inside my head, I told the McDanielses about a fatal car wreck that had happened many years ago; that my partner, Dennis Carbone, and I had been nearby and had responded to the call.

"When we got to the scene, there was about a

half hour left of daylight. It was gloomy with a drizzling rain, but there was enough light to see that a vehicle had skidded off the road. It had caromed off some trees like a two-ton eight ball, crashing out of control through the woods.

"I radioed for help," I said now. "Then I was the one who stayed behind to interview the witness who'd been driving the other car—while my partner went to the crashed vehicle to see if there were survivors."

I told the McDanielses that the witness had been driving the car coming from the opposite direction, that the other vehicle, a black Toyota pickup, had been in his lane, coming at him *fast*. He said that he'd swerved, and so had the Toyota. The witness was shaken as he described how the pickup had left the road at high speed, said that he'd braked—and I could see and smell the hundred yards of rubber he'd left on the asphalt.

"Response and rescue vehicles showed up," I said. "The paramedics pulled the body out of the pickup, told me that the driver had been killed on impact with a spruce tree and that he'd had no passengers.

"As the dead man was taken away, I looked for my partner. He was a few yards off the roadside, and I caught him sneaking a look in my direction. A little odd, like he was trying not to be seen doing something."

There was a sudden flurry of girlish laughter as a bride, surrounded by her maids of honor, passed through the bar to the lounge. The bride was a pretty blonde in her twenties. Happiest day of her life, right?

Barbara turned to see the bridal party, then turned back to look at me. Anyone with eyes could see what she was feeling. And what she was hoping.

"Go on, Ben," she said. "You were talking about your partner with the guilty look."

I nodded, told her that I turned away from my partner because someone called my name and that when I looked back again, he was closing the trunk of our car.

"I didn't ask Dennis what he was doing, because I was already thinking ahead. We had reports to write up, work to do. We had to start with identifying the deceased.

"I was doing all the right stuff, Barbara," I told her now. "I think it's pretty common to block out things we don't want to see. I should have confronted my partner right then and right there. But I didn't do it. Turns out that that sneaky, half-seen moment changed my life."

Chapter 22

A WAITRESS CAME OVER and asked if we wanted to refresh our drinks, and I was glad to see her. My throat was closing up and I needed to take a break. I'd told this story before, but it's never easy to get past disgrace.

Especially when you didn't earn it.

Levon said, "I know this is hard, Ben. But we appreciate your telling us about yourself. It's important to hear."

"This is where it gets *hard*," I told Levon.

He nodded, and even though Levon probably had only ten years on me, I felt his fatherly concern.

My second club soda arrived and I stirred at it with a straw. Then I went on.

"A few days passed. The accident victim turned out to be a small-time drug dealer, Robby Snow, and his blood came back positive for heroin. And now his girlfriend called on us. Carrie Willis was her name. Carrie was crushed by Robby's death, but something else was bothering her. She asked me, 'What happened to Robby's backpack? It was red with silver reflecting tape on the back. There was a lot of money in there.'

"Well, we hadn't found any red backpack, and there were a lot of jokes about Carrie Willis having the nerve to report stolen drug money to the police.

"But Robby's girlfriend was convincing. Carrie didn't know that Robby was a dealer. She just knew that he was buying a piece of acreage by a creek and he was going to build a house there for the two of them. The bank papers and the full payment for the property—a hundred thousand dollars—were in that backpack because he was on his way to the closing. She put all that money in the backpack herself. Her story checked out."

"So you asked your partner about the backpack?" Barbara prompted.

"Sure. I asked him. And he said, 'Well, I sure as hell didn't see a backpack, red or green or sky blue pink.'

"So, at my insistence, we went to the impound, took the car apart, found nothing. Then we drove in broad daylight out to the woods where the accident happened and we searched the area. At least I did. I thought Denny was just rustling branches and kicking piles of leaves. That's when I remembered his face getting foxy the night of the accident.

"I had a long, hard talk with myself that night. The next day I went to my lieutenant for an off-the-record chat. I told him what I suspected, that a hundred thousand dollars in cash might have left the scene and was never reported."

Levon said, "Well, you had no choice."

"Denny Carbone was an old pit bull of a cop,

and I knew if he learned about my conversation with the lieutenant he'd come at me. So I took a chance with my boss, and the next day Internal Affairs was in the locker room. Guess what they found in my locker?"

"A red backpack," said Levon.

I gave him a thumbs-up. "Red backpack, silver reflecting tape, bank papers, heroin, and ten thousand dollars in cash."

"Oh, my God," said Barbara.

"I was given a choice. Resign. Or there would be a trial. *My* trial. I knew that I wasn't going to win in court. It would be 'he said/he said,' and the evidence, some of it, anyway, had been found in my locker. Worse, I suspected that I was getting hung with this because my lieutenant was in on it with Denny Carbone.

"A very bad day, blew up a lot of illusions for me. I turned in my badge, my gun, and some of my self-respect. I could've fought, but I couldn't take a chance I'd go to jail for something I hadn't done."

"That's a sad story, Ben," said Levon.

"Yep. And you know how the story turns out. I moved to L.A. Got a job at the *Times*. And I wrote some books."

"You're being modest," Barbara said, and patted my arm.

"Writing is what I do, but it's not who I am."

"And who would you say you are?" she asked.

"Right now, I'm working at being the best reporter I can be. I came to Maui to tell your daughter's story, and, at the same time, I want you to have that happy ending. I want to see it, report it, be here for all the good feelings when Kim comes back safe. That's who I am."

Barbara said, "We believe you, Ben." And Levon nodded at her side.

Like I said, Nice people.

Chapter 23

AMSTERDAM. FIVE TWENTY in the afternoon. Jan Van der Heuvel was in his office on the fifth floor of the classic, neck-gabled house, gazing out over the treetops at the sightseeing boat on the canal, waiting for time to pass.

The door to his office opened, and Mieke, a pretty girl of twenty with short, dark hair, entered. She wore a small skirt and a fitted jacket, her long legs bare to her little lace-up boots. The girl lowered her eyes, said that if he didn't need her for anything she would leave for the day.

"Have a good evening," Van der Heuvel said.

He walked her to the office door and locked it behind her, returned to his seat at the long drawing table, and looked down at the street running along the Keizersgracht Canal until he saw Mieke get into her fiancé's Renault and speed away.

Only then did Van der Heuvel attend to his computer. The teleconference wasn't for another forty minutes, but he wanted to establish contact early so that he could record the proceedings. He tapped keys until he made the connection and his friend's face came on the screen.

"Horst," he said. "I am here."

At that same time, a brunette woman of forty was on the bridge of her 118-foot yacht anchored in the Mediterranean off the coast of Portofino. The yacht was custom-made, constructed of high-tensile aluminum with six cabins, a master suite, and a video conference center in the saloon, which easily converted to a cinema.

The woman left her young captain and took the stairs down to her suite, where she removed a Versace jacket from the closet and slipped it on over her halter top. Then she crossed the galleyway to the media room and booted up her computer. When the connection was made to the encrypted line, she smiled into the webcam.

"Gina Prazzi checking in, Horst. How are we today?"

Four time zones away, in Dubai, a tall bearded man wearing traditional Middle Eastern clothing passed a mosque and hurried to a hole-in-the-wall restaurant down the street. He greeted the proprietor and continued on through the kitchen, aromatic with garlic and rosemary.

Pushing aside a heavy curtain, he took the stairs down to the basement level and unlocked a heavy wooden door leading to a private room.

In Hong Kong's Victoria Peak section, a young chemist flicked on his computer. He was in his twenties with an IQ in the high 170s. As the software loaded, he looked through his curtains, down the long slope, past the tops of the cylindrical high-rises, and farther below to the brightly lit towers of Hong Kong. It was unusually clear for this time of year, and his gaze had drifted to Victoria Harbour and beyond, to the lights of Kowloon, when the computer signaled and he turned his attention to the emergency meeting of the Alliance.

In São Paulo, Raphael dos Santos, a man of fifty, drove to his home at just past three in his new Wiesmann GT MF5 sports coupe. The car cost 250,000 U.S. dollars and went from zero to sixty in under four seconds with a top speed of 193 miles per hour. Rafi, as he was called, loved this car.

He braked at the entrance to the underground garage, tossed the keys to Tomás, and took the elevator that opened inside his apartment.

There he crossed several thousand square feet of Jatoba hardwood floors, passed ultramodern furnishings, and entered his home office with its view of the gleaming facade of the Renaissance Hotel on Alameda Santos.

Rafi pressed a button on his desk, and a thin screen rose vertically up through the center. He wondered again at the purpose of this meeting. Something had gone wrong. But what? He touched the keyboard and pressed his thumb to the ID pad.

Rafi greeted the leader of the Alliance in Portuguese. "Horst, you old bastard. Make this good. You have our undivided attention!"

Chapter 24

IN THE SWISS ALPS, Horst Werner sat in the upholstered chair in his library. Flames leapt in the fireplace and pin lights illuminated the eight-foot-long scale model of the *Bismarck* he had made himself. There were bookshelves on every wall but no windows, and behind the cherrywood paneling was a three-inch-thick wall of lead-lined steel.

Horst's safe room was linked to the world by sophisticated Internet circuitry, giving him the feeling that this chamber was the very center of the universe.

The dozen members of the Alliance had all signed on to the encrypted network. They all spoke English to greater and lesser degrees, their live pictures on his screen. After greeting them, Horst moved quickly to the point of the meeting.

"An American friend has sent Jan a film as an amusement. I am very interested in your reaction."

A white light filled twelve linked computer screens and then clarified as the camera focused on a Jacuzzi-style tub. Inside the tub was a dark-skinned young girl, lying on her stomach in about four inches of water. Her hands and feet were tied behind her with a rope that also passed around her throat.

There was a man in the video, his back to the camera, and when he half turned, one of the Alliance members said, "Henri."

Henri was sitting on the edge of the tub, the clear plastic mask obscuring his features. He spoke to the camera. "You see there is very little water, but enough. I don't know which is more lethal for Rosa. Whether she will choke or if she will drown. Let's watch and see."

The girl continued to sob, gasping for air every time her legs relaxed and the rope tightened around her throat. She wailed, "*Mama.*" Then her head dropped, her final exhalation causing bubbles to break the surface of the water.

Henri touched the side of her neck and shrugged. "It was the ropes," he said. "Anyway, she committed suicide. A beautiful tragedy. Just what I promised."

He was smiling when the video faded to black.

Gina spoke now, indignant. "Horst, this is in violation of his contract, yes?"

"Actually, Henri's contract only says he cannot take work that would prevent him from fulfilling his obligations to us."

"So. He is not technically in violation. He is just freelancing."

Jan's voice came over the speakers. "Yes. You see how Henri looks for ways to give us the finger? This is unacceptable."

Raphael broke in. "Okay, he is difficult, but let's admit, Henri has his genius. We should work with him. Give him a new contract."

"That says what, for example?"

"Henri has been making short films for us like the one we just saw. I suggest we have him make... a documentary."

Jan jumped in, excited. "Very good, Rafi. Wall-to-wall with Henri. A year in the life, *ja?* Salary and bonuses commensurate with the quality of the action."

"Exactly. And he's exclusive to us," said Raphael. "He starts now, on location with the parents of the swimsuit girl."

The Alliance discussed terms, and they put some teeth into the contract, penalties for failure to perform. That phrase provided a light moment, and then, after they had voted, Horst made the call to Hawaii.

Chapter 25

THE McDANIELSES AND I were still in the Typhoon Bar as dusk dropped over the island. For the past hour, Barbara had sweated me like a pro. When she was satisfied that I was an okay guy, she brought me into her family's lives with her passion and a natural gift for storytelling that I wouldn't have expected from a high school math and science teacher.

Levon could barely string two sentences together. He wasn't inarticulate. He just wasn't with us. I read him as choked up with fear and too anxious about his daughter to concentrate. But he expressed himself vividly with his body language, tightening his fists, turning away when tears welled up, frequently taking off his glasses and pressing his palms over his eyes.

I'd asked Barbara, "How did you learn that Kim was missing?"

At that, Levon's cell phone rang. He looked at the faceplate and walked away toward the elevator.

I heard him say, "Lieutenant Jackson? *Not tonight?* Why not?" After a pause, he said, "Okay. Eight a.m."

"Sounds like we have a date with the police in the morning. Come with us," Barbara said. She took my phone number, patted my hand. And then, she kissed my cheek.

I said good night to Barbara, then ordered another club soda, no lime, no ice. I sat in a comfortable chair overlooking the hundred-million-dollar view, and in the next fifteen minutes the atmosphere at the Typhoon Bar picked up considerably.

Handsome people in fresh suntans and translucent clothing in snow-cone colors dropped into chairs at the railing while singles took the high-backed stools at the long bar. Laughter rose and fell like the warm breeze that gusted through the wide-open space, riffling hairlines and skirt hems as it passed.

The piano player uncovered the Steinway, then turned sideways on the piano seat and broke into an old Peter Allen standard, delighting the crowd as he sang "I Go to Rio."

I noted the security cameras over the bar, dropped several bills on the table, and walked down the stairs and past the pool, lit now so that it looked like aqua-colored glass.

I continued past the cabanas, taking a walk that Kim might have taken two nights ago.

The beach was nearly empty of people, the sky still light enough to see the shoreline that ringed the whole of Maui like a halo around an eclipse of the moon.

I pictured walking behind Kim on Friday night. Her head might have been down, hair whipping around her face, the strong surf obliterating all other sound.

A man could have come up behind her with a rock, or a gun, or a simple choke hold.

I walked on the hard-packed sand, passing hotels on my right, empty chaises and cockeyed umbrellas as far as I could see.

After a quarter mile, I turned off the beach, walked up a path that skirted the Four Seasons, another five-star hotel where eight hundred bucks a night might buy a room with a view of the parking lot.

I continued on through the hotel's dazzling marble lobby and out to the street. Fifteen minutes later I was back sitting in my rented Chevy, parked in the leafy shadows surrounding the Wailea Princess, listening to the rush of waterfalls.

If I'd been a killer, I could've dumped my victim into the surf or slung her over my shoulder and carried her out to my car. I could've left the scene without anyone noticing.

Easy breezy.

Chapter 26

I STARTED MY engine and followed the moon to Stella Blues, a cheerful café in Kihei. It has high, peaked ceilings and a wraparound bar, now buzzing with a weekend crowd of locals and cruise ship tourists enjoying their first night in port. I ordered a Jack Daniel's and mahimahi from the bar, took my drink outside to a table for two on the patio.

As the votive candle guttered in its glass, I called Amanda.

Amanda Diaz and I had been together for almost two years. She's five years younger than me, a pastry chef and a self-described biker chick, which means she takes her antique Harley for a run on the Pacific Coast Highway some weekends to blow off the steam she can't vent in the kitchen. Mandy is not only smart and gorgeous, but when I look at her, all those rock-and-roll songs about booming hearts and loving her till the day I die make total sense.

Right then I was aching to hear my sweetie's voice, and she didn't disappoint, answering the phone on the third ring. After some verbal high fives, and at my request, she told me about her day at Intermezzo.

"It was Groundhog Day, Benjy. Rémy fired Rocco, again," Amanda said, going into a French accent now. 'What I have to say to you to make you think like chef? This confit. It looks like pigeon *poop*.' He put about twelve *ooohs* in *poop*."

She laughed, said, "Hired him back ten minutes later. As usual. And then I scorched the crème brûlée. '*Merde, Ahmandah, mon Dieu*. You are making me *craaaaa-zy*.'" She laughed again. "And you, Benjy? Are you getting your story?"

"I met with the missing girl's folks. They're talking to me."

"Oh, boy. How grim was that?"

I caught Mandy up on the interview with Barbara, told her how much I liked the McDanielses and that they had two other kids, both boys adopted from Russian orphanages.

"Their oldest son was almost catatonic from neglect when the police in Saint Petersburg found him. The younger boy has fetal alcohol syndrome. Kim decided to become a pediatrician because of her brothers."

"Ben, honey?"

"Uh-huh. Am I breaking up?"

"No, I can hear you. Can you hear me?"

"Totally."

"Then listen. Be careful, will you?"

I felt a slight burr of irritation. Amanda was uncommonly intuitive, but I was in no danger.

"Careful of what?"

"Remember when you left your briefcase with all of your notes on the Donato story in a diner?"

"You're going to bring up the bus again, aren't you?"

"Since you mention it."

"I was under your spell, goofball. I was looking at you when I stepped off the curb. If you were *here* now, it could happen again—"

"What I'm saying is, you sound the same way *now* as you did then."

"I do, huh?"

"Yeah, you kinda do. So watch out, okay? Pay attention. Look both ways."

Ten feet away, a couple clinked glasses, held hands across a small table. Honeymooners, I thought.

"I miss you," I said.

"I miss you, too. I'm keeping the bed warm for you, so come home soon."

I sent a wireless kiss to my girl in L.A. and said good night.

Chapter 27

AT SEVEN FIFTEEN Monday morning, Levon watched the driver pull the black sedan up to the entrance of the Wailea Princess. Levon got into the front passenger seat as Hawkins and Barb got into the back, and when all the doors had slammed shut, Levon told Marco to please take them to the police station in Kihei.

During the ride, Levon half listened as Hawkins talked, telling him how to handle the police, saying to be *helpful,* to make the cops your friends and not to be belligerent because that would work against them.

Levon had nodded, grunted "uh-huh" a few times, but he was inside his head, wouldn't have been able to describe the route between the hotel and the police station, his mind fully focused on the upcoming meeting with Lieutenant James Jackson.

Levon came back to the present as Marco was parking at the mini–strip mall, and he jumped out before the car had fully stopped. He walked straight up to the shoebox-sized substation, a storefront wedged between a tattoo parlor and a pizzeria.

The glass door was locked, and so Levon jabbed the intercom button and spoke his name, saying to the female voice that he had an appointment at eight with Lieutenant Jackson. There was a buzz and the door opened and they were in.

The station looked to Levon like a small-town DMV. The walls were bureaucrat green; the floor, a buffed linoleum; the long hallway-width room lined with facing rows of plastic chairs.

At the end of the narrow room was a reception window, its metal shutter rolled down, and beside it was a closed door. Levon sat down next to Barbara, and Hawkins sat across from them with his notebook sticking out of his breast pocket, and they waited.

At a few minutes past eight, the shuttered window opened and people trickled in to pay parking tickets, register their cars, God knows what else. Guys with Rasta hair; girls with complicated tattoos; young moms with small, bawling kids.

Levon felt a stabbing pain behind his eyes, and he thought about Kim, wanting to know where she could be right now and if she was in any pain and why this had happened.

After a while, he stood up and paced along the gallery of Wanted posters, looked into the staring eyes of murderers and armed robbers, and then there were the missing-children posters, some of them digitally altered to age the kids to how they might look now, having disappeared so many years ago.

Behind him, Barbara said to Hawkins, "Can you believe it? We've been here two hours. Don't you just want to scream?"

And Levon did want to scream. *Where was his daughter?* He leaned down and spoke to the female officer behind the window. "Does Lieutenant Jackson know we're here?"

"Yes, sir, he sure does."

Levon sat down next to Barb, pinched the place between his eyes, wondered why Jackson was taking so long. And he thought about Hawkins, how he'd gotten in very tight with Barb. Levon trusted Barb's judgment, but, like a lot of women, she made friends fast. Sometimes too fast.

Levon watched Hawkins writing in his notebook and then some teenage girls joined the line at the front desk, talking in high-pitched chatter that just about took off the top of his head.

By ten fifteen, Levon's agitation was like the rumbling of the volcanoes that had raised this island out of the prehistoric sea. He felt ready to explode.

Chapter 28

I WAS SITTING in a hard plastic chair next to Barbara McDaniels when I heard the door open at the end of the long, narrow room. Levon leapt up from his seat and was practically in the cop's face before the door swung closed.

The cop was big, midthirties, with thick black hair and mocha-toned skin. He looked part Jimmy Smits, part Ben Affleck, and part island surfer god. Wore a jacket and tie, had a shield hooked into the waistband of his chinos, a gold one, which meant he was a detective.

Barbara and I joined Levon, who introduced us to Lieutenant Jackson. Jackson asked me, "What's your relationship to the McDanielses?"

"Friend of the family," Barbara said at the same time that I said, "I'm with the *L.A. Times.*"

Jackson snorted a laugh, scrutinized me, then asked, "Do you know Kim?"

No.

"Have any information as to her whereabouts?"

No.

"Do you know these people? Or did you meet them, say, yesterday?"

"We just met."

"Interesting," Jackson said, smirking now. He said to the McDanielses, "You understand this man's job is to sell newspapers?"

"We know that," Levon said.

"Good. Just so you're clear, anything you say to Mr. Hawkins is going directly from your mouths to the front page of the *L.A. Times*. Speaking for myself." Jackson went on, "I don't want him here. Mr. Hawkins, have a seat, and if I need you, I'll call you."

Barbara spoke up. "Lieutenant, my husband and I talked it over last night, and it comes down to this. We trust Ben, and he has the power of the *L.A. Times* behind him. He might be able to do more for us than we can do alone."

Jackson exhaled his exasperation but seemed to concede the point. He said to me, "Anything out of *my* mouth has to be okayed by me before you run with it, understand?"

I said I did.

Jackson's office took up a corner at the back of the building, had one window and a noisy air conditioner; numbers were written on the blue plasterboard walls near the phone.

Jackson indicated chairs for the McDanielses, and I leaned against the doorframe as he flapped open a notepad, took down basic information.

Then he got down to business, working, I thought, off a notion that Kim was a party girl, questioning her late-night habits and asking about men in her life and drug use.

Barbara told Jackson that Kim was a straight-A student. That she had sponsored a Christian

Children's Fund baby in Ecuador. That she was responsible to a fault and the fact that she hadn't returned their call was *way* out of character.

Jackson listened with a mostly bored look on his face before saying, "Yeah, I'm sure she's an angel. I'm waiting for the day someone comes in, says their kid is a meth head or a slut."

Levon sprang to his feet, and Jackson stood up a beat after that, but by then Levon had the advantage. He shoved his palms into Jackson's beefy shoulders, sending him backward into the wall, which shook with a loud crack. Plaques and photos crashed to the floor, which is what you'd expect when 180 pounds or so was used as a wrecking ball.

Jackson was the bigger and younger man, but Levon was mainlining adrenaline. Without pause, he reached down and grabbed Jackson up by his lapels and threw him against the wall again. There was another terrible crashing sound as Jackson's head bounced off the plasterboard. I watched him grab for the arm of his chair, which toppled, and sent him down a third time.

It was an ugly scene even *before* Levon crowned the moment.

He stared down at Jackson, and said, "Damn, that felt good. You son of a bitch."

Chapter 29

A HEAVYSET FEMALE OFFICER BARRELED toward the doorway as I stood there like a stump, trying to absorb that Levon had assaulted a *cop*, shoved him, thrown him down, cursed at him, and said it felt *good*.

Now Jackson was on his feet, and Levon was still panting. The woman cop yelled, *"Hey, what's going on?"*

Jackson said, "We're fine here, Millie. Lost my balance. Gonna need a new chair." And he waved her off. Then he turned back to Levon, who was shouting at him, "Don't you *get* it? I told you last *night*. We got a fricking *phone call* in Michigan. The man said he took my daughter, and you're trying to say Kim's a tramp?"

Jackson straightened his jacket, his tie, righted his chair. His face was red and he was scowling. He jerked the chair around, then shouted back at Levon, "You're *crazy*, McDaniels. You realize what you just did, you stupid *fuck*? You want to be locked up? *Do you*? You think you're a tough guy? You want to find out just how tough *I am*?

I could arrest your ass and have you put away for this, don't you know that?"

"Yeah, throw me in jail, damn you. Do that, because I want to tell the world how you treated us. What a yahoo you are."

"Levon, Levon." Barbara was up, begging her husband, pulling at his arm. "Stop, Levon. Control yourself. Apologize to the lieutenant, please."

Jackson sat down, rolled his chair up to his desk, said, "McDaniels, don't ever put a hand on me again. Due to the fact that you're out of your fucking mind, I'll minimize what just happened in my report. Now sit down before I change my mind and arrest you."

Levon was still blowing hard, but Jackson gestured to the chairs, and Levon and Barbara sat down.

Jackson touched the back of his head, rubbed his elbow, then said, "Half the time, a kid goes missing, one of the parents knows what happened. Sometimes both of them. I had to see where you were coming from."

Levon and Barbara stared. And we all got it. Jackson had provoked them to see how they'd react.

It had been a test. They'd passed. In a manner of speaking.

"We've been investigating this case since yesterday morning. Like I told you when I called," Jackson said, glaring at Levon. "We've met with the *Sporting Life* people, also the desk and bar staff at the Princess. So far, we got nothing from that."

Jackson opened his desk drawer, took out a cell phone, one of those thin, half-human devices that takes pictures, sends mail, and tells you when you're low on oil.

"This is Kim's phone," Jackson said. "We found it on the beach behind the Princess. We've dumped the data and found a number of phone calls to Kim from a man named Doug Cahill."

"Cahill?" Levon said. "Doug Cahill used to date Kim. He lives in Chicago."

Jackson shook his head. "He was calling Kim from *Maui*. Called her every hour until her mailbox filled up and stopped taking incoming calls."

"You're saying Doug is *here*?" Barbara asked. "He's in Maui now?"

"We located Cahill in Makena, worked on him for two hours last night before he lawyered up. He said he hadn't seen Kim. That she wouldn't talk to him. And we couldn't hold him, because we have nothing on him," Jackson said, putting Kim's cell phone back in the drawer.

"McDaniels, here's what we've got. You got a phone call saying Kim was in bad hands. And we have Kim's cell phone. We don't even know if a crime has been committed. If Cahill gets on a plane, there's nothing we can do to stop him from leaving."

I saw Barbara start, shock coming over her face again.

"Doug's not your guy," Levon said.

Jackson's eyebrows shot up. "Why do you say that?"

"I know Doug's voice. The man who called us wasn't Doug."

Chapter 30

WE WERE BACK in the black sedan. This time I was in front, beside the driver. Marco adjusted his rearview mirror, and we exchanged nods, but there was nothing to say. It was all going on in the backseat between Barbara and Levon.

Levon was explaining to his wife, "Barb. I didn't tell you what that bastard said *verbatim* because there was nothing to be gained from it. I'm sorry."

"I'm your wife. You had no right to hold back what he said."

" 'She's fallen into bad hands,' okay? That's the only thing I didn't tell you, and I still wouldn't tell you, but I had to tell Jackson. I tried to spare you, sweetheart, I wanted to spare you."

Barb cried, "Spare me? You lied to me, Levon. You lied." And then Levon was crying too, and I realized that this was what had been binding Levon up, why he'd been so glassy-eyed and removed. A man had said that he was going to hurt his daughter and Levon hadn't told his wife. And now he couldn't pretend anymore that it wasn't true.

I wanted to give them some privacy, so I lowered

the window, stared out at the beachfront whizzing by, at the families picnicking by the ocean, as Kim's parents suffered terribly. The contrast between the campers and the weeping couple behind me was excruciating.

I made a note, then swiveled in my seat and, trying for something comforting, I said to Levon, "Jackson isn't subtle, but he's on the case. He might be a pretty good cop."

Kim's father leveled hard eyes on me.

"I think you're right about Jackson. He nailed you in five seconds. Look at you. You parasite. Writing your story. Selling newspapers on our pain."

I felt the accusation like a gut punch — but there was some truth in it, I guess I swallowed the hurt and found my compassion for Levon.

I said, "You've got a point, Levon But even if I'm exactly what you say, Kim's story could get out of control and eat you alive.

"Think of JonBenet Ramsey. Natalee Holloway. Chandra Levy. I hope Kim is safe and that she's found fast. But whatever happens, you're going to want me with you. Because I'm not going to fan the flames and I'm not going to make anything up. *I'm going to tell the story right.*"

Chapter 31

MARCO WATCHED UNTIL Hawkins and the McDanielses passed between the koi ponds and entered the hotel before he put the car in gear, eased out onto Wailea Alanui Drive, and headed south.

As he drove, he felt under the seat, pulled out a nylon duffel bag, and put it beside him. Then he reached behind the rearview mirror where he'd parked the cutting-edge, wireless, high-resolution, micro–video camera. He ejected the media card and dropped it into his shirt pocket.

He had a thought that maybe the camera had slipped during the drive back from the police station and the angle might have been off, but even if he just got the crying, he had his sound track for another scene. Levon talking about bad hands? Priceless.

Sneaky Marco.

Imagine their surprise when they figure it all out. If they ever do.

He felt a rush as he added up the cash potential of his new contract, the thick stack of euros with the possibility of doubling his take, depending on the vote of the Alliance on the project as a whole.

He would thrill them to the roots of their short hairs, that's how good this film would be, and all he had to do was what he did best. How could a job possibly be better than this?

Marco saw his turn coming up, signaled, got into the right lane, then entered the parking lot of the Shops at Wailea. He parked the Caddy in the southernmost section of the lot, far from the mall's surveillance cameras and next to his nondescript rented Taurus.

Hidden behind the Caddy's tinted glass, the killer stripped himself of all things Marco: the chauffeur's cap and wig, fake mustache, livery jacket, cowboy boots. Then he took "Charlie Rollins" out of the bag. The baseball cap, beat-up Adidas, wraparound shades, press pass, and both cameras.

He changed quickly, bagged the Marco artifacts, then made the return trip to the Wailea Princess in the Taurus. He tipped the bellman three bucks, then checked in at the front desk, lucking out, getting a king-size bed, ocean view.

Leaving the desk, heading for the stairway at the far end of the marble acreage of the lobby, Henri as "Charlie Rollins" saw the McDanieleses and Ben Hawkins sitting together around a low glass table, coffee cups in front of them.

Rollins felt his heart kick into overdrive as Hawkins turned, looked at him, pausing for a nanosecond—maybe his reptilian brain was making a match?—before his "rational" brain, fooled by the Rollins getup, steered his gaze past him.

The game could have been over in that one look, but *Hawkins hadn't recognized him*—and he'd been sitting right beside him in the car for hours.

This was the real thrill, skating along the razor's edge and getting away with it.

So Charlie Rollins, photographer from the non-existent *Talk Weekly,* jacked it up a notch. He raised his Sony—*say cheese, mousies*—and snapped off three shots of the McDanielses.

Gotcha, Mom and Dad.

His heart was still pounding as Levon scowled and leaned forward, blocking his camera's-eye view of Barbara.

Ecstatic, the killer took the stairs to his room, thinking now about Ben Hawkins, a man who interested him even more than the McDanielses did. Hawkins was a great crime writer, every one of his books as good as *The Silence of the Lambs.* But Hawkins hadn't quite made it to the big time. Why not?

Rollins slipped the card key into the slot and got the green light. His door opened onto a scene of casual magnificence that he barely noticed. He was busy turning ideas over in his mind, thinking about how to make Ben Hawkins an integral part of his project.

It was just a question of how best to use him.

Chapter 32

LEVON PUT DOWN HIS COFFEE CUP, the porcelain chattering against the saucer, knowing that Barb and Hawkins and probably the entire gang of Japanese tourists trooping by could see that his hands were shaking. But he couldn't do a thing about it.

That damned bloodsucking paparazzo pointing the camera at him and Barb! Plus he was reeling from the aftershocks of his out-of-control fight with Lieutenant Jackson. He still felt the shove in the balls of his hands, still felt a flush of mortification at the idea that he could be in a jail cell right now, but hell, he'd done it, and that was that.

The bright side: maybe he'd motivated Jackson to bust his ass on Kim's behalf. If not, too bad. They weren't going to be relying entirely on Jackson anymore.

Levon felt someone coming up behind him, and Hawkins was getting out of his chair, saying, "There he is now."

Levon looked up, saw a thirtyish man coming across the lobby in slacks and a blue sports jacket

over a bold Hawaiian-print shirt, his bleached-
blond hair parted in the middle. Hawkins was saying, "Levon, Barbara, meet Eddie Keola, the best
private detective in Maui."

"The *only* private detective in Maui," Keola
said, his smile showing braces on his teeth. God,
Levon thought, he's not much older than Kim. *This*
was the detective who found the Reese girl?

Keola shook hands with the McDanielses,
sat down in one of the richly upholstered rattan-
backed chairs, and said, "Good to meet you. And
forgive me for jumping right in, but I've already got
some feelers out."

"Already?" Barb asked.

"As soon as Ben called me, I reached out. I was
born about fifteen minutes from here and I was on the
force for a few years when I got out of school, University of Hawaii. I've got a good working relationship with the police," he said. He wasn't show-offy
in Levon's opinion, was just stating his credentials.

"They've got a suspect," Keola added.

"We know him," Levon said, and he told Keola
about Doug Cahill being Kim's ex-boyfriend, then
went over the phone call back home in Michigan
that had cracked open his universe like it was a
raw egg.

Barb asked Keola to tell them about Carol Reese,
the twenty-year-old track star from Ohio State
who'd gone missing a couple of years before.

"I found her in San Francisco," Keola said. "She
had a bad-news, violent boyfriend and so she kidnapped herself, changed her name and everything.
She was powerfully mad at me for finding her," he
said, nodding his head as he remembered.

Levon said, "Tell me how this would work."

Keola said he'd want to talk to the *Sporting Life* photographer, see if he might have filmed some bystanders at the shoot, and that he'd talk to hotel security, see the security tapes from the Typhoon Bar the night Kim disappeared.

"Let's hope Kim shows up on her own," Keola went on, "but if not, this is going to be basic, shoe-leather detective work. You'll be my only client. I'll pull in additional help as needed, and we'll work around the clock. It's over when you say it's over and not before. That's the right way to go."

Levon discussed rates with Keola, but it really didn't matter. He thought about the hours posted on the door at the police station in Kihei. Monday through Friday, eight to five. Saturday, ten to four. Kim, in a dungeon or a ditch, helpless.

Levon said, "You're hired. You've got the job."

Chapter 33

MY PHONE RANG as soon as I opened the door to my room.

I said hello to a woman who said, "Ben-ah Hawkeens?" Strong accent.

I said, "Yes, this is Hawkins," and I waited for her to tell me who she was, but she didn't identify herself. "There's a man, staying in the Princess hotel."

"Go on."

"His name is Nils Bjorn, and you should talk to him."

"And why's that?"

My caller said that Bjorn was a European businessman who should be investigated. "He was in the hotel when Kim McDaniels went missing. He could be...you should talk to him."

I pulled at the desk drawer, looking for stationery and a pen.

"What makes this Nils Bjorn suspicious?" I asked, finding the paper and pen, writing down the name.

"You talk to him. I have to hang up now," the woman said—and did.

I took a bottle of Perrier from the fridge and went out to my balcony. I was staying at the Marriott, a quarter mile up the beach from the much pricier Wailea Princess but with the same dazzling ocean view. I sipped my Perrier and thought about my tipster. For starters, how had she found me? Only the McDanielses and Amanda knew where I was staying.

I went back through the sliding doors, booted up my laptop, and when I got an Internet connection I Googled "Nils Bjorn."

The first hit was an article that had run in the London *Times* a year before, about a Nils Bjorn who had been arrested in London, held on suspicion of selling arms to Iran, released for lack of evidence.

I kept clicking and opening articles, all of which were similar if not identical to the first.

I opened another Perrier and kept poking, found another story on Bjorn going back to 2005, a charge of "aggravated assault on a woman," the legal term for rape. The woman's name wasn't mentioned, only that she was a model, age nineteen, and again, Bjorn wasn't indicted.

My last stop on Bjorn's Internet trail was *Skoal,* a glossy European society magazine. There was a photo that had been taken at a reception dinner for a Swedish industrialist who'd opened a munitions factory outside of Gothenburg.

I enlarged the photo, studied the man identified as Bjorn, stared at his flashbulb-lit eyes. He had regular features, light brown hair, straight nose, looked to be in his thirties, and had not one remarkable or memorable feature.

I saved the photo to my hard drive and then I called the Wailea Princess and asked for Nils Bjorn. I was told he'd checked out the day before.

I asked to be put through to the McDanielses.

I told Levon about my phone call from the woman and what I knew about Nils Bjorn: He'd been charged with selling arms to a terrorist nation, and he'd been charged with raping a model. Neither charge had stuck. Two days ago he'd been staying at the Wailea Princess hotel.

I was trying to keep my excitement in check, but I could hear it in my voice.

"This could be a break," I said.

Chapter 34

LEVON WAS HOLDING for Jackson. After five minutes of Muzak, he was told the police lieutenant would call him back. He hung up the phone, turned on the television, a big plasma thing, took up half the wall, as the news was coming on.

First came the flashy graphic intro to *All-Island News at Noon* with Tracy Baker and Candy Ko'alani, and then Baker was talking about the "still-missing model, Kim McDaniels" and cutting to a picture of her in a bikini. Then Jackson's face was on the screen above the word "Live."

He was talking to the press in front of the police station.

Levon shouted, "Barb, come in here, *quick*," as he cranked up the volume. Barb sat next to him on the sofa just as Jackson was saying, "We're talking to a person of interest, and this investigation is ongoing. Anyone with information about Kim McDaniels is asked to call us. Confidentiality will be respected. And that's all I can say at this time."

"They arrested someone or not?" Barb said, clutching his hand.

"A 'person of interest' is a suspect. But they don't have enough on him, or they'd be saying he was in custody." Levon cranked up the volume a little more.

A reporter asked, "Lieutenant, we understand you're talking to Doug Cahill."

"No comment. That's all I have for you. Thank you."

Jackson turned away and the reporters went nuts, and then Tracy Baker was back on the screen, saying "Doug Cahill, linebacker for the Chicago Bears, has been seen on Maui, and informed sources say he was Kim McDaniels's lover." A picture came on the screen of Doug in his uniform, helmet under his arm, huge grin, cropped blond hair, Midwestern good looks.

"I could see him pestering her," Barb said, chewing on her lower lip, snatching the remote out of Levon's hand, dialing the volume down. "But hurt her? I do *not* believe that."

And then the phone rang. Levon grabbed it off the hook.

"Mr. McDaniels, this is Lieutenant Jackson."

"Are you arresting Doug Cahill? If you are, it's a mistake."

"A witness came forward an hour ago, a local who said he'd seen Cahill harassing Kim after the photo shoot."

"Didn't Doug tell you he hadn't seen Kim?" Levon asked.

"Right. So maybe he lied to us and so we're talking to him now. He's still denying any involvement."

"There's someone else you should know about,"

Levon said, and he told Jackson about Hawkins's recent phone call concerning a tip about an international businessman named Nils Bjorn

"We know who Bjorn is," Jackson said. "There's no link between Bjorn and Kim. No witnesses. Nothing on the surveillance tapes."

"You talked with him?"

"Bjorn had checked out before anyone knew Kim was missing. McDaniels, I know you don't buy it, but Cahill is our guy. We just need time enough to break him."

Chapter 35

HENRI, IN HIS Charlie Rollins gear, was having lunch at the Sand Bar, the hotel's exquisite beach-side restaurant. Yellow market umbrellas glowed overhead, and teenagers ran up the steps from the beach, their tanned bodies glistening with water. Henri didn't know who was more beautiful, the boys or the girls.

Henri's waitress brought him liquid sugar for his iced tea and a basket of cheesy breadsticks and said his salad would be coming shortly. He nodded pleasantly, said he was enjoying the view and had no place he'd rather be than here.

A waiter pulled out a chair at the next table, and a pretty, young woman sat down. She wore her black hair in a short, boyish style, was dressed in a white bikini top and yellow shorts.

Henri knew who she was behind her Maui Jim shades.

When she put down her menu, he said, "Julia. Julia Winkler."

She looked up, said, "Sorry. Do I know you?"

"I know *you*," he said, held up his camera to say, I'm in the business. "Are you on a job?"

"I was," she said. "The shoot wrapped yesterday. I'm going back to L.A. tomorrow."

"Oh. The *Sporting Life* job?"

She nodded, her face getting sad. "I've been waiting around, hoping...I was rooming with Kim McDaniels."

"She'll be back," Henri said kindly.

"You think? Why?"

"I have a feeling she's taking a holiday. It happens."

"If you're so psychic, where is she?"

"She's out of my vibrational reach, but I can read you loud and clear."

"Sure. So what am I thinking?"

"That you're feeling sad and a little lonely and you wish you were having lunch with someone who would make you smile."

Julia laughed, and Henri signaled to the waiter, asked him to set Ms. Winkler up at his table, and the beautiful girl sat down next to him so that they were both looking out at the view.

"Charlie," he said, putting out his hand. "Rollins."

"Hi, Charlie Rollins. What am I having for lunch?"

"Grilled chicken salad and a Diet Coke. And here's what else. You're thinking you'd like to stay over another day because a neighbor is taking care of your cat and it's so nice here, so what's the rush to go home?"

Julia laughed again. "Bruno. He's a Rottweiler."

"I knew that," Henri said, sitting back as the waitress brought his salad and asked Julia for her order, grilled chicken and a mai tai.

"Even if I were to stay over another night, I never date photographers," she said, eyeing the camera resting on the table facing her.

"Have I asked you out?"

"You will."

Their grins turned into laughter, and then Rollins said, "All right, I'll ask you out. And I'm taking your picture so the guys in Loxahatchee won't think I made this up."

"Okay, but take off your sunglasses, Charlie. I want to see your eyes."

"Show me yours, I'll show you mine."

Chapter 36

"*WHOOOOOOO,*" JULIA SCREAMED as the chopper yawed into the coral-gold sky. The little island of Lanai grew huge, and then they were dropping softly to the tiny private heliport at the edge of the vast Island Breezes Hotel's greener-than-green golf course.

Charlie got out first and helped Julia to the ground as she held the collar of her Windbreaker closed, her curly hair parting, her cheeks flushed. They ducked under the rotor blades and ran to a waiting car.

"You've got a great expense account, buddy," she said breathlessly.

"Our dream date's on me, Julia."

"Really?"

"What kind of person would expense a date with you?"

"Awww."

The driver opened the doors, and then the car rolled slowly over the carriage road to the hotel, Julia gasping as she entered the lobby, all velvety teal and gold and burgundy, dense Chinese carpets and ancient statuary. The sunset streamed through the open-air space, almost stealing the show.

Julia and Charlie had their twin massages in a bamboo hut open to the ocean's rhythmic pounding on the shore. The masseurs quartered the plumeria-scented sheets that covered them as their strong hands massaged in cocoa butter before proceeding to the long strokes of the traditional *lomi lomi* massage.

Julia, lying on her stomach, smiled lazily at the man she'd just met, saying, "This is too good. I don't want it to ever stop."

"It only gets better from here."

Dinner came hours later at the restaurant on the main floor. Pillars and soft lighting were the backdrop for their feast of shrimp and Kurubuta pork chops with mango chutney and an excellent French wine. And Julia was happy to let Charlie lead her in conversation about herself. She opened up to him, talking about her upbringing on an army base in Beirut, her move to Los Angeles, her lucky break.

Charlie ordered a dessert wine and the entire dessert menu: zuccotto, pralines and milk, chocolate mousse, Lanai bananas caramelized by the waiter at the table. The delicious fragrance of burnt sugar made him hungry all over again. He looked at the girl, and she was a girl now, sweet and vulnerable and available to him.

Four thousand dollars had been well spent, even if he stopped right now.

But he didn't.

They changed into their swimsuits in a cabana by the pool and took a long walk on the beach. Moonlight bathed the sand, turning the ocean into a magical meeting of rushing sound and frothing foam.

And then Julia laughed, and said, "Last one in the water is an old poop, and that will be you, Charlie."

She ran, screamed as the water lapped her thighs, and Charlie snapped off some quick shots before putting his camera back inside his duffel bag and setting it down.

"Let's see who's an old poop."

He sprinted toward her, dove into the waves, and surfaced with his arms around her.

Chapter 37

AFTER A QUICK DINNER out with Keola, I returned to my hotel room, checked for messages, had no new calls from the woman with the accent, or anyone else. I cranked up my computer, and after a while I sent a pretty fine seven-hundred-word story to Aronstein's in-box at the *L.A. Times.*

Work done for today, I turned on the TV and saw that Kim's story was headlining the ten o'clock news.

There was a banner, "Breaking News," and then the talking heads announced that Doug Cahill was a presumed suspect in the presumed abduction of Kim McDaniels. Cahill's picture came on the screen, fully uniformed for a Chicago Bears game, smiling at the camera like a movie star, all 6 feet, 3 inches, and 250 pounds of him.

Anyone would have been able to do the math. Cahill could've easily picked up 110-pound Kim McDaniels and carried her under his arm like a football.

And then my eyes nearly jumped out of my head.

Cahill was shown in a video clip that had been

shot two hours earlier. While I was having pizza with Eddie Keola, the action had taken place right outside the police station in Kihei.

Cahill was flanked by two lawyers, one of whom I recognized. Amos Brock was dapper in his pearl gray suit, a New York criminal defense attorney with a history of representing celebrities and sports stars who'd gone too far over to the dark side. Brock had turned into a star himself, and now he was defending Doug Cahill.

Station KITV had cameras trained on Cahill and Brock. Brock stepped to the microphone, said, "My client, Doug Cahill, hasn't been charged with anything. The accusations against him are preposterous. There's not a speck of evidence to support any of the allegations that have been going around, which is why my client hasn't been charged. Doug wants to speak publicly, this one and only time."

I grabbed the phone, woke Levon out of what sounded like a deep sleep. "Levon. It's Ben. Turn on the TV. Channel four. Hurry."

I stayed on with Levon as Cahill stood front and center. He was unshaven, wearing a blue cotton button-down shirt under a well-cut sports jacket. Without the pads and the uniform, he looked relatively tame, like a kid in a Wall Street management training program.

"I came to Maui to see Kim," Doug said, his voice shaking, thick with the tears that were also wetting his cheeks. "I saw her for about ten minutes three days ago and never saw her after that. I *didn't* hurt her. I love Kim, and I'm staying here until we find her."

Cahill handed the mic back to Brock: "To repeat,

Doug had nothing to do with Kim's disappearance, and I will absolutely, unequivocally bring action against anyone who defames him. That's all we have to say for the moment. Thank you."

Levon said to me, "What do you make of that? The lawyer? Doug?"

"Doug was pretty convincing," I said. "Either he loves her. Or he's a very good liar."

I had another thought, one I didn't share with Levon. Those seven hundred words I'd just sent to Aronstein at the *Times*?

They were old news.

Chapter 38

I E-MAILED MY EDITOR, told him that Doug Cahill was going to be chum for the media feeding frenzy and why: that a mystery witness had seen him coming on strong with Kim, and that Cahill was being represented by Amos Brock, the current champion bully of defense attorneys.

"Here's an updated version of my article," I wrote Aronstein. "If nothing else, I'm fast."

And then I called our sports chief, Sam Paulson. He keeps odd hours, and I knew he'd be up.

Paulson likes me, but he doesn't trust anyone. I said, "Look, Sam, I need to know what kind of person Doug Cahill is. My story isn't going to mess with yours."

It was a wrestling match that went on for fifteen minutes, Sam Paulson protecting his position as the sports world's premiere "in" guy, while I tried to get something out of Paulson that would tell me if Cahill was dangerous *off* the playing field.

At last Sam gave me a tantalizing lead.

"There's a PR girl. I got her a job working for the Bears. Hawkins, I'm not kidding. This is off the record. This girl's a friend of mine."

"I understand."

"Cahill got this girl pregnant a couple months back. She's told her mother about the baby. She also told Cahill and me. She's giving Cahill a chance to do the right thing. *Whatever* the hell that might be."

"He was dating Kim when this happened with the other woman? You're certain?"

"Yep."

"Does he have any history of violence?"

"They all do. Sure. Bar fights. One zesty one when he played at Notre Dame. Crap like that."

"Thanks, Sam."

"Don't mention it," he said back. "I mean *really*. Don't mention it."

I sat on this bombshell for a few minutes, thinking through what this meant. If Kim knew Cahill had cheated on her, that was reason enough for her to dump him. If he wanted her back, if he was desperate, a confrontation could have led to something physical that might have gotten out of hand.

I called Levon. And I was startled by his reaction.

"Doug is a testosterone machine," he told me. "Kim said he was strong-willed, and we all know he was a killer on the field. How do we know what he's capable of doing? Barb still believes in him, but as for me, I'm starting to think maybe Jackson is right. Maybe they've got the right guy after all."

Chapter 39

JULIA FELT WEIGHTLESS in Charlie's arms, like an angel. Her long legs locked around his waist, and all he had to do was raise his knees, and she was sitting on his lap.

He did just that as they bobbed in the waves. She lifted her face to him, saying, "Charlie, this has been the most. The best."

"It gets better from here," he said again, his theme song for their date, and she grinned at him, kissed him softly, then deeply, a long salty kiss followed by another, electricity arcing like heat lightning around them.

He undid the string tie at her neck, jerked loose the tie behind her back, said, "You do a lot for a simple white bikini."

"What bikini?"

"Never mind," he said, and the swimsuit top drifted away, a ribbon of white on the black waves, until it was gone, and she didn't seem to care.

Julia was too busy licking his ear, her nipples as hard as diamonds against his chest. She groaned as he shifted her so she was pressed even tighter to him, rubbing like an eager beaver against his dick.

He reached around and ran his fingers under the elastic of her bikini bottoms, touched the tender places, making her squeal and squirm like a kid.

She pushed down at the waistband of his swim shorts with the backs of her feet.

"Wait," he said. "Be good."

"I plan to be *great*," she said breathily, kissing him, pulling at his shorts again. "I'm dying for you." She sighed.

He unhooked her legs and pulled off the bottom half of her swimsuit. Carrying the naked girl in his arms, he walked out of the waves as water streamed off their bodies, silver in the moonlight.

Charlie said, "Hang on to me, monkey."

He brought her over to where he'd left his duffel bag next to a mound of black lava rock. He stooped and unzipped the bag, pulled out two enormous beach towels.

Still balancing the girl in his arms, he spread out one towel and laid Julia softly down, covered her with the second towel.

He turned away briefly, set the Panasonic camera on top of the duffel, and switched it on, angling it just so.

Then he faced Julia again, shucked his swim trunks, smiled when she said, "Oh my God, oh my *God*, Charlie."

He knelt between her legs, tonguing her until she cried out, "Please, I can't stand it, Charlie. I'm begging you, please," and he entered her.

Her screams were washed away by the ocean's roar, just as he had imagined they would be, and when they were done, he reached into the duffel bag and took out a knife with a serrated blade. Put the knife down on the towel beside them.

"What's that for?" Julia asked.

"Can't be too careful," Charlie said, shrugging off the question. "In case some bad guy is creeping around."

He raked back her short hair, kissed her closed eyes, put his arms around the naked girl, and warmed her up with his skin. "Go to sleep, Julia," he said. "You're safe with me."

"It gets better from here?" she teased.

"Piggy."

She laughed, snuggled against his chest. Charlie pulled the towel up over her eyes. Julia thought he was talking to her when he said into the camera lens, "Is everybody happy?"

"Totally, completely happy," she said with a sigh.

Chapter 40

ANOTHER WRENCHING TWENTY-FOUR hours passed for Levon and Barbara, and I felt helpless to ease their despair. The news shows were running the same old clips when I went to bed that night, and I was somewhere deep in a troubling dream when the phone rang.

Eddie Keola spoke to me, saying, "Ben, *don't* call the McDanielses on this. Just meet me in front of your hotel in ten minutes."

Keola's Jeep was running when I jogged out into the warm night, then quickly climbed up into the passenger seat.

"Where are we going?" I asked him.

"A beach called Makena Landing. The cops may have found something. Or somebody."

Ten minutes later, Eddie parked along the curving roadside behind six police cruisers, vans from the Special Response Team and the coroner's office. Below us was a semicircle of beach, a cove that was bounded by fingers of lava rock before tapering out into the ocean.

A helicopter hovered noisily overhead, beaming

its spotlight on the scramble of law enforcement people moving like stick figures along the shoreline.

Keola and I made our way down to the beach, and I saw that a fire department rescue vehicle had backed down to the water's edge. There were inflatable boats in the water, and a scuba team was going down.

I was sickened at the thought that Kim's body was submerged there and that she had disappeared to get away from an old boyfriend.

Keola interrupted my reverie to introduce me to a Detective Palikapu, a heavyset young cop in a Maui PD jacket.

"Those campers over there," Palikapu said, pointing to a cluster of children and adults on the far side of the lava-rock jetty. "They saw something floating during the day."

"A body, you mean," said Keola.

"They thought it was a log or garbage at first. Then they saw some shark activity and called it in. Since then, the tides took whatever it is under the bubble rock and left it there. That's where the divers are now."

Keola explained to me that the bubble rock was a shelf of lava with a concave undersurface. He said that sometimes people swam into caves like this one at low tide, didn't pay attention when the tide came in, and drowned.

Was that what had happened to Kim? Suddenly it seemed very possible.

TV vans were pulling up on the shoulder of the road, photographers and reporters clambering down to the beach, the cops stringing up yellow tape to keep the scene intact.

One of the photographers came up to me, introduced himself as Charlie Rollins. He said he was freelance and if I needed photos for the *L.A. Times* he could provide them.

I took his card, then turned in time to see the first divers coming out of the water. One of them had a bundle in his arms.

Keola said, *"You're with me,"* and we skirted the crime scene tape. We were standing on the lip of the shore when a boat came in.

The bright light from the chopper illuminated the body in the diver's arms. She was small, maybe a teenager or maybe a child. Her body was so bloated that I couldn't tell her age, but she was bound with ropes, hand and foot.

Lieutenant Jackson stepped forward and used a gloved hand to move the girl's long, dark hair away from her face.

I was relieved that the victim wasn't Kim McDaniels and that I didn't have to make a call to Levon and Barbara.

But my relief was swamped with an almost overwhelming sorrow. Clearly another girl, someone else's daughter, had been savagely murdered.

Chapter 41

A WOMAN'S HIGH-PITCHED scream cut through the chopper's roar. I turned, saw a dark-skinned woman, five feet two or so, maybe a hundred pounds, make a run toward the yellow tape, crying out, *"Rosa! Rosa! Madre de Dios, no!"*

A man running close behind her shouted, *"Isabel, don't go there. No, Isabel!"* He caught up and pulled the woman into his arms and she beat at him with her fists, trying to break free, the cords in her neck stretched out as she cried, *"No, no, no, mi bebé, mi bebé."*

Police surrounded the couple, the woman's frantic cries trailing behind as she was hustled away from the scene. The press, a pack of them, ran toward the parents of the dead child. You could almost see light glinting in their eyes. Pathetic.

Under other circumstances, I could've been part of that pack, but right then I was behind Eddie Keola, scrambling up the rocky slope to where media setups dotted the upper ledge. Local TV correspondents fed the breaking news to the cameras as the small, twisted body was transferred by stretcher into the coroner's van. Doors slammed and the van sped away.

"Her name was Rosa Castro," Keola told me as we got into the Jeep. "She was twelve. Did you see those ligatures? Arms and legs tied back like that."

I said, "Yeah. I saw."

I'd seen and written about violence for nearly half my life, but this little girl's murder put such ugly pictures into my mind that I felt physically sick. I swallowed my bile and yanked the car door closed.

Keola started up the engine, headed north, saying, "See, this is why I didn't want to call the McDanielses. And if it *had* been Kim—"

His sentence was interrupted by the ringing of his cell phone. He patted his jacket pocket, put his phone to his ear, said, "Keola," then "Levon, *Levon*. It's not Kim. Yes. I saw the body. I'm *sure*. It's not your daughter." Eddie mouthed to me, "They're watching the news on TV."

He told the McDanielses we would stop by their hotel, and minutes later we pulled up to the main entrance to the Wailea Princess.

Barb and Levon were under the breezeway, zephyrs riffling their hair and their new Hawaiian garb. They were holding each other's white-knuckled hands, their faces pale with fatigue.

We walked with them into the lobby. Keola explained, without going into the unspeakable details.

Barbara asked if there could be a connection between Rosa's death and Kim's disappearance, her way of seeking assurances that no one could give her. But I tried to do it anyway. I said that pattern killers had preferences, and it would be rare for one of them to target both a child and a woman. *Rare, but not unheard of*, I neglected to add.

I wasn't just telling Barbara what she wanted to hear; I was also comforting myself. At that time, I didn't know that Rosa Castro's killer had a wide-ranging and boundless appetite for torture and murder.

And it never entered my mind that I'd already met and talked with him.

Chapter 42

HORST TASTED THE Domaine de la Romanée-Conti, bought at Sotheby's for $24,000 per bottle in 2001. He told Jan to hold out his glass. It was a joke. Jan was hundreds of miles away, but their webcam connection almost made it seem as if they were in the same room.

The occasion of this meeting: Henri Benoit had written to Horst saying to expect a download at nine p.m., and Horst had invited Jan, his friend of many years, to preview the newest video before sending it out to the rest of the Alliance.

A ping sounded from Horst's computer, and he walked to his desk, told his friend he was downloading now, and then forwarded the e-mail to Jan in his office in Amsterdam.

The images appeared simultaneously on their screens.

The background was a moonlit beach. A pretty girl was lying faceup on a large towel. She was nude, slim-hipped, small-breasted, and her short hair was finger-combed in a boyish fashion. The black-and-white images of form and shadow gave the film a moody quality, as though it had been shot in the 1940s.

"Beautiful composition," said Jan. "The man has an eye."

When Henri entered the frame, his face was digitally pixilated to a blur, and his voice had been electronically altered. Henri talked to the girl, his voice playful, calling her a monkey and sometimes saying her name.

Horst commented to Jan, "Interesting, yes? The girl isn't the least bit afraid. She doesn't even appear to be drugged."

Julia was smiling up at Henri, reaching out her arms, opening her legs to him. He stepped out of his shorts, his cock large and erect, and the girl covered her mouth as she stared up at him, saying. *Oh my God, Charlie.*

Henri told her she was greedy, but they could hear the teasing and the laughter in his voice. They watched him kneel between her thighs, lift her buttocks, and lower his face until the girl squirmed, grinding her hips, digging her toes into the sand, crying out, *"Please, I can't stand it, Charlie."*

Jan said to Horst, "I think Henri is making her fall in love. Maybe he is falling in love, too? Wouldn't that be something to watch."

"Oh, you think Henri can feel love?"

As the two men watched, Henri stroked, teased, plunged himself into the girl's body, telling her how beautiful she was and to give herself to him until her cries became sobs.

She reached her hands around his neck, and Henri took her in his arms and kissed her closed eyes, her cheeks and mouth. Then his hand became large in front of the camera, almost blocking the image of the girl, and reappeared again, holding a hunting knife. He placed the blade beside the girl on the towel.

Horst was leaning forward, watching the screen intently, thinking, *Yes, first the ceremony, now the ultimate sacrifice,* when Henri turned his digitally obscured face to the camera and said, "Is everybody happy?"

The girl answered, yes, she was completely happy, and then the picture went black.

"What is *this?*" Jan asked, jerked out of what was almost a trance state. Horst reversed the video, reviewed the last moments, and he realized it was over. At least for them.

"Jan," he said, "our boy is teasing us, too. Making us wait for the finished product. Smart. Very smart."

Jan sighed. "What a life he is having at our expense."

"Shall we make a wager? Just between you and me?"

"On what?"

"How long before Henri gets caught?"

Chapter 43

IT WAS ALMOST FOUR IN THE MORNING, and I hadn't slept, my mind still burning with the images of Rosa Castro's tortured body, thinking of what had been done to her before her life ended under a rock in the sea.

I thought about her parents and the McDanielses and that these good people were suffering a kind of hell that Hieronymus Bosch couldn't have imagined, not on his most inspired day or night. I wanted to call Amanda but didn't. I was afraid I might slip and tell her what I was thinking: *Thank God we don't have kids*.

I swung my legs over the bed, turned on the lights. I got a can of POG out of the fridge, a passion fruit, orange, and guava drink, and then I booted up my laptop.

My mailbox had filled with spam since I'd checked it last, and CNN had sent me a news alert on Rosa Castro. I scanned the story quickly, finding that Kim was mentioned in the last paragraph.

I quickly typed Kim's name into the search box

to see if CNN had dragged any new tidbits into their net. They had not.

I opened a can of Pringles, ate just one, made coffee with the complimentary drip coffeemaker, then pecked away at the Internet some more.

I found Doug Cahill videos on YouTube: frat house clips and locker-room antics, and a video of Kim sitting in the stands at a football game, clapping and stomping. The camera went back and forth between her and shots of Cahill playing against the New York Giants, nearly decapitating Eli Manning.

I tried to imagine Cahill killing Kim, and I couldn't rule out that a guy who could slam into three hundred pounders was a guy who could get physical with a resistant girl and accidentally, or on purpose, break her neck.

But, in my heart, I believed that Cahill's tears were real, that he loved Kim, and, logically, if he *had* killed her he had the means to get lost anywhere in the world by now.

So I sent my browser out to search for the name the female tipster had whispered in my ear, the suspected arms trader, Nils—middle name, Ostertag—Bjorn. The search returned the same leads I'd gotten the day before, but this time I opened the articles that were written in Swedish.

Using an online dictionary, I translated the Swedish words for "munitions" and "body armor," and then I found another photo of Bjorn dated three years earlier.

It was a candid shot of the man with the regular, almost forgettable, features getting out of a Ferrari in Geneva. He was wearing a handsome chalk-striped suit under a well-cut topcoat, carrying a Gucci briefcase. Bjorn looked different in this photo from the way he looked at the industrialist's black-tie dinner, because Bjorn's hair was now blond. White blond.

I clicked on the last of the articles about Nils Ostertag Bjorn, and another photo filled my screen, this one of a man in a military uniform. He looked about twenty or so, had wide-spaced eyes and a boxy chin. But he looked nothing like the other photos of Nils Bjorn I'd seen.

I read the text beneath the photo and made out the Swedish words for "Persian Gulf" and "enemy fire," and then it hit me.

I was reading an obituary.

Nils Ostertag Bjorn had been dead for fifteen years.

I went to the shower, let the hot water beat down on my head as I tried to fit the pieces together. Was this simply a case of two men with the same unusual name? Or had someone using a dead man's identity checked into the Wailea Princess?

If so, had he abducted and possibly murdered Kim McDaniels?

Chapter 44

HENRI BENOIT WOKE UP between soft, white layers of bedding in an elegant four-poster bed in his room at the Island Breezes Hotel on Lanai.

Julia was snoring gently under his arm, her face warm against his chest. Late morning sunlight filtered through the filmy curtains, the whole wide Pacific only fifty yards away.

This girl. This setting. This inimitable light. It was a cinematographer's *dream*.

He brushed Julia's hair away from her eyes with his fingers. The sweet girl was under the spell of the kava kava, plus the generous lacing of Valium he'd put in her cup. She'd slept deeply, but now it was time to wake her for her close-up.

Henri shook Julia's arm gently, said, "Wakey, wakey, monkey face."

Julia cracked open her eyes, said, "Charlie? What? Is it time for my flight?"

"Not yet. Want another ten minutes?"

She nodded, then dropped off against his shoulder.

Henri eased out of bed and got busy, turning on

lamps, replacing the media card in his video camera with a new one, setting the camera on the dresser, blocking out the scene. Satisfied, he removed the silk tassel tiebacks from the curtains, letting the heavy drapery fall closed.

Julia mumbled a complaint as he turned her onto her stomach. He said, "It's okay. It's just Charlie," as he tied her legs to the posts at the foot of the bed, making a clove hitch knot with the cords, and then he tied her arms to the headboard using an exotic Japanese chain knot that photographed beautifully.

Julia threw a sigh as she slipped into another dream.

Henri went to his duffel bag, sorted through the contents, put on the clear plastic mask and blue latex gloves, unsheathed the hunting knife.

Masked and gloved but otherwise naked, Henri straddled the sleeping girl, twirled her short hair around the fingers of his left hand, and lifted her head a few inches off the pillow.

"Ow," Julia said, opening her eyes. "You hurt me, Charlie."

"I'm sorry. I'll be more careful."

He waited a moment before drawing the blade lightly across the back of Julia's neck, leaving a thin red line.

Julia only flinched, but with Henri's second cut, her eyelids flew open wide. She twisted her head, her eyes growing huge as she took in the mask, the knife, the blood. She sucked in her breath, shouted, *"Charlie! What are you doing?"*

Henri's mood shattered. He'd been filled with love for this girl, and now she was defying him, wrecking his shot, ruining everything.

"For God's sake, Julia. Show a little class."

Julia filled her lungs and let loose a long, undulating, horror-movie screech.

She'd left Henri no choice. It wasn't graceful, but it was ultimately the best means to the end. He closed his hands around Julia's throat.

Henri was panting by the time he got off the bed and crossed the floor to the camera.

He leaned toward the lens, put his hands on his knees, said with a grin, "Better than I planned. Julia went off script and ended our time together with a real flourish. I just love her. Is everybody happy?"

Chapter 45

HENRI WAS STEPPING OUT of the shower when he heard a knock at the door. *Had someone heard Julia screaming?* A voice called out, "Housekeeping."

"Go away!" he shouted. "Do not *disturb*. Read the *sign,* huh?"

Henri tightened the sash of his robe, walked to the glass doors at the far end of the room, opened them, and stepped out onto the balcony.

The beauty of the grounds spread out before him like the Garden of Eden. Birds chirped their little hearts out in the trees, pineapples grew in the flower beds, children ran along the walks to the pool as hotel staff set up lounge chairs. Beyond the pool, the ocean was bright blue, the sun beat down on another perfect Hawaiian day.

There were no sirens. No men in black. No trouble on the horizon for him.

All was well.

Henri palmed his cell phone, called for the helicopter, then went to the bed and pulled the comforter over Julia's body. He wiped down the room, every knob and surface, and turned on the TV as he dressed in his Charlie Rollins gear. Rosa Castro's face grinned at him from the TV screen, a sweet little girl, and then there was the continuing story of Kim McDaniels. No news, but the search went on.

Where was Kim? Where, oh, where could she be?

Henri packed his gear, checked the room for anything he might have overlooked, and when he was satisfied he put on Charlie's wraparound sunglasses and ball cap, swung his large duffel onto his shoulder, and left the room.

He passed the housekeeper's cart on his way to the elevator, said to the stout brown woman vacuuming, "I'm in Four-twelve."

"I can clean now?" she asked.

"No, no. A few more hours, please."

He apologized for the inconvenience, said, "I've left something for you in the room."

"Thank you," she said. Henri winked at her, took the stairs down to the marvelous velvet jewel box of a lobby with birds flying through one side and out the other.

He settled his bill at the desk, then asked a groundskeeper for a lift out to the helipad. He was already thinking ahead as the hotel's oversize golf cart ran smoothly alongside the green, the wind picking up now, blowing clouds out to the sea.

He tipped the driver and, holding down his cap, ran toward the chopper.

After buckling in, he raised his hand to say hello to the pilot. He pulled on headphones and, as the chopper lifted, he snapped off shots of the island with his Sony, what any tourist would do. But it was all for show. Henri was well beyond the magnificence of Lanai.

When the helicopter touched down in Maui, he made an important call.

"Mr. McDaniels? You don't know me. My name is Peter Fisher," he said, brushing his speech with a bit of Aussie. "I have something to tell you about Kim. I also have her watch—a Rolex."

Chapter 46

THE KAMEHAMEHA HOSTEL on Oahu had been built in the early 1900s, and it looked to Levon like it had been a boardinghouse, with small bungalows surrounding the main building. The beach was right across the highway. Out on the horizon, surfers crouched above their boards, skimming the waves, waiting for the Big One.

Levon and Barbara stepped over backpackers in the dark lobby, which smelled musty, like mildew with a touch of marijuana.

The man behind the desk looked like he'd washed up on the beach a hundred years ago. He had bloodshot eyes, hair in a white braid even longer than Barb's, and a stained "Bullish on America" T-shirt with a name patch: "Gus."

Levon told Gus that he and Barb had a reservation for one night, and Gus told Levon that he'd need to be paid in full before he handed over the keys, those were the rules.

Levon gave the man ninety bucks in cash.

"No refunds, checkout at noon, no exceptions."

"We're looking for a guest named Peter Fisher,"

Levon said. "He has an accent. Australian or South African maybe. 'Pee-ta Fish-a.' You have his room number?"

The clerk flipped pages of the guest book, saying, "Not everyone signs in. If they come in a gang, I only need the one signature of whoever's paying. I don't see any Peter Fleisher."

"Fisher."

"Either way, I don't see him. Most people eat in our dining room at dinner. Six dollars, three courses. Ask around later, and you might find your man."

Gus looked hard at Levon, said, "I know you. You're the parents of that model got killed over on Maui."

Levon felt his blood pressure rocket, wondered if today was the day he would be cut down by a fatal myocardial infarction. "Where'd you hear that?" he snapped.

"Whad'ya mean? It's on TV. In the newspapers."

"She's not dead," Levon said.

He took the keys. With Barb behind him, they climbed to the third floor, opened the door to an appalling room: two small beds, mattress springs poking at grimy sheets. The shower stall was black with mold, there were years of crud in the blinds, and the scatter rug looked damp to the touch.

The sign tacked over the sink read, *"Please clean up after yourselfs. There's no maid service here."*

Barbara looked helplessly at her husband.

"We'll go downstairs for dinner in a while and talk to people. We don't have to stay here. We could go back."

"After we find this Fisher person."

"Of course," Levon said. But what he was thinking was, *If Fisher hadn't checked out of this hellhole. If the whole thing wasn't a hoax like Lieutenant Jackson warned him from the day they met.*

Chapter 47

HENRI DIDN'T RELY on the costume, the cowboy boots or the cameras or the wraparound shades. The trappings were important, but the *art* of disguise was in the gestures and the voice, and then there was the X Factor. The element that truly distinguished Henri Benoit as a first-class chameleon was his talent for becoming the man he was pretending to be.

At half past six that evening, Henri strolled into the rustic dining room of the Kamehameha Hostel. He was wearing jeans, a summer-weight blue cashmere sweater, sleeves pushed up, Italian loafers, no socks, gold watch, wedding band. His hair, streaked gray, was combed straight back, and his rimless glasses framed the look of a man of sophistication and means.

He gazed around the rough-hewn room, at the rows of tables and folding chairs and at the steam table. He joined the line and took the slop that was offered before heading toward the corner where Barbara and Levon sat behind their untouched food.

"Mind if I join you?" he asked.

"We're about to leave," Levon said, "but if you're brave enough to eat that, you're welcome to sit down."

"What the heck do you think this is?" Henri asked, pulling out a chair next to Levon. "Animal, vegetable, or mineral?"

Levon laughed, "I was told it's beef stew, but don't take my word for it."

Henri put out his hand, said, "Andrew Hogan. From San Francisco."

Levon shook his hand, introduced Barb and himself, said, "We're the only ones here in the over-forty crowd. Did you know what this pit was like when you booked your room?"

"Actually, I'm not staying here. I'm looking for my daughter. Laurie just graduated from Berkeley," he said modestly. "I told my wife that Laur's having the time of her life camping out with a bunch of other kids, but she hasn't called home in a few days. A week, actually. So Mom is having fits because of that poor model who went missing, you know, on Maui."

Henri turned his stew over with his fork, looked up when Barbara said, "That's *our* daughter. Kim. The model who is missing."

"Oh, *Jesus,* I'm sorry. I'm so *sorry.* I don't know what to say. How're you holding up?"

"It's been awful," said Barb, shaking her head, eyes down. "You pray. You try to sleep. Try to keep your wits together."

Levon said, "You're willing to chase any scrap of hope. What we're doing here, we got a call from some guy named Peter Fisher. He said he had Kim's watch and if we met him here he'd give it to us and tell us about Kim. He knew that Kim wore a Rolex. You said your name is Andrew?"

Henri nodded his head.

"Cops told us the call was probably bull, that there are nut jobs who love to screw with people's heads. Anyway, we've talked to everyone here. No one's heard of Peter Fisher. He's not registered at the fabulous Kamehameha Hilton."

"You shouldn't stay here, either," said the man in blue. "Listen, I rented a place about ten minutes from here, three bedrooms, two baths, and it's *clean*. Why don't you two stay with me tonight? Keep me company."

Barbara said, "Nice of you to offer, Mr. Hogan, but we don't want to impose."

"It's Andrew. And you'd be doing me a *favor*. You like Thai food? I found a place not far from here. What do you say? Get out of this hole, and we'll go looking for our girls in the morning."

"Thanks, Andrew," said Barbara. "That's a nice offer. If you let us take you out to dinner, we'll talk about it."

Chapter 48

BARBARA WOKE UP in the dark, feeling sheer, naked terror.

Her arms were tied behind her back and they ached. Her legs were roped together at her knees and ankles. She was crammed into a fetal position against the corner of a shallow compartment that was moving!

Was she blind? Or was it just too dark to see? Dear God, what was happening? She screamed, *"Levon!"*

Behind her back, something stirred.

"Barb? *Baby?* Are you *okay?*"

"Oh, honey, thank God, thank *God* you're here. Are you all right?"

"I'm tied up. Shit. What is this?"

"I think we're in the trunk of a car."

"Christ! A trunk! It's Hogan. Hogan did this."

Muffled music came through the backseat to where the couple lay trussed like hens in a crate.

Barbara said, "I'm going crazy. I don't understand any of this. What does he want?"

Levon kicked at the trunk's lid. *"Hey! Let us*

out. Hey!" His kick didn't budge the lid, didn't make a dent. But now Barbara's eyes were growing accustomed to the dark.

"Levon, look! See that? The trunk release."

The two turned painfully by inches, scraping cheeks and elbows against the carpeting, Barb working off her shoes, pulling at the release lever with her toes. The lever moved, but there was no resistance, no release of the lock.

"Oh, God, please," Barbara wailed, her asthma kicking in, her voice trailing into a wheeze, then a burst of coughs.

"The cables are cut," said Levon. "The *back-seat*. We can kick through the backseat."

"And then what? We're tied up!" Barb gasped.

Still they tried, the two of them kicking without full use of their legs, getting nowhere.

"It's latched, goddammit," said Levon.

Barb was fighting to take one breath and then another, trying to stop herself from going into a full-blown gag attack. Why had Hogan taken them? Why? What was he going to do with them? What was to be gained from kidnapping them?

Levon said, "I read somewhere, you kick out the taillights and you can stick a hand out, wave until someone notices. Even if we just bust the lights, maybe a cop will pull the car over. Do it, Barb. *Try*."

Barb kicked, and plastic shattered. "Now you!" she shouted.

As Levon broke through the taillight on his side of the trunk, Barbara turned so that her face was near the shards and wires.

She actually could see blacktop streaming below

the tires. If the car stopped, she'd scream. They weren't helpless, not anymore. They were still alive and dammit, they would fight!

"What's that sound? A cell phone?" Levon asked. "In the trunk with us?"

Barb saw the glowing faceplate of a phone by her feet. "We're getting out of here, honey. Hogan made a big mistake."

She struggled to position her hands as the first ring became the second, thumbing the buttons blindly behind her back, hitting the Send key, turning on the phone.

Levon yelled, "Hello! Hello! Who's there?"

"Mr. McDaniels, it's me. *Marco*. From the Wailea Princess."

"Marco! Thank God. You've got to find us. We've been kidnapped."

"I'm sorry. I know you're uncomfortable back there. I'll explain everything momentarily."

The phone went dead.

The car slowed to a stop.

Chapter 49

HENRI FELT BLOOD charging through his veins. He was tense in the best possible way, adrenalized, mentally rehearsed, ready for the next scene to play itself out.

He checked the area again, glancing up to the road, then taking in the 180 degrees of shoreline. Satisfied that the area was deserted, he hauled his duffel bag out of the backseat, tossed it under a tangle of brush before returning to the car.

Walking around the all-wheel-drive sedan, he stooped beside each tire, reducing the air pressure from eighty to twenty pounds, slapping the trunk when he passed it, then opening the front door on the passenger side. He reached into the glove box, tossed the rental agreement to the floor, and removed his ten-inch buck knife. It felt like it was part of his hand.

He grabbed the keys and opened the trunk. Pale moonlight shone on Barbara and Levon. Henri, as Andrew, said, "Is everyone all right back here in coach?"

Barbara launched a full-throated, wordless scream

until Henri leaned in and held the knife up to her throat. "Barb, *Barb*. Stop yelling. No one can hear you but me and Levon, so call off the histrionics, okay? I don't like it."

Barb's scream became a wheeze and a cry.

"What the hell are you doing, Hogan?" Levon demanded, wrenching his body so he could see his captor's face. "I'm a reasonable man. Explain yourself."

Henri put two fingers under his nose to resemble a mustache. He lowered his voice and thickened it, said, "Sure, I will, Mr. McDaniels. You're my number one priority."

"My dear Christ. You're *Marco?* You're him! I don't believe it. How could you scare us like this? What do you want?"

"I want you to behave, Levon. You, too, Barb. Act up, and I'll have to take strong measures. Be good and I'll move you up to first class. Deal?"

Henri sawed through the nylon ropes around Barbara's legs and helped her out of the car and into the backseat. Then he went back for Levon, cutting the restraints, walking the man to the back of the car, strapping them both in with the seat belts.

Then Henri got into the driver's seat. He locked the doors, turned on the dome light, reached up to the camera behind the rearview mirror, and switched it on.

"If you like, you can call me Henri," he said to the McDanielses, who were staring at him with unblinking eyes. He reached into the pocket of his Windbreaker, pulled out a dainty, bracelet-style wristwatch, and held it up in front of them.

"See? As I promised. Kim's watch. The Rolex. Recognize it?"

He stuffed it into Levon's jacket pocket.

"Now," Henri said, "I'd like to tell you what's going on and why I have to kill you. Unless you have questions so far."

Chapter 50

WHEN I WOKE UP that morning and snapped on the local news, Julia Winkler was all over it. There, filling the TV screen, was her achingly beautiful face and a headline in bold italics running under her picture: *Supermodel Found Murdered.*

How could Julia Winkler be dead?

I bolted upright in bed, goosed up the sound, stared at the next shot, this one of Kim and Julia posing together for the *Sporting Life* photo-story, their lovely faces pressed together, laughing, both absolutely radiant with life.

The TV anchors were going back over the breaking news "for those who've just tuned in."

I stared at the tube, gathering in the stunning details: Julia Winkler's body had been found in a room at the Island Breezes Hotel, a five-star resort on Lanai. A housekeeper had run through the hotel shouting that a woman had been strangled, that there were bruises around her neck, blood all over the linens.

Next up, a waitress was interviewed. Emma Laurent. She'd waited on tables in the Club Room last night and recognized Julia Winkler. She'd been having dinner with a good-looking man in his thirties, Laurent said. He was white, brown-haired with a good build. "He definitely works out."

Winkler's date signed the check with a room number, 412, registered to Charles Rollins. Rollins left a good tip, and Julia had given the waitress her autograph. Personalized it. *To Emma from Julia*. Emma held up the signed napkin for the camera.

I got a POG out of the fridge, guzzled it, watched the camera cut now to live shots outside the Island Breezes Hotel. Cruisers were everywhere, the loud garble of police radios squawked in the background. The camera held on a reporter with the local NBC affiliate.

The reporter, Kevin de Martine, was well respected, had been embedded with a military unit in Iraq in '04. He was now standing with his back to a sawhorse barrier, rain falling softly on his bearded face, palm fronds waving dramatically behind him.

De Martine said, "This is what we know. Nineteen-year-old supermodel Julia Winkler, *former roommate* of the still-missing top model Kimberly McDaniels, was found dead this morning in a room registered to a Charles Rollins of Loxahatchee, Florida."

De Martine went on to say that Charles Rollins was not in his room, that he was sought for questioning, that any information about Rollins should be phoned in to the number at the bottom of the screen.

I tried to absorb this horrendous story. Julia Winkler was dead. There was a suspect—but he was missing. Or how the police like to describe it—*he was in the wind*.

Chapter 51

THE PHONE RANG next to my ear, jarring the hell out of me. I grabbed the receiver. "Levon?"

"It's Dan Aronstein. Your paycheck. Hawkins, are you on this Winkler story?"

"Yep. I'm on the case, Chief. If you hang up and let me work, okay?"

I glanced back at the TV. The local anchors, Tracy Baker and Candy Ko'alani, were on-screen, and a new face had been patched in from Washington. Baker asked the former FBI profiler John Manzi, "Could the killings of Rosa Castro and Julia Winkler be connected? Is this the work of a serial killer?"

Those two potent and terrifying words. "Serial killer." Kim's story was now going global. The whole wide world was going to be focused on Hawaii and the mystery of two beautiful girls' deaths.

Former agent Manzi tugged at his earlobe, said serial killers generally had a signature, a preferred method for killing.

"Rosa Castro was strangled, but with ropes," he said. "Her actual manner of death was *drowning*. Without speaking to the medical examiner, I can only go by the witness reports that Julia Winkler was manually strangled. That is, she was killed by someone choking her with his hands.

"It's too soon to say if these killings were done by the same person," Manzi continued, "but what I can say about manual strangulation is that it's personal. The killer gets more of a thrill because unlike a shooting, it takes a long time for the victim to die."

Kim. Rosa. Julia. Was this coincidence or a wildfire? I wanted desperately to talk to Levon and Barbara, to get to them before they saw Julia's story on the news, prepare them somehow — but I didn't know where they were.

Barbara had called me yesterday morning to say that she and Levon were going to Oahu to check out what was probably a bum lead, and I hadn't heard from them since.

I turned down the TV volume, called Barb's cell phone number, and when she didn't answer, I hung up and called Levon. He didn't answer, either. After leaving a message, I called their driver, and when I got forwarded to Marco's voice mail, I left my number and told him that my call was urgent.

I showered and dressed quickly, collecting my thoughts, feeling an elusive and important *something* I should pay attention to, but I couldn't nail it down.

It was like a horsefly you can't swat. Or the faint smell of gas, and you don't know where it's coming from. What was it?

I tried Levon again, and when I got his voice mail I called Eddie Keola. He had to know how to reach Barbara and Levon.

That was his job.

Chapter 52

KEOLA BARKED HIS name into the phone.

"Eddie, it's Ben Hawkins. Have you seen the news?"

"Worse than that. I've seen the real thing."

Keola told me he'd been to the Island Breezes since the news of Julia Winkler's death had gone over the police band. He'd been there when the body was taken out and he had spoken with the cops on the scene.

He said, "Kim's roommate was murdered. Do you believe it?"

I told him I'd had no luck reaching the McDanielses or their driver and asked if he knew where Barb and Levon were staying.

"Some dive on the eastern shore of Oahu. Barb told me she didn't know the name."

"Maybe I'm paranoid," I told Keola, "but I'm worried. It isn't like them to be incommunicado."

"I'll meet you at their hotel in an hour," Keola said.

I arrived at the Wailea Princess just before eight a.m. I was heading to the front desk when I heard

Eddie Keola calling my name. He came across the marble floor at a trot. His bleached hair was damp and wind-combed, and fatigue dragged at his face.

The hotel's day manager was a young guy wearing a smart hundred-dollar tie and a blue gabardine jacket with a nametag reading "Joseph Casey."

When he got off the phone, Keola and I told Casey our problem—that we couldn't locate two of the hotel guests and we couldn't locate their hotel-comped driver, either. I said that we were concerned for the McDanielses' safety.

The manager shook his head, and said, "We don't have any drivers on staff and we never hired anyone to drive Mr. and Mrs. McDaniels. Not somebody named Marco Benevenuto. Not anyone. We don't do that and never have."

I was stunned into an openmouthed silence. Keola asked, "Why would this driver tell the McDanielses he'd been hired and paid for by your hotel?"

"I don't know the man," said the manager. "I have no idea. You'll have to ask him."

Keola flashed his ID, saying he was employed by the McDanielses, and asked to be let into their room.

After clearing Keola with the head of security, Casey agreed. I took a phone book to a plush chair in the lobby. There were five limousine services on Maui, and I'd worked my way through all of them by the time Eddie Keola sat down heavily in the chair beside me.

"No one's ever heard of Marco Benevenuto," I told him. "I can't find a listing for him in all of Hawaii."

"The McDanielses' room is empty, too," Keola said. "Like they were never there."

"What the hell is this?" I asked him. "Barbara and Levon left town, and you didn't know where they were going?"

It sounded like an accusation. I didn't mean it that way, but my panic had risen to the high-water mark and it was still climbing. Hawaii had a low crime rate. And now, in the space of a week, two girls were dead. Kim was still missing, and her parents and driver were missing, too.

"I *told* Barbara it should be me following that lead on Oahu," Keola said. "Those backpacker joints are remote and kind of rough. But Levon talked me out of it. He said that he wanted me to spend my time *here* looking for Kim."

Keola was snapping his wristband, chewing his lip. The two of us, ex-cops without portfolio, were trying desperately to make sense out of thin air.

Chapter 53

IT WAS BECOMING a three-ring circus in the lobby of the Wailea Princess. A queue of German tourists had lined up at the desk, a flock of little kids were begging the gardener to let them feed the koi, even a presentation on tourist attractions was going on thirty feet away, slides and film and native music.

Eddie Keola and I might as well have been invisible. No one even looked at us.

I started ticking off the facts, linking Rosa to Kim, Kim to Julia, and to the driver, Marco Benevenuto, who had lied to me and the McDanielses — who were missing.

"What do you think, Eddie? Do you see the connection? Or am I fanning the flames of my overheated imagination?"

Keola sighed loudly, and said, "Tell you the truth, Ben, I'm in over my head. Don't look at me like that. I do cheating husbands. Insurance claims. What do you think? Maui is Los Angeles?"

I said, "Work on your friend, Lieutenant Jackson. why don't you?"

"I will. I'll get him to reach out to the PD in Oahu, get a serious search going for Barb and Levon. If he won't do it, I'll go over his head. My dad's a judge."

"That must come in handy."

"Damned right it does."

Keola said he'd call me, then left me sitting with my phone in my lap. I stared across the open lobby to the dark aqua sea. I could see the outline of Lanai through the morning mist, the small island where Julia Winkler's life had been snuffed out.

It was five a.m. in L.A., but I had to talk to Amanda.

"Wassup, buttercup?" she slurred into the phone.

"Bad stuff, honeybee."

I told her about this latest shocker, how it felt like spiders were using my spine as a speedway, and no, I hadn't had anything stronger to drink than guava juice in three days.

"Kim would have shown up by now if she could do it," I told Amanda. "I don't know the who, where, why, when, or how, but honest to God, honey, I think I know the what."

"'Serial Killer in Paradise.' The story you've been waiting for. Maybe a book."

I hardly heard her. The elusive fact that had been bothering me since I turned on the TV two hours before lit up in my mind like it was made of bright red neon. *Charles Rollins.* The name of the man last seen with Julia Winkler.

I knew that name.

I told Amanda to hold on a sec, got my wallet out of my back pocket, and, with a shaking hand, I sorted through the business cards I'd stashed behind the small plastic window.

"Mandy."

"I'm here. Are you?"

"A photographer named Charles Rollins came up to me at the Rosa Castro crime scene. He was from a *Talk Weekly* magazine, Loxahatchee, Florida. The cops think he may have been the last person to have seen Julia Winkler alive. He's nowhere to be found."

"You talked to him? You could identify him?"

"Maybe. I need a favor."

"Boot up my laptop?"

"Please."

I waited, my cell phone pressed so hard against my ear that I could hear the toilet flush in L.A. Finally, my beloved's voice came back on the line.

She cleared her throat, said, "Benjy, there are forty pages of Charles Rollinses on Google, gotta be two thousand guys by that name, a hundred in Florida. But there's no listing for a magazine called *Talk Weekly*. Not in Loxahatchee. Not anywhere."

"For the hell of it, let's send him an e-mail."

I read her Rollins's e-mail address, dictated a message.

Seconds later Amanda said, "It bounced back, Benjy. 'Mailer-Daemon. Unknown e-mail address.' What now?"

"I'll call you later. I've got to go to the police."

Chapter 54

HENRI SAT TWO rows back from the cockpit in a spanking new charter jet that was almost empty. He watched through the window as the sleek little aircraft lifted smoothly off the runway and took to the wide blue and white sky above Honolulu.

He sipped champagne, said yes to caviar and toast points from the hostess, and when the pilot made his all-clear announcement Henri opened his laptop on the tabletop in front of him.

The miniature video camera he'd affixed to the rearview mirror of the car had been sacrificed, but before it was destroyed by the flooding seawater, it had sent the video wirelessly to his computer.

Henri was dying to see the dailies.

He put in his earbuds and opened the MPV file.

He almost said "wow" out loud. The pictures unfurling on his computer screen were *that* beautiful. The interior of the car glowed from the dome light. Barbara and Levon were softly lit, and the sound quality was excellent.

Because Henri had been in the front seat, he was not in the shot—and he liked that. No mask. No

distortion. Just his disembodied voice, sometimes
as Marco, sometimes as Andrew, at all times rea-
soning with the victims.

"I told Kim how beautiful she was, Barbara, as I
made love to her. I gave her something to drink so
she wouldn't feel pain. Your daughter was a lovely
person, very sweet. You don't have to think she did
anything to deserve being killed."

"I don't believe you killed her," Levon said.
"You're a freak. A pathological liar!"

"I gave you her watch, Levon.... Okay, then,
look at this."

Henri had opened his cell phone, and showed
them the photo of his hand holding Kim's head by
the roots of her wild blond hair.

"Try to understand," he said, talking over Barb
and Levon's insufferable wailing and snuffling.
"This is business. The people I work for pay a lot
of money to see people die."

Barbara was gagging and sobbing, telling him
to stop, but Levon was in a different kind of hell,
clearly trying to balance his grief and horror with a
desire to keep the two of them alive.

He'd said, "Let us go, Henri. We don't know
who you really are. We can't hurt you."

Henri had said, "It's not that I *want* to kill you,
Levon. It's about the money. Yes. I make money by
killing *you*."

"I can get you money," Levon said "I'll beat
their offer. I will!"

And now there on his laptop, Barbara was pleading for her boys. Henri stopped her, saying it was
time for him to go.

He'd stepped on the gas, the soft tires rolling

easily over the sand, the car plowing into the surf.
When it had good momentum, Henri had gotten
out of the car, walked alongside it, until the water
rose up to the windshield.

Inside, the camera on the rearview had recorded
the McDanielses begging, the water sloshing over
the window frames, rising up the seats where the
McDanielses' arms were locked behind them, their
bodies lashed in place with the seat belts.

Still he'd given them hope.

"I'm leaving the light on so you can record your
good-byes," he heard himself saying on the small
screen. "And someone on the road *could* see you.
You could be rescued. Don't count it out. But if I
were you, I'd pray for that."

He had wished them luck, then waded back up to
the beach. He'd stood under the trees and watched
the car sink completely in only about three minutes. Faster than he would have guessed. Merciful.
So maybe there was a God after all.

When the dome light winked out, he'd changed
his clothes, then walked up the highway until he
caught a ride.

Now he closed his laptop, finished the champagne as the hostess handed him the lunch menu.
He decided on the duck *à l'orange,* put on his Bose
speakers, and listened to some Brahms. Soothing.
Beautiful. Perfect.

The last few days had been exceptional, a fantastic drama every minute, a highlight of his life.

He was quite sure everybody would be happy.

Chapter 55

HOURS LATER, HENRI Benoit was in the washroom of the first-class flight lounge at Honolulu International. The first leg of his flight had been a pleasure, and he was looking forward to the same for his flight to Bangkok.

He washed his hands, checked out his new persona in the mirror. He was a Swiss businessman based in Geneva. His white-blond hair was short, his eyeglass frames were large and horn-rimmed, giving him an erudite look, and he wore a five-thousand-dollar suit with some fine handmade English shoes.

He had just sent a few frames of the McDanielses' last moments to the Peepers, knowing that by this time tomorrow, there would be a good many more euros in his bank account in Zurich.

Henri left the washroom, went to the main waiting area in the lounge, set his briefcase beside him, and relaxed in a soft gray chair. Breaking news was coming over the television, a cable news special. The anchorwoman Gloria Roja was reporting on a crime that she said "evoked horror and outrage."

She went on, "A young woman's decapitated

body has been found in a rental cabin on a beach in Maui. Sources close to the police department say the victim has been *dead for several days.*"

Roja turned to the large screen behind her and introduced a local reporter, Kai McBride, on the ground in Maui.

McBride said into the camera, "This morning, Ms. Maura Aluna, the owner of this beach camp, found the decapitated head and body of a young woman inside. Ms. Aluna told police that she had rented her house to a man over the telephone and that his credit card cleared. Any minute now, we expect Lieutenant Jackson of the Kihei PD to make a statement."

McBride turned away briefly from the camera, then said, "Gloria, Lieutenant James Jackson is coming out of the house *now.*"

McBride ran, and her cameraman ran right alongside her, the picture jiggling. McBride shouted, "Lieutenant, Lieutenant Jackson, can you give us a minute?"

The camera closed in on the lieutenant.

"I have nothing to say to the press at this time."

"I have just *one* question, sir."

Henri leaned forward in his seat in the flight lounge, transfixed by the dramatic scene that was unfolding on the large screen.

He was witnessing the endgame in real time. This was just too good to be true. What he'd do later is lift the broadcast from the network's Web site, cut it into his video. He'd have the whole Hawaiian saga, the beginning, middle, phenomenal ending, and now—this epilogue.

Henri quashed a giddy desire to say to the guy

sitting two seats away, "Look at that cop, would you? That Lieutenant Jackson. His skin is *green*. I think he's going to throw up."

On-screen, the reporter persisted.

"Lieutenant Jackson, is it Kim? Is the body you found that of the supermodel Kim McDaniels?"

Jackson spoke, tripping over his words. "No comment at this, *on* this. We're right in the middle of something," he said. "We've got a lot of moves we have to make. Will you turn that thing off? We never comment on an ongoing investigation, McBride. You *know* that."

Kai McBride turned back to the camera.

"I'm going to take a wild flying leap and say that Lieutenant Jackson's no-comment dodgeball was a confirmation, Gloria. We're all waiting now for a positive ID that the victim *was* Kim McDaniels. This is Kai McBride, reporting from Maui."

Chapter 56

THAT MORNING AT low tide the roof of a car had looked at first to the passing jogger like the shell of a giant sea turtle. When he realized what it was, he'd called the police and they'd responded in force.

Now the crane had lowered the waterlogged car to the beach. The fire department crew, search and rescue, and cops from two islands were standing in groups on the sand, watching the Pacific flow out of the chassis.

A cop opened one of the back doors and called out, "Two DBs wearing their seat belts. I recognize them. Jesus God. It's the McDanielses. The parents."

My stomach dropped, and I spewed a string of curse words that didn't make any literal sense, just me venting all the bile I could without getting physically violent or sick.

Eddie Keola was standing beside me outside the yellow tape that ran from a branch of driftwood to a chunk of lava rock thirty yards away. Keola was not only my ticket to police intel and crime scenes, but I was starting to think of him as the younger brother I never had.

Actually, we looked nothing alike, except that we both looked like shit right now.

More vehicles pulled up, some with sirens, some without, all braking on the potholed asphalt running above and parallel to the beach, a road that had been closed for repairs.

These new additions to the law enforcement fleet were black SUVs, and the men who got out of them wore jackets stenciled "FBI."

A cop friend of Eddie's came over to us, said, "Only thing I can tell you is that the McDanielses were seen having dinner at the Kamehameha Hostel. They were with a white man, six foot or so, grayish hair and glasses. They left with him, and that's all we've got. Based on that description, the guy they had dinner with could've been anyone."

"Thanks," said Eddie.

"It's okay, but now you guys really have to leave."

Eddie and I walked up a sandy ramp to Eddie's Jeep.

I was glad to go.

I didn't want to see the corpses of those two good people I'd come to care about so very much. Eddie drove me back to the Marriott, and we sat in the lot for a while just chewing it over.

The deaths of everyone attached to this crime spree had been premeditated, calculated, almost artistic, the work of a very smart and practiced killer who'd left no clues behind. I felt sorry for the people who had to solve this crime. And now Aronstein was terminating my all-expenses-paid Hawaiian holiday.

"When's your flight?" Keola asked.

"Around two."

"Want me to drive you? I'd be happy to do it."

"Thanks, anyway. I've got to return my car."

"I'm sorry how this turned out," said Keola.

"This is going to be one of those cases, if it gets solved at all, it'll be like...seventeen years from now. A deathbed confession," I said. "Or a deal with a jailhouse snitch."

A little while later, I said good-bye to Eddie, threw my things together, and checked out of the hotel. I was going back to L.A. unresolved and disconsolate, feeling like I'd left a big piece of myself behind. I would've bet anything I owned that for me, at least, the story was over.

I was wrong again.

Part Three

BODY COUNT

Chapter 57

THE VERY GOOD-LOOKING gentleman with the white-blond hair walked down a red, silk-lined corridor ending in a breeze-swept lobby. A stone desk rose out of the floor at the far end of the room, and a young clerk received the guest with a smile and lowered eyes.

"Your suite is ready for you, Mr. Meile. Welcome back to the Pradha Han."

"Delighted to be here," Henri said. He pushed his horn-rimmed glasses to the top of his head as he signed the credit card slip. "Did you keep the gulf warm for me, Rahpee?"

"Oh, yes sir. We would not disappoint our precious guest."

Henri opened the door to the luxury suite, undressed in the lavish bedroom, tossing his clothes onto the king-size bed under the mosquito netting. He wrapped himself in a silk robe and sampled chocolates and dried mango as he watched *BBC World News,* thrilling to the update on "the killing spree in Hawaii that continues to confound police."

He was thinking, *That* should make the Peepers happy.

Chapter 58

HENRI'S WELL-EARNED HOLIDAY continued in Bangkok, one of his favorite cities in all the world.

He met the Swedish girl in the night market, where she was struggling to translate baht into euros so that she could decide whether to buy a small wooden elephant. His Swedish was good enough that she spoke to him in her own language until, laughing, he said, "I've used up all of my Swedish."

"Let's try this," she said in perfect, British-inflected English. She introduced herself as Mai-Britt Olsen, telling Henri that she was on holiday with classmates from Stockholm University.

The girl was striking, nineteen or twenty and nearly six feet tall. She wore her flaxen hair cut straight at the shoulders, drawing his attention to her lovely throat.

"You have remarkable blue eyes," he said.

She said, "Oooh," and batted her lashes comically, and Henri laughed. She waggled her little elephant, and said, "I'm looking for a monkey, also."

She took Henri's arm and they strolled down the

aisles of colorfully lit stalls of fruit and costume jewelry and sweets.

"My girlfriends and I went to the elephant polo today," Mai-Britt told him, "and tomorrow we're invited to the palace. We are volleyball players," she explained. "The 2008 Olympics."

"Truly? That's fantastic. Hey, I hear the palace is really stupendous. As for me, tomorrow morning I'm going to be strapped into a projectile heading to California."

Mai-Britt laughed. "Let me guess. You're flying to L.A. on business."

Henri grinned. "That's a very good guess. But that's tomorrow, Mai-Britt. Have you had dinner?"

"Just little bites in the market."

"There's a place close by that few people know. Very exclusive and a little risqué. Are you up for an adventure?"

"You are taking me to dinner?" Mai-Britt asked.

"Are you saying yes?"

The street was lined with open-air restaurants. They passed the boisterous bars and nightspots on Selekam Road and headed to an almost hidden doorway that opened into a Japanese restaurant, the Edomae.

The maitre d' walked Henri and Mai-Britt into the glowing, green-glass-lined interior, partitioned with aquariums of jewel-colored fish from floor to ceiling.

Mai-Britt suddenly grabbed Henri's arm, making him stop so she could really see.

"What are they *doing*?"

She jutted her chin toward the naked girl lying gracefully on the sushi bar and a customer drinking from the cup made by the cleft of her closed thighs.

"It's called *wakesame*," Henri explained. "It means 'floating seaweed.' "

"Hah! That is quite new to me," she said. "Have you done that, Paul?"

Henri winked at her, then pulled out a chair for his dinner companion who was not just beautiful, but had a daring streak, was willing to try the horsemeat sashimi and the edomae, the raw, marinated fish that the restaurant was named for.

Henri had already fallen half in love with her — when he noticed the eyes of a man at another table fixed on him.

It was a shock, as though someone had dumped ice down the back of his shirt. *Carl Obst*. A man Henri had known many years ago, now sitting with a lady-boy, a high-priced, very polished, transvestite prostitute.

Henri was sure that his own looks had changed so much that Obst wouldn't recognize him. But it would be very bad if he did.

Obst's attention swung back to his lady-boy, and Henri let his eyes slip away from Obst. Henri thought he was safe, but his good mood was gone.

The enchanting young woman and the rare and beautiful setting faded as his thoughts were hurled back to a time when he was dead — and yet somehow he still breathed.

Chapter 59

HENRI HAD TOLD Marty Switzer that being in an isolation cell was like being inside his own bowel. It was that dark and stinking, and that's where the analogy ended. Because nothing Henri had ever seen or heard about or imagined could be compared to that filthy hole.

It had started for Henri before the Twin Towers came down, when he was hired by Brewster-North, a private military contractor that was stealthier and deadlier than Blackwater.

He'd been on a reconnaissance mission with four other intelligence analysts. As the linguist, Henri was the critical asset.

His unit had been resting in a safe house when their lookout was gutted outside the door where he stood guard. The rest of the team was taken captive, beaten just short of death, and locked away in a prison with no name.

By the end of his first week in hell, Henri knew his captors by name, their tics and preferences. There was the Rapist, the one who sang while hanging his prisoners like spiders, their arms chained above their heads for hours. Fire liked to use burning cigarettes; Ice drowned prisoners in freezing cold water. Henri had long conversations with one soldier, Cocktease, who made tantalizing offers of phone calls, and letters home, and possible freedom.

There were the brutes and the ones who were more refined, but all the guards were sadistic. Had to give credit where it was due. They all really enjoyed their work.

One day Henri's schedule was changed.

He was taken from his cell and kicked into the corner of a windowless room—along with the three remaining men from his unit, all bloodied, with broken bones and oozing sores.

Bright lights flashed on, and when Henri could finally see, he took in the cameras and the half-dozen hooded men lined up against a wall.

One of those men grabbed his cellmate and friend Marty Switzer, pulled him to the center of the room, and hauled him to his feet.

Switzer answered their questions, saying that he was Canadian, twenty-eight, that his parents and girlfriend lived in Ottawa, that he was a military operative. Yes, he was a spy.

He lied as expected, saying that he was being treated well, and then one of the hooded men threw Switzer to the ground, lifted his head by his hair, and drew a serrated knife across the back of his neck. Blood spouted, and there was a chorus of the *takbir: Allahu Akbar.* Allah is great.

Henri was transfixed by how easily Switzer's head had been severed with a few saws of the blade, an act both infinite and quick.

When the executioner held up Switzer's head for

the camera, his friend's expression of despair was fixed on his face. Henri had thought to call out to him—as though Marty could still speak.

There was one other thing that Henri could never forget. How as he waited to die, he felt a flush of excitement. He couldn't understand the emotion, and he couldn't put it down. As he lay on the killing floor, he had wondered if he was elated because soon he'd be free of his misery.

Or maybe he'd just realized who he really was, and what was at his core.

He got a thrill from death—even his own.

Chapter 60

FRESH TEA WAS POURED into his cup at the Edomae, and Henri came back to the present; he thanked the waiter automatically. He sipped the tea but couldn't entirely pull himself back from the memory.

He thought of the hooded tribunal, the headless body of a man who'd been his friend, the stickiness of the killing floor. His senses had been so acute then; he could hear the electricity singing in the light fixtures.

He had kept his eyes on the remaining men in his unit as they were separated from the heap. Raymond Drake, the former marine from Alabama who screamed for God to help him. The other boy, Lonnie Bell, an ex-SEAL from Louisiana, who was in shock and never said a word, never even screamed.

Both men were beheaded to exultant cries, and then Henri was dragged by his hair to the bloody center of the room. A voice came out of the darkness beyond the lights.

"Say your name for the camera. Say where you are from."

He answered in Arabic, "I will be armed and waiting for you in hell. Send my bottomless contempt to Saddam."

They laughed. They mocked his accent. And then, with the smell of shit in his nostrils, Henri was blindfolded. He waited to be shoved to the ground, but instead a coarse blanket was thrown over his head.

He must have passed out because when he awoke, he was tied with ropes and folded into the rear of a vehicle in which he rode for hours. Then he was dumped at the Syrian border.

He was afraid to believe it, but it was true.

He was alive. He was *alive*.

"Tell the Americans what we have done, infidel. What we *will* do. At least you try to speak our language."

A boot struck him hard in the lower back, and the vehicle sped away.

He returned to the United States through an underground chain of friendly back doors from Syria to Beirut, where he got new documentation, and by cargo plane from Beirut to Vancouver. He hitched a ride to Seattle, stole a car, and made his way to a small mining town in Wisconsin. But Henri didn't contact his controller at Brewster-North.

He never wanted to see Carl Obst again.

Still, Brewster-North had done great things for Henri. They'd eradicated his past when they hired him, had thoroughly expunged his real name, his fingerprints, his entire history from the records. And now he was presumed dead.

He counted on that.

Across from him now, inside an exclusive Japanese club in Thailand, the lovely Mai-Britt had noticed that Henri's mind had drifted far away from her.

"Are you okay, Paul?" she asked. "Are you angry that that man was staring at me?"

Together they watched Carl Obst leave the restaurant with his date. He didn't look back.

Henri smiled, said, "No, I'm not angry. Everything is fine."

"Good, because I was wondering if we should continue the evening more privately?"

"Hey, I'm sorry. I wish I could," Henri told the girl with the most elegant neck since Henry VIII's second wife. "I really wish I had the time," he said, taking her hand. "I have that early flight tomorrow morning."

"Screw business," Mai-Britt joked. "You're on holiday tonight."

Henri leaned across the table and kissed her cheek.

He imagined her nakedness under his hands—and he let the fantasy go. He was already thinking ahead to his business in L.A., laughing inside at how surprised Ben Hawkins would be to see him.

Chapter 61

HENRI SPENT a three-day weekend at the airport Sheraton in L.A., moving anonymously among the other business travelers. He used the time to reread Ben Hawkins's novels and every newspaper story Ben had written. He'd purchased supplies and made dry runs to Venice Beach and the street where Ben lived, right around the corner from Little Tokyo.

At just after five that Monday afternoon, Henri took his rental car onto the 105 Freeway. The yellowing cement walls lining the eight-laner were illuminated by a golden light, randomly splashed with spiky vines of red and purple bougainvillea and gothic Latino gang graffiti, giving the drab Los Angeles highway a Caribbean flavor, at least in his mind.

Henri took the 105 to the 110 exit at Los Angeles Street, and from there he made his way through stop-and-go traffic to Alameda, a major artery running to the heart of downtown.

It was rush hour, but Henri was in no rush. He was keyed up, focused on an idea that over the last three weeks had taken on potential for life-changing drama and a hell of a finale.

The plan centered on Ben Hawkins, the journalist, the novelist, the former detective.

Henri had been thinking about him since that evening in Maui, outside the Wailea Princess, when Ben had stretched out his hand to touch Barbara McDaniels.

Henri waited out the red light, and when it changed he took a right turn onto Traction, a small street near the Union Pacific tracks that ran parallel to the Los Angeles River.

Following the poky SUV in front of him, Henri trawled down the middle of Ben's homey neighborhood, with its L.A. hipster restaurants and vintage clothing shops, finding a parking spot across from the eight-story, white-brick building where Ben lived.

Henri got out of the car, opened the trunk, and took a sports jacket from his bag. He stuck a gun into the waistband of his slacks, buttoned his jacket, and raked back his brown and silver-streaked hair.

Then he got back into the car and found a good music station, spent about twenty minutes watching pedestrians meander along the pleasant street, listening to Beethoven and Mozart, until he saw the man he was waiting for.

Ben was in Dockers and a polo shirt and was carrying a beat-up leather briefcase in his right hand. He entered a restaurant called Ay Caramba, and Henri waited patiently until Ben emerged with his take-out Mexican dinner in a plastic bag.

Henri got out of his car, locked it, followed Ben across Traction right up the short flight of stairs to where Ben was fitting his key into the lock.

Henri called out, "Excuse me. Sorry. Mr. Hawkins?"

Ben turned, a look of mild alertness on his face.

Henri smiled and, pulling aside the front of his jacket, showed Ben his gun. He said, "I don't want to hurt you."

Ben spoke in a voice that still reeked of cop. "I've got thirty-eight dollars on me. Take it. My wallet's in my back pocket."

"You don't recognize me, do you?"

"Should I?"

"Think of me as your godfather, Ben," Henri said, thickening his speech. "I'm gonna make you an offer—"

"I can't refuse? I know who you are. You're Marco."

"Correct. You should invite me inside, my friend. We need to talk."

Chapter 62

"SO, WHAT THE fuck is this, Marco?" I shouted. "Suddenly you have information about the McDanielses?"

Marco didn't answer my question. He didn't even flinch.

He said, "I mean it, Ben," and standing with his back to the street, he drew the gun from his waistband and leveled it at my gut. "Open the door."

I couldn't move my feet, I was that stuck. I'd known Marco Benevenuto a bit, had spent time sitting next to him in a car, and now he'd taken off the chauffeur's cap, the mustache, put on a six-hundred-dollar jacket, and completely skunked me.

I was ashamed of myself and I was confused.

If I refused to let him into my building, would he shoot me? I couldn't know. And I was having the irrational thought that I *should* let him in.

My curiosity was overriding caution big-time, but I wanted to satisfy my curiosity with a gun in *my* hand. My well-oiled Beretta was in my nightstand, and I was confident that once I was inside with this character, I could get my hands on it.

"You can put that thing away," I said, shrugging when he gave me a bland, you-gotta-be-kidding smile. I opened the front door, and with the McDanielses' former driver right behind me, we climbed up three flights to the fourth floor.

This building was one of several former warehouses that had gone residential in the past ten years. I loved it here. One unit per floor, high ceilings, and thick walls. No nosy neighbors. No unwanted sounds.

I unlocked the heavy-duty dead bolts on my front door and let the man in. He locked the door behind us.

I put my briefcase down on the cement floor, said "Have a seat," then headed into the kitchen area. Perfect host, I called out, "What can I get you to drink, Marco?"

He said from behind my shoulder, "Thanks anyway. I'll pass."

I quashed my jump reflex, took an Orangina out of the fridge, and led the way back to the living room, sitting at one end of the leather sectional. My "guest" took the chair.

"Who are you really?" I asked this man who was now looking my place over, checking out the framed photos, the old newspapers in the corner, every title of every book. I had the sense that I was in the presence of a highly observant operator.

He finally set his Smith & Wesson down on my coffee table, ten feet from where I was sitting, out of my reach. He fished in his breast pocket, took out a business card held between his fingers, slid it across the glass table toward me.

I read the printed name, and my heart almost stopped.

I knew the card. I'd read it before: Charles Rollins. Photographer. *Talk Weekly.*

My mind was doing backflips. I imagined Marco without the mustache, and then envisioned Charles Rollins's half-seen face the night when Rosa Castro's twisted body had been brought up from the deep.

That night, when Rollins had given me his card, he'd been wearing a baseball cap and, maybe, shades. It had been another disguise.

The prickling at the back of my neck was telling me that the slick, good-looking guy sitting on my sofa had been *this* close to me the whole time I was in Hawaii. Almost from the moment I arrived.

I'd been completely unaware of him, but he'd been watching me.

Why?

Chapter 63

THE MAN SITTING in my favorite leather chair watched my face as I desperately tried to fit the pieces together.

I was remembering that day in Maui when the McDanielses had gone missing and Eddie Keola and I had tried to find Marco, the driver who didn't exist.

I remembered how after Julia Winkler's body was found in a hotel bed in Lanai, Amanda had tried to help me locate a tabloid paparazzo named Charles Rollins because he'd been the last person seen with Winkler.

The name Nils Bjorn jumped into my mind, another phantom who'd been staying at the Wailea Princess at the same time as Kim McDaniels. Bjorn had never been questioned—because he had conveniently disappeared.

The police hadn't thought Bjorn had anything to do with Kim's abduction, and when I'd researched Bjorn, I was sure he was using a dead man's name.

Those facts alone told me that at the very least, Mr. Smooth on my chair was a con artist, a master of disguise. If that were true, if Marco, Rollins, and maybe Bjorn were all the same man, what did it mean?

I fought off the tsunami of black thoughts that were swamping my mind. I unscrewed the top of the soda bottle with a shaking hand, wondering if I'd kissed Amanda for the last time.

I thought about the messiness of my life, the overdue story Aronstein was waiting for, the will I'd never drawn up, my life insurance policy—had I paid the latest premium?

I was not only scared, I was furious, thinking, *Shit, this can't be the last day of my life. I need time to put my damned affairs in order.*

Could I make a break for my gun?

No, I didn't think so.

Marco-Rollins-Bjorn was two feet from his Smith & Wesson. And he was maddeningly relaxed about everything. His legs were crossed, ankle over knee, watching me like I was on TV.

I used that fearful moment to memorize the prick's bland, symmetrical face. In case somehow I got out of here. In case I had a chance to describe him to the cops.

"You can call me Henri," he said now.

"Henri what?"

"Don't worry about it. It's not my real name."

"So what now, Henri?"

He smiled, said, "How many times has someone said to you, 'You should write a book about my life'?"

"Probably at least once a week," I said. "Everyone thinks they have a blockbuster life story."

"Uh-huh. And how many of those people are contract killers?"

Chapter 64

THE TELEPHONE RANG in my bedroom. It was probably Amanda. Henri shook his head, so I let my sweetheart's voice send her love to the answering machine.

"I've got a lot of things to tell you, Ben. Get comfortable. Tune in to the present only. We could be here for a while."

"Mind if I get my tape recorder? It's in my bedroom."

"Not now. Not until we work out our deal."

I said, "Okay. Talk to me," but I was thinking, *Was he serious? A contract killer wanted a contract with me?*

Henri's gun was a half second away from Henri's hand. All I could do was play along with him until I could make a move.

The worst of amateur autobiographies start with "I was born...," so I leaned back in my seat, prepared myself for a saga.

And Henri didn't disappoint. He started his story from *before* he was born.

He gave me a little history: In 1937 there was a

Frenchman, a Jewish man who owned a print shop in Paris. He was a specialist in old documents and inks.

Henri said that very early on, this man understood the real danger of the Third Reich and that he and others got out before the Nazis stormed Paris. This man, this printer, had fled to Beirut.

"So this young Jew married a Lebanese woman," Henri told me. "Beirut is a large city, the Paris of the Middle East, and he blended in fairly well. He opened another print shop, had four children, lived a good life.

"No one questioned him. But other refugees, friends of friends of friends, would find him. They needed papers, false identification, and this man helped them so that they could start new lives. His work is excellent."

"*Is* excellent?"

"He's still living, but no longer in Beirut. He was working for the Mossad, and they've moved him for safekeeping. Ben, there's no way for you to find him. Stay in the present, stay with me, my friend.

"I'm telling you about this forger because he works for me. I keep food on his table. I keep his secrets. And he has given me Marco and Charlie and Henri and many others. I can become someone else when I walk out of this room."

Hours whipped by.

I turned on more lights and came back to my seat, so absorbed by Henri's story that I'd forgotten to be afraid.

Henri told me about surviving a brutal imprisonment in Iraq and how he'd determined that he would no longer be constrained by laws or by morality.

"And so, what is my life like now, Ben? I indulge myself in every pleasure, many you can't imagine. And to do that, I need lots of money. That's where the Peepers come in. It's where you come in, too."

Chapter 65

HENRI'S SEMIAUTOMATIC WAS KEEPING me in my seat, but I was so gripped by his story that I almost forgot about the gun. "Who are the Peepers?" I asked him.

"Not now," he said. "I'll tell you next time. After you come back from New York."

"What are you going to do, muscle me onto a plane? Good luck getting a gun on board."

Henri pulled an envelope from his jacket pocket, slid it across the table. I picked it up, opened the flap, and took out the packet of pictures.

My mouth went dry. They were high-quality snapshots of *Amanda*, recent ones. She was Rollerblading only a block from her apartment, wearing the white tank top and pink shorts she'd had on when I met her for breakfast yesterday morning.

I was in one of the shots, too.

"Keep those, Ben. I think they're pretty nice. Point is, I can get to Amanda anytime, so don't even think about going to the police. That's just a way of committing suicide and getting Amanda killed, too. Understand?"

I felt a chill shoot from the back of my neck all the way down my spine. A death threat with a smile. The guy had just threatened to kill Amanda and made it sound like an invitation to have lunch.

"*Wait a minute,*" I said. I put the pictures down, shoved my hands out, as if pushing Henri and his gun and his damned life story far, far away. "I'm wrong for this. You need a biographer, someone who's done this kind of book before and would see it as a dream job."

"Ben. It *is* a dream job, and *you're* my writer. So turn me down if you want, but I'll have to exercise the termination clause for my own protection. See what I mean?

"Or, you could look at the upside," Henri said, affable now, selling me on the silver lining while pointing a 9-millimeter at my chest.

"We're going to be *partners*. This book is going to be *big*. What did you say a little while ago about blockbusters? Yeah, well that's what we're looking at with my story."

"Even if I wanted to, I can't. Look, Henri, I'm just a writer. I don't have the power you think. Shit, man, you have no idea what you're asking."

Henri smiled as he said, "I brought you something you can use as a sales tool. About ninety seconds of inspiration."

He reached inside his jacket and pulled out a gizmo hanging from a cord around his neck. It was a flash drive, a small media card used to save and transfer data.

"If a picture's worth a thousand words, I'm guessing this is worth, I don't know, *eighty* thousand words and several million dollars. Think about

it, Ben. You could become rich and famous...or...
you could die. I like clear choices, don't you?"

Henri slapped his knees, stood, asked me to walk
him to the door and then to put my face against the
wall.

I did it—and when I woke up sometime later,
I was lying on the cold cement floor. I had a painful lump at the back of my head and a blinding
headache.

Son of a bitch pistol-whipped me before he
took off.

Chapter 66

I PULLED MYSELF to my feet, bumped against walls all the way to the bedroom, yanked open the drawer to my nightstand. My heart was clanging in my chest like a fire alarm until my fingers curled around the butt of my gun. I stuck the Beretta into my waistband and went for the phone.

Mandy answered on the third ring.

"Don't open your door for anyone," I said, still panting, perspiring heavily. Had this really happened? Had Henri just threatened to kill me and Mandy if I didn't write his book?

"Ben?"

"Don't answer the door for a neighbor or a Girl Scout or the cable guy, or anyone, okay, Mandy? Don't open it for the *police*."

"Ben, you're scaring me to death! Seriously, honey. What's going on?"

"I'll tell you when I see you. I'm leaving now."

I staggered back to the living room, pocketed the items Henri had left behind, and headed out the door, still seeing Henri's face and hearing his threat.

That's just a way of … getting Amanda killed …

*I'll have to exercise the termination clause...
Understand?*

I think I did.

Traction Avenue was dark now, but alive with honking horns, tourists buying goods from racks, gathering around a one-man band on the sidewalk.

I got into my ancient Beemer, headed for the 10 Freeway, worried about Amanda as I drove. Where was Henri now?

Henri was good-looking enough to pass as a solid citizen, his features bland enough to take on any kind of disguise. I imagined him as Charlie Rollins, saw a camera in his hand, taking pictures of me and Amanda.

His camera could just as easily have been a gun.

I thought about the people who'd been murdered in Hawaii. Kim, Rosa, Julia, my friends Levon and Barbara, all tortured and so skillfully dispatched. Not a fingerprint or a trace had been left behind for the cops.

This wasn't the work of a beginner.

How many other people had Henri killed?

The freeway tailed off onto 4th and Main. I turned onto Pico, passed the diners and car repair shops, the two-level crappy apartments, the big clown on Main and Rose—and I was in a different world, Venice Beach, both a playground for the young and carefree and a refuge for the homeless.

It took me another few minutes to circle around Speedway until I found a spot a block from Amanda's place, a former one-family home now split into three apartments.

I walked up the street listening for the approach

of a car or the sound of Italian loafers slapping the pavement.

Maybe Henri was watching me now, disguised as a vagrant, or maybe he was that bearded guy parking his car. I walked past Amanda's house, looked up to the third floor, saw the light on in her kitchen.

I walked another block before doubling back. I rang the doorbell, muttered, *"Please, Mandy, please,"* until I heard her voice behind the door.

"What's the password?"

" 'Cheese sandwich.' Let me in."

Chapter 67

AMANDA OPENED THE door, and I grabbed her, kicked the door closed behind me, and held her tight.

"What is it, Ben? What *happened?* Please tell me what's going on."

She freed herself from my arms, grabbed my shoulders, and inventoried my face.

"Your *collar* is bloody. You're *bleeding.* Ben, were you *mugged?*"

I threw the bolts on Amanda's front door, put my hand at her back, and walked her to the small living room. I sat her down in the easy chair, took the rocker a few feet away.

"Start talking, okay?"

I didn't know how to soften it, so I just told it plain and simple. "A guy came to my door with a gun. Said he's a contract killer."

"What?"

"He led me to believe that he killed all those people in Hawaii. Remember when I asked you to help me find Charlie Rollins from *Talk Weekly* magazine?"

"The Charlie Rollins who was the last one to see Julia Winkler? That's who came to see you?"

I told Amanda about Henri's other names and disguises, how I had met him not only as Rollins, but that he'd also masqueraded as the McDanielses' driver, calling himself Marco Benevenuto.

I told her that he'd been sitting on my couch and pointing a gun, telling me that he was a professional assassin for hire and had killed many, many times.

"He wants me to write his autobiography. Wants Raven-Wofford to publish it."

"This is unbelievable," Amanda said.

"I know."

"No, I mean, it's *really* unbelievable. Who would confess to murders like that? You've got to call the police, Ben," she said. "You know that, don't you?"

"He warned me not to."

I handed Mandy the packet of pictures and watched the disbelief on her face change to shock and then anger.

"Okay, the bastard has a zoom lens," she said, her mouth clamped into a straight line. "He took some pictures. Proves nothing."

I took the flash drive out of my pocket, dangled it by the cord. "He gave me this. Said it's a sales tool and that it will inspire me."

Chapter 68

AMANDA LEFT THE LIVING ROOM, then came back with her laptop under her arm and holding two glasses and a bottle of Pinot. She booted up while I poured, and when her laptop was humming, I inserted Henri's flash drive into the port.

A video started to roll.

For the next minute and a half, Amanda and I were in the grip of the most horrific and obscene images either of us had ever seen. Amanda clutched my arm so hard that she left bruises, and when it was finally over she threw herself back into the chair, tears flowing, sobbing.

"Oh, my God, Amanda, what an *ass* I am. I'm so sorry. I should have looked at it first."

"You couldn't have known. I wouldn't have believed it if I hadn't seen it."

"That goes for me, too."

I put the media card into my back pocket and went down the hall to the bathroom, sluiced cold water over my face and the back of my scalp. When I looked up, Amanda was standing in the doorway. She said, "Take it all off."

She helped me with my bloody shirt, undressed herself, and turned on the shower. I got into the tub and she got in behind me, put her arms around me as the hot water beat down on us both.

"Go to New York and talk to Zagami," she said. "Do what Henri says. Zagami can't turn this down."

"You're sure about that?"

"Yeah, I'm sure. The thing to do is keep Henri happy while we figure out what to do."

I turned to face her. "I'm not leaving you here alone."

"I can take care of myself. I know, I know, famous last words. But really, I can."

Mandy got out of the shower and disappeared for long enough that I turned off the water, wrapped myself in a bath towel, and went looking for her.

I found her in the bedroom, on her tiptoes, reaching up to the top shelf of her closet. She pulled down a shotgun and showed it to me.

I looked at her stupidly.

"Yeah," she said. "I know how to use it."

"And you're going to carry it around with you in your purse?"

I took her shotgun and put it under the bed.

Then I used her phone.

I didn't call the cops, because I knew that they couldn't protect us. I had no fingerprint evidence, and my description of Henri would be useless. Six foot, brown hair, gray eyes, could be anyone.

After the cops watched my place and Mandy's for a week or so, we'd be on our own again, vulnerable to a sniper's bullet—or whatever Henri would or could use to silence us.

I saw him in my mind, crouched behind a car, or standing behind me at Starbucks, or watching Amanda's apartment through a gun sight.

Mandy was right. We needed time to make a plan. If I worked with Henri, if he got comfortable with me, maybe he'd slip, give me convictable evidence, something the cops or the Feds could use to lock him up.

I left a voice-mail message for Leonard Zagami, saying it was urgent that we meet. Then I booked tickets for me and Mandy, round trip, Los Angeles to New York.

Chapter 69

WHEN LEONARD ZAGAMI TOOK ME on as one of his authors, I was twenty-five, he was forty, and Raven House was a high-class specialty press that put out a couple dozen books a year. Since then, Raven had merged with the gigantic Wofford Publishing, and the new Raven-Wofford had taken over the top six floors of a skyscraper overlooking Bloomingdale's.

Leonard Zagami had moved up as well. He was now the CEO and president, the crème de la cheese, and the new house brought out two hundred books a year.

Like their competition, the bulk of RW's list either lost money or broke even, but three authors—and I wasn't one of them—brought in more revenue than the other 197 combined.

Leonard Zagami didn't see me as a moneymaker anymore, but he liked me and it cost him nothing to keep me on board. I hoped that after our meeting he'd see me another way, that he'd hear cash registers ringing from Bangor to Yakima.

And that Henri would remove his death threat.

I had my pitch ready when I arrived in RW's spiffy modern waiting room at nine. At noon, Leonard's assistant came across the jaguar-print carpet to say that Mr. Zagami had fifteen minutes for me, to please follow her.

When I crossed his threshold, Leonard got to his feet, shook my hand, patted my back, and told me it was good to see me but that I looked like crap.

I thanked him, told him I'd aged a couple of years while waiting for our nine o'clock meeting.

Len laughed, apologized, said he'd done his best to squeeze me in, and offered me a chair across from his desk. At five feet six, almost child-sized behind the huge desk, Leonard Zagami still radiated power and a no-bullshit canniness.

I took my seat.

"What's this book about, Ben? When last we spoke, you had nothing cooking."

"Have you been following the Kim McDaniels case?"

"The *Sporting Life* model? Sure. She and some other people were killed in Hawaii a few...Hey. You were covering that story? Oh. I see."

"I was very close to some of the victims—"

"Look, Ben," Zagami interrupted me. "Until the killer is caught, this is still tabloid fodder. It's not a book, not yet."

"It's not what you're thinking, Len. This is a first-person tell-all."

"Who's the first person? You?"

I made my pitch like my life depended on it.

"The killer approached me incognito," I said. "He's a very cool and clever maniac who wants to do a book about the murders, and he wants me to write it. He won't reveal his identity, but he'll tell how he did the killings and why."

I expected Zagami to say *something*, but his expression was flat. I crossed my arms over his leather-topped desk, made sure my old friend was looking me in the eyes.

"Len, did you hear me? This guy could be the most-wanted man in America. He's smart. He's at liberty. And he kills with his *hands*. He says he wants me to write about what he's done because he wants the money and the notoriety. Yeah. He wants some kind of credit for a job well done. And if I won't write the book, he'll kill *me*. Might kill Amanda, too.

"So I need a simple yes or no. Len. Are you interested or not?"

Chapter 70

LEONARD ZAGAMI LEANED back in his chair, rocked a couple of times, smoothed back what remained of his white hair, then turned to face me. When he spoke, it was with heartbreaking sincerity, and that's what really hurt.

"You know how much I like you, Ben. We've been together for what, twelve years?"

"Almost fifteen."

"Fifteen good years. So, as your friend, I'm not going to bullshit you. You deserve the truth."

"Agreed," I said, but my pulse was booming so loudly that I could hardly hear what Len said.

"I'm verbalizing what any good businessman would be *thinking*, so don't take this wrong, Ben. You've had a promising but quiet career. So now you think you've got a breakout book that'll raise your profile here at RW and in the industry. Am I right?"

"You think this is a stunt? You think I'm that desperate? Are you kidding?"

"Let me finish. You know what happened when Fritz Keller brought out Randolph Graham's so-called true story."

"It blew up, yeah."

"First the 'startling reviews,' then Matt Lauer and Larry King. Oprah puts Graham in her book club—and then the truth starts leaking out. Graham wasn't a killer. He was a petty thug and a pretty good writer who embellished the hell out of his life story. And when it exploded, it exploded all over Fritz Keller."

Zagami went on to say that Keller got late-night threats at home, TV producers calling his cell phone. His company's stock went down the toilet, and Keller had a heart attack.

My own heart was starting to fibrillate. Leonard thought that either Henri was lying or I was stretching a newspaper article beyond reality.

Either way, he was turning me down.

Hadn't Leonard heard what I said? *Henri had threatened to kill me and Amanda*. Len took a breath, so I seized the moment.

"Len, I'm going to say something very important."

"Go ahead, because unfortunately, I only have five more minutes."

"I questioned it, too. Wondered if Henri was really a killer, or if he's a talented con man, seeing in me the grift of a lifetime."

"Exactly," Len said.

"Well, Henri is for real. And I can prove it to you."

I put the media card on the desk.

"What's that?"

"Everything you need to know and more. I want you to meet Henri for yourself."

Len inserted the flash drive, and his computer

screen went from black to a shot of a dusky yellow room, candles burning, a bed centered on a wall. The camera zoomed in on a slender young woman lying belly-down on the bed. She had long, pale blond hair, wore a red bikini and black shoes with red soles. She was hog-tied with intricately knotted ropes. She seemed drugged or sleeping, but when the man entered the frame she began crying.

The man was naked except for a plastic mask and blue latex gloves.

I didn't want to see the video again. I walked to the glass wall that looked straight down the well of the atrium, from the forty-third floor to the tiny people who crossed the plaza on the ground floor below.

I heard the voices coming from the computer, heard Leonard gag. I turned to see him make a run for the door. When he returned a few minutes later, Leonard was as pale as a sheet of paper, and he was changed.

Chapter 71

LEONARD DROPPED BACK into the seat behind his desk, yanked out the flash drive, stared at it like it was the snake in the Garden of Eden.

"Take this back," he said. "Let's agree that I never saw it. I don't want to be any kind of accessory after the fact or God knows what. Have you told the police? The FBI?"

"Henri said that if I did, he'd kill me, kill Amanda, too. I can't take that chance."

"I understand now. You're sure that the girl in that video is Kim McDaniels?"

"Yeah. That's Kim."

Len picked up the phone, canceled his twelve-thirty meeting, and cleared the rest of his afternoon. He ordered sandwiches from the kitchen, and we moved to the seating area at the far side of his office.

Len said, "Okay, start at the beginning. Don't leave out a bloody period or comma."

So I did. I told Len about the last-minute Hawaiian boondoggle that had turned out to be a murder mystery times five. I told him about becoming friends with Barbara and Levon McDaniels and about being deceived by Henri's alter egos, Marco Benevenuto and Charlie Rollins.

Emotion jammed up my voice box when I talked about the dead bodies, and also when I told Len how Henri had forced me into my apartment at gunpoint, then showed me the pictures he'd taken of Amanda.

"How much does Henri want for his story? Did he give you a number?"

I told Len that Henri was talking about multimillions, and my editor didn't flinch. In the past half hour, he had gone from skeptic to inside bidder. From the light in his eyes, I thought he'd sized up the market for this book and saw his budget gap being overwhelmed by a mountain of cash.

"What's the next step?" he asked me.

"Henri said he'd be in touch. I'm certain he will be. That's all I know so far."

Len called Eric Zohn, Raven-Wofford's chief legal counsel, and soon a tall, thin, nervous man in his forties joined our meeting.

Len and I briefed Eric on "the assassin's legacy," and Zohn threw up objections.

Zohn cited the "Son of Sam" law that held that a killer can't profit from his crimes. He and Len discussed Jeffrey MacDonald, who had sued his ghostwriter, and then the O.J. book, since the Goldman family had claimed the book's earnings to satisfy their civil suit against the author.

Zohn said, "I worry that we'll be financially responsible to each and every one of the victims' families."

I was the forgotten person in the room, as loopholes

and angles were discussed, but I saw that Len was fighting for the book.

He said to Zohn, "Eric, I don't say this lightly. This is a guaranteed monster bestseller in the making. Everyone wants to know what's actually in the mind of a killer, and this killer will talk about crimes that are current and *unsolved*. What Ben's got isn't *If I Did It*. It's *I Damn Well Did It*."

Zohn wanted more time to explore the ramifications, but Leonard used his executive prerogative.

"Ben, for now, you're Henri's anonymous ghostwriter. If anyone says they saw you in my office, say you came to pitch a new novel. That I turned it down.

"When Henri contacts you, tell him that we're fine-tuning an offer I think he'll like."

"That's a yes?"

"That's a yes. You have a deal. This is the scariest book I've ever taken on, and I can't wait to publish it."

Chapter 72

THE NEXT EVENING, in L.A., the unreality was still settling in. Amanda was cooking a four-star dinner in her minuscule kitchen while I sat at her desk working the Internet. I had indelible pictures in my mind of the execution of Kim McDaniels, and that led me to multiple Web sites that discussed personality disorders. I quickly homed in on the description of serial killers.

A half-dozen experts agreed that serial killers almost always learn from their mistakes. They evolve. They compartmentalize and don't feel their victims' pain. They keep upping the danger and increasing the thrill.

I could see why Henri was so happy and self-satisfied. He was being paid for doing what he loved to do, and now a book about his passion would be a kind of victory lap.

I called out to Mandy, who came into the living room with a wooden spoon in her hand.

"The sauce is going to burn."

"I want to read you something. This is from a

psychiatrist, a former Viet Nam vet who's written extensively on serial killers. Here. Listen, please.

" 'All of us have some of the killer in us, but when you get to the proverbial edge of the abyss, you have to be able to take a step back. These guys who kill and kill again have jumped right into the abyss and have lived in it for years.' "

Mandy said, "But Ben, what's it going to be like to work with this...*creature?*"

"If I could walk away from it, Mandy, I'd run. I'd run."

Mandy kissed the top of my head and went back to her sauce. A moment later, the phone rang. I heard Mandy say, "Hang on. I'll get him."

She held out the phone to me with a look on her face that I can describe only as one of pure horror.

"It's for *you.*"

I took the phone, said, "Hello."

"So how did our big meeting in New York go?" Henri asked me. "Do we have a book deal?"

My heart almost jumped out of my chest. I did my best to keep calm as I told him, "It's in the works. A lot of people have to be consulted for the kind of money you're asking."

Henri said, "I'm sorry to hear that."

I had a green light from Zagami, and I could have told Henri that, but I was looking at the twilight coming through the windows, wondering where Henri was, how he'd known that Amanda and I were here.

"We're going to do the book, Ben," Henri was saying. "If Zagami isn't interested, we'll have to take it somewhere else. But either way, remember your choices. Do or die."

"Henri, I didn't make myself clear. We have a deal. The contract is in the works. Paperwork. Lawyers. A number has to be worked up and an offer made. This is a big corporation, Henri."

"Okay, then. Break out the champagne. When will we have a solid offer?"

I told him I expected to hear from Zagami in a couple of days and that a contract would follow. It was the truth, but still my mind was reeling.

I was going into partnership with a great white shark, a killing machine that never slept.

Henri was watching us right now, wasn't he?

He was watching us all the time.

Chapter 73

HENRI HADN'T GIVEN me my final destination when he mapped out my drive, just said, "Get on the Ten and go east. I'll tell you what to do after that."

I had the papers in my briefcase, the contract from Raven-Wofford, the releases, signature lines with flags marked "sign here." I also had a tape recorder, notepads, and laptop, and in the zipped pocket at the back of the briefcase, right next to my computer's power pack, was my gun. I hoped to God I would get the chance to use it.

I got into my car and headed out to the freeway. It wasn't funny, but the situation was so weird that I wanted to laugh.

I had a contract for a "guaranteed monster best-seller," what I'd been looking for and dreaming about for years, only this contract had a very literal termination clause.

Write it or die.

Had any author in modern history had a book deal attached to a death penalty? I was pretty sure this was unique, and it was all mine.

It was sunny, a Saturday in mid-July. I set off on

the freeway, checking my rearview mirror every minute or so, looking for a tail, but I never saw one. I stopped for gas, bought coffee, a doughnut, got back on the road.

Fifty miles and an hour later, my cell phone rang.

"Take the One-eleven to Palm Springs," he said.

I'd put another twenty miles on the odometer when I saw the turnoff for the 111. I took the exit ramp and continued on the highway until it became Palm Canyon Drive.

My phone rang again, and again I got directions from my "partner."

"When you get to the center of town, turn right on Tahquitz Canyon, then a left on Belardo. Don't hang up the phone."

I made the turns, sensing that we were near our meeting spot, when Henri said, "You should be seeing it now. The Bristol Hotel."

We were going to be meeting in a public place.

This was good. It was a relief. I felt a burst of elation.

I pulled up to the hotel, handed my keys to the valet at the entrance of this famous old luxury resort and spa, known for its high-end amenities.

Henri spoke into my ear. "Go to the restaurant out by the pool. The reservation is in my name. Henri Benoit. I hope you're hungry, Ben."

This was news.

He'd given me a last name. Real or fictitious, I didn't know, but it struck me as an offering of trust.

I headed through the lobby to the restaurant, thinking, Yes. This was going to be very civilized.

Break out the champagne.

Chapter 74

THE DESERT ROSE RESTAURANT was situated under a long blue canopy near the swimming pool. Light bounced off the white stone patio, and I had to shield my eyes from the glare. I told the maitre d' that I was having lunch with Henri Benoit, and he said, "You're the first to arrive."

I was shown to a table with a perfect view of the pool, the restaurant, and a path that wound around the hotel and led to the parking lot. I had my back to the wall, my briefcase open by my right side.

A waiter came to the table, told me about the various drinks, including the specialty of the house, a cocktail with grenadine and fruit juice. I asked for a bottle of San Pellegrino, and when it came I slugged down a whole glass, refilled it, and waited for Henri to appear.

I looked at my watch, saw that I'd been waiting for only ten minutes. It seemed at least twice that long. With an eye on my surroundings, I called Amanda, told her where I was. Then I used my phone to do an Internet search, looking for any mention of Henri Benoit.

I came up with nothing.

I called Zagami in New York, told him I was waiting for Henri, got a crackly connection. I killed another minute as I filled Len in on the drive into the desert, the beautiful hotel, the state of my mood.

"I'm starting to get excited about this," I said. "I'm just hoping he signs the contract."

"Be careful," said Zagami. "Listen to your instincts. I'm surprised he's late."

"I'm not. I don't like it, but I'm not surprised."

I took a bathroom break and then went back to the table with trepidation. I was expecting that while I was gone, Henri would have arrived and would be sitting across from my empty chair.

I wondered whether Henri was donning a new disguise, whether he was undergoing another metamorphosis—but the seat was still empty.

The waiter came toward me again, said that Mr. Benoit had phoned to say he was delayed and that I was to start without him.

So I ordered lunch. The Tuscan bean soup with black kale was fine. I took a few bites of the penne, ate without tasting what I imagined was excellent cuisine. I'd just asked for an espresso when my cell phone rang.

I stared at it for a moment, then, as if my nerves weren't frayed down to the stumps, said, "Hawkins" into the mouthpiece.

"Are you ready, Ben? You've got a little more driving to do."

Chapter 75

COACHELLA, CALIFORNIA, is twenty-eight miles east of Palm Springs and has a population of close to forty thousand. For a couple of days every year in April, that number swells during the annual music festival, a mini-Woodstock, without the mud.

When the concert is over, Coachella reverts to an agricultural flatland in the desert, home to young Latino families and migrant workers, a drive-through for truckers, who use the town as a pit stop.

Henri had told me to look for the Luxury Inn, and it was easy to find. Off by itself on a long stretch of highway, the Lux was a classic U-shaped motel with a pool.

I pulled the car around to the back as directed, looked for the room number I'd been given, 229.

There were two vehicles in the parking lot. One was a late-model Mercedes, black, a rental. I guessed that Henri must've driven it here. The other was a blue Ford pickup hitched to an old house trailer about twenty-six feet long. Silver with blue stripes, air conditioner on top, Nevada plates.

I turned off my engine and reached for my briefcase, opened the car door.

A man appeared on the balcony above me. It was Henri, looking the same as the last time I saw him. His brown hair was combed back, and he was clean-shaven, wore no glasses. In short, he was a good-looking Mr. Potato Head of a guy who could morph into another identity with a mustache or an eye patch or a baseball cap.

He said, "Ben, just leave your briefcase in the car."

"But the contract—"

"I'll get your briefcase. But right now, get out of your car and please leave your cell phone on the driver's seat. Thanks."

One part of me was screaming, *Get out of here. Jam on the gas and go.* But an opposing inner voice was insisting that if I quit now, nothing would have been gained. *Henri would still be out there. He could still kill me and Amanda at any time, for no reason other than that I'd disobeyed him.*

I took my hand off my briefcase, left it in my car along with my cell phone. Henri jogged down the stairs, told me to put my hands on the hood. Then he expertly frisked me.

"Put your hands behind your back, Ben," he said. Very casual and friendly.

Except that a gun muzzle was pressed against my spine.

The last time I turned my back to Henri, he'd coldcocked me with a gun butt to the back of my head. I didn't even think it through, just used instinct and training. I sidestepped, was about to whip around and disarm him, but what happened next was a blur of pain.

Henri's arms went around me like a vise, and I went airborne, crashing hard on my shoulders and the back of my head.

It was a hard fall, painfully hard, but I didn't have time to check myself out.

Henri was on top of me, his chest to my back, his legs interwoven with mine. His feet were hooked into me so that our bodies were fused, and his full weight crushed me against the pavement.

I felt the gun muzzle screw into my ear.

Henri said, "Got any more ideas? Come on, Ben. Give me your best shot."

Chapter 76

I WAS SO IMMOBILIZED by the takedown, it was as if my spinal cord had just been cut. No weekend black belt could have thrown me like that.

Henri said, "I could easily snap your neck. Understand?"

I wheezed "yes," and he stood, grasped my forearm, and hauled me to my feet.

"Try to get it right this time. Turn around and put your hands behind your back."

Henri cuffed me, then yanked upward on the cuffs, nearly popping my shoulders out of their joints.

Then he shoved me against the car and set my briefcase on the roof. He unlatched the case, found my gun, tossed it into the footwell. Then he locked the car, grabbed my case, and marched me toward the trailer.

"What the hell *is* this?" I asked. "Where are we going?"

"You'll know when you know," said the monster.

He opened the trailer door, and I stumbled inside.

The trailer was old and well used. To my left was

the galley: a table attached to the wall, two chairs bolted to the floor. To my right was a sofa that looked like it doubled as a foldaway bed. There was a closet that housed a toilet and a cot.

Henri maneuvered me so one of the chairs clipped me at the back of my knees and I sat down. A black cloth bag was dropped over my head and a band was cinched around my legs. I heard a chain rattle and the snap of a lock.

I was shackled to a hook in the floor.

Henri patted my shoulder, said, "Relax, okay? I don't want to hurt you. I want you to write this book more than I want to kill you. We're partners now, Ben. Try to trust me."

I was chained down and essentially blind. I didn't know where Henri was taking me. *And I definitely didn't trust him.*

I heard the door close and lock. Then Henri started up the truck. The air conditioner pumped cold air into the trailer through a vent overhead.

We rolled along smoothly for about a half hour, then took a right turn onto a bumpy road. Other turns followed. I tried to hang on to the slick plastic seat with my thighs, but got slammed repeatedly against the wall and into the table.

After a while, I lost track of the turns and the time. I was mortified by how thoroughly Henri had disabled me. There was no way around the bald and simple truth.

Henri was in charge. This was his game. I was only along for the ride.

Chapter 77

MAYBE AN HOUR, hour and a half, had gone by when the trailer stopped and the door slid open. Henri ripped off my hood, and said, "Last stop, buddy. We're home."

I saw flat, uninviting desert through the open door: sand dunes out to the horizon, mop-headed Joshua trees, and buzzards circling on the updraft.

My mind also circled around one thought: *If Henri kills me here, my body will never even be found.* Despite the refrigerated air, sweat rolled down my neck as Henri leaned back against the narrow Formica counter a few feet away.

"I've done some research on collaborations," Henri said. "People say it takes about forty hours of interviews to get enough material for a book. Sound right?"

"Take off the cuffs, Henri. I'm not a flight risk."

He opened the small fridge beside him, and I saw that it was stocked with water, Gatorade, some packaged food. He took out two bottles of water, put one on the table in front of me.

"Say we work about eight hours a day, we'll be here for about five days—"

"Where's here?"

"Joshua Tree. This campsite is closed for road repairs, but the electric hookup works," Henri told me.

Joshua Tree National Park is eight hundred thousand acres of desert wilderness, miles of nothing but yucca and brush and rock formations in all directions. The high views are said to be spectacular, but normal folk don't camp here in the white heat of high summer. I didn't understand people who came here at all.

"In case you think you can get out of here," Henri said, "let me save you the trouble. This is Alcatraz, desert-style. This trailer is sitting on a sea of sand. Daytime temperatures can climb to a hundred and twenty. Even if you got out at night, the sun would fry you before you reached a road. So, please, and I mean this sincerely, stay put."

"Five days, huh?"

"You'll be back in L.A. for the weekend. Scout's honor."

"Okay. So how about it?"

I held out my hands, and Henri took off the cuffs. Then he removed the cinch around my legs and unshackled me.

Chapter 78

I RUBBED MY wrists, stood up, drank down a bottle of cold water in one continuous swallow, those small pleasures giving me a boost of unexpected optimism. I thought about Leonard Zagami's enthusiasm. I imagined dusty old writing dreams coming true for me.

"Okay, let's do this," I said.

Henri and I set up the awning against the side of the trailer, put out a couple of folding chairs and a card table in the thin strip of shade. With the trailer door open, cool air tickling our necks, we got down to business.

I showed Henri the contract, explained that Raven-Wofford would only make payments to the writer. I would pay Henri.

"Payments are made in installments," I told him. "The first third is due on signing. The second payment comes on acceptance of the manuscript, and the final payment is due on publication."

"Not a bad life insurance policy for you," Henri said. He smiled brightly.

"Standard terms," I said to Henri, "to protect

the publisher from writers crashing in the middle of the project."

We discussed our split, a laughably one-sided negotiation.

"It's my book, right?" Henri said. "And your name's going on it. That's worth more than money, Ben."

"So why don't I just work for free?" I said.

Henri smiled, said, "Got a pen?"

I handed one over, and Henri signed his nom de jour on the dotted lines, gave me the number of his bank account in Zurich.

I put the contract away, and Henri ran an electric cord out from the trailer. I booted up my laptop, turned on my tape recorder, gave it a sound test.

I said, "Ready to start?"

Henri said, "I'm going to tell you everything you need to know to write this book, but I'm not going to leave a trail of breadcrumbs, understand?"

"It's your story, Henri. Tell it however you want."

Henri leaned back in his canvas chair, folded his hands over his tight gut, and began at the beginning.

"I grew up in the sticks, a little farming town on the edge of nothing. My parents had a chicken farm, and I was their only child. They had a crappy marriage. My father drank. He beat my mother. He beat me. *She* beat me, and she also took some shots at him."

Henri described the creaking four-room farm-house, his room in the attic over his parents' bedroom.

"There was a crack between two floorboards," he told me. "I couldn't actually see their bed, but

I could see shadows, and I could hear what they were doing. Sex and violence. Every night. I slept over that."

Henri described the three long chicken houses— and how at the age of six, his father put him in charge of killing chickens the old-fashioned way, decapitation with an axe on a wooden block.

"I did my chores like a good boy. I went to school. I went to church. I did what I was told and tried to duck the blows. My father not only clocked me regularly, but he also humiliated me.

"My mom. I forgive her. But for years I had a recurring dream about killing them both. In the dream, I pinned their heads to that old stump in the chicken yard, swung the axe, and watched their headless bodies run.

"For a while after I woke up from that dream, I'd think it was true. That I'd really done it."

Henri turned to me.

"Life went on. Can you picture me, Ben? Cute little kid with an axe in my hand, my overalls soaked with blood?"

"I can see you. It's a sad story, Henri. But it sounds like a good place to start the book."

Henri shook his head. "I've got a better place."

"Okay. Shoot."

Henri hunched over his knees and clasped his hands. He said, "I would start the movie of my life at the summer fair. The scene would center on me and a beautiful blond girl named Lorna."

Chapter 79

I CONSTANTLY CHECKED the recorder, saw that the wheels were slowly turning.

A dry breeze blew across the sands, and a lizard ran across my shoe. Henri raked both hands through his hair, and he seemed nervous, agitated. I hadn't seen this kind of fidgety behavior in him before. It made me nervous, too.

"Please set the scene, Henri. This was a county fair?"

"You could call it that. Agriculture and animals were on one side of the main path. Carnival rides and food were on the other. No breadcrumbs, Ben. This could have happened outside Wengen or Chipping Camden or Cowpat, Arkansas.

"Don't worry about where it was. Just see the bright lights on the fairgrounds, the happy people, and the serious animal competitions. Business deals were at stake here, people's farms and their futures.

"I was fourteen," he continued. "My parents were showing exotic chickens in the fowl tent. It was getting late, and my father told me to get the truck from the private lot for exhibitor's vehicles, upfield from the fairgrounds.

"On the way, I cut through one of the food pavilions and I saw Lorna selling baked goods," he said.

"Lorna was my age and was in my class at school. She was blond, a little shy. She carried her books in front of her chest, so you couldn't see her breasts. But you could see them anyway. There was nothing about Lorna I didn't want."

I nodded, and Henri went on with his story.

"That day I remember she was wearing a lot of blue. Made her hair look even more blond, and when I said hi to her, she seemed glad to see me. Asked me if I wanted to get something to eat at the fairgrounds.

"I knew my father would kill me when I didn't come back with the truck, but I was willing to take the beating, that's how crazy I was about that beautiful girl."

Henri described buying Lorna a cookie and said that they'd gone on a ride together, that she'd grabbed his hand when the roller coaster made its swooping descent.

"All the while I felt a wild kind of tenderness toward this girl. After the ride," Henri said, "another boy came over, Craig somebody. He was a couple of years older. He looked right past me and told Lorna that he had tickets to the Ferris wheel, that it was unreal how the fairgrounds looked with the stars coming out and everything lit up down below.

"Lorna said, 'Oh, I'd love to do that,' and she turned to me, and said, 'You don't mind, do you?' and she took off with this guy.

"Well, I did mind, Ben.

"I watched them go, and then I went to get the truck and my beating. It was dark up in that lot, but I found my dad's truck next to a livestock trailer.

"Standing outside the trailer was another girl I knew from school, Molly, and she had a couple of calves with show ribbons on their halters. She was trying to load them into the trailer, but they wouldn't go.

"I offered to help her," Henri told me. "Molly said, 'No, thanks. I've got it,' something like that, and tried to shove those calves up the ramp by herself.

"I didn't like the way she said that, Ben. I felt she had crossed a line.

"I grabbed a shovel that was leaning against the trailer, and as Molly turned her back to me, I swung the shovel against the back of her head. There was the one loud smack, a sound that thrilled me, and she went down."

Henri stopped speaking. A long moment dragged on, but I waited him out.

Then he said, "I dragged her into the trailer, shut the tailgate. By now she'd started to wail. I told her no one would hear her, but she wouldn't stop.

"My hands went around her neck, and I choked her as naturally as if I was reenacting something I'd done before. Maybe I had, in my dreams."

Henri twisted his watchband and looked away into the desert. When he turned back, his eyes were flat.

"As I was choking her, I heard two men walking by, talking. Laughing. I was squeezing her neck so hard that my hands hurt, so I adjusted my grip and choked her again until Molly stopped breathing.

"I let go of her throat, and she took another breath, but she wasn't wailing anymore. I slapped her—and I got hard. I stripped off her clothes, turned her over, and did her, my hands around her throat the whole time, and when I was done, I strangled her for good."

"What went through your mind as you were doing this?"

"I just wanted it to keep going. I didn't want the feeling to *stop*. Imagine what it was like, Ben, to climax with the power of life and death in your hands. I felt I had earned the *right* to do this. Do you want to know how I felt? *I felt like God.*"

Chapter 80

I WAS AWOKEN the next morning when the trailer door rolled open, and light, almost white sunlight, poured in. Henri was saying, "I've got coffee and rolls, for you, bud. Eggs, too. Breakfast for my partner."

I sat up on the foldaway bed, and Henri lit the stove, beat the eggs in a bowl, made the frying pan sizzle. After I'd eaten, we began work under the awning. I kept turning it over in my mind: Henri had confessed to a murder. Somewhere, a fourteen-year-old girl had been strangled at a county fair. A record of her death would still exist.

Would Henri really let me live knowing about that girl?

Henri went back to the story of Molly, picked up where he'd left off the night before.

He was animated, using his hands to show me how he'd dragged Molly's body into the woods, buried it under piles of leaves, said that he was imagining the fear that would spread from the fair-grounds to the surrounding towns when Molly was reported missing.

Henri said that he'd joined the search for Molly, put up posters, went to the candlelight vigil, all the while cherishing his secret, that he'd killed Molly and had gotten away with it.

He described the girl's funeral, the white coffin under the blanket of flowers, how he'd watched the people crying, but especially Molly's family, her mother and father, the siblings.

"I wondered what it must be like to have those feelings," he told me.

"You know about the most famous of the serial killers, don't you, Ben? Gacy, BTK, Dahmer, Bundy. They were all run by their sexual compulsions. I was thinking last night that it's important for the book to make a distinction between those killers and me."

"Wait a minute, Henri. You told me how you felt raping and killing Molly. That video of you and Kim McDaniels? Are you telling me now that you're not like those other guys? How does that follow?"

"You're missing the point. Pay attention, Ben. This is critical. I've killed dozens of people and had sex with most of them. But except for Molly, when I've killed I've done it for money."

It was good that my recorder was taking it all down because my mind was split into three parts: The writer, figuring out how to join Henri's anecdotes into a compelling narrative. The cop, looking for clues to Henri's identity from what he told me, what he left out, and from the psychological blind spots he didn't know that he had. And the part of my brain that was working the hardest, the survivor.

Henri said that he killed for money, but he'd

killed Molly out of anger. He'd warned me that he would kill me if I didn't do what he said. He could break his own rules at any time.

I listened. I tried to learn Henri Benoit in all of his dimensions. But mostly, I was figuring out what I had to do to survive.

Chapter 81

HENRI CAME BACK to the trailer with sandwiches and a bottle of wine. After he uncorked the bottle, I asked him, "How does your arrangement with the Peepers work?"

"They call themselves the Alliance," Henri said. He poured out two glasses, handed one to me.

"I called them 'the Peepers' once and was given a lesson: no work, no pay." He put on a mock German accent. "You are a bad boy, Henri. Don't trifle with us."

"So the Alliance is German."

"One of the members is German. Horst Werner. That name is probably an alias. I never checked. Another of the Peepers, Jan Van der Heuvel, is Dutch.

"Listen, that could be an alias, too. It goes without saying, you'll change all the names for the book, right, Ben? But these people are not so stupid as to leave their own breadcrumbs."

"Of course. I understand."

He nodded, then went on. His agitation was

gone, but his voice was harder now. I couldn't find a crack in it.

"There are several others in the Alliance. I don't know who they are. They live in cyberspace. Well, one I know very well. Gina Prazzi. She recruited me."

"That sounds interesting. You were recruited? Tell me about Gina."

Henri sipped at his wine, then began to tell me about meeting a beautiful woman after his four years in the Iraqi prison.

"I was having lunch in a sidewalk bistro in Paris when I noticed this tall, slender, extraordinary woman at a nearby table.

"She had very white skin, and her sunglasses were pushed up into her thick brown hair. She had high breasts and long legs and three diamond watches on one wrist. She looked rich and refined and impossibly inaccessible, and I wanted her.

"She put money down for the check and stood up to leave. I wanted to talk to her, and all I could think to say was, 'Do you have the time?'

"She gave me a long, slow look, from my eyes down to my shoes and back up again. My clothes were cheap. I had been out of prison for only a few weeks. The cuts and bruises had healed, but I was still gaunt. The torture, the things I'd seen, the afterimages, were still in my eyes. But she recognized something in me.

"This woman, this angel whose name I did not yet know, said, 'I have Paris time, New York time, Shanghai time... and I also have time for *you*.'"

Henri's voice was softened now as he talked about Gina Prazzi. It was as if he'd finally tasted fulfillment after a lifetime of deprivation.

He said that they'd spent a week in Paris. Henri still visited every September. He described walking with her through the Place Vendôme, shopping with her there. He said that Gina paid for everything, bought him expensive gifts and clothing.

"She came from very old money," Henri told me. "She had connections to a world of wealth I knew nothing about."

After their week in Paris, Henri told me, they cruised the Mediterranean on Gina's yacht. He called up images of the Côte d'Azur, one of the most beautiful spots in the world, he said.

He recalled the lovemaking in her cabin, the swell of the waves, the wine, the exquisite meals in restaurants with high views of the Mediterranean.

"I had nineteen fifty-eight Glen Garioch whisky at twenty-six hundred dollars a bottle. And here's a meal I'll never forget: sea urchin ravioli, followed by rabbit with fennel, mascarpone, and lemon. Nice fare for a country boy and ex–Al Qaeda POW."

"I'm a steak and potatoes man myself."

Henri laughed, said, "You just haven't had a real gastronomic tour of the Med. I could teach you. I could take you to a pastry shop in Paris, Au Chocolat. You would never be the same, Ben.

"But I was talking about Gina, a woman with refined appetites. One day a new guy appeared at our table. The Dutchman — Jan Van der Heuvel."

Henri's face tightened as he talked about Van der Heuvel, how he had joined them in their hotel room, called out stage directions from his chair in the corner as Henri made love to Gina.

"I didn't like this guy or this routine, but a couple of months before I'd been sleeping in my own shit, eating bugs. So what wouldn't I do to be with Gina, Jan Van der Heuvel or not?"

Henri's voice was drowned out by the roar of a helicopter flying over the valley. He warned me with his eyes not to move from my chair.

Even after the silence of the desert returned, it was several moments before he continued his story about Gina.

Chapter 82

"I DIDN'T LOVE GINA," Henri said to me, "but I was fascinated by her, obsessed with her. Okay. Maybe I did love her in some way," Henri said, admitting to having a human vulnerability for the first time.

"One day in Rome, Gina picked up a young girl—"

"And the Dutchman? He was out of the picture?"

"Not entirely. He'd gone back to Amsterdam, but he and Gina had some strange connection. They were always on the phone. She'd be whispering and laughing when she spoke with him. You can imagine, right? The guy liked to *watch*. But in the flesh, she was with *me*."

"You were with Gina in Rome." I prompted him to continue with the main narrative.

"Yes, of course. Gina picked up a student who was screwing her way through college, as they say. A first-semester prostitute from Prague, at Università degli Studi di Roma. I don't remember her name, only that she was hot and too trusting.

"We were in bed, the three of us, and Gina told

me to close my hands around the girl's neck. It's a sex game called 'breath play.' It enhances the orgasm, and yes, Ben, before you ask, it was exciting to revisit my singular experience with Molly. This girl passed out, and I loosened my grip so that she could breathe.

"Gina reached out, took my cock in her hand, and kissed me. And then she said, 'Finish her, Henri.'

"I started to mount the girl, but Gina said, 'No, Henri, you don't understand. *Finish* her.'

"She reached over to the bedside table, held up the keys to her Ferrari, swung the keys in front of my eyes. It was an offer, the car for the girl's life.

"I killed that girl. And I made love to Gina with the dead girl beside us. Gina was electrified and wild under my hands. When she came, it was like a death and a rebirth as a softer, sweeter woman."

Henri's body language relaxed. He told me about driving the Ferrari, a leisurely three-day ride to Florence with many stops along the way, and about a life he believed was becoming his.

"Not long after that trip to Florence, Gina told me about the Alliance, including the fact that Jan was an important member."

The travelogue of Western Europe had ended. Henri's posture straightened, and the tempo of his voice changed from languid to clipped.

"Gina told me that the Alliance was a secret organization composed of the very best people, by which she meant wealthy, filthy rich. She said that they could use me, 'make use of my talents' is the way she put it. And she said that I would be rewarded handsomely.

"So Gina didn't love me. She had a purpose for me. Of course, I was a little hurt by that. At first, I thought I might kill her. But there was no need for that, was there, Ben? In fact it would have been stupid."

"Because they hired you to kill for them?"

"Of course," Henri said.

"But how would that benefit the Alliance?"

"Benjamin," Henri said patiently. "They didn't hire me to do *hits*. I film my work. I make the films for *them*. They pay to *watch*."

Chapter 83

HENRI HAD SAID he killed for money, and now his story was coming together. He had been killing and creating films of these sexual executions for a select audience at a premium price. The stage-like setting for Kim's death made sense now. It had been a cinematic backdrop to his debauchery. But I didn't understand why Henri had drowned Levon and Barbara. What could possibly explain that?

"You were talking about the Peepers. The assignment you took in Hawaii."

"I remember. Well, understand, the Peepers give me a great deal of creative freedom," Henri said. "I picked Kim out from her photos. I used a ploy to get information from her agency. I said I wanted to book her and asked when would she be returning from—where was she shooting?

"I was told the location, and I worked out the rest: which island, her time of arrival, and the hotel. While I was waiting for Kim to arrive, I killed little Rosa. She was a tidbit, an *amuse-bouche*—"

"*Amuse* what?"

"It means an appetizer, and in her case, the

Alliance hadn't commissioned the work. I put the film up for auction. Yes, there's a market for such things. I made some extra money, and I made sure the film got back to the Dutchman. Jan especially likes young girls, and I wanted the Peepers to be hungry for my work.

"When Kim arrived in Maui for the shoot, I kept watch on her."

"Were you going under the name of Nils Bjorn?" I asked.

Henri started. Then he frowned.

"How did you know that?"

I'd made a mistake. My mental leap had connected Gina Prazzi to the woman who'd phoned me in Hawaii telling me to check out a guest named Nils Bjorn. This connection had apparently struck home—and Henri didn't like it.

Why would Gina betray Henri, though? What didn't I know about the two of them?

It felt like an important hook into Henri's story, but I gave myself a warning. *For my own safety, I had to be careful not to tick Henri off. Very careful.*

"The police got a tip," I said. "An arms dealer by that name checked out of the Wailea Princess around the time Kim went missing. He was never questioned."

"I'll tell you something, Ben," Henri said. "I *was* Nils Bjorn, but I've destroyed his identity. I'll never use it again. It's worthless to you now."

Henri got up from his seat abruptly. He adjusted the awning to block the lower angle of the sun's rays. I used the time to steady my nerves.

I was swapping out the old audiotape for a new one when Henri said, "Someone is coming."

My heart started tap-dancing in my chest again.

Chapter 84

I SHIELDED MY eyes with my hands and looked in the direction of the trail stretching through the desert to the west, saw a dark-colored sedan coming over a hill.

Henri said, "Right now! Take your things, your glass and your chair, and go inside "

I did what I was told, hustled back into the trailer with Henri behind me. He unhooked the chain from the floor, put it under the sink. He handed me my jacket and told me to go into the bathroom.

"If our visitor gets too nosy," Henri said, hiding the wineglasses, "I may have to dispose of him. That means you'll have witnessed a murder, Ben. Not good for you."

I squeezed into the tiny washroom, looked at my face in the mirror before flicking off the light. I had a three-day beard, rumpled shirt. I looked disreputable. I looked like a bum.

The bathroom wall was thin, and I could hear everything through it. There was a knock on the trailer door, which Henri opened. I heard heavy footsteps.

"Please come in, Officer. I'm Brother Michael," Henri said.

A woman's authoritative voice said, "I'm Lieutenant Brooks. Park Service. This campsite is closed, sir. Didn't you see the roadblock and the words 'Do Not Enter' in giant letters?"

"I'm sorry," Henri said. "I wanted to pray without being disturbed. I'm with the Camaldolese monastery. In Big Sur. I'm on retreat."

"I don't care if you're an acrobat with the Cirque du Soleil. You have no business being here."

"*God* led me here," said Henri. "I'm on *His* business. But I didn't mean any harm. I'm sorry."

I could feel the tension outside the door. If the ranger used her radio to call for help, she was a dead woman. Years ago, back in Portland, I'd backed my squad car into a wheelchair, knocked over an old man. Another time, I put a little kid in my gun sights when he'd jumped out from between two cars, pointing a squirt gun at me.

Both times I thought my heart couldn't beat any harder, but honest to God, this was the worst.

If my belt buckle clanked against the metal sink, the ranger would hear it. If she saw me, if she questioned me, Henri might feel he had to kill her, and her death would be on me.

Then he'd kill me.

I prayed not to sneeze. I prayed.

Chapter 85

THE RANGER TOLD HENRI that she understood about desert retreats, but that the campsite wasn't safe.

"If the chopper pilot hadn't seen your trailer, there would be no patrols out this way. What if you ran out of fuel? What if you ran out of water? No one would find you, and you would die." Lieutenant Brooks said. "I'll wait while you pack up your gear."

A radio crackled, and I heard the ranger say, "I got him, Yusef."

I waited for the inevitable gunshot, thought of kicking open the door, trying to knock the gun out of Henri's hand, save the poor woman somehow.

The lieutenant said to her partner, "He's a monk. A hermit. Yeah. He's by himself. No, it's under control."

Henri's voice cut in, "Lieutenant, it's getting late. I can leave in the morning without difficulty. I'd really appreciate one more night here for my meditation."

There was silence as the park ranger seemed to

consider Henri's request. I slowly exhaled, took in another breath. *Lady, do what he says. Get the hell out of here.*

"I can't help you," she said.

"Sure you can. Just one night is all I ask."

"Your gas tank is full?"

"Yes. I filled up before I drove into the park."

"And you have enough water?"

The refrigerator door squealed open.

The ranger said, "Tomorrow morning, you're outta here. We have a deal?"

"Yes, we do," Henri said. "I'm sorry for the trouble."

"Okay. Have a good night, Brother."

"Thank you, Lieutenant. And bless you."

I heard the ranger's car engine start up. A minute later, Henri opened my door.

"Change of plans," he said, as I edged out of the washroom. "I'll cook. We're pulling an all-nighter."

"No problem," I said.

I looked out the window and saw the lights of the patrol car heading back to civilization. Behind me, Henri dropped hamburger patties into the frying pan.

"We've got to cover a lot of ground tonight," he said.

I was thinking that by noon of the next day, I could be in Venice Beach watching the bodybuilders and the thong girls, the skaters and bikers on the winding concrete paths through the beach and along the shore. I thought of the dogs with kerchiefs and sunglasses, the toddlers on their trikes, and that I'd have huevos rancheros with extra salsa at Scotty's with Mandy.

I'd tell her everything.

Henri put a burger and a bottle of ketchup in front of me, said, "Here ya go, Mr. Meat and Potatoes." He started making coffee.

The little voice in my head said, *You're not home yet.*

Chapter 86

THE KIND OF LISTENING you do when interviewing is very different from the casual kind. I had to focus on what Henri was saying, how it fit into the story, decide if I needed elaboration on that subject or if we had to move along.

Fatigue was coming over me like fog, and I fought it off with coffee, keeping my goal in sight. *Get it down and get out of here alive.*

Henri backtracked over the story of his service with the military contractor, Brewster-North. He told me how he'd brought several languages to the table and that he'd learned several more while working for them.

He told me how he'd formed a relationship with his forger in Beirut. And then his shoulders sagged as he detailed his imprisonment, the executions of his friends.

I asked questions, placed Gina Prazzi in the timeline. I asked Henri if Gina knew his real identity, and he told me no. He'd used the name that matched the papers his forger had given him: Henri Benoit from Montreal.

"Have you stayed in contact with Gina?"

"I haven't seen her for years. Not since Rome," he said. "She doesn't fraternize with the help."

We worked forward from his three-month-long romance with Gina to the contract killings he did for the Alliance, a string of murders that went back over four years.

"I mostly killed young women," Henri told me. "I moved around, changed my identity often. You remember how I do that, Ben."

He started ticking off the bodies, the string of young girls in Jakarta, a Sabra in Tel Aviv.

"What a fighter, that Sabra. My God. She almost killed *me*."

I felt the natural arc of the story. I felt excited as I saw how I would organize the draft, almost forgot for a while that this wasn't some kind of movie pitch.

The murders were real.

Henri's gun was loaded even now.

I numbered tapes and changed them, made notes that would remind me to ask follow-up questions as Henri listed his kills; the young prostitutes in Korea and Venezuela and Bangkok.

He explained that he'd always loved film and that making movies for the Alliance had made him an even better killer. The murders became more complex and cinematic.

"Don't you worry that those films are out in the world?"

"I always disguise my face," he told me. "Either I wear a mask as I did with Kim, or I work on the video with a blur tool. The software that I use makes editing out my face very easy."

He told me that his years with Brewster-North had taught him to leave the weapons and the bodies on the scene (Rosa was the one exception), and that even though there was no record of his fingerprints, he made sure never to leave anything of himself behind. He always wore a condom, taking no chances that the police might take DNA samples from his semen and begin to link his crimes.

Henri told me about killing Julia Winkler, how much he loved her. I stifled a smart-ass comment about what it meant to be loved by Henri. And he told me about the McDanielses, and how he admired them as well. At that point, I wanted to jump up and try to strangle him.

"Why, Henri, why did you have to kill them?" I finally asked.

"It was part of a film sequence I was making for the Peepers, what we called a documentary. Maui was a big payout, Ben. Just a few days' work for much more than you make in a year."

"But the work itself, how did you feel about taking all of those lives? By my count, you've killed thirty people."

"I may have left out a few," Henri said.

Chapter 87

IT WAS AFTER THREE IN THE MORNING when Henri told me what fascinated him most about his work.

"I've become interested in the fleeting moment *between* life and death," he said. I thought about the headless chickens from his childhood, the asphyxiation games he played after killing Molly.

Henri told me more, more than I wanted to know.

"There was a tribe in the Amazon," he continued. "They would tie a noose high under the jaws of their victims, right under their ears. The other end of the rope was secured around the tops of bent saplings.

"When they cut off a victim's head, it was carried upward by the young tree snapping back into place. These Indians believed this was a good death. That their victim's last sensation would be of flying."

"Henri, are you saying the moment between life and death is what makes you want to kill?"

"I think so. About three years ago, I killed a couple in Big Sur. I knotted ropes high up under their jaws," he said, demonstrating with the V between thumb and index finger of his hand. "I tied the other end of the ropes to the blades of a ceiling fan. I cut their heads off with a machete, and the fan spun with their heads attached.

"I think the Peepers knew that I was very special when they saw that film," Henri said. "I raised my fee, and they paid. But I still wonder about those two lovers. I wonder if they felt that they were flying as they died."

Chapter 88

EXHAUSTION DRAGGED ME down as the sun came up. We'd worked straight through the night, and although I heavily sugared my coffee and drank it down to the dregs, my eyelids drooped and the small world of the trailer on the rumpled acres of sand blurred.

I said, "This is important, Henri."

I completely lost what I was going to say—and Henri prompted me by shaking my shoulder. "Finish your sentence, Ben. *What* is important?"

It was the question that would be asked by the reader at the beginning of the book, and it had to be answered at the end. I asked, "Why do you want to write this book?"

Then I put my head down on the small table, just for a minute.

I heard Henri moving around the trailer, thought I saw him wiping down surfaces. I heard him talking, but I wasn't sure he was talking to me.

When I woke up, the clock on the microwave read ten after eleven.

I called out to Henri, and when he didn't answer

I struggled out of my cramped spot behind the table and opened the trailer door.

The truck was gone.

I left the trailer and looked in all directions. The sludge began to clear from the gears in my brain, and I went back inside. My laptop and briefcase were on the kitchen counter. The piles of tapes that I'd carefully labeled in sequence were in neat stacks. My tape recorder was plugged into the outlet— and then I saw the note next to the machine.

Ben: Play this.

I pushed the Play button and heard Henri's voice.

"Good morning, partner. I hope you had a good rest. You needed it, and so I gave you a sedative to help you sleep. You understand. I wanted some time alone.

"Now. You should take the trail to the west, fourteen miles to Twenty-nine Palms Highway. I've left plenty of water and food, and if you wait until sundown, you will make it out of the park by morning.

"Very possibly, Lieutenant Brooks or one of her colleagues may drop by and give you a lift. Be careful what you say, Ben. Let's keep our secrets for now. You're a novelist, remember. So be sure to tell a plausible lie.

"Your car is behind the Luxury Inn where you left it, and I've put your keys in your jacket pocket with your plane ticket.

"Oh, I almost forgot the most important thing. I called Amanda. I told her you were safe and that you'd be home soon.

"*Ciao,* Ben. Work hard. Work well. I'll be in touch."

And then the tape hissed and the message was over.

The bastard had called Amanda. It was another threat.

Outside the trailer, the desert was cooking in the July inferno, forcing me to wait until sundown before beginning my trek. While I waited, Henri would be erasing his trail, assuming another identity, boarding a plane unhindered.

I no longer had any sense of security, and I wouldn't feel safe again until "Henri Benoit" was in jail or dead. I wanted my life back, and I was determined to get it, whatever it took.

Even if I had to put Henri down myself.

Part Four

BIG GAME HUNTING

Chapter 89

ON MY FIRST DAY back from my desert retreat with Henri, Leonard Zagami called to say he wanted to publish fast so we'd get gonzo press coverage for breaking Henri's first-person story before the Maui murders were solved.

I'd called Aronstein, taken a leave from the *L.A. Times,* turned my living room into a bunker and not just because of the pressure from Zagami. I felt Henri's presence all the time, like he was a boa constrictor with a choke hold on my rib cage, peering over my shoulder as I typed. I wanted nothing more than to get his dirty story written and done, and get him out of my life.

Since my return, I'd been working from six in the morning until late at night, and I found transcribing the interview tapes educational.

Listening to Henri's voice behind a locked door, I heard inflections and pauses, comments made under his breath, that I'd missed while sitting next to his coiled presence and wondering if I was going to make it out of Joshua Tree alive.

I'd never worked so hard or so steadily, but by

the end of the second full week at my laptop, I'd finished the transcription and also the outline for the book.

One important item was missing: the hook for the introduction, the question that would power the narrative to the end, the question Henri hadn't answered. *Why did he want to write this book?*

The reader would want to know, and I couldn't understand it myself. Henri was twisted in his particular way, and that included being an actual survivor. He dodged death like it was Sunday traffic. He was smart, probably a genius, so why would he write a tell-all confession when his own words could lead to his capture and indictment? Was it for money? Recognition? Was his narcissism so overpowering that he'd set a trap for himself?

It was almost six on a Friday evening. I was filing the transcribed audiotapes in a shoe box when I put my hand on the exit tape, the one with Henri's instructions telling me how to get out of Joshua Tree Park.

I hadn't replayed the tape because Henri's message hadn't seemed relevant to the work, but before I boxed it up, I dropped tape number 31 into the recorder and rewound it to the beginning.

I realized instantly that Henri hadn't used a fresh tape for his message. He'd recorded on the tape that was already in the machine.

I heard my drugged and weary voice coming through the speaker, saying, "This is important, Henri."

There was silence. I'd forgotten what I wanted to ask him. Then Henri's voice was saying, "Finish your sentence, Ben. *What* is important?"

"Why...do you want to write this book?"

My head had dropped to the table, and I remembered hearing Henri's voice as through a fog.

Now he was coming in loud and clear.

"Good question, Ben. If you're half the writer I think you are, if you're half the cop you used to be, you'll figure out why I want to do this book. I think you'll be surprised."

I was going to be *surprised?* What the hell was that supposed to mean?

Chapter 90

A KEY TURNED in the lock, and bolts thunked open. I started, swiveled in my chair. *Henri?*

But it was only Amanda coming across the threshold, hugging a grocery bag. I leapt up, took the bag, and kissed my girl, who said, "I got the last two Cornish game hens. Yea! Also. Look. Wild rice and haricots verts—"

"You're a peach, you know that?" I said.

"You saw the news?"

"No. What?"

"Those two girls who were found on Barbados. One of them was strangled. The other was *decapitated*."

"What two girls?"

I hadn't turned on the TV in a week. I didn't know what the hell Amanda was talking about.

"The story was all over cable, not to mention the Internet. You need to come up for air, Ben."

I followed her into the kitchen, put the groceries on the counter, and snapped on the under-cabinet TV. I tuned in to MSNBC, where Dan Abrams was talking to the former FBI profiler John Manzi.

Manzi looked grim. He was saying, "You call it 'serial' when there've been three or more killings with an emotional cooling-off period in between. The killer left the murder weapon in a hotel room with Sara Russo's decapitated body. Wendy Emerson was found in a car trunk, bound and strangled. These crimes are very reminiscent of the killings in Hawaii a month ago. Despite the distances involved, I'd say they could be linked. I'd bet on it."

Pictures of the two young women appeared on a split screen as Manzi talked. Russo looked to be in her late teens. Emerson in her twenties. Both young women had big, expectant, life-sized smiles, and Henri had killed them. I was sure of it. I'd bet on it, too.

Amanda edged past me, put the birds in the oven, banged pots around, and ran water on the veggies. I turned up the volume.

Manzi was saying, "It's too soon to know if the killer left any DNA behind, but the absence of a *motive,* leaving the murder weapons *behind,* these form a picture of a very practiced killer. He didn't just get started in Barbados, Dan. It's a question of how many people he's killed, over how long a time, and in how many places."

I said to Mandy over the commercial break, "I've been listening to Henri talk about himself for weeks. I can tell you absolutely, he feels no remorse whatsoever. He's happy with himself. He's *ecstatic.*"

I told Mandy that Henri had left me a message telling me that he expected me to figure out why he was doing the book.

"He's challenging me as a writer, and as a cop. Hey, maybe he wants to get *caught*. Does that make any sense to you?"

Mandy had been solid throughout, but she showed me how scared she was when she grabbed my hands hard and fixed me with her eyes.

"*None* of it makes sense to me, Benjy. Not why, not what he wants, not even why he picked you to do this book. All I know is he's a freaking *psycho*. And he knows where we live."

Chapter 91

I WOKE UP in bed, my heart hammering, my T-shirt and shorts drenched with sweat.

In my dream, Henri had taken me on a tour of his killings in Barbados, talked to me while he sawed off Sara Russo's head. He'd held up her head by her hair, saying, "See, this is what I like, the fleeting moment between life and death," and in the way of dreams, Sara became Mandy.

Mandy looked at me in the dream, her blood streaming down Henri's arm, and she said, "Ben. Call Nine-one-one."

I threw my arm over my forehead and dried my brow.

It was an easy nightmare to interpret. I was terrified that Henri would kill Mandy. And I felt guilty about those girls in Barbados, thinking, *If I'd gone to the police, they might still be alive.*

Was that dream-thinking? Or was it true?

I imagined going to the FBI now, telling them how Henri had put a gun on me, took photos of Amanda, and threatened to kill us both.

I would have to tell them how Henri chained me to a trailer in the desert and detailed the killings of thirty people. But were those confessions? Or bullshit?

I had no proof that anything Henri had told me was true. Just his word.

I imagined the FBI agent eyeing me skeptically, then the networks broadcasting "Henri's" description: a white male, six feet, 160 pounds, mid-thirties. That would piss Henri off. And then, if he could, he'd kill us.

Did Henri really think I'd let that happen?

I stared at headlights flickering across the ceiling of the bedroom.

I remembered names of restaurants and resorts Henri had visited with Gina Prazzi. There were a number of other aliases and details Henri hadn't thought important but that might, if I could figure them out, unwind his whole ball of string.

Mandy turned over in her sleep, put her arm across my chest, and snuggled close to me. I wondered what *she* was dreaming. I tightened my arms around her, lightly kissed the crown of her head.

"Try not to torment yourself." she said against my chest.

"I didn't mean to wake you."

"That's a joke, right? You almost blew me out of bed with all your heaving and sighing."

"What time is it?"

"It's early. Too early, or late, for us to be up. Benjy, I don't think obsessing is helping."

"Oh. You think I'm obsessing?"

"Get your mind on something else. Take a break."

"Zagami wants—"

"Screw Zagami. I've been thinking, too, and I have an idea of my own. You won't like it."

Chapter 92

I WAS PACING in front of my building with an overnight bag when Mandy roared up on her gently used Harley Sportster, a snappy-looking bike with a red leather saddle.

I climbed on, put my hands around Mandy's small waist, and with her long hair whipping across my face we motored to the Ten and from there to the Pacific Coast Highway, a dazzling stretch of coastal road that seems to go on forever.

To our left and below the road, breakers reared up and curled toward the beach, bringing in the surfers who dotted the waves. It struck me that I had never surfed—*because it was too dangerous.*

I hung on as Mandy switched lanes and gunned the engine. She shouted to me, "Take your shoulders down from your ears."

Huh?

"Relax."

It was hard to do, but I willed myself to unclench my legs and shoulders, and Mandy shouted again, "Now, make like a *dog.*"

She turned her head and stuck out her tongue,

pointed her finger at me until I did it, too. The fifty-
mile-an-hour wind beat on my tongue, cracking me
up, making both of us laugh so hard that our eyes
watered.

I was still grinning as we blew through Malibu
and crossed the Ventura County line. Minutes later,
Mandy pulled the bike over at Neptune's Net, a sea-
food shack with a parking lot full of motorcycles.

A couple of guys called out, "Hey, Mandy," as I
followed her inside. We picked out two crabs from
the well, and ten minutes later we picked them up
at the take-out window, steamed and cracked on
paper plates with small cups of melted butter. We
chased the crabs down with Mountain Dew, then
climbed aboard the Harley again.

I felt more at home on the bike this time, and
finally I got it. Mandy was giving me the gift of
glee. The speed and wind were blowing the snarls
out of my mind, forcing me to turn myself over to
the excitement and freedom of the road.

As we traveled north, the PCH wound down
to sea level, taking us through the dazzling towns
of Sea Cliff, La Conchita, Rincon, Carpinteria,
Summerland, and Montecito. And then Mandy
was telling me to hang on as she took the turn off
the freeway onto the Olive Mill Road exit to Santa
Barbara.

I saw the signs, and then I knew where we were
going—a place we had talked of spending a weekend at, but we had never found the time.

My whole body was shaking when I dismounted
the bike in front of the legendary Biltmore Hotel,
with its red tiled roofs and palm trees and high
view of the sea. I took off my helmet, put my arms

around my girl, and said, "Honey, when you say you have an *idea,* you sure don't mess around."

She told me, "I was saving my Christmas bonus for our anniversary, but you know what I thought at four this morning?"

"Tell me."

"No better time than now. No better place than this."

Chapter 93

THE HOTEL LOBBY GLOWED. I'm not one of those guys who studies the "House Beautiful" channel, but I knew luxury and comfort, and Amanda, prancing in place beside me, filled in the details. She pointed out the Mediterranean style, the archways and beamed ceilings, the plump sofas and logs burning in a tiled fireplace. The vast, rolling ocean below.

Then Mandy warned me—and she was serious.

"If you mention what'-s-his-name, even once, the bill goes on your credit card, not mine. Okay?"

"Deal," I said, pulling her in for a hug.

Our room had a fireplace, and when Mandy started tossing her clothes onto the chair, I pictured us rolling around in the king-size bed for the rest of the afternoon.

She read the look in my eyes, laughed, and said, "Oh, I see. Wait, okay? I've got another idea."

I was becoming a big fan of Mandy's ideas. She stepped into her leopard-print bikini, and I put on my trunks, and we went out to a pool in the center of the main garden. I followed Mandy's lead.

diving in, and heard—I couldn't quite believe it—
music playing underwater.

Back in our room, I untied the strings of Mandy's
swimsuit, pushed down the bikini bottoms, and
she climbed up on me, her legs around my waist. I
walked her into the shower and not too many minutes later we tumbled onto the bed, where goofi-
ness became heart-pounding lovemaking.

Later we napped, Mandy falling asleep while
lying on my chest with her knees tucked up along my
sides. For the first time in weeks, I slept deeply without my eyes flying open at some bloody nightmare.

At sundown, Mandy slipped into a small black
dress and twisted up her hair, making me think of
Audrey Hepburn. We took the winding stairs down
to the Bella Vista and were shown to a table near
the fire. There was marble underfoot, mahogany-
paneled walls, a billion-dollar view of whitecaps
below, and a glass-paned ceiling showing cobalt
twilight over our heads.

I glanced at the menu, put it down when the
waiter came over. Mandy ordered for us both.

I was grinning again. Amanda Diaz knew how
to take a day out of the dumper and light up memories that could take the two of us into old age.

We started our five-star dinner with sautéed
jumbo scallops and continued with scrumptious
honey-cilantro-glazed sea bass with mushrooms
and snow peas. Then the waiter brought dessert
menus and chilled champagne.

I turned the bottle so I could read the label: Dom
Pérignon.

"You didn't order this, did you, Mandy? This is
about three hundred dollars."

"Wasn't me. We must've got somebody else's bubbly."

I reached for the card the waiter had left on a small silver tray. It read, "The Dom is on me. It's the good stuff. Best regards, H.B."

Henri Benoit.

Fear shot right up my spine. How had that fucker known where we were when I hadn't known where we were going myself?

I got to my feet, knocking over my chair. I pivoted around, a full 360 and then back again in the other direction to be sure. I scanned every face in the room: the old man with soup on his whiskers, the bald tourist with his fork poised over his plate, the honeymooners standing in the entranceway, and every one of the waitstaff.

Where was he? *Where?*

I stood so that I blocked Mandy with my body, and I felt the scream tearing out of my throat.

"Henri, you bastard. Show yourself."

Chapter 94

AFTER THE SCENE in the dining room, I locked and chained the door to our suite, checked the latches on the windows, closed the drapes. I hadn't brought my gun, a gross mistake I wouldn't make again.

Mandy was pale and shaking as I sat her down next to me on the bed.

"Who knew we were coming here?" I asked her.

"I made the reservation when I went home to pack this morning. That's all."

"You're sure?"

"Except for calling Henri on his private line, you mean?"

"Seriously. You talk to anyone on your way out this morning? Think about it, Mandy. He knew we'd be here."

"I just told you, Ben, really. I didn't tell anyone. I just called in my credit card to the reservation clerk. That's all I did. That's *all*."

"Okay, okay," I said. "I'm sorry."

I had been thorough. I was sure of it. I revisited that night when I'd just returned from New

York, and Henri called me at Amanda's apartment
minutes after I'd walked in the door. I'd checked
Mandy's phones and mine, checked both of our
apartments for bugs.

I hadn't noticed anything unusual around us on
the highway this afternoon. There was no way anyone could have followed us when we took the off-
ramp to Santa Barbara. We had been alone for so
many miles that we'd practically owned the road.

Ten minutes ago, after the maitre d' escorted us
out of the dining room, he'd told me that the champagne had been phoned in, charged to a credit card
by Henri Benoit. That explained nothing. Henri
could have called from any point on the globe.

But how had he known where we were?

If Henri hadn't tapped Mandy's phone, and if he
hadn't tailed us—

A stunning thought cracked through my mind
like a lightning strike. I stood up, and said, "He
put a tracking device on your bike."

"Don't even think about leaving me in this room
alone," Amanda said. I sat back down beside her,
took her hand between both of mine and kissed it.
I couldn't leave her in the room, and I couldn't protect her in the parking lot either.

"As soon as it's light tomorrow, I'm dismantling
your bike until I find the bug."

"I can't believe what he's doing to us," Mandy
said, and then she started to cry.

Chapter 95

WE HELD ON to each other under the bedcovers, our eyes wide open, listening to every footstep overhead, every creak in the hallway outside the room, every groan and pitch of the air conditioner. I didn't know if I was being rational or extremely paranoid, but I felt Henri watching us now.

Mandy had me tightly wrapped in her arms when she started crying out, "Oh, my God, oh, my God."

I tried to comfort her, saying, "Honey, stop. This isn't such bad news. We'll find out how he's tracking us."

"Oh, my God—*this,*" she said, poking me hard high on my right buttock. "This thing on your hip. I've told you about it. You always say it's nothing."

"That thing? It *is* nothing."

"*Look at it.*"

I threw off the blankets, switched on the lights, walked to the bathroom mirror with Mandy close behind me. I couldn't *see* it without contorting myself, but I knew what she was talking about: a welt that had been tender for a few days after Henri had clubbed me in my apartment.

I'd thought it was a bruise from the fall, or a bug bite, and after a few days the soreness went away.

Mandy had asked me about the bump a couple of times, and, yes, I'd said it was nothing. I reached around and touched the raised spot, the size of two grains of rice lying end-to-end.

It didn't seem so nothing, not anymore.

I rifled through my toiletry kit, dumped it out on the vanity, and found my razor. I beat it against the marble sink until the shaving head broke into parts.

"You're not going to...Ben! You don't want *me* to do it?"

"Don't worry. It'll hurt me more than it hurts you."

"Wow, you're funny."

"I'm fucking terrified," I said.

Mandy took the blade from my hand, poured Listerine over it, and dabbed at the spot on my rump. Then she pinched a fold of skin and made a quick cut.

"I've got it," she said.

She dropped the bloody bit of glass and metal into my hand. It could only be one thing: a GPS tracking device, the kind that are implanted into the necks of dogs. Henri must've injected it into my hide when I was lying unconscious on the floor. I'd been wearing this damned bug for *weeks*.

"Flush it down the toilet," Amanda said. "That'll keep him busy."

"Yeah. *No*. Tear some tape off that roll, would you?"

I pressed the device against my side, and Mandy ripped off a length of adhesive tape with her teeth.

I patted the tape across the chip, securing it to my body again.

"What's the point of keeping it?" Mandy asked.

"As long as I'm wearing it, he won't know that I know that he's tracking me."

"And...what good is that?"

"It starts the ball rolling in the other direction. We know something he doesn't."

Chapter 96

FRANCE.

Henri stroked Gina Prazzi's flank as his breathing slowed. She had a wonderful peach-shaped ass, perfect rounded haunches with a dimple on each cheek at the small of her back.

He wanted to fuck her again. Very much so. And he would.

"You can untie me now," she said.

He patted her, got up, reached under a chair and into his bag, then went to the camera that was clipped to the heavy folds of the curtains.

"What are you doing? Come back to bed, Henri. Don't be so cruel."

He turned on the floor lamp and smiled into the lens, then went back to the canopied bed, said, "I don't think I caught the part when you were calling out to God. Too bad."

"What are you doing with that video? You're not sending it? You're crazy, Henri, if you think they'll pay."

"Oh, no?"

"I assure you, they will not."

"It's for my private collection, anyway. You should trust me more."

"Untie me, Henri. My arms are tired. I want a new game. I demand it."

"You always think of your own pleasure."

"Suit yourself," she said. "But there will be a price to pay for this."

Henri laughed. "Always a price."

He picked up the remote control from the ornate night table, turned on the television set. He clicked past the hotel welcome screen, found the channel guide, pressed the buttons for the BBC.

First there were sports scores, then a market wrap-up, and then there were the faces of the new girls, Wendy and Sara.

"I absolutely loved Sara," he told Gina, who was trying to loosen the knots binding her wrists to the headboard. "She never begged for her life. She never asked any stupid questions."

"If I had use of my, ah, hands, I could do some nice things for you," Gina said.

"I'll think about it."

Henri clicked off the remote, rolled over, and straddled Gina's fantastic ass. He put his hands on her shoulders, rubbed his thumbs in circles at the base of her neck. He was getting hard again. Very hard, painfully so.

"This is becoming boring," she said. "Maybe this reunion was a bad idea."

Henri closed his fingers gently around her throat, still just playing a game. He felt her body tense and a film of sweat come over her skin.

Good. He liked her to be afraid. "Still bored?"

He squeezed until she coughed, pulled at the restraints, wheezing his name as her lungs fought for air.

He released her, and then, as she gulped for breath, he untied her wrists. Gina shook out her hands and rolled over, still panting, said, "I knew you couldn't do it."

"No. I couldn't do that."

She got out of the bed and flounced toward the bathroom, stopping first to wink at the camera. Henri watched her go, then he got up, reached into his bag again, and walked into the bathroom behind her.

"What do you want now?" she asked, making eye contact with him in the mirror.

"Time's up," he said.

Henri pointed the gun at the back of Gina's neck and fired, watched in the blood-spattered mirror as her eyes got large, then followed her body as she dropped to the floor. He put two more slugs into her back, checked her pulse, wiped down the gun and the silencer, placed the weapon at her side.

After his shower, Henri dressed. Then he downloaded the video to his laptop, wiped down the rooms, packed his bag, and checked that everything was as it should be.

He stared for a moment at the three diamond wristwatches on the nightstand and remembered the day he met her.

I...have time for you.

Together, the watches were worth a hundred thousand euros. Not worth the risk, though.

He left them on the table. A nice tip for the maid, no?

Gina had used her credit card, so Henri left the room, closing the door behind him. He walked across the forecourt without incident, got into his rented car, and drove to the airport.

Chapter 97

BY SUNDAY AFTERNOON, I was back in my bunker, back to my book. I had a month's supply of junk food in the cupboard and was bent on finishing the expanded chapter outline for Zagami, who was expecting it in his e-mail box by morning.

At seven p.m., I turned on the tube: 60 *Minutes* had just started, and the Barbados murders were headlining the show.

Morley Safer was speaking: "Forensic experts say that when combined with the five Maui murders, the deaths of Wendy Emerson and Sara Russo are part of a pattern of brutal, sadistic killings, with no end in sight.

"Right now, detectives around the world are reexamining unsolved murder cases, looking for anything that can lead to a serial murderer who has left no known witnesses, no living victims, not a trace of himself behind. CBS correspondent Bob Simon talked with some of those detectives."

Film clips came on the screen.

I watched retired cops interviewed in their homes and was struck by their somber expressions and quavering voices. One cop in particular had tears in his eyes as he displayed photos of a murdered twelve-year-old whose killer had never been found.

I turned off the set and screamed into my hands.

Henri was living inside my brain—in the past, the present, and the future. I knew his methods, his victims, and now I was adapting my writing to the cadence of his voice.

Sometimes, and this really scared me—sometimes I thought that I was him.

I uncapped a beer and drank it down in front of the open fridge. Then I wandered back to my laptop. I went online and checked my e-mail, something I hadn't done since leaving with Mandy for the weekend.

I opened a dozen e-mails before I came to one with the subject heading "Is everybody happy?" The e-mail had an attachment.

My fingers froze on the keys. I didn't recognize the sender's address, but I blinked at the heading for a long time before I opened the message: "Ben, I'm still working like a madman. Are you?"

The note was signed "H.B."

I touched the strip of bandage stuck to my left side and felt the small device that was beaming my location to Henri's computer.

Then I downloaded the attachment.

Chapter 98

THE VIDEO OPENED with a burst of light and an extreme close-up of Henri's digitally blurred face. He turned and walked toward a canopied bed in what looked to be a very expensive hotel room. I noted the elaborate furnishings, the traditional European fleur-de-lis pattern that was repeated in the draperies, carpet, and upholstery.

My eyes were drawn to the bed, where I saw a naked woman lying facedown, hands stretched out in front of her, tugging at the cords that tied her wrists to the headboard.

Oh no, here we go, I thought as I watched.

Henri got into bed next to her, and the two of them spoke in offhand tones. I couldn't make out what they were saying until she raised her voice sharply, asking him to untie her.

Something was different this time.

I was struck by the lack of fear in her voice. Was she a very good actor? Or had she just not figured out the climax?

I hit the Pause button, stopping the video.

Henri's ninety-second cut of Kim McDaniels's

execution flashed into my mind in sharp detail. I would never forget Kim's postmortem expression, as if she was in pain even though her head had been detached from her body.

I didn't want to add another Henri Benoit production to my mental playlist.

I didn't want to see *this*.

Downstairs, an ordinary Sunday night was unfolding on Traction Avenue. I heard a street guitarist playing "Domino" and tourists applauding, the whoosh of tires on pavement as cars passed under my windows. A few weeks ago, a night like this, I might have gone down, had a couple of beers at Moe's.

I wished I could do it now. But I couldn't walk away.

I pressed the Play button and watched the moving pictures on my computer screen: Henri telling the woman that she cared only about her own pleasure, laughing, saying, "Always a price." He picked up the remote control and turned on the TV.

The hotel welcome screen flashed by, and then an announcer on *BBC World News* gave a sports update, mostly football. Another announcer followed with a summary of various international financial markets, then came the breaking news of the two girls who'd been killed in Barbados.

Now, on my computer screen, Henri shut off the TV. He straddled the naked woman's body, put his hands around her neck, and I was sure that he was going to choke her—and then he changed his mind.

He untied her wrists, and I exhaled, wiped my eyes with my palms. He was letting her go—but why?

On screen, the woman said to Henri, "I knew you couldn't do it." Her English was accented. She was Italian.

Was this *Gina?*

She got out of the bed and strolled toward the camera, and she winked. She was a pretty brunette in her late thirties, maybe forty. She headed to an adjoining room, probably the bathroom.

Henri got out of the bed, reached down, and pulled a gun from a bag that looked to be a 9-millimeter Ruger with a suppressor extending the muzzle.

He walked behind the woman and out of camera range.

I heard muffled conversation, then the *phfffft* sound of the gun firing through the suppressor. A shadow passed over the threshold. There was a soft, heavy thud, two more muffled shots, then the rush of running water.

Except for the empty bed, that's all I saw or heard until the screen went black.

My hands shook as I played the video again. This time I was looking for any detail that could tell me where Henri had been when he had surely killed this woman.

On my third viewing, I saw something I'd missed before.

I stopped the action when Henri turned on the TV. I enlarged the picture and read the welcome screen with the name of the hotel at the top of the menu.

It had been shot on an angle, and it was damned hard to make out the letters, but I wrote them down and then went out to the Web to see if such a place existed.

It did.

I read that the Château de Mirambeau was in France, in the wine country near Bordeaux. It had been built on the foundations of a medieval fortress founded in the eleventh century, reconstructed in the early 1800s, and turned into an expensive resort. Pictures on the hotel's Web site showed fields of sunflowers, vineyards, and the château itself, an elaborate fairy-tale construction of vaulted stone, capped with turrets surrounding a courtyard and formal gardens.

I searched the Web again, found the football scores and the market closings that I'd seen on the TV in Henri's room.

I realized that this video had been shot on Friday, the same night Amanda had brought home Cornish game hens and I had learned about the deaths of Sara and Wendy.

I put my hand over the bandage against my ribs and felt the banging of my heart. It was all clear to me now.

Two days ago, Henri was in France, about a five-hour drive from Paris. This coming week marked the beginning of September. Henri had told me that he always went to Paris in September.

I had a pretty good idea where he might be.

Chapter 99

I SLAMMED DOWN the lid of my laptop, as if I could actually shut out the images Henri had left to my imagination.

Then I called Amanda, talking rapidly as I threw clothes into a suitcase.

"Henri sent me a video," I told her. "Looks like he killed Gina Prazzi. Maybe he's doing cleanup. Getting rid of people who know him and what he's done. So we have to ask ourselves, Mandy, when the book is finished, what's he going to do to us?"

I told her my plan, and she argued with me, but I got the last word. "I can't just *sit* here. I have to *do* something."

I called a cab, and once we were rolling I ripped the adhesive tape from my rib cage and stuck the tracking device underneath the cab's backseat.

Chapter 100

I CAUGHT a direct flight to Paris—midcabin coach, next to the window. As soon as I put the seatback down, my eyes slammed shut. I missed the movie, the precooked meals, and the cheap champagne, but I got about nine hours of sleep, waking only as the plane started its descent.

My bag shot down the luggage chute like it had missed me, and within twenty minutes of landing I was sitting in the backseat of a taxi.

I spoke to the driver in my broken French, told him where to take me: the Hôtel Singe-Vert, French for "Green Monkey." I'd stayed there before and knew it to be a clean two-and-a-half-star lodging popular with journalists on location in the City of Lights.

I walked through the unmanned lobby door, passed the entrance to the bar called Jacques' Américain on my left, then crossed into the dark inner lobby with its worn green couches, racks of folded newspapers in all languages, and a large, faded watercolor of African green monkeys behind the front desk.

The concierge's nametag read "Georges." He

was flabby, fiftyish, and pissed that he had to break off his phone conversation to deal with me. After Georges ran my credit card and locked my passport in the safe, I took the stairs, found my room on the third floor at the end of a frayed runner at the back of the hotel.

The room was papered with cabbage roses and crowded with century-old furniture, jammed in wall to wall. But the bedding was fresh, and there was a TV and a high-speed Internet connection on the desk. Good enough for me.

I dropped my bag down on the duvet and found a phone book. I'd been in Paris for an hour, and before I did another thing, *I had to get a gun.*

Chapter 101

THE FRENCH TAKE handguns seriously. Permits are restricted to police and the military and a few security professionals, who have to lug their guns in cases, carry them in plain sight.

Still, in Paris, as in any big city, you can get a gun if you really want one. I spent the day prowling the Golden Drop, the drug-dealing sinkhole around the Basilica of Sacré-Coeur.

I paid two hundred euros for an old snub-nosed .38, a ladies' pistol with a two-inch barrel and six rounds in the chamber.

Back at the Green Monkey, Georges took my key off the board and pointed with his chin to a small heap on one of the sofas. "You have a guest."

It took me a long moment to take in what I was seeing. I walked over, shook her shoulder, and called her name.

Amanda opened her eyes and stretched as I sat down beside her. She put her arms around my neck and kissed me, but I couldn't even kiss her back. She was supposed to be home, safe in L.A.

"Gee. Pretend you're glad to see me, okay? Paris is for lovers," she said, smiling cautiously.

"Mandy, what in God's name are you thinking?"

"It's a little rash, I know. Look, I have something to tell you, Ben, and it could affect everything."

"Cut to the chase, Mandy. What are you talking about?"

"I wanted to tell you face-to-face—"

"So you just got on a plane? Is it about Henri?"

"No—"

"Then, Mandy, I'm sorry, but you have to go back. No, don't shake your head. You're a liability. Understand?"

"Well, thank you."

Mandy was pouting now, which was rare for her, but I knew that the further I pushed her, the more obstinate she'd get. I could already smell the carpet burning as she dug in her heels.

"Have you eaten?" she asked me.

"I'm not hungry," I said.

"I am. I'm a French chef. And we're in Paris."

"This is *not* a vacation," I said.

A half hour later, Mandy and I were seated at an outdoor café on the Rue des Pyramides. Night had blotted up the sunlight, the air was warm, and we had a clear view of a gilded statue of Saint Joan on her horse where our side street intersected with the Rue de Rivoli.

Mandy's mood had taken an upturn. In fact, she seemed almost high. She ordered in French, put away course after course, describing the preparation and rating the salad, the pâté, and the *fruits de mer*.

I made do with crackers and cheese and I drank

strong coffee, my mind working on what I had to do, feeling the time rushing by.

"Just try this," Mandy said, holding out a spoonful of crème brûlée.

"Honestly, Amanda," I said with frank exasperation. "You shouldn't be here. I don't know what else to say to you."

"Just say you love me, Benjy. I'm going to be the mother of your child."

Chapter 102

I STARED AT Amanda; thirty-four years old, looking twenty-five, wearing a baby blue cardigan with ruffled collar and cuffs and a perfect Mona Lisa smile. She was astonishingly beautiful, never more so than at this very moment.

"Please say that you're happy," she said.

I took the spoon out of her hand and put it down on her plate. I got out of my chair, placed one hand on each of her cheeks, and kissed her. Then I kissed her again. "You are the craziest girl I ever knew, *très étonnante*."

"You're very amazing, too," she said, beaming.

"Boy, do I love you," I said.

"*Moi aussi. Je t'aime* you to pieces. But are you, Benjy? Are you happy?"

I turned to the waitress, said to her, "This lovely lady and I are going to have a baby."

"It is your first baby?"

"Yes. And I love this woman so much, and I'm so happy about the baby I could fly circles around the *moon*."

The waitress smiled broadly, kissed both my cheeks

and Mandy's, then made a general announcement that I didn't quite understand. But she made wing motions with her arms, and people at the next table started laughing and clapping and then others joined in, calling out congratulations and bravos.

I smiled at strangers, bowed to a beatific Amanda, and felt the flush of an unexpected and full-blown joy. Not long ago I was thanking God that I have no children. Now I was lit up brighter than I. M. Pei's glass pyramid at the Louvre.

I could hardly believe it.

Mandy was going to have our child.

Chapter 103

AS QUICKLY AS my expanding love for Mandy sent my heart to the moon, my happiness was eclipsed by an even greater fear for her safety.

As we trekked back to our little hotel, I told Amanda why she had to leave Paris in the morning.

"We'll never be safe as long as Henri is calling the shots. I have to be smarter than he is, and that's saying something, Amanda. Our only hope is for me to get out in front of him. Please trust me about this."

I told Mandy that Henri had described walking with Gina around the Place Vendôme.

I said, "It's like looking for one needle in a hundred haystacks, but my gut is telling me that he's here."

"And if he is, what are you going to do about it, Benjy? Are you really going to kill him?"

"You've got a better idea?"

"About a hundred of them."

We took the stairs to our room, and I made Amanda stand back as I drew my dainty Smith &

Wesson and opened the door. I checked the closets and the bath, pushed aside the curtains, and looked out into the alley, seeing pop-up monsters everywhere.

When I was sure the room was clear, I said, "I'll be back in an hour. Two hours at most. Sit tight, okay? Watch the tube. Swear to me you won't leave the room."

"Oh please, Benjy, call the police."

"Honey. One more time. They can't protect us. We're not protectable. Not from Henri. Now promise me."

Mandy reluctantly held up the three-fingered Girl Scout salute, then locked the door behind me as I headed out.

I'd done some homework. There were a handful of first-class hotels in Paris. Henri might stay at the Georges V or the Plaza Athénée. But I was betting on my hunch.

It was an easy walk to the Hôtel Ritz on the Place Vendôme.

Chapter 104

HENRI POPPED HIS knuckles in the backseat of a metered Mercedes taxi heading north from Orly toward the Rue de Rivoli and from there to the Place Vendôme. He was hungry and irritated, and the ridiculous traffic was barely crawling across the Pont Royal on the Rue des Pyramides.

As the taxi idled at a traffic light, Henri shook his head, thinking again about the mistake he'd made, a genuine amateur boner, not knowing that Jan Van der Heuvel would be out of town when he visited Amsterdam earlier that day. Rather than leave immediately, he'd made a decision on the fly, something he rarely did.

He knew that Van der Heuvel had a secretary. He'd met her once, and he knew she'd be locking up Van der Heuvel's office at the end of the day.

So he'd watched and waited for Mieke Helsloot, with her cute little body and her short skirt and lace-up boots, to lock Van der Heuvel's big front door at five on the nose. Then he'd followed her in the intense silence of the canal district, only the sound of church bells and seabirds breaking the stillness.

He followed quietly, only yards behind her, crossing the canal after her, turning down a winding side street. Then he called out, "Hello, excuse me," and she'd turned to face him.

He'd apologized right away, falling in step beside her, saying he'd seen her leaving Mr. Van der Heuvel's office and had been trying to catch up to her for the last couple of blocks.

He'd said, "I'm working with Mr. Van der Heuvel on a confidential project. You remember me, don't you, Mieke? I'm Monsieur Benoit. I met you once in the office," Henri had said.

"Yes," she said doubtfully. "But I don't see how I can help you. Mr. Van der Heuvel will be back tomorrow."

Henri had told her that he'd lost Mr. Van der Heuvel's cell phone number, and that it would really help him if he could explain how he'd gotten the date of their meeting wrong. And Henri had continued the story until Meike Helsloot had stopped at the front door to her flat.

He thought of her now, holding the key in her hand, impatience showing on her face, but in her politeness and willingness to help her employer she'd let him into her flat so that she could make the call for him to her boss.

Henri had thanked her, taken the one upholstered chair in Meike's two-room flat that had been built under a staircase, and waited for the right moment to kill her.

As the girl rinsed out two glasses, Henri had looked around at the sloping bookshelves, the fashion magazines, the mirror over the fireplace that was almost completely covered with photos of Mieke's handsome boyfriend.

Later, when she understood what he was going to do, she'd wailed, *no-no-no,* and begged him, please not to, she hadn't done anything wrong, she would never tell anyone, no, *never.*

"Sorry. It's not about you, Mieke," he'd said. "It's about Mr. Van der Heuvel. He's a very wicked man."

She'd said, "So why do this to me?"

"Well. It's Jan's lucky day, isn't it? He was out of town."

Henri had bound her arms behind her back with one of her own bootlaces and was undoing his belt buckle when she said, "Not that. Please. I'm supposed to get married."

He hadn't raped her. He hadn't been in the mood after doing Gina. So he'd told her to think of something nice. It was important in the last moments of life to have good thoughts.

He looped another bootlace around her throat and tightened it, holding her down with his knee in the small of her back until she stopped breathing. The waxed shoelace was as strong as wire, and it cut through her thin neck and she bled as he killed her.

Afterward, he arranged the pretty girl's body under blankets and patted her cheek.

He was thinking now, he'd been so angry at himself for missing Jan that he hadn't even thought to videotape the kill.

Then again—Jan would get the message.

Henri liked thinking about that.

Chapter 105

STILL SITTING IN THE INTERMINABLE SLOG of traffic, Henri's mind turned back to Gina Prazzi, thinking of her eyes getting huge when he shot her, wondering if she'd really understood what he'd done. It was truly significant. She was the first person he'd killed for his own satisfaction since strangling the girl in the horse trailer more than twenty years ago.

And now he'd killed Mieke for the same reason. It wasn't about money at all.

Something inside him was changing.

It was like a light slipping beneath a door, and he could either open it to its full blinding brightness, or slam the door shut and run.

The horns were blaring now, and he saw that the taxi had finally *crept* to the intersection of Pyramides and Rivoli, and then stopped again. The driver turned off the air-conditioning and opened the windows to save gas.

Disgusted, Henri leaned forward, tapped on the glass.

The driver took a break from his cell phone to tell Henri that the street was jammed because of the French president's motorcade, which was just leaving the Elysée Palace on its way to the National Assembly.

"There's nothing I can do, Monsieur. My hands are tied. Relax."

"How long will it be?"

"Perhaps another fifteen minutes. How should I know?"

Henri was more furious at himself than before. It had been stupid to come to Paris as some kind of ironic postscript to killing Gina. Not only stupid, but self-indulgent, or maybe self-destructive. Was that it? *Do I want to be caught now?* he wondered.

He watched the street through the open window, desperate for the absurd politician's motorcade to come and go, when he heard shouts of laughter coming from a brasserie at the corner.

He looked that way.

A man wearing a blue sports jacket, a pink polo shirt, and khakis, an American of course, made a comic bow to a young woman in a blue sweater. People began clapping, and as Henri looked more closely, the man seemed familiar and then— Henri's mind stopped cold.

In fact, he couldn't believe it. He wanted to ask the driver, *Do you see what I see? Is that Ben Hawkins and Amanda Diaz?* Because I think I've lost my mind.

Then Hawkins wiggled the metal frame chair, turning it, sitting so that he faced the street, and Henri knew without a doubt. *It was Ben.* When he'd last checked, Hawkins and the girl had been in L.A.

Henri's mind flashed back over the weekend to late on Saturday night, after he'd shot Gina. He'd e-mailed the video to Ben, but he hadn't checked the GPS tracker, not then. Not for a couple of days.

Had Ben discovered and discarded the chip?

For a moment, Henri felt something completely new to him. He was *afraid*. Afraid that he was getting sloppy, losing his hard-won discipline, losing his grip. He couldn't let that happen.

Never again.

Henri barked at the driver, saying that he couldn't wait any longer. He pushed a wad of bills into the driver's hand, grabbed his bag and briefcase, and got out of the cab on the street side.

He walked between cars, before doubling back to the sidewalk. Moving quickly, he ducked into an alcove between two storefronts only ten yards or so from the brasserie.

Henri watched, his heart racing, as Ben and Amanda left the restaurant and walked arm in arm, east up Rivoli.

When they had gone far enough ahead, Henri fell in behind them, keeping them in view as they reached the Singe-Vert, a small hotel on Place André Malraux.

Once Amanda and Ben disappeared inside, Henri went into the hotel bar, Jacques' Américain, adjacent to the lobby. He ordered a Scotch from the bartender, who was actively putting the moves on a horse-faced brunette.

Henri sipped his drink and viewed the lobby through the bar's back mirror. When he saw Ben come downstairs, Henri swiveled in the stool, watched as Ben handed his key to the concierge.

Henri made a mental note of the number under the key hook.

Chapter 106

IT WAS ALREADY half past eight p.m. by the time I reached the Place Vendôme, an enormous square with traffic lanes on four sides and a tall bronze memorial to Napoléon Bonaparte in the center. On the west side of the Place is Rue St.-Honoré, shopping paradise for the wealthy, and across the square was the drop-dead-fantastic French Gothic architecture of the Hôtel Ritz, all honey-colored stone and luminous demilune awnings over the doorways.

I stepped onto the red carpet and through a revolving door into the hotel lobby and stared at the richly colored sofas, chandeliers throwing soft light on the oil paintings, and happy faces of the guests.

I found the house phones in an alcove and asked the operator to ring Henri Benoit. My heartbeats counted off the seconds, and then the operator came back on and told me that Monsieur Benoit was expected but had not checked in. Would I care to leave a message?

I said, "I'll call back. *Merci.*"

I had been right. *Right.*

Henri was in Paris. At least he would be very soon. *He was staying at the Ritz.*

As I hung up the phone I had an almost violent surge of emotion as I thought about all the innocent people Henri had killed. I thought about Levon and Barbara and about those suffocating days and nights I'd spent chained in a trailer, sitting face-to-face with a homicidal madman.

And then I thought about Henri threatening to kill Amanda.

I took a seat in a corner where I could watch the door, ducked behind the pages of a discarded copy of the *International Herald Tribune,* thinking this was the same as a stakeout in a squad car, minus the coffee and the bullshit from my partner.

I could sit here forever, because I'd finally gotten ahead of Henri, that freaking psychopath. He didn't know I was here, but I knew he was coming.

Over the next interminable two hours, I imagined Henri coming into the hotel with a suit bag and checking in at the desk, and that whatever disguise he was in, I would recognize him immediately. I would follow him into the elevator and give him the same heart-attack surprise he'd once given me.

I was still unsure what I would do after that.

I thought I could probably restrain him, call the police, have them hold him on suspicion of killing Gina Prazzi.

Or maybe that was too chancy. Maybe I'd put a bullet in his head and turn myself in at the American embassy, deal with it after the fact.

I reviewed option one: The cops would ask me, "Who is Gina Prazzi? How do you know she's dead?" I imagined showing them Henri's film in which Gina's dead body was never seen. If Henri had disposed of the body, he wouldn't even be arrested.

But I'd be under suspicion. In fact, I would be suspect number one.

I ran through the second option, saw myself pulling the .38 on Henri, spinning him around, saying, "Hands against the wall, don't move!" I liked the idea a lot.

That's how I was thinking when, among the dozens of people crossing the lobby, I saw two beautiful women and a man pass in front of me, heading toward the front door. The women were young and stylish, English-speaking, laughing and talking over each other, directing their attention to the man sandwiched between them.

Their arms were entwined like school buddies, breaking apart when they reached the revolving door, the man hanging back to let the very attractive women go through first.

The rush I felt was miles ahead of my conscious thought. But I registered the man's bland features, his build, the way he dressed.

He was very blond now, wearing large, black-framed eyeglasses, his posture slightly stooped.

This was exactly how Henri disguised himself. He'd told me that his disguises worked because they were so simple. He adopted a distinct way of walking or speaking, and then added a few distracting, but memorable visual cues. He *became* his new identity. Whatever identity he'd assumed, this much I knew.

The man with those two women was none other than Henri Benoit.

Chapter 107

I DROPPED THE newspaper to the floor and followed the threesome with my eyes as the revolving door dispensed them one at a time into the street.

I headed for the main door, thinking I could see where Henri was going, buy some time to come up with a plan. But before I reached the revolving door, a clump of tourists surged in front of me, staggering and giggling and bunching up inside the blades of the door as I stood by wanting to scream, *"You assholes, get out of my way!"*

By the time I got outside, Henri and the two women were far ahead of me, walking along the arcade that lined the west side of the street.

They were now heading down the Rue de Castiglione and toward the Rue de Rivoli. I just caught a glimpse of them turning left when I reached the corner.

Then I saw the two pretty women standing with their heads together in front of a designer shoe store, and I saw Henri's white-blond hair far up ahead.

As I tried to keep him in sight, he disappeared

down into the Tuileries Métro station at the end of the street.

I ran across the stream of traffic, ran down the stairs to the platform, but the station is one of the Métro's busiest, and I couldn't see Henri.

I tried to look everywhere at once, my eyes piercing the clots of travelers weaving through the station.

And there he was, at the far end of the platform. Suddenly he turned toward me, and I froze. For one eternal minute, I felt completely vulnerable, as if I'd been illuminated with a spotlight on a black stage.

He had to see me.

I was in his direct line of sight.

But he didn't react, and I continued to stare at him while my feet behaved as though they were glued to the cement.

Then his image seemed to shift and clarify. Now that I was looking at him straight on, I saw the *length* of his nose, the *height* of his forehead, his *receding* chin.

Was I this crazy?

I'd been so sure—but I was just as sure now that I'd gotten it all wrong. That I was a dumb-ass, a total jerk, a failure as a sleuth. The man I had just followed from the Ritz? He wasn't Henri at all.

Chapter 108

I CLIMBED UP out of the Métro, remembering that I'd told Mandy I'd be back in an hour or so but had now been gone for three.

I walked back to the Hôtel Singe-Vert empty-handed, no chocolates, no flowers, no jewelry. I had nothing to show for my Ritz-to-Métro escapade except one scrap of information that could turn out to be critical.

Henri had booked a room at the Ritz.

The lobby of our small hotel was deserted, although a cloud of cigarette smoke and loud conversation floated out from the bar and into the shabby main room.

The concierge desk was closed.

I went behind the desk and grabbed my key from the hook.

I took the stairs to my room, more than anything wanting to sleep.

I knocked on the door, called Mandy's name, and when she didn't answer, I turned the knob, ready to tell Mandy that she had no right to be girlish and irresponsible anymore. She had to be careful for two.

I opened the door and felt instantly that something was wrong. Mandy wasn't in bed. Was she in the bathroom? Was she okay?

I stepped into the room, calling her name, and the door slammed behind me. I swung around and tried to make sense of the impossible.

A black man was holding Mandy, his left arm crossing her chest, his right hand with a gun to her head. He was wearing latex gloves. Blue ones. I'd seen gloves exactly like those before.

My eyes went to Mandy's face. She was gagged. Her eyes were wild, and she was grunting a wordless scream.

The black man grinned at me, tightened his hold on her, and pointed the gun at me.

"Amanda," the man said. "Look who's home? We've been waiting for a long time, haven't we, sweetheart? But it's been fun, right?"

All the fragments of information came together: the blue gloves, the familiar tone, the pale gray eyes, and the stage makeup. I wasn't mistaken this time. I'd heard hours of his voice piped directly into my ear. It was Henri. But how had he found us here?

My mind spun in a hundred directions, all at once.

I'd gone to Paris out of fear. But now that Henri had come to my door, I wasn't afraid anymore. I was furious, and my veins were pumping a hundred percent adrenaline, lifting-a-car-off-a-baby-carriage kind of adrenaline, the running-into-a-burning-building kind of damn-it-to-hell rush.

I whipped the .38 out of my waistband, pulled back the hammer, yelled, *"Let her go."*

I guess he didn't believe I would fire. Henri

smirked at me, said, "Drop your gun, Ben. I just want to talk."

I walked up to the maniac and put the gun's muzzle against his forehead. He grinned, gold tooth winking, part of his latest disguise. I got off one shot at the exact moment that he kneed me in the thigh. I was sent crashing backward into a desk, the wooden legs shattering as I went down.

My first thought—*had I shot Mandy?* But I saw blood flowing from Henri's arm and heard the clatter of his gun sliding across the wooden floor.

He shoved Mandy away from him, hard, and she fell on me. I rolled her off my chest, and as I tried to sit, Henri pinned me—with his foot on my wrist, looking down with contempt.

"Why couldn't you just do your job, Ben? If you'd just done your job, we wouldn't be having this little problem, but now I can't trust you. I only wish I'd brought my camera."

He leaned down, bent my fingers back, and peeled the gun from my hand. Then he aimed it— first at me, and then at Mandy.

"Now, who wants to die first?" Henri said. "*Vous* or *vous?*"

Chapter 109

EVERYTHING WENT WHITE in front of my eyes. This was it, wasn't it? Amanda and I were going to die. I felt Henri's breath on my face as he screwed the muzzle of the .38 into my right eye. Mandy tried to scream through her gag.

Henri barked at her, *"Shut up."*

She did.

Water filled my eyes then. Maybe it was from the pain, or the fierce regret that I'd never see Amanda again. That she would die too. That our child would never be born.

Henri fired the gun—directly into the carpet next to my ear, deafening me. Then he yanked my head and shouted into my ear.

"Write the fucking *book*, Ben. Go home and do your *job*. I'm going to call you every night in L.A., and if you don't pick up the phone, I *will* find you. You know I'll do it, and I promise you both, *You won't get a second chance.*"

The gun was pulled away my face. Henri grabbed up a duffel bag and a briefcase with his good hand

and arm, slammed the door on his way out. I heard his footsteps receding down the stairs.

I turned to Mandy. The gag was a pillowcase pulled across the inside of her mouth and was knotted at the back of her head. I plucked at the knot, my fingers trembling, and when she was free, I took her into my arms and rocked her back and forth, back and forth.

"Are you okay, honey? Did he hurt you?"

She was crying, saying she was fine.

"You're sure?"

"Go," she said. "I know you want to go after him."

I crawled around, feeling under the spindly legs and ruffled skirts of the wall-to-wall collection of antique furniture, saying, "You know I've got to. He'll still be watching us, Mandy."

I found Henri's Ruger under the dresser and wrapped my hand tightly around the grip. I twisted open the blood-slicked doorknob and shouted to Mandy that I'd be back soon.

Leaning heavily on the banister, I walked off the pain in my thigh as I made my way down the stairs, trying to hurry, knowing that I had to kill Henri somehow.

Chapter 110

THE SKY WAS BLACK, but the streetlights and the large and perpetually booked Hôtel du Louvre next door had just about turned night into day. The two hotels were only a few hundred yards from the Tuileries, the huge public garden outside the Louvre.

This week some kind of carnival was going on there: games, big rides, oompah music, the works. Even at this late hour, giddy tourists and folks with kids flowed out onto the sidewalk, adding their raucous laughter to the sharp shocks of fireworks and blaring car horns. It reminded me of a scene from a French movie, maybe one that I'd watched somewhere.

I followed a thin trail of blood out to the street, but it disappeared a few yards from the front door. Henri had done his disappearing act again. Had he gone into the Hôtel du Louvre to hide? Had he lucked out and caught a taxi?

I was staring through the crowds when I heard police sirens coming up the Place André Malraux.

Obviously, shots had been reported. Plus, I'd been seen running around with a gun.

I stuffed Henri's Ruger into a potted planter outside the Hôtel du Louvre. Then I gamely limped into the lobby, sat in an overstuffed chair, and thought about how I would approach the *agents de police*.

Finally, I was going to have to explain Henri and everything else to the cops.

I wondered what the hell I was going to say.

Chapter 111

THE SIRENS GOT louder and louder, my shoulders and neck stiffened, and then the looping wail passed the hotel and continued on toward the Tuileries. When I was sure it was over, I reclaimed Henri's gun, made my way back to the Singe-Verts, and climbed the stairs like an old man. I knocked on the door to my room, said, "Mandy, it's me. I'm alone. You can open the door."

Seconds later, she did. Her face was tear-stained, and there were bruises at the corners of her mouth from the gag. I opened my arms to her, and Mandy fell against me, sobbing like a child who might never be soothed again.

I held her, swayed with her for a long while. Then I undressed us both and helped her into bed. I shut off the overhead light, leaving on only a small boudoir lamp on the night table. I slid under the covers, and took Mandy into my arms. She pressed her face to my chest, tethered herself to my body with her arms and legs.

"Talk to me, honey," I said. "Tell me everything."

"He knocked on the door," she finally said. "He

said he had flowers. Is that the most simpleminded trick ever? But I believed him, Ben."

"He said they were from me?"

"I think so. Yeah, he did."

"I wonder—how did he know we were here? What tipped him? I don't get it."

"When I unlocked the door, he kicked it open and grabbed me."

"I wish I'd killed him, Mandy."

"I didn't know who he was. A black man. He wrenched my arms behind my back. I couldn't move. He said...oh, this makes me *sick*," she said, crying again.

"What did he say?"

" 'I love you, Amanda.' "

I was listening to Mandy and hearing echoes at the same time. Henri had told me that he'd *loved* Gina. He'd *loved* Julia. How long would Henri have waited to prove his love to Mandy by raping her and strangling her with those blue gloves on his hands?

I whispered, "I'm so sorry. I'm so sorry."

"I'm the jerk who came here, Benjy. Oh, God, how long was he here? Three hours? *I'm* sorry. I didn't understand until now what those three days with him must have been like for you."

She started crying again, and I hushed her, told her over and over that everything would be all right.

"Don't take this the wrong way," she said, her voice ragged and strained. "But what makes you so sure?"

I got out of bed, opened my laptop, and booked two morning flights back to the States.

Chapter 112

IT WAS WELL after midnight, and I was still pacing the room. I took some Tylenol, got back under the covers with Amanda, but I couldn't sleep. I couldn't even shut my eyes for more than a few seconds.

The TV was small and old, but I turned it on and found CNN.

I watched the headline news, bolted upright when the talking head said, "Police have no suspects in the murder of Gina Prazzi, heiress to the Prazzi shipping fortune. She was found murdered in a room at the exclusive French resort Château de Mirambeau."

When Gina Prazzi's face came on the screen, I felt as though I knew her intimately. I'd watched her pass in front of the camera in the hotel room, not knowing that her life was about to end.

I said, "Mandy, Mandy," shook her arm. But she turned away, settled even more deeply into the feather bed and sleep.

I watched the police captain brief the press on TV, his speech translated and recapped for those just tuning in. Ms. Prazzi had checked into the

Château de Mirambeau alone. The housekeepers believed that two people stayed in the room, but no other guest was seen. The police were not releasing any further information about the murder at this time.

That was enough for me. I knew the full story, but what I hadn't known was that Gina Prazzi was a *real name*, not an alias.

What other lies had Henri told me? For what possible reason? Why had he lied — *in order to tell me the truth?*

I stared at the TV screen as the anchor said, "In the Netherlands, a young woman was found murdered this morning in Amsterdam. What brings this tragedy to the attention of international criminalists is that elements of this girl's death are similar to elements of the murders of the two young women in Barbados, and also to the famous American swimsuit models who were murdered this spring in Hawaii."

I dialed up the volume as the faces came on the screen: Sara Russo, Wendy Emerson, Kim McDaniels, and Julia Winkler, and now another face, a young woman whose name was Mieke Helsloot.

The announcer said, "Ms. Helsloot, twenty years old, was the secretary to the well-known architect Jan Van der Heuvel of Amsterdam, who was at a meeting in Copenhagen at the time of the murder. Mr. Van der Heuvel was interviewed at his hotel minutes ago."

Jesus Christ. I knew his name.

The picture cut away to Van der Heuvel leaving his hotel in Copenhagen, suitcase in hand, journalists crowding around him at the bottom of a rounded staircase. He was in his early forties, had gray hair and angular features. He looked genuinely shocked and *scared*.

"I have only just now learned of this terrible tragedy," he said into the clutch of microphones. "I am shocked and devastated. Mieke Helsloct was a proper, decent young lady, and I have no idea why anyone would harm her. It is a terrible day. Mieke was to be married."

Henri had told me that Jan Van der Heuvel was an *alias* for one of the members of the Alliance, the man Henri called "the Dutchman." Van der Heuvel was the third wheel who'd joined up with Henri and Gina during their romp through the French Riviera.

And now, soon after Henri had killed Gina Prazzi, Van der Heuvel's secretary had also been murdered.

If I hadn't once been a cop, I might have dismissed these two killings as a coincidence. The women were different types. They were killed hundreds of miles apart. But what I saw were two more flags on a grid, a part of a pattern.

Henri had loved Gina Prazzi, and he killed her. He'd hated Jan Van der Heuvel. Maybe he'd wanted to kill him, too, so, just thinking it out...what if Henri hadn't known that Van der Heuvel was in Denmark that day?

What if he'd decided to kill his secretary instead?

Chapter 113

I WOKE UP to sunlight seeping in through a small window. Amanda was lying on her side, facing away from me, her long, dark hair fanned out over the pillow. And in a flash, I was enraged as I remembered Henri in blackface, his gun pointed at Amanda's head, her eyes wild with fear.

Right then, I didn't care why Henri had killed anyone, what he was planning to do next, why the book was so important to him, or why he seemed to be spinning out of control.

Only one thing was important to me. I had to keep Mandy safe. And the baby, too.

I grabbed for my watch, saw that it was almost seven thirty. I shook Mandy's shoulder gently, and her eyes flew open. She gasped, then saw my face and sagged back into the bedding.

"I thought for a moment—"

"That it was a dream."

"Yeah."

I put my head very gently on her belly, and she stroked my hair.

"Is that the baby?" I asked.

"You dummy. I'm hungry."

I pretended she was speaking for the baby. I made a little megaphone with my hands, called out, "Hellloooo in there, Foozle. This is Dad," as though the tiny clump of our combined DNA could hear me.

Mandy cracked up, and I was glad she could laugh, but I cried in the shower, where she couldn't see me. If only I'd killed Henri when I had him in my gun sight. If only I had done that. Then it would all be over now.

I kept Mandy close to me as I paid the bill at the front desk and then hailed a cab and told the driver to take us to Charles de Gaulle airport.

Mandy said, "How can we go back to L.A.?"

"We can't."

She turned her head and stared at me. "So what are we doing?"

I told Mandy what I'd decided, gave her a short list of names and numbers on the back of my business card, and told her that she'd be met when the plane landed. She was listening, not fighting with me, when I told her that she couldn't phone me, or send me e-mail, nothing. That she had to rest and eat good food. "If you get bored, think about the dress you want to wear."

"You know I don't wear dresses."

"Maybe you'll make an exception."

I took a ballpoint pen out of my computer case and drew a ring on Mandy's left ring finger with lines radiating out from a big sparkly diamond in the center.

"Amanda Diaz, I love every bit of you. Will you marry me?"

"Ben."

"You and Foozle."

There were happy tears rolling down our cheeks now. She threw her arms around me, said, "Yes, yes, yes," and swore she wouldn't wash off the ring I'd drawn until she had a real one.

I bought breakfast for us at the airport, chocolate croissants and café au lait, and when it was nearly time to board, I walked with her as far as I could go. Then I wrapped my arms around her, and she sobbed against my chest until I was crying again, too. Could anything be scarier than this? The thought of losing someone you love so much? I didn't think so.

I kissed Mandy's poor bruised mouth again and again. If love counted for anything, she would be safe. Our baby would be safe. And I would see them both soon.

But the opposing thought went through me like a lance. *I might never see Amanda again. This could be the end for us.*

I dried my eyes with the palms of my hands, then watched Mandy go through the checkpoint. She looked back, waved, threw kisses, then turned away.

When I couldn't see her any longer, I left the airport, took a cab to the Gare du Nord, and boarded a high-speed train to Amsterdam.

Chapter 114

FOUR HOURS AFTER I boarded the train in Paris, I disembarked in the Centraal Station in Amsterdam, where I used a public phone to call Jan Van der Heuvel. I had contacted him before I left Paris about our getting together as soon as possible. He asked me again what made this meeting so urgent, and this time I told him, "Henri Benoit sent me a video I think you should see."

There was a long silence; then Van der Heuvel gave me directions to a bridge that crossed the Keizersgracht Canal only a few blocks from the train station.

I found Van der Heuvel standing by a lamppost, looking into the water below. I recognized him from the news clip that had been shot of him in Copenhagen, the journos asking him to comment on Mieke Helsloot's murder.

Today he was wearing a smart gray gabardine suit, a white dress shirt, and a charcoal-colored tie with a silken sheen. The part in his hair was as crisp as if it had been drawn with a knife, and it highlighted his angular features.

I introduced myself, saying that I was a writer from Los Angeles.

"How do you know Henri?" he asked after a long pause.

"I'm writing his life story. His autobiography. Henri commissioned it."

"You met with him?"

"I did, yes."

"All of this surprises me. He told you my name?"

"In publishing, this type of book is called a 'tell-all.' Henri told me everything."

Van der Heuvel looked extremely uncomfortable out on the street. He appraised my appearance, seemed to weigh whether or not to take this meeting further, then said, "I can spare a few minutes. My office is right over there. Come."

I walked with him across the bridge to a handsome five-story building in what appeared to be an upscale residential area. He opened the front door, indicated that I should go first, and I took the four well-lit flights of stairs to the top floor. My hopes rose as I climbed.

Van der Heuvel was as twisted as a snake. As part of the Alliance, he was as guilty of multiple murders as if he'd killed people with his own hands. But as despicable as he was, I wanted his cooperation, and so I had to control my anger, keep it hidden from him.

If Van der Heuvel could lead me to Henri Benoit, I would get another chance to bring Henri down.

This time, I wouldn't blow it.

Van der Heuvel took me through his design studio, a vast uncluttered space, bright with blond wood and glass and streaming sunlight. He offered me an uncomfortable-looking chair across from him at a long drawing table near the tall windows.

"It is hilarious that Henri is telling you his life story," Van der Heuvel said. "I can only imagine the lies he would say."

"Tell me how funny you find this," I said. I booted up my laptop, turned it around, and pushed the Play button so that Van der Heuvel could see the last minutes of Gina Prazzi's life.

I didn't think he had seen the video before, but as it ran, his expression never changed. When it was over, Van der Heuvel said, "What is funny is…I think he loved her."

I stopped the video, and Van der Heuvel looked into my eyes.

I said, "Before I was a writer, I was a cop. I think Henri is doing *mop-up*. He's killing the people who know who he is. Help me find him, Mr. Van der Heuvel. I'm your best chance for survival."

Chapter 115

VAN DER HEUVEL'S back was to the tall windows. His long shadow fell across the blond table, and his face was haloed by the afternoon light.

He took a pack of cigarettes from his drawer, offered me one, then lit one for himself. He said, "If I knew how to find him, there would no longer be a problem. But Henri has a genius for disappearance. I don't know where he is. I have never known."

"Let's work on this together," I said. "Kick around some ideas. There must be something you know that can lead me to him. I know about his imprisonment in Iraq, but Brewster-North is a private company, closed tight, like a vault. I know about Henri's forger in Beirut, but without the man's name—"

"Oh, this is too much," Van der Heuvel said, laughing, a terrible laugh because there was actual humor in it. He found me amusing. "He is psychopathic. Don't you understand this man at all? He's delusional. He's narcissistic, and most of all he lies. Henri was never in Iraq. He has no forger other than himself. Understand something, Mr. Hawkins. Henri is *glorifying* himself to you, inventing a better life story. You're like a small dog being pulled along—"

"Hey!" I said, slapping the table, jumping to my feet. "Don't screw with me. I came here to find Henri. I don't care about you or Horst Werner or Raphael dos Santos or the rest of you sick, pathetic motherfuckers. If you can't help me, I have no choice but to go to the police and give them everything."

Van der Heuvel laughed again and told me to calm down, take a seat. I was rocked to my core. Had Van der Heuvel just answered the question of why Henri wanted to write the book? To glorify his life story?

"The Dutchman" opened his laptop, said, "I got an e-mail from Henri two days ago. The first one he ever sent to me directly. He wanted to sell me a video. I think I just saw it for free. You say you have no interest in us?"

"I don't care about you at all. I just want Henri. He's threatened my life and my family."

"Maybe this will help your detective work."

Van der Heuvel ran his fingers over the keyboard of his laptop as he talked, saying, "Henri Benoit, as he calls himself, was a juvenile *monster*. Thirty years ago, when he was six years old, he strangled his infant sister in her crib."

The shock showed on my face as Van der Heuvel nodded, smiling, tapping ashes into a tray, assuring me that this was true.

"Cute little boy. Fat cheeks. Big eyes. He murdered a baby. He was diagnosed with psychopathic personality disorder, very rare that a child would have all the hallmarks. He was sent to a psychiatric facility, the Clinic du Lac in Geneva."

"This is documented?"

"Yes, indeed. I did the research when I first met him. According to the chief psychiatrist, a Dr. Carl Obst, the child learned a lot during his twelve years in the crazy house. How to mimic people, of course. He picked up several languages and learned a trade. He became a printer."

Was Van der Heuvel telling me the truth? If so, it explained how Henri could become anyone, forge documents, slip through the cracks at will.

"After he was released at age eighteen, our boy got busy with casual murders and robberies. He stole a Ferrari, anyway. Whatever else, I don't know. But when he met Gina four years ago, he didn't have to dine on scraps anymore."

Van der Heuvel told me that Gina "fancied Henri," that he opened up to her, told her how he liked his sex and that he had committed acts of extreme violence. And he said he wanted to make a lot of money.

"It was Gina's idea to have Henri provide entertainment for our little group and Horst went along with this plan for our sex monkey."

"This is where you came in."

"Ah. Yes. Gina introduced us."

"Henri said you sat in a corner and watched."

Van der Heuvel looked at me as though I was an exotic bug and he hadn't decided whether to smash me or put me under glass.

"Another lie, Hawkins. He took it up the ass and squealed like a girl. But this is what you should know because it is the truth. We didn't make Henri who he is. We only fed him."

Chapter 116

VAN DER HEUVEL'S fingers flew across the keyboard again. He said, "And now, a quick look, for your eyes only. I'll show you how the young man developed."

Delight brightened his face as he turned the screen toward me.

A collection of single frames taken from videos of women who'd been tied up, tortured, decapitated, flickered across the computer screen.

I could hardly absorb what I was seeing as Van der Heuvel flashed through the pictures, smoking his cigarette, providing blithe commentary for a slide show of absolute and, until now, unimaginable horror.

I felt light-headed. I was starting to feel that Van der Heuvel and Henri were the same person. I hated them equally. I wanted to kill Van der Heuvel, the worthless shit, and I thought I could even get away with it.

But I needed him to lead me to Henri.

"At first I didn't know that the murders were real," he was saying, "but when Henri began to cut off heads, then, of course, I knew....In the last year, he began writing his own scripts. Getting a little too drunk with attention. Getting too greedy.

"He was dangerous. And he knew me and Gina, so there was no easy way to end it."

Van der Heuvel exhaled a plume of smoke and went on.

"Last week, Gina planned to either pay Henri off or make him disappear. Obviously, she misjudged him. She never told me how she contacted him, so once again, this is the truth, Mr. Hawkins, I have no idea where Henri is. None at all."

"Horst Werner signs Henri's paychecks, doesn't he?" I said. "Tell me how to find Werner."

Van der Heuvel stubbed out his cigarette. His delight was gone. He spoke to me with dead seriousness, emphasizing every word.

"Mr. Hawkins, Horst Werner is the last person you ever want to meet. In your case in particular. He will not like Henri's book. Take my meaning. Don't let it out of your hands. Scrub your computer. Burn your tapes. Never mention the Alliance or its members to anyone. This advice is worth your life."

It was too late to scrub my hard drive. I'd sent my transcripts of the Henri interviews and the outline of the book to Zagami in New York. The transcripts had been photocopied and passed around to editors and Raven-Wofford's outside law firm. The names of the Alliance members were all over the manuscript. I had planned to change the names, as I'd promised Henri, in the final draft.

I bulled ahead. "If Werner helps me, I'll help him."

"You have the brain of a brick, Hawkins. Listen

to what I'm telling you. Listen. Horst Werner is a powerful man with long arms and steel fists. He can find you wherever you are. Do you hear me, Hawkins? Don't be afraid of Henri, our little windup toy.

"Be afraid of Horst Werner."

Chapter 117

VAN DER HEUVEL abruptly called our meeting to an end, dismissed me, saying that he had a flight to catch.

My skull felt like a pressure cooker about to blow. The threat against me had been doubled, a war on two fronts: If I didn't write the book, *Henri* would kill me. If I did write the book, *Werner* would kill me.

I still had to find Henri, and now I had to stop Van der Heuvel from telling Horst Werner about Henri's book, and about me.

I dug Henri's Ruger out of my computer case and aimed it at the Dutchman. My voice was hoarse from the stress of unexpressed fear and fury when I said, "You remember I said I didn't care about you and the Alliance? I've changed my mind. I care a lot."

Van der Heuvel looked at me with scorn.

"Mr. Hawkins, if you shoot me, you will be in a prison for the rest of your life. Henri will still be alive and living in luxury somewhere in the world."

"Take off your coat," I said, hefting the gun in my hand. "And everything else."

"What is the point of *this*, Hawkins?"

"I like to watch," I said. "Now shut up. Take off all your clothes. The shirt, the shoes, the pants, every stitch you have on."

"You are really a fool," he said, obeying me. "What have you got on me? Some pornography on my computer? This is Amsterdam. We are not prudes like your citizens of the United States. You can't tie me to any of it. Did you see me in any of those videos? I don't think so."

I stood with the gun clasped in both my hands, leveled at Van der Heuvel, and when he was naked, I told him to grab the wall. Then I whacked him on the back of his head with the gun butt, the same treatment Henri had given me.

Leaving him unconscious on the floor, I lifted Van der Heuvel's tie from the pile of clothes on the chair and used it to secure his wrists tightly behind his back.

His computer was connected to the Internet, and I worked fast, attaching the Henri Benoit videos to e-mails that I addressed to myself. *What else?*

There was a box of marking pens on his desk, and I dropped one of them into my coat pocket.

Then I walked through Van der Heuvel's immaculate, full-floor flat. The man was house-proud. He had beautiful things. Expensive books. Drawings. Photographs. His closet was like a clothes museum. It was sickening that a man this base, this vile, could have such a carefree and luxurious life.

I went to Van der Heuvel's magazine-quality kitchen and turned on the gas burners on his stove.

I set dish towels and two-hundred-dollar ties on fire, and as flames reached for the ceiling, the overhead sprinkler system opened.

An alarm rang out in the stairwell, and I was sure another alarm was ringing in a firehouse nearby.

As water surged across the fine wooden floors, I returned to the main room, packed away the computers, slinging both mine and Van der Heuvel's over my shoulder.

Then I slapped Van der Heuvel's face, yelled his name, jerked him to his feet. "Up! Get up. Now!" I yelled.

I ignored his questions as I marched him down the stairs to the street. Smoke billowed from the windows and, as I'd hoped, a thick crowd of witnesses had congregated around the house: men and women in business attire, old people and children on bicycles that the city provided free to residents.

I sat Van der Heuvel down on the curb and uncapped the marking pen. I wrote on his forehead, "Murderer."

He called out to people in the crowd, his voice shrill. He was pleading, but the only word I could understand was "police." Cell phones came out and numbers were punched.

Soon sirens screamed, and as they came closer I wanted to howl along with them. But I kept Henri's gun trained on Van der Heuvel and waited for the police to arrive.

When they finally did, I set down the Ruger on the sidewalk, and I pointed at Van der Heuvel's forehead.

Chapter 118

SWITZERLAND.

Two cops were in the front seat, and I sat in the back of a car speeding toward Wengen, a toylike Alpine town in the shadow of the Eiger. Despite the ban on cars in this idyllic ski resort, our armored vehicle twisted around the narrow and icy roads. I clenched the armrest, leaned forward, and stared straight ahead. I wasn't afraid that the car would sail over a guardrail. I was afraid that we wouldn't get to Horst Werner in time.

Van der Heuvel's computer had yielded his contact list, and in addition to the complete playlist of Henri Benoit's videos, I'd turned over my transcripts of Henri's confessions in the trailer. I'd explained to the police the connection between Henri Benoit, serial killer for hire, and the people who paid him.

The cops were elated.

Henri's trail of victims, dozens of horrific killings in Europe and America and Asia, had been linked only since the recent murders of the two young women in Barbados. Now the Swiss police were optimistic that with the right kind of pressure, Horst Werner would give Henri up.

As we sped toward Werner's villa, law enforcement agents were moving in on members of the Alliance in countries around the world. These should have been triumphant hours for me, but I was in a state of raw panic.

I'd made calls to friends, but there were no phones where Amanda was staying. I didn't know if it would be hours or days before I would know if she was safe. And although Van der Heuvel had referred to Henri as a toy, I had more evidence than before of his ruthlessness, his resourcefulness, his lust for revenge. And I finally understood why Henri had drafted me to write his book. He wanted the Alliance, his puppeteers, to be caught so that he could be free of them, to change his identity again and lead his own life.

The car I was riding in braked, wheels shimmying on ice and gravel, the heavy vehicle sliding to a stop at the foot of a stone wall. The wall fronted a fortresslike compound built into the side of a hill.

Car doors opened and slammed, radios chattered. Armored commando units flanked us, dozens of men in flak jackets who were armed with automatic weapons, grenade launchers, and high-tech equipment I couldn't even name.

Fifty yards away, across a snowy field, glass shattered. A window had been knocked out in a corner room of the villa. Bullets flew, and grenades boomed as they exploded inside the target area.

Under covering fire, a dozen agents charged the villa, and I heard the rumble of snow cracking loose from the steep grade behind Horst's stronghold. There was shouting in German, more small-arms fire, and I visualized Horst Werner's dead body coming out on a stretcher, the final act of this takedown.

With Horst Werner dead, how would we find Henri?

The massive front door opened. The men who were leaning against the wall aimed their weapons.

And then I saw him.

Horst Werner, the terror who Van der Heuvel had described as a man with long arms and steel fists. "the last man you'd ever want to meet," came out of his house of stone. He was barrel-chested, with a goatee and gold wire-framed glasses, and he wore a blue overcoat. Even with his hands folded on top of his head, he had a confident "military" bearing.

This was the twisted man behind it all, the master voyeur, the murderer's murderer, the Wizard of some hellacious, perverted Oz.

He was alive, and he was under arrest.

Chapter 119

HORST WERNER WAS BUNDLED into an armored car, and Swiss cops piled in behind him. I went with two Interpol investigators in another. An hour after the takedown, we arrived at the police station in Bern, and the questioning of Horst Werner began.

I watched anxiously from a small observation chamber with a window onto the interrogation room.

As Werner waited for his lawyer to arrive, his face streamed with sweat. I knew that the heat had been turned up, that the front legs of Werner's chair were shorter than the back, and that Captain Voelker, who was questioning him, was not getting much information.

A young officer stood behind my chair and interpreted for me. "Herr Werner says, 'I do not know Henri Benoit. I haven't killed anyone! I watch, but I do nothing.' "

Captain Voelker left the interrogation room briefly and returned holding what looked like a CD. Voelker spoke to Werner, and my interpreter told me that this disc had been found inside a DVD player, along with a cache of other discs in Werner's library. Werner's face stiffened as Voelker inserted the disc into a player.

What video was this? The Gina Prazzi murder? Maybe some other killing by Henri?

I angled my chair so that I could see the monitor, and I took a deep breath.

A man's bowed head came on the screen. I could see him from the crown of his skull to the middle of his T-shirt. When he lifted his swollen and bloodied face, he turned away from the camera, away from me.

From the one brief glimpse, the man looked to be in his thirties and had no distinguishing features.

An interrogation was clearly in progress. I felt the most extreme tension as I watched. Off camera, a voice said, "Onnn-reee, say the words."

My heart jumped. Was it him? Had Henri been caught?

The bloodied prisoner said to his questioner, "I'm not Henri. My name is Antoine Fascal. You've got the wrong man."

"It's not hard to say, is it, Henri?" asked the voice from the wings. "Just say the words, and maybe we will let you go."

"I tell you, *I'm not Henri*. My identification is in my pocket. Get my wallet."

The interrogator finally came into view. He looked to be in his twenties, dark-haired, had a spiderweb tattooed on his neck and the inked netting continued to his left cheek. He adjusted the camera lens so that there was a wide shot of the bare, windowless room, a cellar lit by a single bulb. The subject was hog-tied to a chair.

The tattooed man said, "Okay, 'Antoine.' We've

seen your ID, and we admire how you can become someone else. But I am getting tired of the game. Say it or don't say it. I give you to the count of three."

The tattooed man held a long, serrated knife in his hand, and he slapped it against his thigh as he counted. Then he said, "Time is up. I think this is what you've always wanted, Henri. To know that moment between life and death. Correct?"

The voice I'd heard from the hostage was familiar. So was the look in his pale gray eyes. It *was* Henri. I knew it now.

Suddenly I was filled with horror as I realized what was going to happen. I wanted to shout out to Henri, express some emotion that I didn't understand myself.

I had been prepared to kill him, but I was not capable of *this*. I couldn't just watch.

Henri spit at the lens, and the tattooed man grabbed a hank of his brown hair. He pulled his neck taut. "Say the words!" he yelled.

Then he made four powerful sawing strokes at the back of Henri's neck with the knife. Blood spurted and poured everywhere. On Henri. On his killer. On the camera lens.

I backed away from the glass, but I couldn't stop watching the video. It seemed to me that Henri was making eye contact with me through the monitor, through the glass. His eyes were still open—and then he *blinked*. He actually did that—*blinked*.

The executioner bent to the camera, his chin dripping sweat and blood, smiling with satisfaction, as he said, *"Is everybody happy?"*

Chapter 120

INSIDE THE SILENT interrogation room, Horst Werner's unfeeling expression hadn't changed, but then he looked up and smiled sweetly as the door opened, and a man in a dark suit came in, put a hand on his shoulder.

My interpreter confirmed what I'd guessed; Werner's lawyer had arrived.

The conversation between the lawyer and Captain Voelker was a short, staccato volley that boiled down to one unalterable fact: the police didn't have enough to hold Werner at this time.

I watched in shock as Werner strolled from the interrogation room with his lawyer, a free man.

A moment later, Captain Voelker joined me in the observation room, told me emphatically that it wasn't over yet. Warrants for Werner's bank and phone records had been obtained. Alliance members around the world would be squeezed, he said. It was just a matter of time before they had Werner locked up again. Interpol and the FBI were on the case.

I walked out of the police station on unsteady legs, but into clean air and daylight. A limo was waiting to drive me to the airport. I told the driver to hurry. He started the engine and raised the glass divider. But still, the car took off and maintained only a moderate speed.

Inside my mind, Van der Heuvel was saying, *"Be afraid of Horst Werner"*—and I was. Werner would find out about my transcripts of Henri's confession. It was admissible evidence against him and the Peepers. I had replaced Henri as the Witness, the one who could bring Werner and the rest of them down on multiple murder charges.

My brain sped across continents. I slapped at the divider, shouted to the driver, *"Go faster. Drive faster."*

I had to get to Amanda, by plane, by helicopter, by pack mule. I had to get to her first. We had to draw the walls around us and stay hidden, I didn't know for how long, and I didn't care.

I knew what Horst Werner would do if he found us.

I knew.

And I couldn't stop myself from wondering one other thing. Was Henri really dead?

What had I just watched back there at the station?

That *blink* of his eye—was it a wink? Was the film some kind of video trick he'd played?

"Drive faster."

Epilogue

By Benjamin Hawkins

A letter to my readers.

When this book came out, the sales far exceeded my publisher's expectations, but it had never occurred to me that it would be in thousands of bookstores around the world—and that I would be living in a shack on the side of a mountain in a country not my own.

Some would say, "Be careful what you wish for because you may get it." And I would answer, "I got what I wished for in a way I could not have imagined."

I am with Amanda, my love, and she has adapted easily to the breathtaking beauty and solitude of our new life together. She is bilingual, and has taught me to speak another language, and to cook. From the start, we planted a vegetable garden and took weekly hikes down the mountain to a charming village for bread and cheese and supplies.

Amanda and I were married in this village, in a small church made by devout hands, blessed by a priest and a congregation of people who have taken Amanda and me into their hearts. The Foozle will be baptized here when he comes into the world, and I can hardly wait for him to be born. Our son.

But what is his birthright? What promises can I make him?

The first time I saw the off-road vehicle climbing the rut that winds up from the valley, I armed my bride and lined up guns on the table near the window.

The car was a private carrier that my publisher had hired to bring me mail and news of the world. After I searched the driver and let him go, I read everything Zagami sent me. I learned that the Peepers had been rounded up, that every one of them will go to trial for murder, and for conspiracy to commit murder, and for lesser crimes that will keep them in prisons for as long as they live.

Some days, my mind fastens on Horst Werner, his long arms and steel fists, and as his trial drags on, I think, *At least I know where he is*.

And then I think about Henri.

Sometimes I run the images of Henri's death through my mind like a length of film through the sprockets of an old-time film projector. I watch his horrific execution and convince myself that he really is dead.

At other times, I'm just as sure that he has fooled everyone. That he is living his life under an assumed name—as I am. And, one day, he will find us.

I thank my loyal readers for your letters, your concern, and your prayers for our safety. Life is good here. Sometimes I am very happy, but I can't quite dismiss my fear of the psychopathic monster I knew too well—and I cannot ever forget the McDaniels family: Levon, Barbara, and Kim.

Acknowledgments

The authors are grateful to these fine professionals for giving generously of their time and expertise: Dr. Humphrey Germaniuk, Capt. Richard Conklin, Clint Van Zandt, Dr. David Smith, Dr. Maria Paige, and Allison Adato.

We also thank our excellent researchers: Rebecca DiLiberto, Ellie Shurtleff, Kai McBride, Sage Hyman, Alan Graison, Nick Dragash, and Lynn Colomello.

Special thanks to Michael Hampton, Jim and Dorian Morley, Sue and Ben Emdin, and to Mary Jordan, who makes it all possible.

About the Authors

JAMES PATTERSON has had more *New York Times* bestsellers than any other writer, ever, according to *Guinness World Records*. Since his first novel won the Edgar Award in 1976, James Patterson's books have sold more than 205 million copies. He is the author of the Alex Cross novels, the most popular detective series of the past twenty-five years, including *Kiss the Girls* and *Along Came a Spider*. Mr. Patterson also writes the bestselling Women's Murder Club novels, set in San Francisco, and the top-selling New York detective series of all time, featuring Detective Michael Bennett.

James Patterson also writes books for young readers, including the award-winning Maximum Ride, Daniel X, and Witch and Wizard series. In total, these books have spent more than 200 weeks on national bestseller lists, and all three series are in Hollywood development.

His lifelong passion for books and reading led James Patterson to launch a new website, ReadKiddoRead.com, to give adults an easy way to locate the very best books for kids. He writes full-time and lives in Florida with his family.

MAXINE PAETRO is a novelist and journalist. She lives with her husband in New York.

Books by James Patterson

FEATURING ALEX CROSS

Cross Fire

I, Alex Cross

Alex Cross's Trial
    (with Richard DiLallo)

Cross Country

Double Cross

Cross

Mary, Mary

London Bridges

The Big Bad Wolf

Four Blind Mice

Violets Are Blue

Roses Are Red

Pop Goes the Weasel

Cat & Mouse

Jack & Jill

Kiss the Girls

Along Came a Spider

THE WOMEN'S MURDER CLUB

The 9th Judgment (with Maxine Paetro)

The 8th Confession (with Maxine Paetro)

7th Heaven (with Maxine Paetro)

The 6th Target (with Maxine Paetro)

The 5th Horseman (with Maxine Paetro)

4th of July (with Maxine Paetro)

3rd Degree (with Andrew Gross)

2nd Chance (with Andrew Gross)

1st to Die

FEATURING MICHAEL BENNETT

Tick Tock (with Michael Ledwidge)

Worst Case (with Michael Ledwidge)

Run for Your Life (with Michael Ledwidge)

Step on a Crack (with Michael Ledwidge)

FOR READERS OF ALL AGES

Angel: A Maximum Ride Novel

Witch & Wizard: The Gift (with Ned Rust)

Daniel X: The Manga 1

Maximum Ride: The Manga 3 (with NaRae Lee)

Daniel X: Demons and Druids (with Adam Sadler)
FANG: A Maximum Ride Novel
Witch & Wizard (with Gabrielle Charbonnet)
Maximum Ride: The Manga 2 (with NaRae Lee)
Daniel X: Watch the Skies (with Ned Rust)
MAX: A Maximum Ride Novel
Maximum Ride: The Manga 1 (with NaRae Lee)
Daniel X: Alien Hunter (graphic novel; with Leopoldo Gout)
The Dangerous Days of Daniel X (with Michael Ledwidge)
The Final Warning: A Maximum Ride Novel
Saving the World and Other Extreme Sports: A Maximum Ride Novel
School's Out—Forever: A Maximum Ride Novel
Maximum Ride: The Angel Experiment

OTHER BOOKS

Don't Blink (with Howard Roughan)
The Postcard Killers (with Liza Marklund)
Private (with Maxine Paetro)
The Murder of King Tut (with Martin Dugard)
Swimsuit (with Maxine Paetro)
Against Medical Advice (with Hal Friedman)
Sail (with Howard Roughan)
Sundays at Tiffany's (with Gabrielle Charbonnet)
You've Been Warned (with Howard Roughan)
The Quickie (with Michael Ledwidge)
Judge & Jury (with Andrew Gross)
Beach Road (with Peter de Jonge)
Lifeguard (with Andrew Gross)
Honeymoon (with Howard Roughan)
santaKid
Sam's Letters to Jennifer
The Lake House
The Jester (with Andrew Gross)
The Beach House (with Peter de Jonge)
Suzanne's Diary for Nicholas
Cradle and All

For previews of upcoming books by
James Patterson and more information about the author, visit
www.JamesPatterson.com.

Exceptional intelligence...super-human strength...two beautiful children...Hays and Lizbeth Baker will lose their perfect life—unless they use their extraordinary abilities to save their family *and* the entire human race.

Please turn this page
for a preview of

TOYS

Available in March 2011

"MY, MY. THE *PRESIDENT* wants to meet us," Lizbeth whispered in my ear as we followed Jax Moore farther into the mansion.

"Of course he does," I said with a wink.

Actually, Lizbeth and I *were* considered stars at that particular moment in time. We'd just returned from Vegas where we had saved countless lives while arresting a gang of moderately clever human bank robbers who had been terrorizing the West.

Anyway, Jax Moore whisked us through eight-foot-tall carved oak doors that led to the mansion's private living area. Well-concealed scanners examined every pore of our bodies as we walked to the entrance of the president's oval-shaped office, which was modeled after the famous original in the now-sunken city of Washington, DC.

I was immediately reminded that humans had created some good things in the past, such as this fine neoclassic style of architecture. But they'd also severely ravaged the planet, hadn't they? A couple decades ago, the first generation of Elites had barely managed to save it from total destruction.

Washington, DC, was one of many cities on the casualty list, along with most of the low-lying eastern seaboard, including New York City, Boston, and Philadelphia, all of which had been swallowed up long ago by the rising oceans.

When we stepped into the Oval Office, President Hughes Jacklin was standing in front of a full-length mirror, fumbling with his cravat. At his side was his faithful bodyguard and supposed lover, a behemoth named Devlin.

Seeing us, the president let the tie go and strode across the room to greet Lizbeth and me, as if we were old friends. He was a hugely impressive man, classically educated, firm-jawed and broad-shouldered, and his thick dark hair was just beginning to gray at the temples.

"My dear, the sun is down and it's still as bright as day around you," he said to Lizbeth, kissing her perfect cheeks, one, then the other.

"Mr.—Mr. President," Lizbeth stammered ever so slightly, "I'm speechless—almost anyway."

"What you are is incredibly charming," countered the president.

He turned to me and gave a firm handshake. "Hays Baker, this is a great pleasure. *You're* beautiful too. Look, I'm late for my own party—we'll have time to get better acquainted later. But I want you to know I've followed your careers at the Agency closely. And I'm a big fan. That operation in Vegas was pure genius. Efficient and effective. Just what I like."

"We're proud to help, Mr. President," Lizbeth said, actually blushing a little now.

"Then would you help me out with *this* thing?"

He flapped the loose ends of his cravat with good-humored exasperation. "I never could get the hang of it. Or the significance of ties, damn them."

"I could do that," said Devlin, but the president waved the bodybuilding guard away.

"Lizbeth?" he said, exposing his throat to her. "Let's see how you would *garrote* a world leader."

"IT WOULD BE my pleasure, sir!"

Lizbeth laughed like an impressionable school-girl and took over. As her nimble fingers arranged the president's tie into an expert knot, he gave us a conspiratorial wink. Off to the side, Devlin was grimacing and fidgeting, and I hoped we hadn't made an enemy of the giant bodyguard.

"I will tell you this much about my future plans," the president said. "My best people have developed a program to—let's just say—*complete* the work of making our world a safer, cleaner place with respect to the human strain. We'll be launching it soon. In *days,* actually."

Lizbeth and I had heard rumors that a sweeping human-containment initiative had been taking shape. It was hard not to be relieved. The fool-hardy and dangerous humans had only themselves to blame. They had blown their chance to make the world a better place. It was undeniable that they had accomplished quite the opposite.

"I'm counting on you both for important help with the launch of the human cleanup. Meantime, you're the best we have at holding the gross and undesirable elements in check. Please keep up the good work. Bigger, better things are coming for you two. For all Elites, actually." He checked himself in the mirror. "Come to think of it—humans are responsible for *ties!*"

President Jacklin smiled, then he said goodbye with effusive warmth—he was obviously an expert at it, perhaps aided by the prototype Cyrano 3000 implant he was rumored to have. I'd only read about the device, but what I knew was that it was surgically attached to a person's inner ear and could offer guidance through any social interaction. The amazing appliance had wireless access to a database of pretested social cues, pertinent information about whatever person you were talking to, and other useful facts, names, quotes, and quips that might fit a given situation. The irony: a human had also invented it.

Jax Moore took my elbow, then Lizbeth's, and walked us back to the oak doors. He lit up another of his cigars and puffed contentedly.

"Not a word about this. There can be no security leaks. Check with me first thing tomorrow." he said. "I have classified information we need to discuss. The president specifically asked for you two on the 'human problem.' You're both—*beautiful,*" Moore closed, giving us an icy grin that could have frozen vegetables. I doubted he'd undergone a Cyrano 3000 implant, or even heard of them.

After the doors closed, Lizbeth took my arm and said, "One of the best nights of our lives, don't you think?" She'd handled the president with perfect poise—and charm—but she was also clearly starstruck after meeting the great man in person. To be honest, so was I. I just didn't let on.

"Definitely in the top hundred or so," I teased her.

"*Really,*" she said archly. "You'll have to remind me of the others. Such as?"

"How about the night when we met? Michigan Avenue, New Chicago."

She laughed. "Hmmm. Well, that *might* be in the top hundred."

"I guess I asked for that," I said as we exchanged a kiss that I'm sure caused a whistle or two in the president's security-camera control room.

WHAT CAUGHT MY attention next was the incredible number of high-ticket toys at the party.

Sometimes it seemed like toys were all the world cared about in the second half of the twenty-first century. Humans and Elites had both fallen under their spell and become addicted to the endless pleasures and nonstop excitement they could provide. And the toys were only getting better, or worse, depending on your point of view.

Even in the presidential mansion—where you might think the serious business of the country would be getting done 24-7—toys were playing a big part in the celebration. Wide-eyed, deep-pocketed guests were crowded around a display where employees from TOYZ Corporation were giving demos of some of the choicer items in the forthcoming, but thus far unreleased, catalog.

As Lizbeth and I reentered the ballroom, we were surrounded by a menagerie of cloned, genetically tamed animals—birds-of-paradise, Galápagos tortoises, enormous butterflies, pygmy hippos—and then we almost got knocked over by a beautiful woman in a gold gown and matching high heels, who was laughing while riding on a thick-maned lion.

"Oops, sorry," she said breathlessly as she raced by. Then she called over her shoulder to Lizbeth, "You've *got* to try this, Liz. You've never felt such *muscles*."

"Now that's certainly not true," Lizbeth whispered as her hand delicately grazed my upper leg. "My beauty."

Other women were draping defanged cobras and wondrously patterned tropical vipers around their necks like mink stoles, and one demented man showed off by thrusting his head into the jaws of a docile baby *Tyrannosaurus rex*. I almost wished the toy would take a bite.

While Lizbeth admired the fauna—Elite and otherwise—I stepped up to a bank of SimStims, the hugely popular, addictive simulators that offered a variety of different experiences, all so intensely real that it was illegal to sell SimStim machines to anyone with a heart condition. You could choose from any number of different simulations—have passionate sex with a movie or government star, for example, rock out onstage surrounded by a vast audience of screaming fans, or fight for your life in the heat of combat.

I slipped on a mood helmet at one of the simulators and scanned the on-screen menu. The range of choices was staggering—Moorish Harem, Eye of a Hurricane Experience, Pagan Barbarities, Tennis Vs the Pro, Pig Out: No Calories, Death Experience: A Final Sixty Seconds, Visit Your Former Lives.

Movie buff that I am, I picked the general heading of Great Moments in Cinema.

I barely glimpsed the words "This Program Has Been Edited for Your Enhanced Pleasure," and then I was *there*. Bogie in *Casablanca*.

I gazed into the liquid blue eyes of Ingrid Bergman sitting across from me—then I raised my whiskey glass to touch hers.

"Here's looking at you, kid," I said, losing myself in her answering smile.

Then the door of the noisy café burst open and a toadlike little man ran in, looking around in panic. The great human character actor Peter Lorre had arrived.

"Rick, you have to help me," he gasped in a heavy accent, thrusting a sheaf of papers at me. "Hide these!"

I strode to the piano as he rushed out the back door, and I had just managed to shove the papers under the lid when gunshots sounded in the street outside. Suddenly, jackbooted soldiers stormed in—

My heart raced, and I felt myself instinctively backing away toward the bar. There was a Luger right there under the counter.

This was amazing. I was living Bogie's part in the great film masterpiece. And then—surprise of surprises...

From the imagination of
James Patterson,
here's a behind-the-scenes
look at
illustrations from
TOYS

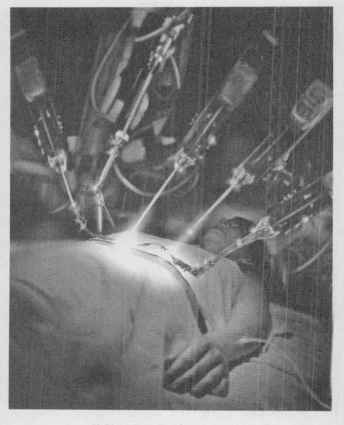

60-Year Part Replacement Plan
Replace all or most of your body parts at sixty years,
guaranteed for another sixty.

The World-Famous Jessica and Jacob Dolls
Only 12" tall, they do everything that we can—*everything*.

Fold-Out Phone
This four-screen communications model is the rage
among young, idle, rich Elites.

iJeeves Butlers
Want to feel like lord of your English manor? These straight-backed bastions of old-world service will make you feel like a viscount.

My Little Ponies 4.0
Artificially intelligent, 9-inch-tall toy horses that walk, trot,
canter, gallop, or stay still to have their flowing manes and
tails brushed—all at your little princess's command.

Robot Call Girl
She (or he) morphs to meet your every desire.

Synthetic Jewelry
Synthetic diamond jewelry that looks like it costs millions,
but is in every Elite woman's price range.

ZX-740 Airpod
All-environments model. Works on-road, off-road, airborne, and can safely dive to 1,000 meters underwater. Gull-wing doors, ultrasound massage seats, and THX 6.3 holographic surround sound.

WE DISAGREE.

Go to READKIDDOREAD.com

• Over 120 of the best and coolest children's books ever, books kids will absolutely gobble up • Snappy Reviews • Interviews with James Patterson, Jeff Kinney, Rick Riordan, Julie Andrews, Carl Hiaasen • And a lot more!

James Patterson's
READKIDDOREAD.com
Dedicated to making kids readers for life.